THE INTERNATIONAL SURVEY OF FAMILY LAW

2000 EDITION

PUBLISHED ON BEHALF OF
THE INTERNATIONAL SOCIETY OF FAMILY LAW

THE INTERNATIONAL SURVEY OF FAMILY LAW

2000 EDITION

Covering developments since publication of
The International Survey of Family Law 1997

Edited by

Andrew Bainham

Fellow of Christ's College, Cambridge
Lecturer in Law, University of Cambridge, UK

Family Law

EXETER COLLEGE
OXFORD

Published by Family Law
a publishing imprint of
Jordan Publishing Limited
21 St Thomas Street
Bristol
BS1 6JS

British Library Cataloguing-in-Publication Data

A catalogue record for this book is available from the British Library.

ISBN 0 85308 634 6

This volume is produced in-house by Jordans.
Printed in Great Britain by MPG Books Ltd, Bodmin, Cornwall

THE INTERNATIONAL SURVEY OF FAMILY LAW

PUBLISHED ON BEHALF OF
THE INTERNATIONAL SOCIETY OF FAMILY LAW

A   THE HISTORY OF THE SOCIETY

On the initiative of Professor Zeev Falk, the Society was launched at the University of Birmingham, UK in April 1973. The Society's first international conference was held in West Berlin in April 1975 on the theme *The Child and the Law*. There were over 200 participants, including representatives of governments and international organisations. The second international conference was held in Montreal in June 1977 on the subject *Violence in the Family*. There were over 300 participants from over 20 countries. A third world conference on the theme *Family Living in a Changing Society* was held in Uppsala, Sweden in June 1979. There were over 270 participants from 26 countries. The fourth world conference was held in June 1982 at Harvard Law School, USA. There were over 180 participants from 23 countries. The fifth world conference was held in July 1985 in Brussels, Belgium on the theme *The Family, The State and Individual Security*, under the patronage of Her Majesty Queen Fabiola of Belgium, the Director-General of UNESCO, the Secretary-General of the Council of Europe and the President of the Commission of the European Communities. The sixth world conference on *Issues of the Ageing in Modern Society* was held in 1988 in Tokyo, Japan, under the patronage of H.I.H. Takahito Mikasa. There were over 450 participants. The seventh world conference was held in May 1991 in Croatia on the theme, *Parenthood: The Legal Significance of Motherhood and Fatherhood in a Changing Society*. There were 187 participants from 37 countries. The eighth world conference took place in Cardiff, Wales in June/July 1994 on the theme *Families Across Frontiers*. The ninth world conference of the Society was held in July 1997 in Durban, South Africa on the theme *Changing Family Forms: World Themes and African Issues*. The Society's tenth world conference will be held in July 2000 in Queensland, Australia on the theme *Family Law: Processes, Practices and Pressures*. The Society has also increasingly held regional conferences including those in Lyon, France (1995); Quebec City, Canada (1996); Seoul, South Korea (1996); Prague, Czech Republic (1998); Albuquerque, New Mexico, USA (June 1999); and Oxford, UK (August 1999).

B   ITS NATURE AND OBJECTIVES

The following principles were adopted at the first Annual General Meeting of the Society held in the Kongresshalle of West Berlin on the afternoon of Saturday 12 April 1975.

(1)   The Society's objectives are the study and discussion of problems of family law. To this end the Society sponsors and promotes:

    (a)   International co-operation in research on family law subjects of world-wide interest.

    (b)   Periodic international conferences on family law subjects of world-wide interest.

    (c)   Collection and dissemination of information in the field of family law by the publication of a survey concerning developments in family law throughout the world, and by publication of relevant materials in family law, including papers presented at conferences of the Society.

    (d)   Co-operation with other international, regional or national associations having the same or similar objectives.

    (e)   Interdisciplinary contact and research.

    (f)   The advancement of legal education in family law by all practical means including furtherance of exchanges of teachers, students, judges and practising lawyers.

    (g)   Other objectives in furtherance of or connected with the above objectives.

C   MEMBERSHIP AND DUES

In 1997 the Society had approximately 540 members in some 56 countries.

(a)   Membership:
- Ordinary Membership, which is open to any member of the legal or a related profession. The Council may defer or decline any application for membership.
- Institutional Membership, which is open to interested organisations at the discretion of, and on terms approved by, the Council.
- Student Membership, which is open to interested students of law and related disciplines at the discretion of, and on terms approved by, the Council.
- Honorary Membership, which may be offered to distinguished persons by decision of the Executive Council.

(b)   Each member shall pay such annual dues as may be established from time to time by the Council. At present, dues for ordinary membership are *Hfl*. 180 (or equivalent) for three years or *Hfl*. 75 (or equivalent) for one year, plus *Hfl*. 15 (or equivalent) if cheque is in another currency.

D   DIRECTORY OF MEMBERS

A Directory of Members of the Society is available to all members.

E   BOOKS

The proceedings of the first world conference were published as *The Child and the Law* (F. Bates, ed, Oceana, 1976); the proceedings of the second as *Family Violence* (J. Eekelaar and S. Katz, eds, Butterworths, Canada, 1978); the proceedings of the third as *Marriage and Cohabitation* (J. Eekelaar and S. Katz, eds, Butterworths, Canada, 1980); the fourth, *The Resolution of Family Conflict* (J. Eekelaar and S. Katz, eds, Butterworths, Canada, 1984); the fifth, *Family, State and Individual Economic Security (Vols I & II)* (M.T. Meulders-Klein and J. Eekelaar, eds, Story Scientia and Kluwer, 1988); the sixth, *An Ageing World: Dilemmas and Challenges for Law and Social Policy* (J. Eekelaar and D. Pearl, eds, Clarendon Press, 1989); the seventh *Parenthood in Modern Society* (J. Eekelaar and P. Sarcevic, eds., Martinus Nijhoff, 1993); the eighth *Families Across Frontiers* (N. Lowe and G. Douglas, eds, Martinus Nijhoff, 1996) and the ninth *The Changing Family: Family Forms and Family Law* (J. Eekelaar and T. Nhlapo, eds, Hart Publishing, 1998). These are commercially marketed but are available to Society members at reduced prices.

F   THE SOCIETY'S PUBLICATIONS

The Society regularly publishes a newsletter, *The Family Letter*, which appears twice a year and which is circulated to the members of the Society and reports on its activities and other matters of interest. *The International Survey of Family Law* provides information on current developments in family law throughout the world and is received free of charge by members of the Society. The editor is currently Andrew Bainham, Christ's College, Cambridge, CB2 3BU, UK. The Survey is circulated to members or may be obtained on application to the Editor.

PREFACE

The International Survey of Family Law (2000 Edition) is the next edition to follow *The International Survey of Family Law 1997* which was published in 1999. It mainly covers developments in the various jurisdictions up to and including the end of the calendar year 1998. The International Society felt that in future it would be more appropriate for the title of the Survey to reflect the year of *publication* rather than the time period covered by the individual articles, and that it was fitting to give effect to this change at the start of the new millennium.

The Survey begins with the usual annual review of international developments affecting family law and this is followed by articles from 29 jurisdictions. Sixteen contributions are from Europe, with four from the Americas, and three each from Africa, Asia and Australasia. It is particularly pleasing that this volume should contain the first ever Palestinian contribution to the Survey. It remains difficult to secure articles from South America and Central America and from most parts of Asia with the exception of the Far East. At the same time, it is fair to say that considerable progress has been made in Africa with some 14 countries being covered in the first five volumes of the International Survey.

As always, I am dependent in my editorial role on the support and advice which I receive from others regarding potential contributors. I remain very grateful to all those who have assisted me with contacts in this way. It is encouraging that I now receive the occasional unsolicited approach from those wishing to write for the Survey. In this respect, I would like to repeat what I have said in previous years. I am always glad to receive such approaches and to explore the possibilities for participation in the Survey which they represent.

As in previous years, I have received the indispensable help of Peter Schofield with translation of the French and Spanish texts and Carol Dowling with the preparation of the manuscript. I would also like to acknowledge with thanks the work of others who occasionally assist with translation and of James Hurst in particular who translates the Swedish contribution. As ever, I am grateful to all those who have written articles for the current volume.

Regular readers of the Survey will be aware that this is the first volume to be published by Jordan Publishing Ltd of Bristol. I would like to take this opportunity of thanking, on behalf of the International Society, the former publishers of the Survey, Kluwer Law International, for providing the Society with the opportunity of publishing the first four International Surveys as annual volumes. The Society now looks forward to a fruitful association with Jordans as it takes the Survey confidently forward into the twenty-first century.

ANDREW BAINHAM
Christ's College, Cambridge
May 2000

INTERNATIONAL SOCIETY OF FAMILY LAW
SUBSCRIPTION FORM

☐ I prefer to communicate in ☐ English ☐ French

☐ Please charge my credit card ☐ **MASTERCARD or EUROCARD** ☐ VISA

　　☐ for 3 years　　(NGL 180)

　　☐ for 1 year　　(NGL 75)

Name of Card Holder: _____

Card no.　|_|_|_|_|_|　|_|_|_|_|_|　|_|_|_|_|_|　|_|_|_|_|_|

Expiry date:　____ / ____

Address of Card Holder:　_____

_____

_____

_____

☐ I pay *NGL 180*[1] (three years) or *NGL 75* (one year), plus *NGL 15* if cheque is in another currency, by *postgiro* to **63.18.019** from

The International Society of Family Law,
Den Hooiberg 17
4891 NM Rijsbergen
The Netherlands

(We have a bank account at the Postbank, Amsterdam, The Netherlands.)

☐ Payment enclosed *by cheque* to the amount of *NGL 195* (three years) or *NGL 90* (one year)

Date: _____　Signature: _____

☐ *New member, or*

☐ *(Change of) name/address:*　_____

_____

　　　　　　　　　　Tel:　_____
　　　　　　　　　　Fax:　_____
　　　　　　　　　　e-mail:

Comments:　_____

_____

_____

To be sent to the treasurer of the ISFL:
Prof. Paul Vlaardingerbroek
International Society of Family Law
Den Hooiberg 17
4891 NM Rijsbergen
THE NETHERLANDS (or by fax: +31-13-466 2323;
e-mail address P.Vlaardingerbroek@kub.nl)

---

[1] Or its countervalue in US Dollars (in March 2000: 87 US$).

ASSOCIATION INTERNATIONALE DE DROIT DE LA FAMILLE
FORMULAIRE DE COTISATION

☐ Pour la communication avec ISFL je préfère la langue ☐ française ☐ anglaise

☐ Je vous prie de charger ma carte de crédit: ☐ **MASTERCARD/EUROCARD** ☐ VISA

   ☐ pour 3 ans

   ☐ pour 1 an

Le nom du possesseur de la carte de crédit: _____

Card no. ⏐_⏐_⏐_⏐_⏐ ⏐_⏐_⏐_⏐_⏐ ⏐_⏐_⏐_⏐_⏐ ⏐_⏐_⏐_⏐_⏐

Date d'expiration: _____ / _____

L'adresse du possesseur de la carte de crédit: _____

_____

_____

_____

☐ Je payerai *Hfl. 180,-*[1] (trois ans) ou: ☐ *Hfl. 75,-* (un an), plus *Hfl. 15,-* surcharge si paiement est en autre cours, *par postgiro* à **63.18.019**

(du)
The International Society of Family Law
Den Hooiberg 17
4891 NM Rijsbergen
The Netherlands
(Nous avons un crédit au Postbank, Amsterdam, les Pays-Bas)

☐ Paiement est inclus avec un chèque de ☐ *Hfl. 180,-* (trois ans) ou *Hfl. 75,-* (un an), plus *Hfl. 15,-* surcharge si paiement est en autre cours.

La date: _____ Souscription: _____

☐ *Nouveau membre, ou*

☐ *(Changement de) nom/adresse:* _____

_____

            Tel: _____

            Fax: _____

            e-mail: _____

Remarques: _____

_____

_____

Veuillez envoyer ce formulaire au trésorier de l'Association:
Prof. Paul Vlaardingerbroek
International Society of Family Law
Den Hooiberg 17
4891 NM Rijsbergen
LES PAYS BAS (ou par fax: +31-13-466 2323; e-mail address P.Vlaardingerbroek@kub.nl)

---

[1] Ou la contrevaleur en francs français ou US dollars.

TABLE OF CONTENTS

CONTRIBUTORS

International	*Geraldine Van Beuren and Randini Wanduragala* Queen Mary and Westfield College Faculty of Law Mile End Road London E1 4NS England
Argentina	*Cecilia P. Grosman and Delia Iñigo* C/o Corrientes 1515 PISO 60 "B" 1042 Buenos Aires Argentina
Australia	*Frank Bates* Faculty of Law The University of Newcastle University Drive Callaghan Newcastle 2308 Australia
Belgium	*Thierry Moreau* Faculté de Droit de l'Université Catholique de Louvain Place Montesquieu 2 B–1348 Louvain La Neuve Belgium
Botswana	*Athaliah Molokomme* Private Bag 00470 Gaborone Botswana
Cameroon	*E.N. Ngwafor* Faculty of Law University of Yaounde II B.P. 1365 Yaounde Cameroon
Canada	*Martha Bailey and Nicholas Bala* Faculty of Law Queen's University Kingston Canada

Chile

Inés Pardo de Carvallo
Catholic University of Valparaiso
Fundacion Isabel Caces de Brown
Avenida Brazil 2950
Casilla 4059
Valparaiso
Chile

China

Michael Palmer
School of Oriental and African Studies
Department of Law
Thornhaugh Street, Russell Square
London WC1H OXG
England

Croatia

Dubravka Hrabar
Family Law Department
Trg M. Tita 14
10 000 Zagreb
Croatia

Czech Republic

Jiří F. Haderka
Jan Werich Street 2a
CZ 736 01 Havirov
Czech Republic

England and Wales

Gillian Douglas
Cardiff Law School
P.O. Box 427
Law Building
Museum Avenue
Cardiff CF1 1XD
Wales

France

Jacqueline Rubellin-Devichi
L'Université Jean Moulin
40 Quai Gailleton
69002 Lyon
France

Germany

Rainer Frank
Direktor des Institus für ausländisches und
internationales Privatrecht - Abt. II
Europlatz 1
D-7800 Freiburg 1
Germany

Greece

Efie Kounougeri-Manoledaki
University of Thessaloniki
7 Vironos St.
546 22 Thessaloniki
Greece

Republic of Ireland

Paul Ward
University College Dublin
Faculty of Law
Roebuck Castle
Belfield
Dublin 4
Republic of Ireland

Italy

Elena Urso
Dipartmento di Diritto Comparato
Facoltà di Giurisprudenza
Università degli studi di Firenze
Via Benedetto Vardi 2
50132 Firenze
Italy

Japan

Satoshi Minamikata and Teiko Tamaki
Niigata University Faculty of Law
8050 Igarashi Zonocho
Niigata-shi 950-21
Japan

The Netherlands

Caroline Forder
Rijksuniversiteit Limburg
Faculteit der Rechtsgeleerdheid
Vakgroep Privaatrecht
Postbus 616
Maastricht 6200 MD
The Netherlands

New Zealand

Bill Atkin
Reader in Law
Faculty of Law
Victoria University
PO Box 600
Wellington
New Zealand

Palestine

Lynn Welchman
School of Oriental and African Studies
Department of Law
Thornhaugh Street, Russell Square
London WC1H 0XG
England

ANNUAL REVIEW OF INTERNATIONAL FAMILY LAW

Geraldine Van Bueren[*] *and Randini Wanduragala*[**]

I INTRODUCTION

The focus of the cases concerning the family under the European Convention on Human Rights concerns the application and the non-application of the criminal law. The studying and the teaching of family law can no longer be considered in isolation from the criminal law.

The European Court also considered the impact of security forces violations in relation to family life.

Although there are only a few international cases which directly concern the family, it is possible to see that, particularly in relation to international human rights law, there are emerging trends which will have an impact on the family. Broadly, the areas concern the competing interests of individual members within the family and cover such issues as access to medical treatment, the elderly and the role of the family in the eradication of child labour.

II THE FAMILY, CRIMINAL LAW AND THE EUROPEAN CONVENTION ON HUMAN RIGHTS

A v United Kingdom

The United Kingdom's ancient and cherished freedom of parental corporal punishment was once again tested before the European Court of Human Rights. In *A v United Kingdom* the applicant, a child, was beaten with a garden cane by his stepfather.[1] The stepfather was tried before a criminal court but successfully pleaded 'reasonable chastisement', a statutory defence under English Law. The applicant brought a case under Article 3 of the European Convention on Human Rights alleging that the United Kingdom had failed to protect him from degrading and inhuman punishment. He also alleged breaches of Article 8 (privacy), Article 13 (lack of effective remedy) and Article 14 (unjustifiable discrimination).

The case was slightly unusual in that, before the Court hearing, the Government in the light of the European Commission of Human Rights' decision, had accepted that there had been a violation under Article 3 but the Court considered it necessary to examine the issues itself.[2]

The Court observed that in order for there to be a violation of Article 3 the punishment has to reach a minimum level of severity. A was only 9 years old at the time

---

[*] Professor of International Human Rights Law and Director of the Programme on International Rights of the Child, University of London, Queen Mary College.

[**] Child Rights Officer at World Vision UK and a Research Associate of the Programme on International Rights of the Child, University of London, Queen Mary College. The comments and observations made in this article are those of the author and do not in any way reflect the policy of World Vision UK.

[1] *A v United Kingdom* 27 EHRR 1999, 611.

[2] See *Findlay v United Kingdom* 1997 24 EHRR 221.

of the caning. The paediatrician who examined him found him to have been beaten with a garden cane on a number of occasions with considerable force. This, the Court found, fell within the Article 3 test. The assessment of the level is relative and must depend on all the factors of the case including the context and the nature of the punishment, its duration, the physical and mental consequences and where relevant the gender, the age and the health of the victim. The Court found that children and other vulnerable family members are entitled to state protection not only after the event but also in the form of effective deterrence against serious breaches of personal integrity. In accordance with English law it is a defence to a charge of assault on a child that the treatment amounted to 'reasonable chastisement'. The burden of proof is upon the prosecution to establish beyond reasonable doubt that any assault falls outside of such chastisement. In *A* the Court observed that the applicant had suffered such a serious assault as to fall within the prohibition of degrading and inhuman treatment and punishment but that the jury had been able to acquit the stepfather. The Court therefore found that the law did not sufficiently protect against treatment and punishment prohibited by Article 3 and the failure to provide such adequate protection amounted to a breach of Article 3 itself. Hence in relation to all vulnerable members of the family, not only children, the prohibition on degrading and inhuman treatment and punishment places a strict duty of effective deterrence on the State. This same duty is applicable to all forms of domestic violence which fall within prohibited treatments and punishments.

In the light of the breach of Article 3 and in accordance with its well-established practice the Court found it unnecessary to deal with the other Articles.

The strict duty of effective deterrence is welcome but the Court's avoidance of determining whether a State should be held responsible for the beating by the stepfather without giving further reasoning was disappointing.[3] The Court also avoided citing Article 19 of the UN Convention on the Rights of the Child which had been cited by the majority of the European Commission and which obliges States to 'protect the child from all forms of physical or mental violence, injury or abuse.' The UN Committee on the Rights of the Child had expressed concern about the 'imprecise nature of the expression of reasonable chastisement ... [which] may pave the way for it to be interpreted in a subjective and arbitrary manner.'[4] This continuing non-reference by both the European Court of Human Rights and the UN Committee on the Rights of the Child and the avoidance of reconciliation of each other's different approach in relation to corporal punishment does not serve the interests of either family law or justice.

T and V v United Kingdom (1998)

The increasing rate of adoption by international human rights law of family principles to criminal cases concerning children is exemplified in the decision by the European Commission of Human Rights in the cases of *T and V v United Kingdom* and its approach to trial and fact-finding procedures.[5] The case concerned the trial and punishment of T and V who were convicted of the murder of another young child, James Bulger.

---

[3]   Para. 22.

[4]   Initial Report of the United Kingdom UN Doc CRC/C/15 Add 34 para.16.

[5]   Report of the European Commission of Human Rights adopted December 4, 1998. This report focuses on the trial procedures but the applicants also brought complaints under Articles 3, 6 and 14, 5(1) and 5(4).

Although the bipartite procedures in Strasbourg of the European Commission and Court of Human Rights have been merged with the creation of one full-time Court, cases already lodged with the Commission will continue to be heard first by them.

The Commission considered the nature of the public trial and the modifications which were taken. The applicants were provided with defence counsel and the assistance of social workers; the court sittings were shortened and, whilst the Commission recognised that these were 'not inconsiderable safeguards', the Commission did not find the necessity of public trial for eleven-year-old children in an adult court to be in the interests of justice.[6] The Commission found that the children were unable to give evidence. Although there is a right to silence the Commission decided to apply family law principles, and arguably Articles 12 and 13 of the UN Convention on the Rights of the Child, and found that where an alleged offender is a child the trial procedures must be 'conducive to active participation as opposed to passive presence'.[7] This far reaching approach arguably applies to all family proceedings concerning children within the Council of Europe regardless of whether States are party to the newer European Convention on the Exercise of Children's Rights. The Commission by a majority of 14 to 5 therefore found a violation of Article 6 in relation to the trial.

The parents of James Bulger, quite correctly, have been granted the right to lodge an amicus curiae brief when the case is heard before the European Court of Human Rights.

III SECURITY FORCES AND FAMILY LIFE

Selcuk and Asker v Turkey

In *Selcuk and Asker v Turkey*[8] the applicants lived in one of the ten Turkish provinces which have been subject to emergency rule since 1987. They complained that their homes had been burnt down by the security forces and that they had been forced to leave their village.[9]

Turkey raised a preliminary objection as the applicants had not exhausted domestic remedies in accordance with the Convention. The European Court of Human Rights, however, observed that it was understandable that the applicants had felt that, in this particular case, it was pointless for them to pursue national legal remedies and there existed special circumstances which cancelled the obligation upon the applicants first to exhaust such remedies.

The Court also found that it was established that the security forces intentionally destroyed the applicants' homes and domestic property and forced them to leave their village. In addition to giving rise to violations of Article 3, these acts constituted particularly grave and unjustified interferences with the applicants' right to respect for family and private lives and homes and to their right to peaceful possession of property.[10]

---

6   Para. 104.
7   Para. 105.
8   26 EHRR 1998, 477.
9   The applicants relied upon Articles 3, 5, 6, 8, 13, 14, and 18 of the Convention and upon Article 1 of Protocol 1.
10 Hence, inter alia, the Court found a violation of Article 8 and Article 1, Protocol 1.

IV   INTERNATIONAL LAW AND THE FAMILY – A FOCUS ON COMPETING INTERESTS

A   Medical treatment

The question of consent to medical treatment has been one issue which has highlighted the competing interests of family members. The issue of consent for children is significant because it is the key to accessing health care and the question remains at what point is a child considered to have sufficient legal capacity under international law to consent to treatment.[11] Thus, whilst very young children may require their parents, guardians or other parties standing in this capacity to make that judgement, older children may find themselves in a different position. A basic presumption is that, in order to give consent, children have the right to be informed of their medical condition.

With conditions like HIV/AIDS, there are a number of problems which are posed which affect different members of the family. The prevalence of mother-to-child (vertical) transmission of HIV/AIDS has raised questions about medical decisions which affect individual members of the family in differing ways. UNICEF have long advocated breast-feeding as the best means of ensuring the nutritional health of new-born babies. However, UNAIDS have accepted that this is a major cause of transmission of HIV where the mother is HIV positive. The use of antiretroviral drug therapy, if used pre-natally and post-natally, can reduce the likelihood of transmission. However, the long term effects on babies and young children is not known.

The United Nations Programme on HIV/AIDS recognises that testing for HIV/AIDS should be voluntary and 'done with the informed consent of the person involved … if children's parents or guardians are involved, they should pay due regard to the child's views if the child is of an age or maturity to have such views'.[12] This must be viewed in the context of giving due regard to children's rights to confidentiality and privacy in regard to their HIV status. However, children are sometimes prevented by their parents or guardians from receiving information about their HIV status, even when the children have undergone testing, and are therefore not placed in a position to give their informed consent to treatment[13] or to take active steps concerning their treatment.

Access to healthcare and consent to treatment are major issues in determining the effectiveness of Articles 5, 12(1) and 24 of the Convention on the Rights of the Child which deal with the evolving capacities of the child, freedom of expression and the right to health including the right to access appropriate health care. The right of children to seek medical treatment or advice without parental consent will be the subject of forthcoming discussions by the Committee on the Rights of the Child to assess the impact of the Convention on the Rights of the Child.[14]

Children are not the only persons who may require consent from other family members for medical treatment. The question of women having to seek their partner's consent for family planning and sterilisation techniques is an issue which has concerned the Committee on the Elimination of Discrimination against Women. The Committee has recently expressed its concern in recent concluding observations on the need for women to obtain spousal consent in order to undergo tubal ligation. It declared such practices

---

[11]   G. Van Bueren, *International Law on the Rights of the Child*, Kluwer.
[12]   UNAIDS Briefing Paper on HIV/AIDS: *Children and HIV/AIDS*, February 1999.
[13]   European Forum on HIV/AIDS Children and Families: *HIV, AIDS and Schooling Briefing*, Winter 1998.
[14]   Committee on the Rights of the Child: Notes on the twenty-first session.

'unacceptable'[15] and similar concerns were expressed where wives required the consent of their husbands to obtain sterilisations or abortions even when their health was in danger.[16]

This aspect has been highlighted in the most recent General Comment issued by the Committee on the Elimination of Discrimination. General Comment No. 24[17] on Article 12[18] of the Convention on the Elimination of Discrimination against Women recognises that women's health issues are of central importance to the family as a whole but accepts that competing interests within family structures may create an imbalance of power such that it affects the ways in which women can access health care. The General Comment states that in interpreting Article 12 of the Convention there should be 'no restrictions on the ground that women do not have the authority of husbands, partners, parents or health authorities.'

By including parents and health authorities, the Committee has sought to maximise access to healthcare and consent to treatment for women who may otherwise have been excluded.

B   Child labour – a family matter

The eradication of child labour has often been seen as requiring sanctions, boycotts and legislation. This ignores the complex issues surrounding child labour including the role of the family in determining the extent of child labour. For example, a significant finding of recent research is that the composition of the family has a major impact on the incidence of child labour.[19] Thus, where there was a greater proportion of adult females, there was a reduction in the hours worked by both boys and girls. Where there was a greater proportion of adult males in the household, there was a significant reduction in the hours worked by boys only. The main theme underlying this is that if child labour is a consequence of meeting the survival needs of the family then any interventions must take into account the role the family plays in the decision-making process. Whilst not all aspects of child labour are driven by family poverty, families are an important component in determining the nature of the intervention.

Whilst sanctions and boycotts like those proposed by US Senator Harkin may protect jobs in developed countries and attract attention to the more formal sectors of work, they are unlikely to enhance child welfare and can result in harming children and their families, particularly if the reason for child labour is to meet the survival needs of the family. Thus, trade sanctions are likely to drive children into lower wage occupations and can have the effect of impoverishing families. Sanctions also fail to take into account that a significant number of children work for their families in family enterprises or in agricultural work. The International Labour Organisation (ILO) believes that the largest proportion of child workers is in economic activities and occupations related to agriculture. It estimates that the average proportion is 70 to 74 per cent but can go as high

---

[15]   State Report.

[16]   UN Doc A53/38/Rev.1 .

[17]   General Recommendation No. 24 of February 2, 1999 UN Doc, 'On Article 12 – Women and Health'.

[18]   Article 12 of CEDAW deals with women's right to health without discrimination.

[19]   S. Bhalotra, 'Is Child Work Necessary?', 1999, Department of Economics, University of Bristol (unpublished).

as 90 to 95 per cent in some countries[20] with many working in family agricultural concerns.[21]

If the income from child labour is necessary for family subsistence, policy measures need to be devised which reduce child work but do not increase family poverty.[22] Thus a balancing act is necessary if child labour is to be eradicated and the new ILO Convention on the Immediate Abolition of the Worst Forms of Child Labour 1999 (which was agreed in July 1999 but has yet to be ratified) seeks to have a more holistic approach to the eradication of child labour. It acknowledges that the eradication of child labour is a lengthy process but one in which priority action such as an immediate stop to the worst forms of child labour is possible. It recognises that simply taking children out of such forms of work without providing them with alternatives is equally intolerable and that children will have to undergo a form of reintegration if the process is to be successful. For the first time it acknowledges, at an international legislative level, the crucial role that the family plays both in preventing child labour and in reintegrating children who have been employed in the worst forms of child labour.

The main thrust of the Convention is to identify the worst forms of child labour, namely slavery or debt bondage, the sexual exploitation of children in prostitution or pornography and engaging in dangerous or hazardous work.[23] Article 7 of the Convention provides for States to take time-bound measures to prevent children from engaging in the worst forms of child labour and to provide the necessary means of taking children out of such work and providing them with alternatives such as education. If child work is to be truly eradicated then policies (like access to opportunities for saving and access to credit for families) which would alleviate the transitional nature of poverty, together with interventions which improve the quality of life for children and their families, should form part of those time-bound measures.[24]

The Convention provides for each State to draw up a Plan of Action which should aim at the rehabilitation and social integration of children taken out of hazardous employment through measures which address their educational, physical, emotional and psychological needs. This envisages involving the families of such children in this process. Further paragraph 2(e) specifically requires the Plan of Action to inform, sensitise and mobilise public opinion and concerned groups, including children and their families. The role of the family in this process is vital.

C   The elderly

The increasing concern for the protection of the elderly under international law has been previously referred to in this Survey.[25] The United Nations Population Fund has confirmed that 'a gradual ageing of the global population in the decades to come is all but certain'.[26] This has far reaching consequences for States who are facing the task of adapting their policies to take into account an ageing population. Specifically, the

---

[20]   ILO: *Facts and Figures on child labour*, 1999.

[21]   ILO 1999 *Targeting the intolerable: A new international convention to eliminate the worst forms of child labour.*

[22]   See note 19.

[23]   Article 3, ILO Convention on the Immediate Abolition of the Worst Forms of Child Labour 1999.

[24]   See note 19.

[25]   See A. Bainham, *The International Survey of Family Law 1995*, Annual Review of International Family Law.

[26]   United Nations Population Fund: *The State of the World Population* (1999) at 22.

protection of ageing individuals within the family and the support and assistance required by the family to respond to the needs of members, will be of importance as States respond to challenges in providing support and medical care including assistance to keep the elderly at home or at institutions.

An additional factor is that women are likely to outnumber men in an ageing population and, as many women would have spent part or all of their lives caring for their families (which is unremunerated) and with constraints on engaging in remunerated work because of their family responsibilities, the consequence of elderly women suffering poverty is very real.

Recent case law has indicated that, as the population grows older, the nature of the support offered by States and the composition of family units may well be of significance. Whilst the Human Rights Committee recommended in General Comment No. 6[27] that there be no discrimination against the elderly, the question of discrimination between groups of elderly people may also be relevant at an international level.

The case of *J. Snijders and others v The Netherlands*[28] brought before the Human Rights Committee under Article 26 of the International Covenant on Civil and Political Rights concerned alleged discrimination suffered by single people in relation to contributions made towards their long term medical care in institutions. The contributions made by married or cohabiting couples were significantly less. The single people had to pay income related contributions towards the cost of hospitalisation whereas married or cohabiting persons where one partner was not hospitalised only had to pay a minimal non-income related contribution. The contributions therefore appeared to relate to marital status.

The State argued that such a distinction was reasonable as married or cohabiting people leave behind a partner who continues to live in their common household and therefore does not save the same amount of money as does a single person in residential care. This is based on the notion that when a person is taken into care, there is a saving in household expenses. The State argued that a single person was likely to remain in residential care, must be deemed incapable of maintaining a household and therefore would be saving the expenses of maintaining such a household. The same would apply if both parties to a marriage (or cohabitants) were also in residential care although their joint contribution would not exceed that of a single person. In relation to married or cohabiting couples, where only one of the partners is in care, the saving is minimal, mainly food and care and is a lower amount than a single person in residential care.

The Committee concluded that whilst contributions should be calculated objectively, the distinction in levels of contribution was objective and reasonable and did not amount to discrimination given that there was a factual difference in the level of savings.

The Committee also concluded that as the complainants had not actually been levied the full single person contribution, (they had been asked for a lesser sum), they failed to show that they were victims of a violation under Article 26.

The Committee failed to consider whether in so doing, single people were in effect denied the right and the choice of keeping an independent household which was not the case for married or cohabiting couples. The Committee also failed to give due consideration to the argument that even where both partners may be taken into care, the chances of married or cohabiting couples being able to return to their households was

---

[27] Committee on Economic and Social and Cultural Rights General Comment No. 6 UN Doc. E/C.12/1995/16/Rev.1 (1995).

[28] *J. Snijders, A.A. Willemen and Ch.C.M. Van der Wouw v The Netherlands* – Communication No. 651/1995, UN Doc CCPR/C/63/D/651/1995 (27 July 1998).

greater as their contribution was the same as that of single persons and they could therefore afford to maintain their homes even whilst both were in residential care, an option not open to single persons.

In reaching this decision the Committee did not address the recommendations of the Committee on Economic Social and Cultural Rights[29] which included encouragement and support for the elderly who wished to live at home. A clear distinction was being drawn here on the basis of marital status but ostensibly based on the question of costs.

The other significant development in this case is that the question of contributions relating to long term health care could be strictly construed as falling within the ambit of the International Covenant on Economic Social and Cultural Rights. This instrument does not have a mechanism for individual rights of petition. Therefore by bringing the case as one of discrimination under Article 26 of the International Covenant on Civil and Political Rights it has theoretically paved the way for other issues relating to family life to be scrutinised by the Human Rights Committee on the grounds of discrimination even though the normative right arises under the former Convention.

V   NEW AREAS FOR INTERNATIONAL FAMILY LAW

It is undoubtedly the case that the pandemic of HIV/AIDS will raise crucial and complex issues in relation to international family law as it affects the complete structure of family life.

Whilst the common theme has been to view the elderly as recipients of care, whether in a family or institutional context, increasingly they are also becoming the primary care givers for their families as many elderly people are left to care for their grandchildren who are orphaned as a result of HIV/AIDS. Moreover, in developing countries, the prohibitive cost of caring for people diagnosed with HIV/AIDS means that families are now the focus of care and reintegration programmes. According to Naomi Honigsbaum of the European Forum on HIV/AIDS, Children and Families, 'family systems in developing countries and in many European countries are coming under pressure because of changing social structures and demography'.[30] Children orphaned by AIDS are also at risk of losing their property rights and the rights to inheritance.[31] It is also likely to have an important influence on issues such as guardianship, adoption, fostering, and the right to access medical treatment. The Committee on the Rights of the Child has recognised that HIV/AIDS is an issue which many countries have yet to grapple with and its effect on families is and will continue to be profound.

---

[29]   See note 27.
[30]   See note 12 above.
[31]   Ibid.

ARGENTINA

THE 'OVERRIDING INTEREST OF THE CHILD' IN LEGISLATIVE POLICY AND IN JUDICIAL DECISIONS IN ARGENTINA

Cecilia P. Grosman and *Delia Iñigo*

Cecilia P. Grosman[*] and Delia Iñigo[**]

I   INTRODUCTION

In recent years there has been a manifest concern in Argentina to bring our legislation into line with the International Convention on the Rights of the Child which our country approved in 1990. We see this at two levels: at that of legislation, in laws passed and proposed with the aim of conforming to that Treaty; and, in the courts, in judicial interpretation to that end.

II   LAWS AND PROPOSED LAWS

A   *The comprehensive protection of the child*

Various laws recently enacted in different parts of the country have been directed at providing comprehensive protection for the rights of the child or adolescent, taking account of the principles of the International Convention on the Rights of the Child. It is worth noting that these laws, formulating and applying public policy in relation to putting into effect the rights of childhood, were given priority in the allocation of available public resources. It has to be remembered that the 'overriding interest of the child' must be a paramount responsibility of the State when it is a question of working out priorities between public policies.

We may cite as an example the law of the child and adolescent of Mendoza Province and the new law for the comprehensive protection of the rights of the child and adolescent, enacted by the autonomous city of Buenos Aires on December 3, 1998. This last enactment defines the standard of the 'overriding interest of the child' in terms of the set of rights children are considered to possess (Article 2). It indicates that the family, society and the government are responsible for making these effective with absolute priority.

While maintaining that the social policy of the State must give protection and support to the family unit at all levels, it is emphasised that the absence or inadequacy of material resources on the part of father, mother or carer cannot be a ground for removing a child from the family group. Likewise, as an ideological position, the exclusion of poverty as a judicial consideration is established. This means that when the rights of the child are endangered or violated as a result of a lack of economic resources, of a job or of a home,

---

[*]   Titular Consultant Professor of Family Law and Succession, Faculty of Law, University of Buenos Aires.

[**]   Professor of Family Law in the Faculty of Legal and Social Sciences of the Universidad Nacional del Litoral, Argentina.

Translated by Peter Schofield.

rather than take the child out of the family, steps should be taken by way of social programmes to strengthen the family, giving advice and assistance, including economic support. In view of the needs presented by alternative family structures, these rights are directed at parents and other community members, while always taking account of the wishes and feelings of the child or adolescent. A child may only be taken into care as an exception, and for a limited period, during which measures are to be taken to facilitate his return to his family and community (Articles 42, 43 and 44). Along the same lines, a project is being debated in the National Congress to create a Regime for the Comprehensive Protection of the Rights of the Child and Adolescent applying to the entire country.

B   *Establishing the office of Defender of the rights of the child and adolescent*

The National Chamber of Deputies has approved a project, now being considered in the Senate, to create the office of Defender of the rights of the child and adolescent to take responsibility for protecting and furthering the rights of the child as laid down in the National Constitution, in the Convention on the Rights of the Child and Adolescent and in international treaties. Among the functions of the Defender, we mention:

(a) to investigate anything done or omitted by the Public Administration or by non-governmental organisations that threatens, disregards or violates the overriding interests of children;

(b) to promote and protect children's rights by means of action and by recommendations made to the competent public authorities, and to propose law reform and other necessary measures to bring the legislation into line with the Convention on the Rights of the Child and other international norms;

(c) to supervise public and private institutions concerned with children and adolescents, and to bring any irregularities to the notice of the authorities; and

(d) to make known the situation and the requirements of children in various ways and to receive complaints made by children and others, which are to be promptly investigated on receipt of the request.

C   *Child abuse*

Since 1995 a law of protection against family violence has been in force in Buenos Aires city. It enables anyone who has suffered physical or psychological abuse at the hands of another member of his or her family to lay a complaint before the family court about the matter. The judge, on proof of the risk, is to take the necessary protective steps and arrange a hearing, at which he will instruct the parties to attend educative or therapeutic programmes based on diagnosis of the family situation (Law 24.4170). This law, on which we have commented more extensively elsewhere, has made the problem far more visible, as there has been a notable increase in the number of complaints. Laws passed in other provinces have followed the same lines. Some of these apply sanctions to the perpetrator if he refuses to take part in the treatment programme or drops out from it. These include warnings, fines, community service orders, informing the perpetrator's professional or trade union organisation of the facts (Santa Cruz and Rio Negro Provinces).

As is well known, one essential element in ensuring that rights are effective is to make the citizens, adults, young persons, adolescents or children in whose favour they have been created aware that they can claim and defend them. Various legislative initiatives have sought to do this in relation to child abuse. Thus a law of Prevention of Abuse of Children and Adolescents and of Family Violence has been enacted (Law 25.072), which provides for an official campaign of information and prevention of abuse consisting of the transmission of short broadcast announcements ten times a day with particular frequency at times of maximum audiences. The announcements concentrate on giving information about the ways and procedures for making complaints about abuse. The Senate has approved a Project for a law, currently being considered in the Chamber of Deputies, which will compel all bodies dependent on the public administration to display copies of the International Convention on the Rights of the Child. The obligation will cover particularly public and private educational establishments, juvenile courts, police stations, public and private hospitals and the nation's children's homes. Provision is made for court orders, and for fines to be imposed on institutions that fail to comply, as well as for sanctions on their directors.

III   IN THE COURTS

Here, we shall focus on the interpretation which our courts have placed on the criterion of the 'overriding interest of the child' laid down in Article 3 of the International Convention on the Rights of the Child. The place of this in the hierarchy of norms is assured by the Constitution (Article 75, inc. 22).

The meaning and contents of the notion are being developed in judicial decisions based on the particular facts of the cases that come to court. Over time, rules of construction evolve, defining the import of the governing criterion in specific institutions of family law.

Also, the notion has often allowed gaps in the law to be filled. And it has shown its ability to derogate from the old rules, when these could be detrimental to the needs and to the welfare of the child. To exemplify the creative power of the notion of the 'overriding interest', we examine a number of judgments in various aspects of family law.

A   Adoption

Several judgments relating to adoption have set aside legal demands and prohibitions where these, in the instant case, would have run counter to the interests of the child. That is to say the consideration of the welfare of the child was given precedence over the requirements of the legal rule.

As an example of this we could take the so-called integrative adoption. This is where the adopter is the spouse of, or cohabits with, the genetic parent. Judges have, in the interest of the child, allowed the adoption even where the applicant did not meet the legal criteria in respect of age, or of the difference in age between adopter and person adopted. Thus, the benefit to the child which could result from the adoption was considered to justify putting aside the express terms of the law, because the intention was to integrate the child into the new family.[1]

---

[1]   See, inter alia, CNCiv., Sala J, F.JO94546, 8/5/95; C.Apelaciones del Uuguy, Sala Civ. y Com., 9/9/98, *Jurisprudencia Argentina*, July 7, 1999.

Likewise, in another case, despite the rule prohibiting the adoption of a grandchild by a grandparent, adoption was approved, because it was considered that refusal based on the legal rule would be detrimental to the child.[2]

Also, treating the benefit to the child as paramount has made it possible for courts to overcome the prejudices and doubts that the personality or particular problems of a petitioner can often arouse. So, in one case, a court was willing to overlook the fact that a woman who wished to adopt had used drugs, she having by then got over the problem. It was held that she was able to care for the child, and that to refuse her application on the ground that she had used drugs at one period in her life would be 'tantamount to refusing to let her rehabilitate herself, subjecting her for the rest of her life to a reservation that, on medical evidence, she has now overcome'.[3] In essence, the court held that there was a firm and sufficient emotional bond, the child's psychological and physical development was good, as was the socio-economic situation and the acceptance by the family was positive. On the other hand, it was judged that it would be detrimental to remove the child from his current family environment. This was likely to revive the sense of rejection already experienced when his biological mother had abandoned him.

Judges carry with them the baggage of the different values and beliefs they derive from their personal history, experience and social situation. In other words, their judgment does not represent absolute reality as an objective and external phenomenon. They construe reality in line with their own perception.[4] The ideological differences and divergent perceptions can be seen in the way they interpret the principle of 'the overriding interest of the child', influencing the criteria they apply to decide what is good for the child. In relation to adoption, it has been held that the interest of the child takes precedence over the wishes of the adults involved – of the biological parents and the would-be adopters.[5] However, while some judges emphasise the benefit to the child of staying close to his family of origin and only approve an adoption when all measures to keep the child in this family have been exhausted,[6] others give no priority to this consideration. Their view is that, according to the circumstances, it is for the judge to define the way in which the 'overriding interest of the child' is best served. That is, they do not consider that precedence can be given on an 'a priori' basis either to the blood family or to those who want to adopt. We can see these divergent perceptions in a single judgment. The child's mother, a minor, and the grandmother had consented, by notarial act, to adoption of the child by a married couple. A few days after signing, the child's mother, represented by her own mother and assisted by the Official Defender, applied for the act to be annulled and to have the child returned. The child's father, who had married the mother and recognised the child, joined in this demand. The Civil Appeals Chamber of the Province of San Juan (bear in mind Argentina is a federal state in which each of the provinces has its own court system) ordered the return of the child to the birth family, which was to receive psychological and educational support. But a higher court overturned that decision, deciding that the child should stay with the would-be adopters. Among other considerations, the first judges held that the child's personality would be able better to develop in the context of the biological family. The others, on the contrary, thought the 'interest of the child' lay in preserving the status quo – staying with the

---

2   CCiv. y Com. Santa Fé, Sala 3a., 21/12/95, JA, 27/3/96.
3   CNCiv., Sala F, September 10, 1998.
4   Cecilia P. Grosman, 'El interés superior del niño', in *Los Derechos del niño en la familia. Discurso y realidad*, Editorial Universidad, Buenos Aires, 1998, p. 23.
5   CNCiv., Sala L, 13/10/94, La Ley, 1995-D-421.
6   CNCiv., Sala L, 10/3/93, La Ley, 1993-C-407.

family that had cared for the child from birth – since returning the child could cause psychological harm. Consequently, the order that the child be returned to the biological parents was reversed by the higher court, which declared it unconstitutional for arbitrariness, on the ground that account had not been taken of the child's 'overriding interest'.[7]

B   The exercise of parental authority

In the same way, the ruling criterion of the 'overriding interest of the child' has enabled the judges to act creatively in a significant way in relation to the exercise of parental authority.[8] Our courts have ruled that the notion of the 'overriding interest of the child', laid down in Articles 3.1 and 9.1 of the Convention on the Rights of the Child, must be given precedence over other rights given to the parents and to the family when the judges are dealing with disputes about the upbringing of minors. Equally, they have maintained that '"the overriding interest of the child" is also an interest of society and governs the entire field of the care of children, whether on a temporary or a permanent basis, just as is the proper exercise of patria potestas, as this represents the right of the child to a proper physical, psychological and spiritual upbringing'.[9]

Thus it was decided that, on the death of a parent, the exercise of this function did not automatically pass to the other, unless this was what for the benefit of the child. It was held in one case that the court has power to restrain patria potestas if its uncontrolled exercise would be detrimental to the child.[10] Likewise, in the name of the overriding interest, the right of children to communicate with third parties has been extended, despite parental opposition.[11]

As is well known, the increasing instability of the conjugal pair has given rise to the principle of co-parenthood as a way of ensuring that the rearing and education of children remains the responsibility of both parents, even if their relationship fails. Opinion is that ensuring the involvement of both parents is the most conducive to the best interests of the child's care and upbringing. A number of decisions in our courts affirm this principle. In this way, one ruling held that 'the person most suitable to be with the children is the one who reduces the level of conflict in the family and who best facilitates communication with the other parent'.[12] In another, it was said that a parent who hinders contact with the other violates the right of the child to full and harmonious personal development, since a child needs to have contact with both parents. Consequently, it was held that where one parent encouraged the children to reject the other, custody should be given to the parent who best guaranteed that the children kept in contact with both parents.[13]

In our legislation, on divorce or separation the exercise of parental authority (patria potestas) goes to the parent with care of the children, usually the mother. The other parent has the right to communicate with the child and to supervise his education (Article 264

---

[7]   CJ. San Juan, Sala I, 1/4/98, La Ley, T.1998-F-64.

[8]   In fact, in our country, this is still referred to as 'patria potestas', an expression that ill describes the content of that institution under our current laws. It is now no longer a 'power', but rather a 'function' of both parents.

[9]   ST Tierra del Fuego, Antarctic and South Atlantic Islands, October 8, 1998, B.,S.B. c/T., M.H., La Ley, 1998-F-571.

[10]   Cciv. y Com. San Nicolas, 5/7/94, *Jurisprudencia Argentina*, 6/9/65.

[11]   CNCiv. Sala F, 18/5/93, La Ley, 1994-B-240.

[12]   CNCiv. Sala L, 12/9/91, La Ley, 1991-E-503.

[13]   CNCiv. Sala F. 22/9/98.

inc.2). On this point, the courts have held that, despite the legal rule, parents can agree to the exercise of patria potestas by both of them, even if one alone has custody.[14]

There is also a change in the evaluation of parental agreements whereby custody is shared or alternates, that is to say the child stays at one time with the mother and at another with the father. Formerly such agreements were frowned on and even rejected, but now our judges are more ready to approve them. In a recent case, on the basis of the 'overriding interest of the child', it was held that parents have the right to enter into such agreements, by which they seek to share more or less equally in the care and responsibility for the education of their children, with the aim of following as closely as possible the model of the intact family. What is more, it was the court itself, seeing the conflict between the parents, that decided to 'grant to both the shared care of the child, who would spend alternate periods with each, during which the other should enjoy generous visitation rights'.[15] In the judgment, it was held that the proposed model would assist and encourage dialogue between the parents, increasing the exchange of information about the child. The judgment also pointed out that 'both would have the right to talk to the schoolmistress, take the child to the psychologist, help with homework, take him to sports training ... etc'. Both parents, the judgment continues, 'must set aside selfish attitudes and remember that the child cannot do without either father or mother'.[16]

We should note that a project was presented in the Chamber of Deputies which would amend the law so that, on separation de facto, judicial separation, divorce or nullity, father and mother would together exercise patria potestas (Article 3). Also, by another rule, the judge would be empowered, either of his own motion or on the application of either party, to give shared custody to both parents, always taking into account the overriding interest of the child and the maintaining of a regular and balanced relation with both parents (Article 1).

Under the doctrine of the overriding interest of the child, where the parent with care of children, generally the mother, has resisted the father's access to the children, courts have ordered family therapy, under an order whereby failure to comply becomes a ground for changing the custody. Such intervention is accepted as a way of protecting the welfare of children, notwithstanding the restriction it imposes on the autonomy of the individual. The State, it is affirmed, 'must ensure the psycho-social health of the children and remove the obstacles which impede their normal bonding with all other family members'.[17] Of course, there is no question of forced treatment, or of physical compulsion, since the parties must, in the end, consent. The parents are offered merely a way out of the family conflict.

Deserving of attention is a judgment in which it was held to be 'an absolute obligation of both parents to resume the psychotherapeutic treatment that the minor needs in accordance with professional advice'. Hence, the court ordered them to fulfil this duty for the protection of the interest of the child, who had a 'right to develop his personality, aptitudes and mental and physical capacities as far as possible and to have a satisfactory life, free from pathological tensions'. According to the judgment, lack of resources was

---

[14]   (13)CNCiv. Sala F. 22/9/98.
[15]   (13)CNCiv. Sala F. 22/9/98.
[16]   (13)CNCiv. Sala F. 22/9/98.
[17]   CNCiv. Sala E, 31/5/88, La Ley, 1990-A-70.

not an excuse as there were public institutions which would, at reduced cost, provide suitable therapy for family conflict.[18]

C   *A voice for the child in judicial proceedings*

Formerly, hearing what the child wanted to say in a case affecting his person was only a possibility depending on the decision of the judge. That is to say the judge could, at his discretion, give the child a hearing. Now, the status of the Convention on the Rights of the Child, Article 12, in the constitutional hierarchy imposes on judges a duty to hear a child who is capable of forming his own opinion and of expressing it freely. So, it has been judicially stated that the intervention of the child in legal proceedings is a right that must be respected. This does not mean, the judgment states, that this is just an additional part of the process, but rather 'it is a matter of giving it its own place, and, when reaching a decision, taking his point of view and opinion into account as a criterion of evaluation'; however, the judgment goes on, the decisive criterion – 'the best interests of the child' – will not always coincide with his wishes.[19] So the opinion of the child is not of itself decisive and it is still up to the judge to adjudicate on the matters in issue. Thus the case makes clear that 'even if the opinion of the minor does not have binding force in determining which parent shall have care, it must still be given due weight when he is twelve years old and has expressed himself freely.'[20] On similar lines, it is decided that 'the opinion and wishes of an adolescent minor must be listened to, for therein lies the exercise of his right to justice'.[21]

In other words, his opinion must be given due weight along with the other elements of the case.[22] That is to say, in accordance with the judicial guidelines, the child ceases to be a mere object of the court's decision, and becomes a person whose interests must be considered. Thus, the hearing allows the needs of the one most directly affected by the court's decision to be more effectively assessed.[23]

As can be seen, there is no precise rule as to the exact age from which minors have to be given a hearing, however a review of the cases indicates that they can be heard from the age of 14 years, the onset of adolescence, when it is thought they can act with discernment, intention and freedom. Nonetheless, sometimes it is envisaged that they can be heard at an even younger age, 'in cases where minors are able to give reasoned opinions in relation to the issues which involve them in the forensic contest'.[24]

D   *Maintenance payment*

In relation to maintenance, we refer to a judgment which held that an interim order for support should be made, pending the judgment in affiliation proceedings, if a prima facie

---

18   CNCiv. Sala A, 7/10/97, La Ley, December 14, 1998.
19   CNCiv. Sala A, 7/10/97, La Ley, December 14, 1998.
20   CNCiv. Sala E, November 7, 1995, La Ley, 1997-E-690.
21   CCiv. y Com. San Isidro, Sala I, October 15, 1996 B., S.E. c/ C., R.T., La Ley, Buenos Aires 1997-229.
22   CNCiv. Sala H, 20/10/97, La Ley, t. 1998-D-261.
23   CNCiv. Sala I, 20/10/98, El Derecho, February 8, 1999.
24   (24)CCiv. y Com. Morón, Sala II, October 23, 1997, B. De T., M. c/ T.D., La Ley, Buenos Aires 1998-243.

case had been made out, based on DNA tests, establishing the likelihood of the respondent's paternity.[25]

One problem seriously affecting children's rights is the behaviour of divorced fathers who fail to meet their support obligations, and often take no further interest in the child. Various legislative proposals have been made to deal with this by improving execution and collection proceedings, and by giving publicity to the failure to pay. The National Senate has approved a law, now before the Chamber of Deputies, which would set up a National Register of 'Morosos' (people in arrears) with their maintenance obligations. Persons failing to meet an interim order would be placed on the register. The taking up of a new contract of employment, or starting a new self-employed activity would have to be notified to the register. Likewise escribanos (public writers) will have to check whether the grantor is on the register and, if so, to inform the judge forthwith of the transaction which is about to be recorded before drawing up a public document formalising a disposition or creation of rights of property (derechos reales). The judge will thereupon take steps to give proper protection to the rights of the maintenance creditor.

Another frequent question before the courts is the petition of the mother, to whom custody is usually given, to have the absent parent's visitation rights suspended, when he fails to meet his support obligation. Judges normally refuse to grant this request, regarding contact with the father as the child's right not to be used as a sanction against a non-payer. This would, in effect, only further disadvantage the child and reinforce abandonment by the parent. That is why it was held: 'Visitation rights belong to the minor, so their suspension or denial based on maintenance arrears amounts to a violation of the rights of children and a failure to take account of their interests, whereas they are not responsible for the father's conduct. To interrupt any regime of visits in view of the conduct of a parent towards a child or children is a measure to be used sparingly, even though the right is not absolute, to the extent that the exercise of the right should only be blocked for reasons so serious as to pose a threat to the children's safety or to their physical or mental health.'[26]

E   The right to identity

The child's right to an identity, recognised in Articles 7.1 and 8.1 of the Convention on the Rights of the Child, has, let us emphasise it again, the status of a constitutional provision in Argentina and it has repeatedly come before the courts. This has given the courts various opportunities to protect that right. Thus, it has been held 'there is a social duty to guarantee the child's right to know his origins'.[27] It has also been held that 'the right to identity is a fundamental right with constitutional ranking, because it concerns personal dignity and, what is more, one's own identity is central to any notion of personal freedom'.[28]

To establish the child's true identity in affiliation cases it is necessary to have recourse to biological evidence, whereas the taking of blood is currently regarded as humiliating or degrading. On this, in a case where the issue was whether a minor had, at birth, been a victim of the suppression of his true identity by being handed over to a married couple who had adopted him, the National Supreme Court decided that 'the proof

---

[25]   CNCiv., Sala M, 30/6/97, *Jurisprudencia Argentina*, June 9, 1999.

[26]   CCiv. y Com., Sala I, San Isidro, 15 April 1997, R., G.R. c/ C., A.L., La Ley, Buenos Aires, 1997-1060.

[27]   Suprema Corte de Mendoza, Sala I, 29/8/96, La Ley 1996-B-546.

[28]   CNCiv., Sala H, October 4, 1996, T.M. c/ V.G.H., La Ley 1998-D-69.

of histocompatibility – when the identity of a minor is in issue – does not affect fundamental rights, such as life, health or the inviolability of the person, because the taking of a few cubic centimetres of blood, performed according to normal medical procedures, is an infinitessimal interference in comparison with the overriding interests of protecting the freedom of others, the defense of society and the prosecution of crime'.[29] For the protection of the child's right to know his origins, the court rejected the arguments of a putative father who refused to give blood for testing, on the grounds that he could not submit to this, as a Jehovah's Witness. The court said 'the rights of others, in this case, the rights of a child to know his origins, a fundamental right having constitutional ranking, impose limits on that of conscientious objection'.[30]

With a view to facilitating the implementation of the right to identity, Article 40 of Law No 23.511 lays down that, in court proceedings, refusal to submit to blood tests to examine DNA (deoxyribonucleic acid) or HLA (histocompatibility) to establish the existence or otherwise of a biological link between a child and the alleged father, should be admitted as evidence against the latter. The National Supreme Court of Justice held that 'when a minor's right to identity is in issue, to allow one accused of falsifying civil status to refuse to give blood for the purpose of medical immunogenetic tests for histocompatibility would amount to disregarding the requirements of the Convention on the Rights of the Child'.[31] Likewise, in another case, to establish a child's identity, the compulsory taking of blood was ordered on the argument that 'the judicial power extends to the enforced carrying out of blood testing, if the measure is proportional to the risk of harm, and it is performed by appropriate persons so as to avoid unnecessary harm to health'.[32]

In order to give effect to the child's right to identity in affiliation cases, the following direction has been given by the National Supreme Court of Justice: 'The Judicial Authority will pay in advance for histocompatibility (HLA) and immunogenetic (DNA) investigations which have to be carried out to reach a result in a case, when these are ordered by the court of its own motion or on the application of a party who sues with the benefit of litigation without payment.'[33]

F   The right to occupy the home

Our law forbids the selling or imposition of an encumbrance on immovable property in which a parent resides with minor or incapacitated children of whom s/he has had custody awarded, by reason of judicial separation or divorce, unless both spouses consent to it (Civil Code, Article 1277). This is, therefore, a law protecting the home of children of a marriage.

As we have explained elsewhere, there is in our country, no specific regulation for de facto couples (concubines). As a result of this, doctrinal writers discuss whether the above rule should be applied – by analogy – for the benefit and assistance of extramarital

---

[29]   Corte Suprema de Justicia de la Nación, Guarino Mirta Liliana, s/ querella, December 27, 1996, Fallos 319-3370.

[30]   CNCiv, Sala H, October 4, 1996, G., T.M. c/ V., G.H., La Ley 1998-D-69 cited above at note 13.

[31]   Corte Suprema de la Nación 'H.G.S. y otro', Fallos 318-2518; the various Provincial Superior Courts have expressed a similar view, including Corte Suprema de Justicia de Santa Fé, La Ley 1992-D-536, Supremo Tribunal de Entre Ríos, Sala Civ. y Com. April 29, 1994, C., M.M. y otra, *Jurisprudencia Argentina* 1995-III-311.

[32]   Juzgado Federal de San Carlos de Bariloche, Causa 1727/94, El Derecho 161-224.

[33]   Acordada No 23/92 of July 7, 1992.

children. In the most recent judgments, courts have made room for the claim to render the home inalienable, in case of de facto unions or cohabitation, on the ground that the rule is concerned with protecting the homes of children and that, for this, there should not be 'any discrimination by reason of their birth or their condition (Article 2, Convention on the Rights of the Child, Law 23.849; Articles 240 and 241, Civil Code)'.[34] In another decision, it is said 'bearing in mind that the status of extramarital children is equal to that of those conceived in wedlock, we see no reason why – faced with an identical situation arising from the breakdown of their parents' cohabitation – the one should enjoy a protection denied to the others'.[35] Both of these correctly interpret the legal text, which protects the interests of minors, regardless of the personal condition of their parents (Convention on the Rights of the Child, Article 2).

G   Compensation for psychological harm

While there is no express legal rule, judges have repeatedly allowed claims for psychological harm based on refusal to recognise paternity voluntarily. This is seen as an unlawful act which violates the child's right to know his origins and to enjoy his proper filial status. Such conduct on the part of a father, it has been held, causes damage to the child for which he is entitled to redress, without prejudice to other legal sanctions which may exist, including the declaration that the father is unworthy of succession rights to the child (Civil Code, Article 3296 bis). Thus it was held 'unjustified refusal to recognise a child causes psychological harm to the latter which must be made good. Parents have a series of duties and obligations to their children, and these have a set of rights, including that of personal identity, a surname, to know their identity, etc., failure to fulfil which gives rise to responsibility'.[36]

---

[34] CCiv. y Com. Primera, Sala III La Plata, February 4, 1997, Scalabrini Guillermo F. c/ Eschemberg Cristina s/ División de Condominio, *Revista del Colegio de Abogados de La Plata*, July 1997, p. 27.

[35] Juzgado de Primera Instancia Civ. y Com. No 2 de Zárate, Guzman L.R. c/ Rodriguez R.G s/ División de condominio, *Rev. Interdisciplinaria de Derecho de Familia*, No 15, Abeledo-Perrot, Buenos Aires.

[36] Suprema Corte de Justicia de la Provincia de Buenos Aires, April 28, 1998, P., M.D. c/ A., E. s/ filiación e indemnización por daños y perjuicios.

AUSTRALIA

'FAST FOLD THY CHILD'[1] – AUSTRALIAN FAMILY LAW IN 1998

Frank Bates[*]

Australian family law in 1998 has seen a number of cases, especially in relation to children, which will be of global interest. Some break new ground, another is something of a disappointment, whilst another confuses an already uncertain area.

I   A LEADING DECISION ON SURROGACY

There is, though, no doubt that the starting point for any discussion of Australian family law in 1998 is the decision of the Full Court of the Family Court of Australia in *Re Evelyn*.[2] This case, which is of central importance, involved an appeal against parenting orders concerning the child in question.[3] The appellants were the child's biological father and his wife, Mr and Mrs Q, who lived in the State of Queensland with their adopted son. The respondents were Mr and Mrs S, who lived in South Australia with their three children. Mrs S was the child's biological mother. The child was born in consequence of a surrogacy arrangement between the couples. It appeared that the couples had been close for many years and, in the latter part of 1995, Mrs S offered to assist Mr and Mrs Q by conceiving and bringing to full term a child fathered by Mr Q. Mrs Q was, owing to a total hysterectomy necessitated by ovarian cancer, infertile and the couple were aware of that fact prior to their marriage. The child was born in December 1995 and she and Mrs Q returned to Queensland.

However, by this time, tensions had developed between the two families; particularly, Mrs S found it difficult to cope with having to relinquish the child. In July 1997, she arrived at Mr and Mrs Q's house and, after a confrontation with Mr Q, took the child and returned to South Australia on the same day. After various convolutions,[4] the trial judge decided that the child should live with Mr and Mrs S, who should have responsibility for the day-to-day welfare and development. In addition, it was ordered that the child have specified contact with Mr and Mrs Q and that both couples share responsibility for her long-term care, welfare and development. The orders provided for a

---

*   LL.M., Professor of Law, University of Newcastle (NSW).
1   Gerard Manley Hopkins, *Poems* (No 60), 'The Blessed Virgin Compared to the Air We Breathe', line 124:

> 'World-mothering air, air wild
> Wound with thee, in these isled,
> Fold home, fast fold thy child.'

2   (1998) F.L.C. 92-807.
3   Referred to as 'Evelyn' for the sake of anonymity.
4   Proceedings were originally begun in South Australia but were then transferred to Queensland. There was a contested interim hearing there where the child was placed with Mr and Mrs Q pending application, which was dismissed. The hearing of the substantive matter was expedited as a preferred opinion to an appeal against the interim order, the Court's having regard to the nature of the issues involved and the age of the child.

timetable of contact leading to his orders coming into effect in February 1998. The trial judge relied on the evidence of five experts.[5] The parties also had support from expert testimony,[6] although there was no family report.[7]

At trial, the judge at first instance had commented that the various experts were in fundamental disagreement in their recommendations, but that many of those differences were differences of emphasis rather than incompatible differences of opinion. In reaching his conclusion, the trial judge emphasised, first, the long-term implications which any orders might have for the child, as contrasted with short-term implications. Second, the importance of the biological mother in respect of the child, particularly in relation to the child coping with her special situation and the risk of her having a sense of rejection. Third, a perception that, as a result of events in the case, Mr and Mrs Q would be less able to meet the needs of the child, especially taking into account the involvement of Mr and Mrs S. Finally, the relatively greater significance of losing an opportunity to be raised with biological siblings, in comparison with separation from Mr and Mrs S's adopted son.

The grounds of appeal essentially attacked the evidentiary aspects of the decision: thus, first, it was argued that, at the trial, the expert evidence was deficient; second, that the judge ought to have appointed a court expert; third, that the trial judge was in error, '… in that he ought to have found that Evelyn's interests were best served by placing greater weight on immediate realities in the short term, as opposed to future hypothetical issues in the longer term'. Fourth, that the trial judge had erred in his treatment of certain expert evidence.[8] In the event, the Full Court of the Family Court of Australia[9] dismissed the appeal. In doing so, the Court applied[10] their earlier decision in *Rice v Miller*,[11] to the effect, in their own words that, '… while the fact of parenthood is an important and significant factor in considering which of the proposals best advance a child's welfare, the fact of parenthood does not establish a presumption in favour of a natural parent nor generate a preferential position in favour of that parent from which the Court commences the decision making process'. In *Evelyn*, the Court noted that, even though it was concerned with the issue of surrogacy, that did not change the application of that general principle nor did it provide any presumption in favour of a biological mother where the child was female. Although it appeared that the trial judge had given the biological mother a preferential position, he had done so on the basis of the facts of the particular case and the expert evidence which had been presented to him.

The Court did, though, express[12] some doubt about the trial judge's conclusion that there were advantages to the child in growing up with her biological siblings rather than

---

[5]   In relation to such matters as, '… the circumstances surrounding Evelyn's birth, the parties involved in the arrangement and, most importantly, the implications of separation from adults and siblings for Evelyn, both in the short term and longer term'.

[6]   Mr and Mrs Q relied on the evidence of a clinical psychologist, a Professor of Psychiatry and a consultant psychiatrist. Mr and Mrs S were supported by a clinical psychologist and a consultant psychologist.

[7]   See *Family Law Act* 1975 section 62G.

[8]   There was also an application for leave to admit fresh evidence from a United States psychologist who had practised for some fifteen years in the area of surrogate parenting. That expert had been discovered through the Internet by a new firm of solicitors for the appellants who had been instructed for the purposes of the appeal. That application was refused.

[9]   Nicholson C J, Ellis and Lindenmayer JJ.

[10] (1998) F.L.C. 92-807 at 85, 106.

[11] (1993) F.L.C. 92-415. See also *Re Hodak; Newman; Hodak* (1993) F.L.C. 92-421. It is worthy of note that Lindenmayer J was involved in all three decisions.

[12] (1998) F.L.C. 92-807 at 85, 107.

with her adopted brother. However, they thought it was 'quite apparent' that that was merely another factor which he had thought supported the natural mother's case. But they considered that he would have reached the same conclusion, regardless of that finding.

It had also been argued, on behalf of Mr and Mrs S, that various statutory provisions, both in State and Commonwealth law, required a conclusion that a decision in their favour was inevitable. That proposition had been rejected and the trial judge's decision was squarely based on the notion, as it appears in the *Family Law Act*,[13] that the best interests of the child remained the paramount consideration.

In one sense, *Re Evelyn* breaks new ground in that it is the first reported appellate decision on the vexed topic of surrogacy. In another, the only mention of legal and social policy in respect of the issue occurs towards the end of the judgment[14] where attention was drawn to the part of the judgment at first instance, in which the trial judge had said that he was comforted in his decision by the law's public policy of discouraging surrogacy.[15]

II   PART VII AND THE PRINCIPLES OF CONTACT

Another rather disappointing decision of the Full Court is *Re C and D*,[16] which might have provided an opportunity for a discussion of the provisions of the new Part VII of the Act introduced in 1995. As in *Re Evelyn*, the Full Court[17] elected to deal with the matter, which of itself was not without interest, in very general terms. *C and D* involved an appeal from orders made at first instance in relation to a child. The child had been born in 1992 during the subsistence of the marriage of Mr and Mrs C and had been regarded as their child until their separation in 1995. Following that separation, paternity testing showed that the husband could not have been the father of the child and also established that D was the father. The husband made an application seeking orders that the husband and wife be joint guardians, that the wife have custody of the child and that the husband have substantial access: conversely, the wife sought orders granting her sole custody and guardianship and that the husband be refused access.[18]

The wife and D then began living together and were planning to marry when free to do so. Prior to the trial, the husband filed an amended application based on the 1995 amendments: he sought a residence order in respect of the child, or extensive and defined contact. At the trial, D was granted the right to intervene[19] and supported the orders sought by the mother. The child's representative[20] supported orders for extensive contact to the husband. The psychologist who prepared the family report[21] had originally concluded that contact with the husband ought to be phased out, although continued

---

[13]   *Family Law Act* 1975 section 67Z(2)).

[14]   (1998) F.L.C. 92-807 at 85, 107.

[15]   Surrogacy agreements are illegal in all Australian jurisdictions. However, the decision was not to be the end of the matter: in *Re Evelyn (No. 2)* (1998) F.L.C. 92-187, the issue of an appeal to the High Court of Australia was considered by a differently constituted Full Court (Baker, Finn and Chisholm JJ) as well as application for a continuance of a stay. In those proceedings Mr and Mrs Q were wholly unsuccessful.

[16]   (1998) F.L.C. 92-815.

[17]   Nicholson C J, Baker and Fogarty JJ.

[18]   These orders were sought prior to the 1995 amendments to the Act coming into force.

[19]   See *Family Law Act* 1975 section 92. This meant that he could be treated as a party to the proceedings.

[20]   See *Family Law Act* 1975 section 68L.

[21]   *Family Law Act* 1975 section 62G.

presently. In her later report and evidence, she was, however, of the view that contact should continue at the level which had been prescribed in earlier interim orders. Her conclusion was substantially based on the good relationship which apparently existed between the husband and the child.

The trial judge made three relevant orders: first, that the child should live with the wife and the intervener who should have daily responsibility for the welfare and development of the child. Second, that the child and the husband have contact on alternate weekends and one weekday evening per fortnight and for half of school holidays. Third, that, until further order, the wife be restrained from using the intervener's surname in respect of the child and also be restrained from discouraging the child from using the husband's surname.

The grounds of the appeal were essentially based around the weight which the trial judge had attached to various items of evidence, especially those concerned with the relationships between the child, the parties and the husband's family.[22] The appeal was unsuccessful, except in relation to the issue of the child's surname. As regards the matter of weight, Nicholson C J and Baker J were of the view[23] that issues as to weight of evidence and credibility of witnesses were within the province of the trial judge[24] and it was open to him to draw the conclusions which he had.

A further issue which had arisen in *C and D*, as in *Evelyn*, was the position of biological parents relative to others. Applying *Rice v Miller*[25] and *Re Evelyn*,[26] Nicholson C J and Baker J emphasised[27] that a biological parent did not stand in any preferred position and that fact does not, in any way, impinge on the principle that the best interests of the child were paramount.

On the general issue of contact, Fogarty J ultimately agreed with Nicholson C J but adopted a somewhat different approach: he was of the opinion[28] that there was some substance in the submissions made on behalf of the wife that confusion could result from the contact ordered by the trial judge because it was too expansive, especially given the dispute as to which male party had the proper paternal relationship with the child. This was exacerbated by the attitude of the husband and his family and, especially, as the husband had not always made himself available for contact periods. However, he was of the view[29] that the initial orders ought not to be disturbed because of, in his own words, 'the tyranny of time'; in other words, given the length of time which had elapsed[30] between the hearing at first instance and the appeal. In addition, the trial at first instance had, itself, been lengthy where the trial judge had devoted considerable time to the assessment of the character and credibility of the witnesses.

There remained the issue of the child's surname: all three judges agreed that the child be permitted to adopt the surname of his biological father. Nicholson C J and Baker J noted[31] that the circumstances of the wife and the intervener had changed since the

---

[22] As in *Re Evelyn*, note 8 above, there was an application to adduce fresh evidence. As in *Evelyn*, that was refused.

[23] (1998) F.L.C. 92-815 at 85, 242.

[24] See *House v The King* (1936) 55 C.L.R. 499; *Gronow v Gronow* (1979) 144 C.L.R. 513.

[25] Note 11 above.

[26] Note 2 above.

[27] (1998) F.L.C. 92-815 at 85, 243.

[28] *Ibid* at 85, 246.

[29] *Ibid* at 85, 244.

[30] The orders had been made on April 29, 1997 and the judgments in the appeal delivered on July 1, 1998.

[31] (1998) F.L.C. 92-815 at 85, 243.

hearing at first instance. Again, the husband had, apparently, made it clear that, although he would rather the child retained his original surname, he did not consider it a matter of great moment, when compared to the issue of contact. Fogarty J took an identical view,[32] though emphasising that that course of action might assist in preventing further litigation.

Whatever the merits of the decision in relation to the child and the parties, this commentator considers it to be something of a disappointment. There was scant discussion of the nature of the 1995 amendments to the Act and less of prior case law. Given the nature of the factual situation which gave rise to *Re C and D*, one might have thought that a more conceptual approach would have been desirable and have provided a pointer towards the directions which ought to be taken in relation to the new Part VII.

III DOMESTIC VIOLENCE AND CONTACT

One particular issue which was emphasised in the amendments was that of domestic violence[33] and this arose, in quite graphic form, in the Full Court's decision in *A v A*.[34] In that case, the parties had married in 1985 and finally separated when the husband left in August 1996. The wife and the three children of the marriage (aged eleven, nine and seven) continued to live in the matrimonial home and, by agreement, the husband had contact with his children. However, overnight in December 1996, when the children were in contact with their father, the wife was seriously assaulted in the home in what seemed to be an attempt to kill her. She suffered serious injuries and was hospitalised for approximately two months. The evidence suggested that her injuries included a sexual assault. During the time when she was in hospital, the children lived with their maternal grandparents with the husband having supervised contact. After she had been discharged from hospital, the wife lived with her parents but, in April 1997, she returned to the matrimonial home with the children.

The wife, not surprisingly, had no recollection of the events which surrounded the assault, but she believed that the husband was the assailant and it seemed that there was some additional, and objective, evidence to support that belief. The husband denied any involvement in the incident and no charges were laid against him. The wife, though, had given evidence of various assaults which had been committed upon her by the husband during the course of the marriage.

In June 1997, the husband applied for unsupervised contact, including weekends and school holidays. His case was substantially supported by the child's representative. The wife was opposed to any contact because she believed that the children might be in danger if they were to be within the husband's control, especially were it to be unsupervised.

At first instance, the judge concluded that it was not the role of the Family Court to '... investigate criminal activity, even though such activity may have a direct bearing upon the issues which the Court is called upon to decide'. Thus, the trial judge approached the matter on the basis that he should determine whether the wife believed that the husband was her assailant and whether there were reasonable grounds for such a belief. On both of those issues, he concluded in the wife's favour. There was evidence, given by a Court appointed psychiatrist, to the effect that the children, who appeared to

---

[32]   *Ibid* at 85, 248.
[33]   *Family Law Act* 1975 sections 43(ca), 68F(2)(g).
[34]   (1998) F.L.C. 92-800.

be unaware of the wife's belief that the husband was her assailant, had a good relationship with their father and strongly wished to maintain contact with him. However, the psychiatrist attached significance to the likely sexual nature of the assault and concluded that, were the husband the perpetrator, there was a risk that he would re-offend, especially against the mother, but the possibility existed that the children might also be assaulted.

The trial judge ordered contact at weekends and school holidays; the contact being supervised for nine months and, thereafter, not being supervised. The judge also ordered that the psychiatrist and the child's representative explain the orders to the children and also that the wife and her family believed that the husband was responsible for the assault, whilst the husband and his family believed that he was not. The trial judge also restrained the parties, and the maternal grandparents, from discussing the events of December 1996 with the children. The wife appealed, arguing that there should be no contact and that she should be entitled to inform the children of those events. The husband, supported by the child's representative, opposed the appeal. The child's representative claimed that the assault was an occasional matter, as there was no evidence of previous assaults by the husband on the children and, hence, that there was no unacceptable risk to them. It was also agreed, if the appeal was to be allowed, that the Full Court should re-exercise its discretion rather than order a new trial. The Full Court allowed the appeal.

In so doing, the Court[35] were of the opinion[36] that the trial judge had adopted a 'basically incorrect' approach to the issues involved in the case. They encapsulated their view[37] by saying that, 'Whilst it is correct to say that the Family Court is not a criminal court and that its primary task is not to determine guilt or innocence, that is entirely different from an approach which declines to examine the issue at all'. The basis of that comment was, inevitably, the decision of the High Court of Australia in *M v M*.[38] That case, which has been far from uncriticised,[39] proposed that the test, in custody and access[40] cases where child sexual abuse was an issue, was whether there was an '*unacceptable risk* to the child of such abuse occurring'. In *A*, the Full Court were of the view[41] that the trial judge had misapplied that, and another,[42] case. Particularly, the Court had stated that nowhere in *M* was it said that the Family Court *must not*[43] investigate or form a conclusion about the question whether a respondent committed the acts in question.

Of course, as is now notorious, *M v M* was concerned with child sexual abuse, but there is no reason to suggest that the test therein enunciated might not be more generally applicable. Indeed, the High Court had stated[44] that, 'The existence and magnitude of the risk of sexual abuse, as with other risks of harm to the welfare of a child, is a fundamental matter to be taken into account in deciding issues of custody and access'.

---

35 Fogarty, Kay and Brown JJ.
36 (1998) F.L.C. 92-800 at 84, 993.
37 *Ibid* at 84, 995.
38 (1998) 166 C.L.R. 69.
39 See, for example, F. Bates, 'Evidence, Child Sexual Abuse and the High Court of Australia' (1990) 39 *ICLQ* 413.
40 Prior to the 1995 amendments to the *Family Law Act* 1975.
41 (1998) F.L.C. 92-800 at 84, 994.
42 *In the Marriage of B.* (1993) F.L.C. 92-357.
43 The Court's emphasis.
44 (1989) 166 C.L.R. 69 at 77.

What, then, ought the trial judge to have done? The Full Court were of the opinion[45] that the task which the trial judge was required to carry out was to determine whether the evidence was such as to establish that there would be an unacceptable risk to the children were they to have contact or supervised contact with the husband. In reaching that conclusion, the Court stated, 'on that issue, it is necessary for the Court to form some opinion about the connection between the assailant and the husband. It would not be necessary in this exercise to reach a positive conclusion that the husband was the assailant. On the other hand, if the Court reached a comfortable conclusion that the husband was not the assailant, that would be likely to have a profound effect upon the approach to the question of contact.'

The Court continued[46] by commenting that the primary question which the trial judge ought to have considered was, when looking at the whole of the evidence, whether contact (or, at any rate, contact which was not strictly supervised) might expose the children to an unacceptable risk because, although it might be impossible to quantify in any precise way, it might place the children in jeopardy were they in their father's care. There then arose the issue of the nature of the wife's belief as to the events of the case: the Court were of the view that, if the wife did have particular beliefs as to them, it was not necessary that any such belief should be objectively or reasonably based. The position was, as represented by earlier case law,[47] that, '… if the wife genuinely holds that belief that may so impinge upon her capacity as the primary carer of the children to look after them that the question arises whether in the interests of the children contact should continue and/or whether it should be supervised to allay those apprehensions'. Hence, the trial judge's approach that it was necessary for the belief to have been reasonable or objective was erroneous. To this commentator, it must be said, the view of the Full Court does not have much to commend it: thus, it would seem that the more vehement and irrational the belief held, the more the chance of successful opposition to contact might be. A paradox indeed! Although it is a paradox far from unknown in cases where child sexual abuse is alleged.[48]

The Court then turned their attention[49] to the trial judge's discussion of section 68F(2)(g) of the *Family Law Act* which requires the Court to take account of the need to protect children from physical or psychological harm, an issue which, of course, was crucial in the present case. The Court were cognisant of a dilemma which had faced the trial judge, in that section 68F(2)(g) of the Act required account to be taken of the wishes of the children. In the present case, it appeared that the children had an excellent relationship with their father and did wish to spend time with him and, ordinarily, that would be a very important factor. However, two problems immediately arose: first, it appeared that the children had not been informed by any appropriate agency that it was the wife's belief that her husband was her assailant. Second, they had not been told that their father denied any involvement in the incident, and it also appeared that the maternal grandparents had been restrained, at an early stage from discussing these matters with the children. The Court specifically commented that, '… the wife has exercised great restraint in not doing so and the husband apparently has not done so'.

---

[45]   (1998) F.L.C. 92-800 at 84, 995.

[46]   *Ibid* at 84, 996.

[47]   See, particularly, *In the Marriage of Russell and Close*, unreported June 25, 1993; *Re Andrew* (1996) F.L.C. 92-692.

[48]   See, for example, the decision of Carr J of the Manitoba Court of Queen's Bench [Family Division] in *Plesh v Plesh* (1992) 41 R.F.L. (3d)/102.

[49]   (1998) F.L.C. 92-800 at 84, 997.

The Court, after considering an expert's report on the matter, concluded[50] that supervision of the husband's contact with the children was necessary to ensure that the unacceptable risk of harm eventuating to the children did not so eventuate. In that context, the Court were of the view[51] that the children ought to receive basic information regarding the situation from an objective person and that the injunction restraining the maternal grandparents from discussing the matter with the children was inappropriate, '… not simply because it was open-ended in its operation but also because it curtails the rights of children to know essential facts about their life, even though that information may be initially disturbing to them'.

Further, the Court refused to accept the suggestion by the child's representative that there was no evidence of violence by the husband towards the children, that there was no unacceptable risk to them and that benefits from unsupervised access would flow to them. The Court emphatically stated that, '… this was a case where there was clearly an unacceptable risk to the children. The nature of the assault bespeaks a violent and disturbed person. As there is a possibility that the husband is that person, it seems to us to be unacceptable for this Court to place these children in any position of risk arising from these circumstances'.

A is an interesting case which may go some way towards rehabilitating the *unacceptable risk* test, albeit in a somewhat different context from that in which it was initially devised. The circumstances of the assault on the wife were obvious and medically documented, unlike the situation in many of the alleged sexual abuse cases. Nonetheless, this writer cannot conceal his suspicion of the test at large.

IV   RESIDENCE: INTERIM PROCEEDINGS

More, perhaps, mundane matters relating to children were considered by the Full Court of the Family Court of Australia in *Cowling v Cowling*[52] although the case raises issues which are of general importance in relation to the 1995 amendments. The parties had been married for some twelve years and there were three children of the marriage; the two older children[53] lived with their father whilst the youngest, aged ten, lived with the wife who had left the matrimonial home taking that child with her. However, the youngest child had contact with his father and siblings. The trial judge ordered that, until further order, the youngest child should live with the husband. The wife appealed, unsuccessfully, to the Full Court.

In reaching his decision, the trial judge had considered the wishes of the child and had given them such weight as was appropriate, having regard to the child's age and all the surrounding circumstances of the case. The trial judge found that the wife had been the youngest child's primary caregiver during the subsistence of the marriage and after separation, but then referred to the fact that, were the child to live with his father, he would be reunited with his older siblings and would be living in the environment to which he had become accustomed in his earlier life. The trial judge, was satisfied that each parent was capable of exercising parental responsibility in respect of the child, who, until separation, had always lived in the home where his parents and siblings had always

---

[50]   *Ibid* at 84, 999.
[51]   *Ibid* at 85, 000.
[52]   (1998) F.L.C. 92-801.
[53]   Aged sixteen and fifteen respectively.

lived. The trial judge, hence, concluded that it was in the child's best interests to be reunited, and live, with his siblings.

The wife, in her appeal, argued some seven grounds: first, that the judge had attached inappropriate weight to the child's wishes and the circumstances which surrounded the expression of those wishes. Second, that he had placed insufficient weight on the mother's uncontested role as primary caregiver and her availability to care for the child on a full-time basis. Third, that inappropriate weight had been placed on allegations that the wife had been violent towards the husband and one of the older children. Fourth, that the judge had failed to take the husband's working hours into account and consequent child care arrangements. Fifth, that the trial judge had placed inappropriate weight on the necessity of the children living together and for the youngest child to reside in the former matrimonial home. Sixth, that he had failed to consider, or place insufficient weight on, the fact that the youngest child had resided with the mother since the parties' separation. Finally, that the judge was in error in the way in which he had treated the decision in *In the Marriage of Cilento*.[54]

To deal with the last ground first, the Full Court[55] noted[56] the submission that, had *Cilento* been properly applied, the trial judge ought to have determined, '... whether there was a relevant status quo, found what that status quo was and then made orders to preserve it unless there was convincing proof that to do so would endanger the child's physical or mental health or moral welfare'. On that issue, the Court commented[57] that the relationship of the child with his primary caregiver was but one factor to be taken into account in making any determination. In the Court's view, the child was not living in a settled environment.

In deciding whether a child was living in such a settled environment, the Court considered[58] that, *inter alia*, six factors ought to be taken into account: first, the wishes, age and level of maturity of the child. Second, the current and proposed arrangements for the day to day care of the child. Third, the period during which the child had lived in the environment. Fourth, whether the child has any siblings and where they reside. Fifth, the nature of the relationship between the child, each parent, any other significant adult and her or his siblings and, last, the educational needs of the child.

The Court also discussed[59] the principles which ought to govern the determination of an interim residence application. Their Honours, first, stated that the *Family Law Act* did not draw any distinction between the principles to be applied in determining interim and final orders. 'The essential difference,' they considered, 'is one of procedure. Interlocutory proceedings do not determine the long term rights and obligations of the parties and their children. The issue for determination at an interim hearing involves a consideration of what orders should be made to regulate properly the position of the children pending the final determination of the matters. Such proceedings are an abridged process where the scope of the inquiry is necessarily significantly curtailed. As a consequence, the Court needs to exercise considerable caution against being drawn into matters properly dealt with in the trial process'. It followed, the Court continued, that the Court ought not, at interim hearings, to be drawn into issues of fact as matters relating to

---

[54]   (1980) F.L.C. 90-847.
[55]   Ellis, Lindenmayer and Jordan JJ.
[56]   (1998) F.L.C. 92-801 at 85, 007.
[57]   *Ibid* at 85, 008.
[58]   *Ibid* at 85, 006.
[59]   *Ibid* at 85, 006.

the merits of the substantive cases of each of the parties. The Court will, thus, look at less contentious matters such as the agreed facts, the care arrangement prior to separation, the parties' current circumstances and their relative proposals for the future.

Taking those matters into account, the Court sought to summarise[60] the relevant criteria for the determination of interim proceedings. In so doing, the best interests of the child were the paramount consideration and those interests would normally best be met by ensuring stability in the child's life, pending a full hearing of all of the relevant issues. Where, at the date of the hearing, the child is well settled in his environment, that stability would usually be promoted by an order which provided for a continuation of that arrangement, unless there were overriding considerations, relevant to the child's welfare, to the contrary. These overriding considerations might include convincing proof that the child's welfare would be genuinely endangered by the child's remaining in that environment.

At the same time, the Court was entitled to place such weight on the importance of retaining the child's living arrangements as it saw fit in the circumstances. In determining that weight, the Court may take account of the circumstances which have given rise to the current status quo and might examine whether the living arrangements arose by reason of some agreement between the parties, arose as a result of acquiescence or having been unilaterally imposed by one party on the other, the duration of the current arrangements and whether there had been any delay in instituting proceedings or in the proceedings being listed for hearing.

Cowling is an interesting and valuable case: although there had been previous Australian authority relating to interim proceedings,[61] the Full Court have taken the opportunity to synthesise[62] that authority and to relate it to the 1995 amendments to the *Family Law Act* 1975. The criteria set out in *Cowling* will be of especial value as a guide to practitioners in their conduct of interim hearings.

V   RELOCATION: THE UNACCEPTABLE RISK TEST

Another decision of interest in relation to children and one which again involves the 'unacceptable risk' test enunciated by the High Court of Australia in *M v M*[63] in relation to child sexual abuse is the Full Court's decision in *R v R*.[64] There, a mother of four children wished to relocate to Scotland where her family of origin lived. The three eldest children, who had little relationship with their father wanted to go and, in support of her application, she asserted that she had family support in Scotland, had employment and free accommodation and that she would be in a better financial situation. At first instance, the application was rejected on the grounds that there was a risk of emotional damage to the youngest child were he to be deprived of contact with his father. In reaching that conclusion, the trial judge found that the risk to the child was 'unacceptable'. The wife's appeal to the Full Court was dismissed.

---

[60]   *Ibid* at 85, 006.

[61]   See *In the Marriage of Cilento* (1980) F.L.C. 90-847; *In the Marriage of Griffiths* (1981) F L C/91-064; *In the Marriage of Rainer* (1982) F.L.C. 91-239; *In the Marriage of D and Y* (1995) F.L.C. 92-581; *In the Marriage of C* (1996) F.L.C. 92-651; *Tate v Tate* (1996) F.L.C. 92-724.

[62]   (1998) F.L.C. 92-801 at 85, 005.

[63]   (1989) 16 C.L.R. 69 at 78.

[64]   (1998) F.L.C. 92-820.

In essence, the Full Court[65] found that the findings which the trial judge had made in relation to the contact issues were legitimately open to him.[66] As regards the contention that the mother would not be able to function appropriately were the application not to be granted, the Court said[67] that there were, '... frequently what may be termed as compelling cases where the evidence relating to such unhappiness and the capacity of the unchallenged residence parent to function becomes so overwhelming that other aspects have to give way to the needs of that parent. It is not hard to envisage cases in which such circumstances would exist. Strong evidence of an inability to function due to homesickness or a real or perceived need to escape from what is thought to be a hostile environment are but some examples of such circumstances'. The Court considered that, in the instant case, the evidence fell far short of establishing those circumstances. In making that statement, the Court were adopting the view which had been expressed by the Full Court in the important case of *B and B; Family Reform Act*,[68] where it had been said that, 'Ordinary common experience indicates that long term unhappiness by a residence parent is likely to impinge in a negative way upon the happiness and best interests of children who are part of that household. Similarly, where the parent is able to live a more fulfilling life this may reflect in a positive way in the children ...' It must be said that, unlike the *B* case where the relocation was permitted, there appeared to be scant evidence regarding expressed wishes and there was no evidence,[69] and nor was there any suggestion, that the children were malfunctioning in their existing environment.[70]

Perhaps more controversial was the adoption by the trial judge of the 'unacceptable risk' test: even in the area where it had originally been enunciated – the area of child sexual abuse – it has been criticised as being manifestly too subjective and open-ended[71] and there had been attempts both in Australia[72] and England[73] to devise a more specific formula. In *R*, the Court said[74] that 'there is nothing which limits the formulation to abuse cases and it is a useful test in many circumstances. The Court is required to chart a course which it perceives will best advance the child's best interests. Almost invariably one would expect such a course to avoid any unacceptable risk to the child's welfare, irrespective of how that risk might manifest itself. The risk of sexual abuse is an obvious example. However lesser risks can still be measured by the same standards'. It may be, it is suggested, that the test may be more applicable to, so-called, lesser risk than to sexual abuse in that consequences of a finding of an unacceptable risk of sexual abuse may be considerably damaging to a person against whom such allegations are made, the more so if they are found to be untrue.[75] However, only time will tell what the fate of the 'unacceptable risk' test will be.

---

[65] Finn, Kay and Burton JJ.

[66] (1998) F.L.C. 92-820 at 85, 331.

[67] *Ibid* at 85, 330.

[68] (1997) F.L.C. 92, 755 at 84, 222 *per* Nicholson C J, Fogarty and Lindenmayer JJ.

[69] (1998) F.L.C. 92-820 at 85, 331.

[70] At its highest, *ibid*, the evidence was that the children might be 'disappointed and angry' were they not to be allowed to relocate.

[71] See F. Bates, note 39 above.

[72] *In the Marriage of D and Y* (1995) F.L.C. 92-581.

[73] *Re H and Others (Minors) (Sexual Abuse: Standard of Proof)* [1996] 1 All E.R. 1.

[74] (1998) F.L.C. 92-820 at 85, 330.

[75] For a discussion of the decision of the Full Court of the Supreme Court of South Australia in *Hillman v Black* (1996) 67 S.A.S.R. 490, see F. Bates, 'Child Sexual Abuse, the Fact-Finding Process and Negligence: An Opportunity Lost?' (1998) 6 *Tort L.R.* 125.

VI   CHILD ABDUCTION: JURISDICTION

At the beginning of this commentary, I noted that one decision confused an already uncertain area – that case is the decision of Kay J in *Karides v Wilson*.[76] By way of background, in the case of *Z.P. v P.S.*,[77] the High Court of Australia held that their earlier decision in the case of *Voth v Matildra Flour Mills*[78] did not apply in cases involving children. Thus, *Z.P. v P.S.* overruled a considerable body of case law decided in the Family Court of Australia[79] and made cases involving children who had been abducted to or from jurisdictions which were not parties to the *Hague Convention on Civil Aspects of International Child Abduction*, at the very least, difficult to litigate outside Australia[80]. In *Karides v Wilson*, the parties had married in the United States in 1992, the relevant child having been born there in 1994. Shortly after the birth, the mother and child, without the father's consent, left the United States and went, first, to New Zealand and, then, to Australia where they went into hiding. In 1996, they were located by police and, at that point, Kay J made orders for the child to be returned to the State of Virginia in the United States pursuant to the Hague Convention.

The mother then applied for orders[81] for her to have telephone contact with the child. It appeared that a court in Virginia had made interim orders granting custody (residence) to the husband and visitation (contact) to the wife. The mother indicated that she was unwilling or unable to attend any further proceedings in Virginia and asked for contact issues to be adjudicated in the Family Court of Australia. The threshold issue which arose before Kay J was whether the Court should entertain the mother's application or summarily dismiss it on the grounds that the matter should properly be dealt with by the courts in Virginia. Not wholly surprisingly, Kay J dismissed the mother's application but, in so doing, discussed the surrounding law in some detail.

Kay J quoted[82] extensively from *Z.P. v P.S.* and concluded[83] that, 'the issue of whether a decision of this Court assuming or declining jurisdiction over a child outside of the jurisdiction is to be governed entirely by the "best interests" principle remains as yet undecided at the highest level'.[84] The dilemma raised by those cases was that the Court might be asked to make an order which was incapable of enforcement and, hence, looking at the question entirely from the point of view of the best interests test, how could it be in the child's best interests to require that the parents litigate in respect of an order which would have no binding effect? In the present case, the judge thought, there was no doubt that the Court had jurisdiction to hear an application in respect of a child

---

[76]   (1998) F.L.C. 92-823.

[77]   (1994) 181 C.L.R. 639.

[78]   (1990) 171 C.L.R. 538.

[79]   *In the Marriage of Scott* (1991) F.L.C. 92-241; *In the Marriage of Chong* (1992) F.L.C. 92-113; *In the Marriage of Erdal* (1992) F.L.C. 92-292; *In the Marriage of Gilmore* (1993) F.L.C. 92-391.

[80]   For comment on *Z.P. v P.S.*, see F. Bates, 'Australian Family Law in International Context: A Recent Development' (1995) 4 *Asia Pacific L.R.* 100.

[81]   The mother had come, once again, before Kay J and the mother argued that he should not hear the matter because he had initially ordered the return of the child to the United States. Kay J, however, decided to continue with the case on the basis of authorities relating to perceived bias: see, *In the Marriage of Kennedy and Cahill* (1995) F.L.C. 92-605; *Livesey v New South Wales Bar Association* (1983) 151 C.L.R. 288; *Re J.R.L; Ex Parte C.J.L.* (1986) F.L.C. 91-738.

[82]   (1998) F.L.C. 92-823 at 85, 356-8.

[83]   *Ibid* at 85, 359.

[84]   The same situation also pertained in England; see *Re S (Residence Order: Forum Conveniens)* [1995] 1 F.L.R. 314.

who was not within the jurisdiction. At the same time, though, existing authority[85] suggested that great care should be taken before any attempt is made to exercise the jurisdiction.

After having examined[86] relevant United States[87] and Virginian law,[88] Kay J concluded[89] that all indications – whether by the application of the best interests principle, or the broader principle that courts ought not to exercise jurisdiction by making futile orders, or by the application of principles of comity, or by the application of whether Australia was a clearly inappropriate forum – pointed to Virginia as being the jurisdiction to decide the relevant issues. So long as the child remained in Virginia and, so long as the courts in that jurisdiction remained available to determine issues relating to the child's best interests, then those courts were where the litigation should continue.

It will readily be apparent that *Karides v Wilson* is a case of considerable interest; how far it is likely to undermine the general thrust of *Z.P. v P.S.* remains to be seen, especially as the later case can clearly be distinguished on the grounds that the United States is a party to the Hague Convention whereas, when *Z.P. v P.S.* was decided, Greece was not.

VII PROPERTY DISTRIBUTION

On the issue of property distribution, the decision of the Full Court of the Family Court of Australia in *Campbell v Kuskey*[90] is of global interest. This case involved an appeal against a finding that, although the parties' contributions were equal, the wife should receive a 15 per cent adjustment[91] in her favour, taking into account the husband's superannuation entitlement and long service leave, his greater income available because of his control of the parties' company as well as his possible tax liability for the parties' loan accounts[92]. The trial judge had not taken that liability into account as a liability of the husband and had ordered him to indemnify the wife in respect of any liability which she might incur arising from her association with the company. In addition, a joint report by the parties' accountants[93] had noted that the parties' loan accounts with their company incurred a possible income tax liability[94]. Accordingly, they had recommended that the parties reduce their loan accounts by the payment of fully franked dividends so as to reduce their tax liability[95]. Counsel for both parties had submitted that they both should be ordered to follow the recommendations of the accountants.

On appeal, the husband submitted, *inter alia*, that, having been ordered to indemnify the wife, the trial judge should have ordered the parties to enter into the scheme

---

[85] *In the Marriage of Taylor* (1998) F.L.C. 91-943; *In the Marriage of Soares* (1989) F.L.C. 92-024; *In the Marriage of Scott* (1991) F.L.C. 92-241.

[86] (1998) F.L.C. 92-823 at 85, 360-85, 365.

[87] *Uniform Child Custody Jurisdiction Act.*

[88] *Middleton v Middleton; Lyons v Lyons* 314 S.E. 2d 362 (1984). This case involved two simultaneous appeals both involving Virginian and English proceedings.

[89] (1998) F.L.C. 92-823.

[90] (1998) F.L.C. 92-795.

[91] See *Family Law Act* 1975 section 75(2).

[92] *Income Tax Assessment Act* 1936 section 108.

[93] See *Family Law Rules* 030A.

[94] Amounting to $193, 724.

[95] To $86, 328.

recommended by the accountants and to have brought the tax liability of the husband into account. On the hearing of the appeal, it was agreed that the trial judge was in error in failing to take the wife's employment into account as well as taking into account a tax liability in relation to the transfer of land from the parties' company to the wife where, in fact, the transaction had never occurred. The Full Court[96] allowed the appeal.

First, in so doing, the Court emphasised[97] that a trial judge '... has the clear responsibility to identify the assets and liabilities of the parties before considering and making the necessary findings as to the respective contributions which the parties have made to them'.[98] The Court were also of the view[99] that, as a general rule, trial judges should make a finding, on the balance of probabilities, as to whether or not a taxation liability existed and, if so, in what amount.

Second, owing to the extent of the indemnity granted to the wife by the husband and the fact that the parties had adopted the joint statement of their accountants, the Full Court considered[100] that the trial judge was in error in failing to recognise the husband's potential tax liability[101]. The Full Court, in consequence, re-exercised their discretion, and ordered[102] the parties to enter into the scheme recommended by the accountants and the net assets were adjusted to take account of the husband's tax liability. Contributions were assessed as being equal, though an adjustment of 7.5 per cent was made in favour of the wife.[103] *Campbell v Kuskey* is of interest in that it provides an appellate example of tax liability being taken into account in property distribution.

VIII FORMALITIES OF MARRIAGE

There was, by way of diversion, an eccentric factual situation which arose in relation to the formalities of marriage. In *W v T*[104], the Full Court[105] was required to consider an appeal from an initial decision which had dismissed an application for a decree of nullity but had granted a decree of dissolution. The facts of this strange case were that the parties had begun cohabiting in the late 1980s when they were both aged in their early thirties. There were two children of the relationship, born in 1991 and 1993. At about that time, as Baker J described[106] the history of the relationship, they became adherents of the Assemblies of God Australia Church and became regular attenders.[107] In early 1994, they were advised by members of the Church that they were 'leading a sinful life' and that they should marry. Accordingly, they were married in a religious ceremony in August 1994 and, later, separated in January 1995.

---

[96]   Baker, Lindenmayer and Maxwell JJ.

[97]   (1998) F.L.C. 92-795 at 84, 918.

[98]   See, for example, *In the Marriage of Pastrikos* (1980) F.L.C. 90-897; *In the Marriage of Ferraro* (1993) F.L.C. 92-235.

[99]   (1998) F.L.C. 92-795 at 84, 917.

[100] *Ibid* at 84, 925.

[101] See *NRMA Insurance Ltd v B and B Shipping and Marine Salvage Co Pty Ltd* (1947) 47 SR (NSW) 273; *David Syme and Co Pty Ltd v Lloyd* (1985) 1 N.S.W.L.R. 416.

[102] (1998) F.L.C. 92-795 at 84, 928.

[103] See *Family Law Act* 1975 section 75(2).

[104] (1998) F.L.C. 92-808.

[105] Fogarty, Baker and Lindenmayer JJ.

[106] (1998) F.L.C. 92-808 at 85, 110.

[107] Previously, it appeared that the wife had been of the Unitarian persuasion and the husband a Catholic.

In February 1997, the husband filed an application for dissolution of marriage and, in reply, the wife sought a decree of nullity on the grounds that the parties had never been validly married. The wife's argument was based around section 41 of the *Marriage Act* 1961 that the marriage had not been '... solemnized ... in the presence of an authorized celebrant'. The wife argued that there was no authorised celebrant present at the marriage or, if there was, his 'presence' was insufficient for the purposes of section 41 and section 5(2) of the same Act, which requires that the authorised celebrant consents to being present for the solemnisation of the marriage.

The relevant facts were that the ceremony had been conducted by the celebrant of the parties' choice, whom they knew was not an authorised celebrant for the purposes of the Act, but whom, they believed, had taken the necessary steps to ensure that the formalities were complied with. There was no issue that the clergyman who conducted the ceremony was not an authorised celebrant, but the issue was whether another clergyman, who was an authorised celebrant, was present for the purposes of ensuring that the ceremony was properly solemnised. The wife argued that section 41 required, not only the close physical presence of the authorised celebrant, but that the celebrant be visibly present to the parties, so as to be regarded as having taken a significant part in the ceremony.

At first instance, the judge having taken account of all of the evidence, including photographs and video footage, concluded that the authorised celebrant was present when the ceremony took place even though he had been standing inconspicuously at the rear of the church, that it was he who had signed the marriage certificate and had consented to be present for that purpose. Although neither party knew that that clergyman was present for the purpose, the trial judge held that the requirements of the *Marriage Act* had been satisfied. The wife appealed unsuccessfully to the Full Court of the Family Court.

The Full Court's decision is notable for the lengthy and scholarly historical judgment of Fogarty J, with whom Baker and Lindenmayer JJ agreed.[108] In essence, the Court held that, provided that authorised celebrants have consented to attend the ceremony for the purpose of ensuring its validity, their mere physical presence, rather than any active participation is sufficient for the purposes of the Act. The words 'in the presence of' therein found, should be given their ordinary meaning and, hence, the trial judge had been correct in his initial finding. In reaching that conclusion, Fogarty J had relied on, and apparently followed, such well-known authorities as *R v Millis*,[109] *Beamish v Beamish*[110] and the South Australian case of *Purins v Klismets*.[111] It should be said that, without canvassing the whole issue,[112] the present writer considers that the judges in *W v T* have rather oversimplified the matter and that authority can be found in the older cases, including those relied on, for the view that more active participation is required. That apart, *W v T* remains an intriguing curiosity: one wonders why the wife would rather never have been married, in law at any rate, than have been divorced.[113] We shall, in all distinct probability, never know.

---

108 Baker J, though reaching the same ultimate conclusion as Fogarty J, adopted a slightly different approach to the same materials.

109 (1844) 10 Cl.W. Fin 534.

110 (1861) 9 H.L.C. 274.

111 (1973) 6 S.A.S.R. 493.

112 See F. Bates, 'The History of Marriage and Modern Law', (Unpublished Conference Paper, 1999).

113 That was the comment of Baker J, with whom the author had the benefit of discussing the case at a conference in October 1998.

In the end, 1998 has presented some features of interest in Australian family law, although there also seem to have been opportunities not taken and it is likely to be some time before the effects of the 1995 amendments to the *Family Law Act* are genuinely felt.

BELGIUM

THE EFFECT OF THE TRAGIC EVENTS OF AUGUST 1996 ON CHILD PROTECTION IN BELGIUM

*Thierry Moreau**

I   IMPORTANT DEVELOPMENTS IN THE BATTLE AGAINST SEXUAL ABUSE OF CHILDREN SHORTLY BEFORE THE EVENTS UNFOLDED

In the early spring of 1995, Belgium had added to its criminal law armoury stronger measures against sexual offences, particularly where the victims were minors.

First, a law of March 27, 1995 widened significantly the range of offences relating to advertisements offering sexual services for reward directly or indirectly, whether addressed to minors or relating to services provided by minors (Article 380 *quinquies* of the Penal Code); advertisements of any kind relating to prostitution are prohibited; the offence is still punishable if the author conceals the nature of the offer by using coded language; offers of services made by means of telecommunications are also forbidden. Further, the penalties applying to these offences have been increased.

The law of April 13, 1995, containing provisions aimed at trafficking in human beings and child pornography, widened the effect of provisions of the Penal Code relating to the corruption and prostitution of young people and increased the penalties applicable to both sorts of offences (Articles 379 and 380 *bis* of the Penal Code). This law also created a new specific offence of child pornography covering not only sale, hire and distribution of any form of pornographic material, but also the mere possession of representations of a pornographic nature involving minors under 16, in whatever form (Article 383 *bis*). The law added to the Belgian legal arsenal an extraterritorial element, allowing prosecution of anyone, be it a Belgian or a foreigner, found in Belgium, who commits an offence of a sexual nature abroad (a limited list of such offences having been set out in the legislation), whether or not the authorities of Belgium or of the relevant foreign country have had any official complaint or notification of it (Article 10 *ter* of the preliminary title of the *Code d'instruction criminelle*). In particular this is intended to increase the effectiveness of the battle against sexual tourism.

A second law of April 13, 1995, dealing with sexual abuse of minors, was enacted to adapt certain criminal procedure rules to the specific requirements of this matter.

Thus, this law was aimed at changing two procedural rules to help children. On the one hand, the period of prescription by which prosecution for a range of offences set out in legislation becomes time-barred will now start to run only when the victim has reached legal majority at the age of 18 (Article 21 *bis* of the preliminary title of the *Code d'instruction criminelle*). The Legislature took the view that, once having reached majority, the victim was not subject to the authority of the abuser, particularly when the latter was a family member. Moreover, it was hoped that this would mean that children who had been abused at a very young age would not be penalised when they became old

---

*   Avocat au Barreau de Nivelles, Assistant at the Catholic University of Louvain. Translated by Peter Schofield.

enough to speak out. On the other hand, the law also gave any minor victim of a sexual offence the right to be accompanied by an adult of his or her choice at any hearing arranged by the judicial authority, unless a reasoned decision to the contrary was given by a magistrate conducting the enquiry, in the interests of the minor or in those of discovering the truth (Article 91 of the *Code d'instruction criminelle*).

To ensure an adequate response to sexual offences against minors the Legislature has provided for the *correctionalisation* of all such offences (law of October 4, 1867 on mitigating circumstances, Article 2). Previously, *le viol*, ie any act of penetration against a child under 10, fell under the exclusive jurisdiction of the *cour d'assises*, and thus of the *jury populaire*. This was a very difficult procedure, with the result that many files were classed as not to be taken forward, or ended with the accused committed to hospital, ie with a declaration that he could not be held criminally responsible, on the grounds that his mental state was unbalanced to such an extent that he could not control his actions. This is a step that an examining magistrate can order before the case is submitted to a jury.

The law also increased the punishment applicable to sexual offenders. A new discretionary penalty is provided for a person convicted of a sexual offence against a minor. The criminal court can ban the person, for a period of from one to 20 years, from taking part in any capacity in teaching given in a public or a private establishment receiving minors, as well as taking part as a voluntary worker, as a member of the statutory or of the contractual personnel, or as a member of the administration or management, in any institution or association whose activities have to do with minors (Article 382 *bis* of the Penal Code). Parole is made more difficult for sexual offenders against minors; in addition to the conditions applying to other convicted persons, they must not be released without the approval of a service specialising in the guidance and treatment of such offenders and, once released, they are subject to guidance or to a treatment plan specified in their parole conditions (Articles 5 and 8 of the law of May 31, 1888 on conditional release).

Finally, the law increased the punishment for failing to come to the assistance of a person in danger when that person is a minor, as the Legislature wanted to combat the guilty silence of one who knows and says nothing (Article 422 *bis* of the Penal Code).

II   MATTERS TAKE A TURN IN AUGUST 1996

A few weeks after these new laws were voted, a dramatic turn of events was to call in question the whole system of protection of children against abduction and abuse.

On June 24, 1995, two 8-year-old girls, Julie and Melissa, disappeared at Liège. Failure to find them soon gave rise to the conclusion that they had been abducted. On August 22, two teenage girls, Ann and Eefje disappeared on the Belgian coast. At the end of May 1996, a 12-year-old girl disappeared. At the beginning of August, a 14-year-old was abducted.

The 12-year-old and the 14-year-old were found alive on August 14, 1996 in a house belonging to Marc Dutroux. He was arrested along with his wife and some suspected accomplices. Three days later, in the garden of the house, the bodies of Julie and Melissa were discovered. At the beginning of September, those of Ann and Eefje were found.

Subsequently, in March 1997, the body of a 9-year-old girl of Moroccan origin missing since 1992 was recovered. The person on whose property she was found had, like

Dutroux, a record of convictions for improper conduct (*faits de moeurs*) in relation to children.

Enquiries quickly revealed that all these children had, in addition to their abduction, suffered cruelty and sexual abuse.

The horror of these events gave rise to a public emotional response of considerable intensity. The macabre discoveries were the subject of international repercussions.

The parents of these children called in question the manner in which the magistrates responsible for the enquiries had dealt with the search for their children. One of their main complaints against the judicial authorities was that they were excluded from the investigation, and particularly from seeing the enquiry records, which might have enabled them to suggest lines for the investigating officers to pursue and, perhaps, to get back their children alive. They got a lot of public support which showed itself most impressively in the 'white march' of three hundred thousand people through the streets of Brussels under the slogan 'Never again'. On the evening of the white march the Prime Minister met the parents of the children who had disappeared and promised that he would press forward reforms to meet their demands.

Already in October 1996, Parliament had set up a parliamentary commission charged with looking into the manner in which the judicial, police and administrative authorities had conducted the investigations, and with taking up the various questions raised by the cases from a structural point of view.

Both the action of the parents of the children and of their many supporters and the work of the parliamentary commission were to have a profound influence on the legislative reforms and the various initiatives which followed.

III   THE REFORM OF THE JUDICIAL AND POLICE SYSTEM

An important finding of the parliamentary commission was the disfunction of the judicial and police systems. For instance, some police officers were found to have worked without reporting to the investigating magistrates. Also the collaboration between magistrates and police officers in different districts was less than perfect. Finally, the lack of training of personnel and of means of communication in the various levels of the judicial system were identified.

A law of March 4, 1997 set up a *collège des procureurs généraux*. This brought together the five *procureurs généraux* of the country under the Minister of Justice (Article 143 *bis* ff. of the *Code judiciaire*). The main task of this institution is to coordinate criminal law policy across the whole of the country. It provides for the function of national magistrate, of whom there are three. This involves a magistrate of the *parquet* (*ministère public*) responsible for coordinating the activities of the public authorities and facilitating international cooperation with one or more *procureurs du Roi*.

A law of November 20, 1998 established a *conseil supérieure de la justice* made up of equal numbers of judges and officials of the *ministère public* elected directly by their colleagues, on one side and, on the other, of other members, particularly of university teachers and practising advocates, nominated by the Senate by a two-thirds majority of votes cast (Article 151 of the Constitution). The task of this council involves the nomination and training of magistrates and of officials of the *ministère public*, the giving of advice and making proposals as to the general functioning of the judicial profession and, excluding all disciplinary and penal matters, to receive complaints about the work of the judicial profession and to ensure they are followed up, and to investigate the functioning of the judicial profession. Currently, the council has not yet been set up. The law also provides for the regular assessment of the chief officers of the bench and of the *ministère public*.

A further reform of the judicial system is still in course of development. This is to integrate vertically the *parquets* (sections of the *ministère public*) so that the official dealing with a case on appeal would be the same one as handled it at first instance.

A law of December 7, 1998 reformed the police landscape of Belgium. Formerly, three separate and independent police services operated side by side: *la police communale* responsible for administrative and investigative (*judiciaire*) policing at local level; *la police judiciaire* responsible for investigative work in each judicial district; and *la gendarmerie* responsible for administrative and investigative policing locally and nationally. In the framework of their investigative functions, these three police services were supposed to collaborate under the direction of the magistrate in charge of the investigation. Events showed that this did not always happen in practice and that there could be rivalry between the police services. The law abolishes the separate services and creates an integrated police service working on two levels: local and federal – each level being responsible for administrative and for investigative policing. Currently this law is not yet in force. The date of its implementation is to be fixed by the King, but the law provides this must be not later than January 1, 2001.

IV   NEW MEASURES IN THE SEARCH FOR MISSING CHILDREN

An internal directive of the Ministry of Justice, dated July 22, 1997, sent to the magistrates of each *parquet* and to the police, governs the search for missing persons. In each *parquet* a designated magistrate is responsible for coordinating the cases of disappearance. The circular provides the procedure to follow whenever a disappearance is reported. It also governs the relations between the judicial and the police authorities on the one hand and the victims and the press on the other. Finally, it provides for what to do when a missing person is found.

On the evening of the white march, the Prime Minister had promised to create a centre specialised in missing child enquiries, comparable with the American 'National centre of missing and exploited children'. Named 'Child Focus', the centre became operational in March 1998. It is an establishment to which the public have access, in which the public authorities have only a minority representation on the council of administration of one member in eleven, and that with a consultative role only, which ensures a measure of independence. Financially, it benefits from public subsidies and from sponsorship by a variety of private companies and societies. The centre provides a 24-hour manned telephone answering service. A Freephone number is allocated to it, obtainable from anywhere in the country. There is, signed by the centre and the Ministry of Justice, an intervention protocol by which, save in exceptional circumstances, the centre directs its attention to disappearances of minors under 18. Its principal functions are to receive and pass on to the judicial authorities information relating to a disappearance, to distribute messages in relation to the enquiry (by posters, televised announcements etc.) and to mobilise volunteers to conduct area searches and give support to the family of the missing child. As a rule, the centre only acts after checking that a missing person report has been lodged with a police service, and with the consent of the parents. It can be called on to act by the magistrate in charge of an investigation.

V   A NEW PLACE FOR THE VICTIM IN CRIMINAL CASES

Two laws of 17 and 18 February 1997 improve the law of August 1, 1985 on compensating victims of acts of wilful violence. The aim of the legislation is to enable a commission to award financial help from public funds to victims of intentional violence on the part of persons who cannot be traced or who are insolvent. The award is discretionary, taking into account the resources and the needs of the victim. The two new laws extend considerably the list of forms of harm for which compensation can be given, so as to recognise the longer term effects suffered by victims of child abuse. They also give additional machinery to the commission responsible for giving effect to this legislation.

By a law of March 12, 1998, Parliament also reformed criminal procedure. In so doing, it relied on the work of a commission of experts set up as early as 1991 chaired by Bâtonnier Franchimont. The new law (*loi Franchimont*) only seeks to reform procedure up to the point of judgment, ie the stages of the laying of the information and the drawing up of the case (*instruction*). In the light of the failures revealed by the work of the parliamentary commission, it has in particular strengthened the control that magistrates exercise over investigations as well as legislating for and regulating proactive police investigations.

In response to the demands of parents of child victims, the *loi Franchimont* accords a more important role to the victim in the preparatory stages of criminal procedure. In future, like any other person questioned, the victim can receive a copy of his evidence (Article 28 *quinquies* and 57 of the *Code d'instruction criminelle*). The victim also acquires the right to be treated fairly, to receive information and to be put in touch with legal assistance (Article 3 *bis* of the preliminary title of the *Code d'instruction criminelle*). If the victim is dead, next-of-kin have the right to see the body in case of autopsy (Article 44 of the *Code d'instruction criminelle*). Without being joined as a civil party, a victim can make a declaration of damage suffered in the form of a simple declaration at the secretariat of the *parquet*. This gives the victim the right to be kept informed as to what becomes of the case, and to have documents added to it (Article 5 *bis* of the preliminary title of the *Code d'instruction criminelle*). A victim who becomes a civil party has the right to ask the examining magistrate for access to the case file. It can be refused. If it is, the civil party has an appeal to the *chambre des mises en accusation* of the appeal court (Article 61 *ter* of the *Code d'instruction criminelle*). Finally, the victim has the right to call on the examining magistrate to carry out the supplementary duties of the preparation of the case (Article 61 *quinquies* of the *Code d'instruction criminelle*).

In regard to the taking of evidence in cases of sexual abuse of minors, for some years there has been a growing use of video recording in the presence of psychologists as well as of police.

In contrast, nothing has been done to provide minor victims with legal representation. No legal aid scheme has been set up, whereas minors are by definition without means to pay. Likewise, no particular training has been provided for advocates willing to take on the representation of child victims.

VI RESTRICTIONS ON PAROLE FOR PERSONS CONVICTED OF CHILD ABUSE

At the time of the offences for which he stands accused, Marc Dutroux was subject to the conditions of parole for earlier convictions. The work of the parliamentary commission showed up many gaps in the law then in force, in particular the fact that decisions about parole were left to the absolute discretion of the Minister of Justice.

In future, decisions on parole will be taken by parole boards (*commissions de libération conditionelle*), with recourse to the appeal court, as set out in a law of March 18, 1998. The chair of these boards is taken by a first instance judge who is specifically allocated to this role on a full-time basis. They have one assessor concerned with the carrying out of punishments and another concerned with reintegration into the community. As well as deciding who should be freed, they are responsible for the after-care of convicts on parole.

The law of March 5, 1998 on parole repeals the old law which dated from 1888. While not appreciably changing the proportion of the term that a convicted person must serve before being able to be considered for parole, it makes many procedural changes.

First, it sets out the conditions a convict must satisfy to be given parole once the date when he can receive it arrives. It also specifies the way in which the case is referred to a parole board: proposal from the prison staff conference sent to the Minister of Justice, enquiries by the Ministry of Justice, case submitted to the parole board by the Ministry of Justice. For those convicted of sexual abuse of children, the law requires also the opinion of a service specialising in the guidance and treatment of sexual offenders. Note that the prison staff conference has power to hold back the case for eighteen months at this stage. The law allows the Minister of Justice, during the administrative stage, to obtain information from the victims as to special conditions that could be imposed on parole in their interests.

The law provides for adversary procedure before the parole boards. The prisoner can be assisted by counsel and can consult his file before the hearing. The *ministère public* and the prison governor also have the right to be heard. In some circumstances, the victim may ask to be heard in relation to the conditions that should be imposed in his own interests. The parole board sets out the conditions when granting parole. In the case of sexual offenders, these must include guidance or treatment by a specialised service. If parole is refused, the board specifies a date when the case can be reconsidered by the conference of prison staff. A freed prisoner is, at his request, informed by the board and receives by registered post a statement of the conditions protecting his interests.

It was intended that the parole boards would start work on March 1, 1999.

The law of March 5 also completes the law of social defence. In future the *commission de la défense sociale* cannot authorise the release of persons who have committed sexual offences without having consulted a specialised centre. Moreover, the commission can, during the period it specifies, impose on a detainee freed on probation a prohibition on involvement in any capacity, whether as a volunteer, member of the statutory or contractual personnel, or as a member of the administrative organs, in any institution or association whose activities are involved with minors.

VII STRENGTHENING CHILD PROTECTION

On August 30, 1996, the Council of Ministers set up the National Commission Against the Sexual Exploitation of Children, composed of six independent experts. The Commission has three aims: to ascertain the true extent and significance of the phenomenon of child sexual abuse; to assess current policy in Belgium concerning this; and to make concrete proposals in response to the facts as found. The Commission has organised extensive consultation with professionals and with the children themselves. Its final report was submitted on October 23, 1997. In it were many concrete proposals on a wide range of matters, such as prevention including strengthening the social and legal status of children, providing aid and assistance both to child victims and to perpetrators of sexual abuse, the approach to the problem in civil and criminal law as well as in social child protection, and the recognition of children's rights.

A decree of the Communauté Française, of March 16, 1998, reformed aid to child victims of maltreatment in the French speaking part of the country. It obliges anyone who is in charge of children to help them if they become aware of the fact that they are being physically mistreated. If unable to do anything personally, the person is required to inform the authorities specified in the decree as competent in the matter. Such disclosure is obligatory in any case where the perpetrator is a third party in the family household. These obligations of disclosure are backed by criminal penalties. Nonetheless, they do not apply to those who are subject to professional confidentiality. Additionally, the decree sets up a commission to coordinate assistance to child victims of maltreatment in each judicial district. It requires social workers working with children to undergo training on the approach to cases of maltreatment. It establishes the conditions to be satisfied by the telephone help-lines and by multidisciplinary 'S.O.S.-Enfants' teams specialising in the management of child abuse cases. Finally the decree sets up a permanent child abuse commission to give advice and to make proposals on the matter.

Last of all, in December 1998, the Government set out a draft of a law on the protection of minors in criminal law. It drew heavily on the work of the National Commission Against the Sexual Exploitation of Children and on various studies commissioned by the Government in universities.

This project had, inter alia, the objective of protecting children against abduction and hostage-taking, abandonment, neglect and physical cruelty. In the field of sexual exploitation, it filled out the laws of March and April 1995, extending to 16- and 17-year-olds the protection already given to those under 16 in relation to debauchement, prostitution and child pornography. To make the extraterritorial element more effective, the draft eliminates the requirement of double criminality. This will also apply to improper conduct (*faits de moeurs*) committed against minors under 16.

The draft also seeks to make the system of prohibitions imposed on those convicted of *faits de moeurs* more effective. It makes the opinion of a centre specialising in the guidance and treatment of sexual offenders a requirement in other circumstances than questions of conditional liberty.

It also proposes to re-examine the offences relating to *faits de moeurs* with a view to imposing penalties for all forms of abuse committed against minors in order to obtain their consent to sexual acts. It envisages special penalties for genital mutilation. It introduces a possible exception to professional confidentiality in the case of violence against children under 14. Last, to give fuller recognition to changes in family structure, it extends the principle of aggravating circumstances applying to violence committed by family members against a minor, to cover acts of any adult residing on an occasional or on a regular basis in the minor's household.

BOTSWANA

OVERVIEW OF FAMILY LAW IN BOTSWANA

*Athaliah Molokomme**

I INTRODUCTION

A *Scope of the Review*

The fact that this is the first contribution to the International Survey on Botswana reflects to a large extent the limited legal reforms that have taken place in the field of family law over the past two decades. As a result, this article presents a brief overview of the state and sources of family law in Botswana, and the trends in its development since the 1970s. It observes that there has been very little real reform in the field of family law, or any other field of law for that matter, except for piecemeal amendments of specific statutes in response to specific problems or demands. It also notes that these amendments have tended to be ad hoc, reactive rather than proactive, with little attention paid to their effect on existing Roman-Dutch and customary laws.[1] Most of these were transplants from English statutes, and include the Affiliation Proceedings Act 1970; the Married Persons Property Act 1971; and the Matrimonial Causes Act 1973.

However, the article acknowledges that there have been some important developments, especially reflected in the decisions of the courts, in the areas of child maintenance, matrimonial property and custody of children. These are discussed with a special focus on the Affiliation Proceedings (Amendment) Bill of 1999.

B *The sources of family law in Botswana*

In common with other former colonies and protectorates, Botswana operates a plural legal system comprising various types of customary laws, Roman-Dutch law received during the colonial period, and legislation passed by the Botswana Parliament. In Botswana legal parlance, the combination of Roman-Dutch law and statutes is normally referred to as common law, which should be distinguished from its English law meaning. The relationship between these various sources is not always clear, especially in the matters or categories of people to whom they apply. However, it can generally be said that common law mainly applies to the field of public law, such as constitutional and administrative law, criminal law and employment law. In the private law areas, including family law and inheritance, customary law applies to persons who are subject to it, usually those who are affiliated to one of the tribes to be found in Botswana, while

---

* Senior Lecturer, University of Botswana, Head of the Gender Unit of the Southern African Development Community.

[1] See Molokomme, 'The Reception and Development of Roman Dutch Law in Botswana' (1982) *Lesotho Law Journal* Vol. 1 No. 1 and Molokomme, 'Disseminating Family Law Reforms: Some Lessons from Botswana', (1990) *Journal of Legal Pluralism* Nos 30 and 31.

common law applies to the rest of the population. However, persons can choose to opt out of either system in private law matters, either explicitly or implicitly.[2]

In practice customary law applies to the majority of the population who live in the rural and peri-urban centres of Botswana although, with changing lifestyles, a steadily increasing number are opting for the common law in some cases.

The contemporary sources of family law in Botswana therefore include customary law, Roman-Dutch law and legislation passed by the Botswana Parliament since independence.

The next sections review developments in the field of maintenance, matrimonial property and custody of children.

II   THE LAW OF MAINTENANCE: THE AFFILIATION PROCEEDINGS ACT OF 1970

A   Background

The Affiliation Proceedings Act of 1970 laid down a judicial procedure by which a single woman could bring a paternity and maintenance action against a man alleged to be the father of her child. Hailed as a landmark statute at the time, the Act has been plagued by problems ranging from its restricted procedures to its weak enforcement mechanisms. During the past three decades the courts, researchers and women's organisations have called for its amendment, especially with a view to removing the restrictions and clarifying its relationship with customary law and common law.[3]

The question whether a claim for maintenance can be brought outside the Act, under Roman-Dutch law, came before the High Court in the case of *Moremi and others v Mesotlho*.[4] In that case, a single mother and her children applied for an order directing the father of the children to pay P1,000 per month for their maintenance. The father opposed the application, raising a point *in limine* that the application was before the wrong court, and that it should have been brought before a Magistrate's Court under the Affiliation Proceedings Act. He further argued that, under that Act, the time within which the application should have been brought had lapsed.

The mother responded by arguing that children have a common law right to support, and that Botswana was obliged by the UN Convention on the Rights of the Child, as well as the African Charter on Human and People's Rights, to ensure non-discrimination of children born outside marriage. Agreeing with the mother, the High Court took the position that the Constitution gives it unlimited jurisdiction in all civil and criminal cases, that it was the upper guardian of all minors, and that the Affiliation Proceedings Act did not deprive it of its jurisdiction. It further held that the P40 per month, laid down as the upper limit for maintenance under the Affiliation Proceedings Act, was insufficient for

---

[2]   See the Customary Law and Common Law Act 1992, which lays down certain rules of application. For example by marrying under the statute, or writing a will, a person subject to customary law can have common law apply.

[3]   See Emang Basadi, *Report of the Proceedings of a Conference on Women and the Law in Botswana,* Gaborone (1987); Molokomme, 'Children of the Fence: The Maintenance of Extramarital Children under Law and Practice in Botswana', (1991) Africa Studies Center Research report No 41/91, Leiden Ph.D. thesis; 'Maintenance Laws and Practices in Botswana', National Institute of Research, University of Botswana, Gaborone, *Women and Law in Southern Africa* (1992).

[4]   MISCA 13/1996 (High Court, unreported). See also Ministry of Labour and Home Affairs, *Report on a Review of all Laws Affecting the Status of Women in Botswana,* Gaborone.

the maintenance and education of a child, and expressed the hope that this would be removed 'to leave the Magistrate unfettered to award an amount of money for the maintenance and education of a child that reflects the true needs of the child in this present age.'

This was indeed a landmark case which settled once and for all the question whether a maintenance claim can be brought outside the Affiliation Proceedings Act, and meant that the restrictions of the Affiliation Proceedings Act could be avoided by women bringing claims under the common law.

B   Amendments to the Affiliation Proceedings Act in 1999

In response to some of the problems experienced in the administration of the Act, a number of amendments were introduced by the Affiliation Proceedings (Amendment) Bill of 1999.[5] These are briefly presented below.

1   Gender-neutral application

Section 3 marks a departure from the previous position where action could only be brought by a single mother against the alleged father of the child. The word 'mother' is substituted with 'parent', and proceedings may now be instituted by someone other than the mother of the child. Moreover, maintenance proceedings can also be brought against her by the father, or any person having the care and custody of the child. This is a significant development, which recognises the common law position that the duty of support rests on both parents. In addition, it is a recognition of the variety of arrangements and changing conditions under which children are being raised in Botswana.

2   Separation of paternity from maintenance actions

Under the previous law, the action to establish paternity was combined with that for maintenance, which resulted in the untenable situation in which a woman had to adduce evidence of paternity even in the case of an admission by the defendant. The amendment separates the two actions, and requires the complainant to state whether he or she seeks a paternity or maintenance order. This has also been made necessary by the inclusion of the mother as a potential defendant since paternity actions cannot obviously be brought against her.

According to section 7(a) a court may make a paternity or maintenance order against the alleged father, or a maintenance order against the mother, where it is satisfied 'as to the sufficiency of the evidence adduced'. This is a welcome departure from the previous position which required material corroboration of the mother's allegation by other evidence.

3   Extension of the time period

The Bill in section 5 responds to one of the most common complaints that were made against the old Act, that of restricting actions to the first 12 months following the birth of the child. This period has been extended to five years, and the exceptions have been

---

[5]   Bill No 4 of 1999, Supplement B – *Botswana Government Extraordinary Gazette* dated March 8, 1999. These amendments all passed through the June 1999 session of Parliament, and will become law after the presidential assent, expected during July 1999.

widened. Previously, an action could be brought outside the 12-month period where the father had been outside Botswana, or where he had influenced the mother, through words or conduct, not to report the matter within the 12-month period. The strict interpretation of these provisions by the courts had resulted in a number of late complaints being dismissed and children going without maintenance.[6]

Where the child has a physical or mental disability preventing him or her from being independent, the paternity complaint can be brought at any subsequent time after the expiry of five years. In the case of maintenance, complaints may be brought at any subsequent time after obtaining a paternity order where the defendant is the male parent. Where the defendant is the female parent, a maintenance action may be brought at any time before the child turns 18 years.

Another related departure from the old law is the duration of maintenance orders which were restricted to 13 years in the first instance, and could not be extended beyond 16 years. The amendment lays down a general rule of 18 years, which may be extended to 21 years in the case of a child who is pursuing education. Where a child has a disability which prevents him from ever being independent, the parent may be ordered to maintain the child until the death of the parent or the child, whichever comes first.[7]

4   Courts with jurisdiction

While previously only Magistrates Grade 1 had jurisdiction to entertain actions under the Act, section 3(b) includes all ranks of magistrates and customary courts which have been authorised by any instrument to hear such proceedings. In addition, section 6 provides that a complaint shall be made to a court having jurisdiction in the administrative district in which the complainant resides, or in which it is convenient for him or her to bring the suit. This is a good development in view of the fact that very few places in Botswana, a vast country, are serviced by a Magistrate Grade 1. It will be especially welcomed by many rural women who previously had to travel long distances to bring complaints before courts in which the defendant was ordinarily resident or employed.

The extension of jurisdiction to customary courts will make the Act more accessible to the rural public, since customary courts are spread around the country and are less intimidating than magistrates' courts. Chiefs and other tribal authorities are likely to especially pleased, as they have demanded this extension of their jurisidction over the past few years.[8] However, in view of the technical nature of the Act, the fundamental differences in ideology and solutions, an educational programme for customary court personnel on the operation of the Act would seem to be in order.

Another related question is that of the link between the customary law action for seduction and the Act. Section 13 of the Act has been considered to be rather vague on this relationship and courts have been at a loss as to how to deal with it. The amendment is surprisingly silent on this issue, which has caused a lot of uncertainty in legal circles.[9] The only reference to customary law is in section 7(b), which provides for cases where the parent against whom an action is brought has no income from which deductions for maintenance and education can be made. In such cases a social worker can be ordered to

---

6   See the following cases: *Sichinga v Phumetse* 1981 BLR 161; *Makwati v Ramohago* Civil Appeal 10/83 (High Court).

7   Section 10 of the Bill.

8   See Ministry of Labour and Home Affairs 1998, note 4 above.

9   See Molokomme, 'The Mosaic of Botswana Maintenance Law' *Botswana Notes and Records* Vol. 19 (1986) and *Makwati v Ramohago* (earlier cited).

assess his estate or socio-economic standing, to determine how he can contribute to the child's maintenance. The social worker's report and the complaint can then be referred to a customary court, 'which shall apply customary law thereto'.

While this is an interesting innovation, it does not clarify the long-standing doubts surrounding the precise nature of the customary law applicable to paternity and maintenance. Is the action seduction, maintenance or both? Moreover, it does not answer the major question, which has been posed over the years, whether an action under the Act prevents the father of an unmarried woman from suing a man who makes her pregnant for damages for seduction.[10]

5   *Amounts of maintenance payments*

Under the previous law, a maximum of P40 per month or P10 per week could be ordered for maintenance and, in some cases, a lump sum could be awarded. These amounts had last been reviewed in 1979 and, with the rising inflation rate, had led to increasing demands for their revision during the past decade. In section 7(b), the Bill introduces the rule that the parent will be required to pay not less than P100 per month for the maintenance and education of the child. The proviso to this section however suggests that this is not intended to be an inflexible minimum: a parent may be ordered to pay such lesser or greater amount as the court considers appropriate taking into account the financial circumstances and ability of the parent to pay.

This provision is likely to be received with mixed feelings. On the one hand, the upward revision of the P40 maximum as such will be welcomed as long overdue. However, the figure of P100 seems rather arbitrary, and the criteria used to reach the amount are not clear. In fact, this issue generated a lot of argument during the parliamentary discussions of the Bill. Most previous recommendations from researchers and the general public had preferred a flexible situation where no amounts were stated in the legislation. Rather, it was felt desirable to leave the determination of the amount to the courts in cases before them, as echoed by Justice Gittings in the case of *Moremi v Mesotlho* (earlier cited).

6   *Persons entitled to payment*

Another innovation introduced by the amendment is the use of social workers in cases where the recipient of payments is no longer able to receive them, or is misusing them.[11] In such cases, the court may order a social worker to identify and assess another person to whom payments shall be made, who may be appointed in the place of the parent. Social workers are also given powers to monitor the use to which payments are applied and report to the court every three months.

Finally, the Act removes the discriminatory reference by the old law to an illegitimate child, and simply makes reference to a child. This is consistent with the provisions of the Convention on the Rights of the Child which Botswana acceded to in 1995.

---

[10]   See Molokomme 1986 and 1991, notes 9 and 3 above.

[11]   Section 8(b).

III   THE LAW OF MATRIMONIAL PROPERTY: THE MARRIED PERSONS PROPERTY ACT OF 1971

A   Background

This Act was apparently intended to redress the disabilities suffered by women married in community of property, an institution of Roman-Dutch law which gives them limited decision-making power over the joint estate[12]. But as I have argued elsewhere, this Act only introduced cosmetic reforms into the law, and did not achieve these objectives.[13]

This is because it merely reversed the previous Roman-Dutch law presumption that all marriages were in community of property, unless otherwise indicated. Community of property gives the husband the marital power over the joint estate, which means that he is its sole administrator, making final decisions over it without the necessary consent of his wife. The wife, on the other hand, may not enter significant contracts with respect to the joint property without her husband's consent, and requires his assistance to borrow money from financial institutions.

The Married Persons Property Act did not interfere with the husband's marital power, nor did it do anything to remove the disabilities suffered by a wife married in community of property. Instead, it introduced a presumption in favour of the marriage without community, unless otherwise indicated. Moreover, the Act provided different forms to be completed by marrying partners to indicate their desire to marry in or out of community which have been misunderstood by both their administrators and consumers.

Like the Affiliation Proceedings Act, the past three decades have witnessed increased demands for reform of the law of matrimonial property, especially a removal of the restrictions imposed on women married in community of property. Instead of amending the Married Persons Property Act, and abolishing the husband's marital power, Parliament responded by amending section 18 of the Deeds Registry Act in 1996.

B   Amendments to the Deeds Registry Act in 1996

The old section 18 of the Deeds Registry Act previously codified the common law position by providing that immovable property could not be transferred or ceded to a woman married in community of property. It also required that a woman married in community be assisted by her husband in executing any deed or other document.

In the Memorandum to the Bill, it is stated that its principal object is to 'enable women, whether married in or out of community, and whether or not the marital power has been excluded, to execute deeds and other documents... without their husband's assistance'.[14] The final amendment however fell short of these objectives in several respects.

First, the amendment simply makes it possible for immovable property to be transferred or ceded to a woman married in community 'as if she were married out of community and the marital power did not apply'. Similarly, it makes it possible for immovable property to be bequeathed or donated to such a woman, and provides that

---

[12]   See National Assembly, *Official Report of the Parliamentary Debates, Hansard* 34.

[13]   Molokomme, 'Disseminating family law Reforms: Some Lessons from Botswana', *Journal of Legal Pluralism* Nos 30 and 31.

[14]   *Government Gazette*, September 20, 1996.

such property shall not form part of the joint estate if it is excluded from the community and the marital power.[15]

The major problem with this provision is that, like the Married Persons Property Act before it, it does not go far enough in introducing equality of rights to the matrimonial assets between husband and wife.[16] By leaving the husband's marital power intact, it treats only the symptoms (the requirement that wives be assisted) and not the root cause of the disease (the husband's marital power over the joint property). The result is an untenable situation where, while immovable property may be transferred or ceded to a woman married in community of property, the husband can still frustrate her efforts by refusing to assist her to obtain a loan to purchase it, which remains a requirement under common law.

Secondly, because the amendment is targeted at the Deeds Registry Act, and not the law of matrimonial property, it introduces changes only with respect to immovable property. As a result, it leaves out of its application other property such as livestock, crop produce, cash/money/income, vehicles and other movables which are often the only property an average Botswana couple may have. This means that women married in community of property remain unprotected from husbands who may continue to deal in any way whatsoever with joint movables without consultation or consent.

However, a welcome provision is section 2(c), which provides that neither spouse may alone deal with immovable joint property unless s/he has the written consent of the other spouse, or has been authorised by a court order to do so. This will come as a relief for wives who have previously complained that the law allows husbands married in community literally to sell the roof over their families' heads without consulting them.

IV   CUSTODY OF CHILDREN

A number of interesting decisions in this field were handed down by the High Court during the 1990s, especially with respect to custody of children born outside marriage.

A   *Extra-marital children*[17]

Before the introduction of the best interests principle by statute into the law of Botswana in 1969,[18] the common law rule which favoured mothers of extra-marital children over their biological fathers was applicable. This reflects the different treatment of children based on their birth status, and violates Article 2 of the Convention on the Rights of the Child. It also reflects discrimination against the biological fathers of extra-marital children who, while required by the common law to maintain their children, were not given automatic rights of access to them.

It must be pointed out however that there are very few cases which have come before the superior courts in which fathers have sought custody of their extra-marital children; thus the courts had little opportunity to pronounce on this matter. Such an opportunity

---

[15]   See section 2(a) and (b) of the Amendment.

[16]   The Namibian Equality in Marriage Act of 1996 is an example of reforms that went much further.

[17]   This section is extracted from Molokomme and Mokobi, 'Custody and Guardianship of Children in Botswana: Customary Laws and Judicial practice within the Framework of the Children's Convention' in Ncube (ed), *Law, Culture, Tradition and Children's Rights in Southern Africa*, Ashgate, Dartmouth (1998).

[18]   See section 6, Customary Law (Application and Ascertainment) Act.

first arose in the landmark case of *Chiepe v Sago*[19] where the mother of an extra-marital child sought an order against the father of the child to return the child to her. The four-year-old boy had been living with the father, since his parents' break-up, by arrangement with the mother. She contended that the common law recognised her as the child's legal guardian, and that she was entitled to his custody unless good cause was shown why she should be deprived of this right.

The father responded that she was unfit to raise the child because she had been indifferent to him, given him inadequate supervision, and planned to have him adopted by a relative. In addition, she had recently served a long prison sentence for dishonesty.

The court reviewed the common law and accepted that the mother's contention was supported by very strong authority, but the judge noted that statute law had since 1969 modified this position. He stressed that the welfare of the child was paramount over any other legal provisions and, applying that principle, granted interim custody to the father with the following remarks:

> 'Even without regard to section 6 of the Customary Law Act I would hold that the father has in his affidavit made out a prima facie case such as might, if the facts therein alleged were established, warrant the court, as upper guardian of this four year old boy, interfering with the custody of the mother ... If the father's allegations are correct then can it possibly be said that this child of tender years would be better off in the care and control of a mother who is indifferent to his welfare rather than in the care of a concerned father who is in the position to provide for all his needs? ... In the meantime I am firmly of the view that the child should remain with his father, the respondent. His ability to care for the child and the arrangements he has made for him have not been questioned in the affidavit evidence before me. On the other hand serious allegations have been made against the mother. Unless there is some good reason not to do so, the court, when dealing with interim custody, will prima facie preserve the status quo as at the institution of the proceedings.'

It took almost a decade before a case raising similar issues came before the High Court. In *Langebacher v Thipe*[20] a man who had lived together with the mother of his two extra-marital children aged seven and two years claimed their custody after they broke up, on the grounds that this would be in the children's best interests. Previous attempts by the father to adopt the children had failed, and he subsequently changed his custody claim to access to the children over weekends.

The mother opposed this on the ground, among others, that she feared that the father, a foreigner, would take the children out of the country for good. The court found no evidence to support the mother's allegations and instead found that the father loved the children, maintained and entertained them very well, including paying their school fees at private schools.

Granting the father access to the children every weekend, from Friday to Sunday, Justice Aboagye had the following to say:

> It has been held that in determining questions of access, the welfare of the child is the first and paramount consideration although, as a general rule, the court is slow to deprive a parent of all contact with his or her child ... And in *M v M* (1973) 2 All ER 81 it was stated at pages 85 and 88 by Wrangham J. and Latey J., respectively, that access should be regarded as a basic right of the child rather than a basic right of the

---

[19]   1982 (1) BLR 25.
[20]   MISCA F 58/1990, High Court, Unreported.

parent and save in exceptional circumstances to deprive a parent of access is to deprive a child of an important contribution to his emotional and material growing up in the long term. In my view, for the purpose of access, "parent" includes the biological father of an illegitimate child.'

This passage contains some very important remarks for the development of the law regarding the biological father's access to his extra-marital child. First, the judge makes it clear that the best interests principle is applicable to questions of access, and not only to custody cases.

Secondly, by concluding that the father of an extra-marital child is a parent for purposes of access, the judge breaks away from the discriminatory approach of Roman-Dutch law, preferring instead to use English precedents. Thirdly, and most importantly, this approach recognises the superiority of children's rights by making the observation that access is not a basic parental right but rather a basic right of the child.

In yet another landmark case brought by the father for access to his extra-marital child, the High Court rejected the mother's argument that he had no rights of access because she had sole rights of guardianship. This is the case of *Phiri v Dintsi and Dintsi*,[21] in which the mother was actually given a suspended prison sentence for contempt of a court order granting the father access to the child on school holidays. As a reflection of the concern for the best interests of the child the court also ordered that the most senior social welfare officer should supervise the child when in his father's custody.

These cases suggest that the courts are beginning to develop a jurisprudence on the concept of the best interests of the child, as well as changing attitudes towards extra-marital children.

B   Custody of children born within marriage

In this area, two contradictory decisions were handed down by the High Court in 1998 and 1999. In the first case, *Masego Sello v Lefatlhe Sello and Another*,[22] a mother sought the return of her two minor children, as well as their interim custody. She also sought an order interdicting the father, who had removed the children from Botswana, from interfering with and having access to them. The father opposed the application on the basis that without instituting an action for divorce or judicial separation, the applicant cannot bring any application for an order *pendente lite*. Judge Aboagye relied on section 28(1) of the Matrimonial Causes Act and upheld the respondent's contention that questions of custody, maintenance and education of the children can only be considered in the course of proceedings for divorce, nullity or judicial separation.

The applicant subsequently instituted divorce proceedings and launched proceedings before Judge Dow on an urgent basis seeking the return of the children. Judge Dow concluded as follows:

'I conclude that children are not chattels, subject to relocation at the instance of the whims of any one parent, but are individuals with rights. I also conclude that whether or not the 1st Respondent succeeds in due course, the immediate return of the children to Botswana is in their best interest. I arrive at this conclusion having considered that the children's continued separation from their home, mother and youngest sibling is not in their best interest. In addition, it would not be in the best

---

[21]   MISCA F45/1995, (High Court, Unreported).

[22]   MISCA 322/98, (High Court, Unreported).

interest of the children to have them establish roots in Lesotho, only to be removed to Botswana, should the Applicant prevail. I note that the children were removed from Botswana in July 1998, an act that would have disrupted their schooling. Any decision of this court must attempt to limit any further schooling disruptions to the minimum. I note that schools in Botswana re-open for the year in January and this ruling has taken that in consideration.'

An interim order for the father to return the children to the mother was issued which he failed to comply with. As a result, he was ordered to show cause why he should not be found in contempt of court. In an interesting twist of events, the father responded by applying for Judge Dow's recusal. The basis for the recusal was that he felt that he had upset the judge, and was apprehensive that 'she may not divorce her mind from the fact that his conduct, which seemingly went against the grain of the order, would prejudice any explanation in the contempt proceedings'.

Judge Dow dismissed the application, and set the date for hearing the contempt proceedings on September 21, 1999. The result was awaited at the time of writing.

A similar case came before Judge Dow soon thereafter, in which she differed with Judge Aboagye's approach in *Sello's* case. In *Mnqibisa v Mnqibisa*,[23] a mother who had left the matrimonial home sought an order confirming an earlier custody order in her favour. Judge Dow noted that no divorce proceedings were pending and that the applicant's papers were 'sadly lacking in the type of details necessary to support a custody order'. However, she was of the view that simply to dismiss the rule would not serve the child's best interests. She therefore decided that pending the hearing of oral evidence, the custody of the child should remain with the mother. Her reasoning was as follows:

'It is my view that having been forced by the behaviour of the Respondent to flee, she did not have to file for divorce before she could place the issues of the best interest of the child before the court for litigation and determination. Whether or not she finally files for divorce, the disruption in the home had affected the child Vuyani in such a way that his custody and support were clearly matters the two parents could not deal with without the intervention of the Court. It seems to me then that Applicant need not have claimed to be planning to sue for divorce when she might not have been so minded at the time. It may well be that the marriage relationship between the parties deteriorates further and ends in divorce. Still, it may well be that their problems are resolved and a marriage relationship is rebuilt. However things end up, the interest of the child Vuyani must be safeguarded and clarity must prevail as to his custody and support.'

Although Judge Dow does not make any reference to the decision in *Sello* (cited above), she clearly took a different view of the matter, and put the best interests of the child above the provisions of section 28(1) of the Matrimonial Causes Act as interpreted by Judge Aboagye. It remains to be seen what direction future decisions of the High Court will take in such cases.

---

23   MISCA 380/1998, (High Court, Unreported).

V   CONCLUSION

This overview of the situation in certain areas of family law in Botswana shows that there have been some significant legislative and judicial developments. However, as earlier pointed out, these have not taken place in the context of a properly planned law reform programme, and have tended to be ad hoc, reactive rather than proactive. As a result, a number of gaps remain in areas such as the law of maintenance, despite the existence of research findings over the years pointing these out. The failure of recent statutory amendments to close these gaps is partly the result of the lack of strong links between research and the legislative process.

Similarly, the amendments to the Deeds Registry Act in 1996 amount to half-way measures rather than a full-scale reform that ensures equality of rights to joint matrimonial assets. Because the field of family law is generally a difficult one to reform, it requires a planned and comprehensive approach which identifies the gaps and develops interventions to address them. Unfortunately, the law reform process in Botswana generally does not adopt this approach, and this is reflected in the state of family law.

CAMEROON

CUSTOMARY LAW VERSUS STATUTORY LAW
AN UNRESOLVED SECOND MILLENNIUM MORAL QUAGMIRE

E.N. Ngwafor[*]

I   INTRODUCTION

The application of customary law in Anglophone Cameroon[1] received legislative recognition in Section 27(1) of the Southern Cameroons High Court Law 1955, wherein it is provided that:

> 'The High Court shall observe, and enforce the observance of every native law and custom which is not repugnant to natural justice, equity and good conscience, nor incompatible with any law for the time being in force, and nothing in this law shall deprive any person of the benefit of any such native law or custom.'

Indeed, customary law and statutory law operate in well-defined jurisdictions throughout our national territory.[2] It is only at the level of an Appeal Court that issues on both statutory law and customary law can be canvassed, coming in the form of appeals from the High Court and the Customary Court respectively. It is at this second level that a serious conflict has emerged. The spirited debates and slogans proffered by feminist groups in Cameroon[3] have resulted in watering down recognized principles which presiding judges ought to follow before passing judgment in any case. In support of this worry, this paper seeks to demonstrate, among other things, the striking inconsistencies in court judgments within the last few years on matters emanating from conflicts that exist between customary law and statutory law.

II   RE-IMBURSEMENT OF THE BRIDE PRICE

It is not my intention in this paper to discuss all the intricacies that surround a customary law marriage. I will merely refer to the issues which have some connection with the

---

[*]   Professor of Law at the University of Yaounde II, Soa.

[1]   For the evolution of the legal system in Cameroon, see E.N. Ngwafor, 'The Law Across the Bridge : Twenty Years (1972–1992) of Confusion', (1995) 26 R.G.D. 69; E.N. Ngwafor, 'Nullity : The Squaring Of A Questionable Dilemma', (1994) *Int. Surv. Fam. Law.*101.

[2]   Under statutory law, original jurisdiction to try and hear matrimonial matters is vested in the High Court as indicated in Section 16(1)(b) of the Judicial Organization Ordinance No.72/4 of August 26, 1972 as modified by Law No.89/019 of December 29, 1989, Section 16(1)(c). However, customary law matters are dealt with in customary courts and it has been emphatically stated in Section 9(1)(b) of the Southern Cameroons High Court Law, 1955 that: 'Subject to the provisions of the Land and Native Right Ordinance and any other written law, the High Court shall not exercise original jurisdiction in any suit or matter which is subject to the jurisdiction of a native court relating to marriage, family status, guardianship of children, inheritance or the disposition of property on death.'

[3]   ACCOLAGIG; The Association of Cameroon Commonwealth Ladies for Gender-in-Development; ACAFEG; FIDA.

subject under consideration. In traditional society parental consent is a pre-requisite to the formation of a valid marriage. This is especially so because a customary law marriage unites two families and not two spouses.[4] It is equally relevant to add that the payment of a bride price is essential for a valid customary law marriage. It therefore goes without saying that it would be virtually impossible to pay the bride price in a case where parental consent is absent. This is because the payment must be made to the family (represented by a family head) and not to the bride.

This explains why, in the event of any divorce, the bride price must be refunded to indicate a complete severance of the cord that united the two families. So, in *Esther Guta v. Alex Guta Musi*,[5] Justice Nfobin had to decide on the consequence of a phrase in an earlier judgment namely: 'Divorce granted, £25 part dowry deposit. Defendant to accept assessed dowry refund. No order as to costs'. The learned judge took the view that since part payment of £25 had been made and the only reason why more money had not been paid was because the defendant had failed to assess the refund, the decree of divorce could not be challenged. It implies that if the defendant had done so and the petitioner's family failed to make the payments, she would still have been considered the respondent's wife. Indeed, customary law dictates that in such a case any children she bears with any other man belong to the first husband.[6] However, Justice Monekosso once took the view that no order as to return of bride price would be made in the case where the couple had been married for a long time. He argued that the woman should be compensated for her long-standing services to the family.[7]

The 1981 Ordinance[8] has also explicitly provided that the total or partial settlement of dowry shall under no circumstances give rise to natural paternity.[9] Indeed, even before the coming into force of this Ordinance, Chief Justice Gordon had held in *Ngeh v. Ngome*[10] that a custom which permits a husband to claim paternity of a child which his run-away wife begot with another man, simply because she has failed to pay back the bride price, was repugnant to natural justice.[11]

III   THE POLEMICS OF *PAUL TEH v. KEDZE REGINA MBEI*[12]

Underneath this customary law principle of repayment of a bride price upon divorce as proof that the link between the two families has been severed lie stormy legal waters which need close exploration. Customary courts in Anglophone Cameroon are limited to a civil jurisdiction of 69.200 FCFA (about £69).[13] One is immediately confronted with a

---

[4]   E.T. Nwogugu, *Family Law in Nigeria* (1974) Heineman Press, Nigeria, 44.

[5]   The unreported judgment of the Court of Appeal No.BCA/3/85. See also *Jacob Sama Ntumvi v. Mary Ndibabonga*, the unreported judgment of Appeal, No.BCA/50/84.

[6]   *Mary Buck v. Lucas Mume Kubong*, the unreported judgment of Appeal No.BCA/15/85.

[7]   *Anje Rosyline Buma v. Clement Buma*, the unreported judgment of Appeal No.BCA/20/81.

[8]   Ordinance No.81-02 of June 29, 1981 to organize Civil Status Registration.

[9]   *Ibid*, Section 72.

[10]   (1962–64) WCLR 321.

[11]   The Southern Cameroons High Court Law, 1955, Section 27(1).

[12]   The unreported judgment of Appeal No.BCA/2187 of December 14, 1988.

[13]   Customary Courts Ordinance, Cap 142 of the 1948 edition of the Revised Laws of Nigeria, Section 8, as amended by the Southern Cameroons Customary Court Law, 1956 and the Schedule to that Section. See also Ordinance No.72/4 of August 26, 1972, Section 26 as amended. Some helpful cases where complainants tailored their claims to suit these provisions are: *Isidore Ngueukmason Yamacam v. Hannah Nelle*, the unreported judgment of Appeal No.CASWP/CC/13/83 of December 17, 1982; *Marcus A.*

legal quandary in the case where the plaintiff maintains that the dowry paid was above 69.200 FCFA. He could, for example, have paid 500.000 FCFA (about £500). Has the Customary Court jurisdiction to entertain the matter? Should the matter go on appeal? Has the Court of Appeal the locus standi to pass judgment in favour of the plaintiff? In other words can the Court of Appeal give redress on an issue which the customary court did not have jurisdiction to entertain?

In *Paul Teh v. Kedze Regina Mbei*[14] the appellant had filed a claim of 410.000 FCFA against the respondent in the Wum Court of First Instance. He maintained that the respondent and himself had contracted a customary law marriage in 1979. The respondent sued him and obtained a divorce in the Customary Court in September 1984. Surprisingly, the appellant did not ask for a refund of dowry at this level but did so in a fresh action in the Wum Court of First Instance.[15] Indeed, Section 13(1) of Ordinance No.72/4 of August 26, 1972 spells out the civil jurisdiction of the Court of First Instance and this does not include jurisdiction in matrimonial and divorce causes. This right, as earlier indicated, is reserved exclusively to the High Court. Small wonder that the presiding Magistrate, Mr. Paul Ayah, did not hesitate to rule that the Wum Court of First Instance did not have jurisdiction to hear the matter. This position was upheld at the Court of Appeal in Bamenda.

In reading out the unanimous judgment of the Court of Appeal, Justice P.E.N. Ebung, in a very laconic statement, declared that the Customary Court could entertain a claim for a refund of dowry, notwithstanding the fact that this figure was above 69.000 FCFA. He remarked :

'The order for the refund is therefore incidental to the substantive cause of action, the divorce. It does not therefore constitute a separate and independent claim per se as in civil claims as founded on a debt, a civil wrong, a contract and others. It should not therefore be limited to the civil jurisdiction of the Court which is 69.000 FCFA ...'

These are very strong words indeed. And if left unqualified they could go a long way in eroding Section 8 of the Customary Courts Ordinance, Cap.142 of the 1948 edition of the Revised Laws of Nigeria or in making a new Law.

IV   SENTIMENTALISM OR TRESPASS TO THE LAW

The judgment in *Paul Teh v. Kedze Regina Mbei* should not be read alone. A comparative study vis-à-vis other judgments along the same lines may be helpful.

In *Ngnitedem Etienne v. Tashi Lydia Sinaga*[16] the Court of Appeal in Bamenda listened to an appeal from the decision of the Mankon Customary Court whereby the

---

Abanda v. Bertha Enanga, the unreported judgment of Appeal No.CASWP/CC/163/183 of December 16, 1981; *Atem David Nonjong v. Efuetaka Mbe Ngu & 4 others*, the unreported judgment of Suit No.CASWP/CC/51/81, of December 30, 1982.

[14]   Note 12 above.

[15]   In Cameroon, the civil jurisdiction of the Court of First Instance, formerly known as the Magistrate's Court, is laid down in Section 8(1) of the Magistrate's (Southern Cameroons) Law 1955. Section 18(2)(iii) and 18(2)(a) of that Law state that :
  'Subject to the provisions of paragraph (2) of sub-section (1) and of any written law a Chief Magistrate shall not exercise original jurisdiction in any suit or matter which :
  – is subject to the jurisdiction of a native court relating to marriage, family status, guardianship of children, inheritance or disposition of property on death.'

[16]   The unreported judgment of Appeal No.BCA/46/86 of March 31, 1988.

marriage was dissolved and the Court awarded an uncompleted house to the respondent (wife) and the following household articles: a standing fan, a baby's bed and mattress, a family bed and mattress, all the kitchen utensils, drinking glasses, plates and one hand radio. Citing Section 8 of the Customary Courts Ordinance, Justice O.M. Inglis underlined the fact that Customary Courts have ' jurisdiction in all matrimonial causes other than those arising from or connected with Christian marriage'. He then went on to note that matrimonial causes in the customary law context include: 'marriage, divorce and nullity, and those incidental causes as refund of dowry ...'. Since the question at stake was the sharing of property (which customary law does not countenance) especially landed property between husband and wife, the judge went on to accept the appeal. This judgment was given barely nine months before that of *Paul Teh v. Kedze Regina Mbei* and emanated from a court of equal standing. Yet, Justice Ebung did not cite it, let alone distinguish it from his own case.

The very cryptic statement by Justice Inglis in the *Ngnitedem Etienne* case that matrimonial causes include such incidental causes as 'refund of dowry' begs the question whether or not an independent claim can be made for refund of dowry, thus casting doubts on Justice Ebung's opinion in *Paul Teh v Kedze Regina Mbei* that it cannot constitute a separate and independent claim.

In a divorce suit under customary law it is easy to visualise a scene whereby the husband and wife are the only parties involved. But when you continue in your stream of consciousness and look at the consequences flowing from the pronouncement of the dissolution of the marriage it becomes clear that the number of people concerned increases. It was remarked above that the bride cannot receive the bride price. This is done on behalf of the family by the family head or his representative. One can therefore argue with maximum conviction that two different scenarios can be conjured in a legal expert's mind – first, a divorce suit concerning the husband and wife and secondly, a claim for a refund of the dowry in which the husband will include the head of the bride's family as a co-defendant.[17] In this connection it becomes unimaginable that the Customary Court will be able to offer the plaintiff more than 69.000 FCFA.

Another argument which weakens Justice Ebung's view that no separate claim on a refund of dowry is justifiable can be seen in the case where it is the wife who petitions for divorce and the husband challenges it. Should the wife win her divorce suit could the husband not bring an independent claim a few months later in the Customary Court for a refund of the dowry? This could be a proper approach to follow.[18]

Facts similar to the Bamenda Court of Appeal case of *Ngnitedem Etienne v. Tashi Lydia Sinaga*[19] were heard by the Court of Appeal in Buea in the case of *Gaius Ebande v. Elizabeth Neh Ebande.*[20] This was an appeal from a Customary Court judgment where the wife, the respondent, left the matrimonial home with property worth about

---

[17] CF/*Ronaté Tupong v. Joshua Mobit.* The unreported Bamenda Court of Appeal judgment in Suit No.BCA/31/74 which concerned a breach of promise to marry. The appeal failed simply because the groom-to-be did not personally sue the bride-to-be. Instead the action was brought by the groom-to-be's elder brother whom the court considered to be a stranger in the action. The question is, had the parties been married, would the court have accepted that the groom's brother who had paid the bride price could be a party to the suit? Or, could this 'stranger', in the case where the marriage had failed to take place, bring an action for mental distress? See Nelson Enonchong, 'Breach of Contract and Damages for Mental Distress' (1999) *Oxford Journal of Legal Studies* vol.16, No.4, 617–640.

[18] In *Ayuk Etang Elias Bechgem v. Manyi Agbor Serah and Agbor Simon*, the unreported judgment of Case No.44/85-86 CRA 2/85/86 p.37 it was held that the Kumba Customary Court had jurisdiction to hear a case based on the refund of dowry.

[19] Note 16 above.

[20] The unreported judgment of Suit No.CASWP/CC/50/95.

4.677.000 FCFA (£5000). Justice Bawak held that the respondent had to return the items or pay the equivalent value.

In 1996, the Buea High Court in *Kang Sume Née Aboh v. Kang Sume David*,[21] had to face up to the same legal difficulties encountered by the Wum Court of First Instance in *Paul Teh v. Kedze Regina Mbei*. The parties were married under customary law and on September 19, 1994 the wife successfully petitioned for divorce in the Buea Customary Court.[22] In 1995 the wife then appealed to the Buea Court of Appeal asking for ancillary orders. She knew that the Customary Court did not have jurisdiction to entertain such matters. Justice Deba dismissed the appeal.[23] Less than a year later, the appellant (wife) through the mechanism of an originating summons[24] at the Fako High Court in Buea applied for custody of the children, alimony, maintenance and property rights pursuant to Sections 23, 24 and 42(2) of the Matrimonial Causes Act 1973, as read with Sections 11, 15 and 27 of the Southern Cameroons High Court Law, 1955. On July 20, 1998, the High Court judge, in an unprecedented first, not only entertained the matter but determined it in favour of the applicant (the wife).

Once more the judicial clock was set to work backwards. This judgment was founded on no legal basis. I dare say that it harps on recklessness. And where did the judge place Section 8 of the Customary Law Ordinance which spells out the jurisdiction of Customary Courts? Customary law is not statutory law. The mere mention of Sections 22, 24 and 42(2) of the MCA 1973 as applied in a customary law marriage destroys the very invitation for any legal debate. Statutory law rules do not apply when matters concerning customary law are evoked.[25]

There was authority for the dismissal of this case from the highest Court of the Land, the Supreme Court. In *Daniel Nyancho v. Joan Nana Nyanch*,[26] a similar set of facts were examined by the Supreme Court in Yaounde. It was an appeal against the judgment of Justice Kesiro whereby the appellant was adjudged to pay 189.000 FCFA as allowances to two children of his marriage with the respondent. The parties had been married under customary law. The wife filed her action at the High Court alleging that the appellant had not been maintaining the two children of the marriage. The Honourable Mr. Justice S.M.L. Endeley, who read the unanimous judgment of the Supreme Court, held that the trial judge erred in law in holding that the High Court had jurisdiction to entertain maintenance proceedings on a marriage founded on customary law principles. On this score alone, one can say, without fear of any legal contradiction, that *Kang Sume Née Aboh v. Kang Sume David* is bad law.

---

21 The unreported judgment of Suit No.HCF/38/96 of July 23, 1996.

22 *Kang Sume Née Aboh v. Kang Sume David*, the unreported judgment of Customary Suit No.178/93-94.

23 *Kang Sume Née Aboh v. Kang Sume David*, the unreported judgment of Customary Suit No.CASWP/CC/70/95.

24 The unreported judgment of Suit No.HCF/38/96.

25 E.N. Ngwafor, 'Nullity : The Squaring of a Questionable Dilemma', in *The International Survey of Family Law 1994*, ed. A. Bainham, at 101–108; E.N. Ngwafor, 'Property Rights for Women – A Bold Step in the Wrong Direction?' 29, *J. Fam.L.* 297 (1990–91).

26 The unreported judgment of the Supreme Court in Civil Appeal No.29, judgment No.67/CC of May 3, 1973.

V   EQUALITY OF THE SEXES: OR HAVE YOUR CAKE AND EAT IT?

It is trite knowledge that Cameroon still lags behind Western countries in the field of family law.[27] A long-standing bone of contention has been created by the application of certain customary law principles which feminist groups regard as vexatious and discriminatory. For example, under customary law, a woman cannot own property. And what is more, she is looked upon as the husband's property. This point of view has been vividly expressed by a Ghanaian author as he quotes an example of a will written by an African :

> 'If I die my brother (i.e., a close relative) will inherit my possessions including my wife. In my absence my family has a right to guard her in (the) same way as they will guard my other possessions against trespasses.'[28]

Another illustration of a 'vexing' customary law principle is that a woman cannot own landed property. The reason is simple: under customary law, the administration of any piece of land is carried out by a family head on behalf of the community he represents. No sale of any parcel of land can be carried out without the blessing of the said family head. A recorded utterance by a Nigerian Chief, the Elesi of Odogbow, loudly explains this traditional set-up. He said:

> 'I conceive that land belongs to a vast family of which many are dead, few are living and countless members are still unborn.'[29]

On the face of it, these principles are discriminatory and inequitable. What proper approach should be adopted in the fight launched by feminist groups, family lawyers and judges against these 'regrettable' customary law tenets. It should be noted that Cameroon does not stand alone on this issue of gender discrimination. It has been a consistent fight all over the world and the examples abound: Zimbabwe,[30] Switzerland,[31] Korea,[32] Canada,[33] Botswana,[34] Peru[35] and the United States of America where the problem has taken a wider dimension.[36]

The public outcry and debates launched by feminist groups have tended to blur acceptable legal principles instead of solving the very problems against which they are directed. Common sense would dictate that the surest platform for redress would have been to lobby for a change of the law through Parliament. In fact, even in Pakistan where over 96 per cent of the citizens are followers of Islam, legislation has made a significant

---

[27]   This seems to be the same story in Japan: Ichiro Shimazu, 'Trailing the West in Family Law', 27 *J. Fam.L.* 185n (1988–89).

[28]   K. Mensah, 'Marriage in Sefwi-Akan Customary Law: A Comparative Study in Ethno-Jurisprudence', (1968).

[29]   *West African Lands Commission Report*, Commd. 1078 at 183 (1912). Cited with approval by V. Ngoh, 'The Juridical Nature of Native Land Right in the Anglophone Provinces of Cameroon', 6 *Annales de la Faculté de Droit du Cameroun*, 50 (1973).

[30]   Alice Armstrong, 'Away from Customary Law', *J.Fam.L.* 339 (1988–89).

[31]   Jacques Michel Grossen, 'Further Steps Towards Equality', 25, *J.Fam.L.* 255 (1986–87).

[32]   Mi-Kyung Cho, 'The 1990 Family Law Reform And The Improvement of The Status of Women', 335 *Fam.L.* 431 (1994–1995).

[33]   Nicholas Bala, 'Struggling To Find a Balance On Gender Issues' 33 *J.Fam.L* 30 (1994–95).

[34]   M.D.A. Freeman, 'Bucking The Backlash', 33 *J.Fam.L.* 293 (1994–95).

[35]   C.F. Sessarego, 'Toward Equality in Marriage', 32 *J.Fam.L.* 395 (1993–94).

[36]   The United States has gone beyond the problem of gender discrimination, to recognize the legal rights of heterosexual and homosexual couples. See Rebecca L. Melton, 'Legal Right of unmarried Heterosexual and Homosexual couples and Evolving Definitions of Family', 29 *J.Fam.L.* 497 (1990–91).

inroad in the fight for the protection of women. In Pakistan today the custom of dowry has been abolished by making its practice an offence.[37] In the event of any resistance in Parliament, then the law courts if properly exploited could also be helpful. It was noted in Professor Freeman's article cited above that a Botswanan Court of Appeal declared a law to be unconstitutional because it discriminated against women.[38] It does not mean that a judge has to take the law into his hands. Feminist groups know that in Cameroon today spouses are given the liberty to choose the type of law which would govern their marriage: statutory law (for monogamous marriages) or customary law (for potentially polygamous marriages).[39] You cannot opt for the two types of law simultaneously, nor will the inclusion of the magic word 'monogamy' change the choice of law for those who have opted for a customary law marriage.[40] Unfortunately the attempts made to protect the rights of women have resulted in turning out a string of inconsistent judgments which have not only gone a long way to cast doubts on our legal system but have also led critics to charge the judges with sentimentalism. If you opt for a customary law marriage that is your legal cake which you have baked and, as you eat it, you should remember that you cannot have it back by opening the doors of a statutory law bakery. A few examples immediately spring to mind. What is the rôle of Sections 23, 24 and 42(2) of the MCA 1973 in trying a case that is founded in a marriage celebrated under customary law? We saw in one case that, this legal incongruity notwithstanding, a High Court judge in Buea went ahead to entertain and determine the matter.[41] Again, which court has jurisdiction when the evidence shows overwhelmingly that the marriage was celebrated according to the native laws and customs of a particular tribe?[42] But less than a year ago the High Court in Buea entertained a matter concerning issues arising from a customary law marriage.[43]

Interpretation becomes all the more difficult when one looks at the importance that the citizens themselves attach to customary law. And these citizens do not necessarily exclude women. It is noted en passant that even in Canada, the first female Prime Minister, Kim Campbell, was brought down after a brief term in office because feminists held the view that her approach was conservative.[44] In Cameroon even those who choose statutory law to regulate their marriage (monogamy) find themselves crossing into customary law waters on issues of bride price and parental consent. This unexplained attitude needs elucidation.

Under the Cameroonian Civil Status Ordinance (1981) once the spouses-to-be have capacity and have fulfilled the necessary formalities they can contract a statutory law

---

[37]   Tahir Mahmood, 'Family Law and The Protection of Women', 28 *J.Fam.L.* 578 (1989–90).

[38]   *Dow v. Attorney General* (1992) LRC (Cons) (623, July 3, 1992) cited by Professor M.D.A. Freeman in 'Bucking The Backlash', above.

[39]   Ordinance No.81-02 of June 29, 1981, Section 49.

[40]   *Kukmbongsi v. Kukmbongsi*, the unreported judgment of the Court of Appeal No.CASWP/4/84; *ASA'AH*, the unreported judgment of Suit No.HCF/66/94 of December 21, 1994.

[41]   *Kang Sume Née Aboh v. Kang Sume David*, above.

[42]   There is a proliferation of authorities which show that the customary court is the only court which has original jurisdiction: *Kemgue v. Kemgue*, the unreported judgment of Suit No.HCB/16MC/83; *Ngwa v. Ngwa*, the unreported judgment of Suit No.HCB/100 MC/87; *Tufon v. Tufon*, unreported judgment of Suit No.HCSW/42MC/83; *Ebako v. Ebako*, the unreported judgment of Suit No.HCSW/42MC/77; cf/ *Mokwe v. Mokwe*, the unreported judgment of Suit No.HCB/14MC/89.

[43]   *Kang Sume Née Aboh v. Kang Sume David*, the unreported judgment of Suit No.HCF/38/96 of July 20, 1998.

[44]   Nicholas Bala : 'Struggling To Find a Balance On Gender Issues', 33 *J.Fam.L.* 301 (1994–95), above.

marriage without the consent of their parents.[45] One recognizes the fact that this has not been the practice. Respect for one's parents in Africa in general and Cameroon in particular cannot be over-emphasized. This explains why it is an uphill task, speaking loosely, to draw a line between a statutory law marriage and a customary law marriage in Cameroon.

Examples abound of spouses who before the celebration of their marriage in the Civil Status Registration Office[46] begin by discussing the bride price. What is more, payments even continue after the celebration of the marriage, in keeping with the custom that the dowry is never paid in one instalment. And because, as explained above, it is the father or family head of the woman who receives the bride price, the bride-to-be may refuse to be a party in the celebration of a statutory law marriage simply because her parents have failed to give the necessary consent. Her fears are usually heightened by the fact that failure to receive such consent and its incidental blessings may result in calamities against her, her children and the husband. For example, she may not be able to procreate, her children may die, she may become insane, etc. Indeed, Justice S.M.L. Endeley had once used this argument, of lack of consent, as justification for the dissolution of a monogamous marriage in the case of *Evelyn Fese Njotsa v. Michael Nkongcha Njotsa*.[47]

In the above trial the petitioner based her case on only one of the old grounds for divorce, namely, cruelty.[48] She alleged persistent assaults on her person by the respondent. She called one witness whose evidence, unfortunately, did not help her case. The relevant part of Justice Endeley's judgment read :

> 'The evidence so far led to support the charge on which this petition is being prosecuted falls short of the above standards laid down in law. I therefore find no evidence sufficient to justify my finding that the respondent was cruel to the petitioner.
>
> From what I have seen of the petitioner, I feel satisfied that she honestly believes that continued marital relations with the respondent will be injurious to her health. The marriage as far as the parties are concerned is broken.
>
> *I am satisfied that the failure of this marriage has been sealed by the fact that it did not when it was being solemnized, and does not even now, enjoy the blessings of the married couple's respective parents. In these circumstances, it will not be in the interest of the parties to keep it on.*' (emphasis added)

How Endeley J. could 'feel satisfied that he honestly believes that continued marital relations with the respondent will be injurious to her health' and yet not find cruelty is very difficult to comprehend. However, that is not the fact in issue in this paper. The fact remains that, in the absence of proof of one of the five grounds for divorce, Endeley J. got caught in the perversion of that silent cause for divorce (borrowed from customary law) namely, the absence of parental consent with its incidental blessings.

VI   CONCLUSION

Family law in Cameroon has not witnessed rapid changes as is the case in Western countries. However, with the acceptance of democratic practices by our various socio-

---

[45]   Ordinance No.81/02 of June 29, 1981, see generally Part VI.

[46]   As required by Section 48 of the 1981 Ordinance, above.

[47]   (1971-73) U.Y.L.R.5.

[48]   This petition was heard when the Divorce Reform Act, 1969 was still in force.

political structures, there has been a sudden awareness amongst the citizenry throughout the national territory. There is therefore room for hope. At this stage of our development, the question is no longer whether or not there should be a change, but rather, how we should go about it without destroying those customs that continue to portray our enigmatic character.

CANADA

REFORMING THE DEFINITION OF SPOUSE AND CHILD RELATED LAWS

*Martha Bailey and Nicholas Bala**

I   INTRODUCTION

Canada is going through a slow but significant period of reform of its laws governing children and families. Both judges and politicians have had a role in this process.

In one controversial area, the definition of 'spouse', politicians have been reluctant to act. Judges have taken the lead, invoking the *Charter of Rights*,[1] a part of Canada's constitution, to expand the definition of 'spouse' to cover same-sex and unmarried opposite-sex partners for certain purposes, though the courts have not fully equated these to the married.

In regard to important areas of child-related laws, politicians have taken the initiative to change legislation to structure more clearly how judges make decisions about children. New legislation has come into effect to introduce child support guidelines, largely to meet the concerns of mothers about the inconsistencies between judges and the inadequacy of the amount of child support. An important Supreme Court decision helped clarify and extend the liability of step parents (usually step fathers) for child support. Fathers' groups claim that judges are biased against them, and in 1998 there were controversial Parliamentary hearings to consider reforms to the child-related provisions of the *Divorce Act*.

There have also been concerns that some judges may have placed too much emphasis on parents' rights, and, as a result, Ontario enacted legislation to increase the power of child welfare agencies to remove children from parental care in situations of abuse or neglect. A 1998 Supreme Court of Canada decision also emphasized the welfare of children over the right of parents to maintain contact with their children in long-term State care. Although beyond the scope of this article, the federal government has also introduced new legislation to increase the accountability of adolescents who violate the criminal law.[2]

This article concludes by considering some issues that have arisen in Canada with regard to intercountry adoption and the *Hague Convention* that deals with that issue.

---

[*]   Martha Bailey is an Associate Professor at the Faculty of Law at Queen's University, Kingston, Canada, and Nicholas Bala is a Professor at the same Faculty. The authors wish to acknowledge the editorial assistance of Mandy Aylen, Queen's Law '00 and support from the Social Sciences and Humanities Research Council of Canada.

[1]   *Canadian Charter of Rights and Freedoms*, Part I of the *Constitution Act, 1982*, being Schedule B to the *Canada Act 1982* (U.K.), 1982, c.11 [hereinafter *the Charter*].

[2]   *Criminal Youth Justice Act*, Bill C-68, 1st Sess., 36th Parl., First Reading March 11, 1999; see also Department of Justice Canada, *A Strategy for the Renewal of Youth Justice* (Ottawa, May 1999) online: http://canada.justice.gc.ca/Orientations/jeunes/yoas1_en.html.

II   THE CHANGING DEFINITION OF SPOUSE

The most politically contentious family law issues in recent years in Canada have related to the definition of 'spouse'. Politicians have been reluctant to act, but the courts are using the *Charter of Rights* to extend to same-sex partners and unmarried cohabitants many of the same rights and obligations as those attaching to the legally married.

In the late 1970s and early 1980s most Canadian jurisdictions enacted legislation to give partners in unmarried opposite-sex relationships (often called 'common law marriage' in English Canada) limited statutory recognition as 'spouses', for example for spousal support purposes. The definition of 'common law spouse' varies between jurisdictions, and often within jurisdictions with different periods of cohabitation required by different statutes in the same province. Some (but not all) statutes require that the couple both cohabit *and* be parents of a child, while other statutes only require a specified period of cohabitation.

In 1995 the Supreme Court of Canada ruled in *Miron v. Trudel* that a law excluding an unmarried opposite-sex partner from the benefits of an automobile insurance provision available to a 'spouse' violated the *Charter* by discriminating on the basis of marital status.[3] Despite this ruling, there remain many legislative distinctions between opposite-sex partners who are unmarried and those who are married, as legislators did not react quickly to the implications of *Miron*.

An important decision of the Alberta Court of Appeal, *Rossu v. Taylor*,[4] addressed this issue in 1998. The Court of Appeal held that Alberta's spousal support provisions were unconstitutional because they failed to include an unmarried opposite-sex partner as a 'spouse', discriminating on the basis of marital status contrary to the *Charter*. The Court of Appeal suspended the declaration of invalidity for one year to give the government time to draft new legislation.[5]

No province includes unmarried couples in its scheme of marital property division, although the common law doctrine of unjust enrichment is applied in all of the common law provinces to allow a division of property based on contributions to the acquisition of assets.[6] Quebec (Canada's only civilian jurisdiction) has the highest rate of unmarried opposite-sex cohabitation in Canada, but it has not yet extended spousal support rights to cohabiting couples. Unmarried parties are not entitled to marital property division on breakdown of the relationship under the *Civil Code*,[7] although unmarried parties may obtain a share of their former partners' property if they are able to prove an implied partnership, a contract or unjust enrichment.[8]

On June 18, 1998 Quebec's Justice Minister, then Serge Menard, announced that the province would enact legislation to harmonize its public laws relating to unmarried couples to ensure that the criteria for legal recognition of unmarried couples would be uniform, and to extend that legal recognition to same-sex couples. Thus, the laws relating

---

[3]   *Miron v. Trudel*, [1995] 2 S.C.R. 418.

[4]   *Rossu v. Taylor* (1998), 161 D.L.R. (4th) 266 (Alta. C.A.).

[5]   The Northwest Territories and Prince Edward Island are the other common law jurisdictions that have yet to include unmarried opposite-sex partners in their spousal support legislation.

[6]   See, e.g., *Peter v. Beblow*, [1993] 1 S.C.R. 980.

[7]   *The Civil Code of Quebec*, S.Q., 1991.

[8]   *Beaudoin-Daigneault v. Richard*, [1984] 1 S.C.R. 2, confirmed the existence of the partnership as a possible remedy for unmarried cohabitants. A claim based on partnership, contract or unjust enrichment was accepted in *De L'Isle v. Carton*, [1997] Q.J. No. 1693 (Q.C.A.) (QL), leave to appeal dismissed, [1997] S.C.C.A. No. 451 (QL).

to such issues as pensions, automobile insurance, and employment rights are to be amended to harmonize the definition of spouse and to include same-sex couples within that definition.

A proposal to amend the relevant public laws to equalize the position of same-sex couples and unmarried opposite-sex couples was put before the National Assembly of Quebec on October 21, 1998. Bill 32, which is to amend the 28 relevant laws and 11 regulations of Quebec, was introduced in the Quebec Assembly in the spring of 1999,[9] making Quebec the first jurisdiction in Canada to extend equal treatment to same-sex couples and unmarried opposite-sex couples for public law purposes.[10] Bill 32 does not, however, extend spousal support or property rights to unmarried cohabitants.

Quebec is one of the provinces still to exclude unmarried opposite-sex cohabitants from the right to spousal support. In June 1998, it was announced that Quebec would consider recognizing the right of unmarried couples to family patrimony, spousal support, and inheritance rights, but that any amendments to the *Civil Code* would be preceded by public consultations.[11] The Quebec government planned to proceed more slowly with amendments to extend private marital rights and obligations to unmarried couples, though the *Charter* litigation may push the province to respond more quickly.

Quebec's initiatives to eliminate discrimination against same-sex couples with Bill 32 are important, though some other provinces have already extended some rights and obligations to same-sex couples on a piecemeal basis.[12] British Columbia has made substantial legislative reforms in this regard.[13] As well, the British Columbia Law Institute published a report in 1998 recommending further legal recognition for non-traditional relationships,[14] including enactment of a *Domestic Partner Act*, which would allow two people to make formal declaration of their partnership and thereby obtain rights and obligations similar to those of married spouses.[15]

In its 1998 judgment in *Rosenberg v. Canada,*[16] the Ontario Court of Appeal declared that the definition of 'spouse' in the *Income Tax Act,*[17] as it applies to the registration of pension plans, was unconstitutional because it discriminates on the basis of sexual orientation contrary to section 15 of the *Charter*. The Court's remedy for this violation was to read members of same-sex couples into the definition of 'spouse'. The federal

---

9   Debates, National Assembly of Quebec, October 21, 1998; Quebec, Bill 32, 1st Sess., 36th Leg., 2nd reading May 19, 1999.

10   Conférence de presse de Mme. Linda Goupil ministre de Justice, May 6, 1999, available online: http://www.assnat.qc.ca/fra/conf-presse/9905061g.htm. Some journalists adopted Goupil's self-congratulatory tone. For example, Lysiane Gagnon wrote of Bill 32 that 'this Quebec law marks a first step toward the recognition of same-sex couples throughout Canada': 'Vive le Québec gai', *Globe and Mail*, May 22, 1999.

11   Gouvernement du Québec, Communiqué, June 18, 1998. Quebec's current Justice Minister also suggested that these amendments might be made: Conférence de presse de Mme. Linda Goupil ministre de Justice, May 6, 1999, available online: http://www.assnat.qc.ca/fra/conf-presse/9905061g.htm.

12   For example, in Ontario, a same-sex partner may give consent to health care treatment for a person who lacks capacity: *Health Care Consent Act*, S.O. 1996, c. 2, section 20(9).

13   See, for example, *Adoption Act*, R.S.B.C. 1996, c. 5; *Medicare Protection Act*, R.S.B.C. 1996, c. 286; *Family Relations Amendment Act, 1997*, S.B.C. 1997, c. 20.

14   British Columbia Law Institute, *Report on the Recognition of Spousal and Family Status* (Vancouver, 1998), available online: http://www.bcli.org.

15   *Ibid.*, at 11. Registered domestic partnerships are also under consideration in Alberta: 'Alberta government decides to say no to same-sex marriages', *Globe and Mail*, March 19, 1999; Registered domestic partnerships were also recommended by the Ontario Law Reform Commission in its *Report on the Rights and Responsibilities of Cohabitants under the Family Law Act* (Toronto, 1993) at 53–56.

16   *Rosenberg v. Canada* (1998), 38 O.R. (3d) 577 (C.A.).

17   *Income Tax Act*, R.S.C. 1985 (5th Supp.), c.1, section 252(4) [enacted 1993, c.4, section 140(3)].

government decided not to appeal this judgment, although it did not announce plans to amend the *Income Tax Act* and the *Canada Pension Plan Act* until March 1999.[18] As a result of the federal government's decision not to appeal the *Rosenberg* decision, the provisions of the *Income Tax Act* that permitted registration of a private pension plan only if the plan restricts survivor benefits to spouses of the opposite-sex were no longer effective. The *Rosenberg* decision also means that provincial pension legislation that defines 'spouse' in accordance with the federal *Income Tax Act* definition must be amended to comply with the *Charter*. British Columbia was the first province to introduce legislation to extend equal rights in regard to the provincial pension benefits to same-sex couples to comply with *Rosenberg*, and Nova Scotia announced that it will also enact legislation to extend the definition of 'spouse' to same-sex spouses for the purpose of provincial pension and medical benefits.[19]

At the beginning of January 1999, the Foundation for Equal Families brought an 'omnibus' lawsuit challenging dozens of federal statutes that discriminate against same-sex couples. The motivation for this lawsuit was to require the federal government to change its laws to reflect court rulings: 'Gays and lesbians are fed up with bringing legal challenge after legal challenge – which they have done consistently over the past decade – to fight discriminatory laws'.[20]

On the same day that the omnibus lawsuit was launched, Immigration Minister Lucienne Robillard announced proposed changes to the immigration and refugee system that would include expanding the definition of 'spouse' to include cohabiting couples of the same or opposite sex. At the same time, the Minister announced that 'a national federal strategy is being formulated to deal with a number of court decisions, including one that allows same-sex partners to receive survivor benefits from pension plans'.[21]

In March 1998, the Supreme Court of Canada heard the appeal of *M. v. H.*, and reserved judgment.[22] In *M. v. H.*, one member of a lesbian couple applied for spousal support after the relationship broke down. The definition of 'spouse' in Ontario's *Family Law Act*[23] was challenged on the basis that it is limited to opposite-sex couples and therefore violates the *Charter* by discriminating on the basis of sexual orientation.[24] In May 1999, the Supreme Court of Canada, by an 8 to 1 majority, held that this provision is unconstitutional and gave Ontario 6 months to amend its legislation. Ontario may respond by equating same-sex cohabitants with unmarried opposite-sex cohabitants or by providing same-sex partners with the possibility of having a registered domestic partnership.

British Columbia already legislatively extends spousal support rights to members of same-sex couples.[25] Before the Supreme Court handed down its decision in *M. v. H.*, a number of governments were already considering amendments to reduce discrimination

---

18   'Tax act to recognize same-sex couples', *Globe and Mail,* March 23, 1999.

19   *Pension Statutes Amendment Act (No. 2)*, S.B.C. 1998, c. 40; 'N.S. extends same-sex rights,' *Globe and Mail,* May 26, 1998.

20   'Group Hopes Lawsuit Spurs Legislative Action on Gay Rights', *Globe and Mail,* January 8, 1999.

21   'Robillard is Seeking Same-sex Rights for Immigrants', *Globe and Mail,* January 8, 1999.

22   *M. v. H.* (1996), 31 O.R. (3d) 417 (C.A.).

23   *Family Law Act*, R.S.O. 1990, c. F.3.

24   The *Family Law Act, ibid*, section 29, extends the definition of 'spouse' for the purposes of spousal support to include 'either of a man and woman who are not married to each other and have cohabited, (a) continuously for a period of not less than three years, or (b) in a relationship of some permanence, if they are the natural or adoptive parents of a child.'

25   *Family Relations Amendment Act, 1997*, S.B.C. 1997, c. 20.

against same-sex couples and it is likely that legislation extending beyond the issue of spousal support will be introduced.

Over the past decade, politicians have often avoided dealing with the issue of same-sex couples, despite the growing body of jurisprudence indicating that many statutes violate the *Charter*. The strenuous opposition to legal recognition of same-sex couples among some Canadians was illustrated by a 1998 case in the ultimately unsuccessful arguments put forward to support a school board resolution to ban three books for use in kindergarten and grade one classes because the books depicted children with homosexual parents.[26] Because of the political risks involved in extending legal recognition to same-sex couples, 'many politicians are content to let judges make hard social decisions'.[27]

Critics of judicial decisions that uphold the rights of gay and lesbian persons or same-sex couples charge that 'judicial activism' is undermining the role of legislative bodies,[28] but the role of law maker has been thrust upon judges by legislators who have refused to bring statutes into conformity with the *Charter*. Supreme Court of Canada Chief Justice Lamer commented on the limitations of judges as policy-makers in relation to difficult issues such as same-sex benefits:[29]

'A judge cannot approach a case as a legislature would. The scope of the judge's decision is defined by the questions submitted by the parties. The answer which the judge gives is constrained and dictated by the legal context in which the dispute arises.'

The Supreme Court decision in *M. v. H.* may well mark the end of the 'court challenge' era. Canadian legislators are starting to feel the judicial pressure to assume responsibility for crafting family laws and policies that take into account the diversity of Canadian families, and they will be able to take a more consistent approach to the legal regulation of non-traditional families than have judges.

III REFORMING THE CHILD RELATED PROVISIONS OF THE DIVORCE ACT

Canada is in the process of slowly reforming the child-related provisions of its *Divorce Act*. A new child support regime came into effect in Canada in May of 1997. The experience with *Child Support Guidelines*[30] has generally been positive, with lawyers and judges reporting that there is more consistency in the amounts of child support that judges are determining, and greater ease for parents to settle the amount of child support without relying on a judge.[31] However, some provisions of the *Guidelines* remain controversial and are producing significant amounts of litigation and jurisprudence. Further, fathers'

---

[26] *Chamberlain v. Surrey School District No. 36* (1998), 168 D.L.R. (4th) 222 (B.C.S.C.) (resolution to ban the books quashed on the grounds that it was based on religious principles and therefore contrary to the requirement that schools be operated on non-sectarian principles).

[27] James McLeod, 'Annotation', *Taylor v. Rossu* (1998), 39 R.F.L. (4th) 242 at 246 (Alta. C.A.).

[28] See, for example, 'Reform seeks curbs on judicial activism', *Globe and Mail*, June 9, 1998.

[29] Chief Justice Antonio Lamer, Address to the Empire Club in Toronto, April 13, 1995, quoted by Philp J.A. in *Vogel v. Manitoba*, [1995] M.J. No. 235 (C.A.) (QL) at para.1.

[30] The *Divorce Act*, section 2(5) allows provinces to adopt their own version of child support guidelines. Only Quebec has its own child support guidelines, with an income sharing model that utilizes the incomes of both parents in determining the amount of child support, as well as taking account of visitation when it accounts for 20% or more of the child's time. The federal *Guidelines* are in SOR./97-563.

[31] See, for example, Paetsch, Bertrand and Hornick, *Consultation on Experiences and Issues Related to the Implementation of the Child Support Guidelines* (Canadian Research Institute for Law and the Family, for Department of Justice, September 1998).

groups complained that governments were reacting to the concerns of mothers about child support, but not dealing with their concerns about denial of access and lack of involvement in the lives of their children. As a result, the federal Parliament has begun a contentious review of all child-related provisions of the *Divorce Act.*

The federal *Guidelines* have provided more consistency, and in many cases (especially for lower income payers) their application is straight forward. The basic *Guidelines* model provides that child support is determined as a percentage of the payer's income, with judges having a limited discretion to vary the amount payable, for example if there are 'special or extraordinary expenses' or a situation of 'undue hardship.' Some of the provisions lack clarity and have understandably been the subject of differing interpretations; other provisions deal with factually complex situations where it is difficult to know exactly how to apply the *Guidelines.* There are clearly differing judicial approaches, with some judges emphasizing a relatively narrow interpretation that will promote certainty and consistency.[32] Other judges seem more inclined to take a more flexible and discretionary approach, straining to find a fair resolution in individual cases. There may also be some tension between interpretative approaches that tend to favour custodial parents (usually mothers), while other approaches may be more favourable to non-custodial parents (usually fathers).

One of the most frequently litigated issues under the *Guidelines*, especially where there is a middle or higher income payer, concerns the applicability of the 'special and extraordinary' expense 'add-ons'. Section 7 provides that a court may add to the base amount:

> 'an amount to cover the following expenses ... taking into account the necessity of the expense in relation to the child's best interests and the reasonableness of the expenses, for ...
>
> a)   child care expenses ...
> b)   ... medical and dental insurance premiums attributable to the child;
> c)   health-related expenses that exceed insurance reimbursement ...
> d)   extraordinary expenses for primary or secondary school education ...
> e)   expenses for post-secondary education; and
> f)   extraordinary expenses for extracurricular activities.'

The application of section 7 creates an interpretative challenge for the courts. From a conceptual perspective, a major problem is that there is no real information available as to what expenses are 'ordinary' and already reflected in the *Guidelines* and thus determining what expenses are 'special or extraordinary' is bound to be a somewhat speculative exercise.

Some judges have taken a narrow approach, arguing that the cases in which this provision is used should be the exception, not the rule, expressing a concern that if section 7 expenses are granted routinely, the process of determining child support will

---

[32]   There are a number of online and print resources that summarize *Guidelines* jurisprudence, including *Quicklaw* online database, Payne's Digest of Child Support [PDCS]. Looseleaf services are MacDonald and Wilton, *Child Support Guidelines Law and Practice* (Carswell); and Hainsworth, *Child Support Guidelines Service* (Canada Law Book). See also Aston, 'An Update of Case Law under the Child Support Guidelines' (1998), 16 *Can. Fam L. Q.* 261. The Canada Department of Justice (Ottawa) has the *Reference Manual* for which it sends out periodic additions, and a website: http://canada.justice.gc.ca/Orientation/Pensions/Child/guide/intann_en.html.

become too complex. This approach was, for example, taken by the Manitoba Court of Appeal in *Andries v. Andries*,[33] where Twaddle J.A. explained:

'an extracurricular activity is extraordinary only where it is out of proportion to the usual costs associated with that particular activity. For example, if the average costs of downhill skis is $500, then $500 for downhill skis would not be an extraordinary expense, but $1000 would be.'

This approach considers the particular expense rather than the activity or the burden of the expense on this family, and excludes consideration of whether the expenses are extraordinary for parents with the incomes of the individual parents involved. It appears to restrict section 7(1)(f) to situations where a child has 'extraordinary' talents or special needs and concomitant expenses.

Other courts, such as the British Columbia Court of Appeal in *McLaughlin v. McLaughlin,* have taken a more expansive view of section 7, and determined that whether an expense is 'extraordinary' is to be determined by reference to the incomes of the parents. Prowse J.A. wrote that it is:[34]

'... "fundamentally fair" to take an expansive approach to the meaning of 'extraordinary expenses' by viewing the expense or expenses claimed in the context of the parties' joint incomes ... examining the "means" of the parties, taking into account the reality of their separate status and such other factors as their ... capital, income distribution, debt load, third party resources which impact upon a parent's ability to pay, access costs, obligations to pay spousal or other child support orders, spousal support received and any other relevant factors.'

Applying this 'expansive approach' may result in a court concluding that where the total parental incomes were about $60,000, expenses of $170 per month for music, gymnastics, swimming, bowling, cubs and arts were 'extraordinary' and should be divided between the parents.[35]

Determining whether an expense is 'extraordinary' relative to parental incomes in practice gives judges significant discretion, as there is no data available on what expenses are 'ordinary' at different income levels. Whatever approach is taken in the interpretation of section 7, this provision is most likely to be applicable only in middle income situations. As the income of the payer and child support payments rise, an increasing amount of money from the basic Table amount will be available for extra expenses, and courts will be less likely to invoke section 7. For lower income payers, such expenses are unlikely to be viewed as 'reasonable' having regard to the parents' means.

Section 2(2) of the *Divorce Act* provides that in addition to biological parents, a person who 'stands in the place of a parent' will have child support obligations. The imposition of this type of obligation on persons who have no biological relationship with a child is consistent with Canadian laws which may grant a person who is a 'psychological parent' rights of custody or access to a child.[36] The Canadian approach emphasizes the best interests of the child over notions of rights and obligations arising out of biological ties.

In November 1998, the Supreme Court of Canada held in *Chartier v. Chartier* that a step parent could not unilaterally terminate the relationship of standing 'in the place of a

---

[33]   (1998), 36 R.F.L. (4th) 175 (N.S.C.A.).

[34]   (1998), 167 D.L.R.(4th) 39 (B.C.C.A.).

[35]   *Kofoed v. Fichter* (1998), 39 R.F.L. (4th) 348 (Sask. C.A.).

[36]   See e.g. *King v. Low*, [1985] 1 S.C.R. 87.

parent' after separation, and thereby terminate child support obligations.[37] The court rejected arguments that imposing this type of post-separation obligation may make step parents less generous as they will fear that this may give rise to post-separation obligations, with Bastarche J. commenting: 'People do not enter into parental relationships with the view that they will be terminated'. The Court also rejected American jurisprudence that takes a much narrower approach and allows a step parent to terminate unilaterally child support obligations when a marriage to the biological parent ends. The Court did, however, recognize that merely being married to a parent and providing a child with economic support does not make a person 'stand in the place of a parent'. Rather, the court must consider such factors as the nature of the psychological ties, whether the step parent disciplines the child, whether the person 'represents to the child, the family [and the world] either explicitly or implicitly that he ... is responsible as a parent to the child [and] the nature ... of the child's relationship with the ... [non-custodial] biological parent'.

While *Chartier* does not deal directly with the issue of the quantum of the child support obligation of a person who is not a biological parent, Bastarche J. did acknowledge that a step parent facing a child support application could seek 'contribution' from a biological parent. Section 5 of the *Guidelines* provides that where the payer spouse is a person 'who stands in the place of a parent', the amount of child support shall be 'such amount as the court considers appropriate, having regard to these *Guidelines* and any other parent's legal duty to support the child'. This suggests that if a non-custodial biological parent is also paying support, the obligation of the non-biological parent may be reduced. However, there is no provision for any reduction in the child support obligation of a biological parent if there is also a non-biological parent with a support obligation. This would suggest that the support obligation of a biological parent is paramount, provided that parent can be located and has the means to support a child. A number of decisions have held that the obligation of a non-biological parent should be limited as to amount or duration, provided a biological parent is also paying support.[38] Though some judgments have refused to limit the obligations of a non-biological parent, these have generally been cases in which the non-custodial biological parent has limited ability to contribute or is paying no support at all.[39]

While there is now growing acceptance of at least the principle of having child support guidelines, there is continuing bitter controversy over other child-related provisions of the *Divorce Act*. After the House of Commons passed the amendments for the *Child Support Guidelines* in the fall of 1996, fathers began an intensive lobbying campaign of the Senate Committee that was studying the issue of guidelines. Some of their criticisms focused on the *Guidelines*, but most of the concerns that were raised were about the broader child-related issues of custody and access. The fathers' groups were concerned that child support issues were receiving attention while their concerns over access related issues seemed to be ignored by the federal government. Fathers were joined by grandparents who had their own concerns about family law, in particular about their lack of access to grandchildren.

In order to obtain the support of the Senate Committee and secure passage of the *Guidelines* legislation, the government had to make some concessions. A few relatively

---

[37]   Reasons for judgment January 28, 1999 (1999), 43 R.F.L.(4th) 1, revg. (1997), 35 R.F.L. (4th) 255 (Man.C.A.).

[38]   *Bell v. Michie* (1998), 38 R.F.L. (4th) 199 (Ont. Gen Div.).

[39]   *Powell v. Thomas* (1998), 38 R.F.L. (4th) 127 (Ont. Gen. Div.).

small changes were made to the actual *Guidelines,* such as reducing the threshold for a possible exercise of judicial discretion in situations of shared custody from a requirement that there be 'substantially equal' time spent with each parent to a requirement that a parent have care of the child at least 40% of the time. The government also agreed that a Committee with representation from both the Senate and the House of Commons would study the child-related provisions of the *Divorce Act.*

The Special Joint Committee was established and held highly contentious public hearings across Canada in 1998. While the Committee was not deeply divided along party lines, there were profound differences in terms of 'gender politics'. Some of the M.P.s seemed quite sensitive to the concerns of women, but the Committee hearings tended to be dominated by members who were more sensitive to the concerns of fathers and sometimes hostile to women witnesses. Liberal Senator Anne Cools was described by one reporter as a 'dominant and sometimes disruptive force, leaving her chair during testimony to consult with men's groups in the audience' and 'cross-examining' female witnesses.[40] At one point in the hearings Senator Cools remarked: 'Men and women are not treated equally before the law. Children are not the possession of any one parent. They are not the possession of the mother.'[41]

The Committee met 55 times and reported in December 1998. The first witnesses were mainly government officials, representatives of national professional organizations and academics. The Committee listened to their ideas with interest, but the most gripping testimony came from individuals telling their stories about their experiences with the justice system and their former spouses. There were about the same number of men and women witnesses before the Committee, but the stories of men tended to attract more attention from the Committee and dominated the media coverage. Women presenters often raised concerns about wife battering and its effects on children; however, the hearings were not a sympathetic environment for women. Female witnesses were occasionally heckled by men in the audience, even when discussing issues such as spousal abuse and homicide, and the most outspoken Committee members were more aggressive with women witnesses. After one session where women witnesses were treated rudely, one female Senator lamented that the hearings were degenerating into a 'war zone' of gender politics.[42]

Witnesses from fathers' groups focused on denial of access by mothers, arguing that the justice system deals aggressively with default in support payments, but ineffectively with situations where fathers are denied the opportunity to see their children. Fathers also claimed that mothers were making false allegations of wife battering or child sexual abuse in order to deny fathers access rights.

One of the serious limitations of this kind of hearing is that Committee members seemed to accept that witnesses were telling 'the truth' about what happened to them, while in reality most of them were giving their *perspectives* of what happened. As in family law litigation, the stories told by only one parent are often a very limited version of 'the truth'. It is apparent that many of the presenters before the Committee gave very partial and one-sided descriptions of their experiences with their children, which could not be challenged in the context of the hearings.[43]

---

[40] 'Child Custody: The Great Divide', *Globe & Mail*, December 5, 1998.

[41] 'Custody not awarded fairly', *Halifax Daily News*, April 27, 1998.

[42] Senator Ermine Cohen, quoted in 'Women heckled', *Canadian Press,* March 31, 1998.

[43] 'Child custody: The Great Divide', *Globe & Mail*, December 5, 1998.

In the final weeks before the *Report* was released, Cabinet Ministers and representatives of the Department of Justice began to pressure the Committee to back away from some of the most radical 'pro-father' positions. In the end, although the recommendations dealt with a number of the concerns raised by fathers in the hearings, the final *Report* also tried to focus on the interests of children and on diminishing the adversarial nature of the divorce process.

The 48 recommendations are directed to federal and provincial governments, and to various agencies and professional groups involved in the divorce process. As its title – *For the Sake of the Children* – indicates, the *Report* purports to take a child-focused approach.[44] Generally, an effort is made in the *Report* to link the recommendations to the objective of promoting the 'best interests' of children. However, the concept of the 'best interests of the child' is highly malleable and advocates for almost any position in this area can usually cast their arguments in terms of promoting this objective.

Perhaps the most prominent objective of the Report is to encourage parents to resolve their differences without resort to an expensive and embittering judicial process, in a way that continues to have both parents actively involved in their children's lives. A central recommendation is the abandonment of 'custody and access' terminology and the adoption of the concept of 'shared parenting'. Although 'shared parenting' is never clearly defined, it is not intended to be a presumption in favour of joint custody as many fathers urged. The new concept is modeled on similar reforms in jurisdictions such as England and Washington State. Parents are to be encouraged to formulate jointly 'parenting plans' to divide their parental responsibilities between them in a way that they consider appropriate. The Committee also recommended more use of education programs for parents who are separating, and more use of mediation, though recognizing that mediation should not be mandatory as there may be concerns about domestic violence.

A number of recommendations address the concerns of non-custodial parents, though some of the more radical proposals of fathers, such as the creation of a criminal offence for denial of access, were not endorsed. The Committee recommended that the *Divorce Act* should explicitly abolish the 'tender years' doctrine, a judicially created presumption that children of 'tender years' (7 years or under) should be in the custody of their mothers. The reality is that very few judges in Canada, if any, have consciously used this type of explicitly gendered and sexist assumption in the past decade.[45] The Committee also recommended that if a parent with whom the child resides plans a move that might affect the arrangements of a parenting plan, that parent must give the other parent 90 days' notice and seek judicial permission before relocating. The Committee also made a number of recommendations to facilitate and better enforce the rights of non-custodial parents through the 'development of a nationwide co-ordinated response ... involving both therapeutic and punitive elements'.[46] This would include counselling, parenting education and mediation, but for 'persistent intractable cases, punitive solutions' are needed for custodial parents who wrongfully disobey access orders. Although a review of the federal *Child Support Guidelines* was not within its specific

---

[44]   Canada, Special Joint Committee on Child Custody and Access, *For the Sake of the Children* (Ottawa: Government Services Canada, December 1999) available online: http://www.parl.gc.ca/InfoComDoc/ 36/1/SJCA/Studies/Reports/sjcarp02-e.htm.

[45]   See, for example, *R. v. R.* (1983), 34 R.F.L. (2d) 277 (Alta. Ca.) and *Tyabji v. Sandana* (1994), 2 R.F.L. (4th) 265 (B.C.S.C.), rejecting any presumption in favour of mothers, but some judges occasionally still refer to the tender years doctrine as a rule of 'common sense': *S. v. S.* (1991), 35 R.F.L. (3d) 400 (Ont. C.A.).

[46]   Report (1998), Recommendation 19 (p.55).

mandate, the Committee chose to express 'concerns' about some situations in which payer parents believe that the burden of child support is too great.

The *Report* also contains a number of recommendations that are intended to increase the rights and protections afforded to children in the divorce process and Canadian society. The Committee recommended that the views of children should be communicated to the court, but it recognized that children will often be unable or unwilling to appear to 'take sides' by testifying. As such, the Committee recommended that skilled professionals, trusted friends or relatives, and lawyers should communicate a child's views to the courts. The *Report* includes a proposal that judges should have the power to appoint a lawyer to represent a child involved in a divorce proceeding. In Ontario, judges can request that legal representation or assessment services should be provided for a child by the Office of the Children's Lawyer. In most places in Canada, however, there is no legal representation for children in divorce proceedings, and there are limited public resources available for an assessment of the child's needs or views by a social worker or other skilled professional. The Committee also endorsed a recommendation that has been made by others who have studied child-related issues, that there should be a Children's Commissioner appointed to superintend and promote the welfare of children, with the responsibility of reporting to Parliament.[47]

Although the Committee heard from both victims of spousal abuse and those who work with them, the Committee seemed more sympathetic to fathers who appeared before the Committee to raise the issue of false allegations of spousal abuse. The most inadequate part of the *Report* is its treatment of spousal violence issues, which reflects the 'pro-father' sympathies of some Committee members. The *Report* deals more extensively with the issue of false allegations by mothers and abuse perpetrated by women, than with the more prevalent and serious problem of male abuse of women and children. The Committee did recommend that the best interests test should include '*proven* family violence' as a factor in making determinations about children.[48] The qualifier 'proven' is not used to modify any other best interests factors. Clearly the Committee was influenced by the stories of fathers who claimed that mothers frequently make false allegations of spousal abuse. Violence should not be just another 'best interests' factor; courts should be satisfied that any parenting arrangements do not pose a significant risk to the safety of a parent or child.

After the Joint Committee *Report* was released in December 1998, the Minister of Justice, Anne McLellan, was cautiously supportive of the *Report* and of more recognition for the role of fathers: 'We talk about support and ensuring that a custodial parent has rights to enforce his or her rights to support for either themselves or their children. But we haven't as a society focused very much on the rights and responsibilities of the non-custodial parent.'[49] While the *Report* was criticized by some lawyers and women's groups,[50] the Minister's support for the principle of encouraging involvement of fathers after divorce is not politically controversial for a majority of Canadians. Public opinion polls indicate that 70% of Canadians believe that fathers get too little attention in the divorce courts.[51]

---

[47] Report (1998), Recommendation 22.3 , p. 59. A similar recommendation was made by Rix Rogers, *Reaching For Solutions: Report of the Special Advisor to the Minister of National Health and Welfare on Child Sexual Abuse in Canada* (Ottawa: Department Health & Welfare, 1990).

[48] Report (1998), Recommendation 16.11 (p.45).

[49] 'Minister's response is a cautious one', *Lawyers Weekly*, January 15, 1999.

[50] See 'Custody & Access Report Draws Mixed Reaction', *Lawyers Weekly*, February 5, 1999.

[51] 'Needs of children and fathers ignored: poll', *Southam Newspapers*, November 23, 1998.

In May 1999 the Minister issued a formal *Response* giving qualified support to the broad objectives of the *Report*.[52] The *Response* is a relatively brief document, dealing explicitly with only 16 out of the 48 recommendations. The general and non-committal tone of the *Response* reflects the government's sense that it is dealing with a controversial issue, about which 'at present there is no clear consensus'. The federal government also wants to leave itself room to shape more detailed responses in consultation with justice system professionals and with the provincial officials who have responsibility for many of the issues in this area.

According to the *Response*, the introduction of new terminology 'will be a high priority'. Though there was no specific commitment to use the concept of 'shared parenting', there will be 'child-centred' terminology, placing an emphasis on parental responsibilities and reducing the conflict between parents. The *Response* also endorses greater use of a range of measures to reduce the adversarial nature of the divorce process and to encourage greater co-operation between parents. These measures include the use of parenting plans and mediation, as well as parenting education, which the federal government is already starting to fund and evaluate on a pilot project basis. More than the Committee *Report*, the *Response* recognizes that there will be some high conflict situations that cannot be resolved by non-adversarial means. While not as supportive of fathers as the *Report,* the *Response* recognizes the benefit, for most children, of maintaining relationships with both parents as well as members of extended families following separation. The *Response* also pledges to take steps to deal with access denial, emphasizing the non-court responses wherever possible, but recognizing the need 'for persistently intractable cases, [of] punitive solutions for parents who wrongfully disobey parenting orders'.

The *Response* calls for a three-year time frame for consultation and formulation of a coordinated strategy for dealing with child related issues, including child support as well as what is now called custody and access. The three-year time frame would allow for the dovetailing of a detailed response on custody and access issues within the time frame for an expected report to Parliament on the *Child Support Guidelines*. But the government has been heavily criticized for allowing itself to postpone making any decisions in this contentious area until after the next election.

It is important to link the government response on child support to the other child-related issues. Child support is conceptually distinct from custody and access, and there should not be an explicit *quid pro quo* in individual cases. However, all of the child-related issues are psychologically and politically intertwined, as the Committee process revealed.

While it is vitally important to engage the provinces, professionals and the public in the law reform process, there is unlikely to be unanimity among the provinces about how to proceed. In addition, there will never be a consensus among parents who have become embittered with each other. Government action may need to be taken even without a 'clear consensus'. While the broad principles set out in the *Response* are sound, three years seems like a lengthy period to formulate a detailed federal response to a report that was produced in a year.

---

[52]   Government of Canada's Response to the Report of the Special Joint Committee on Child Custody and Access (Ottawa: Department of Justice, 1999) available online: http://canada.justice.gc.ca/publications/sjcarp02.

IV   REFORMING CHILD WELFARE LAWS

In the 1980s, agencies and legislation in Canada moved towards a 'family preservation' approach to child welfare. Children were removed from parental care only as a 'last resort' and the number of children in State care fell. In recent years there has been a sense that the child welfare system is 'in crisis,' with the media filled with stories of child abuse deaths. Child welfare is a provincial and territorial responsibility in Canada, and many governments responded by establishing inquiries or commissions. Ontario and British Columbia recently enacted legislation to increase the power of the State to intervene in families to protect children, and some key decisions have also placed less emphasis on the rights of parents.

The family preservation policies of earlier decades were also premised on a set of political and social beliefs in the importance of social supports for 'the family.' The 1990s have been a conservative time, with more emphasis on individual responsibility and accountability, and less on societal support and responsibility. 'Family values' remain important, but society is prepared to be more judgmental of parents who are seen to be inadequate. Related to a 'law and order' political agenda that has seen growing restraints on welfare eligibility and a growing tendency to treat young offenders as adults, Canadian governments are more prepared to intervene and remove children from the care of parents whose care is considered inadequate.

A number of recent decisions reflect a judicial trend to restrict the substantive custodial rights of parents who clearly pose a significant risk to their children.[53] In its 1998 decision in *New Brunswick Minister of Health and Community Services v. L.(M.)*,[54] the Supreme Court of Canada upheld a trial judge's decision to terminate access rights to the parents of a permanent ward, emphasizing that 'access is a right that belongs to the child, and not to the parents'. Justice Gonthier wrote that 'preserving the family unit only plays an important role if it is in the best interests of the child,' endorsing the view that 'the parents must be worthy of being "visitors in their child's life".' This rhetoric must be understood in the context of the facts of the particular case, where there was significant evidence that the children were disturbed by visits with parents who had a history of marital violence and the children's lawyer was advocating termination of access. However, this decision clearly emphasized children's welfare over parental rights.

One of most significant developments in the child welfare field in Canada in the late 1990s has been the public focus on child abuse deaths, often in situations where the children were known to the agencies but were not removed from parental care. The concern that agencies were not doing enough to protect children resulted in investigations

---

[53]   In *Catholic CAS of Metro Toronto v. M.(C.)* (1994), 9 R.F.L. (4th) 157, the Supreme Court of Canada emphasized the importance of the psychological bonding of a child in agency care with foster parents. The Court considered the psychological harm that would result from removing the child from the care of the long-term foster parents to justify a finding that the child was continuing to be 'in need of protection'. This decision made it substantially more difficult for a biological parent who has lost custody of a child for a period of years due to the parent's mental or emotional problems to regain custody of her child (provided that the agency has placed the child in a stable foster family), even if the parent has undertaken a course of treatment and regained the capacity to parent adequately.

In *Catholic CAS of Metro Toronto v. O. (L.M.)* (1997), 30 R.F.L. (4th) 16 (Ont. CA), the court held that parents who had been found criminally liable for the death of one child could lose all rights in regard to their other children at a 'summary hearing', without any oral testimony. The 'best interests' of the children and the desirability of placing them for adoption took precedence over any parental rights.

The recent Supreme Court of Canada decision in *D.H. v. H.M.*, [1999] S.C.J. 22 (full reasons to follow) rejected the claim of an aboriginal mother to regain custody of her child from the child's adoptive white grandparents, again emphasizing welfare over notions of parental rights and aboriginal culture.

[54]   (1998), 41 R.F.L. (4th) 339 (S.C.C.).

and inquiries in British Columbia, Quebec, Ontario, Manitoba and New Brunswick. The British Columbia public inquiry by Family Court Judge Tom Gove, responding to the tragic death of 5-year-old Matthew Vaudreuil who was killed by his mother, provided the most comprehensive study.[55] The 1995 *Gove Report* resulted in new legislation in British Columbia as well as a substantial change in the administration of child welfare services in that province, with a new Ministry for Children and Families being created.

In Ontario, after a series of Coroners' inquests, a Committee was appointed to recommend legislative reforms. The *Report of the Panel of Experts on Child Protection* was released in June 1998. The Panel, chaired by Family Court Judge Mary Jane Hatton, held no public hearings and had very little time to produce a report. There were no advocates for children or for parents involved with child protection agencies on the Panel.

The *Panel Report* recommended very substantial changes to Ontario's *Child and Family Services Act.* Amendments to the child protection law were introduced in the Ontario legislature in October 1998 and were enacted in May 1999.[56] The amendments were hurriedly enacted before the Ontario elections; the opposition parties agreed to waive any public hearings, as they did not want to appear to be delaying enactment of legislation that would appear to increase protection for children. Although not as interventionist as the *Panel Report,* the amendments widen the grounds for apprehension and require 'permanent decisions' to be made more quickly.

The new law stipulates that: '*The* paramount purpose of this Act is to promote the best interests, protection and well being of the child.' All other objectives, such as preservation of the family or maintaining the child's culture, are to be 'additional purposes'. Agency action to protect children only needs to be 'the least disruptive ... to help a child' instead of the old provision which requires the 'least restrictive or disruptive' to the 'child or family'. The new principles make clear that the central focus of the child welfare system is to be *the child.* Notions of parental rights, culture, or aboriginal status are to be 'secondary' to the focus on the child.

The definition of 'child in need of protection' is expanded to cover clearly physical neglect as well as abuse. The concept of emotional abuse is also widened, so that involuntary agency intervention is justified when there is 'serious emotional abuse or neglect' and there are 'reasonable grounds' to believe that the child's condition 'results from' parental conduct or neglect. The test for intervention based on the possibility of future harm is changed from 'substantial risk' to 'risk of likely harm'.

There are also changes to procedural and evidentiary rules to facilitate agency removal of children from parental care. At the interim care hearing, which is often critical as the proceedings can drag through the courts for months and even years, the standard of proof for the agency will only require the agency to show that there is 'a risk that the child is likely to suffer harm and the child cannot be protected adequately' by an order for agency supervision.

Ontario's Child and Family Services Act had a '24-month rule' as a maximum period for 'temporary' decisions to be made about children. The amendments provide that for children under 6 years of age, there will be a 12-month maximum for temporary care under a court order or agreement. Further, the total period in 'temporary care' is to be

---

[55]   British Columbia, *Gove Inquiry into Child Protection in British Columbia*, [1995] B.C.J. 2483 (Q.L.); Ontario Association of Children's Aid Societies, *Ontario Child Mortality Task Force Recommendations: A Progress Report* (1998); 'Horrific child abuse case reveals deep flaws in system: Commission censures Quebec for failing to protect children', *Globe & Mail*, April 23, 1998; 'Answers sought on child neglect in New Brunswick', *Globe & Mail*, December 29, 1997.

[56]   Enacted as S.O. 1999, c. 2, May 6, 1999.

determined on a cumulative basis for the past five years. To facilitate permanency planning and adoption, the amendments also require that after a permanent wardship order is made, parents will only have access with their children if they can show that their visits are 'beneficial and meaningful' to the child. In addition, parents must show that parental contact will not impair the 'child's *future* opportunities for a permanent or stable placement [i.e. adoption]'.

It is highly desirable to prevent children, especially young children, from 'drifting' in care. Permanent decisions need to be made in a timely fashion. However, the new Ontario regime has the shortest period in Canada of temporary care for children in the aged two to six category, and it is the only province with a 'cumulative' counting provision.

The new legislative scheme seems quite rigid, and in some cases it may be unfair to parents as well as contrary to the best interests of children. The relatively short periods for younger children and the 'cumulative' care provision may discourage parents from seeking voluntary care arrangements. These amendments also have the potential to drive more quickly parents and agencies into an adversarial relationship, with the agency forced to threaten parents with the permanent loss of their children in a relatively short time if the children are under six or have spent time in agency care in the past few years. Judges may be tempted to interpret the legislation in a broad fashion to reduce its rigidity, and may even invoke the *Charter of Rights* to extend statutory limitation periods, based on the argument that requiring a decision that is contrary to a child's best interests would violate the child's 'liberty and security or the person'.[57]

In the past few years, a central theme of criticism of the Canadian child protection legislation has been that children have been endangered because of legal constraints, such as too narrow a definition of 'child in need of protection'. However, the child abuse deaths arose because of difficulties by agency workers with evidence gathering or (at least with hindsight) from the failure to exercise proper judgement. No definition of child in need of protection will eliminate the need for professional judgement and sometimes very difficult individualized decision-making.

It is clear that agencies can change their approach to intervention without a legislative amendment. Even as the *Report* was being released, the number of children being apprehended and taken into care was increasing, without any statutory changes. This was a response to concerns raised by Coroners' reports about the failure to protect children from abuse.[58] There was also a case in Toronto in which a child protection worker was charged with criminal negligence causing death as a result of a mother on her caseload allowing her very young infant son to starve to death. This type of proceeding, which warns that workers may have personal liability if they make a 'wrong decision' – that is by leaving a child who subsequently dies in parental care – has undoubtedly made some workers more aggressive in removing children from parental care.[59] This increase in interventions and apprehensions illustrates that agency practices and interpretations

---

[57] See *Re R.A.J.* [1992] Y.J. 126 (Terr. Ct.) (Q.L.) where Lilles Terr. J. accepted such an argument. The new section 70(4) will give some statutory flexibility, allowing a judge to extend the maximum cumulative periods in temporary care by 'a period' of wardship of up to six months if this is in the child's 'best interests'. *Quaere* whether some judges may be inclined to interpret this as allowing more than one order to be made?

[58] See 'Foster care overflows to college dorm', *Globe & Mail*, June 19, 1998.

[59] 'Charged colleague weighs on case worker', *Globe & Mail*, August 12, 1997. The charges were laid in 1997, but the case was not resolved as of June 1999.

play a very large role in how any legislative scheme is actually implemented, and raise questions about whether dramatic legislative reforms are needed.

V INTERCOUNTRY ADOPTION

Legislative initiatives at the federal and provincial levels and a controversial Federal Court of Appeal decision drew attention to intercountry adoption in 1998. Because of the sharp decrease in healthy infants available for adoption within the country, Canada has become one of the major 'recipient countries'. The majority of non-step parent adoptions in Canada are now intercountry adoptions.[60] Most are adoptions of children from Asia, the USA, Eastern Europe, and Central and South America; of Canada's 2,215 intercountry adoptions recorded in 1998, 894 were from the People's Republic of China, 882 of which involved female adoptees.[61]

Under Canada's federal system, adoption is a matter of provincial legislative jurisdiction, while immigration and citizenship are matters of federal jurisdiction. Each province has its own laws regarding adoption. Immigration and citizenship are governed by federal legislation. The federal government also has constitutional authority to enter into international treaties, but treaties that are not self-executing and in matters of provincial legislative authority must be implemented by provincial statutes.

Canada signed the 1993 *Hague Convention on Protection of Children and Co-operation in Respect of Intercountry Adoption* ('*Hague Convention*') on April 12, 1994 and ratified it on December 19, 1996.[62] By the end of 1998 Alberta, British Columbia, Manitoba, New Brunswick, Ontario, Prince Edward Island, Saskatchewan and the Yukon enacted legislation to implement the *Hague Convention*.[63] Three other provinces (Quebec, Nova Scotia, and Newfoundland) and the Northwest Territories have yet to pass implementing legislation.[64]

On April 1, 1997, the federal *Immigration Act* was amended to comply with the terms of the *Hague Convention*,[65] but under the amended federal legislation, children adopted from abroad still are treated as immigrants. In late 1998, the federal government introduced a Bill to amend the *Citizenship Act*,[66] including provisions to reduce the distinctions made between adopted children and children born abroad of Canadian parents for the purpose of acquisition of citizenship. Under the new Act, children adopted

---

[60] K. Day & M. Sobol, *Adoption in Canada: Final Report* (Guelph: Health & Welfare Canada, 1993) at 12.

[61] Statistics from the Ministry of Citizenship and Immigration Canada.

[62] *Convention on Protection of Children and Co-Operation in Respect of Intercountry Adoption*, The Hague, May 29, 1993. For a discussion of the implications of the Convention for Canada, see Vaughan Black, 'GATT for Kids: New Rules for Intercountry Adoption of Children' (1994) 11 *Canadian Family Law Quarterly* 253.

[63] *Adoption Act*, R.S.B.C. 1996, c. 6; *The Intercountry Adoption (Hague Convention) and Consequential Amendments Act*, S.M. 1995, c. 22; *Intercountry Adoption Act*, S.N.B. 1996, c. I-12.01; *Intercountry Adoption Act*, S.O. 1998, c. 29; *The Intercountry Adoption (Hague Convention) Implementation Act*, S.S. 1995, c. I-10.01.

[64] Quebec, however, has adopted a *Code of Ethics for Certified International Adoption Organizations in Quebec* (Quebec Ministry of Health and Social Services, 1996) available online: http://www.msss.goouv.qc.ca/fr/document/index.htm. The *Code* came into force on January 1, 1997. The General Principles of the *Code* indicate that it is intended to ensure that intercountry adoptions involving accredited organizations take place in accordance with the principles of the *UN Convention on the Rights of the Child* and the *Hague Convention*.

[65] *Immigration Act*, R.S.C. 1985, c. 1-2.

[66] *Citizenship Act*, R.S.C. 1985, c. c-29; Canada, Bill C-63, 1998, *An Act Respecting Canadian Citizenship*, 36th Parl. 1st Sess.

abroad by Canadian citizens will no longer be characterized as immigrants, and instead will be treated as if they are natural-born children of Canadians living abroad.

The original Bill eliminated the need for medical tests and for the child to obtain immigrant status. The Bill was revised in early 1999 to provide that children adopted abroad by Canadian citizens be granted citizenship only if the adoption was:

(1) in the best interests of the child;
(2) created a genuine relationship of parent and child;
(3) was in accordance with the laws of the place where the adoption took place and the laws of the country of residence of the adopting citizen; and
(4) was not intended to circumvent the requirements under any enactment for admission to Canada or citizenship.[67]

Prospective Canadian adopters had been pleased with the prospect of legislative reform that would remove barriers to citizenship for children adopted from other countries. They objected to the revisions to the Bill on the grounds that they would add additional procedural requirements to what is already a lengthy and complex process.[68] The debates surrounding the Bill reveal a tension between the demand by prospective adopters for reduced procedural requirements and the interest of the government in ensuring that intercountry adoptions are genuine and in the best interests of the child.

The proposed amendments to the *Citizenship Act* are of great relevance to the parties in *McKenna v. Canada*.[69] McKenna and her husband are Canadian citizens and permanent residents of Ireland. They adopted two daughters in accordance with the laws of Ireland. The children were born in Ireland in 1974 and 1975 and were Irish citizens. Children born abroad to Canadian citizens obtain 'automatic' Canadian citizenship, but because McKenna's daughters were adopted, they were required to gain admission to Canada as permanent residents, in accordance with the current *Citizenship Act*, which incorporates by reference the requirements imposed by the *Immigration Act*. Because of the differential treatment accorded to birth and adopted children born abroad, and the refusal of the Canadian government to issue passports to her two adopted children, McKenna lodged a complaint with the Canadian Human Rights Commission, alleging discrimination on the basis of family status contrary to sections 3 and 5 of the *Canadian Human Rights Act*.[70]

The Federal Court of Appeal accepted McKenna's argument that the provisions of the current *Citizenship Act* discriminate on the basis of family status in imposing the extra burden on adopted children in order to obtain Canadian citizenship. The onus was then on the government to justify the discriminatory provisions. In this case, the government had not had an opportunity to do so. Therefore the Court dismissed McKenna's appeal but remitted the matter to the Human Rights Tribunal for reconsideration and disposition in accordance with the Federal Court of Appeal's reasons. The proposed changes to the *Citizenship Act* will address the issue of discrimination raised in the *McKenna* case.

---

[67] Bill C-63, *ibid.*, section 8.
[68] 'Immigration plan angers adoptive parents', *Globe and Mail*, May 20, 1999.
[69] *McKenna v. Canada*, [1999] 1 F.C. 401 (C.A.).
[70] *Canadian Human Rights Act*, S.C. 1976-77, c. 33, section 5.

CHILE

IDENTIFYING PARENTAGE AND THE METHODS OF PROOF IN THE NEW CHILEAN LAW

*Inés Pardo de Carvallo**

I   INTRODUCTION

The National Secretariat for Women, an organ of the Chilean State Administration, produced a project aimed at reforming certain institutions of private law. The President of the Republic sent this project to the National Congress in 1993. After protracted discussion, the Parliament approved it subject to certain amendments, and it was promulgated as Law 19.585, and published in the Diario Oficial on October 26, 1998.

The new law fundamentally changes the system of family law in Chile, in particular in such aspects as affiliation, the right to maintenance, custody, parentage, the right of succession etc. replacing and reforming numerous Articles in the Civil Code.

It comes into force on October 27, 1999, so that until that day we have a vacant period.

As it would not be possible to analyse the matters covered by the reforms in their entirety, this article is confined to what we consider to be the fundamental aspects related to affiliation, that is to say the determination of paternity and/or maternity and the methods of proof. From a legal point of view, it is essential to have clarity as to who is, or should be regarded as, descended from whom, and as to how that status is to be proved when the parents have not conferred it of their own volition. Otherwise the whole purpose of the legislation – viz. equality of status for all children born in Chile – is no more than a declaration of intention, worthless to those claiming rights based on affiliation.

II   THE ESTABLISHING OF AFFILIATION

A   The notion of affiliation

Affiliation means, in the words of Lacruz Berdejo and others,[1] 'the establishment in law of the biological fact of procreation'. It is this that gives the child his civil status.

By new Article 33 of the Civil Code, 'The civil status of children of a person belongs to those whose affiliation is established in conformity with Book I, Title VII of this Code'.

Establishment of affiliation varies according to whether it is a case of affiliation in or out of wedlock. In the first case, a legal presumption applies. Article 184 of the Civil Code provides: 'children born after the celebration of the marriage and within 300 days

---

*   Professor of Law, Universidad Católica de Valparaíso-Chile. With the collaboration of Professor María Soledad Quintana. Translated by Peter Schofield.

[1]   Lacruz Berdejo, J.L., Sancho Rebullida, F. y Rivero Hernandez, F., *Elementos de Derecho Civil.IV.*t.II, Bosch, Barcelona (1989), at 40.

after its dissolution or after the spouses divorce are presumed to be the children of the husband'. That is to say that legally a child born after the marriage is celebrated and within 300 days after it is dissolved or the parties divorce[2] is presumed to have been fathered by the husband.

Out of wedlock, however:

–   maternity is established by the fact of giving birth, by recognition, or by court order;
–   paternity is established by recognition or by court order.

Affiliation thus defined is proved and also its certification is performed in the manner set out in new Articles 305 and 309, based on records and other official documents.

B   *Criteria for establishing maternity or paternity*

We must first make it clear that, despite the best efforts of the Legislature to avoid classifying children in this way, reality asserted itself and the difference between affiliation in and out of wedlock had to be recognised when it came to establishing paternity or maternity.

As a result there is matrimonial and extramarital affiliation (Article 179 of the Civil Code).

Under the new law there is only one category of children, but more than one type of affiliation: 'All children are regarded as equal in the law', says the final part of the new Article 33 of the Civil Code, but it is necessary to add that this depends on establishing affiliation in relation to one or both parents. As new Article 37 affirms, 'It is possible for affiliation of children not to be established in relation to the father, to the mother or to both'.

C   *Classes of affiliation*

Affiliation may be either:

–   biological; or
–   by adoption (Article 179 of the Civil Code).

In the case of adoption, rights as between the adopter and adopted and the affiliation established between them will be governed by a special law; namely Article 179 inc. 2 of the Civil Code.

A project for a law to replace the current system of adoption in Chile is under consideration by a mixed Commission of the National Congress, so we cannot take this aspect any further.

Biological affiliation can be either in or out of wedlock (matrimonial or extramarital).

1   *A child whose affiliation is matrimonial*
Such a descendant enjoys a bilaterally linked status. S/he always has a relationship to father and mother. The bond is not independently with either one of the parents, but with both.

A child's matrimonial affiliation can either arise at birth or be acquired subsequently.

---

2   There is no divorce *a vinculo* in Chile.

(i) Matrimonial affiliation arising at birth, or properly so called

Article 180 inc. 1 of the Civil Code applies, 'where, at the time of the birth or the conception of the child, the parents are married to each other'.

It is sufficient if the birth takes place immediately after the wedding ceremony for matrimonial affiliation to arise at birth. The law assumes that, if a man marries a pregnant woman, it is because he is taking responsibility for the child she is carrying, otherwise he would not marry.

However, if the man was unaware of the woman's pregnancy, the law enables him to show that he did not know of it, and to deny paternity (Article 184 inc. 2 of the Civil Code).

So the elements of such affiliation are:

a. that a married woman is delivered of a child and the child's maternity is proved by the birth;
b. that the conception or the birth takes place during the marriage;
c. paternity is attributed to the mother's husband.

a.   The woman who gives birth must be married

Maternity is established by the fact of giving birth (Article 183 of the Civil Code), following the old maxim, Mater semper certa est.

b.   Conception or birth while the marriage is subsisting

Turning to the commencement of the marriage, the requirement is that this must precede the birth, be it only for a moment. But if we consider its dissolution – by nullity or death – or if a divorce has been decreed between the parties, what is required is that the child should at least have been conceived while it was subsisting, or before the divorce decree. We say this, because the Legislature requires birth to take place within 300 days after the dissolution or decree, thus retaining the presumption of Article 76 of the Civil Code, which the new law does not alter.

c.   Paternity of the husband

As a general rule, the establishment of paternal affiliation in wedlock, given the foregoing conditions, follows from the application of the legal presumption that the mother's husband is the child's father.

(ii) Acquired matrimonial affiliation per subsequens matrimonio

Affiliation is acquired if the parents intermarry after the child's birth. It arises in the following circumstances.

a. First, it applies to the child whose extramarital affiliation is already established in relation to both parents when the latter intermarry. It does not matter how affiliation was established, whether by recognition or by court order. Only the valid marriage of the parents is required.

    In this case, the marriage converts the extramarital affiliation into matrimonial affiliation. Article 185 inc. 2 of the Civil Code states 'Concerning the child born before the marriage of the parents, matrimonial affiliation is established by the celebration of the marriage, provided that maternity and paternity have already been established under Article 186 ...'

b. The second case is, we believe, where the parents recognise the child in the registration of their marriage.

This situation is not specifically mentioned in the Civil Code, but on the face of the provisions of the Civil Registration Law:

Article 37: 'The Officer of the Civil Register shall also privately inform the contracting parties that they can recognise children of their union born before the marriage, with the results set out in the following Article.'

Article 38 inc. 1: 'In the record of the marriage the parties can recognise children of their union born to them before the registration containing such declaration, and this shall produce the effects set out in inc. 2 of Article 185 of the Civil Code.'

Taking these two rules into account, we have no doubt that affiliation can be so established.

The same would apply to the child where affiliation was established only in relation to one parent, if the other made such a declaration in the registration of the marriage.

c.   The third possibility is that, at the time of the wedding, affiliation is not already established in relation to one of the parents, nor is a declaration made in the recording of the marriage, but, while the marriage is subsisting, the parents recognise the child in a document described in Article 187 of the Civil Code namely Public Records, Registration before the Officer of the Civil Register and of Wills.

We do not think a joint declaration is required; it can be achieved by separate declarations, in which case affiliation will date from whichever of them is the later.

d.   The fourth possibility is that one or both of the parents, despite having married, do not recognise the child before the marriage and are not willing to do so thereafter.

Would the child have an action to claim affiliation? Doubt arises since Article 180 and Article 185 of the Civil Code both seem only to accept voluntary acts of recognition. But in our view a court could still declare matrimonial affiliation.

2   *The extramarital child*

This is a child whose parents have not intermarried, but who has received in relation to one or both of his parents either recognition or a final judgment of affiliation, or whose maternity has been officially registered on the basis of the fact of the delivery.

Here, the parental link is with father or mother. It is unilateral, purely in personam, subjectively simple or complex as the case may be, received, irrevocable and unconditional (Article 189 inc. 2 of the Civil Code).

The ways of establishing this type of affiliation are set out in Articles 183 and 186 of the Civil Code:

As to maternity:

–   by the fact of giving birth (Article 183 of the Civil Code);
–   by recognition;
–   by court order.

As to paternity:

–   by recognition;
–   by court order.

(i)   The fact of giving birth

Article 183 of the Civil Code provides: 'Maternity is legally established by the birth, when the birth and the identity of the child and of the woman who gave birth to him appear in the records of the Civil Register'. For its part, new Article 31 No 4 of the law of the Civil Register provides: 'The birth records shall contain, as well as the matters common to all registration, the following: … 4th … the given names and family names of the mother, even in the absence of recognition, when the information given by the declarant is confirmed by the doctor who attended the birth, with regard to the identity of the child and of the mother who gave birth to him.'

We note a marked difference between these rules and the former legislation. There is now no need for a special declaration of recognition by the mother. So we can say maternity is established by the fact of birth.

In Chile the mother has no right to remain anonymous, as she can under the French law of January 8, 1993,[3] nor, as under Article 47 of the Spanish law of the Civil Register, has she the right to repudiate her child.[4]

(ii)   Recognition by the father, by the mother, or by both

Before setting out on this aspect, let us clarify the matter of the capacity of the person recognising.

Can a person under incapacity recognise?

We have to distinguish two kinds of incapacity:

- if the incapacity is relative – under age, or a spendthrift under interdict – there is no doubt that the person can recognise;
- if it is absolute – insanity, a deaf-mute unable to communicate in writing – affiliation cannot be established in this way, since the declaration would be null and void. The new rules abolish the exception introduced by law 19.089, which allowed the legal representative of an insane or deaf-mute mother to recognise her extramarital child (Repealed Article 271 No 1 final part, Civil Code).

Does the biological truth of paternity or maternity have to be shown?

It is unnecessary for the person recognising to prove his assertion at the time of recognition. Other means are available to nullify the declaration: it can be impugned or repudiated.

Who can be recognised?

Anyone, alive or dead, may be recognised, so long as affiliation has not been established in relation to both parents, or, at least not to the one of the same sex as the person recognising.

Recognition can take various forms:

a.   an explicit, spontaneous declaration;
b.   by implication from silence;
c.   in response to an inducement.

3   Jean Carbonnier, Droit Civil II *La famille*, Puf, 18th ed., Paris (1997), at 425–426.
4   Manuel Albaladejo, *Curso de Derecho Civil IV Derecho de Familia*, 8th ed., Barcelona (1997), at 230.

a. A declaration is explicit and spontaneous when one or both parents make it with that express intention. It is formal and may be made:

    –   before the Officer of the Civil Register when the child's birth is registered. In this case the officer must note it in the record of the birth; Article 31 No 4 of the Law of the Civil Register. At this point the law erroneously states that such a declaration can be included in the recording of the parents' marriage. However, here it would not be extramarital, but matrimonial affiliation;

    –   in a document drawn up at any time before any Officer of the Civil Register;

    –   in a public document;

    –   in a testamentary instrument.

    The first three forms of recognition can be performed by agency. The agent is appointed formally – by a public and special document.

b. Declaration implied from silence

    The simple fact of registering the name of the father or of the mother, on the application of either, at the time of registering the birth, is a sufficient recognition of affiliation (Article 188 inc. 1 of the Civil Code).

c. In response to an inducement

    If the child brings proceedings against the putative father – or mother – in court, with the aim of obtaining recognition, and the parent attends and confesses on oath, affiliation is established in relation to the person confessing.

D   Judicial competence

During the child's incapacity, this falls to the Judge of Minors of the district in which the child is domiciled; by amendment under Article 3 of Law 14908, Article 6 of Law 19.585.

    When the child has capacity, competence is with the Judge of Letters with civil jurisdiction.

If the respondent fails to appear
The law allows proceedings to be brought again against father or mother within three months.

Frustration of the proceedings
a. If the respondent appears and denies paternity or maternity as the case may be, the proceedings are frustrated. They cannot be restarted.
b. Similarly, if the respondent fails to appear on the second occasion.

E   Repudiation of recognition

Chilean law, unlike its Spanish model,[5] does not require the consent of the person being recognised as a condition of the validity of the legal act of recognition, but it does allow him to repudiate.

The Legislature inappropriately uses the term 'child' in this context, whereas by the fact of repudiating he ceases to be such. That is why we prefer to speak of the 'person recognised'.

In our view, this possibility of repudiating recognition undermines the principle of the dominance of 'biological reality', since it allows the child unilaterally, without giving reasons, to renounce the affiliation conferred on him.

The justification of the rule is to prevent persons from taking advantage, by means of recognition, of rights accorded, under a variety of laws, to parents vis-à-vis their children, e.g. maintenance, custody, succession, etc.

Requirements of repudiation

The law lays down certain requirements for one to be able to repudiate.

By way of formality, it must be made by a public written document, within a year of becoming aware of the recognition – a time which seems to us uncertain, since it requires proof of when the person discovered that recognition had taken place.

The writing must be recorded in the margin of the birth register.

As to essential validity, the person repudiating must be of full age. If he is a minor (at the time of recognition) the same time limit applies, starting from the date of reaching majority. If he is insane, or a deaf-mute unable to communicate in writing, repudiation must be made by his curator, and requires judicial authorisation.

A spendthrift under interdict can act for himself.

The ability to repudiate recognition passes to the heirs of a deceased person recognised.

Limitations of repudiation

Repudiation is not available to one who has, explicitly or tacitly, accepted the recognition (Article 192 of the Civil Code).

Effects

Repudiation is an irrevocable legal act.

It annuls 'retroactively, all effects of the recognition which exclusively benefit the child or his descendants, but does not affect rights already acquired by the parents or third parties, nor does it affect acts or contracts validly executed and made before the relevant annotation' (Article 195 of the Civil Code).

F   Affiliation by court order

Maternity and paternity alike can be established by order of a court made in affiliation proceedings (Articles 183 inc. 2 and 186 of the Civil Code).

To get such a decision, the child must apply to the court with jurisdiction over his father, his mother, or both parents.

---

[5]   Articles 123 y 124, Spanish Civil Code.

The child's application must contain sufficient grounds to establish a prima facie case in his favour.

The judge can, if he considers there are not adequate grounds, reject the application. In giving this power to the judge, the law omitted to say whether rejection was subject to any procedural recourse. Our view is that, considering the effects which follow from the decision to reject the case, the general rules should apply and the interested party should be able to take such recourse as the law normally permits.

To guard against false and malicious claims which could damage the reputation of parties, the law allows those affected to claim compensation for harm suffered in such a case.

III   CERTIFICATION OF AFFILIATION

The person whose affiliation has been established is likely to have to provide certification of it. That is to say, he will have to satisfy third parties thereof. The manner of doing this is prescribed in the Civil Code in Articles 305 and 309, to be found in Title XVII of Book 1.

The first and most effective form of certification of one's civil status, says the law, is by the birth or baptismal certificate. This is quite simply a copy of the corresponding registration issued by the competent officer.

A further form of certification is the registration or annotation of the act of recognition. In the absence of a certificate, or of registration or annotation, affiliation can only be certified by means of the authenticated documents by which it was legally established (public written document, act before the Officer of the Civil Register, testamentary instrument).

The judgment which established the affiliation can also be used to certify it.

Apart from those we have listed, the new law does not accept any other form of certifying affiliation.

IV   THE METHODS OF PROOF

In answer to the question why it is, or may become, necessary to prove one is the child of another person, we must reply that, while any human being has to have a biological father and mother, it is possible that either or both are lacking from a legal point of view. There can be a discrepancy between the biological reality and the legal reality.

The system of investigation of paternity or of maternity is invoked to resolve this uncertainty.

A   *Matrimonial affiliation*

In determining matrimonial affiliation, we draw on an important probative element, the legal presumption of paternity set out in new Article 184 of the Civil Code, which, as such, can be rebutted by proof to the contrary, whereupon the burden of proof reverts, under the general law, to the person whose affiliation is unknown. The Article, to which we referred above, says: 'children born after the celebration of the marriage and within 300 days after its dissolution or after the spouses divorce are presumed to be the children of the husband'.

B Extramarital affiliation

In extramarital affiliation, in contrast, unable to rely on the technical support of the presumption, one who claims to be the child or, as the case may be, the parent of another must, if s/he cannot point to a voluntary recognition, apply to a court for a declaration of the maternal or paternal kinship.

This brings us into the realm of the claim of, or of the challenge to, maternity or paternity, requiring a process of investigation in which the methods of proof prescribed by law come into play.

With regard to the investigation of maternity or paternity, we refer to the ability of a person who claims to be the child or the parent of another to have recourse to a court to ascertain and declare who is his parent, or his child.

With regard to the system of proof, we must remember that, in parallel with the general trend in comparative law to legislate for a broadening of this, to permit the investigation of paternity or maternity without restriction and in various ways, there is at the same time a reduction in the content of the rights of the child and of the parents.

Before the enactment of Law 19.585, the situation in Chile was paradoxical in that, while it provided a highly restrictive system of investigation, the law gave to the so-called natural child (born out of wedlock but recognised by the parents or deemed recognised by virtue of a court order) fewer rights than were enjoyed by a legitimate child (born in wedlock).

Even worse was the situation of the illegitimate child who had taken proceedings against his father or mother under Article 280 of the Civil Code (now repealed) and had won after a long and difficult process. All he could claim, as a general rule, was necessary maintenance.

The new law, in response to widespread doctrinal criticism, substantially alters the system.

C The system of proof

By new Article 198 of the Civil Code: 'In proceedings for the establishment of affiliation, maternity or paternity may be proved in any way, as decreed by the court or on the application of a party'.

This, then, is the general rule and sets the point of departure to analyse the means of proof in this matter.

It is important to note that, not only can the parties to the suit apply for the use of means of proof, but also the judge can, proprio motu, if he sees fit, order such means of proof to be used. Thus the general principle, characteristic of the civil process, is restored, after recent changes had restricted it.

The Legislature has made use of a terminology broad enough to allow us to say that non-traditional means of proof, such as photographs, films, video recordings, recordings in general, fax, e-mail, etc, can all be made use of in the action.

It is also noteworthy that methods of proof by biological expert witnesses are admitted.

In Chile there are currently in use three biological methods of investigating paternity: analysis of blood groups and subgroups, serological analysis of HLA antigens and DNA analysis.

In a case where application is made for – or where a judge orders – proof by a biological expert, this can be done by the Medico Legal Service, or by a suitable laboratory selected by the judge.

The law allows the parties to make a single application for new biological reports. The Legislature considered that allowing for a second opinion would protect the rights of the respondent.

Should either the respondent or the applicant refuse, without justification, to submit to examination by a biological expert, this raises a serious presumption against him. The provision of Article 462 of the Code of Civil Procedure leads to the conclusion that the judge could on this basis find the case proved.

This brings us back to the question of judicial discretion. When will the judge hold a refusal to be unjustified? Would it be held justified, so as not to bring the presumption into play, if the party in question raises problems of conscience or of religion which prevent him from submitting to such tests, on the ground that they constitute manifestations of cannibalism?

This is a question that will only be resolved over the years, as cases fall to be decided.

It will also be for the courts to decide when the presumption is sufficiently serious and precise.

Limitations on the system of proof

The Legislature has once again expressed a lack of confidence in oral testimony. In effect, in Article 198 inc. 2 of the Civil Code we read '… for these matters oral testimony is not of itself enough … there must be other evidence corroborating the testimony of witnesses if the facts alleged are to be held to be fully proved'.

What has been said about the evidence of biological experts shows the importance attached to this. We can see in *el Mensaje* evidence of the wish of the Executive, which commenced the original project, to promote biological considerations above all others. And yet, in the legislative debates an important limitation was placed on this idea. We see this in Article 201 inc. 1 of the Civil Code, by which a relationship amounting to openly acknowledged possession of the civil status of a child of the family is made a mode of proof. In the words of the law 'openly acknowledged possession of the civil status of a child [of the family] if duly proved takes precedence over expert biological evidence, where the two conflict'.

What are we to understand by openly acknowledged possession capable of having this effect? From ancient times, writers have listed three elements; the name, the habitual treatment and the reputation. What Article 200 inc. 2 of the Civil Code says is: 'Openly acknowledged possession means that the father or the mother or both of them have treated the child as their own, suitably providing for his education and establishment and presenting him to family and friends as such; and that among friends, family and the local community in general he is reputed and recognised as such.'

To give the child this civil status, the openly acknowledged possession must have lasted for five continuous years at least. It must be proved 'by a combination of oral testimony and of credible facts and circumstances which uncontrovertibly establish it'.

According to credible accounts of the background history of the passage of the law, this primacy given to openly acknowledged possession as against biological reality is motivated by a wish on the part of the Legislature to show respect for the decision of those who, knowing they were not the real parents, have brought up, educated and generally treated the child as theirs.

Despite this, as this fiction may in a particular case work against the child's interests, inc. 2 of the same Article allows the judge, 'if he finds serious circumstances showing it not to be in the child's interests', to give priority to the biological evidence over that of possession of status.

V FINAL COMMENTS

To conclude this study, it seems appropriate to make a few brief comments on the most important aspects of the new law, besides the equating of the effects of matrimonial and extramarital affiliation (once this is legally established) provided for in Law 19.585. Particularly, we consider how affiliation is determined and the system of proof.

1. As to the determination of affiliation, we consider it an improvement that maternity can now be proved by the fact of giving birth, provided the identities are duly proved, without the need for an express declaration. When an event is as obvious as giving birth to a child we consider it unthinkable that the mother should be able to deny it or to remain silent about it.
2. While biological evidence was admissible in our country before the new law, now we have the great advantage that rules exist for it, and particularly that the consequences, for the father and mother, of refusing to submit to tests are clearly set out.
3. It is also noteworthy that, even against the principle of the primacy of biological reality, the child has the facility of repudiating the recognition accorded to him. Clearly, with this rule, Chilean law departs from the European models, on which it has drawn, but despite which it wishes to retain its own legal tradition in this matter.

Finally, we conclude with the hope that the new law will indeed produce the desired egalitarian results and that, under it, there will not be an increase in the number of children born without a father and mother to see to their due protection, upbringing and education to a worthy adult life in the future.

CHINA

CARING FOR YOUNG AND OLD: DEVELOPMENTS IN THE FAMILY LAW OF THE PEOPLE'S REPUBLIC OF CHINA, 1996–1998

*Michael Palmer**

I   INTRODUCTION

In the period covered by this survey, 1996–1998, changes in the legal framework governing marriage and family relations in the People's Republic of China (PRC) included, in particular, the introduction in 1996 of a law to protect the rights and interests of the elderly and the revision in 1998 of the Adoption Law. There were also a number of changes in the areas of marriage, divorce and population control. The general emphasis on reform and legal construction in the post-Mao period[1] has resulted in the rapid evolution of China's system of family law into a relatively sophisticated system with a fragmented but extensive corpus of rules, a considerable degree of functional specialisation, a more firmly established process of judicial interpretation and a greater role for courts in resolving family disputes. Nevertheless, the system remains still highly politicised in the sense that the policies of the Chinese Communist Party (CCP) continue to have a predominant influence, and many complications are caused by tensions between such policies and the continuing influence of a number of traditional values. The developments outlined in this essay are part and parcel of the general processes of change taking place in post-Mao Chinese family law, and also reflect in various ways the problems that have arisen largely as a result of tension between CCP policies and customary norms.

II   RETHINKING THE MARRIAGE LAW

Looming over the developments noted above are well-advanced plans to revise the 1980 Marriage Law. The modified law, when introduced, will provide a much more unified and comprehensive normative framework for marriage and family relations in the PRC, and a full draft of the revised law has already been prepared by the National People's Congress under the title 'Zhonghua Renmin Gongheguo Hunyin Jiating Fa' or 'Law of the PRC on Marriage and Family'.[2] Pressure for substantial reform appears to have been initiated by the publication in 1990 of the book 'Marital and Family Problems in Contemporary China' compiled by the quasi-official Research Society on the Marriage Law. Among other factors which have encouraged substantial revision has been a general need felt by the Chinese authorities to revise legislation introduced in the late 1970s and

---

*   Senior Lecturer in Law and Chair of the Centre of Chinese Studies, SOAS, University of London.

[1]   Michael Palmer, 'The Re-emergence of Family Law in Post-Mao China: Marriage, Divorce and Reproduction', in Stanley B. Lubman (ed.) *China's Legal Reforms* (Oxford: Oxford University Press (1996) at 110–134).

[2]   Dated October 1997.

early 1980s when the PRC was in the throes of rebuilding its legal institutions and restoring and extending substantive laws, the Chinese leadership's decision to pursue policies of socialist legality in reaction to the disorder and unrest experienced during Cultural Revolution. In the years immediately following the death of Mao, there was a general emphasis on producing law codes which were very general, programmatic, and relatively elementary in nature, inter alia, in order to make them more accessible to 'the people'. These laws are now regarded as inadequate for regulating the much more complex social environment found in China in the late 1990s. Other factors include a growing familiarity with more liberal ideas about marriage, family and related matters found in other parts of the world, behavioural changes reflecting some of these more radical ideas, economic reforms promoting a more commercialised economy and thereby affecting such matters as domestic property relations, China's accession to a number of important international Conventions,[3] and the continuing efforts to control population growth and quality,[4] as well as changes to the system of social welfare.[5]

The draft revised code has generated significant jurisprudential controversy in Chinese legal circles, with some scholars arguing that the PRC should follow the example of the former Nationalist regime and include the marriage law and related legislation in a chapter on 'Relatives' in the general code on Civil Law. Another school of thought argues that there is no real need for major legislative amendment, and that there are more important legislative needs – in particular, in the area of commercial law – which should be given priority. A third school of thought has advocated reform and extension of the law along the lines laid out in the October 1997 draft, and bearing the amended title 'Marriage and Family Law'. Although this latter view appears to have prevailed, disputes over substantive provisions governing such issues as grounds for divorce, reproduction rights and so on have delayed the introduction of the new law, so that neither the 1998 nor the 1999 annual meetings of the National People's Congress considered the revised draft. When it is introduced, however, the reformed code will bring greater clarity and certainty in a number of areas of marriage and family law including: the concept of 'relative' (*qinshu*); family property (*jiating caichan*); invalidity of marriage (*wuxiao hunyin*); reproduction (*shengyu*); and divorce (*lihun*).[6]

III   CRIMINAL LAW REFORMS IN RELATION TO MARRIAGE AND THE FAMILY

One major code of law first introduced in the early post-Mao era that has been successfully reformed in the last few years is the Criminal Law (revised and in force

---

3   In particular, the Convention on the Elimination of All Forms of Discrimination Against Women (1979) and the Convention on the Rights of the Child (1989).

4   The October 1997 draft law contains a full chapter on family planning, whereas the 1980 Marriage Law contains just two articles, and these impose a general obligation on the part of wife and husband to practise birth control.

5   See Gordon White 'Social Security Reforms in China: towards an East Asian Model?', in Roger Goodman, Gordon White and Huck-ju Kwon (eds.) *The East Asian Model: Welfare Orientalism and the State* (London and New York: Routledge (1996) at 175–197).

6   See, generally, 'Hunyin Faxue' (Jurisprudence of Marriage), in Zhongguo Falü Nianjian Bianjibu (Editorial Department of the Law Yearbook of China), *Zhongguo Falü Nianjian, 1998* (Law Yearbook of China 1998) (Beijing: Zhongguo Falü Nianjian Chubanshe (1998) pp 1099–1106, at 1099–1100).

March 14, 1997).[7] To some extent the revision amounts to an incorporation into the main criminal code of various decisions of the Standing Committee of the National People's Congress on such matters as economic crime and public security. Many family-related decisions of the Standing Committee such as those forbidding prostitution and the patronage of prostitutes,[8] and the strict punishment of persons who deal in women and children,[9] remain in force. At first glance, the amended Criminal Law gives less attention to crime within the family context as it does not retain the special part on 'Crimes of Disrupting Marriage and Family' found in the 1979 Law.

However, the revised law does retain in modified form the chapter dealing with 'Crimes of Infringing on Citizens' Rights of the Person and Democratic Rights', and this now includes provisions that continue and extend those contained in the marriage and family crimes part in the 1979 Law. Thus, Article 179 in the old law, which made it an offence to use violence to interfere in the freedom of marriage of others, is repeated in Article 257 of the revised code. Similarly, the provision in Articles 180 and 181 of the 1979 code, prohibiting bigamy and cohabitation with the spouse of a member of the armed forces respectively, are now contained in Articles 258 and 259 of the 1997 Law. However, Article 259 in the amended law introduces the further offence of taking advantage of one's position or authority to coerce the wife of a serviceman on active service into sexual intercourse. Such conduct will henceforth be characterised, by reference to Article 236, as a form of rape. The duty to care for aged parents, sick relatives and other vulnerable persons – which if not performed could result in punishment of up to five years' fixed-term imprisonment – is retained in Article 261 of the revised law.[10] And the offence of abusing or maltreating (*nüedai*) family members contained in 182 of the old law is now to be found in unaltered form in Article 260.

In two important respects, however, the revised code attempts to deal in a more rigorous manner with two family-related problems which are increasingly characterised by the Chinese authorities as serious social issues – violence against women, and juvenile delinquency. Thus, the revised law incorporates a number of the basic features of the Decision of the Standing Committee of the National People's Congress Regarding the Severe Punishment of Criminals who Abduct and Traffic in, or Kidnap Women and Children (while not repealing that Decision). The amended law emphasises that abduction, purchase, and dealing in women and children is a serious offence which is punishable by fixed-term imprisonment, life imprisonment or even death (Article 240). In

---

[7]   Zhonghua Renmin Gongheguo Xingfa (Criminal Law of the People's Republic of China) 1997, in Zhongguo Falü Nianjian Bianjibu (Editorial Department of the Law Yearbook of China), *Zhongguo Falü Nianjian, 1998* (Law Yearbook of China, 1998) (Beijing: Zhongguo Falü Nianjian Chubanshe (1998) at 206–241).

[8]   Quanguo Renmin Daibiao Dahui Changwu Weiyuanhui (Standing Committee of the National People's Congress), 'Quanguo Renmin Daibiao Dahui Changwu Weiyuanhui guanyu yanjin maiyin piaochang de jueding' (Decision of the Standing Committee of the National People's Congress on the strict prohibition of prostitution and the patronising of prostitutes) 1991, in Zhongguo Falü Nianjian Bianjibu (Editorial Department of the Law Yearbook of China), *Zhongguo Falü Nianjian, 1992* (Law Yearbook of China, 1992) (Beijing: Falü Chubanshe, 1992, at 164–165).

[9]   Quanguo Renmin Daibiao Dahui Changwu Weiyuanhui (Standing Committee of the National People's Congress), 'Quanguo Renmin Daibiao Dahui Changwu Weiyuanhui guanyu yancheng guaimai bangjia funü he ertong de fanzui de jueding (Decision of the Standing Committee of the National People's Congress regarding the severe punishment of criminals who abduct and traffic in, or who kidnap, women or children) 1991, in Zhongguo Falü Nianjian Bianjibu (Editorial Department of the Law Yearbook of China), *Zhongguo Falü Nianjian, 1992* (Law Yearbook of China, 1992) (Beijing: Falü Chubanshe, 1992, at 165–166).

[10] Article 183 of the 1979 Criminal Law.

addition, the purchase of an abducted woman or child is also confirmed as an offence which may be punished by public surveillance, criminal detention, or fixed-term imprisonment of not more than three years.

Also confirmed by the revised law is the provision in the 1991 Decision of the Standing Committee that characterises as the offence of rape sexual intercourse with a woman who has been purchased (Article 241). However, the amended code appears to strengthen the provisions in the 1991 Decision which stipulate that no individual or organisation may obstruct state functionaries from rescuing women or children who have been subjected to sale. The leader of an organised group which hinders officials in this manner may be punished by criminal detention or fixed-term imprisonment of not more than five years. The revised code does not, however, contain specific provisions to deal with the issue of domestic violence against women other than the general rule – found at Article 134 of the 1979 Law and now contained in Article 234 of the revised code – prohibiting the intentional injury of another person. The preferred approach in China to the problem of domestic violence is proactive 'people's mediation' (*renmin tiaojie*) in which neighbourhood mediators are expected to 'nip domestic contradictions in the bud' by intervening directly and uninvited in family disputes.[11] And although violence against women is domestically seen as a serious social issue that necessitates firm measures in the criminal law, in international fora representatives of the PRC continue to be reluctant to acknowledge the significance of the problem: 'the [PRC] representative [advised] that violence against women had not been a serious social problem. Respect for women's dignity was stressed by the Government.'[12] In addition, the 1995 White Paper on human rights in the PRC insists that 'the family violence common in some western countries is relatively rare in China'.[13]

The amended Criminal Law 1997 also introduced general changes to the system of juvenile justice in China.[14] First, the revised code, at Article 17, paragraph 2, replaces a number of rather general provisions in the 1979 Law with somewhat clearer albeit still very general characterisations of criminal responsibility, imposing such responsibility in cases of serious crime: 'a person who has reached the age of 14 but not the age of 16 who commits intentional homicide, and who intentionally hurts another person so as to cause serious injury or death of the person, or commits rape, robbery, drug-trafficking, arson explosions or poisoning, shall bear criminal responsibility'. A second area of change concerns the death penalty: the 1979 Criminal Law allowed persons under the relevant age to be sentenced to death with a two-year suspension of execution.[15] The revised code defines the maximum punishment for a person under the age of 18 as life imprisonment. Thus, Article 49 stipulates: 'the death penalty shall not be imposed on persons who have not reached the age of 18 at the time the offence is committed or on women who are

---

[11] See, generally, Michael Palmer 'The Revival of Mediation in the People's Republic of China: (I) Extra-Judicial Mediation,' in W.E. Butler (ed.) *Yearbook on Socialist Legal Systems 1987* (New York, Dobbs Ferry: Transnational Books (1988) at 219–277).

[12] United Nations Commission on Human Rights, *Report of the Special Rapporteur on the ... Promotion and Protection of the Right to Freedom of Opinion and Expression,* January 28, 1998 (E/CN. 4/1998/40), at paragraph 171.

[13] Guowuyuan Xinwen Bangongshi (Information Office of the State Council) 'Zhongguo renquan shiye de fazhan' (Progress regarding human rights in China), in Zhongguo Falü Nianjian Bianjibu (Editorial Department of the Law Yearbook of China), *Zhongguo Falü Nianjian, 1996* (Law Yearbook of China 1996) (Beijing: Zhongguo Falü Nianjian Chubanshe, 1998, at 54–65).

[14] Preparations are also well advanced for a special code for the prevention of juvenile delinquency.

[15] Article 44 of the 1979 Criminal Law – see Michael Palmer 'The Death Penalty in the People's Republic of China,' in Andrew Rutherford and Peter Hodgkinson, (eds.) *Capital Punishment: Global Issues and Prospects* (London: Waterside Press (1996) at 105-141).

pregnant at time of trial'. For many minor offences committed by young persons under the age of 16, the family will remain a critically important sanctioning agent for a young offender's head of household continues to bear an obligation to discipline (*guanjiao*) the delinquent (Criminal Law 1997, Article 17, paragraph 4).

IV MARRIAGE AND DIVORCE

In the PRC marriages are concluded by registration[16] and in recent years efforts have been made to enhance compliance with this requirement by making more efficient the system for administering marriage registration and limiting the discretionary powers of the courts to characterise unregistered, customary unions as de facto marriages.[17] The sometimes ambiguous status of marriages taking place between Chinese citizens working outside China, or between Chinese citizens resident in the PRC and PRC citizens serving abroad, has been a growing problem as a result of China's increased involvement in the international community in the post-Mao era, and in 1997 efforts were made to reform this situation when the Ministry of Civil Affairs and the Ministry of Foreign Affairs introduced new Procedures governing marriage and divorce registration of such persons.[18] In an economic system in which state ownership continues to play an important role, the category of persons covered by the new measures is perhaps wider than might otherwise be imagined. The Procedures restrict the rights of certain categories of such personnel – members of the armed forces, public security personnel, officials dealing with important state secrets and so on – to marry at Chinese embassies or consulates or in the country in which they are resident (Procedures, Article 4). All Chinese personnel residing abroad are required to apply for marriage registration at the place of household registration[19] of one of the parties prior to her or his departure from China unless both parties are abroad – in which case they may marry instead in a Chinese

---

[16] Article 7, Marriage Law 1980; Articles 2, 9, and 10 of the Regulations for the Administration of Marriage Registration 1994.

[17] Michael Palmer, 'The Re-emergence of Family Law in Post-Mao China: Marriage, Divorce and Reproduction' in Stanley B. Lubman (ed.) *China's Legal Reforms* (Oxford: Oxford University Press, 1996, at 118–122).

[18] Chuguo Renyuan Hunyin Dengji Guanli Banfa (Procedures for the Administration of Marriage Registration of Personnel Working Abroad), promulgated May 8, 1997, Wang Hui'an and others (eds.) *Zhonghua Renmin Gongheguo Falü Quanshu, 1997* (Complete Book of Laws of the People's Republic of China, 1997 [Vol. 8]) (Jilin: Jilin Renmin Chubanshe (1998) at 127–128).

[19] Household registers or *hukouji* have been used as an administrative device in China for more than two thousand years, and have been mandatory since the establishment of the PRC in 1949. The principal function of the household registration system is to provide a system of internal domicile and thereby limit population mobility, enabling the authorities to promote public order by restricting and recording the movement of persons – especially strangers to the local community. It is also an important administrative mechanism for restricting the number of children that women may bear. And in order to contain the development of urban social problems, the right to urban residence is made difficult to acquire, and permission from the local *paichusuo* or police station must be obtained before an individual may change her or his household registration status, especially when moving to an urban area. During the period covered by this Survey (1996–1998) the system continued to come under pressure from, in particular, the efforts of the rural unemployed to find work in cities and to move to urban areas in violation of the household registration rules. In an effort to improve matters, several experimental projects were conducted in the countryside designed to introduce greater flexibility to the system: 'Gong'anbu xiao cheng-zhen huji guanli zhidu gaige shidian fang'an he guanyu wanshan nongcun huji guanli zhidu yijian' (Opinion of the Public Security Bureau on pilot projects to reform the administration of household registration in small towns and to perfect the system of household registration in villages), Guowuyuan Fazhiju, *Zhonghua Renmin Gongheguo Xin Fagui Huibian* (New Laws and Regulations of the People's Republic of China), no. 2 for 1997 (Beijing: Zhongguo Fazhi Chubanshe, at 169–176).

embassy or consulate if the law of the country in which they reside at the time of marriage recognises such marriages (Procedures, Article 6). In addition to ordinary documentation, Chinese citizens marrying under the Procedures are required to provide written evidence of their marital status which, if they have been abroad for more than six months, should be notarised. Health certificates are required. Broadly similar rules apply when both parties seek divorce, but if the parties are in dispute, they are expected by the new Provisions to bring suit in a people's court in the place of residence of one of the parties prior to departure from China.[20]

In an earlier Survey[21] the problem of the status of betrothal (*dinghun; hunyue*) in PRC law was noted. Briefly stated, although betrothal is practised it is not afforded legal recognition in Chinese law – primarily because in traditional times it was a 'feudal' institution by means of which parents arranged the marriages of their children. Exchanges of gifts and other property associated with engagement do raise legal issues that the courts have to deal with from time to time, particularly in the south-eastern province of Fujian where relatively well-off Taiwanese men often seek young brides from a similar ethnic background living in the province. The prestations made on the occasion of betrothal are governed by the General Principles of the Civil Law 1986 and Supreme People's Court Opinions 'Regarding the Problems of Dividing Property in Divorce Cases Handled by the People's Courts', 1993.[22] In the case of a broken engagement contracted in China by Taiwanese resident Kao Chih-hsiung with a young girl from Fujian Province, Ms. Weng Meitao, the People's Court of Zhangpu county in Fujian had to deal with such problems after the couple were in dispute following a refusal by the department of civil affairs to register their marriage on the ground that the intended bride had not yet reached the minimum legal age of marriage.[23] Although the couple nevertheless subsequently cohabited, an argument ensued in which Kao sued for dissolution of the betrothal, and return of various gifts made to the girl. The Court could not recognise the betrothal and therefore refused to dissolve it, but it did order Weng to return cash and jewellery to Kao. The principal rule used to determine the issue is found in paragraph 1 of Article 19 of the Supreme People's Court Opinions noted above. This provides that even in cases in which the marriage has taken place, if one party has received substantial amounts of property from the other but the marriage does not last very long, the property should be returned to the original owner. And if the gift has clearly been made a condition of marriage, then it must be returned. On the other hand if the gifts are small in value, or if the nature of the prestation is such that it is difficult to ascertain the true nature of the gift, than the judicial practice is to treat the gift as valid so that the donee retains it. In the instant case, it was clear that a considerable portion of the gift had been made to secure marriage, and the position of Kao was further assisted by Article 61 of the General Principles of the Civil

---

[20] Note also: Waijiaobu, Sifabu, Minzhengbu, 'Guanyu zhu waishi, lingguan jiu Zhongguo gongmin shenqing renmin fayuan chengren waiguo fayuan lihun panjueshu jinxing gongzheng, renzheng de you guan guiding' (Regulations regarding the notarisation and recognition of divorce judgments issued by foreign courts to Chinese citizens in Embassies and Consulates), 1997, in Zhongguo Falü Nianjian Bianjibu (Editorial Department of the Law Yearbook of China), *Zhongguo Falü Nianjian, 1998* (Law Yearbook of China, 1998) (Beijing: Zhongguo Falü Nianjian Chubanshe, 1998, at 801).

[21] Michael Palmer, 'The People's Republic of China: Problems of Marriage and Divorce', in M. Freeman (ed.) *Annual Survey of Family Law: 1987*, vol. 11 (Louisville: The International Society on Family Law (1988) at 57–79).

[22] Michael Palmer, 'Women to the Fore: developments in the family law of the PRC', in A. Bainham (ed.) *International Survey of Family Law: 1994* (Dordrecht: Kluwer [for The International Society of Family Law] (1996) at 155–179).

[23] 'Gao Zhixiong su WengMeitao jiechu hunyue fanhuan caiwu an,' (Gao Zhixiong sues Weng Meitao for dissolution of betrothal and return of gifts), *Zhongguo Falü* (Chinese Law), no. 3 for 1997, pp. 28–29.

Law which was applied to the facts of the case as a result of the failed marriage registration: 'after a civil act has been determined to be null and void or has been rescinded, the party who acquired property as a result of the act shall return it to the [other] party'.

In the ISFL essay on the Women's Protection Law[24] it was noted that women often face serious housing problems at the time of their divorce because much housing in China is allocated by the husband's work unit. As a result, the Women's Protection Law at Article 44 encourages the husband 'to do all he can to help the wife solve her housing problem'. Such exhortation has often been inadequate as a protective mechanism, and in 1996 the Supreme People's Court therefore issued a set of explanations[25] giving guidance to the courts on the manner in which such housing difficulties should be addressed in specific cases. The Supreme People's Court emphasises a number of policy considerations that have to be borne in mind by the courts in the decision-making process: promotion of gender equality, protection of the rights and interests of women and children, the financial circumstances of the parties, and 'equitable considerations' (*heqing heli*). Parties are encouraged to resolve their differences by bilateral negotiations (*zixing xieshang*) or through mediation by the parties' work unit or other relevant organisation. If these efforts fail, then the court is expected to decide matters in terms of the specific circumstances of the original housing allocation, as well as the particular needs of the parties – for example, where one party has been given custody of the children then she or he should be given favourable consideration. In general, these new rules seem to go some way to improving the housing rights of women at the time of divorce, although in keeping with other areas of divorce law, moral considerations are also taken into account – preferential treatment is to be given to 'the innocent party' and the opinions of the work unit which owns the housing are to be taken into account. Both considerations are likely to work against rather than for the interests of women.

V POPULATION CONTROL

In recent years, as I have indicated elsewhere, increasing attention is being given by the Chinese authorities to the question of the 'quality' of the Chinese population. The population growth rate of the PRC has been reduced significantly in the past few years so that the birth rate in 1997 was down to 16.57 births per thousand persons. Chinese demographers predict that the population of the PRC will continue to increase by an average of 13 million a year in the next decade, and by the middle of the twenty-first century will actually begin to drop. Policies are increasingly informed by additional worries which include the problem of an ageing population,[26] imbalances in gender ratio amongst new born children, the need to control the reproduction of China's growing transient population, and possible links between single child families and juvenile delinquency. In particular, the changing policies are giving greater attention to

---

[24] Michael Palmer, 'Women to the Fore: developments in the family law of the PRC', in A. Bainham (ed.) *International Survey of Family Law: 1994* (Dordrecht: Kluwer [for The International Society of Family Law] (1996) at 155–179).

[25] Zuigao Renmin Fayuan, 'Guanyu shenli lihun anjian zhong gongfang shiyong chengzu ruogan wenti de jieda' (Explanation of several issues concerning use of public housing and leaseholding in adjudicating divorce cases), *Zhonghua Renmin Gongheguo Zuigao Renmin Fayuan Gongbao* (Bulletin of the Supreme People's Court of the People's Republic of China), no. 2 for 1996, pp. 59–60.

[26] The PRC currently has more than 120 million persons over the age of 60, and this represents some 9 per cent of the population. The number of elderly persons is growing at 3 per cent per annum.

considerations of eugenics, with emphasis placed on the need to promote health care and environmental welfare, and to institute a nation-wide scheme of pre-marital health checks in order to reduce the birth rate of disabled and retarded children. Worries about population quality are focused on China's relatively backward inland and western provinces, where the benefits of the post-Mao economic reforms have not everywhere been felt, and where strenuous efforts are being made to combine effectively poverty relief work and population control.[27]

VI   ADOPTION

Adoption in its various forms was a highly important social institution in traditional China, and it has continued to be very significant in mainland China under socialist rule. In 1979, shortly after the mainland PRC leadership's decision to give law a significantly greater role in its system of rule, special provision was made for adoption by the Supreme People's Court in an official expression of its views regarding various civil matters – the Supreme People's Court Opinions Concerning the Implementation and Enforcement of Civil Affairs Policy, Cases, and Law, (February 2, 1979) at Section 14. In this section of the 1979 Opinions, the people's courts when handling adoption cases were enjoined to protect lawful adoptive relations, to safeguard the lawful rights and interests of the parties to an adoption, and to prevent maltreatment and desertion. It also stressed requirements of consent and the importance of completing the relevant formalities of adoption and household registration. In addition, the section encouraged the use of mediation in cases of disputes over adoptive arrangements, provided guidance on the residential arrangements that should follow the dissolution of adoptive ties, and specified the basic principles of compensation and maintenance that should be followed if an adoptive relationship was ended.

In order to give major legislative support to these rudimentary provisions, in 1980 the new Marriage Law at Article 20 declared that the state protected lawful adoption and that provisions in the Law governing relations between parents and children also applied to adoptive parent-child ties. In 1991 the PRC introduced a new and comprehensive Adoption Law which came into force in 1992.[28]

Perhaps the most significant feature of the 1991 Adoption Law was that enshrined in Article 1, namely that the purpose of the code is not given the meaning ascribed to adoption in many modern jurisdictions namely, protecting the position of the adopted child. Instead, the law offered protection to the rights of *both* adopted child and adopting parents, and to the 'legitimate adoptive relations' between the parties. In other words, the rights of the adopting parents were defined as being as important – or nearly as important – as those of the child. In Article 2 of the 1998 revised Adoption Law, a clause has been

---

[27]   See: Guojia Jihua Shengyu Weiyuanhui, Guowuyuan Fupin Kaizhan Lingdao Xiaozu Guanyu 95 qijian jin yi bu zuo hao fupin kaizhan yu jihua shengyu xiang jiehe gongzuo Yijian (Opinion of the State Family Planning Commission and the Poverty Relief Leading Small Group of the State Council on improving co-ordination of the development of poverty relief and birth planning in the period 1995–2000), Guowuyuan Fazhiju, *Zhonghua Renmin Gongheguo Xin Fagui Huibian* (New Laws and Regulations of the People's Republic of China), no. 1 for 1997, (Beijing: Zhongguo Fazhi Chubanshe, pp. 254–261). See also Chen Fusheng 'Guanyu fupin gongzuo qingquang de baogao,' (Report of the situation regarding poverty relief) in Zhonghua Renmin Gongheguo Quanguo Renmin Daibiao Dahui Changwu Weiyuanhui Gongbao (Gazette of the Standing Committee of the National People's Congress), no. 3 for 1997, pp. 485–493.

[28]   Michael Palmer, 'Minors to the Fore: juvenile protection legislation in the PRC', in M. Freeman (ed.) *Annual Survey of Family Law: 1991*, vol. 15 (Louisville: The International Society on Family Law (1993), pp. 299–308.

inserted declaring that the amended law has as one of its purposes the safeguarding of the rights and interests of the adopted person *and* the adopting parent or parents, and in so doing it strengthens the *reciprocal* nature of the adoptive relationship in Chinese law. Article 4 stipulates that the adopted person should be a child under fourteen years of age who is disadvantaged in one of three ways: the child must be either an orphan, or a foundling (or have natural parents who cannot be located), or a child whose natural parents cannot raise the child because they are burdened with unusual hardships. These provisions remain unaltered, as do the requirements that an adoptant must be childless and 'capable of rearing and providing education for the adopted child'. However, the requirement that the adoptant must be 35 years or older has been amended so that the adoptant now need have reached only 30 years of age, a very significant change designed to make it easier to create adoptive relations. An additional safeguard has also been introduced, namely, that the adoptant should not suffer from an illness considered inappropriate for the adoption of children.[29] Article 7 is amended in the revised law to confirm that even with the reduced minimum legal age for adoptants, continued recognition will be given in Chinese law to the customary practice of adoption of an agnatic nephew for the purpose of continuing a patriline that would otherwise be extinguished. Changes to Article 8 in the amended law are also intended to make adoption easier – and to enhance the family as a unit of care and welfare – by allowing couples with children or who have already adopted one or more children to adopt an orphan, foundling or handicapped child in the care of a social welfare organ.

The 1991 Adoption Law was surprisingly relaxed on the matter of formalities. It was hoped that the rural population would abandon their use of customary adoption deeds and rely instead on notarial proceedings to create adoptive relations. In this way, the public notary could be satisfied that all the conditions for an adoption had been met, especially those of consent, and a record of the adoption agreement certified and kept for future reference. In the 1991 Adoption Law, however, Article 15 merely required a written agreement between the parties. Notarial proceedings only became obligatory if one party sought this service, with the adoption taking effect from the date of the issue of the notarial certificate (Article 20). As a result, in the countryside most adoptions have not been notarised, but instead continue to be formed as a matter of private agreement between the parties.

The 1991 Adoption Law did not specify any requirement of registration of an adoption, although the fact of an adoption often makes necessary changes in household registration status and food supply credentials (that is, for example, ration cards). Subsequent regulations encouraged registration with the Civil Affairs Department[30] and in order to regulate adoption more effectively Article 15 of the revised Adoption Law 1998 stipulates that 'adoptions should be registered with civil affairs departments at the county level or above', with adoptive relations commencing from the date of registration. Similarly, Article 28 of the revised law encourages parties who wish to dissolve their adoptive relations to register the dissolution with a civil affairs department. Thus, although registration does not appear to be have been made compulsory by the amended law, the general direction of change is clear to see and it is to be expected that in due

---

[29] This parallels Marriage Law provisions which prohibit marriage if one party is deemed to be suffering from a disease rendering her or him unfit for marriage (Marriage Law 1980, Article 6[2]).

[30] Minzhengbu, Zhongguo Gongmin zai Zhongguo Banli Shouyang Dengji de Ruogan Guiding (Certain Provisions [Governing the] Procedures for Registration of Adoptions by Chinese Citizens in China), promulgated April 1, 1992, in Liang Wenshu (ed.) *Zhonghua Renmin Gongheguo Hunyinfa Quanshi* (Explanatory Notes on the Marriage Law of the People's Republic of China) (Beijing: Renmin Fayuan Chubanshe (1995) at 105–108).

course there will be a system of compulsory registration of adoption just as there is for marriage. Article 21 regulates more clearly the processes by means of which foreign parties may adopt Chinese children.[31] Finally, the revised Law strengthens the rules against abandonment of children and their subsequent sale under the guise of adoption.[32]

VII PROTECTION OF THE RIGHTS AND INTERESTS OF THE ELDERLY

Another important development was the introduction in 1996 of the latest in what is becoming a long line of 'protective' legislation,[33] namely, the 1996 Law for the Protection of the Rights and Interests of the Elderly (that is, those aged 60 or above), promulgated at the end of August in 1996 and in force October 1st of that year.[34] Although there is as yet little information available on the manner in which the Elderly Person's Law is operating, it is an important development and it is still possible to assess, in a preliminary way, the significance of this new legislation in China's still rapidly expanding corpus of family law. In my view, its promulgation reflects the state's felt need to protect a particularly vulnerable category of person in modern Chinese society – a need that itself reflects more traditional authoritarian and paternalistic attitudes than it does the emergence of civil society. And such protection is structured so that the principal substantive burdens continue to fall on the family or household rather than the state – and so that traditional ideals of respect for the elderly are significantly reinforced. This is a Law in which in a number of important respects the values and benefits of a gerontocracy are affirmed – reflecting the official view that age itself is a mark of achievement, and that the elderly and their knowledge and experience are inherently superior. The Law is thus firmly consistent with the political realities of China and the official drive for social stability.

In examining the actual provisions of this new item of legislation it is important to address issues of enforcement. Hitherto in PRC legislation offering social protection to such social categories as minors and women, there have been areas of ambiguity in respect of enforcement mechanisms – undermining, potentially at least, the effectiveness of the law. The new Law Protecting the Rights and Interests of the Elderly does not suffer from this problem, for at Articles 43 to 48 it provides a full corpus of the sanctions available in PRC law for dealing with deviant conduct directed against the elderly. Moreover, by the standards of PRC law, it identifies clearly the type of penalties or

---

[31]   Detailed provisions on this process are now provided by Sifabu 'Guanyu Waiguoren shouyang gongzheng ruogan wenti' (Some issues concerning the notarisation of adoptions by foreign parties), 1997, in Zhongguo Falü Nianjian Bianjibu (Editorial Department of the Law Yearbook of China), *Zhongguo Falü Nianjian, 1998* (Law Yearbook of China, 1998) (Beijing: Zhongguo Falü Nianjian Chubanshe (1998) at 806–808).

[32]   Thus, Article 30 specifies that abandonment or sale of an infant is either an administrative offence, punishable by a fine imposed by the Public Security Bureau, or in more serious cases, a criminal offence.

[33]   See: Michael Palmer, 'Minors to the Fore: juvenile protection legislation in the PRC,' in M. Freeman (ed.) *Annual Survey of Family Law: 1991*, vol. 15 (Louisville: The International Society on Family Law (1993) at 299–308); 'The Re-emergence of Family Law in Post-Mao China: Marriage, Divorce and Reproduction,' in Stanley B. Lubman (ed.) *China's Legal Reforms*, (Oxford: Oxford University Press, 1996); 'Women to the Fore: developments in the family law of the PRC,' in A. Bainham (ed.) *International Survey of Family Law: 1994* (Dordrecht: Kluwer [for The International Society of Family Law] (1996) at 155–179).

[34]   Zhonghua Renmin Gongheguo Laonianren Quanli Baozhang Fa (Law of the People's Republic of China for the Protection of the Rights and Interests of the Elderly) in Zhongguo Falü Nianjian Bianjibu (Editorial Department of the Law Yearbook of China), *Zhongguo Falü Nianjian, 1997* (Law Yearbook of China 1997) (Beijing: Zhongguo Falü Nianjian Chubanshe (1997) at 295–297).

corrective action that is to be applied in the event of maltreatment of the elderly. Article 43 provides that the elderly person who feels that his or her rights have been infringed may seek remedies through administrative channels, or by directly bringing suit in a people's court. The administrative body or the court are required by the same Article to handle the case promptly – in Article 45 the enforcement chambers of the People's courts are encouraged to give court rulings in cases centred on the problem of providing financial support and care for the elderly enforcement priority. In order to facilitate access to the courts, the new Law provides that court fees may be postponed or waived, and that legal aid may be made available to the indigent elderly. Two other forms of response to trouble cases involving the elderly are specified in the new Law. As we might expect, at Article 45, the elderly are provided not only with direct access to the courts in disputes over questions of finance and the provision of care with family members but also are encouraged to take up their dispute, with a view to mediation, with their local residents' committee. The latter will, of course, be composed of persons likely to be strongly supportive of the position of the elderly person. In addition, in the case of minor offences against the elderly – when the circumstances are relatively trivial – administrative punishments may be applied by the Public Security Bureau under the provisions of the 1994 Law on Public Security Administrative Penalties. Application of the Criminal Law is reserved for serious instances of conduct which physically or mentally harms the elderly person (including slander and public humiliation), failure to maintain financial support, and theft or other acts against the property of the elderly person. And reflecting the moral pressures that are imposed on family members in respect of the provision of support, family members and relevant officials who fail in their duty may be subjected to *piping jiaoyu* or 'criticism and education' – that is, a severe berating by local worthies (Articles 44 and 45).

The core provisions of the law for the elderly, however, lie in Chapter Two. This deals with the provision of financial support and care within the family. The 1979 Marriage Law, the 1979 Criminal Law (revised 1997), the 1982 Constitution, and the 1991 Adoption Law (revised 1998) all specify that there is an obligation on family members with the means to support other family members to provide such support. Not surprisingly, then, the pivotal role of the family is clearly enunciated in the new Law. Article 10 stipulates that the most important source of support for the elderly – *yanglao* – is the family, and further provides that members of the family should look after the elderly family members. A key term here is *shanyangren* or 'those who provide support' – this is characterised in Article 11 as referring primarily to the children of the elderly and others defined by law as bearing responsibility to provide support. The term *shanyang* has a primarily financial meaning. But the new Law, while laying stress on this form of support, also enjoins younger members of the family to provide emotional support and care, medical expenses, satisfactory accommodation, and so on. Paralleling the provision in the chapter on intestate succession in the 1985 Inheritance Law at Article 12 – that a filial daughter-in-law who has looked after her husband's parents is entitled to a share of the deceased in-law's estate – the Elderly Person's Law at Article 11 also states that the spouse of a person with support responsibilities is expected to assist in the provision of such support. The net of responsibility is further widened by Article 16 to include the spouse of an elderly person – that is, there are mutual obligations of support – and to younger siblings where their older brothers and sisters have brought them up. In addition, again by way of indirect reference to provisions in Article 31 of the 1985 Inheritance Law on 'Agreements for Inheritance and Care', the new Law at Article 15 specifies that persons with obligations of support for an elderly person may not refuse to carry out such duties by renouncing her or his rights of inheritance. Thus, any support and care arrangements made pursuant to Article 31 should supplement rather than substitute for family care. Moreover, Article 17 of the new Law encourages family members themselves to formalise support arrangements between themselves in the form of written agreements or *qianding xieyi* to which the elderly recipient of support must give her or his consent.

A number of provisions in this chapter also affirm in the family context the personal freedoms and rights in property of the elderly. Thus, Article 18 provides: 'the freedom of marriage of the elderly is protected by law. Children or other relatives [*qinshu*] may not interfere in the divorce, remarriage or post-married life [*hunhou*] of the elderly'. This provision refers to various practices, often associated with the exigencies of household registration, by means of which children of widowers and other elderly family members are prevented from remarrying because of fears that remarriage would have an adverse effect on their rights of inheritance. Such obstructionist practices were subject to a Joint Notice put out in the late 1980s by the Public Security Ministry, the Ministry of Civil Affairs, and the Procuracy, the effect of that Notice being severely to discourage such practices. Article 18 also specifies that the obligation to provide support does not diminish with a change in the marital relations of the elderly person. At Article 19 the rights of the elderly to divide lawfully their individual property (*geren caichan*) are protected. According to this provision, children or other relatives may not interfere in this process, nor may they obtain by force the property of the elderly person. The same Article confirms that the elderly have the right to inherit in accordance with the law the heritable property of their parents, their spouse, and their children. In order to make the position clear, Article 19 further declares that the elderly have the right to accept gifts – the fact of a gift may not be used to infer that there is some form of agreement over inheritance rights.

This Chapter, then, clearly locates the family at the centre of the system for providing support and care for the elderly, and anticipates a number of problems that could arise as a result of the interaction of the Inheritance Law with the Elderly Person's Law.

The 1994 Labour Law called for the establishment of a nation-wide pension scheme in the PRC. In Chapter Three of the Elderly Person's Law, a number of provisions are made which provide an interim 'system of old-age security' or *yanglao baoxian zhidu*. Pensions where they are paid are guaranteed, and in rural areas the profits gained from the exploitation of scarce resources – such as arable land which has not been contracted out – are to be devoted to old age support. The Chapter also encourages local governments to develop schemes of medical insurance for the elderly, to give priority to the needs of the elderly in the distribution of housing and residential care, and to provide adequate educational and welfare facilities for the elderly.

At the same time, however, the local community is encouraged to play an active supplementary role as Article 35 provides that 'traditions of mutual assistance between neighbours shall be promoted ... and voluntary social work for the elderly shall be encouraged and supported'. Much of the language used in this section lacks the precise allocation of specific responsibilities found in the Family Chapter, and is probably intended primarily to be exhortatory in nature.

The new law also attempts to lay out some broad social functions that the elderly can undertake in their declining years. Article 40 in the Chapter entitled 'Participation in Social Development' is intended to reinforce the position of the elderly as disseminators of ideas about appropriate conduct – by the Article, State and society are enjoined to respect the revolutionary and reconstruction experiences of the elderly, the fine morality of the elderly, and the knowledge and skills of old people. In Article 41 the elderly are encouraged to educate young people in the proud traditions of socialism, patriotism, collectivism, hard work and so on – more or less the same language as found in one of the General Provisions of the Law on the Protection of Minors which requires that young people be socialised in these values.[35] This superior position is also strengthened by the requirement in Article 7 of the new law that 'youth organisations, schools and nurseries shall educate the young and children to respect and to support the elderly, and conduct legal education in order to protect the legally defined rights and interests of the elderly'. The social control functions are further buttressed by the provisions of Article 41, paragraph 7 – these encourage the participation of elderly persons in public order work – that is, the local committees that are part of the neighbourhood and village apparatus, and which have special responsibility for liaison with the Public Security Bureau in public order issues.

But at the same time, both in this Chapter and elsewhere, a considerable and perhaps surprising degree of emphasis is placed on the continuing involvement of the elderly in economic production. Article 42 protects the income lawfully obtained by the elderly from their employment and related activities, and more generally, considerable stress is placed on the economic contributions that the elderly are able to make both as specialist advisors and as entrepreneurs. Thus, for example, people's governments at all levels are required in their economic planning to make provision for or take into account that there should be a 'gradually increasing involvement' of the elderly in enterprises of one sort or another. In a social and economic system in which the apparatus of government and the role of State-owned enterprises are being scaled down, leaving many persons approaching old age without employment, there is a felt need to anticipate some of the problems involved in the re-employment of laid-off, middle-aged workers.

---

[35] See: Michael Palmer, 'Minors to the Fore: juvenile protection legislation in the PRC', in M. Freeman (ed.) *Annual Survey of Family Law: 1991*, vol. 15 (Louisville: The International Society on Family Law (1993) at 299–308).

CROATIA

THE REFORM OF ADOPTION LAW – A CHANCE FOR BETTER AND MORE ADOPTIONS IN THE LIGHT OF CHILDREN'S RIGHTS

Dubravka Hrabar[*]

I   INTRODUCTION

This report deals with legal changes regarding adoption that have been made within the context of the complete reconstruction of family law in Croatia. There has already been a basic commentary on the expected family law reform,[1] including adoption.

In the meantime, the family law has been passed; it entered into force on December 30, 1998, and it will be implemented on July 1, 1999.[2]

The new adoption law conserves all previous rules that have proved to be a good solution in practice. Changes have been introduced with the intention of improving the quality and the number of adoptions in Croatia.[3] Besides that, since the Convention on the Rights of the Child ranks in Croatia at the constitutional level,[4] there was a requirement to respect and implement some specific children's rights including those in the area of adoption. The Croatian Constitution does not mention adoption at all, but Article 63, section 4 imposes a duty on the Republic of Croatia to take special care of minors without parents and of those who are not under parental care. This provision is the legal basis for working out in detail the protection of such children under family law.

This article will mention all the substantive and procedural provisions on adoption, including where appropriate remarks on those provisions of the Convention of the Rights of the Child that have an impact on children in the adoption process.

II   FORMS OF ADOPTION

The new law retains two forms of adoption – full adoption, called kin adoption, and simple adoption, called parental adoption.

According to their legal effects it is obvious that these two forms, as a consequence of legal changes,[5] have tended to be more and more drawn together. However, some differences are still present giving rise to a variety of legal forms to provide for children

---

[*]   Professor of Family Law, Faculty of Law, University of Zagreb.

[1]   See M. Alinčić and D. Hrabar, 'Family legislation in the period of creating a new legal order', *The International Survey of Family Law 1995*, M. Nijhoff Publishers, The Hague/Boston/London (1995), pp. 117–126.

[2]   The Family Act was reported in the Croatian Official Gazette – *Narodne novine*, No. 162/1998.

[3]   In 1997 in Croatia 157 adoptions took place according to the *Statistical Yearbook 1998*, p. 465; in 1996 there were 131 children adopted according to the internal record of the Ministry of Labour and Social Affairs, pp. 17–18.

[4]   Under Article 134 of the Croatian Constitution, *Narodne novine*, 56/1990.

[5]   The family law, including adoption, was changed after 1947 in 1978 and 1989.

who lack any, or satisfying, parental care. Children who are adopted in the form of full adoption (and their future descendants) have a legal relationship with their adoptive parents and their wider kin. The essence of the legal connection is a complete imitation of the natural, biological link between parents and their children. At the same time adopted children cut their ties with all of their biological relatives. It is impossible ever to revoke such an adoption. In the case of ill-treatment of adopted children by their adoptive parents or even in the case of mutual disregard, the center for social care will operate some of the very same protective measures as those which apply to biological parents.

Contrary to this, in simple adoption, children (and their future descendants) have legal ties only with the adoptive parents. In relation to succession law, there is no longer a possibility for a child adopted in this form to inherit from his biological parents and other blood-relatives. The new law, contrary to the previous law[6] that enabled the adopted child to inherit from both parents, adoptive and biological (the latter could not inherit from the child), provides that biological parents will not usually have any property that might be inherited.

III   THE ADOPTED CHILD AND THE ADOPTIVE PARENTS

Only minors[7] may be adopted. There is no provision that renders it impossible to adopt a child who marries at 16[8] or becomes a parent. In any event, practice shows that there is no interest in adopting older children, especially those who become parents. The child's age plays an important part in the decision of future adopters to adopt a child. Data show a decrease in the number of adoptions with the increase in the child's age.[9] Full adoption is provided only for children who have not reached 10 years of age. The former age limit of 6 years has been extended to enable more couples to enjoy a close legal relationship with the adopted child. Moreover, since potential parents prefer this type of adoption, children above the age of six, often remained in social care institutions for good. By raising the limit for full adoption to 10 years, it is to be expected that many children will find adopters.

Simple adoption is provided for children up to the age of 18. Children are the subject of simple adoption mostly where they exceed the age provided for full adoption and thus may not be adopted in this form. Also, more than half of simple adoptions are carried out by step-parents.[10] It is prohibited to adopt any child in direct parentage as well as a brother or a sister. Of course, in practice a biological father who did not acknowledge his paternity and, thus, was not registered as the father in state registers, could by the act of adoption become the adoptive father. Since there is no difference in rights and duties between adopted children (in this example they are regarded as biological children born

---

6   The Law on Marriage and Family Relations, *Narodne novine*, No. 51/1989.

7   According to Article 121, section 2 minors are persons under 18 years old.

8   The Family Act under Article 26, section 2, enables a minor who is 16 to marry.

9   Of the 102 full adoptions in 1996, 43 children were one–2 years old; 21 were 2–3 years; 16 of them 3–4; 10 were 4–5 and 8 were between 5 and 6 years old. The most sought after children, those aged under one were adopted in only 4 cases. The statistics were compiled according to the legal provisions of the Law on Marriage and Family Relations under which children could be adopted in full adoption up to the age of 6; see note no. 3, p. 109.

10   In 1996 there were 28 simple adoptions; among them 19 by step-parents. Concerning age, among 37 simple adoptions, 21 took place when the child was aged 6–10; 9 where the children were aged between 10–14; 2 children were aged 2–4 and 2 aged 14–18; and 3 children were adopted at the age of 4–6; see note no. 3, p. 109.

in wedlock) and those born out of wedlock, it would be pointless to adopt one's own child.

The view that the blood-relationship is an obstruction to adoption is based on the fact that by changing the blood-relationship to adoption nothing positive would come out of it. On the contrary, there might be a confusion of roles which would not be helpful to the minor. Close relatives (for instance a grandfather) can perform the functions of care and support regardless of the adoption in their existing family relationship. Other blood-relatives and relatives by marriage may adopt freely.[11]

The law provides that a child born to a minor parent cannot be adopted, except when the baby attains one year and there is no prospect that it will be brought up in its grand-parents' or close relatives' family. This is a new provision introduced because in practice such situations have been registered in the past few years. The adoption of minor parents' children might not take place sometimes for as long as 4 years (if a mother was 14 years old when she had the baby). It would be contrary to the child's best interests and his/her right to live in a family environment to wait for many years only because of lack of appropriate legal regulation.

There is no limit to the number of children who may be adopted, singly or together. The practice that siblings ought not to be separated has already been established. An orphan may be adopted after three months from the date of his/her birth or his/her abandonment. It is rather confusing to determine the beginning of the possibility to adopt an orphan. The date of birth will surely not be his/her real birth date, but the date that has been put into state registers as his (approximately) correct birth date. It would be preferable if the date of abandonment were the date of finding the child.

There is a preventative provision. According to Article 124, section 5 it is not permitted for a guardian to adopt his ward until he is no longer guardian. The grounds are connected with the guardian's duty to submit a report on his work as a guardian. The prohibition is aimed at the prevention of possible misuse of the ward's property.

As to the adoptive parents, account is taken of their age and their aptitudes in relation to the child's welfare. This means that the specific interest of the child will be considered as well as the adopters' compatibility with the child. The adopters' aptitude will be assessed with the assistance of expert opinion.

As a rule, the child will be available for adoption by Croatian citizens. Foreigners may adopt children in Croatia only exceptionally where it is of a particular benefit to the child.[12] In the case of intercountry adoption it is necessary to obtain the permission of the Ministry of Labor and Social Affairs. In practice the criterion 'exceptionally' envisages the situation where a step-parent is a foreigner or where a child is handicapped and there is no interest in adopting him in Croatia. The exception is in accordance with Article 21 of the Convention on the Rights of the Child under which intercountry adoption should take place only if the child cannot be placed in a foster or adoptive family or cannot be cared for in any suitable manner in his country of origin.

With regard to the adopters' personal status, all persons who are deprived of parental care or legal capacity are not allowed to adopt a child. As to the deprivation of parental care, this relates to those parents who have neglected or misused parental care towards their own children.

---

[11] As many as 30% of adoptions are by blood-relatives or those related by marriage; see M. Alinčić and A. Bakarić, *Porodično pravo* (Family Law), Zagreb (1989), p. 197.

[12] In spite of rumours about many children being available for adoption as a result of war in Croatia, there were only approximately 4 or 5 children adopted by foreigners every year.

The deprivation of legal capacity refers to the person who, according to Article 182, suffered from mental disease, psychiatric illness, was dependent on narcotics, senile or something similar, and was in need of special protection such as guardianship. Such a person is not capable of taking care of himself, let alone of his (adoptive) child.

Moreover, if the adopter's present behaviour or personal characteristics do not suggest that it would be desirable to allow him to adopt a child, he will be excluded from the possibility of gaining parental care through adoption. With regard to the adopters' previous behaviour, the adopters are usually asked to present a certificate showing absence of a criminal record.[13] Personal characteristics refer to moral, social or health shortcomings which would prevent good upbringing of the child.

Adopters must be aged between 21 and 35 and at least 18 years older than the adoptee. If there is sound justification, a person older than 35 may adopt, but in that case the age difference between him and the adopting child should not exceed 40 years. The statistical data reveal that the exception has become the rule in practice.[14] It has been shown that in Croatia most people try to bear their own children, using medical treatment in the case of infertility problems, and in case of failure, now older than 35, they apply to adopt. That fact illustrates that adoption is a legal institution that exists more for gaining parenthood than for helping children without care. There are not many couples who adopt a child who already have a biological child of their own,[15] although having their own children is not a bar to adoption. With regard to adoption by parents who have biological or other adopted children, there is no provision for hearing the opinion of those children in the adoption proceedings. We hope that the authorities will, in the absence of legal provision, implement Article 12 of the Convention on the Rights of the Child, under which children who are in a position to form a judgement of their own, should be heard.

Full adoption is reserved for couples married for at least 3 years. The duration of marriage is not at issue if the child is adopted by his step-father or step-mother. Persons who are not married, but live in an extra-marital union, are not allowed to adopt. The delay is required because it is to be expected that married couples will go through a period of adaptation as well. Moreover, since the divorce rate in Croatia is not very high,[16] marriage is a reasonable guarantee that a child will be placed in a harmonious union.

The options for simple adoption are more extensive – a couple may adopt a child regardless of the duration of their marriage; a child may be adopted by one of them with the consent of the other; and a single person is also allowed to adopt a child.[17] The existence of marriage is irrelevant in relation to simple adoption. In practice, a child will be adopted by a couple rather than a single person because a two-parent family is a better environment for the harmonious upbringing of the child. If a child is be adopted by only one partner, the consent of the other is required because of the fact that the child enters into a new family. As to the legal consequences, in the case of simple adoption, if the parent who has adopted a child dies, the other partner will share the inheritance and the

---

[13]   It is contrary to the Croatian Constitution's provision on the presumption of innocence.

[14]   In 1996, of 103 full adoptions, 49 adopters (one or both) were older than 40, 11 older than 45; see note 3, p. 109 above.

[15]   For instance, in Zagreb 84% of adopters do not have their own children; see M. Alinčić and A. Bakarić, N. Hlača and D. Hrabar, *Obiteljsko pravo* (Family Law), Zagreb (1994), p. 269.

[16]   In the last few years there have been around 150 divorces per 1,000 marriages: in 1997 there were 159 divorces; in 1996, 146.9; in 1995, 173.7; in 1994, 193.2, etc: see *Statistical Yearbook 1998*, note 3, p. 109.

[17]   Among 28 simple adoptions in 1996 only one adoption was by a single person, 19 by a step-mother or a step-father; see note 3, p 109 above.

pension with the adopted child. During their lives, there are special provisions imposing a duty of mutual maintenance (Article 218).

IV CONSENT TO ADOPTION

Since by adoption a child enters into a new family, breaking his legal and social ties with his biological family, due attention has been paid to the importance of consent to the adoption. The legal concept of consent includes implicitly awareness of the changes that will occur after adoption. Thus, there are strict provisions on a duty to agree to the adoption.

There are several persons who have to give their consent to adoption.

Biological parents (one or both) must consent to the adoption of their child. They must express clearly whether they consent to simple or full adoption. Moreover, they may give their consent in relation to either known or unknown future adopters (so-called *bianco* consent). If they wish to relinquish their interest in their child without having any interest in the identity of the future adopters, they may give consent after their child is 6 weeks old. After that, there is a waiting period, because they can revoke their consent within the next 30 days. Consequently, this means that no child may be adopted before the age of 10 weeks. Parents who have given their *bianco* consent will be excluded from the adoption process.

According to Article 129 parental consent need not be acquired if a parent is deprived of parental care or legal capacity, from a minor parent who does not understand the meaning of adoption, or from a parent whose residence has been unknown for at least 6 months and does not take care of his own child. In many cases parents do not want their children to be adopted although they do not take care of them. To protect the child's right to live in a family environment, according to Articles 9 and 20 of the Convention on the Rights of the Child, it is possible to adopt such a child despite the fact that parents, who do not live together with the child, do not consent to adoption.

Children who are without any, or adequate, parental care have to be under guardianship (Article 177). The guardian is then the child's legal representative and his consent must be given to the adoption of the child.

A child's right to express his own opinion and views (Article 12 of the Convention on the Rights of the Child) results in the child's consent to his/her adoption being required when aged 12 or more.

The consent should be given either to the center for social care which is handling the adoption or to the center for social care of the person's domicile or residence.

V PRIVACY, IDENTITY AND SECRECY OF THE ADOPTION

One of the most sensitive aspects of the adoption process is the regulation of three different rights which might influence the child's position in society and his new family, as well as form his character. By adoption many changes occur in the adoptive parents' family and around the child.

As to this aspect of the adoption, the provisions of several international Conventions have been taken into account as they bear on particular children's rights.

The child's right to information[18] has been widely recognised. Although the Convention on the Rights of the Child and other human rights treaties do not provide for or deal very carefully with the problem of access to (adoption) records,[19] the Family Act has in Article 123 stated as follows: 'The child has the right to find out from his/her adoptive parents the fact that he/she has been adopted, at the latest by the age of seven, or if the child has been adopted later, immediately after the adoption'.

That provision has clearly acknowledged the child's right to know about his origins. In fact, knowledge about adoption necessarily involves a subsequent question about the identity of the child's biological parents. The intention of Article 123 is to make adoptive parents aware of their role in the child's life and to make them responsible for the child's upbringing. In this sense Article 90 states: 'Parents are, before all others, expected and responsible for acquainting the child with his own rights. Parents will teach the child his/her rights as appropriate to his/her age and maturity'.

This provision expresses the psychological experience which dictates the desirability of the child's earliest possible consciousness of the adoption.

The child's right to have access to the adoption registers is guaranteed by the provisions of Article 141, by which the adopted child on attaining majority has the right to have access to the state registers, and also a minor adoptee has the right if the center for social care[20] estimates that it would be in his best interests.

Since it has been necessary to separate two different concepts – the privacy and the secrecy of the adoption process from the truth about the adoption – the Family Act contains particular provisions on third parties' rights and duties in the process of adoption. All data with regard to the adoption are officially secret (Article 141, section 2). At the same time, the Penal Code in Article 132 envisages as a criminal offence the unauthorised revealing of professional secrecy. Access to the adoption records is, according to Article 141, section 3, allowed to the adult adoptee, to the adoptive parents and to the biological parents if they have not given their *bianco* consent to the adoption of their child.

The privacy and the secrecy of the adoption process are protected by the possibility for the adoptee's close relatives to look into the adoption records only if the center for social care obtains the adult adoptee's consent (Article 141, section 5). The close relatives' interest in this information relates to medical issues (transplantation of organs for instance) or succession issues.

All the above-mentioned provisions recognize the right to respect for private life in accordance with the European Convention on Human Rights.[21] As a matter of fact, different rights that arise within and around adoption indicate that adoption as a legal fact is the most private and intimate process. These rights exclude third persons from getting involved with the family (now the adoptive family) as a union protected by the law.

By allowing the adoption, another question arises – the right to identity. The Convention on the Rights of the Child regulates the right to identity in Articles 7 and 8. Although these two provisions relate more to the problem of child abduction and to the actions which might allow third persons or the State to change the child's identity or to diminish the importance of family relations (Article 7), in relation to the adopted child, it

---

[18]   Article 13 of the Convention on the Rights of the Child.

[19]   See D. Hrabar, 'Pravo na privatnost i pravno na saznanje podrijetla' (The Right to Privacy and the Right to Know Origin – New Directives of the Institute of Adoption), *Zbornik Pravnog fakulteta u Zagrebu*, 47, (6), (1997), pp. 685–703.

[20]   Under Article 135 the center for social care is authorised in relation to the adoption procedure.

[21]   This is an issue under Article 8 of the European Convention.

is necessary to regulate the conditions and legal presumptions under which information may be changed during the adoption process.

According to the Family Act, full adoption enables the adoptive parents to change the child's personal name.[22] It is the adoptive parents' obligation to decide upon the child's name (which means that they may, if they wish, leave the name as it was written in the state registers) and his/her family name must be the same as that of the adoptive parents. If they do not have the same family name,[23] the Law on the Personal Name will be applied. This means that they must agree about their (adopted) child's family name; if not the center for social care will decide upon the child's family name.

The inscription of changed personal data is governed by two principles. First the child's right to know his/her origin will be preserved in that the adoption of a child will be registered in a special column called *subsequent inscriptions and notes* (Article 9 section b) point 6 of the Law on State Registers[24]). No data may be erased. All changes will be made in the mentioned column. This means that a child having access to the State register (Article 33 of the Law on State Registers) may reconstruct facts about his/her biological parents, such as personal name, date of adoption, etc.

Adoptive parents will be inscribed in the State register as 'parents' (Article 144 of the Family Act). Since the information in the State register is in a new form, third parties will not be able to discover that an adoption took place. Consequently the child's parents' and family's privacy will be protected.

Among other differences between full and simple adoption, there is an option (not a duty) for parents who have adopted a child under simple adoption to determine the child's first name if they so wish. With regard to the family name, the adoptee may keep his birth family name, add his adopted parents' family name to his own family name or change completely his family name taking only the adoptive parents' family name. As a new solution, there is a provision (Article 147, section 3) which enables adoptive parents to be inscribed in State registers as parents if they so wish. A child older than 12 must agree to changes of his name and the inscription of adopters as parents.

VI THE ADOPTION PROCESS

Adoption is ordered by the center for social care, on the application of the adopters. The adoption process will take place before the center for social care of the child's domicile or residence. Persons who apply for adoption have to enclose an expert opinion on their aptitude for adoption, given by the center for social care of their own residence.

The public will be excluded from the adoption process.

The consents to adoption (see IV above) will be given during the adoption process. If it is necessary, the center for social care will hear the child's close relatives about circumstances relevant to the adoption decision. Hearings are held in private; when the child gives his consent neither his parents nor his adopters must be present.

---

[22] The Law on the Personal Name, *Narodne novine*, no. 69/1992 in Article 3, section 3 provides that the personal name is composed of the name and the family name.

[23] According to Article 32 of the Family Act, a bride and groom have four options with regard to their family name: (1) everyone keeps his/her prior family name; (2) they both have the same (one) family name; (3) they create a new family name made from both of their family names; (4) only one of them adds to his family name the family name of the other.

[24] Law on State Registers, *Narodne novine*, no. 96/1993.

Before deciding on adoption, it is the center's duty to acquaint the child's parents, the adopters and the child over 12 years of age with the consequences of adoption.

Although some children are placed in non-governmental institutions (for instance 'Caritas'), only the center for social care has power to grant an adoption.

Croatian family law has never, including the latest law, provided for the child's temporary trial placement in the adopters' family. Such a period of custody has been avoided because during the period of adaptation the child might become integrated into the family and attached to possible adopters, only for the authority later to proclaim the adoption undesirable. Thus, special attention, during the process of adoption, will be paid to the expert considering the compatibility of the child and the adopters. In practice, all children who are placed in institutions have, immediately after their placement, their 'records' concerning them.

VII SUBSEQUENT ADOPTION

Adopted children may afterwards be adopted by other adopters in the case of the adopters' deprivation of parental care, death of both adopters or dissolution of simple adoption. The status of the new adoption depends on the personal stage of the adopted child (his age and aptitude for subsequent adoption, etc). This is a matter for wide discretion, since there is no single or special provision governing the criteria for subsequent adoption.

VIII SPECIAL PROVISIONS ON FILIATION

In the case of full adoption (Article 145) it is forbidden to initiate, after the order, an action to claim filiation (maternity or paternity).

If, in simple adoption, adoptive parents have decided upon their registration in state registers as parents (Article 147), the prohibition on disputes over filiation applies to that situation too.

The theoretical objection to depriving the child of his right to know his origin is not valid, because the child, according to Article 141 has the right to have access to the adoption records and state registers.

Since the possibility to be registered as a parent is extended to parents in simple adoption, the law-maker has given equal opportunity to adoptions that have taken place under earlier adoption rules.[25] The provision in Article 368 enables the adopters and the adult adoptee, for a period of one year after the law enters into force,[26] to register in the register of births as parents, not as adopters. The child older than 12 must agree to this change if the adopter(s) demand it. Otherwise, it may be demanded by the adopters or the adult adoptee.

---

[25] Previous laws were The Fundamental Law on Adoption of 1947 and The Law on Marriage and Family Relations of 1979 and 1989.

[26] The expiry date will be July 1, 2000.

IX   THE INTERRUPTION OF ADOPTION

Only simple adoption can be interrupted.

If the adoptee is a minor, the interruption order will be made officially or at the adopter's behest. The decision on interruption depends on whether it is justified in the minor's interest.

If the adoptee is an adult, he or the adopters may propose the interruption individually or together. The decision must be justified on welfare grounds.

The interruption of adoption is always, as regards the minor adoptee, in competition with the possibility of providing some child protection measures.

X   CONCLUDING REMARKS

The new Family Law provisions on adoption attempt to achieve a balance between children's rights and quality adoptions. Much attention has been paid to the child's welfare in and after the process of adoption. Children's rights that closely relate to the adoption rules have been taken seriously and by expressly stating that the child's interests must be the centre of every adoption. These rights are clear, beginning with the child's right to know his origin and right to the protection of his privacy. Although practice is the key to every legal provision, the new Family Law provides a real answer to the present situation of children without adequate or any parental care.

CZECH REPUBLIC

A HALF-HEARTED FAMILY LAW REFORM OF 1998

Jiří F. Haderka[*]

I   LEGISLATIVE DEVELOPMENT AND ITS OUTCOME

In my previous contribution to the *International Survey of Family Law 1994*, I mentioned[1] that on January 4, 1995 the Czech Government had issued Ruling No. 1/1995 on Family Law reform and connected matters.

The core of this Ruling was to establish two legislative commissions endowed with the task of preparing two Bills: a Family Law Amendment to the Civil Code and a Children Social and Legal Protection Act. The first Bill should have contained regulation of Family Law relations of all kinds and incorporated them into the frame of the many times reformed Civil Code, 1964. The second Bill should have created a universal new act guaranteeing public participation in ensuring the welfare of the family in a democratic society.

Both the Bills should have been prepared by September 30, 1995. The first commission, at the Ministry of Justice, had completed its task by that date. The second, working under the auspices of the Ministry of Labour and Social Affairs, had not.

Though there should have been numerous coincidences between the two Bills, the Government approved the first one, pardoning the non-existence of the other, and passed it to the Chamber of Deputies of the Parliament in January 1996. The first reactions were positive and the text was submitted to the committees.

At this moment, elections in June 1996 changed the composition of the Chamber and a new Government followed. The mood changed and the Bill was put aside.

Only in July 1997 did the Government go back to the topic, but with more limited objectives. The work of the two legislative commissions was revived. The task of the first commission was restricted to a reform of the present Family Code, 1963, as stated in Government Ruling No. 446/1997 and the commission was required to report by November 30, 1997. The parallel work of the other commission should have been carried out simultaneously.

The first commission submitted the results of its efforts by the due date while the other one staggered on again.

The Chamber of Deputies lost its patience and started working itself. It had at its disposal two Bills drawn up by two groups of deputies: a communist group and a right-wing group. The Constitutional Committee of the Chamber amalgamated them into one text, submitted the result to further reading and finally, on February 13, 1998 the Chamber of Deputies adopted the resulting Bill.

---

[*]   Judge, Professor of the Faculty of Law at the Palacký University in Olomouc, Professor of the Faculty of Economics at the Technical University in Ostrava.

[1]   J.F. Haderka, 'Czech Republic – New Problems and Old Worries', *The International Survey of Family Law 1994*, ed. A. Bainham, Martinus Nijhoff Publishers, The Hague–Boston–London, (1996), 181–197.

In Czech legal practice such a procedure is quite extraordinary, as Bills leading to very important Acts are usually prepared by the Government to guarantee more effectively their quality and systematic coherence with other parts of the legal system.[2] This notwithstanding, the Bill was passed to the Upper House, the Senate. The Bill had such massive support from part of the Lower House that the Senate did not dare to reject it, though voices directing attention to the deficiencies of the Bill were quite loud. The Upper House confined itself to proposing more than 30 changes to the Bill and returned it to the Lower House.

Bearing in mind that pre-term elections were drawing near, the Chamber of Deputies accepted all the proposals of the Senators and on April 3, 1998 approved the amended text by an imposing majority. The new Act was published under No. 91/1998 in the Digest of Laws (hereafter 'D.L.') after the signature of the President of the Republic and entered into force on August 1, 1998.

It introduces changes not only to the Family Code, No. 94/1963 D.L., but also transforms the matrimonial regimes contained in the Civil Code No. 40/1964 D.L. and alters several other not so important matters. A limited number of changes are also made to the Civil Procedure Code No. 99/1963 D.L. and the laws on social security.

The new Act was discussed at the International Conference of the ISFL[3] in Prague in June 1998 perhaps for the first time on an international level.

The purpose of this article is to transmit wider information to interested circles. Within the confines of this article only the basic features of the new legislation can be reported.

In general, we are obliged to confess that the results of this legislative work are far from the desire of most Czech legal theorists to have a really effective Family Law as part of the Civil Law system in the democratic tradition of Continental Europe.

The original intention to separate Private Law and Public Law elements, which were integrated in the original version of the Family Code of 1963 (only slightly modified in 1982 and 1992), and to incorporate Family Law relations in the Civil Law system of the Civil Code (CC) was sound. But the first legislative commission of the Ministry of Justice had a relatively short period of time for its deliberations. Moreover, it was bound by directives of the first Klaus Cabinet contained not only in Ruling No. 1/1995 but also by separately taken decisions about the desired model, where several variants were possible: this method of political determination of legal models would not have done any harm if the Parliament had had enough time to examine the difficult questions raised without haste.[4]

The following legislative commission at the Ministry of Justice was even more limited by Ruling No. 446/1997, worked under undesirable pressures of time and its opportunity for reflection was even more limited. This was because the second Klaus Cabinet was very unstable owing to the fact that it was only a minority Cabinet and depended largely on the goodwill of its coalition partners.

The communist group of deputies put forward their proposal on the basis that it was a minor Family Law amendment intended to retain most features of the old Family Code originating from the totalitarian period of the left in this country.

---

2   After the resignation of the second Klaus Cabinet, the new Cabinet led by J. Tošovský played a very passive role in this respect, perhaps influenced by its own transitory character.

3   International Society of Family Law.

4   J.F. Haderka, 'Ke vzniku a základním problémům novely zákona o rodině z r. 1998' ('On the Origin and Main Problems of the Family Law Amendment Act, 1998'), *Právní praxe*, (46), (1998), 5: 269–297.

The right-wing proposal was not an original work but to a large extent reproduced the governmental Bill from 1996.

The amalgam accepted as a compromise by the Constitutional Committee of the Lower House represented a very incongruous mixture. The elements of the governmental Bill from 1996 prevailed but in important respects it was spoiled by irrational components deriving from the other source. Possibilities for amendment in the Upper House were unrealistic: if the Upper House had over-estimated the willingness of the Lower House to listen to its intentions, the Lower House might very well have rejected the modified version and moreover had a sufficient majority to put through its own unmodified version.

The fact that there were repeated delays in the process of Family Law reform lasting seven years also exerted a more than negligible influence.

In the background there was always the danger that the reform would again end up on the rocks because the Tošovský Cabinet was predestined for several months and it was not certain whether the future social democratic government following the awaited victory of the left would incline towards putting Family Law reform on its agenda.

The first signs reveal that the reform has been greeted with no cheers – with a few exceptions – and that courts, solicitors, social care centre workers and other professionals who have to bear the main burden of applying the Family Law Amendment Act[5] in practice are already rather embarrassed and hesitant.

This report on the content of the new Act will follow the structure of the adapted Family Code and will demonstrate the changes introduced by the Amendment, leaving out those changes which are of lesser interest to the foreign reader.

II MARRIAGE

The Family Law Amendment Bill had to resist two temptations:

- – a not very strongly supported suggestion that a kind of institutionalised concubinage be introduced, or if you prefer another term, a legally recognised heterosexual free union;
- – very strong pressures by a quite loud homosexual lobby to provide for a kind of registered homosexual partnership in the Family Code.

The first temptation was resisted at the beginning of the 1995 legislative commission work under the influences of the former Soviet Union: if you try to equalise cohabitants with spouses in the area of maintenance, property regimes, etc. this is the best way to undermine marriage.

The second dilemma was treated by the first commission purely technically and submitted to the Cabinet, which decided not to incorporate homosexual relationships into the Family Code (FC) but did not oppose partial reforms relating to them outside the frame of the FC. This standpoint led a group of deputies in 1997 to submit a Bill dealing

---

5   The Family Law Amendment Act ('FLAA') was published under No. 91/1998 D.L.

with the so-called 'registered partnership of homosexuals' to the Parliament, which found its way onto the debate list in the Lower House shortly before the final vote on the FLAA.[6]

A   Conclusion of marriage

Since 1992, two marriage ceremonies have been possible: a civil one (which was obligatory in the period 1950–1992) and a religious one before a servant of a registered church or a religious society, the number of which has exceeded 20 in the Czech Republic.

The opinion of legal experts inclined towards the re-introduction of an obligatory civil ceremony, but political reasons have led to retention of the dualism, now embodied in Article 4 and 4a of the FC.

In both cases the ceremony is preceded by a preparatory procedure before a civil registrar and the wedding cannot take place unless this procedure is concluded by the issue of the registrar's written testimony to the effect that there are no obstacles to the performance of the ceremony.

In the case of performance of a religious ceremony without this testimony, the marriage is void. The clergyman is obliged to send the wedding protocol immediately after the ceremony to the civil registrar for registration of the marriage, this registration having importance only for the purposes of records.

A civil wedding may be accompanied by a religious ceremony but not vice versa (Article 10 FC).

For both kinds of wedding, the FLAA stresses that only the union of a man and a woman and nothing else can be understood by the term 'marriage' (Article 1 FC).

Article 8 FC introduces an interesting innovation: besides the existing possibilities of choosing the surname of one of the spouses as the common surname, or of retaining their previous surnames, a spouse who accepts the surname of the other spouse may now join his/her surname to the accepted surname as a second, supplemental surname.

Czech citizens abroad are also entitled to undergo a marriage ceremony at the diplomatic offices of their country (Article 5 FC). In the case of immediate danger to life, the wedding may be performed before the captain of a Czech ship or plane or a commander of a Czech military unit abroad (Article 7, para 2 FC).

Celebration of marriage by a special representative of one of the spouses for important reasons remains possible (Article 9 FC).[7]

B   Nullity and non-existence of marriage

The range of matrimonial impediments remains the same as before the FLAA – bigamy, incest, minimum age and mental health deficiency (Articles 11–14 FC). Only the last of these is more precisely defined.

---

[6]   The female leader of this group was also the communist leader of the communist FC reformers. This effort failed very soon at the first reading (April 2, 1998). Cf. my comment: J.F. Haderka, 'Několik poznámek k nedávnému pokusu o právní institucionalizaci homosexuálního soužití' ('Several Notes on the Recent Attempt Aiming at the Legal Institutionalisation of Homosexual Partnership'), *Správní právo*, (31), (1998), 5: 261–275.

[7]   J.F. Haderka, 'Oddavky, nulity a neexistence manželství od účinnosti zákona č. 91/98 Sb.' ('Conclusion of Marriage, Void and Voidable Marriage According to the FLAA No. 91/98 D.L.'), *Právní praxe*, (46), 1998, 8: 466–481.

A completely new aspect is the express introduction of consequences for defects relating to consent at the wedding. The FLAA creates a limited class of such cases, and removes any uncertainty as to what extent the Civil Code provisions (Article 34 and f.) can be subsidiarily used.

According to Article 15a of FC, a marriage is voidable at the request of one of the spouses within the time limit of one year from the moment he/she learnt of any of the following circumstances:

– vis ac metus;
– error in persona;
– error in negotio.

Sham marriages are not included, in spite of the contrary opinions of legal experts.

According to Article 15a FC, a marriage is not valid if one of the spouses has not attained the age of 16 (between 16 and 18 he/she may marry with the permission of the court), in the case of non-observance of the formalities for the ceremony before the civil or religious authorities competent to perform it, or if the preconditions of marriage are not satisfied by a representative.[8]

C   Mutual rights and duties of husband and wife

Provisions governing the personal and property relations of spouses remain scattered in several places in the FC and in the CC. This is so even now because of conceptual defects in the FLAA of 1998.

For the moment, we will not consider problems of maintenance between spouses and former spouses, since these are inextricably linked to the alimony regulation of other categories of persons.

We will look only at the provisions in Articles 18–21 FC. We can see that there are only minor changes in the provisions relating to the basic mutual rights and duties of husband and wife. But, in Article 19, para 3 FC we can discover a quite new provision. It allows a spouse to sue the other spouse who has not accomplished his/her duty to contribute to the expenses of the common household.

Changes in the provisions governing the property regime of the spouses, contained in Articles 143–151 CC, are very important.

Community of property remains the only legal matrimonial property system, but now it is enlarged to cover all property: not only things and other valuables, but also rights and obligations. Now, it encompasses not only assets, but also liabilities. It relates only to property acquired by the spouses or by one of them in the course of the marriage, with exemptions relating to property acquired by will, gift, or for the personal use of the spouses or that acquired by property restitution.

At present, this legal regime can be largely modified by contract between the spouses, this being possible at any time. Community property can be restricted only to the usual equipment of the household. On the other hand, it can be enlarged without limitation. It can also be postponed until the end of the marriage. The contract must be concluded as a written notarial act and if real estate is its subject, the contract does not enter into force until it is registered at the real estate registration office.

---

[8]   More detailed explanation in: M. Zuklínová, 'Co je nového v zákonu o rodině' ('Changes in the FC'), *Právní praxe*, (46), (1998), 5: 258–268.

Prenuptial contracts are now possible to the same extent. Nevertheless, they become effective only at the conclusion of the marriage.

Special safeguards are introduced in relation to the property of entrepreneurs.

As before, division of the community property is possible by means of a contract of the former spouses or by a court decision, usually after dissolution of the marriage and, exceptionally, earlier.[9]

D Divorce

The FLAA 1998 has profoundly changed the law on divorce.[10]

Two ways to divorce are now possible.

The first is the use of the traditional divorce based on the ground of irretrievable breakdown. There are two obstacles to attaining this goal. The first is the anti-detriment clause relating to minor children born into the marriage: divorce will be refused in exceptional circumstances, if it is contrary to the interests of the children. The second obstacle is the anti-detriment clause relating to a spouse who desires the marriage to continue. In this case there are three cumulative pre-conditions: breakdown of the marriage was not predominantly caused by the respondent, he/she would suffer very grave prejudice, and extraordinary considerations support continuation of the marriage. This clause may not be applied if the spouses have lived apart for a period longer than three years (Article 24, 24 b FC).

Divorce founded on the agreement of the spouses is the second way to divorce. It is also a basis for the ground of irretrievable breakdown; breakdown is presumed if at the start of the procedure the marriage has lasted at least one year and the spouses have lived apart for more than six months (Article 24 a FC).

In this case too, the divorce may be prevented by the anti-detriment clause in favour of the minor children.

It should be stressed that in both these cases the situation of the children must be resolved before the divorce may be granted, a special children court being competent in this regard (Article 25 FC).

Divorce based on the spouses' agreement requires satisfaction of the following conditions:

- before the divorce, the spouses are obliged to make written agreements with attested signatures on division of their property, on the housing situation and on spousal maintenance after divorce;

---

9   Particulars cf. in: J.F. Haderka, 'Osobní a majetková práva manželů od účinnosti zákona č. 91/98 Sb.' ('Personal and Property Rights of Spouses According to the FLAA'), *Právní praxe* (46), (1998), 9: 543–556, J. Salač, 'Společné jmění manželů' ('Community Property of Husband and Wife'), *Právní praxe* (46), (1998), 9: 557–563, J. Veselý, 'Co přináší novela občanského zákoníku do majetkových vztahů manželů' ('What Kind of Transformations of Matrimonial Property Relations has the 1998 Amendment Brought to the Civil Code?'), *Právní rozhledy*, (1998), 6: 299–308, J. Klíma, 'Manželé a podnikání' ('Spouses and Entrepreneurial Activities'), *Rodinné právo*, (1998), 0: 11–15.

10   J.F. Haderka, 'Rozvod a rozvodové řízení odúčinnosti zákona č.91/98 Sb.' ('Divorce and Divorce Proceedings According to the FLAA'), *Právní praxe* (46), (1998), 6: 342–356, J. Nykodým, 'Novela zákona o rodině' ('Family Law Amendment Act 1998'),*Bulletin advokacie*, (1998), 8: 12–23, M. Králík, 'Zamyšlení nad některými novelizovanými ustanoveními zákona o rodině z pohledu soudní praxe' ('Reflections on Selected Family Law Amendment Act Problems from the Viewpoint of Legal Practice'), *Právní rozhledy*, (1998), 7: 352–359.

–   they are also obliged to secure the approval of the children court to their agreement regarding their minor children after divorce as regards custody and financial support by the absent parent.

The new text also mentions the possibility of simultaneous or alternative care by both parents in suitable cases (Article 26 FC). Nevertheless, it seems that in practice such cases will be quite exceptional.

It is to be expected that, normally, one parent will care for the child in his/her household, the other one participating in care during access with the child.

III   RELATIONS BETWEEN PARENTS AND CHILDREN

First it must be mentioned that since 1950 the legal position of a child born in wedlock and one born out of wedlock has been equal in the field of family law.

Since that time, both parents, the father and the mother, have had the same rights and duties towards their children, notwithstanding their origin. In the period from 1950 to 1963 both parents were endowed with the so-called 'parental power'. With the entry into force of the FC, this 'parental power' was abolished and transformed into 'parental rights' belonging to each of the parents to the same extent.[11]

A   Parental responsibility

Disappearance of the concept of parental responsibility turned out to be very disadvantageous for our country in the contemporary world. Czechoslovakia differed from the majority of European legal systems and this fact caused difficulties in the conflicts of laws and in access to international human rights Conventions and recommendations.

Even in the domestic legal context it brought trouble since it was necessary to distinguish between the so-called vested, inalienable parental rights from other rights which did not belong to the parent who did not enjoy full legal capacity or who had been deprived of his/her rights by the court.

Therefore, the FLAA re-introduced the institution of parental power under the changed name of 'parental responsibility'. In this manner, domestic law was adjusted to international terminology (Article 31 and f. FC). Parental responsibility consists of three main components: care for the person of the child, care for his/her property, and his/her representation. The first of these may be conferred by the decision of a court on a parent who has attained the age of 16 if he/she is capable of fulfilling the tasks required. Another important change is that the law incorporates wide directives for the care of the child's property. The FLAA also stresses the principle of the child's well-being and his/her gradual participation in the shaping of his/her own life.

The FC retains the possibilities for imposing educational measures (Article 43 FC), of ordering separation of the child from the parent in cases of necessity and of placing the child in the care of other persons or in foster care. The new Article 44 FC permits suspension of parental responsibility if the parent is hindered in its exercise for certain reasons. The exercise of parental responsibility can also be curtailed in the case of

---

[11]   J.F. Haderka, 'Rodičovská zodpovědnost a související otázky od účinnosti zákona č.91/98 Sb.' ('Parental Responsibility and Related Matters According to FLAA'), *Právní praxe* (46), (1998), 8: 482–495, M. Hrušáková, and Z. Králíčková, *České rodinné právo* (*Czech Family Law*), Brno, Doplněk, (1998).

parental deficiency. Deprivation of parental responsibility for its misuse or negligence is the gravest measure which the court can impose.

In cases of separation of parents, the court decides where the child should live, ensures his/her subsistence, and, if necessary, regulates other matters relating to the exercise of parental responsibility. Parental responsibility however remains vested in the parents (Article 50 FC). Visitation rights can be arranged not only for the other parent, but also for the grandparents and siblings, if living apart (Article 27 FC).

Other provisions concerning the father and mother in relation to children remained mostly unchanged.[12]

B   Affiliation

A new Article 50a FC concerning maternity has been added. It states that the woman who has given birth to the child is always the child's legal mother. All arguments about differences between genetic and gestational mothers are now resolved in this way.

As to paternal affiliation, the existing system of three rebuttable presumptions of paternity has not been changed, subject to small adaptations. The most important of these are:

- during proceedings aiming at denial of paternity by a husband, a common declaration by the husband, the mother and her partner can exclude the paternity of the husband and establish the paternity of the mother's partner, under certain conditions (Article 58, para 1 FC);
- the man claiming paternity of a child born out of wedlock is entitled to assert this before the court against the will of the mother (Article 54, para 1 FC);
- the entitlement of the prosecutor general to seek rebuttal of paternity was enlarged to cases in which the biological link of the man declaring himself father with the consent of the mother is impossible and the interests of the child dictate that, from a human rights perspective, an action should be brought (Article 62a FC).[13]

C   Adoption

The core of the adoption provisions has been retained with several modifications. Their main aim was to remove the obstacles for adherence by the Czech Republic to the European Convention on Adoption of 1967.

Here we should mention that even before August 1998 the Czech FC provided for two types of adoption, both being adoptio plena, making the minor child a member of a new family and suspending all his/her ties to the family of origin. The first type is however revocable under certain conditions by a court decision on important grounds; the other is irrevocable and is accompanied by registration of the adopters (always a married couple, or the spouse of the child's parent) in family registers.

---

[12]   J.F. Haderka, 'Tzv. sociálněprávní ochrana dětí v zákonu o rodině od účinnosti zákona č.91/98 Sb.' ('So-called Social and Legal Protection of Children According to FLAA'), *Právní praxe* (46), (1998), 10: 610–623.

[13]   J.F. Haderka, 'Otázky mateřství a otcovství od účinnosti zákona č.91/98 Sb.' ('Maternal and Paternal Affiliation According to FLAA'), *Právní praxe* (46), (1998), 9: 530–542, S. Radvanová, 'Kdo jsou rodiče dítěte – jen zdánlivě jednoduchá otázka' ('Who Are the Parents of the Child – An Only Seemingly Unequivocal Question'), *Zdravotnictví a právo*, (1998), 5: 7–13, 6: 4–7, 7–8: 9–13.

The most important changes are as follows.

- Where the parent who is the legal representative of the child does not wish to remain so, the child may be adopted quite exceptionally: where the parent has shown a lack of interest in the child without justifiable reasons for a period of six months. These reasons must be proven in a special preliminary (incidental) procedure in which the maxim 'audiatur et altera pars' is fully respected.
- The same result can be achieved where absolutely no interest was demonstrated by the parent towards a newborn child, lasting for an uninterrupted period of two months after the birth; the same procedural guarantees are required.
- The consent of parents who are the legal representatives of the child is not necessary if they have submitted to a court or a specialised child social and legal protection body a written declaration of their agreement to the adoption but without specifying the adopter. This consent cannot be validly given during the first six weeks of the minor's life.
- The so-called pre-adoption care of the child cannot be ordered by the institution in which that child is placed but only by a body entrusted with social and legal protection of the child.
- A child's health deficiencies have ceased to be an obstacle to his/her adoption. Nevertheless, the future adopter must be aware of the child's state of health.[14]

D   Tutorship and curatorship

In 1963, the FC confused the institutions of *tutela* and *cura* and considerably limited the autonomy of parents to influence the choice of the tutor.

In 1998 the FLAA re-established the separation of both these civil law institutions (Articles 78–82 FC).[15]

It also gave back to the father and the mother their right to have a say in the choice of the tutor and also stated that the tutor should be preferably sought in the circle of the child's family or persons close to him/her or to his/her parents.

The amendment enlarged the number of cases in which a tutor must be appointed (death of parents, their legal incapacity, deprivation of their parental responsibility or its suspension).

The new Act also filled the gap in defining the tasks of the tutor in administration of the child's property.

As to curatorship, the position of a curator is now clearly distinguished from that of a tutor. A new type of curatorship is now possible in cases in which the parents are not able to administer the child's property successfully (Article 37b FC).

---

[14]   More details in: J.F. Haderka, 'Osvojení a adopční řízení od účinnosti zákona č.91/98 Sb.' ('Adoption and Adoptional Proceedings According to the FLAA No. 91/98 D.L.'), *Právní praxe* (46), (1998), 7: 402–417, A. Winterová, 'Kritické poznámky k několika posledním novelizacím občanského soudního řádu' ('Critical Notes on the Recent Civil Procedure Code Amendments'), *Právní praxe* (46), (1998), 6: 330–341.

[15]   J.F. Haderka, 'Poručenství a opatrovnictví od účinnosti zákona č. 91/98 Sb.' ('Tutorship and Curatorship According to FLAA'), *Právní praxe* – in print.

IV   MAINTENANCE

From the start, one part of the FC has been concerned with regulation of maintenance between various categories of persons.

The changes in this part of the Code as follows are not very great.[16]

A   *Mutual duty of maintenance between parents and children*

1   *Maintenance of children*

It should be recalled that parents' maintenance obligations towards their children are not limited by their minority but continue until the children are able to support themselves: during this time the standard of living of both the parents and the children should be broadly equivalent.

Major changes added to those principles by the FLAA are the following.

– The principle of the actual resources of the parent bound to pay maintenance to the child is complemented by the principle of his/her earning potential which is important if the parent does not take advantage of it: the child has the right to participate in his/her parent's living standard.

– If the parent has independent business activities, e.g. as an entrepreneur, he/she is obliged to submit to the court accounts giving an estimate of his/her economic situation as far as possible and loses the right to confidentiality regarding this material. If he/she does not fulfil this obligation, the court will presume an income level of 15 times the minimum living rate, i.e. now more than 30,000 CZK, taking account of inflation.

– Maintenance of the child is intended not only to cover his/her current needs but also to serve future needs, e.g. university study.

2   *Maintenance of parents*

As we know, the father and mother if in need have the right to fair maintenance from their children.

In this respect, the only change is a new principle which states that the maintenance is determined not only from the income of the children, but also from their property.

B   *Mutual duty of maintenance between more distant ascendants and descendants*

Changes in this category are as follows.

– In the case of the maintenance duty of ascendants towards descendants (in practice of grandparents towards grandchildren), the prohibition on using maintenance payments for the purposes of long-term savings was cancelled, as it was in relation to parents and children, but only in respect of minor children.

– In both directions, i.e. from ascendants to descendants and vice versa, not only income, but also property is taken into consideration.

---

[16] J.F. Haderka, 'Problematika výživného od účinnosti zákona č.91/98 Sb.' ('Problems of Maintenance in FLAA'), *Právní praxe* (46), (1998), 10: 595–609.

C   Mutual duty of maintenance between husband and wife in the course of marriage

No changes were enacted. The claim under Article 19, para 3 FC looks into the past; the claim under Article 91 FC looks into the future.

D   Mutual duty of maintenance between divorced spouses

The core principles were kept, but there is one important change.

Generally speaking, the divorced spouse's maintenance claim is lower than that of a married spouse, who is entitled to the same living standard as the other spouse. The divorced spouse retains a maintenance claim only to provide for an adequate standard of living.

Nevertheless, if the spouse who was not primarily responsible for the breakdown of the marriage suffered grave hardship as a result of the divorce, he/she is entitled to maintenance to the same extent as a married spouse for a maximum period of three years (Article 93 FC).

The FLAA now gives the divorced spouse the possibility to agree with the other spouse a maintenance payment once and for all, in a lump sum. This must be in writing (Article 94 FC).

E   Maintenance and associated claims of an unmarried mother

The period of maintenance payable to an unmarried mother by the father of the child has been increased from one to two years.

The provisional sum extracted from the probable father for maintenance of a newborn child is now determined by the length of the maternity leave according to the Labour Code, 1965, i.e. usually for 28 weeks.

F   Common provisions

The principle of Article 96, para 1 FC is the most important common provision applying to all categories of maintenance. It states that the court is obliged to take into consideration the justifiable needs of the entitled person on one hand and the resources, potential and economic situation of the liable person on the other hand. In evaluating this, the court considers whether the respondent has resigned a more advantageous employment, earning activity or property gain without good reasons, or if he/she is taking unjustifiable risks endangering his/her property.

The rule in Article 96, para 2 FC has been modified only slightly. Its wording now states that maintenance may not be awarded if this was 'contra bonos mores'.

In the case of maintenance for a minor child, the court may order payment of a lump sum for his or her support for an extended period (Article 97, para 2 FC).

In Article 103 FC maintenance is now clearly distinguished from charges paid to institutions in which the child has been placed by a court decision.

V CONCLUSIONS

We have provided here only a very general picture of the present state of changes to Family Law in the Czech Republic. This report needs to be complemented by direct study of the full texts of FC and CC. Let us hope that an English or French version will be produced.

ENGLAND AND WALES

SUPPORTING FAMILIES

Gillian Douglas[*]

1998 saw the usual mixture of legal developments, policy initiatives and reform proposals in the family law sphere. This chapter focuses on two different topics: first, the enactment of the Human Rights Act 1998; and secondly, measures intended to support families, in particular, provisions concerning finances during separation and divorce.

I   THE HUMAN RIGHTS ACT 1998

Arguably the most important legal reform in many years, the 1998 Act incorporates the European Convention on Human Rights into English law, nearly 50 years after its drafting. Although the Convention has not been part of domestic law until now, courts have sought to construe English law in such a way as to be compatible with its provisions. However, in the event of clear incompatibility, they have had to abide by the terms of English law, leaving the aggrieved party to take the case to Strasbourg. Significant changes to legislation in the field of English family law have been prompted by adverse findings by the European Court of Human Rights, both in relation to complaints against the United Kingdom and complaints against other jurisdictions.[1]

The 1998 Act[2] will enable parties to court proceedings to rely on the terms of the Convention and oblige all public authorities, including the courts, to act in conformity with those terms.[3] All legislation must be read and given effect, so far as possible, in a way which is compatible with the Convention.[4] In order to avoid constitutional clashes between the courts and the legislature, where a court (of High Court level or above) finds a provision of primary legislation to be incompatible with the Convention, it may make a declaration to this effect.[5] This enables Parliament to amend the legislation forthwith. All legislation must henceforth be introduced into Parliament with a statement as to its compatibility with the Convention.[6]

Although it is unlikely that large swathes of English family law will be found to be in breach of the Convention,[7] it is likely to have a significant impact in two ways. First,

---

[*]   Professor of Law, Cardiff University.

[1]   See, for example, Children Act 1989, s 34, providing for contact with children in care, prompted by *R v UK* [1988] 2 FLR 445 and *O v UK* (1987) 10 EHRR 82, and Children Act 1989, s 4, provision for unmarried fathers to acquire parental responsibility, prompted, inter alia, by *Marckx v Belgium* (1979–80) 2 EHRR 330 and *Johnston v Ireland* (1987) 9 EHRR 203.

[2]   Which will be brought into force on 2 October 2000.

[3]   Section 6.

[4]   Section 3.

[5]   Section 4.

[6]   Section 19.

[7]   But some aspects of public child law are open to challenge, in particular, the inability to control the implementation by a local authority of plans for a child which formed part of the basis for the court's granting a care order.

family lawyers have become accustomed to considering issues from the perspective of responsibility rather than rights. The Children Act 1989 has been particularly successful in spreading the philosophy that parents have (and usually share) responsibility for their children and that most judicial decisions in respect of those children are to be taken treating the child's welfare as the paramount consideration. There is little room, in this mode of thinking, for a rights-based approach. When the Act comes into force, this will require reconsideration. One can expect parties to family proceedings to begin to bolster their case by reference to Convention rights and it will be an inadequate and illegitimate response simply to say that these are irrelevant when compared with the child's welfare.[8] It does not follow, of course, that the child's welfare will cease to determine the outcome. Rather, the court will have to determine, where an interference with a Convention right is established, whether this can be justified as proportionate and necessary in the circumstances. The court will also have to weigh *competing* rights – for example, both of parents *and* of the child. Just as the UN Convention on the Rights of the Child has enabled 'rights' to be heard as a legitimate source of justification, so the Human Rights Act 1998 is likely to re-introduce the language of *parental* (and other family members') rights into child law.

Secondly, the *way* in which family disputes are handled may come under scrutiny. There has been a strong trend over the past two decades to encourage the resolution of disputes by means of settlement outside the court. This will be considerably strengthened by the encouragement of mediation which will underpin the new divorce procedure introduced by the Family Law Act 1996.[9] There has been some concern, prompted by research into the handling of financial arrangements on divorce[10] and disputes over children,[11] that parties are worn down, by a process of attrition, to settle disputes rather than be permitted the luxury of a judge deciding them. It may be that procedures which appear to be designed to prevent a dispute finding its way to a judge for adjudication could be subject to challenge under Article 6. Should such a development come to pass, then fundamental rethinking would have to be given to the processing of disputes in the family justice system.

II   SOCIAL SECURITY REFORM AND CHILD SUPPORT

More than one in three children are living in poverty in the United Kingdom, compared with one in 10 in 1979. Couples with children account for the largest group, nearly one-quarter, of all people living in poverty. One-third of children live in a family without a full-time worker, and one-fifth of families are headed by a lone parent.[12] Attempts to improve the plight of children – and their carers – have, perforce, to form a corner-stone of the Government's social welfare policies. However, the Labour Government has opted to follow the basic approach of its predecessor, by seeking to promote work opportunities

---

[8]   Cf the concern that there is a danger that the child's interests and rights might take second place to those of the parents: J. Fortin, *Children's Rights and the Developing Law* (1998) at 51–56.

[9]   For details, see G. Douglas, 'England and Wales: "Family Values" to the Fore?' in A. Bainham (ed) *The International Survey of Family Law 1996* (Martinus Nijhoff Publishers, 1998), at 156.

[10]   G. Davis, S. Cretney and J. Collins, *Simple Quarrels* (Clarendon Press, Oxford, 1994).

[11]   R. Bailey-Harris et al, *Monitoring Private Law Applications Under the Children Act*, Research Report to the Nuffield Foundation (1998).

[12]   (1999) *The Guardian*, March 19, reporting a speech by the Rt Hon Tony Blair MP.

for parents, to 'target' social security benefits on the most needy, and to encourage absent parents to meet their responsibilities by paying child support.

A   Welfare reforms

The Government's strategy is primarily to encourage the unemployed to find work. Hitherto, it has not been regarded as appropriate to expect lone parents with dependent children to seek work, since they may choose, or may be obliged, to remain at home to care for those children. However, it appears that the majority of single parents would wish to work if appropriate provision could be made for child care etc.[13] In 1998, after pilot schemes in selected areas, the Government introduced on a nationwide basis a 'New Deal' for lone parents, whereby those receiving income-related benefits are invited to attend for an interview with an advisor who can help them pursue training or work opportunities and arrange child care provision to enable them to re-enter the job market. The results of this scheme have been positive, though limited. In the Cardiff pilot area, for example, of nearly 4,000 lone parents contacted, only 531 attended an interview, and only 196 obtained jobs.[14] Perhaps not surprisingly, the Government later proposed that the interview cease to be by invitation, and will become compulsory, in line with its philosophy that all those who obtain support from the State should at least consider how they can repay the debt by moving into work.

Alongside the drive to encourage parents back to work, it is also intended that State financial support for children will gradually become channelled through the tax, rather than social security, system. A 'working families' tax credit',[15] influenced by the Earned Income Tax Credit used in the United States, will replace family credit, a low-wage supplement currently paid to mothers (regardless of whether they, or their partner, are the ones in work). The tax credit will operate as an additional tax allowance and thus increase net pay for the working member of the family unit. It has been argued that such a device is open to fraud, and is also likely to divert the extra money away from the mother and children to the father (as the more likely wage-earner in a two-parent household). It also, ironically, recreates the problems which prompted the introduction of 'child benefit' in the 1970s, a benefit paid to the mother (usually), regardless of family income, in respect of each child. Before the introduction of this benefit, tax credits were paid to the wage-earner for each child, but these were abolished because it was feared that the children never saw the benefit of them. The irony is compounded because it has now been proposed to re-introduce child tax credits, for lower-rate tax payers only, phasing out the 'married couple's' tax allowance to pay for these.[16]

---

[13]   A. Bryson, R. Ford and M. White, *Making Work Pay: Lone mothers, employment and well-being* (1997).

[14]   See further, G. Douglas, 'The Family, Gender and Social Security', in N. Harris (ed) *Social Security Law In Context* (Oxford University Press, 1999).

[15]   HM Treasury, *Work Incentives* (1998); HM Treasury, *The Modernisation of Britain's Tax and Benefit System: Number 3, The Working Families Tax Credit and work incentives* (1998).

[16]   HM Treasury, Press Release IR1, March 9, 1999, reporting the 1999 budget speech of the Chancellor, the Rt Hon Gordon Brown MP.

B   Child support – yet more reform

The inadequacies of the child support system have produced a flood of denunciatory reports, media criticism and legislative amendments since its inception in 1993.[17] The Government issued a consultation paper in 1998,[18] suggesting further, fundamental reform, although rejecting a return to the old court-based maintenance system. Since it appears that, due to the complexity of the formula to be applied, 90% of child support officers' time is taken up with assessing how much maintenance is to be paid, and only 10% with ensuring its collection, the Government proposed radically simplifying the formula. It would require the non-resident parent (apart from those on very low earnings, who would pay a minimum, or proportionate amount) to pay a fixed percentage of his net income, depending upon the number of children he is required to support – 15% for one child, 20% for two and 25% for three or more.[19] More recognition would be given to the existence of the non-resident parent's second family, by giving equal weight to the parent's obligation to support them (although it is unclear if this would apply to his *step-children* or only to children of his own).[20] In order to assuage the annoyance of non-resident parents who have their children stay with them at weekends and during holidays, but for whom, at present, no allowance is made where such staying contact amounts to less than 104 nights per annum, a reduction would be given once contact exceeds 52 nights per year.

In order to encourage lone parents to use the system, and thus, in most cases, enable the costs (or a proportion of them) of their social security benefits to be recouped from the non-resident parent, it is proposed to strengthen the requirement on benefit recipients to co-operate with the Child Support Agency, both negatively, by activating reductions in benefit payments for unreasonable non-compliance more speedily than under the current system,[21] and positively, by awarding a 'child maintenance premium' of up to £10 per week. This will enable the benefit claimant to keep this sum before it has an impact on the level of benefit paid to her. It is hoped that this will act as an incentive both to the claimant to comply with the Agency's requests for information about the absent parent, and to that parent to ensure that he pays up, since he will see at least part of his maintenance going directly to the family rather than disappearing into the Government's pocket.[22]

The Government estimate that the revised system will see some 70% of absent parents paying less than under the current formula, and some 75% of lone parents better off also. This win-win situation can only be achieved by the Government in effect picking up the bill – expecting less from non-resident parents and allowing more of that smaller amount to remain with the parent with care. As with the original child support scheme, the devil will be in the detail, and it remains to be seen whether the proposals will finally deliver greater compliance coupled with greater acceptance of the parental responsibility to pay for the children one leaves behind.[23]

---

[17]   For the best account of these and a thorough examination of exactly what has gone wrong, see G. Davis et al, *Child Support in Action* (Hart Publishing, Oxford 1998).

[18]   Department of Social Security, *Children First: a new approach to child support*, Cm 3992 (1998).

[19]   Ibid at 24.

[20]   Ibid at 25.

[21]   Ibid at 17.

[22]   Ibid at 16.

[23]   For detailed criticism of the proposals, see N. Mostyn QC, 'The Green Paper on Child Support – Children First: a new approach to child support' [1999] Fam Law 95.

III   FAMILY POLICY

As part of its commitment to 'joined up thinking', the Government issued what it claimed to be the first ever governmental consultation document[24] devoted to 'the family' (as distinct from, for example, divorce or child care). Although the product of an inter-departmental ministerial committee, it was the Home Office, primarily responsible for public order and the control of crime, which was the lead department. This is, in fact, not as strange as it first seems – the court welfare service which reports to courts in private children cases is part of the Probation Service, and hence falls under the remit of the Home Office. Hence it follows that marriage guidance, which has historical links with divorce court welfare, has come under its sphere of interest in the past – and from this derives its interest in family policy. More cynically, one can discern a clear association in the minds of government ministers (echoing their predecessors) between family breakdown, and increases in juvenile offending. The Home Office thus becomes the *obvious* lead department to produce a document of this sort.

The Government sought, as one commentator has put it,[25] simultaneously to run with the hounds of marriage and the hare of rival family forms, by both recognising that families are formed by private choices and people are generally unresponsive to State preaching, and also sending strong messages that marriage is the best foundation on which to bring up children, whose interests should be paramount when designing family policy. The Government's proposals therefore fall into two basic kinds – those which are designed to help all families – for which read *parents and their children* – and those more overtly directed towards making marriage more popular and less unstable.

A   Support for parents and children

A range of initiatives, from establishing a National Family and Parenting Institute, modelled on (but more modestly funded than) the Australian Institute of Family Studies to developing the role of health visitors, is proposed. The latter are trained nurses and midwives, who periodically visit the parents of all children from birth until age 5, to offer advice and support (and to provide an acceptable, if covert, form of surveillance on the quality of the parenting being provided). It is proposed to expand their role to help parents deal with older children.[26] It is unclear what the consequences of declining such advice and assistance might be, in terms of State intervention and investigation with a view to taking care and protection proceedings.

To encourage a more responsible attitude towards children, it is proposed, alongside the reforms detailed above in relation to child support maintenance, to promote two mechanisms, one voluntary and one by operation of law. First, the Government suggest that, for those parents who do not have a religious affiliation, a 'baby-naming ceremony' akin to a Christian baptism, could be held, performed by a registrar, in which the parents make a public commitment to their child and, if unmarried, might sign a parental responsibility agreement.[27] Presumably, the thinking is that a public symbolic demonstration of commitment to the child might make parents think more carefully

---

24   Home Office, *Supporting Families* (1998).
25   See C. Barton, 'Spending More Time with their Families – The Government's Consultation Document' [1999] Fam Law 136.
26   Home Office, *Supporting Families* (above) paras 1.29–1.35.
27   Ibid, para 4.39. But see further below.

before ending their relationship with each other, or at least might make them more aware of their responsibility to maintain their relationship with the child. But the public demonstration of commitment made in a wedding ceremony does not appear to have deterred couples from divorcing, and there is no evidence to suggest (even if it were amenable to proof) that parents who *have* had their child baptised (or the equivalent for other religions) are any more likely to fulfil their responsibilities to each other or to the child. While a ceremony might be a pleasant family occasion, it is doubtful that it would have much meaningful influence on long-term behaviour.

Indeed, the Government's other proposal suggests that it recognises that responsibility towards children is not something which is particularly willingly assumed. It has suggested[28] that where the name of an unmarried father is entered on his child's birth registration (currently the case in about four-fifths of all births outside marriage, of which about three-quarters of fathers are apparently living at the same address as the mother),[29] he should automatically have parental responsibility, compared to the present situation whereby he must acquire it by formal agreement with the mother or court order.[30] The main reason for adopting this approach is that, contrary to expectation and hope, comparatively few couples have bothered to make agreements, and the use of court orders appears to signal the breakdown of the parental relationship, with the father attempting to maintain a role in the child's life against the mother's wishes.[31] If the large number of unmarried parents are therefore to fulfil their parental role in a suitable manner, responsibility must therefore be imposed upon both of them, and not just on the mother. However, this will still leave some 40,000 children born each year where the father is either unknown, or unwilling to acknowledge his paternity, or the mother will not agree to his registration. One might think that these are precisely the hard core of cases where responsibility – and liability – *ought* to be imposed by law, but they will remain outside the net.

B   Supporting marriage[32]

One of the keys to strengthening marriage, according to the Consultation Paper, is greater education about what marriage entails. Thus, it is suggested that intending spouses be given a statement setting out the rights and responsibilities acquired in marriage (and, for those planning to cohabit, a similiar guide could be produced), to be handed out at register offices, places of worship and advice agencies. This would certainly be a useful exercise which could prove a disturbing revelation to many couples. Attendance at marriage preparation courses is also advocated (but compulsion is not suggested), and it is proposed to make couples seeking a civil wedding wait longer than the bare minimum of one clear day's notice before the ceremony can be performed. But it is doubtful if, in peace-time, many couples meet and decide to marry in the space of a few days, and hard to see how waiting a fortnight will significantly improve the chances of the marriage

---

[28]   Lord Chancellor's Department, *The Law on Parental Responsibility for Unmarried Fathers*, Consultation Paper (1998).

[29]   Ibid, para 52.

[30]   Children Act 1989, ss 2(2) and 4.

[31]   There are around 230,000 births outside marriage each year. In 1996, only some 3,590 agreements were made: Children Act Advisory Committee, *Final Report 1997*, Appendix 2. There were 5,587 parental responsibility orders made in that year: *Judicial Statistics 1996*, Table 5.3. See also I. Butler et al, 'The Children Act 1989 and the unmarried father' (1993) 5 J of Child Law 157.

[32]   See generally Chapter 4 of *Supporting Families* (above).

lasting. Whether marriage registrars should also be required to offer 'more support on a voluntary basis to marrying couples' is doubtful. The support envisaged appears to be limited to giving information about marriage such as a marriage preparation pack to intending spouses, and telling them about the availability of pre-marriage support services. On the other hand, it is hard to see how bureaucrats could be expected to take on the role of relationship counsellors or priests. Finally, the Government suggested that registrars be encouraged to be flexible regarding the format of civil marriage ceremonies, and couples encouraged to add their own music and readings to make the occasion more meaningful to them. Such innovations would be part of the trend, in recent years, to make civil weddings less of a shamefully deviant act to be performed in a squalid government office preferably out of the public gaze, and more of a pleasant and equally romantic alternative to religious ceremonies. Given that civil weddings now form the majority of ceremonies,[33] this is a useful liberalisation.

IV ANCILLARY RELIEF REFORM

Other aspects of the Government's new family policy relate to the process and consequences of marriage breakdown. The new divorce law,[34] as has been discussed in previous volumes, places major emphasis upon mediation and the settlement of disputes. However, the broad discretion given under Part II of the Matrimonial Causes Act 1973 to courts to decide the financial arrangements to be made in any given case makes it difficult for lawyers to advise clients of the likely outcome of litigation (and hence settlements are made in an extremely murky shadow of the law). Just as the child support formula approach was intended to increase certainty and therefore reduce the scope for dispute, so the Government has been reviewing the possibility of limiting discretion in relation to adult support and property reallocation. In particular, it is interested in making pre-nuptial agreements binding, and in the Scottish presumption of equal division of family assets. It established an Ancillary Relief Advisory Group, composed of legal practitioners, judges and academics, inter alia to review these ideas. The Group were generally satisfied with the existing state of the law, and were firmly opposed to adoption of the Scottish model, but the Government suggested that giving pre-nuptial agreements legal recognition:

'… could make it more likely that some people would marry, rather than simply live together. It might also give couples in a shaky marriage a little greater assurance about their future than they might otherwise have had. Nuptial agreements could also have the effect of protecting the children of first marriages, who can often be overlooked at the time of a second marriage – or a second divorce.'[35]

No evidence was provided to support these claims.

The fear that a weaker party might be coerced into a disadvantageous agreement was also addressed by the proposal that no agreement would be legally binding if any of six circumstances was found to apply:

---

[33] 58.7% of all weddings in 1996/97: Office for National Statistics, *First data for marriages at 'approved premises'* ONS (98) 62 (1998).

[34] Family Law Act 1996, discussed in Douglas (above at note 9).

[35] Home Office, *Supporting Families* (above), para 4.22.

(1) the presence of a child of the family (ie a child of both parties to the marriage or treated by them as their child);

(2) where the agreement would be unenforceable under normal rules of contract anyway, eg because it attempted to impose an obligation on a third party;

(3) in the absence of either party having received independent legal advice before entering into it;

(4) where the court considers that the enforcement of the agreement would cause significant injustice to either party or to a child of the marriage;

(5) where either party has failed to make full disclosure of assets; and

(6) where the agreement is made fewer than 21 days prior to the marriage.

Given that over half of divorces involve couples with dependent children, it seems that the scope for reliance on such an agreement will be limited. And where there is reliance, there is huge scope for litigation on whether any of the circumstances listed exist to make the agreement unenforceable. The evidence from other jurisdictions suggests that these kinds of arrangement are more likely where the marriage is a second or subsequent one for one or both parties, and where there are substantial assets to protect. In the former case, the interests of children are quite likely to take priority and render the agreement null (but query if it is appropriate or just to limit considerations of injustice to the interests of a child of the marriage and not include step-children?). In the latter case, the greater the assets the more likely that there will be litigation anyway. Pre-nuptial agreements seem destined to remain a minority pursuit.

For those who will have to continue to work with the statutory list of criteria to be taken into account in arriving at a settlement, contained in the Matrimonial Causes Act 1973, the Government agreed with the Advisory Group that there could be advantages in codifying existing principles. It suggested[36] the re-enactment of an over-arching objective (the previous such objective, which required the court to seek to put the parties into the position they would have been if the marriage had not ended, was removed by the Matrimonial and Family Proceedings Act 1984 because it was unworkable), namely: 'to exercise its powers so as to endeavour to do that which is fair and reasonable between the parties and any child of the family'. It is indeed surprising that no such statutory imperative currently guides the courts, but as an objective this is little more than motherhood and apple pie.

The Government then set out its own list of prioritised factors to be taken into account by a court, along the lines of those recommended by the Advisory Group. The first priority would be:

'... to promote the welfare of any child of the family under the age of eighteen, by meeting the housing needs of any children and the primary carer, and of the secondary carer; both to facilitate contact and to recognise the continuing importance of the secondary carer's role.'

This would reflect current case-law and re-assert the significance attached to the continuing relationship between the child and the absent parent.[37] Secondly, the court would take into account the existence and content of any agreement regarding financial arrangements, reached before or during marriage, but which is not enforceable because of the existence of one or more of the circumstances noted above. This would take practice a

---

[36] Ibid, paras 4.48, 4.49.

[37] See, for example, *M v B (Ancillary Proceedings: Lump Sum)* [1998] 1 FLR 53, CA; *H v H (Financial Provision: Conduct)* [1998] 1 FLR 971.

little further than is currently the case. The courts already give considerable weight to *separation* agreements,[38] and are beginning to take account of pre-nuptial agreements as a factor to be considered.[39] The 'court would then divide any surplus so as to achieve a fair result, recognising that fairness will generally require the value of the assets to be divided equally between the parties'. This re-introduction of the Scottish approach, notwithstanding the Advisory Group's firm view that it is inappropriate to the English context, is perhaps more justifiable as a factor ranked third in the list, since in many instances, the court will have exhausted all assets before it gets this far. It may also reflect – uninformed – public opinion. Finally, the court would try to terminate financial relationships between the parties at the earliest date practicable. This is a re-statement of the well-established clean break principle.[40] It is interesting that it should be placed last in the list, since it has become the main feature of the vast majority of divorce settlements. It is unlikely that the Government in fact expected a revival of on-going liabilities in the form of spousal maintenance, which, though highly important to those women (usually older wives facing retirement age) who receive it, is nowadays comparatively rare.[41] It is more likely that they had in mind the wide range of dispositions possible in relation to the matrimonial home, where there are very broad powers to postpone its disposal, transfer mortgage debts, etc, to accommodate the children and the primary carer most economically.

V   ANCILLARY RELIEF IN THE CASE-LAW

Naturally, the courts have continued to develop the law concerning ancillary relief alongside these policy proposals. Yet arguably the most important decision asserted the limitations of precedent in this field, and the desirability of avoiding the courts altogether. In *White v White*,[42] the spouses were in their sixties with no dependent children. They were equal partners in a farm business valued at some £4.5 million. The wife sought about half of this sum, in order to continue farming on her own account. The trial judge granted the wife a sum of under £1 million, assessed as meeting her 'reasonable requirements',[43] leaving the farm assets with the husband. On appeal, the Court held that the starting point in the case should have been the fact that the parties were in a business partnership. The wife was *entitled* to an appropriate division of the assets of this partnership, irrespective of her requirements. That share should be increased to take account of the contributions she had made as wife and mother, but these were offset, to some extent, by the greater financial contributions made to the business by the husband's family. Equal sharing was therefore inappropriate. She was left with approximately £1.7 million.

---

38   See below.

39   See G. Douglas, 'Family Law Developments in England and Wales: Function not Form?' in A Bainham (ed), *The International Survey of Family Law 1997* (Martinus Nijhoff Publishers, 1999) at 137–152.

40   Matrimonial Causes Act 1973, s 25A.

41   There were only 4,502 orders for periodical payments pending further order, and 5,472 for fixed term payments in 1997, compared with 9,565 applications dismissed (presumably because a clean break settlement was achieved instead) and 31,513 orders relating to property or lump sums: *Judicial Statistics 1997*, Cm 3980, Table 5.7.

42   [1998] 4 All ER 659, CA.

43   The usual approach in cases involving substantial assets: see *Preston v Preston* [1982] Fam 17, CA; *Dart v Dart* [1996] 2 FLR 286, CA, and see the discussion in the 1997 Survey (see fn 39 above) at 150.

While the case is reflective of previous decisions concerning substantial contributions made to the success of a family business,[44] its significance lies in the Court's preference for approaching the issue as one of dividing up a business partnership rather than a marriage. Indeed, Butler-Sloss LJ went so far as to say that parties should not have recourse to the courts in such cases,[45] and Thorpe LJ reiterated his view that the discretionary powers under the Matrimonial Causes Act 1973 should not be exercised unless there is a manifest need for court intervention upon the application of the factors listed in s 25.[46] While it is of course correct that every case turns on its individual facts and that therefore the rigidity of stare decisis is inapplicable in this field, it is much more sweeping to suggest that the courts should not be expected to exercise their powers except where a case for this is clearly made out. As Professor Bailey-Harris has noted,[47] the 1973 Act does not contain a provision akin to s 1(5) of the Children Act 1989, which provides that the court should not make an order unless doing so will be better for the child than not doing so. It is one thing for politicians to deplore resort to the courts with the consequential drain on public finances through court time and legal aid. It is more startling to find the judiciary apparently seeking to make themselves redundant. One must ask if the current animus against litigation and adjudication is not becoming a little exaggerated.

The drive towards settlement outside the court, reflected so strongly in this decision and the Family Law Act 1996, assumes that fair bargains, or at least, bargains acceptable to the parties, will be struck. The problem for the courts is to decide how far to uphold the sanctity of agreements, even where these appear to be unfair, and how far to ensure that the weaker party is protected. It is usual, in divorce proceedings, for the parties to present their agreement to the court for conversion into a 'consent order'. Once embodied in an order, the agreement can be enforced like any other court order, rather than requiring fresh action to be taken for breach of contract. The court is under a duty to scrutinise the terms of the agreement taking account of the s 25 factors. However, 'whilst the court is no rubber stamp nor is it some kind of forensic ferret',[48] the extent of scrutiny is likely to be extremely limited in many cases. Yet where a party has been badly advised, she will not usually be permitted to have the consent order set aside, unless she brings proceedings to do so within the statutory 14-day time-limit.[49] The reason is that it is unfair to the other party to find that an agreement is repudiated because of 'the inadequacy of ... legal advisers, over whom the other party had no control and of whose advice he had no knowledge'.[50] The remedy for the disadvantaged spouse is to sue the advisers for negligence.

However, it has also been held that there may be immunity from such suit, where the settlement was reached at the door of the court. In *Kelly v Corston*,[51] in a conference which took place the day before the final hearing, the client was advised by her barrister to accept a settlement involving transfer to her of the matrimonial home. The next day this was embodied in a consent order. When the client attempted to sue because it appeared that she would be unable to meet the mortgage payments on the home, it was

---

[44]   See, for example, *Gojkovic v Gojkovic* [1992] Fam 40, CA; *Conran v Conran* [1997] 2 FLR 615.

[45]   [1998] 4 All ER 659 at 673j.

[46]   Ibid at 666g.

[47]   In her comment on the case at [1998] Fam Law 522.

[48]   *Harris v Manahan* [1997] 1 FLR 205, CA, at 213, per Ward LJ.

[49]   Ibid.

[50]   *Pounds v Pounds* [1994] 1 FLR 775, CA, at 791, per Hoffmann LJ.

[51]   *Kelly v Corston* [1998] 1 FLR 986, CA.

held that the action should be struck out. According to two of their Lordships, this was because the wider immunity conferred on advocates for their conduct of a case in court extends to work which is closely and intimately connected with such conduct, and this test was held to be satisfied on the facts here. Secondly, all three judges agreed that, because the court has to approve the terms of the proposed settlement before it can be made into an order, the general principle that a judicial decision should not be subjected to collateral attack was applicable, and therefore immunity from suit must be given. This would leave the disadvantaged client with no redress – on the one hand, unable to have the order set aside, and on the other, unable to sue her advisers.[52] Fortunately, it was later held that where the negligence related to events earlier in the process, or to failing to discover non-disclosure by the other spouse, no immunity arose, because the court had been prevented from exercising its discretion properly when considering the proposed settlement.[53] This first instance decision was upheld on appeal, though on rather uncertain grounds.[54] The position appears to be that the question of whether a negligence action may be brought will depend upon the facts of the particular case, the extent of the connection with the conduct of the case in the court and the basis of the error made by the representative, making it difficult to advise when such a claim is worth pursuing.

It is clearly undesirable to leave litigants in a position where it will depend, almost fortuitously, upon when their advisers' failings occurred, and upon which defects arose in the agreement, as to whether they can be compensated or not. Under the Family Law Act 1996, settlements will usually have to be presented to the court before a divorce order can be granted,[55] and it is envisaged that more limited legal assistance will be given in many divorces which will be dealt with through mediation instead. There may be more 'door of the court' settlements where parties and their legal advisers are desperate to conclude matters in order to be able to apply for the divorce, and therefore hurriedly reach a deal in the terms of a mediated agreement which might in fact be unsatisfactory. It is arguable, at least, that courts will have to become rather more like 'forensic ferrets' than they have been in the habit of doing under the current law in order to ensure that both procedural and substantive justice can be done.

VI CONCLUSIONS

With child law in a reasonably settled state, policy-makers' attention has moved back to questions of financial and other support for families. The new divorce law provides an opportunity to re-think approaches to settling financial and property arrangements, but the blanket preference for mediation is likely to cause trouble where parties become dissatisfied with the agreements they have reached. Given the current judicial attitude towards resort to adjudication reflected in *White v White*, an attitude which mirrors a broader view of civil justice which underpins fundamental reforms to the system,[56] it seems that support for families is increasingly to come from outside the legal system.

---

[52]   See the criticism by C. Wagstaffe, 'Consent Orders and Bad Legal Advice in Ancillary Relief Cases' [1999] Fam Law 156.

[53]   *Frazer Harris v Scholfield Roberts & Hill (A Firm)* [1998] 2 FLR 679.

[54]   *Hall & Co v Simons; Barratt v Woolf Seddon; Cockbone v Atkinson Dacre & Slack; Harris v Scholfield Roberts & Hill* [1999] Fam Law 215, CA.

[55]   Sections 3(1)(c), 9(2).

[56]   The Civil Procedure Rules 1998, in force from 26 April 1999, introduce new mechanisms, with a strong thrust towards ADR, for handling non-family civil matters.

This is in many ways wholly desirable and realistic, since family life is influenced by many factors other than law, but it would surely be misguided to assume that law – and even the legal process – has no role to play in constituting family relationships and behaviour. Support for families requires appropriate laws and legal mechanisms – and the Human Rights Act 1998 is likely to affirm the right of all family members to rely on, and make use of, such laws and mechanisms.

FRANCE

HOW MATTERS STAND NOW IN RELATION TO FAMILY LAW REFORM

Jacqueline Rubellin-Devichi[*]

I   INTRODUCTION

Once again, there is no simple answer to the question of how reform of family law has affected and been affected by changes in family life, when looking at the way French law has developed. It is as in the case of our European neighbours; in each country, society retains its peculiarities, which result from its history, its economy and its particular customs.[1]

In France, the recasting of family law had been undertaken from the 1960s. Entrusting it to Dean Carbonnier meant a remarkable unity of authorship was assured for the project, covering tutorship of minors, matrimonial regimes, adults under incapacity, parental authority, affiliation, divorce and even the reform of the law of succession. Before the project was completed (which may happen this year), it has been necessary to enact subsequent laws, which Dean Cornu has called second generation laws.[2] This is because of changes in customs and in society (in particular, because 80% of women now work), and the progress of science in the field of bio-ethics, and the development of information technology. These new laws form a sort of extension of the Carbonnier laws.

When the United Nations adopted the Convention on the Rights of the Child, the French Legislature sought to bring French law into line with the international text. At the same time, it made certain changes which were made possible by very recent biological developments, and some simplifications in procedure to take account of individual autonomy. This was the work of the law of January 8, 1993, 'relating to civil status, to the family and to children's rights, establishing the judge of family affairs'.[3] Of course, the so-called bioethical laws of July 29, 1994 (one 'relating to respect for the human body', the other 'relating to the donation and use of parts and products of the human body, in medically assisted procreation and in antenatal diagnosis') also concerned family law and the rights of the child. The law of July 5, 1996 on adoption[4] was a true modernisation of that institution, bringing more transparency to social work, and itself also taking account more fully of children's rights. One could find it surprising, in these circumstances, that successive governments should have decided on a general reform of family law. In 1996, the Conference on the family, at the request of the government, had

---

[*]   Professor at Jean Moulin University, Director of the Centre for Family Law. Translated by Peter Schofield.

[1]   J. Rubellin-Devichi, 'La permanence des spécificités nationales en droit de la famille' in *La question familiale en Europe*, directed by J. Commaille and François de Singly, L'Harmattan (1997), p. 61.

[2]   G. Cornu, *Droit Civil, La famille*, Montchrestien, 6th ed. (1998) n° 6.

[3]   J. Rubellin-Devichi, 'Une importante réforme en droit de la famille, la loi n° 9322 du 8 janvier 1993', JCP 1993, I 3659.

[4]   J. Rubellin-Devichi, 'Permanence et modernité de l'adoption après la loi du 5 juillet 1996', JCP 1996, I 3979, n° 48.

looked at the question from every angle (the family in civil law, compensation for family expenses, the organization of family life, relations between the generations, the family and work).[5] The Report of Mme, le Procureur général Hélène Gisserot (the publication of which had been delayed by the dissolution of the Assemblée Nationale), had already called attention to the reforms which were considered necessary. After the four reports were presented to the Prime Minister, following the new Conference on the family on June 12, 1998,[6] Mme Guigou set up a working party of university teachers and practitioners in family law, chaired by Professor Françoise Dekeuwer-Défossez, with instructions to report by the end of 1999. Family law is certainly not being returned to the drawing-board, but what can be expected – or at least hoped for – is that failings in the operation of some recent laws will be corrected and that totally new legislation will be confined to those areas in which it is truly necessary.

The latest Congress of French Notaries ('Demain, la famille', Marseilles, May 1999) once more stressed the need to stop penalising children on the grounds of their being conceived in adultery. It unanimously called for reform of the rights of the surviving spouse to be undertaken urgently (the French surviving spouse is the worst treated in Europe).[7] Moves which propose giving legal recognition to the status of unmarried couples – even same sex ones – will doubtless bear fruit in the autumn. On the other hand it seems that account has not been taken of the need to improve the provisions concerning respect for children's rights and the right to be heard, which is where we see French law and judicial practice at their most timid.[8]

For the family, the most important reforms have been in the field of social law. The law of July 29, concerning the fight against exclusions,[9] the texts on family mediation voted on 18 and 22 December, 1998 and universal health insurance (CMU: couverture-maladie universelle) adopted – at last – on June 30, 1999, show clearly French interest in family matters. Changes in family structure are marked by increasing acceptance of a number of different models. Marriage is alive and well (since 1998 the annual figure is around 280,000), but out of twelve million couples, two million live in concubinage. Births (at 730,000 a year – a very satisfactory index of 1.72 per woman) include over 40% out of wedlock, two-thirds of which are recognised before or soon after birth, and in most cases the parents live together.

With some qualifications, we could say there is an increasing unity in the legal situation of children, be they born in or out of wedlock, and that of couples shows a robust diversity.

---

[5] The working party on family law (chairman J. Rubellin-Devichi, rapporteurs J. Commaille, T. Fossier, P. Strobel) had proposed, beside the necessary major reforms, a series of changes amounting rather to a tidying-up.

[6] I. Théry, 'Couple, filiation et parenté aujourd'hui', ed. O. Jacob/La Documentaton Française; C. Thélot et M. Villac, 'Politique familiale: bilan et perspectives'; D. Gillot, 'Pour une politiique de la famille rénovée'; M. André, 'La politique des familles'.

[7] See also J. Carbonnier, 'Droit de la famille, état d'urgence', in *Flexible droit, pour une sociologie du droit sans rigueur*, 9th ed. (1999).

[8] See the report of the Commission d'enquête n° 871 (chaired by L. Fabius, rapporteur J.-P. Bret) 'Droits de l'enfant en France, de nouveaux espaces à conquérir', recorded on May 5, 1998, ed. *Documents d'information de l'Assemblée Nationale*.

[9] La lutte contre les exclusions, *Revue droit sanitaire et social*, n° spécial directed by F. Monéger.

II   CHILDREN

Most of the recent reforms in child law come from the law of January 8, 1993:

- Henceforth parents choose freely their child's forenames; the reference to calendars and historical personages has been abolished. Further, whereas formerly a registrar could refuse to record names chosen by parents, he now has to record them and, if they appear to him to be detrimental to the interests of the child or of third parties, he must inform the juge aux affaires familiales (JAF) without delay. The judge decides if a name chosen by the parents is against the child's interests (as for example Babar, Jani-Vercise-Onasis, Folavril) and, if so, failing a new choice by the parents, he himself names the child. Also it is for the JAF, and not the court as a whole, now to authorise or refuse a change of forename, where there is a legitimate interest (Article 57, Civil Code).
- As to family names, if born in wedlock a child takes that of the father; if out of wedlock, that of the first parent to recognise or, if both recognise together, that of the father, by the analogy with the legitimate family. If the mother is the first to recognise, the two parents can, by declaration before the registrar of the tribunal de grande instance, give the child the father's family name. A petition can also be made to the JAF to give the child the family name of the father, or that of the mother if the father recognised first (Articles 372 and 374, Civil Code).[10]
- Changing a name by the administrative route has been made simpler. Usually this is done because the person concerned has a ridiculous or odious surname, or because he wants to prevent a family name (for example that of the mother) from dying out. Most significantly, the change now only extends automatically to children under 13 years old. Others are unaffected unless they consent in person. In general, even if a change of family name results from a change in a person's affiliation by proof of parentage or amendment of the civil status register, it will not affect that person's issue who have reached majority unless they consent to it (Article 61-3, Civil Code). This change is welcomed. It was traumatising for an adult, often with children of his own, to lose a family name (for instance his mother's) which he had borne hitherto and passed on to his children, just because his (true or false) father had married his mother and recognised him at this late stage. This is, however, a further inroad on the principle that in French law the family name goes with the person's affiliation.
- As to the civil status of children, we note that there has been added to the Civil Code a measure to soften the pain of the parents of a child who dies, after a live birth, before the declaration of birth, which must take place within the first three days after delivery. Where a medical certificate can be produced, this can now be recorded as a registered birth followed by a registered death, not as a stillbirth.

The most innovative – and long-awaited – legislation has been the law of January 8, 1993. Aimed at bringing French law into line with the United Nations Convention on the Rights of the Child, this law has made establishing affiliation out of wedlock more like establishing a legitimate affiliation.

In provisions applying to both types of affiliation, the law of July 29, 1994 prohibits the judicial calling into question of affiliation lawfully obtained through medically assisted procreation, using a third party donor, whether the parental couple were or were not married, unless the pregnancy was taken not to be the result of the medical procedure

---

[10]   See Dalloz-Action, *Droit de la famille*, directed by J. Rubellin-Devichi, (1999), n° 1704 ff. by M. Farge.

(Article 311-20, Civil Code; which gives the mother the advantage of being able to chose between the legal father and the true father).

In establishing legitimate affiliation there is little obvious change, save that Article 16-10 of the Civil Code (reformed by L. 29 July, 1994) applies to both forms of affiliation. This forbids the identification of a person by genetic sequencing unless it is undertaken in the context of judicial proceedings (including affiliation proceedings).[11]

As to investigating paternity out of wedlock, the law of 1993 abolished the famous cases for receiving a claim (set out in Article 340)[12] as well as the grounds for rejection (notorious misconduct of the mother, intercourse with another). From now on, paternity can be proved by any evidence supporting serious presumptions or indications of it. Only the demonstration of non-paternity can cause the action to fail. Also, now that positive evidence of paternity, by blood tests or by DNA sequencing, carries all the desired certainty, a claim for maintenance can no longer be rejected on the basis of the mother's dissolute behaviour. This permits a child to claim against a man who had a sexual relationship with the mother at the presumed time of conception. This action remains useful, as the child can claim at any time during minority, whereas an action to establish paternity is barred by lapse of time after two years.

This liberalisation of the law of evidence has not produced the expected surge of actions. We can see this in the result of the case in which the heirs of Y. Montand were opposed by Aurore Drossard. In his lifetime, the singer had always, on somewhat irrelevant grounds, resisted the maintenance claim brought by the girl's mother, and in due course also that of the girl herself, on reaching majority, for a declaration of paternity. Montand had refused to submit to blood tests at the order of the court, which eventually declared he was the father three years after his death. He had used a multiplicity of delaying tactics to prevent the reaching of a decision, when it would have been simpler to have the tests carried out if he was confident on the issue of paternity. On July 4, 1996 the appeal court ordered further tests of blood taken from surviving relatives. The result was a 0.1% probability of paternity of the alleged daughter, against 99% for the natural son, and on November 6, 1997 the court ordered exhumation of the body for genetic examination.[13] The result was made known in June 1998 and, on 1 and 7 December, 1998, the Cour de Paris confirmed that, beyond any doubt, Montand was not the father. Who would have thought it? It really was essential in the interest of the parties to reach biological certainty.

The insertion in the Civil Code of the woman's right to give birth under anonymity was an apparent rather than a real change in relation to out-of-wedlock affiliation, for it did already exist under the Code de la famille et de l'aide sociale (Article 47).[14] This law creates a ground for rejecting an action (Article 341, para. 1), so ending a controversy

---

[11] Civil Code, article 16-11, para. 1: 'The identification of a person by his genetic imprints can only be investigated in the context of means of enquiry or of preparation of a case ordered by a court, or for medical purposes, or for those of scientific research'. This makes it impossible, in France, to ask a laboratory to investigate on an 'out-of-court' basis for the sake of what my colleague Jean Hauser rightly terms 'expertise [reference to expert witness] de curiosité': so you have to ask a laboratory in a neighbouring country, say Switzerland or Belgium.

[12] Rape or abduction at the time of conception, abusive seduction, letters or other writings of the father showing his paternity, open concubinage of the mother and putative father, acceptance of responsibility by contributing to the child's support or establishment as a father.

[13] On the problems this raises, particularly as to consent, see, for example, JCP ed. G, (1998) I, 101 and references cited.

[14] B. Trillat, 'L'accouchement anonyme, de l'opprobre à la consécration', *Liber amicorum à la mémoire de Danièle Huet-Weiller*, LITEC/PUS (1994) p. 527.

which had sharply divided the parliament. Whatever view one takes of this possibility,[15] we must point out on the one hand that it applies as much to the married as to the unmarried woman, since the presumption of paternity relies on maternity (conception or birth in marriage); to the extent that it is impossible to establish maternity, there could be no legitimate affiliation. On the other hand, it is erroneous to affirm that this text is contrary to Article 7 of the United Nations Convention on the Rights of the Child. In effect, the mother's right to anonymity precisely makes impossible the child's right to know his parents.

It would appear that our Minister of Justice wants to suppress this freedom of the woman to prevent her attachment to the child. Despite strong pressure, mainly from former 'pupilles' (roughly translated as wards of the State) and some adopted persons, who claim the right to know their origin, it is doubtful that the parliament will vote for what many see as a backward step, in that the law on adoption of July 5, 1996, desirous of finding an appropriate response to the wish of everyone to know his origins,[16] provided that, in the written report drawn up when the child is received, mention must be made of the possibility of giving information about origins which do not compromise the secrecy of the mother's identity. The information is available to the child on reaching majority, to his adult descendants if he is dead, to his legal representative if he is a minor; in such a case he can even have it communicated to himself, if he has reached the age of understanding, with the consent of his representative. (Now one knows how pressing is the demand of adopted adolescents. Perhaps it was not useful, save as a gesture to fashion, to require capability to understand – the approval of the representative should have been enough.) The text also requires the written report to include the demand for secrecy and the possibility of making the mother's identity known eventually to the child on attaining majority, to his adult descendants if he is dead, and to his legal representative if he is a minor (CFAS, Article 62, para 7). There was no need for a text to affirm this right to lift the secrecy, but finally it might be reassuring for a mother who still hesitates to make the painful decision which is, one way or another, to abandon her child: short of knowing the identity of his biological authors, the child will know part of his history and the detailed explanation regarding secrecy should put an end to aberrant practices.

For the first time, the law has concerned itself also with the woman who gives birth. She will in future have psychological and social support (CFAS, Article 47, para. 2). Regarding the given names of the child, the Legislature was so out of touch with the reality of the matter that, in 1993, it inadvertently suppressed a provision which allowed a woman who gave birth as 'Ms. X' to have the declarant name the child. Until then, in the case of an anonymous delivery or secret maternity, the officer of the hospital made the declaration of the birth, giving the child the names chosen by the biological mother when she had expressed a wish to do so; many regretted the disappearance of a measure which had many advantages, in particular at the psychological level.[17] The new text, inserted at Article 57 of the Civil Code, restores the rule, giving 'the woman who has demanded that

---

[15] Some, rightly, see this freedom as a benefit for the child as well as for the mother, as it avoids abortion, infanticide and mistreatment (for this view see J. Rubellin-Devichi, 'Droits de la mère et droits de l'enfant. Réflexions sur les formes de l'abandon', RTD civ. (1991) p. 695); others refer to the need of the individual, when he is constructing his identity, to know his progenitors, without realising that the individual in question will have largely passed the age at which he constructs his identity when he sets out in search of his origins.

[16] A desire that society has taken upon itself to exacerbate, which explains the impressive growth of requests for information about origins received by social services (26,296 in the 91 départements in five years).

[17] B. Trillat, 'L'accouchement anonyme, de l'opprobre à la consécration,' cited above at fn 14, p. 527 and note 80.

her identity be kept secret at the time of delivery [the facility] of making known the names she desires', and indicating explicitly that the choice only reverts to the registrar 'by default, or where the parents are unknown'; this will in future eliminate an abuse on the part of certain registering officers, who arrogated to themselves the right to give the most freakish names.

Ought we to go further in pursuit of equality between in-wedlock and out-of-wedlock affiliation so as to achieve the negation of the 'pluralism of affiliations'?[18] No doubt a tidying up is called for here and there, there are hold-ups to be reduced or brought to uniformity,[19] but there is no advantage in seeking to assimilate the affiliation of the child of married parents to that of those who are unmarried, still less of those who are married, but not to each other, which is what the government seems to want to do.[20] Better to keep the terms 'filiation légitime' and 'filiation naturelle' in the Code, than to close one's eyes to the differences in the situations or to try, in the words of a quip containing more than a grain of truth, to abolish marriage so as to abolish the presumption of paternity. These comments, moreover, are not based on any value judgement as to forms of family – concubinage is fully accepted in our society. But although some countries, such as Belgium, have suppressed the distinctive terms, while still discriminating between the means of establishment in important ways,[21] French law has gone just about as far as possible towards equality in this area – given that there is no possible equivalent to the presumption of paternity where there is no marriage.

We could not say that about the effects of affiliation.

There are two legislative changes in relation to the exercise of parental authority. First, Article 387 of the Civil Code lays down the principle that after divorce parents continue to exercise authority in common. The court only intervenes to settle the habitual residence of the child if the parents are unable to agree this, or if what they agree appears not to be in the interest of the child. In fact, all the law of 1993 does here is to endorse judicial practice. Judges were only making orders giving parental authority exclusively to one party in limited situations and for very specific reasons. Article 372 reorganises the basic rule for the child of parents who are (or have been) married and for the child of persons living in concubinage (or who have been so living). Parents of a legitimate child exercise parental authority in common. So do those of an extramarital child, only on two conditions. They must both have recognised the child before his first birthday. (This seems logical. Fathers intending to take responsibility for their children mostly recognise before their birth. Recognition after the first year is usually given reluctantly.) And they must be living together at the time of recognition by the second parent to do so, which can – and in the prevailing interpretation in national education must – be proved by writing witnessed by the JAF. This second condition results from a compromise between the Senate and the National Assembly and has been unanimously criticised by doctrinal writers, because it is unworkable and actually contradicts the automatic attribution of authority to both parents. If they are to prevent authority from going exclusively to the mother (Article 374, para. 2) and choose to exercise it in common, they can either make a

---

[18] F. Dekeuwer-Défossez, 'À propos du pluralisme des couples et des familles', *Petites Affiches*, n° spéc. 95th Congress of French Notaries, April 28, 1999, p. 29.

[19] See Y. Favier, 'Précarité des filiations et variété des modes de contestation', JCP (1999) I, 165.

[20] P. Murat, 'L'égalité des filiations légitime et naturelle quant à leur mode d'établissement: jusqu'où aller?' Dr. famille (1998) n° 10, p. 4.

[21] Under the Belgian law of March 31, 1987, the father of a minor child, if he is not married to the mother, can only recognise with the latter's consent. On December 2, 1990 and October 8, 1992, the Cour d'arbitrage belge declared this provision unconstitutional.

joint declaration before the chief registrar of the tribunal d'instance (Article 374, para. 3, law of February 8, 1995), or one or other of them can take the case to the JAF.

The rules in relation to parental authority certainly need to be changed by the suppression of the requirement for living together – recognition by both parents within a specified time should be enough – and by a new provision regarding authority going by default to the mother. Some, mistakenly one may think, want authority in common to take effect immediately on the second act of recognition, whenever this occurs, through to coming of age. The better way would be to decide, as under the law before 1970, but for other reasons, that authority should be exercised by the one who first recognises (unless there is a declaration before the greffier or reference to the judge). The real problems lie elsewhere, not so much as some very active pressure groups would have it in the preference given to the mother (out of wedlock or divorced), for the courts do not in fact prefer either parent,[22] but in the fact that no one has yet discovered how to make a parent, who neglects his visiting rights and leaves the child waiting for him in vain, take seriously the responsibility he has himself claimed.

Far less comprehensible, or far more surprising nowadays, is the position of the child in defending his interests and being given a hearing in court. The law of January 8, 1993 was based on the United Nations Convention on the Rights of the Child. In future, generally, under Article 388-1 of the Civil Code, a minor if, but only if, 'capable of understanding' is allowed, 'in any proceeding concerning him', to be heard by the judge or by a person designated by the judge. The demand of the minor, who may wish to be heard with an advocate or other person chosen by him, may only be set aside 'by a specially reasoned decision'. But there is no appeal against the judge's decision, which, as has been shown in a number of cases, leaves room for much arbitrary decision making. Article 388-2 also provides for the appointment of an ad hoc administrator where the interests of a minor and his legal representatives conflict. This is tremendous progress for French law, which sees the minor only as a person under incapacity whose protection and representation rest with the parents. But still the minor cannot initiate proceedings (saisir le juge) on his own account in place of, or even in opposition to, his parents.[23] Unlike some colleagues,[24] we still think that the right of recourse to a court, which the European Convention on Human Rights gives to every individual, should be given to the child – which does not mean the judge will always agree with him – and that the reform introduced by the law of January 8, 1993, which is content merely to follow the United Nations Convention on the Rights of the Child, is clearly inadequate.

As is generally known, and as we never tire of recalling, France was among the first signatories of the Convention, on January 2, 1990, and one of the first to ratify on August 6, 1990, so as to permit its rapid implementation. One might expect that our country – cradle of the rights of man – would have had the heart to advance the rights of children, inasmuch as France, like for instance Belgium, Luxemburg, Holland, Portugal, to confine ourselves to Europe, and contrary to the United Kingdom, Ireland, Iceland, Sweden, among others, incorporates treaties directly into internal law under Article 55 of the

---

[22] H. Fulchiron and A. Gouttenoire-Cornut, 'Réformes législatives et permanence de pratiques à propos de la généralisation de l'exercice en commun de l'autorité parentale par la loi du 8 janvier 1993', D. 1997, p. 363 ff.

[23] Except for the case of 'assistance éducative', where Article 375 of the Civil Code ('If the health, safety or morality of a minor who is not emancipated are in danger, or if the conditions of his education are gravely compromised ...') lets the minor make application directly to the juge des enfants.

[24] See in particular the brilliant article of Jean Hauser, 'L'enfant et la famille: de l'hexagone à l'ensemble vide? Éloge du compromis', *Petites Affiches* (1995) n° 94, p. 17.

Constitution. One would have expected the Cour de cassation to apply the provisions of the UN Convention wherever there was a gap in French law, or where the latter conflicted with the Convention.

Nothing of the sort. As early as March 10, 1993,[25] the Cour de cassation ruled that 'the provisions of the Convention on the rights of the child ... cannot be invoked before the courts, this Convention, which creates obligations for which only the states which are parties are responsible, not being directly applicable in internal law.' This formula has not changed subsequently.[26] The Conseil d'État, the highest administrative court (same level as the Cour de cassation on the civil side), in judgments of February 17, and June 30, 1993, did agree to consider arguments based on violation of the Convention, and held that they did not in fact succeed.[27] On July 29, 1994,[28] it declared that Article 9 of the Convention (not the whole Convention) creates obligations only between signatory States and does not give rights to individuals; on March 10, 1995,[29] that Article 16 of the Convention is directly applicable and on July 3, 1996,[30] that Articles 12 and 14-1 were not, which shows that each Article of the Convention has to be examined individually. On September 22, 1997, for a four-year-old Turk,[31] and on November 9, 1998, for a 14-year-old Algerian,[32] the Conseil d'État annulled decisions to return them to their country of origin, applying Article 3-1, which makes the overriding interest of the child the paramount consideration when the Administration reviews the regularity of regrouping a family; on June 30, 1999,[33] in a case where the father complained that the mother, who had sole parental authority over a child aged 17 months, had taken the child to Canada, the Conseil d'État once again had to say both that Articles 2-1 and 2-2 do not produce direct effects with regard to individuals, and that the provisions of Article 374, on the exercise of parental authority over an extramarital child are not incompatible with the stipulations of Articles 3-1 and 16 of the Convention which proclaim the overriding interest of the child and his right to the protection of the law.

Can we hope for a change of direction in this line of cases by the Cour de cassation? Many have thought so on reading the declarations of the highest judges, however discreet. Yet, on June 25, 1996,[34] when it was asked to say that Article 760 of the Civil Code was contrary to the European Convention on Human Rights and to the United Nations Convention on the Rights of the Child, because it deprived the child conceived in

25   Cass. 1re civ. March 10, 1993, Bull. civ. I, n° 103.

26   See also Cass. 1re civ. June 2, 1993, Bull. Civ. I, n° 195; July 15, 1993 (two judgments), Bull. civ. I, n° 259; Cass. soc. July 13, 1994, Bull. civ. V, n° 236; Cass. 1re civ. January 4, 1995, Bull. civ. n° 2; Cass. crim. June 18, 1997, Bull. crim. n° 244. On this question and the references, see H. Bosse-Platière, *Dalloz-Action Droit de la famille*, directed by J. Rubellin-Devichi, n° 282 ff.

27   CE February 17, 1993 (interested party cannot use Articles 8, 9 and 10 of the Convention on the Rights of the Child to challenge refusal to issue a 'titre de séjour' [temporary residence permit] to him), *Journal du droit des jeunes*, June 1994, n° 136; 30 June 1993 and 28 July 1993 (grounds, based on Articles 9 and 12 of the Convention, relied on by a boy from Mali to have an order to return him to the frontier annulled, held not to succeed in fact), *Journal du droit des jeunes*, November, 1993, p. 333, and Rec. Lebon, tables, p. 778.

28   CE July 29, 1994, AJDA Nov. 20, 1994, p. 341, concl. Mme. Denis-Lindon; Gaz. Pal. 8 July 1995, p. 24, note Y. Benhamou: the case concerned a Tunisian couple, parents of eight children, who wished to have an order for their return to the frontier annulled, having failed to get annulment at first instance.

29   CE March 10, 1995 (Demirpence), D 1995, p. 617, concl. R. Abraham, note Y. Benhamou.

30   CE July 3, 1996 (Paturel), JCP (1996) ed.G, IV, 2279, obs. M. Ch. Rouault.

31   CE September 22, 1997 (Melle Cinar), JCP (1998) I, 101, obs. T. Fossier.

32   CE November 9, 1998 (Hellal), unreported.

33   CE June 30, 1999, D. 1999, N° 22, Actu, (or summary), p. 2.

34   Cass. 1re civ. June 26, 1996, Bull. civ. 1, n° 268.

adultery of half of his share in an inheritance and gave it to the legitimate children born in the marriage against which the adultery was committed, the court replied first, that Article 8 of the European Convention on Human Rights does not apply to succession rights, and secondly, that the Convention on the Rights of the Child concerned only the child, defined as a human being who has not reached the age of majority. An appeal is pending before the European Court, and it seems certain that France, as other countries have been, will be found to be in breach of the Convention. How can the Cour de cassation be 'forced' to change its line? I see no direct way, as the separation of powers, fortunately, prevents Parliament from giving orders to the Court.

All the same, it seems that the inequality of inheritance that strikes the adulterine child is doomed to disappear, and soon, in changes of the succession law, about which discussion should begin shortly. But with regard to the right to be heard and to access to justice, there is still much to do. The solution – partial but effective – lies in the amendment of certain laws applying to children, specifically those which have given rise to most of the decisions of the Cour de cassation – that is, in essence, Articles 388-1 and 388-2 of the Civil Code. But more must be done; we must stop placing such narrow limits on the child's right to be heard – if he is capable of understanding, if the judge thinks fit, if the proceedings concern him; we must stop denying his right to take part in or become a party to the proceedings; we must stop believing in the absolute virtue of legal representatives of children, and it would be a good idea, in any case, for a minor to be merely protected by having to apply before a family judge (JAF, juge des enfants or juge des tutelles) for authority to take action. Anyway, it is time to end the abusive paternalism, which, in the name of respect for the interests of the child, protects adults against children.

It will be hard to overcome the resistance, wherever it comes from,[35] since we are so committed to the idea that the child's best protection is the family. What if there is none, or not much?

III COUPLES

Today, the founding couple of a family consists of two persons living together, in wedlock (de jure), or out of wedlock (de facto). To examine the reforms, in progress or expected, we must consider marriage, and then cohabitation, whether of a man and a woman, or between persons of the same sex.

In fact, there is only one kind of marriage, but an infinite diversity of de facto situations meet the description of an unmarried couple. As Dean Cornu put it, concubinage is an irreducibly polymorphic phenomenon. Each time the Legislature, or some public or private undertaking, wants something to be a consequence of living together, it specifies the elements to be taken into account and these vary according to the desired object. So – 'concubinages' in the plural.[36]

---

[35] Surprisingly, one sees the Minister of social affairs, who had called for a report on termination of pregnancy which came down in favour of abolishing the requirement to obtain the consent of a parent in cases involving minors, deciding to take a year to consider. (On this, see J. Rubellin-Devichi, 'Le droit et l'interruption volontaire de la grossesse: Vingt ans après la loi Veil', *Petites Affiches* (1996) n° 69, p. 19.)

[36] See *Les concubinages, Approche socio-juridique*, 2 vols, Preface J. Carbonnier, Postscript Jacques Commaille, ed. CNRS (1986); *Les concubinages en Europe, Aspects sociojuridiques*, Preface M.A. Glendon, ed CNRS (1989); *Des concubinages dans le monde*, Preface J. Commaille and J.F. Perrin, Postscript M.-T. Meulders-Klein (1990).

The, usually benevolent, neutrality of the Legislature means we cannot now speak of advantages being given to one or other. The legal and the de facto situations are not in competition, and are a matter of individual choice. There is one legal status of a spouse, a variety of types of concubinage, and the latter situation can be constructed to taste by the couple, and depends particularly on the law that covers it.

A   Marriage

Contract or institution, marriage creates an objective legal situation, as Dean Roubier put it: it binds the spouses at the moment of their union, and entails reciprocal rights and duties (fidelity, support, assistance), failure to respect which can result in divorce; one cannot freely leave marriage. It entails the application of a matrimonial regime (in 90% of cases community as defined by law, fed by the earnings and incomes of the spouses), and of a series of mandatory laws aimed at ensuring their protection and independence.

Clearly, at least in appearance, marriage remains unchanged. As Dean Carbonnier said: 'The winds of change that have blown on family law have left marriage intact, governed, with minor exceptions, by the original texts of the Code Napoleon. Marriage itself, the union of persons, is what it was in 1804, secular: unitary, without any possibility of derogation from the rules it engenders'. The duties and the rights of the spouses (fidelity, support, assistance, living together) are unchanged.

And yet, certain reforms have been found necessary in the effects of marriage, that is to say the marital status: in the view of those for whom marriage is not just the most frequent, but also the best means of founding a family, what is needed is to prevent this favoured form of union from being penalised in fact. Wider reform would be necessary, beside the civil law, so as to ensure at least equality between married and unmarried couples and between those with two incomes and those with just one breadwinner,[37] doubtless with a view to abolishing the family quotient, and by government departments concerned seeking other ways of taking account of the homemaker spouse and children.[38]

Gifts between spouses benefit from a very advantageous fiscal regime, because the Legislature wishes to favour families based on marriage; thus, in relation to rights of mutation, a significant allowance (which went from 330,000 francs to 400,000 francs for the year 1999, and is to rise to 500,000 francs in January 2000) is applied between spouses, with progressive taxation of fractions above that. Meanwhile, in civil law, the surviving spouse is a legitimate heir, but in respect of a very small share, and gifts between spouses are revocable at any time. Reform is called for on both points, and consideration given already to the matter points to its urgency.

As to gifts between spouses, their peculiar rules date from a time when contracts between spouses were just about forbidden, because it was thought that uniting to found a family was not compatible with a professional relationship, precisely on the egalitarian footing inherited from the revolutionary period. Since 1985, sales between spouses are allowed, they are free to sign a contract of partnership together, can employ each other –

---

[37]   J. Commaille, 'Les stratégies des femmes, travail, famille et politique', *La découverte*, 1993; 'Misères de la famille, question d'État', *Presses de Sciences* Po (1996); 39.4% of women work in the European Union; this proportion is 80% for the under 30 age-group.

[38]   In 1996, the report of group I of the mission Gisserot contained the following thought: 'it must be remembered that as long as we do not abandon the present system of assessing married couples jointly for tax purposes, questions will go on being raised as insistently about equality, and there will be a strong demand on the part of or in the name of concubines, to be included in the joint system.' This demand is on the way to being met as a result of the latest turn of the PACS mill (see p 163 below).

the law even contains provisions in favour of the co-worker spouse, but this is in an effort to protect the wife. Meanwhile, gifts between spouses are still revocable, and indirectly void if they are disguised. The reasons put forward for revocability have lost their relevance: genuine independence of the spouses and the possibility of divorce have consigned to oblivion the time when a husband could get hold of his wife's fortune and then mistreat her for the rest of her life; the immutability of matrimonial regimes is no longer an absolute principle; and the informing of third parties is more or less assured by rules of publicity.

Gifts between spouses are now common, particularly at the time of buying a house (56% of French homes are owner-occupied). The unacceptable result of revocability, which subsists after divorce, is that an ex-spouse can revoke a gift made by him, while insisting on receiving one made by his spouse, if the latter died without thinking of revoking it. Worse, the free revocability of gifts between spouses is accompanied by the nullity of disguised gifts to which they may have agreed to get round the rule: it often happens that a spouse, or his reserve heirs, denounce the disguise and invoke the nullity. Of course, courts when possible reclassify so-called gifts, deciding it is a matter of recompense for the spouse's help in her husband's profession. But it is not always possible to argue thus, and in a written-law system such as ours, it is not for the courts to make up the rules as this could lead to arbitrariness.

The French Legislature seems to have no desire to reform this at present, which leaves a lot of spouses surprised and dispossessed[39]. This injustice to married persons is too shocking, and the fact that the latest Congress of notaries (9 to 12 May 1999) adopted by a large majority a resolution calling for the abandonment of revocability of gifts between spouses, even if they risked having less contracts to make, is to be welcomed seeing the notariat is not accustomed to staying inactive when it comes to pressing a proposed reform in the Parliament.

The inheritance rights of the surviving spouse also need to be examined and quickly reformed; another resolution of the Congress of notaries, but one on which everyone agrees. Very many couples still think that marriage entails full community of assets, that is that the union of persons entails the uniting of property. This is almost true for the legal regime of community; but many believe that the spouse inherits in the first line, whether or not there are children of the marriage. They risk a rude awakening. The legal rights of the surviving spouse who was regarded as a stranger in blood to the family, even though he had founded it, were initially very mediocre and have only slightly improved as time passed; even now, to take the commonest case, when the deceased leaves a spouse and children, the spouse gets nothing outright, and takes only a usufruct over a quarter of the assets in the estate (Article 767, Civil Code). He takes nothing outright if there are children, unless they are all adulterine children (Article 759), in which case he is regarded as victim of an outrage against the marriage. Truth to tell, this compromise solution is probably also due to the fact that public opinion would not readily accept that the adulterine child, who got nothing until the law of January 3, 1972 gave him legal status as such, could supplant the surviving spouse altogether. Nowadays, if we are more sensitive to the fact that children ought not to pay for the misdeeds of their parents, hence the desire to put all on an equal footing and abolish discrimination based on birth status, we

---

[39] The answer of the Keeper of the Seals to a parliamentarian who called his attention to this in 1994 was that revocability of gifts was explained by 'concern to protect the giver both from himself making an ill-considered gift and from undue influence on the part of the recipient spouse', Answers to written questions, n° 17168, JOAN, September 19, 1994, p. 4684.

are also conscious that surviving spouses, even without adulterine children, ought to have an increased share of the inheritance.

This is, as Dean Carbonnier wrote, urgent: France, as champion of the rights of the child, as well as of human rights, can no more let herself mistreat a child – even adulterine – than she can leave the surviving spouse – four times out of five, the wife – practically naked where the deceased has left no will. It is highly likely that the reform of the rights of both the surviving spouse and the adulterine child will be taken up in autumn 1999.

The surviving spouse should inherit a meaningful part; under the future Article 757, 'if the deceased leaves children or descendants, the spouse takes, at his option, either the usufruct of all the property, or a quarter of the deceased's assets at death outright.' For the first time in our law, the surviving spouse will inherit – if the reform is passed – a share outright where there are children.[40] The project has not set out to give the surviving spouse a reserved share, unlike some foreign countries, yet it does create a sort of reserve, by guaranteeing a sort of 'legal minimum inheritance' for a spouse totally disinherited by the deceased.[41] This reform, when enacted, will give back to marriage a significant advantage as against the other form of conjugality, concubinage.

Another characteristic of marriage, the fact that, at least for the time being, one cannot get out of it at will, brings us to the question of divorce – society protecting marriage by organising separation according to rules it controls.

B   Divorce

Regarding divorce, the report of the group nominated by Madame Guigou is long-awaited, for studies and proposals have flowed in from all sides over several years, such is the perceived need for reform, at least on certain points. Divorce is still governed by the law of July 11, 1975, which created, beside divorce for fault, divorce mutually agreed (petition presented jointly or by one party with the consent of the other) and divorce for breakdown of marriage (based on separation or on severe disturbance of mental faculties). The basic rules have stayed the same since then, apart from the treatment of children after divorce, which has been the subject of later revision, by the law of January 8, 1993. Bringing all family litigation together under the jurisdiction of the JAF enables him to make a divorce decree on his own, unless he considers that a collegial court is necessary or unless the parties demand it, which it seems they do in defended divorce cases. The fact that the JAF has become, as it is often said, 'judge of all divorces' is an advantage. The same judge drawing up the proceedings, ruling on interim measures (which often end up being, unchanged, the ancillary orders) and finally making the divorce decree, is well placed to advise which form of divorce is the most suitable for the parties.

This apart, in setting up so many varieties of divorce, the 1975 reforms had achieved their purpose: to introduce divorce by mutual consent for those who could agree to end their marriage, either by reaching a settlement of all the consequences, or by leaving

---

[40]   Still to be decided is the share to be inherited by the surviving spouse where there are children of another marriage, a situation which arises more and more often.

[41]   Under the heading 'Of the contribution of the inheritance to the conditions of existence and standard of living of the spouse', the project provides, in the future Article 764, that 'The contribution can be specifically enforced in the form of occupancy [of property], or in money or in a combination of both forms'. It can be seen that the situation is not unlike that of the consequences of divorce, and that the Legislature is remaining true to its policy of not leaving the surviving spouse or the divorcee in need.

these to the judge to dispose of in a second stage of the case; to enable a spouse who was willing to assume responsibility for the costs and for the future support of his ex-spouse to become free to remarry; and finally to retain divorce for fault for those who could not bring themselves to regard the marriage they had entered into as a mere contract, to be terminated at will. Annual judicial statistics for 1996 show 117,716 divorces pronounced, of which 49,463 were by joint petition, 15,876 by unilateral petition with consent, 75 for mental disturbance, and 1,708 for de facto separation, as against 50,490 divorces for fault.

Twenty years on, divorce as we know it needs modifications; the law was well accepted, but not always well applied; it was necessary, in 1975, to break some old habits. Also society has changed, and readily accepts divorce as enabling each spouse to make a new life without losing touch with the children born in the marriage.[42]

But it would be regrettable to succumb to the desire to oversimplify and, so as to come into line with other countries in Europe, to get rid of the varieties of divorce, which match the varied concepts of marriage held by our fellow citizens, or, on the other hand, to add a new form of divorce before the civil status registrar, like getting married.

There has been much discussion of creating 'extrajudicial' divorce, but, in envisaging 'administrative divorce', the dream of those who think the present system excessively favourable to women, those who can believe in the miracle of spouses in perfect agreement and fully able to resolve their differences and the division of assets, and of the judges harassed by overwork, one overlooks the fact that the civil status registrar, in celebrating a marriage, brings the spouses into a particular condition, the married state, which takes effect immediately so that they take on the status of married persons. Divorce in contrast brings that status to an end, and it is necessary to look into the causes and work out the consequences, otherwise marital status makes no sense, and is hardly distinguishable from concubinage. Besides, it is for the State, in the person of the judge and of the advocate, to see to the protection of the weakest, usually the wife and the children. The idea of divorce without a judge looks likely to be dropped.

But it is right to improve certain rules affecting divorce and its financial consequences.

Divorce on joint petition (Civil Code, Article 230) is divorce 'all included' in the apt formula of Dean Cornu. Spouses agree on the principle of divorce, keeping the reasons secret, and on the consequences, presented to the judge as an agreement which he ratifies, in pronouncing the decree. But the procedure has become too slow, and puts one spouse at the mercy of the other, should he change his mind and refuse to come before the judge; then all has to start again using a different route. There is, of course, no advantage in speeding divorce up excessively, as some over-eager couples might find they had got divorced without really wanting to, but it might be appropriate to follow the advice of the Coulon report[43] and abolish one of the hearings, when the judge considers that the agreement presented to him deserves to be ratified without further delay.[44]

---

[42]   In the apt words of Jacques Commaille ('Familles sans justice?'), the dissolution of the conjugal couple more and more often leaves the parental couple to continue. But when speaking of the children, rather than talking of 'reconstructed families' (recomposées), which risks disregarding the parent with whom the child no longer lives, we should speak of 'second families' (see 'L'enfant, sa première et ses secondes familles', colloquium of the Association Louis Chatin, *Petites Affiches*, n°s 118 et 121, October 1997).

[43]   J.-M. Coulon, 'Réflexions et propositions sur la procédure civile', *La documentation française*, 1997.

[44]   The commission of the Order of advocates of the Paris Bar makes the more cautious proposal, that the spouses, by common agreement expressed in their initial petition, request the judge to proceed in a single hearing, so as to exempt them from the 3 months' delay of Article 231 of the Civil Code; thus leaving the judge with the choice between the two forms.

In any event, a text is needed to bring the agreement within the general rule for judicially ratified agreements; in fact, for fear of seeing the revival of litigation after divorce, the Cour de cassation has decided that the ratified agreement was incorporated into the judgment of divorce, and the court based on that 'undesirable indivisibility'[45] its refusal to allow an action for gross unfairness (lésion), omission of an asset, or even fraud on one of the spouses.[46]

Divorce requested by one spouse and accepted by the other (Article 233), more correctly named by Dean Carbonnier as 'divorce on double avowal', has two stages; in the first, the spouses confirm before the judge that they recognise the need for separation, and in the second, which is the adversarial stage, the judge rules on the consequences. Once the first stage is completed, the principle is secured,[47] and one spouse is no longer at the mercy of the other, who might decide not to go forward with the divorce.

For these reasons, in some towns advocates prefer to use divorce on demand accepted, rather than on joint request; and they are also the reasons why there is no obvious need for reform, unless perhaps to let spouses present their petition together.

Divorces for breakdown of conjugal life, that is divorce on the ground of mental disturbance for over six years (Civil Code Article 238) and divorce for de facto separation for over six years (Article 237), have become the residual cases; the second is practically unused except where there is no other way to get one's matrimonial freedom – which would explain the high proportion of petitions by wives (42%).

The hardship clause of Article 240, aimed at preventing divorce from being automatic on proof that the conditions are met, is subject to the first instance judge's sovereign power to evaluate; in 95% of cases it is the wife who invokes it; this usually involves an abandoned wife who wants above all to stop her husband's remarriage; it rarely succeeds and the fear that judges, in the exercise of their sovereign power, may give divergent interpretations according to their beliefs and convictions has proved unfounded; decisions are consistently uniform.

This form of divorce is rarely applied for, now that socially no one much minds living in concubinage, even adulterous, because it is very difficult to obtain. Some authors would like to see it abolished, but many others think it better to retain it, but to reduce the time requirement to three years, after which it is certain that the marriage has no chance of reviving.

Divorce for de facto separation leaves many of the benefits of marriage intact for the spouse who is unwillingly divorced, in particular the right to support, as if the marriage continued, or rather, as under the old alimony provision before 1975; maintenance under Article 281 can always be revised, according to the resources and requirements of each of the (ex-)spouses, and ceases to be payable if the recipient remarries or lives in notorious concubinage (Article 283).

A reform 'in the wind' regarding divorce for breakdown of conjugal life is particularly interesting; it would replace the alimony payments of Article 281 with a compensatory payment, as in all other types of divorce. This is an excellent idea, and would remove the sense of injustice of the unwillingly divorced spouse, who does not understand why he does not enjoy the security of a compensatory payment. But, to

---

[45] A. Tisserand, 'L'indésirable indivisibilité du divorce sur demande conjointe', *Liber amicorum à la mémoire de Danièle Huet-Weiller* (1991) p. 409.

[46] Since Cass. 1re civ. 6 May 1987 (Bull. civ. II, n° 102), there has been no change in the line of decisions, despite unanimous criticism from doctrinal writers (see 'Le contentieux suscité par la convention définitive dans le divorce sur requête conjointe', *chron. Droit de la famille*, JCP (1997) I, 4045).

[47] See also Cass. 2e civ, January 15, 1997 (Bull. civ. II n° 9).

respect the philosophy of divorce for breakdown of conjugal life, it would also be appropriate to revive in its initial tenor the text of Dean Carbonnier, which proposed 'to keep, at least in the background, to back up the maintenance, the present technique of essentially variable alimony, on the rational basis of preserving the support obligation for the benefit of the respondent'.[48]

There is an abundance of decisions on divorce for fault, mainly on two lines: first, adultery is no longer seen as a peremptory cause for divorce and courts quite often assess the circumstances of its commission and reject the petition.[49] Secondly, for some time the Cour de cassation has exercised strict control over the double condition of Article 242 of the Civil Code, condemning without mercy decisions that do not specify exactly how the faults proved made it intolerable to continue conjugal life and how they constituted a grave or persistent violation of the duties of marriage.[50] This recent attitude of the court, which not long ago left it to the sovereign power of the first instance judge to rule on whether the double condition of Article 242 was satisfied, represents, no doubt, the concern to combat the practice of disguising an agreed divorce as a divorce for fault; pluralism of forms of divorce ought to maintain the purity of divorce for fault,[51] and should also prevent slippage towards a generalised divorce on objective grounds. From this point of view, the attitude of the Cour de cassation deserves commendation; numerous authors believe that the abolition of divorce for fault would deeply hurt those of our fellow citizens who value the integrity of marriage and do not want it reduced to a contract of indefinite duration. Divorce for fault must be maintained. If we look at the cases on fault, we see that most of the breaches of conjugal obligations complained of are grave: adultery, drunkenness, and domestic violence, apart from some particular ones which show a certain lack of concern for the family, such as an immoderate passion for computers, or for the restoration of a boat.

The financial effects of divorce are in the greatest need of reform, and most urgently. After 20 years of operation, the law of 1975 has no doubt achieved much of its purpose, and the precautions taken by the Legislature to prevent a return to the former system have proved unnecessary, at least in such a strict form. Criticism has been mainly directed at the fact that the compensatory payment takes the form of a lump sum, which can be revised up or down only in cases of exceptional gravity (Civil Code, Article 273).[52]

The principle of a lump sum compensatory payment, fixed once and for all on the day of dissolution of the marriage and wherever possible paid as capital, was established to make a clean break with the past with no delayed-action litigation. The rule is a hard one: under Article 273 there can be no revision, 'even in the event of unforeseen changes in the means or the needs of the parties'. But the notion of the lump sum has not been taken to its logical conclusion and has been tempered by a sort of hardship clause: revision becomes possible 'if the lack of it would have exceptionally grave consequences

---

[48]   J. Carbonnier, *Essais sur les lois*, 2nd ed. (1995) p. 154.

[49]   See H. Bosse-Platière, *chron. Droit de la famille*, JCP 1997: e.g. Cass. civ. January 22, 1997, March 12, 1997, April 29, 1997, JCP 1997, I. 4045; for example a decision which showed – only – that the husband was guilty of violence and of carrying on a hurtful liaison had to be quashed.

[50]   Ibid.

[51]   Cornu, *Cours de droit civil, Les cours de droit* (1976) p. 91.

[52]   See e.g. A. Bénabent, 'Assainer l'après-divorce', *Liber amicorum à la mémoire de Danièle Huet-Weiller*, PUS/LITEC (1991) p. 19; 'Quelques réformes en matière de divorce', D. (1997) p. 225.

on one of the spouses'; in line with the intention of the Legislature, courts have always taken a very restrictive attitude.[53]

The principle of making a compensatory payment as a capital lump sum comes from Article 274. The payment of a sum of money, eventually over three years, the giving up of the usufruct over specific assets and the deposit of securities with a third party are specifically cited in the law as ways of paying; only if there is no capital will the payment be paid as an annuity, under Article 276. The law, however, has not been applied correctly, the recipient preferring an income so as not to be short of resources after spending the capital, the payer finding an annuity easier to fund than a capital sum, so the courts have gladly reverted to the familiar idea of alimony.[54] It must be added that for the highest level of payments, the adoption of a capital payment is 'confiscatory'.[55]

Among a number of proposals, the one voted for by the Senate on February 25, 1998 best represents the essential changes, as corrections without upheaval. The two main changes would, on the one hand, open the way to revision in case of substantial change in the parties' needs or resources[56] and, on the other, permit either of the ex-spouses to call for the annuity fixed at divorce to be commuted into a lump sum.[57] The first merit of the proposal is that it goes to the technical aspects of the texts that have produced problems; the possibility of revision, open also to the heirs of the debtor, where there has been a substantial change in parties' resources and needs; making it possible to give up property interests outright; a right to claim capitalisation of an annuity at any time; the ending of the payment of the annuity on death of the creditor; all are technical improvements precisely matching the hopes of the legal profession – improvement, not general confusion – so it is to be hoped the deputies will accept it without waiting for the reform of family law on a grand scale to materialise.

C   Concubinages

The couple in concubinage has become part of modern social life. It appears that the reasons for the present social recognition of diverse forms of conjugal life, and the removal of the disapproval that attended those who did not base their family on marriage, are very complex; they probably include the growing neutrality of the State which, as Jacques Commaille stresses, 'tends to give couples a legal status that is not differentiated by reference to the way in which they are constituted';[58] but also the total control of

---

[53]   There are many reported cases: unemployment is taken into account, but not reduction of resources on retirement, as that is foreseeable; a totally incapacitating illness or accident, but not liquidation of a business by the court when the debtor has prospects of returning to work, or refuses to disclose his current income. For an overview of the cases on dismissal for economic reasons, see *chron. Droit de la famille,* JCP (1996), I, 3946, obs. H. Bosse-Platière.

[54]   J. Carbonnier, *Droit civil, La famille,* n° 176.

[55]   D. Grillet-Ponton, *La famille et le droit fiscal,* PUF 198. Article 757A of the Code général des impôts makes transfers of the debtor's own capital taxable as gifts, whereas annuities he pays are deductible for the purposes of income tax.

[56]   Until now, the acquisition of a vast fortune (e.g. a win on the lottery) does not stop the debtor from continuing to pay alimony as ordered, as an annuity, often until the death of the recipient; the debtor of a modest annuity, even if he becomes very rich, will owe no more than was set at the time of the divorce.

[57]   Until now, debtors who divorced in 1977, and have been ordered to pay a life annuity of 1,000 francs a month, which comes to a quarter of their salaries, continue to pay and to watch miserably the blooming financial health of their ex-spouses.

[58]   J. Commaille, 'Nouvelle légalité et mode d'analyse des comportements familiaux', *Colloque INED* préc. n. 40 ; see also 'La régulation politique de la famille', *La famille, l'état des savoirs,* directed by F. de

procreation, so that an extramarital child is no longer seen as punishment for his mother's misconduct, and the existence of divorce, which makes it as easy for married as for unmarried couples to separate – though no less painful. We should add the numbers involved – there are now nearly two million unmarried couples, that is 20% of the total number of couples, as against 3.6% in 1975.[59] Above all, these concubinages produce families.[60] As we have already indicated, extramarital births account for 40% of the total today, compared to 6% in 1965.[61] Further, thanks to the laws on parental authority and the establishment of affiliation, these children do not suffer as a result of their parents' mode of conjugality.

Curiously, social recognition of concubinage may well lead to recognition in civil law, by putting into the Civil Code a definition of this de facto situation. Very soon, in fact, unless the Conseil constitutionel on a reference by the opposition invalidates it (which is unlikely), the text adopted by the National Assembly on June 15, 1999 will become a 'Law relating to the Pacte civil de solidarité [PACS]', and including in the Civil Code an Article 515-8 whereby: 'Concubinage is a union of fact characterised by a common life presenting a character of stability and continuity between two persons, of the same or of different sex, who live as a couple'.

Defining a de facto situation in the Code is an odd thing to do;[62] does it mean the persons in question cannot consider themselves concubines if their life in common is not stable and continuous enough? Adding living as a couple is clumsy as well as redundant, and in any case this attempt to break the trend of decisions in the Cour de cassation which refuses to call same-sex cohabition 'concubinage' will not achieve much; almost every legal provision giving advantages to concubinage call for a specific period of time.[63] We might see same-sex concubinage – hitherto inoperative – taken into account as a ground for ending the right to occupy a home or to payment of alimony agreed after divorce for breakdown of conjugal life (Civil Code Articles 283 and 285-1); to rebut the presumption of single parenthood that gives rise to a benefit claim (C. Séc. soc. Article L. 524-1); in assessing the wealth tax (C.G.I. Article 885-E, para. 2); or to fix the amount of the compensatory payment bearing in mind that the spouse claiming it lives in concubinage, enabling her to economise, or bringing her additional resources. The result would not be what is being sought in the recognition of same-sex concubinage.

It is hard to see the need for legal definition; concubinage is a de facto situation and when the Legislature, or a public or private undertaking, wish to give it consequences, they lay down the relevant conditions. This apart, there is no reason not to subject any person to the general law applying to him, as an individual, whether or not living in a couple.

Thus, since 1970 the Cour de cassation has not required a legitimate interest protected by law in order to compensate a woman for the death of her concubine (even if adulterous) through the fault of a third party, marital infidelity being a matter concerning only the spouses. On the same lines, on July 25, 1995, the Belfort court logically

Singly, ed. La découverte 1991, p. 265; L'esprit sociologique des lois (Essai de sociologie politique du droit), PUF 1994, *coll. Droit Éthique et Societé.*

[59] G. Desplanques et M. de Saboulin, 'Les familles aujourd'hui', *Données sociales* (1990) p. 276.

[60] B. Rabin, 'De plus en plus de naissances hors mariage', *Économie et Statistiques*, n° 251, February 1992; C. Aussay, *Les naissances en 1992*, INSEE 1944 N° 397.

[61] F. Munoz Perez and F. Prioux, 'Naître hors mariage', *Population et Sociétés* n° 342, January 1999.

[62] The reason is political jousting between the National Assembly and the Senate over the PACS.

[63] E.g. Civil Code Article 340-4; law of July 6, 1989, Articles 14 and 15 (on tenancy); Code de la santé publique Article L. 152-2, réd L. July 29, 1994 (on medically assisted procreation).

admitted a woman's claim to compensation for the death of her female companion, against the motorist who had caused the fatal accident.[64]

Concubinage as a de facto state, creates no obligation. The principle is still that concubinage has no effects; judges have to say more and more often that rules written for spouses have no application to concubines, in particular that they can leave freely, and this raises no claim for indemnity in the absence of an element of wrongdoing; the Cour de cassation censures courts that forget this;[65] first instance courts often have to reject the claim for damages of a concubine unable to show such an element.[66] The Colmar appeal court, in awarding 50,000 francs for damages and loss under the heading of compensation for psychological harm, was careful to record 'that the break-up had been brutal and sudden, after about six years of concubinage with the promise of marriage, without prior discussion, and that it involved removal of personal effects without warning and in the concubine's absence'.[67] The manner of separating could be wrongful, and lead to an award of damages, if it was brutal, a response to announcement of pregnancy, or sudden after insisting that the concubine give up her job; where all these circumstances were found the former concubine was condemned to pay 500,000 francs for the damage caused.[68]

On separation, with or without damages, each concubine takes his own assets; one who leaves with nothing, having spent the time helping the other in a professional activity, or having shouldered the whole of the household expenses, can sue in unjust enrichment or partnership created de facto, which the courts often allow, if the required elements are there.[69]

Concubinage has long been a subject of legislation: since 1939 some laws treat a dead soldier's concubine as a war widow;[70] in 1948, the law protecting occupiers, then in 1982 and 1986 laws on rents and the continuation of a lease on abandonment by, or death of the tenant, make the concubine a beneficiary of the protection of occupancy or continuation of the lease; the law of July 6, 1989, in Article 15, provides that renewal can be in favour of 'the tenant, his spouse, his notorious concubine of at least a year at the date of termination, his ascendants, his descendants or those of his spouse or his notorious concubine' (it is perhaps the first step towards recognising collaterals related through concubinage).[71] Since the law of January 2, 1978 on social security generally, 'a person who lives conjugally with the person covered by social insurance' succeeds to the rights of the latter and benefits from the sickness and maternity insurance (C. Séc. soc. Article 161-4, para. 1). Since 1995, Article 434-1 of the new Penal Code which sets out who is protected by immunity for failure to report crime, provides not only for the culprit's spouse, but also for 'the person who lives notoriously in a marital situation with him'.

We should also recall that, since the law of January 8, 1993, the Civil Code gives parental authority in common to concubines who have recognised their child before his

---

[64] TGI Belfort, July 25, 1995, JCP 1996, II, 22724, note C. Paulin, *Petites Affiches*, March 2, 1998, p. 13, note I. Corpart.

[65] E.g. Cass. 1re civ. June 30, 1992, Bull. civ. 1, n 204.

[66] E.g. Bordeaux, January 23, 1992 (Juris-Data n° 40070); Dijon May 27, 1993 (Juris-Data n° 44999); Orléans October 19, 1993 (Juris-Data n° 46418); Bordeaux October 27, 1993 (Juris-Data n° 45247).

[67] Colmar September 18, 1992 (Juris-Data n° 447971).

[68] Cass. 1re civ. April 7, 1998, JCP (1998) I 151, *chron. Droit de la famille*, obs. H. Bosse-Platiére.

[69] See H. Bosse-Platière, *chron. Droit de la famille*, JCP (1999), I 101 and ref. cit.

[70] M. Granier, 'Épouse, concubine ou compagne?' JCP (1959), I 1929.

[71] See J. Rubellin-Devichi, 'La famille et le droit au logement', RTD civ. 1991, p. 254.

first birthday (Article 372, para. 2), thus assimilating their position practically to that of a married couple. But it is particularly in the so-called 'bioethics' laws of July 29, 1994 that we find the most developed example of an obligation to treat concubines as if they were a married couple, placing 'a man and a woman forming a couple' on more or less the same footing with regard to access to medically assisted procreation, married or not: Article L. 152-2 of the Code de la santé publique provides that the man and the woman forming the applicant couple must be 'married or able to show at least two years' life in common'.

On the other hand, some texts deny a benefit to those living in concubinage.[72] In fiscal matters, concubines are greatly disadvantaged as compared to spouses, at least when one is maintained by the other, as they have to make separate tax returns; when both work, each keeps the advantages of a single person.[73] Gifts between concubines, inter vivos or mortis causa, are taxable at 60% of their value, as they are legally strangers to each other. For this reason, when buying a home, they often draw up a tontine contract so that the asset will become the property of the survivor, or they take out a policy of insurance to cover the inheritance tax.

Were it not for this exorbitant taxation, one could say that concubines were better off than spouses in relation to gifts, or rather that one who is abandoned after having received a gift is in a stronger position than in marriage, because gifts in marriage are always revocable.

Gifts between concubines obey the general law; as gifts, they are irrevocable and can only be annulled for illicit cause or for immorality; since 1927, the courts have held that a gift or a legacy made to establish or to maintain sexual relations must be revoked, but that where such motives are not proved, or where gifts are made to repair a detriment suffered, even where the concubinage is adulterous, they must be upheld. Now, by its judgment of February 3, 1999,[74] they have decided to abandon the distinction based on the cause of gifts between concubines which are now all valid, in principle, even those made to keep going an adulterous relationship.[75]

D   The question of same-sex concubinage and the PACS

When individuals of the same sex live together, assume together the duties of support and assistance that the Code places on spouses, and own property in common, notably through tontine contracts, they form a union which validates itself by its duration.[76] The

---

[72]   The divorce law, for the occupancy of the home and alimony after divorce for breakdown of conjugal life; the law of reversionary pensions in public life, etc.

[73]   The fiscal law for 1996 has happily reduced the income tax advantage constituted by the fact that both parents, not being married to each other, could each pass for a 'lone' parent and declare the child as in his care for the family quotient. Now it is only the genuine lone parent who can rely on the fact of being a 'monoparental' family.

[74]   Cass. 1re civ. February 3, 1999, Dr. famille 1999, comm. n° 54, obs. B. Beignier; JCP 199, ed. G., II, 10083, note M. Rilliau and G. Loiseau; *Defrénois* 1999, article 36998, n° 30, obs. J. Massip and article 37008, obs. D. Mazeaud; JCP 1999, ed G. I, 143, F. Labarthe; RJPF 1999, 2/52, obs. J. Casey; see also Angers, February 23, 1998 (Dr. famille 1999, comm. N° 54, obs B. Beignier); here it is in fact the wife who is condemned to pay significant damages (80,000 francs) for the damage caused by delay in clearing up the succession.

[75]   So we associate ourselves even more strongly with the notaries' resolution, in favour of – at least – making gifts between spouses as secure as those between concubines.

[76]   It seems difficult, as Professor Leveneur stresses (L. Leveneur, *Situations de fait et droit privé*, LGDJ, 1990, p. 443 n° 363, ff.) to decide that two individuals who live together (cum cubare), who live 'as if in marriage', by reference to the adage of Loysel, do not live in concubinage.

alarming AIDS epidemic, which struck first and hardest against homosexuals has accentuated the parallels between heterosexual and homosexual unions; fidelity, once said not to be an essential duty in the homosexual couple, is now assumed as a moral obligation to one's partner, and the fate of the survivor is a paramount preoccupation.

Until the mid-1980s, the question of difference of sex in concubinage did not arise, first because few, if any, persons in homosexual relationships came, as such, before the courts, and secondly because nobody thought to ask if concubinage did or did not imply a difference of sex: some texts assumed heterosexuality (e.g. the investigation of paternity based on the notorious concubinage between mother and putative father), others did not, for example the application of the rent laws; when it came to applying the general law, concubinage itself was not important; many wills were made in favour of a same sex concubine;[77] gifts between homosexual couples have been annulled for immorality, because they were considered to have been made as a way of maintaining sexual relations.[78] After the judgment (referred to above) of February 3, 1999, it seems the Cour de cassation will no longer be able to decide that a gift to a homosexual concubine is invalid for that reason, as the court had previously decided on November 21, 1995.[79]

Meanwhile, the Cour de cassation has excluded homosexual couples from advantages given to unmarried couples, in two judgments of the Chambre Sociale on July 11, 1989, where, following the conclusions of their advocate general, the court refused to rule that a steward and his male companion were entitled to the free flights their company, Air France, gave to married couples and concubines, or that a woman could be entitled to benefit from the sickness and maternity insurance of the woman with whom she lived in concubinage.[80] This view was reiterated on December 17, 1997, when the court refused to transfer a tenancy to the companion of a deceased tenant, in spite of the conclusions of their advocate general.[81]

By disregarding homosexual concubinage, not only has the Cour de cassation given recognition and legitimacy to heterosexual concubinage and raised it to being a second tier marriage,[82] but, by marginalising homosexual couples and so rousing homosexual rights groups to militancy, it has forced the Legislature to move towards giving a legal framework to those unable to marry. After the setback of the contract of civil partnership, on which a proposition for a law was laid before the Senate on June 25, 1990, and of a proposition for a law registered with the presidency of the National Assembly on

---

[77] Sometimes these were annulled, but for immorality; thus the Tribunal de grande instance de Paris, on 25 June 1985 (Rép. Defrénois 1985, obs. G. Champenois, p. 1161) annulled legacies made by a man to other younger men with whom he lived in concubinage for some years, or maintained sexual relations which helped him to find other partners.

[78] Bordeaux December 9, 1992, Juris-Data n° 048581; Orléans October 26, 1993, Juris-Data n° 045310.

[79] Cass. 1re civ. November 21, 1995 Dr. et patrimoine, March 1917, p. 72, obs. A. Bénabent.

[80] J. Rubellin-Devichi, obs. RTD civ. 1990 p. 43 and ref. cit.; 'Les concubinages: mise à jour', *Liber amicorum à la mémoire de Danièle Huet-Weiller*, p. 389.

[81] Cass. 3e civ. December 17, 1997, D, 1998. p. 111, concl. J.-F. Weber, note J.-L. Aubert; D 1998, p. 215, Com. A. Bénabent, Defrénois 1998 n° 40 p. 405, which shows how pointless discrimination is in regard to the law of July 6, Article 14. The Paris court followed the decision of the Cour de cassation (CA Paris, April 27, 1989, JCP IV 341: death of tenant; May 10, 1990, D 1990 somm. 306, obs Ph. Bihr; June 9, 1995, RTD civ. 607, obs. J. Hauser; appeal rejected Cass. December 3, 1997).

[82] This entails some contradictions, notably by protecting same-sex couples from the consequences visited on 'true' concubinage: no notorious concubinage putting an end to the right to occupy the home or to receive alimony after divorce for breakdown of conjugal life under Articles 283 and 285 of the Civil Code; no rebutting of the presumption of lone parenthood so as to stop the lone parent's benefit.

November 25, 1992, which would have created a contract of civil union,[83] two Articles only of this proposition, picked out in the form of amendments had been voted. Article 15, inserted into Article 78 of the law of January 27, 1993, making various changes in the social order, extends sickness and maternity benefit rights to the same-sex concubine fully and permanently maintained by the person assured;[84] Article 7, inserted into Article 62 of the same law, authorises transfer of a tenancy, when the tenant dies, to any person who has been living with the tenant for at least a year; this text was declared not in conformity with the Constitution, for want of connection with the text submitted to the assemblies,[85] but must be voted on again one day, as, like the new Article L. 174 of the Social Security Code, it has more to do with solidarity than with a wish to create some sort of status for couples who may wish to be recognised as concubines, or rather as 'partners' – which would entail the resurgence of 'true concubinages, the wildcat concubinages of couples who refuse to make the declaration'.[86] Meanwhile, on July 17, 1993, another proposition was registered at the presidency of the Senate, which would create a 'civil partnership contract', in terms very close to those of the civil union contract;[87] on July 23, 1997, two propositions, one for a contract of social union (CUS) and one for a contract of civil and social union (CUCS) were deposited; on September 30, 1997, a proposition 'relating to the rights of unmarried couples' was again submitted. At the same time, at the request of the government, a commission headed by Professor Hauser was preparing a Pact of interests in common, binding two persons and offered, among others, to same sex couples.

Out of this legislative ferment and the confrontation between all these propositions, there has come one text, that of the civil solidarity pact (Pacte civil de solidarité, or PACS), which has been the subject of full frontal combat between the National Assembly and the Senate. The Assembly had begun to debate it in November 1998; it will be presented for the last time at the end of September 1999, the last word resting with the Assembly.

Fundamentally, the PACS, allowing two persons to arrange their life in common does not do much, with two exceptions; partners in a civil solidarity pact will be jointly assessed for tax (like a married couple), but more importantly, in relation to succession, there will be an abatement of 375,000 francs from January 1, 2000, which makes it like that for the married couple (400,000 francs from that date); the second advantage is the possibility of unilaterally ending the pact, a possibility that Dean Carbonnier rightly describes as 'thunderbolt divorce'.

The homosexual couple had to be recognised, and the PACS was necessary, because of the decisions of the Cour de cassation; but it is highly regrettable, politically speaking, to include in its application, besides the 50,000 homosexual couples, two million or more heterosexual couples. The law allows heterosexual couples, who could marry but choose not to, to benefit from the PACS, by saving themselves from the cost of divorce, and from the tax liability. The second tier marriage is not being offered to homosexual

---

[83]   Likewise in Belgium, in autumn 1993, an advance project for a 'contract for common life' was presented by three deputies to allow two natural persons, regardless of sex, to establish between themselves a community of life and provide a material community for themselves.

[84]   Article L. 161-14 of the Social Security Code and decree of application of March 27, 1993.

[85]   Decision of the Conseil constitutionnel of January 21, 1993, JO January 23, 1993, p. 1240.

[86]   J. Carbonnier, *Le droit entre le droit et le non-droit, Conclusion juridique pour un colloque de démographie sur la nuptialité*, cited above, p. 754.

[87]   See J.-M. Florand and K. Achoui, 'Vers un nouveau modèle d'organisation familiale: le contrat d'union civile', *Les Petites Affiches*, April 9, 1993, n° 43, p. 11.

couples, but to heterosexual ones, who will achieve a legally recognised union 'for better, without the worse' in Évelyne Sullerot's phrase. The PACS ought to have been kept for homosexual couples, leaving the others the freedom to choose between the legal – marriage – and the nonlegal – concubinage.

Short of a miracle, that is not going to happen. Might we seek consolation in the thought that we have not often seen couples choosing the form of their union according to the financial advantages their choice might bring them?

GERMANY

LEGAL PROBLEMS REGARDING THE REPRESENTATION OF PERSONS WITH REDUCED MENTAL CAPACITY OR INCAPACITY

Rainer Frank[*]

I   INTRODUCTION

Reports of the past years[1] were concerned with the parentage law reform which was passed in 1997 and came into effect in 1998. The reform concerned in particular the Equal Status in Inheritance Act,[2] which has been in operation since April 1, 1998, as well as the Guardianship Act,[3] the Parentage Law Reform Act[4] and the Child Maintenance Act,[5] which have been in effect since July 1, 1998. The Marriage Law Act[6] also became effective on July 1, 1998. This legislation, which drastically changed family law, is no longer the subject of this annual report.

This year's report focuses on the representation of persons with a limited or no capacity to form an intent: first of all it takes into consideration the contractual and tortious liability of minors. Parental custody, regarding medical treatment of a child, poses a problem if the minor child wishes for an abortion against the parents' will. The report finally deals with the issue of permissible representation of will regarding euthanasia: can a long-term comatose patient be represented by an uninvolved third party in his decision to abandon all medical treatment? If yes, then the question arises as to whether this consent of the representative requires approval by the Guardianship Court. Beside the so-called advanced healthcare directive and enduring powers of attorney, civil guardianship rights have a role to play here.

II   CONTRACTUAL AND TORTIOUS LIABLILITY OF MINORS

The passing of the Limitation of Liability of Minors Act,[7] within the past parliamentary term, on August 25, 1998, comes as a surprise. The draft Bill of September 24, 1996[8] by the Federal Government has been adopted almost in its original version and was effected

---

[*]   Professor of Law, Albert-Ludwigs-University, Freiburg.

[1]   See the reports in *The International Survey of Family Law* for the years 1994, 1995, 1996 and 1997 under Germany.

[2]   Statute regulating the equal status in succession of children born out of wedlock, BGBl. I 1997, p. 2968.

[3]   Statute for the abolition of statutory guardianship and reformation of the Law of Guardianship, BGBl. I 1997, p. 2846.

[4]   Statute for the reformation of Parentage Law, BGBl. I 1997, p. 2942.

[5]   Statute for the standardization of Maintenance Law for minors, BGBl. I 1998, p. 666.

[6]   Statute for the reformation of Marriage Law, BGBl. I 1998, p. 833.

[7]   Gesetz zur Beschränkung der Haftung Minderjähriger, BGBl. I 1998, p. 2487.

[8]   BT-Drucks. 13/5624; for more on this see the German report in *The International Survey of Family Law* 1997.

on January 1, 1999. It aims at protecting minors from heavy indebtedness on reaching adulthood.

The main concern in this regard was how to limit parental authority over the child's property, in the interest of the latter. Two proposals were made. The first provided for a number of legal transactions which, if performed in the child's name, would require an express authorisation by the Guardianship Court. According to the second proposal, liability for contractual obligations would be limited to the amount of the child's estate at the time of reaching adulthood. The first proposal was rejected by the legislature for the reason that it would be difficult to define the category of transactions requiring authorisation and that, furthermore, the Guardianship Courts would barely be in a position to make decisions based on economic predictions regarding contracts concluded in the child's name.[9] The Limitation of Liability of Minors Act therefore provides for a general limitation of liability (§ 1626a BGB[10]), which is complemented by the child's option to cancel involvement in any existing business partnership when reaching adulthood (§ 723 sec. 1 sent. 2 No. 2 BGB). In the very worst case, therefore, the child will own no property at the time of coming of age but will at least have the opportunity of a new beginning financially.

In order to reduce a creditor's risk of denied access to the child's estate, accrued after the latter has reached adulthood, the dates of birth of partners in a commercial partnership must be entered in the register of companies (§ 125 sec. 3 sent. 2 FGG[11]) and the cancellation of the involvement in the partnership must be announced by the child having reached adulthood, three months after learning about his position as a partner (§§ 723 sec. 1 sent. 3, 1629a sec. 4 BGB). Financial partners of a minor may also protect themselves contractually through the agreement of securities and a commitment by the parents.

The Limitation of Liability of Minors Act therefore has a considerable impact on the German law of contract;[12] it does not however affect the extent of the minor's liability in tort. This differentiation is justified, given that in the contractual sphere the obligation incurred by the minor has been voluntarily assumed by his parents, while tortious liability is based on damage to another's legal interest, caused by the minor's own discerning and wrongful conduct. In German law a minor does not incur delictual liability for a delict committed by his guardian against a third party.

§ 828 sec. 2 sent. 1 BGB provides that a child above the age of seven years is liable for damage caused by his wrongful conduct, provided he has the necessary discerning ability when failing to comply with his duty. As long as the child demonstrates this understanding, he is legally responsible for the damage caused and is liable to compensate the damage to its full extent. The parents are liable alongside the child, but only if they neglected their duty of supervision (§ 832 BGB).

The law of tort presently does not provide for limitation of a minor's liability where he shows the necessary discernment for his actions. This unlimited liability can in certain cases result in considerable hardship. A typical example of adolescent misconduct, which the LG[13] Dessau had to decide upon, demonstrates this clearly: a 16-year-old boy took his 13-year-old girlfriend for a spin on his moped. The boy neither had a driver's licence, nor was the moped insured. He caused a serious accident, whereby his girlfriend was badly

---

9   See report by the legal committee BT-Drucks. 13/10831, p.8.
10   BGB (Bürgerliches Gesetzbuch) = German Civil Code.
11   FGG = Act governing non-contentious matters.
12   See for more detail Habersack/Schneider, *FamRZ* 1997, 649 (655).
13   LG (Landgericht) = Regional Court.

injured. The girl's medical insurers sued the boy for 153.000 DM. The LG Dessau suspended the proceedings, questioning the constitutionality of § 828 sec. 2 BGB and submitted the issue to the Federal Constitutional Court.[14]

§ 828 sec. 2 BGB is concerned only with the minor's intellectual capacity to understand the wrongfulness of his conduct and to take responsibility for it. The provision disregards the issue as to whether the child has the ability also to act in accordance with this understanding. § 276 BGB is merely concerned with the minor's required maturity, which is judged against the general developmental stage of minors in his age, in order to affirm negligence. In the individual case, however, the minor is considered less blameworthy than an adult. Besides, due to his lacking legal capacity, a minor has no possibility of taking precautions by taking out third party liability insurance. If a minor has acted negligently, and if the victim's damage has been covered by the insurer and the recourse by the latter towards the minor offender leads to a liability endangering his financial existence, then the imbalance between the wrongful conduct and its legal consequences is intensified.

In order to solve this problem, it has been suggested that the age limit contained in § 828 BGB should be raised and to impose a legal duty on the parents to take out insurance in their child's name.[15] Others propose that the rigidity of the German law of damages ought to be made more flexible by a liability-quota[16] or – as is the case in other European countries – by introducing considerations of equity.[17] Another option to be considered might be an expansion of parental liability, envisaged in § 832 BGB, excluding the possibility of exculpation or by providing a maximum limit to the insurer's claim against the minor.[18] According to the present state of the law, there are however no legal foundations on which to allow for the protection of a delictually responsible minor from liability.[19]

The catalyst for these considerations was a decision handed down by the German Constitutional Court on May 13, 1986. The court held that minors are to be protected from an unreasonable financial burden. In particular, the situation must be avoided where a minor is deprived of the possibility of leading an independent life, on attaining maturity, due to pre-existing debts.[20] The necessary consequence of this is the Limitation of Liability of Minors Act (see above) which seeks to limit parental authority to incur contractual obligations on behalf of a minor.

Delictual liability in the above case, decided by the LG Dessau, was however not caused through parental influence but was the result of the conduct of the delictually responsible minor himself. The aim of the law of tort is fair compensation for violation of another's legal interest. In the case of fault-based liability, the principle of total compensation applies, i.e. there are no provisions setting a maximum limit of liability.[21]

---

[14]   LG Dessau, *VersR* 1997, 242; contrary Ahrens, *VersR* 1997, 1064; compare also the submission report by the OLG (= Higher Regional Court) Celle (which was however not decided by the Federal Constitutional Court, due to settlement out of court), *JZ* 1990, 294; see Canaris, *JZ* 1990, 679 and Kuhlen, *JZ* 1990, 273.

[15]   Scheffen, *ZRP* 1991, 458 (461ff.); *FuR* 1993, 82 (88).

[16]   LG Osnabrück, *NJW-RR* 1991, 544.

[17]   Compare the draft report by the Federal Ministry of Justice from 1967, printed by Staudinger (Oechsler), § 828 no. 45.

[18]   Scheffen, *FuR* 1993, 82 (88); *Festschrift für Steffen* 1995, 387 (394f.).

[19]   However compare LG Bremen, *NJW-RR* 1991, 1432.

[20]   *BVerfGE* 72, 155; compare the German report in *The International Survey of Family Law 1997* under 'Limitation of Liability of Minors Bill'.

[21]   This is different though with regard to strict liability, for which there exist maximum limits to compensation, compare e.g. § 9 *HPflG*, § 12 *StVG*, § 31 *AtomG*.

With this system of compensation, any decision to the benefit of the tortfeasor is ultimately detrimental to the aggrieved party, provided that there is no collective ultimately to bear the damage. Even then, however, the aggrieved party will ultimately carry the loss through an increase in his insurance premium. Since the claim for damages arises because all elements of liability have been satisfied, the compensation of the damaged party takes priority. This claim is not enforceable, however, where in the instance of insolvency, the minor purports to make an application for the remission of debts (§§ 286ff. InsO[22]). This, in the present state of the law, provides a satisfying option of avoiding unreasonable hardship in an individual case and makes it possible to protect the minor from an exorbitantly heavy burden, endangering his or her financial existence.[23]

III   MEDICAL TREATMENT OF MINORS

In German law, parental guardianship comprises both the administration of the child's property on the one hand and custody of the minor's person on the other hand (§ 1626 sec. 1 sent. 2 BGB). The administration of the minor's property involves its preservation and investment in the child's interest. The custody of the minor's person concerns his education, supervision, the issue of residence and further measures of care and safety including the minor's medical care. § 1629 BGB provides that the parents, fulfilling their duties of custody, act as the minor's representative regarding issues concerning both his person and assets.

In recent years the public's interest has been caught by a number of cases where parents objected on religious grounds to their children receiving medical treatment.[24] An example of such a case in 1995 was that of five-year-old cancer patient Olivia Pilhar, whose parents objected to their child's treatment with orthodox medicine. More recent is the case of eight-month-old Mukarim Emil, who was suffering from a life-threatening tumour of the eye. His parents likewise refused to have him hospitalised in January 1999.

Child custody is as much a right as a duty. It is a duty, the fulfilment of which is ensured by the State (Article 6 sec. 2 GG[25]). §§ 1666f BGB empowers the Family Court to order measures necessary to avert any risk to the child's well-being where the parents demonstrate no willingness to do so. It was for this reason that in the case of Mukarim Emil the parents' guardianship was renounced for a period of time. They regained their rights on April 16, 1999 – excluding however the right to decide on the child's residence – in order to secure further treatment of the child.[26] In cases such as the above, the parents' duty towards their child takes precedence over their right to freedom of religion (Article 4 GG). The extent of this duty is defined by the objectively ascertainable best interest of the child; its fulfilment is safeguarded by the State.

In the above-mentioned cases, both Mukarim Emil and Olivia Pilhar were too young to make their own decisions with regard to the necessity and kind of medical treatment to be employed. If, at this stage they had been 18 years of age, their own views would have

---

[22]　Insolvency Act.

[23]　See also MüKo (Mertens) § 828 no. 14; Staudinger (Oechsler) § 828 no. 2, 41ff.

[24]　See e.g. OLG Hamm *FamRZ* 1968, 221; OLG Celle, *NJW* 1995, 792; AG Meschede, *FamRZ* 1997, 958.

[25]　GG = Grundgesetz (Constitution); Article 6 Abs. 2 GG: 'The care and upbringing of children are the natural right of parents and a duty primarily incumbent on them. It is the responsibility of the State to ensure that they perform this duty'.

[26]　AG Augsburg (decision of 16.4.1999), see Frankfurter Allgemeine Zeitung 17.4.1999, p. 9.

been decisive, since the rights to custody cease when the child reaches maturity.[27] The legal position however, during the intermediate stage where the minor's discerning ability begins to develop, proves to be difficult: § 1626 sec. 2 BGB provides a guideline for the upbringing of a child, i.e. respect for a child's growing independence. Parental authority in guardianship decreases in a dynamic process as the child's personal autonomy grows. The minor's right to self-determination as part of his general personality rights (Article 1 sec. 1, Article 2 sec. 1 GG) gains equal importance to the parent's will ('right' in the sense of Article 6 sec. 2 GG) and the objectively required 'duty' (in the sense of Article 6 sec. 2 GG) for the realisation of the child's welfare. Even though consensus between parents and child with regard to medical treatment is worth striving for, the question arises as to whether the dynamics of § 1626 sec. 2 BGB represent a mere internal educational maxim, or whether this 'third dimension' is also carried outside, in the instance of dissent, so as to affect legal relations.

German law distinguishes between the making of a contract to receive medical treatment on the one hand, and consent by the minor to the intrusion on his bodily integrity, on the other hand.

A person of full age has legal capacity and can therefore independently conclude a valid contract for medical treatment. A child, according to § 104 no. 1 BGB, has no legal capacity before his seventh birthday and, therefore, the parents' consent to treatment is obligatory. Conceivable conflicts during the period of limited legal capacity are avoided in the area of contract law in order to secure legal relations, by making the parent's consent a precondition to every legal transaction which is not concluded exclusively for the minor's benefit (§ 107 BGB). The minor has no capacity to conclude a contract for medical treatment without assistance, as it imposes an obligation on the patient to remunerate the medical service rendered. If parents abusively refuse consent the Family Court, according to § 1666 BGB, has the power to authorise the treatment instead. Parents on the other hand may, within the limits of § 1666 BGB, also conclude a contract for medical treatment against the wishes of their child.

The question as to whether medical treatment is justified, irrespective of how the contract was brought about, arises with regard to the doctor's civil, or even criminal, liability.

There is some controversy as to whether a medically indicated and proficiently performed medical procedure actually satisfies the legal requirements for the offence of bodily injury.[28] The courts however tend to affirm in order to prevent the patient's incapacitation and to safeguard his constitutional right to self-determination.[29] Accordingly, the informed consent of the person whose personality rights are invaded is required, both in criminal law as well as in private law, provided the person has the necessary mental capacity. In determining the mental capacity to consent, it is not possible to fall back on the age limits applicable in contract law (§§ 104 ff. BGB) as these would prove too rigid for a matter with such personal consequences.[30] Of decisive relevance, however, is the specific capacity of the child in each individual case to discern and judge the consequences of his decision, even though this might have negative implications regarding the certainty of legal relations.[31]

---

[27]   The age of majority was reduced from 21 to 18 years by the Reformation of the Age of Majority Act of 31.7.1974 (BGB1 I, p. 1713).

[28]   For present legal opinion see Lackner, *StGB* § 223 no. 8ff. (21. edition München 1995).

[29]   *BGHSt* 11, 111.

[30]   Contrary *RGZ* 68, 431; *JW* 1911, 748; MüKo (Gitter) before § 104 no. 89.

[31]   *BGHZ* 29, 33 (36); *BGH FamRZ* 1959, 200; OLG München *NJW* 1958, 633.

If the minor, however, is mentally and morally mature enough to appreciate fully the implications of his decision, then the question arises as to whether the parents' custody rights should take second place to the child's decision or whether they should, in case of conflict, take precedence over the child's right to self-determination.

German law does not offer any solution to this problem with the exception of § 41 no. 3 AMG,[32] according to which the joint decision of both parents and child is necessary regarding the clinical testing of a pharmaceutical product on a minor. It follows that an exceptionally dangerous procedure requires the consent of the discerning minor, even though his legal custodian has already approved it. It would be wrong, however, to conclude that the sole consent of the parents would be insufficient in all cases, since the clinical testing of a pharmaceutical product is not to be equated with a medically indicated treatment.[33]

Some legal writers commend the competence of the discerning minor to decide for himself, while rejecting the need to obtain the parents' approval.[34] A Bill of the Federal Government of 1974 reforming § 1626a BGB (Consent to Medical Treatment by Minors) provided that a discernible minor, above the age of 14 years, should have the sole right to consent to medical treatment. This power would have been qualified by the parent's right of veto.[35] The Bill was never implemented because of fear that the parents' responsibility for the child's personal welfare would be undermined to an unreasonable degree.[36] The Federal Supreme Court[37] considers that the parents' additional consent is dispensable in cases where the medical procedure cannot be postponed, or in instances where it cannot be obtained.[38] The parents' additional approval is however required if the procedure is of great relevance and if the custodians' consent can be obtained without risk to the child's health.

It seems reasonable to differentiate according to the nature of the medically indicated treatment, i.e. its severity and urgency, the risks involved and the possibility of permanent consequences. It is plausible also to acknowledge the exclusive consent of a discerning and competent minor with regard to routine treatment of minor importance.[39]

The difficulty in finding a solution to the problem can ultimately be put down to the dynamics of § 1626 sec. 2 BGB. A child's growing autonomy as a person with fundamental rights does not categorically exclude his need for help and protection. Even though in individual cases a child might demonstrate the required discernment, the parents' legal duty contained in Article 6 sec. 2 sent. 1 GG however renders the necessity of a joint consent by both child and parents indispensable. The protection by the State, as provided for in Article 6 sec. 2 sent. 2 GG, remains unsatisfactory since there is no legal provision offering a solution apart from § 1666 BGB.

The problem even gains a fourth dimension if the medical procedure indicated for the minor constitutes an abortion; in addition to the above-mentioned conflicting interests (the parent's opinion, the objective well-being of the child, a minor's right to self-determination) the concern here is also for the right to life of the unborn child.

---

[32]   (= Arzneimittelgesetz) Pharmaceutical Products Act.

[33]   In this sense see also Staudinger (Peschel-Gutzeit), § 1626 no. 96.

[34]   See Belling, *FuR* 1990, 68 (76); Reuter, *FamRZ* 1969, 622 (625); Laufs, Arztrecht p. 202 (5. ed. München 1993); Laufs/Uhlenbruck, Handbuch des Arztrechts, § 139 no. 32 (München 1992).

[35]   BT-Drucks. 7/2060, p. 4, 17ff.

[36]   BT-Drucks. 8/2788, p. 45.

[37]   Bundesgerichtshof (BGH).

[38]   *BGHZ* 29, 33 (37); *BGH NJW* 1972, 335 (337); see also *BayObLG FamRZ* 1987, 87.

[39]   Flume, Allg. Teil des Bürgerlichen Rechts, 2. Bd. (Das Rechtsgeschäft), p. 219f. (4. ed. Berlin 1992).

The Higher Regional Court in Hamm[40] had to decide the following case on July 16, 1998. A 16-year-old schoolgirl was 11 weeks' pregnant. The biological father of the child was allegedly a 15-year-old scholar. The girl wished to abort the child but her mother refused her consent. She indicated her intention to support her daughter with all necessary means.

The question at hand is whether the child requires her mother's approval in order to have an abortion.[41] An abortion in German law is sanctioned if it is performed by a doctor within 12 weeks of conception and if the pregnant woman produces a document certifying that she has received counselling, at least three days prior to the abortion. This system of mandatory counselling, bound to a time limit, is complemented by the following indicators for an abortion. Under the criminal law, an abortion does not require prior counselling, but has to be performed within the 12-week limit in order to be lawful. After this time limit has elapsed, an abortion still remains lawful if it was performed for medical or social reasons.

An abortion in all cases nevertheless requires the consent of the pregnant woman who is mature enough to appreciate the facts and to judge accordingly. In this regard, the woman has to be capable of medical self-determination and of weighing up her own legal interests and the right to life of the unborn child. In accordance with these increased requirements, the Higher Regional Court in Hamm held that the 16-year-old schoolgirl, even though she had the capacity to consent to the abortion, nevertheless required the additional approval of her custodian as an abortion would constitute an impairment of her physical integrity with far-reaching, physical and psychological effects. The fact that the custodial rights of the parents take priority is justified by the minor's need for protection regarding a decision 'that demands too much of her in respect of its ethical and moral meaning, even though at that moment she might think herself capable of taking such a decision'.[42]

The local court in Schlüchtern, in a case with similar facts, had previously found the custodians' approval to be unnecessary. This decision followed a thorough examination which had indicated that the minor girl was mentally and morally mature enough to appreciate the nature and implications of an abortion.[43]

This view is not acceptable. An abortion, according to the above criteria constituting an operation possibly inducing physical and psychological harm, demands the additional approval of the parents. An absolute lack of parental guidance is to be regarded as utterly irresponsible considering that abortion involves a decision over the life and death of another human being. The legal interests in question further require absolute certainty in the law regarding the validity of consent; the minor's maturity, however, remains an issue to be determined in each individual case by the respective consultant. In the above case decided by the Higher Regional Court in Hamm, the 16-year-old girl required her mother's approval in order to render her own consent to the abortion legally effective.

---

[40] OLG Hamm, *NJW* 1998, 3424.

[41] There is general consensus, however, that if the minor on the other hand intends to carry her child to term, the minor's parents cannot force her to have an abortion. In order to protect the minor's right to self-determination, the Family Court may take the necessary steps, in accordance with § 1666 BGB, against measures taken by the parents and doctors. See AG Dorsten *DA Vorm* 1978, 131; Staudinger (Peschel-Gutzeit) § 1626 no. 99; Reiserer, *FamRZ* 1991, 1136 (1140).

[42] OLG Hamm *NJW* 1998, 3424 (3425); similar *AG Celle MedR* 1988, 41 (41f.); Reiserer, *FamRZ* 1991, 1136 (1141), which considers the approval of one parent as sufficient.

[43] AG Schlüchtern *FamRZ* 1998, 968 (969); also LG München *FamRZ* 1979, 850; Staudinger (Peschel-Gutzeit) § 1626 no. 100; Belling/Eberl, *FuR* 1995, 287 (292).

According to § 1666 BGB, the Higher Regional Court however has the authority to dispense with the required parental approval if the denial of consent poses a direct threat to the physical and mental well-being of the child, thus constituting an abuse of parental guardianship. The German Constitutional Court, in 1993, stated that unborn life constitutes an independent legal interest which warrants protection by the Constitution.[44] It is therefore also protected from its mother. Even though an abortion can in certain circumstances be lawful, it is nevertheless considered as wrongful during the entire duration of the pregnancy and is therefore regarded as legally prohibited. If a parent, according to the Higher Regional Court in Hamm, asks its child to carry on with the pregnancy, then this alone does not constitute an impairment of the child's well-being since she herself is obliged to respect the right to life of the unborn child.[45] An impairment of the child's well-being, in accordance with § 1666 BGB, can be considered at best if the parents refuse to provide their pregnant daughter with the necessary help and support.[46] This, however, did not occur in the above case. Apart from the reason brought forward by the OLG Hamm, an impairment of the child's well-being is to be considered present, in accordance with § 1666 BGB, if the abortion is justifiable for criminal, social or medical reasons.[47]

Even though § 1626 sec. 2 BGB promotes a balance between the parents' rights and the child's growing fundamental rights, it merely has the effect of an internal educational maxim, bound by the limits of § 1666 BGB. A certain degree of interference by the custodian is unavoidable and necessary for minor's own protection, as soon as her conduct involves the legal interest of a third party, such as the life of an unborn child.

IV   REPRESENTATION OF MENTALLY INCAPACITATED PERSONS REGARDING THE TERMINATION OF MEDICAL TREATMENT

The Higher Regional Court in Frankfurt had to decide the following case on July 15, 1998.[48] An 85-year-old woman, as the result of a cerebral infarct, fell into a permanent coma, involving a complete loss of mobility and an inability to communicate. The woman was hospitalised and received artificial alimentation by means of a nasogastric tube. An improvement of her condition was not to be expected. She had lost the ability to express her will and the treating physicians were not certain as to whether the woman had to endure pain and suffering. Her daughter wished to stop the treatment by withdrawing the gastric tube. As a consequence of the energy deficiency – while maintaining a constant supply of liquid – the patient would however die in a matter of weeks or months.

Against the historic background of crimes committed by the National Socialists, the German public today takes a very critical stand regarding the issue of euthanasia. The absolute right to life, contained in the German Constitution,[49] is in direct conflict with the inhumane concept of an 'unworthy life'. Advances in medical technology and intensive care, on the other hand, threaten to degrade the patient who may become no more than an object of advancing medical technology. Euthanasia in Germany has not been regulated by the legislature. The judicial trend at present is towards favouring an extension of

---

44   The so called 'Fristenlösungsurteil', *BVerfGE* 88, 203 (255f.).

45   OLG Hamm *NJW* 1998, 3424 (3425).

46   See LG Berlin *FamRZ* 1980, 285 (286f.).

47   Similar Scherer, *FamRZ* 1997, 589 (592f.); opposing Siedhoff, *FamRZ* 1998, 8 (11).

48   OLG Hamm *NJW* 1998, 3424 (3425).

49   Article 2 sec. 2 sent. 1 GG: 'Everybody has a right to life and physical integrity'.

legally permitted euthanasia, while trying to find an appropriate solution to the conflict between the patient's right to self-determination[50] and the State's duty to safeguard human life. The position is that mankind should benefit from medical progress without becoming its victim.

A killing, within the meaning of § 212 StGB,[51] is every causation of death, including every insignificant shortening of life. It follows therefore, that strictly speaking, any hastening of the dying process constitutes a killing. § 216 StGB (voluntary euthanasia) provides that every deliberate and active shortening of life constitutes the criminal offence of manslaughter – even if the victim has previously expressed a wish for it.

Certain activities, however, are directed at alleviating the process of dying for the patient and as such do not constitute a criminal offence.[52] The easing of pain of a dying patient, for example, which has an unintended and inevitable life-shortening effect, is not considered a criminal offence, if performed with the express or presumed wish of the patient (indirect euthanasia).[53] To let the patient die, by abstaining from or abandoning treatment already instituted only to prolong further the natural process of dying, likewise does not seem worthy of punishment (passive euthanasia). The abandonment of treatment may be effected by the patient's express or presumed refusal; it is orientated in the right of a terminally ill person to die in dignity, while respecting his claim to self-determination. Both types of legalised euthanasia, however, require that the process of dying has already begun and that death, in the physician's view, is inevitable and will occur within a short time.

The facts of the above case (OLG Frankfurt) indicated that the process of dying had not yet begun; the concern here was therefore not to assist a person, already in the process of dying, but rather to allow him to die. In a controversial judgement in 1995, the Federal High Court of Justice (BGH) held that the termination of life-sustaining treatment for long-term comatose patients constitutes a legal form of euthanasia.[54] In these cases, the presumed will of the incompetent, terminally ill patient is decisive. There are however strict conditions attached to determination of the patient's presumed wishes. The court in the above case, for example, refused to deduce the patient's presumed will from a statement she had made ten years before; in the presence of her son she had said in response to a certain television programme reporting on patients in need of permanent medical care, that she would not want to end this way.[55] A patient's presumed will, is rather to be inferred from a conflation of his past oral and written statements, his religious and moral convictions, the age-related life expectancy and the degree of pain suffered. In the case of doubt, the protection of human life has priority.

The OLG Frankfurt was confronted with the task of determining the presumed will of the 85-year-old woman. The court, in searching for the patient's presumed will, tries to balance the conflict between the absolute sanctity of life on the one hand, and the right to dignity and personal autonomy, on the other hand. In doing so, the issue of substitution or representation of the patient's will by a third party, increases in relevance. To facilitate such representation, German civil law provides adults, unable to express their will, with

---

50   As an expression of fundamental rights to human dignity (Article 1 sec. 1 GG) and the free development of the personality (Article 2 sec. 1 GG).

51   German Criminal Code.

52   There is a general consensus on this issue. Its dogmatic justification however is controversial, see Lackner *StGB* (21. ed. 1995) preliminary statement to § 211 no. 7 with further notes.

53   E.g. the injection of morphine; see also *BGH NJW* 1997, 807 discussed by Verrel, *MedR* 1997, 248.

54   *BGH NJW* 1995, 204; see Schön, *NStZ* 1995, 153; Vogel, *MDR* 1995, 337; Merkel, *ZStW* 107 (1995), 545.

55   *BGH NJW* 1995, 204 f.

the legal institution of guardianship for persons of full age (§§ 1896-1908k BGB). Since the 85-year-old woman, as a result of her illness, was incapacitated, the Guardianship Court had appointed her daughter as legal guardian. The guideline for the guardian in the fulfilment of his duties is the well-being of the patient (§ 1901 sec. 2, 3 BGB) which is ascertained by the patient's wishes and convictions in life. In determining the 'whether' and 'how' of medical treatment, the guardian is to exercise the incompetent's right to self-determination on his behalf. The guardian becomes spokesman for the patient's presumed will which, in cases where treatment is terminated, must be ascertained carefully and in accordance with the above-mentioned criteria set out by the BGH.

While the respective contracts with the physician or hospital can easily be concluded by the third party with his power of representation, the consent to interfere with the patient's physical integrity protects the physician from incurring delictual and criminal responsibility. In the case of a risky and possibly also life-threatening procedure, the representative needs, according to § 1904 sec. 1 sent. 1 BGB, the additional authorisation by the guardianship court to consent on behalf of the patient. An exception to this rule is contained in § 1904 sec. 1 sent. 2 BGB. According to this provision, authorisation by the court is not required in cases where any delay of the treatment would endanger the life and health of the patient. Situations of indirect euthanasia, where the dying process has already begun, satisfy this condition.[56] This kind of imminent danger was however not present in the case before the OLG Frankfurt and § 1904 sec. 1 sent. 2 BGB therefore did not apply.

It is questionable, however, whether the termination of life-sustaining treatment actually falls within the scope of § 1904 sec. 1 sent. 1 BGB. If this question is answered in the negative, then the daughter's decision, to withdraw her mother's treatment, is definitely binding. By demanding the additional authorisation by the guardianship court for justification of the infringement of a patient's physical integrity, the provision thus strengthens the personal element of guardianship and the patient's self-determination.[57] The provision further expresses a certain degree of distrust for the unsupervised co-operation between guardian and physician. This, in any case, cannot be effectively supervised as in the end even the Guardianship Court is forced to orientate itself on the opinion of the medical expert.[58] Apart from diagnostic treatment, § 1904 sec. 1 sent. 1 BGB, according to its exact wording, also includes therapeutic treatment which is aimed at restoring the patient's health, the palliation of the illness, its prevention and other forms of treatment which are not necessarily medically indicated.[59]

Conceptually, though, this presupposes an act as opposed to an omission. Furthermore, the guardian's refusal of any of the treatments expressly mentioned in § 1904 sec.1 sent. 1 BGB, does not require any additional authorisation by the guardianship court.[60] § 1904 BGB finally presupposes medical treatment with inevitable and unintended life-endangering side-effects. The purpose of the treatment is supposed to be the restoration of health and not – as is the case with the cessation of treatment – an intended shortening of life.[61] As a result of the above, the AG Hanau[62] decided, in a case

---

[56]   Assion, BtPrax 1998, 162 (163).
[57]   BT-Drucks. 11/4528, p. 70ff., 140ff.
[58]   MüKo-Schwab § 1904 no. 1.
[59]   Included are plastic surgery and abortion without medical indication, compare MüKo-Schwab § 1904 no. 10.
[60]   Wagenitz/Engers, comment on OLG Frankfurt *FamRZ* 1998, 1256 (1257).
[61]   See AG Ratzeburg SchlHA 1999, 50 (51); Laufs, *NJW* 1998, 3399 (3400).
[62]   AG = Amtsgericht, local court.

with similar facts, against the analogous application of § 1904 BGB, on the basis that this would force the judge to make a decision over life or death. This was not intended by the legislature and it could not be expected from a judge, for legal ethical reasons and legal history.[63] It was further reasoned that the representation of the patient in his will to die is questionable, since this constitutes a highly personal decision comparable with the type of action,[64] listed in § 1903 sec. 2 BGB, for which there may be no representation. This argument is strengthened by the consideration that even the consent by a third party regarding a life-endangering infringement of a patient's physical integrity is not possible without qualification.[65]

The BGH, on the other hand, argues with the degree of risk involved regarding the medical treatment. Consequently, the termination of treatment which would surely cause the patient's death in due time, deprives the representative of his exclusive authority to decide.[66] This teleological approach of interpreting the provisions of the guardianship law, to safeguard the patient's autonomy, is in accordance with the intention of the legislature.[67] The OLG Frankfurt, assuming an unintended loophole in the law, likewise approves of an analogous application of § 1904 BGB with regard to the withdrawal of treatment.[68]

After all, the aim of withdrawing medical treatment is not to end the patient's life but to exercise his will instead, even if this results in his death. The issue here is thus not primarily the unconscious patient's right to life, but instead his right to self-determination. It follows from this that the patient himself decides over life or death and not the judge. The court rather purports to establish the patient's will, in order to guarantee representation by the guardian, which is orientated in the patient's well-being.[69] A course of conduct with the foreseeable causation of death may well be in the patient's best interest if the concept of well-being balances the conflicting claims between human dignity and the sanctity of life.[70] The patient's will determines the physician's mandate and it is a limitation on life-prolonging treatment. An analogous application of § 1904 BGB effects an official determination of the patient's will, carried out by the court, functioning as a neutral body and thereby guaranteeing a high degree of objectivity and rationality. Thereby, arbitrary decisions to withdraw or withhold palliative care and a disrespect for the patient's wishes for fear of legal consequences are avoided.[71] The decision by the representative may not disregard the patient's will, as subsequent criminal sanctioning would, in this regard, be of no avail.[72]

The patient's right to self-determination has been strengthened by the legislature through the implementation of the Act reforming the existing guardianship law[73] which provides for so-called advanced healthcare directives and the appointment of proxy-

---

[63] AG Hanau, *BtPrax* 1997, 82 (83); see also LG München (judgment of 22.4.1999), *Frankfurter Allgemeine Zeitung*, 23.4.1999, p. 9.

[64] E.g. entering into a marriage and the execution of a will.

[65] § 1904 sent. 1 BGB; see in comparison the bonos mores as limitation to one's own declaration of intent in § 228 *StGB*.

[66] *BGH NJW* 1995, 204 (205).

[67] BT-Drucks. 11, 4528, p. 52, 142.

[68] OLG Frankfurt *NJW* 1998, 2747 (2748).

[69] See Rehborn, *MDR* 1998, 1464 (1466f.).

[70] Contrary, Jürgens, *BtPrax* 1998, 159.

[71] Verrel, *JR* 1999, 5 (8); Coeppicus, *NJW* 1998, 3381 (3383); Knieper, *BtPrax* 1998, 160f.

[72] Knieper, *NJW* 1998, 2720.

[73] Betreuungsrechtsänderungsgesetz, BGBl. I 1998, p. 1580; compare Government draft BR-Drucks. 960/96; Wagenitz/Engers, *FamRZ* 1998, 1273; Schellhorn, *FuR* 1997, 139.

decision makers.[74] Today, numerous institutions exist that offer printed forms and law firms increasingly regard advance directives and mandates for proxy-decision makers as a growing alternative to the officially appointed guardian. The German Medical Association likewise, in its directives on euthanasia of 1998, draws attention to the likelihood of a physician's commitment to the advanced declaration by the patient.[75]

The appointment of a proxy-decision maker generally requires no formalities. Risky medical procedures or institutionalisation, however are an exception. Therefore, according to §§ 1904 sec. 2, 1906 sec. 5 sent. 1 BGB, a written statement describing the purported measure is required. For this purpose, both agent and guardian need the additional authorisation by the guardianship court. This requirement, with regard to the above considerations, must also apply to situations where palliative care is terminated.

The mandate for representation as an alternative to guardianship, however, does not solve the dilemma of the situation. It merely places the decision in the hands of the authorised agent and the guardianship court. Even the anticipatory decision made by the patient, while still competent, can after all only serve as evidence for his presumed will. The strength of this evidence depends very much on the likelihood that the patient has changed his mind in the meantime.

Although the analogous application of § 1904 BGB is to be approved regarding the termination of medical treatment, there is a need for specific legislation regulating the determination of a patient's will by the guardianship court, and with regard to its qualitative demands.[76] The present legal vacuum in the areas of criminal and civil law mirrors the complexity of the issue, with which Germany has a particularly hard time in coping, as a consequence of its recent history.

---

[74]   §§ 1896 sec. 2 sent. 2, 1904 sec. 2, 1906 sec. 5, 1908f sec.1 no. 2a *BGB*.

[75]   Copy of the directives in *NJW* 1998, 3406; these were influenced by the respective provisions of the Swiss Academy for Medical Sciences (SAMW), see *NJW* 1996, 767.

[76]   Similar Bienwald, comment on *OLG Frankfurt FamRZ* 1998, 1138f.

GREECE

SPERM, OVUM, AND FERTILISED OVUM OUTSIDE THE HUMAN BODY: THEIR LEGAL STATUS AND TREATMENT IN MODERN GREEK CIVIL LAW

(Problems relating to *in vitro* fertilisation)

*Efie Kounougeri-Manoledaki**

I   INTRODUCTION

By contrast with what happens in *in vivo* fertilisation, where human reproductive material is created, moves, and functions inside the body, in *in vitro* fertilisation the sperm, the ovum, and the fertilised ovum are outside the human body at some stage. The human reproductive material[1] thus acquires a certain independent existence that is maintained for the whole time from when the sperm and the ovum are taken from the man's and the woman's bodies respectively to when the fertilised ovum is implanted in the woman's uterus, whereupon conception takes place and pregnancy begins. In this final stage, the legal problems that arise are the same as when fertilisation takes place *in vivo*; for instance, the question of the civil protection afforded the *nasciturus*, which has been resolved in Greek law, as indeed it has in the law of other countries. The difficulties lie, therefore, in the stage *before* implantation, which can also be very long, owing to the possibility of cryopreservation.[2] During this stage, what is the legal status of the sperm, the ovum, and the fertilised ovum outside the human body, and what legal treatment should civil law reserve for them?

In Greece to date, there is no legislative text nor legal precedent regarding this issue. There has been a great deal of theoretical discussion, however, and it is possible, on the basis of these discussions and the general precepts of Greek civil law and of Greek law in general, to arrive at the following conclusions.

---

[*]   Professor of Civil Law, Faculty of Law, University of Thessaloniki.

[1]   The term '*genetic* material' is usually used in the legal literature, but it is incorrect when referring to *reproductive* cells, i.e. sperm and ovum. These constitute *reproductive* material, whereas 'genetic material' is DNA, which is precisely the primary genetic material of all cells and contains in codified form all the information that defines inherited characteristics. See British Medical Association, *Our Genetic Future: The Science and the Ethics of Genetic Technology*, translated into Greek by K. Stamatopoulos, published by Lexima (1998), 23, 47ff.

[2]   It must be clarified here that, even when fertilisation takes place within the body (*in vivo*), rather than outside the body (*in vitro*), the moment of *fertilisation* (when sperm and ovum unite), which takes place in one of the Fallopian tubes, is to be distinguished from the later phase of the *implantation* of the fertilised ovum in the uterus, which is when *conception* occurs.

II   THE LEGAL STATUS AND TREATMENT OF THE SPERM

The prevailing view in Greece is that any member or element of the human body that is definitively separated from the body becomes a self-existent thing. Such things belong thereafter to the person from whom they were separated, by analogy with the stipulation regarding the acquisition of fruits, which states that the ownership of products or other component parts of a thing still belongs to the owner of the thing after their separation (Civil Code 1064).[3] On this basis, it is not hard to accept that human sperm outside the body is a thing, since it does present all the attributes that characterise a thing in Greek law: it is corporeal (i.e. it has material substance); it is self-existent, since, when it is separated from the man's body, it constitutes an independent entity in space; and it is impersonal, since, when it is dissociated from the person of its donor, it loses its personal nature, nor, certainly, can it acquire a personal nature from the fact that, if a number of actions and natural events take place (fertilisation, implantation-conception, pregnancy, birth), it may lead in the future to the creation of a human being. This creation is, unquestionably, the *natural purpose* of the sperm; but it is so distant and uncertain and depends on so many other factors that it does not suffice to give extracorporeal sperm a personal character.

Lastly, sperm is certainly susceptible of control: it is not inaccessible to a person, and that person may restrict and control it. The very possibility of *in vitro* fertilisation by a donor other than the husband, who *donates* his sperm to the couple, shows that sperm is susceptible of consistent delimitation, control, and transfer, thus presenting all four specific characteristics of a thing as defined in law.[4]

On the other hand, of course, since sperm constitutes reproductive material, it unquestionably expresses the donor's ability to acquire natural offspring, and, insofar as the ability to acquire natural offspring is an expression of the right to develop freely one's personality, sperm is also an aspect of the donor's personality,[5] which is certainly assaulted when, for instance, the sperm is destroyed against his will. Therefore, the legal status of sperm as a thing that belongs to the donor, by analogy with Article 1064 of the Civil Code, does not preclude its also being defined as an aspect of the donor's personality. This is also the case, after all, with other objects, such as a painting, for instance, which has a dual status for the painter – i.e. it is both a thing (belonging to him/her) and an aspect of his/her personality, so that its destruction, apart from being an assault on the painter's ownership, may also constitute an assault on the painter's personality.

From all this, finally, it follows that sperm is an *object* of rights and duties. In other words, in no circumstances may sperm be regarded as a person, i.e. a subject of rights and duties, but it is certainly an element that is controlled and defined by a person, without being identified with him.

Apart from the nature of the donor's claims in the event of its destruction, the legal status of sperm as a thing, as defined above, also means that it may constitute an object of juridical acts concluded by the donor. One initial such act is the contract for the deposition and cryopreservation of the sperm in a clinic or an independent sperm bank.

---

[3]   Sourlas, in *Interpretation of the Civil Code* (in Greek), Introductory article 57s–60, No. 50; Dimakou, in *Civil Code* by Georgiadis and Stathopoulos (in Greek) article 947, No. 18.

[4]   See, for example, A. Georgiadis, *Property Law* (in Greek), vol. I (1991), 78.

[5]   Christakakou-Fotiadi, 'Genetics and Protection of the Personality (Thoughts Provoked by the BGH Decision of 9 Nov. 1993)' (in Greek), *Kritiki Epitheorissi* 1994/2, 353ff., 358ff., 364; Christodoulou, 'Genetic Truth and Law in Parentage' (in Greek), *Kritiki Epitheorissi* 1995/1, 263, 264 n. 23.

Opinion is divided over the legal nature of this contract; but the best approach is to accept that its nature depends on the individual circumstances. If, for instance, the donor deposits his sperm simply for conservation in the frozen state, because he is afraid that he may lose his reproductive ability at some future date, it must be regarded as a mixed work and deposit contract (CC 681, 822). If, however, the sperm is handed over for cryopreservation with a view to its being used in the immediate future in successive attempts at *in vitro* fertilisation directed at the donor's wife, then it is simply a work contract, i.e. a contract with the doctor who will carry out the *in vitro* fertilisation, the terms of which include the incidental obligation to freeze the sperm.

In the former case, particularly, the status of the sperm as a thing is a *basic premise* underlying the concept of conservation and the deposit contract (CC 822: 'the depositary takes delivery from another person of a movable thing with a view to keeping it'). If, however, the sperm is culpably destroyed while it is in the clinic or the sperm bank, then, apart from constituting a refusal to perform the contract and an unlawful act, the offence being an assault on the ownership of the sperm, this also constitutes an unlawful assault on the personality of the donor, who is deprived of the possibility of acquiring natural offspring and is thus entitled to seek reparation for moral injury under the terms of CC 59, which asserts that when one's personality is unlawfully assaulted one may seek reparation for non-material damage due to moral injury.

Another juridical act which the sperm donor may draw up is the *donation* of the sperm to another couple, with a view to *in vitro* fertilisation being performed on their behalf, i.e. the fertilising of the woman with sperm that does not belong to her husband. Here the provider of the sperm is termed the *donor* and the couple the *donee* (if the donor is known, of course). In this case, the couple seeking *in vitro* fertilisation draws up a work contract with the doctor who is to undertake the whole process, and a contract with the donor of the sperm, which, though it is difficult to regard it as the kind of 'donation' discussed in CC 496 (which regulates the transfer of 'property'), may be described as a *peculiar donation or gratuity* and lead to the analogous implementation of certain provisions regarding donations, such as that in CC 499¨1, for instance, which states that the donor shall be liable only for wilful misconduct and gross negligence. Furthermore, it goes without saying that after the sperm has been donated its ownership passes to the donees, and it is now *their* personality which is expressed through the sperm, which will lead to the acquisition of their own offspring (in the case of the husband, in law only (CC 1463¨2 para. 1 and 1465¨1), and in the case of the wife biologically too). It is the donees, therefore, who may henceforth have a claim for damages or reparation for moral injury on the basis of the provisions covering either culpable non-performance of a contract or unlawful acts (CC 914, 932) or unlawful assault on the personality (CC 57, 59).

However, in the case of artifical fertilisation by donor, the latter is usually anonymous,[6] which is to say that the couple have direct contact only with the doctor and the clinic which owns or liaises with the sperm bank from which the couple will obtain the sperm. In this case, the 'donation' of the sperm has already been made, by the donor to the clinic; but at all events, the premise remains that the sperm is a thing that is 'donated' by its owner–donor. And of course the possibility of 'transferring' the sperm to a third party is quite in keeping with its status as an aspect of the donor's personality too,

---

[6] Opinion is sharply divided over whether or not the donor should be anonymous. Persuasive arguments are presented both for and against anonymity: see Kriari-Katrani, *Biomedical Developments and Constitutional Law* (in Greek) (1994), 100, 130ff., 132ff., who also discusses the question of the child's right to know his/her antecedents, which is connected with the issue of anonymity.

in the context of the free development of which the donor has the right to self-determination and therefore may make a 'gift' of his sperm with a view to expressing his personality in *this* way. However, without the parallel definition of the sperm as a thing also, it would be difficult to find provisions regulating the donor's responsibility for actual defects in his sperm. At this point, however, it should be stressed that, if it is fair that the donor's own responsibility for defects in the sperm should be lessened (i.e. that there should be no liability in the event of slight negligence on his part, by analogy with Article 499¨1),[7] the same does not apply to the doctor, who (regardless of whether the donor is known or anonymous) is under the obligation to *examine* the sperm before using it, and may himself be held accountable, during the execution of the work contract, for slight negligence. Another point that must be made clear is that during the period when the sperm, having been given to the clinic, is still in the clinic and has not been selected by the clinic for use by a specific couple, it is only *in the ownership* of the clinic and does not, of course, express anyone's right to acquire offspring. Therefore, the sperm is *also* an aspect of its owner's personality only insofar as that owner is a natural person who is going to use it to acquire offspring.

Some people also link the legal status of sperm with the question of whether it can be the subject of a juridical act drawn up with a view to financial gain, and more specifically whether, apart from donating it, it would be possible to draw up a contract by which the donor *sold* his sperm. Scruples about the validity of such a contract naturally reflect the fear that it might be immoral. But where exactly would the immorality lie in this case? Sperm is an impersonal thing, as the foregoing analysis has shown, so the immorality of selling it is not connected with that.[8] As far as the donor is concerned, the possibility of his disposing of it as he wishes, and to his own advantage moreover, certainly does not constitute an immoral assault on his personality. So if the sale of sperm is indeed an immoral act in law, this is not because of its legal status as a thing that is also an aspect of the donor's personality, but obviously because of *the donor's relationship with the purchaser*. It is an *exploitative* relationship, because the donor is demanding financial gain in order to satisfy the purchaser's existential need to acquire offspring, despite the fact that he, the donor, is simply 'disposing' of his own *natural* substance without being burdened by having to perform any task and without losing any capability, different from or the same as the one he is offering.[9]

Any contract for the sale of sperm to an individual who wishes to have children must therefore be deemed invalid (CC 178), because it is not socially acceptable to seek remuneration for helping one's fellow beings to correct a fault of nature and have children. It is also significant that the donor is offering this assistance without himself shouldering any obligation, as is apparent from the fact that it is certainly not considered immoral to draw up juridical acts relating to sperm which also help people to acquire offspring, but include *medical services* offered to them (such as the contract for cryopreservation, for instance, or for the whole process of *in vitro* fertilisation), with a view to gain. Payment for medical services is, after all, commonplace in the world of the free market; and it is worth noting here that, precisely in the context of the liberal economic system, it has been suggested by some legal scholars that the sale of sperm should be considered valid, because its prohibition would lead to the creation of a black

---

[7]   Papadopoulou-Klamari, in *Civil Code* by Georgiadis and Stathopoulos, articles 1463–4, No. 107.

[8]   But see Katroungalos, *The Right to Life and to Death* (in Greek) (1993), 126–30; Marinos, 'Genetic Engineering and the Law' (in Greek), *Elliniki Dikaiossini*, 39 (1998), 1229.

[9]   Compare Kounougeri-Manoledaki, 'Establishing Parentage in the Case of Surrogate Pregnancy: A Legislative Proposal' (in Greek), *Harmenopoulos* 48 (1994), 1234.

market in sperm. But this argument may easily be turned around, because a prohibition on the sale of sperm could also encourage 'donations' of sperm, and that would be desirable. So *also* on the grounds that someone is unlikely to give away something he can sell, it is advisable not to permit sperm to be sold to someone who wishes to have children.

From what has been said above, it is clear that the invalidity of the sale of sperm is related not to its *legal status* but to its *natural purpose*, which is (via other processes as well) the eventual creation of human life. This natural purpose may well raise further debate about juridical acts relating to sperm: questions such as whether some of these acts genuinely serve or fundamentally conflict with the interests of any child that might be born. From this point of view, it is true, one might express qualms even about the admissibility of *donating* sperm, i.e. whether it is advisable to permit *in vitro* fertilisation using a donor other than the husband or whether this too should be prohibited, or at least controlled, in case, given certain specific circumstances, it is not in the child's interests to be born by this means. Certainly, Greek law has not, at least so far, been influenced by these considerations; on the contrary, *in vitro* fertilisation using sperm donated by a third party seems to be recognised – indirectly but clearly – by the Greek legislator, since Article 1471"2 No. 2 of the Civil Code (which stipulates that a husband who has given his consent for his wife to undergo artificial fertilisation cannot disclaim paternity) is of practical significance precisely when donated sperm has been used. But even in the hypothetical event of a change in Greek legislation on this point at some future date – perhaps prohibiting or in some way restricting *in vitro* fertilisation by third-party donor, in the context, for instance, of a new internationally more conservative attitude to assisted reproduction – any prohibition or restrictions imposed would spring not from the *legal status* of the sperm but from an assessment of the interests of the future child, which interests are associated with the *natural purpose* of the sperm.

Finally, the child's interests are a criterion that is supplementary to the legal status of the sperm with regard to another sperm-related issue: whether fertilisation is permissible using the (obviously frozen) sperm of the donor after his death. Here too there is no specific regulation in Greek law. However, within the framework of Greek civil law as it currently stands, the following thoughts come to mind. First of all, it is clear that the question of the fate of the sperm after the donor's death is bound up with the question of whether or not it can be inherited. This in turn is connected with the legal status of the sperm; but the problem that arises here is that the sperm has a dual legal status, relating to two diametrically opposed solutions. On the basis of the status of sperm as a thing, we have to accept that it is an inheritable object and that after the death of the donor, it is his heirs who should decide what should be done with it. But, on the basis of the status of sperm as an aspect of the donor's personality, and given that specific manifestations of the personality are not inheritable,[10] we have to accept that sperm cannot be inherited.[11] Of the two views, I think we have to uphold the second: insofar as the acquiring of offspring is a thoroughly personal matter, it does not seem acceptable that the donor's heirs should decide about it as such; so with regard to the question of whether or not sperm can be inherited, its legal status as an aspect of its donor's personality should take precedence.

---

[10] See, for example, Papantoniou, *Law of Succession* (in Greek), 5th ed. (1989), 44.
[11] Papachristou, 'Artificial insemination *post mortem*' (in Greek), in *Afieroma ston N. Papantoniou* (1996), 649.

This conclusion, however, gives rise to further questions. If, for instance, the sperm has been frozen as part of the whole contract for *in vitro* fertilisation, in which the wife too has entered into an agreement with the doctor, what part does she play in the decision about the fate of the sperm? Will she alone decide, as the only remaining party to the contract, since, because the sperm is not inheritable, any contractual obligation regarding the husband will no longer exist? Should account be taken, in any case, of any specifically declared or hypothetical desire on the part of the husband in the event of his death, as specified in Article 7¨3 of law 1383/1983 regarding the *post mortem* removal of tissues and organs, which also are not inheritable? Or should the overriding criterion be the interests of the child, in which case many people would argue that it is not in its interests to be born as a designated orphan, particularly in view of the 'morbid' aspect of *post mortem* fertilisation?

It is clear that this last factor, the necessity of ensuring the interests of the child that may be born, is crucial; and the opinion is very often expressed that the child's interest in not being born at all in such circumstances takes precedence over *both* the woman's interest in bearing a child by her deceased husband *and* the husband's interest in perpetuating his species posthumously. Certainly, it is not totally unfounded from a legal point of view to argue that the wife also should have a say in the *post mortem* fate of the sperm, if she too is a party to the cryopreservation contract.[12] Neither is it to accept, particularly in this case, the need to protect posthumously the personality of the deceased 'in life', so that his position on this specific issue 'in life' is also of interest (which, on the one hand, is not irreconcilable with the fact that the manifestations of the personality may not be inherited and, on the other, complements the rule that the right to a personality does, after all, presuppose the existence of a person and may be exercised only by living people). All the same, the interests of the child itself should probably carry special weight in the decision about *post mortem* fertilisation, and it is another question whether those interests should be assessed by the doctor or some other body (the court, for instance) or whether in the end, precisely in order to protect the child's interests, we should move towards a complete legislative ban on *post mortem* fertilisation (as is the case in Germany and France).[13] But be that as it may, two things are certain: first, that sperm is not inheritable, by virtue of its nature *as an aspect of personality*, and therefore the deceased donor's heirs, as such, may not decide about it; and second, that, if it is eventually decided that the child's interests dictate that it should not be born by fertilisation with the sperm of a deceased donor, the doctor may destroy the sperm after the donor's death with no moral qualms, because sperm is *also a thing*.

III   THE LEGAL STATUS AND TREATMENT OF THE OVUM

As far as defining the ovum as a thing is concerned, there is one consideration that may give us pause: the ovum is separated from the woman's body, certainly, but it is destined to re-enter her body, so that in fact it is not definitively separated from it. When it re-

---

[12]   It might be argued that the wife may legitimately have a say in the fate of her dead husband's sperm, whether or not she is a party to the cryopreservation contract, simply in view of the natural purpose of the sperm, which is to fertilise the ovum, which, when the donor is married, may reasonably be expected to be his wife's.

[13]   §4 (1) of the ESchG (Embryonenschutzgesetz, 1991). See also French laws 94/653 and 94/654 of July 29, 1994, and Dreifuss-Netter, 'Adoption ou assistance médicale à la procréation: quelles familles?', *Dalloz,* 1998, *Chronique,* 103.

enters the woman's body, however, it has been fertilised, and therefore is no longer the same as the unfertilised ovum, which has therefore, in fact, been definitively separated. On the basis of this latter observation, then, it may be argued that, in the framework of Greek law, the ovum too is a thing, since it too is impersonal, corporeal, self-existent, and susceptible of human control, and certainly it too is *also* an aspect of its donor's personality,[14] since it expresses her ability to acquire offspring. What has been said about the sperm applies equally to the ovum.

Certainly, as regards juridical acts that concern reproductive material as an object of rights and duties, a cryopreservation contract is almost never drawn up for ova that have not yet been fertilised, because the medical process involved is not free of risks for these: both the freezing and the reheating process may cause serious chromosomal abnormalities. Moreover, a contract for the sale of ova must be deemed immoral and therefore invalid (CC 178), for the same reason (as argued above) as the sale of sperm is immoral. Lastly, qualms should be expressed regarding the acceptability of the *donation* of an ovum as well, such as those expressed, for instance, in the German 'law for the protection of embryos' promulgated in 1991, which, in order to protect the interests of the child who may be born, permits *in vitro* fertilisation only in order to bring about pregnancy in the woman from whom the ovum was taken.[15] In all these cases, however, we are talking about weaknesses or prohibitions that relate not to the legal status of the ovum but either to its natural properties (with which the risks of cryopreservation are associated) or to its natural purpose, which, since this is the creation of offspring, connects it either with a third-party recipient (donee or purchaser) or with the potential child itself, in which case the questions of immorality and the child's interests arise again.

IV   THE LEGAL STATUS AND TREATMENT OF THE FERTILISED OVUM

Without a doubt, the most difficult legal definition is that of the fertilised ovum, because fertilisation moves the process one more step along the way to the creation of human life, and justifiably raises the question of whether the fertilised ovum is as entirely impersonal as the sperm or the ovum separately. In other words, after fertilisation, the problem arises whether some personal element begins to emerge in relation to the human being who will be born, and not simply with regard to the donors of the sperm and the ovum.

In this respect, it must first of all be made clear that, in Greek law, the fertilised ovum is not itself a 'person', because, according to Article 35 of the Civil Code, 'a person begins to exist as soon as he/she is *born* alive' (my italics), and this leaves no way for any other view that might place the start of a person's existence at some point in time other than birth.[16] Further, it is difficult to equate the fertilised ovum – prior to implantation in the uterus – with the *nasciturus*, or even to apply an intermediate legal definition to it, such as 'a developing person' or 'a potential person',[17] insofar as there are two fundamental differences, according to medical science, between the pre-implantation and the post-implantation stage. The first is that after implantation the likelihood of miscarriage is comparatively small, whereas the chances that the fertilised ovum will not

---

[14]   Christakakou-Fotiadi, 353ff., 358ff., 364; Christodoulou, *op. cit.*

[15]   ESchG § 1 para. 1, No. 2.

[16]   But see Christodoulou, 263; Androulidaki-Dimitriadi, 'Legal Problems in Artificial Fertilisation (Problems of Civil Law)' (in Greek), *Nomiko Vima* 34 (1986), 15.

[17]   See Païsidou, 'Cryopreserved Embryo: A Multidimensional Legal Issue in Biotechnology' (in Greek), *Elliniki Dikaiossini* 35 (1994), 1474.

even implant itself in the uterus are fifty-fifty,[18] which shows that the mere fertilisation of the ovum is not a decisive step even on the way to the creation of human life in general. The second difference is more crucial: only after implantation does 'individual human life' start to develop, because up to that point the fertilised ovum may split and produce twins or triplets, for instance.[19] This means that the mere fact of fertilisation is not sufficient for us to consider that the creation of individual human life has begun. This presupposes the development of the specific person's central nervous system – a process which takes place only within the uterus. Before implantation (which, starting on about the sixth day – in *in vivo* fertilisation – is achieved by the end of the thirteenth day after fertilisation),[20] medical science regards the fertilised ovum as merely a zygote, not yet an embryo. So it is wrong at this stage to use the term 'embryo' rather than 'fertilised ovum' or 'zygote', which terms better render the actuality of the initial mere synthesis or joining of the sperm and the ovum. The term 'embryo' refers to a more advanced stage, at which the creation of individual human life does in fact begin.

The fact that there is no individual human life, nor has it even begun to develop, before implantation – and therefore there is no embryo yet, only a fertilised ovum – accounts for the view that now fully prevails in the Greek theory of criminal law, namely that any acts performed before implantation do not not constitute abortion.[21] The same medical perception also lies behind the regulation in foreign legislation to the effect that experiments may be performed on fertilised ova only up to, and no later than, the fourteenth day after fertilisation (which is the period of time within which – in *in vivo* fertilisation – implantation takes place). After this, the fertilised ovum must be destroyed, even if the experiment has begun.[22] This regulation shows the sensitivity of foreign legislators towards the point at which individual human life begins. But there is no individual human life prior to implantation; the fertilised ovum may therefore be destroyed before this.

Does all this mean, then, that the fertilised ovum is a thing, just like the unfertilised ovum or the sperm? As regards this question (which also concerns the relationship of the fertilised ovum to the sperm or to the unfertilised ovum), no one can fail to accept that, apart from the differences between the stages before and after implantation, differences also exist between the stages before and after fertilisation. The first of these differences is that fertilisation is the point at which all the reproductive material required (according to the canons of medical science, so far at least) for the creation of human life comes together. Before fertilisation, the sperm alone or the ovum alone is not enough for the reproduction of the human species. This does not mean, however, that the fertilised ovum may not be defined as a thing, because this coming together of two things does not mean (far from it) that the composite element is not itself a thing. More important, therefore, is the second difference, which consists of the fact that the fertilisation of the ovum is the start of a dynamic development, or, to put it another way, a creative process that contrasts

[18]   See Nagler and Sämmer, 'Die In-Vitro-Fertilisation (IVF) und der Embryo-Transfer', in: Arthur Kaufman (ed.), *Moderne Medizin und Strafrecht* (1989), 191.

[19]   See previous note.

[20]   Nagler and Sämmer, *op. cit.*

[21]   See, for example, Filippidis, *Lessons of Criminal Law, Special Part II* (in Greek) (1981), 122; Symeonidou-Kastanidou, *Abortion as a Criminal Law Problem* (in Greek) (1984), 180, 181, 251; I. Manoledakis, *The 'Legal Good' as a Fundamental Concept of Criminal Law* (in Greek) (1998), 292. See also StGB § 218.1 para. 2: 'Handlungen, deren Wirkung vor Abschluß der Einnistung des befruchteten Eies in der Gebärmutter eintritt, gelten nicht als Schwangerschaftsabbruch im Sinne dieses Gesetzes'.

[22]   Swedish Act (1991) concerning measures for purposes of research or treatment involving fertilised human ova: section 2 § 1 para 1, section 2 § 2; Human Fertilisation and Embryology Act (1990), sections 3–3a, 4.

sharply with the static state of the reproductive cells, i.e. the sperm and the ovum, before they unite. But if this development is still in its initial stage, when it is far from certain whether human life (and how many human lives) will be created, the fact that the development starts in this stage is not enough, in my opinion, to invest the fertilised ovum with even the slightest personal character, even in the most general terms. And this means only one thing: that the fertilised ovum, as totally impersonal, and, of course, corporeal, self-existent, and susceptible of human control, may be defined in Greek civil law as a thing.

Quite apart from the correctness of this conclusion at the level of medical and legal principle, its expediency is obvious. To reject the legal status of the fertilised ovum as a thing in civil law would conflict with the modern and now fully prevailing view in Greek criminal law which holds that acts performed before implantation do not in any circumstances constitute abortion. In other words, even when fertilisation takes place within the body, before implantation the fertilised ovum is not regarded as a specific 'potential human being'. If, then, it were not accepted that the fertilised ovum is a thing, either civil law would appear to be out of step with criminal law, or the debate over abortion would have to recommence on a more conservative basis and the ground gained on this issue would be at risk. Furthermore, while we are on the subject of criminal law, if it were not accepted that the fertilised ovum is a thing, then its 'theft' would have to go unpunished, since it could not be defined as a 'movable thing belonging to another' with a view to applying Article 371 (relating to theft) of the Greek Penal Code (PC) to anyone who might unlawfully appropriate it, nor, certainly, could PC Article 324, relating to 'the kidnapping of minors', be applied to the perpetrator, since the fertilised ovum is certainly not a 'minor' (and the provisions of the Penal Code may not be applied by analogy). Lastly, there is another reason to define the fertilised ovum as a thing: so that it may be the subject of scientific research, which may prove exceptionally beneficial to the human race, on condition, of course, that there is no violation of the time limit beyond which specific human life begins, i.e. the fertilised ovum becomes, as discussed above, an embryo.

It will now have become clear, I think, that it is not only permissible, but imperative, to conclude that the fertilised ovum outside the human body is – just like the sperm or the unfertilised ovum – a thing, and, naturally, is also an aspect of the personality of the donors of the ovum and the sperm that constitute it. The man and the woman, then, may be regarded as having co-ownership – not parental care – of the fertilised ovum (by analogy with CC 1064), and, furthermore, as expressing through it their right to acquire offspring, as a part of their general right to develop freely their personality (also having the associated capacity for self-determination). This means that they may jointly decide (as long as they are married: CC 1387) to enter into a cryopreservation contract regarding the fertilised ovum and, certainly, demand compensation if the fertilised ovum is destroyed by a third party, on the grounds of either culpable non-performance of a contract (for cryopreservation, for instance) or committing an unlawful act, or unlawful assault on their personality. The donors of the sperm and the ovum may also decide freely (that is, with absolutely no restrictions or conditions) to discontinue the process of *in vitro* fertilisation and request the destruction of the fertilised ovum.

That the spouses may 'donate' the fertilised ovum to another couple is also in complete accord with the legal status of the fertilised ovum as a thing and at the same time an aspect of personality, regardless of whether or not restrictions may be placed on the permissibility of such a donation. An example is the restrictions included in the French legislation of 1994, which stipulates that a fertilised ovum may be donated only following a judicial decision, under certain specific conditions, and with the further proviso that the donors remain anonymous. In this case, it is obvious that the specific restrictions are not connected with the legal status of the fertilised ovum (that is, they are not imposed because it is considered to be a 'person' or a 'potential person', so that 'donation' of it essentially constitutes 'adoption' or 'pre-adoption'), but are imposed in order to safeguard the interests of the child who may be born. As we said above in connection with the sperm, the child's interests are bound up with the *natural purpose* of the fertilised ovum, which is unquestionably the creation of offspring, and also, like the legal status of the fertilised ovum, influence the legal treatment of the latter. Furthermore, the child's interests are also a very important criterion in the decision about what happens to the (usually frozen) fertilised ovum after the death of the sperm donor, i.e. whether or not it will be implanted in the woman's uterus despite her husband's death after the *in vitro* fertilisation (and subsequent freezing of the ovum).[23] All the debate outlined above with regard to *post mortem* fertilisation applies equally to the question of *post mortem* implantation.

Finally, since its natural purpose, the creation of offspring, connects the fertilised ovum not only with the child to be born, thus activating the principle of safeguarding the child's interests, but also with third-party recipients who want to have children, it is naturally necessary to ensure that the juridical acts 'transferring' the fertilised ovum to the latter are compatible with social ethics. From this point of view, the sale of fertilised ova must in every case be deemed invalid because it is immoral (CC 178), the immorality lying in precisely the same point as mentioned above with regard to sperm. So in no circumstances may the spouses sell any of their surplus fertilised ova, not because these are not things, for they are, but because it would be an immoral juridical act.

V   CONCLUSION

In this study it has been argued that, according to Greek civil law, the sperm, the ovum, and the fertilised ovum, when outside the human body, constitute things and at the same time aspects of their donors' personality, and are therefore to be treated as such. This dual legal status in itself provides a basis for resolving only some (in fact most) of the problems relating to the legal treatment of the sperm, the ovum, and the fertilised ovum. These include compensation or reparation for moral injury suffered by the donor if reproductive material is destroyed by a third party; the legal definition of a contract for cryopreservation; whether reproductive material may be inherited; whether the fertilised ovum is the object of parental care or co-ownership; whether the spouses are free to decide not to proceed with implantation and to destroy the fertilised ovum; and the question of the liability of the 'donors' of reproductive material. As far as other issues are concerned, such as the permissibility of 'donating' or selling reproductive material or the fate of reproductive material after the death of the donor, apart from defining the legal status of the material, we must also draw on other criteria or principles, such as the invalidity of immoral juridical acts or the safeguarding of the child's interests, in order to reach socially acceptable conclusions. The reason for this is that, apart from their legal status, sperm, ovum, and fertilised ovum also have a specific natural purpose. However, the natural purpose of the reproductive material (which is undeniably the creation of

---

[23]   As an aspect of its donor's personality, the fertilised ovum must be deemed non-inheritable, just like sperm (see above).

offspring) is one thing, and its legal status is quite another. An awareness of this distinction enables us to address the subject of the legal status of reproductive material outside the human body in a rational manner, without being carried away by religious or metaphysical notions that might induce us to 'personify' it. As lawyers, we thus have the satisfaction of knowing that our views neither hinder scientific research and activity nor allow it to proceed unchecked, but keep it within the bounds imposed by the natural purpose of reproductive material.

REPUBLIC OF IRELAND

JUDICIAL AND LEGISLATIVE FAMILY LAW DEVELOPMENTS

*Paul Ward**

I   INTRODUCTION

Most of my contributions to this journal in previous years have had a central or main theme. I have been fortunate in this regard over the past few years that judicial developments have enabled me to write on select and often interesting developments.[1] This year's contribution cannot be confined to a select topic but is rather a rounding up operation. This, I hope, will not detract from what are a number of interesting family law cases and legislative developments.

II   RECOGNITION OF FOREIGN DIVORCES AND JUDICIAL LEGISLATING

G.McG. v. D.W. and A.R. (notice party)[2] has to be one of the most unusual decisions of our High Court not just because of the bizarre and somewhat complicated facts but because of the nature of the problem and how the court resolved it.

This case originated as a nullity petition brought by the husband, G.McG. who was seeking to have annulled his second marriage to his wife, D.W. whom he married in London in 1985. The basis for the petition was that G.McG. was not legally capable of marrying D.W. in 1985 as he was already legally married to his first wife A.R. In essence G.McG. was seeking to have declared unrecognisable his uncontested divorce, granted on the grounds of A.R.'s adultery with her now current husband, Mr. R. His first wife was a British citizen and the 1985 divorce was based upon her one-year residency in the UK. At no time was G.McG. either resident or domiciled in the United Kingdom. At the time of the proceedings, all four parties, G.McG., D.W., A.R. and Mr. R. were resident in the Irish Republic.

The proceedings were converted from a nullity petition to declaratory proceedings as to marital status under section 29(1) of the Family Law Act, 1995 by agreement of the parties, and after an understandable change of heart by G.McG., when the Master of the High Court refused a routine application. The Master refused to fix a time and mode of trial for the nullity petition and took the view that the English divorce was of no effect as the parties to the divorce could not establish joint domicile at the time of the divorce proceedings.[3] He concluded that the parties to both marriages had committed bigamy and

---

*   College Lecturer in Family Law and Tort, University College, Dublin.

[1]   Ward, 'Children: Detention and Abortion', *The International Survey of Family Law* 1997, 355–377; 'Defective Knowledge: A New Ground for Nullity?', *The International Survey of Family Law* 1996, 215–235 and 'Abortion: 'X' + 'Y' =?!' (33) *University of Louisville J. Fam. Law* (1994–95) at 385–407.

[2]   Unreported High Court, January 14, 1999, McGuinness J.

[3]   As the divorce preceded the introduction of the Domicile and Recognition of Foreign Divorces Act, 1986 which by section 5 changed the requirement for recognition from joint domicile to single domicile of the parties after the commencement of the Act on October 2, 1986.

he forwarded the papers to the Director of Public Prosecutions. This order was successfully appealed with a specific direction that the criminal investigations of all the parties then underway cease forthwith.[4]

McGuinness J. decided that the divorce was capable of recognition and that both marriages subsequent to that decree were valid. Whilst the result reached in this case is perhaps correct and just in the circumstances, the manner in which it was achieved is somewhat dubious. To place this in context, a brief outline of the law on recognition of foreign divorces may be instructive.

Article 41 of the Constitution relates to the family and its position in law and society. The notion of the family in Irish constitutional law is that which is based upon marriage. The institution of marriage is highly regarded and Article 41 affords it the appropriate constitutional protection against attack.[5] In this regard, the marital family was constitutionally protected against dissolution by the ban on divorce.[6] Article 41 also governs the law relating to the recognition of foreign divorces. When originally drafted, Article 41.3.3 was perhaps intended to achieve a similar ban on the recognition of foreign divorces.[7] The first interpretation of this provision was considered by the Supreme Court in *Mayo-Perrott v. Mayo-Perrott*[8] where the majority held that it precluded an Irish court from recognising a divorce and specifically enforcing an order for costs in favour of the wife obtained in England. The dissenting opinion of Kingsmill Moore J. in *Mayo-Perrott v. Mayo-Perrott*[9] formed the basis for the overturning of the majority view in subsequent cases resulting in the recognition of foreign divorces provided they complied with *the law then in force*. The position prior to the enactment of the 1937 Constitution, as correctly noted by Kingsmill Moore J., was to recognise a foreign divorce if both the parties to the divorce were domiciled in the jurisdiction granting the decree at the time when the decree was applied for. There had been numerous cases to this effect[10] and, as no legislation had been introduced to the contrary, the common law joint domicile rule prevailed. The joint domicile rule for recognition was rigorously applied in subsequent cases.[11] The joint domicile rule worked favourably for an Irish woman who married an English man in having a foreign divorce recognised owing both to the then valid dependent domicile rule[12] and the notorious difficulty for the husband or any individual to lose or change one's domicile of origin.

A change in the law became evident following the obiter comments of Barr J. in *C.M. v. T.M. (No.2)*[13] where he described a wife's domicile of dependency as:

---

4   Ibid at 5 but note the earlier view of Budd J. who indicated that there was nothing he could do concerning the transfer of the papers to the Director of Public Prosecutions.

5   See generally Shatter *Family Law* (Butterworths) (1997) ch 1.

6   Article 41.3.2 amended by the Fifteenth Amendment to the Constitution and the subsequent introduction of divorce legislation in the form of the Family Law (Divorce) Act, 1996.

7   Article 41.3.3. provides: 'No person whose marriage has been dissolved under the civil law of any other State but is a subsisting valid marriage under the law for the time being in force within the jurisdiction of the Government and Parliament established under this Constitution shall be capable of contracting a valid marriage within that jurisdiction during the lifetime of the other party to the marriage so dissolved'.

8   [1958] I.R. 336.

9   Ibid.

10   *Shaw v. Gould* (1868) LR 3, HL 55, *Le Mesurier v. Le Mesurier* [1895] A.C. 517; *Bater v. Bater* (1906) P. 209; *Sinclair v. Sinclair* [1896] 1 I.R. 603.

11   *Bank of Ireland v. Caffin* [1971] I.R. 123, *Counihan v. Counihan* unreported, High Court, July 1973; *Gaffney v. Gaffney* [1975] I.R. 133.

12   *T. v. T.* [1983] I.R. 29 and *KED (orse KC) v. MC* [1985] I.R. 697.

13   [1990] 2 I.R. 52, a decision handed down in February 1988.

'a relic of female matrimonial bondage which was swept away by the principles of equality before the law and equal rights in marriage as between men and women which are enshrined in the Constitution.'[14]

The result was the introduction of the Domicile and Recognition of Foreign Divorces Act, 1986. The effect of this Act was twofold: first, to abolish prospectively the wife's domicile of dependency rule from October 2, 1986 and, secondly, to alter the recognition rule from joint domicile to one of either party's domicile for divorces granted after October 2, 1986. The rationale for distinguishing between pre- and post-October 2, 1986 was, presumably, to ensure that decrees granted and recognised prior to that date would remain valid with the abolition of the dependent domicile rule. The temporal distinction, whilst it may have had necessary practical advantages, also had glaring theoretical disadvantages[15] and an appropriate case was all that was necessary for the courts to abolish *ab initio* the dependent domicile rule.

The case in question was *W. v. W.*[16] which was an attempt by the husband to annul his marriage on the basis that his wife's divorce in 1972 from her first husband, who had an English domicile, could not be recognised as both parties were not domiciled in England at the relevant time. To achieve this result, the husband had to argue that the dependent wife domicile rule was unconstitutional in holding women unequal before the law. All five members of the Supreme Court readily accepted this argument with the result that the wife's divorce was not capable of recognition, as both parties were not domiciled in England at the time the divorce was applied for. The consequence of this was to render invalid her marriage to the plaintiff husband, as she would have been validly married to her first husband at the time she married her second husband.

This scenario created grave difficulties for the majority of the Supreme Court.[17] The court could either refuse to recognise the divorce and declare the second marriage a nullity or intervene and alter the common law rules for recognition of foreign divorces and bring them in line with the post-October 2, 1986 statutory position of recognition on the basis of either party's domicile. The Supreme Court opted for the latter approach and justified it on the basis that as the common law rules were judge-made it was within their competence to alter such rules despite there having been statutory intervention in this regard.[18] Hederman J. was so vigorously opposed to such a course of action that he considered it to amount to the judiciary assuming the role of legislator.[19] Hederman J. acknowledged that his stance on this issue called into question the constitutionality of the 1986 Act.[20]

Egan J. identified succinctly the practical reason for the court's intervention in altering the common law rules. He stated:

'The defendant in this case participated in a solemn ceremony with the plaintiff which quite clearly they treated as being a valid marriage and the consequence of

---

[14] Ibid at 63. See also *Gaffney v. Gaffney* [1975] I.R. 133 at 152, Walsh J.; *KED (orse KC) v. MC* [1985] I.R. 697, McCarthy J. at 705.

[15] In the light of the clear judicial opinion as to its unconstitutionality, it could not have been validly carried over as a valid rule following the enactment of the Constitution in 1937.

[16] [1993] 2 I.R. 476.

[17] Finlay CJ, Egan J., Blayney J., Denham J. and Hederman J. dissenting on the court's ability to alter the common law position in the light of legislative intervention.

[18] [1993] 2 I.R. 476, at 504–506, Blayney J.

[19] Ibid at 486–487.

[20] Ibid at 468–469.

which four children were born. He ought not, now, in any event, be entitled to argue that it was a nullity.'[21]

Underlying this is also the implicit and valid argument of the court defending and vindicating the plaintiff's wife's constitutional right to equality before the law.[22] Simply put, the wife here would be discriminated against by the non-retrospective effect of the 1986 Act whereby her marriage would be void, whereas a woman in identical circumstances whose divorce was granted after the commencement of the 1986 Act would be entitled to have her divorce recognised and in turn have rendered valid any subsequent marriage celebrated on foot of that divorce and its recognition. As indicted by Hederman J.[23] such a position was constitutionally unjustifiable.

W. v. W.[24] is a rare example of the Supreme Court intervening to do practical, natural and constitutional justice to one of the parties. In other family law cases where a legislative omission has given rise to an injustice, the Supreme Court has been happy to acknowledge the harsh effect of its decision and invite the legislature to intervene. The most notable example is *O'D. v. O'D.*[25] where Keane J. expressed sentiments to this effect.[26]

Whilst the result and the manner in which it was achieved in *W. v. W.*[27] might offend purists, the decision did resolve a potential constitutional anomaly affecting the constitutional rights of individuals in the wife's position. It is doubtful whether the same can be said of the *G.McG. v. D.W. and A.R. (notice party)*[28] decision. McGuinness J. reviewed the current common law position[29] and the Domicile and Recognition of Foreign Divorces Act, 1986. From the case law she concluded that the main objective of the recognition rules was the avoidance of limping marriages under the overall guise of the policy of the comity of Courts. This primary objective was in turn supportable, first by the fact that the rules were judge-made and malleable according to, secondly, the policy of the court in recognising the validity of foreign courts' jurisdiction. This reasoning enabled McGuinness J. to reconsider the foreign recognition rules. She relied upon the speech of Lord Justice Diplock in *Indyka v. Indyka*[30] where he stated that if the English Courts had been given the jurisdiction to grant decrees of divorce, the courts should as a matter of public policy likewise extend the recognition rules to give effect to the validity of the jurisdiction of foreign courts. Had that been the basis for decision, it might have avoided the scepticism that surrounds this decision.

The main impediment to altering the common law rules of recognition was the fact the legislation had superseded the common law position and any anomaly therein had

---

21   Ibid at 495.

22   Article 40.3.1 provides: 'The State guarantees in its laws to respect, and, as far as practicable, by its laws to defend and vindicate the personal rights of the citizen'. It is thus incumbent upon the courts to give effect to this provision.

23   [1993] 2 I.R. 468–469.

24   [1993] 2 I.R. 476.

25   [1998] I.L.R.M. 543, noted by Ward in 'Children: Detention and Abortion', *The International Survey of Family Law 1997*, 355–377 at 376, and in 'Separation Agreements – A Binding Alternative to Judicial Separation' [1998] Fam Law 490.

26   [1998] 1 I.L.R.M. 543 at 558.

27   [1993] 2 I.R. 476.

28   Unreported, High Court, January 14, 1999, McGuinness J.

29   *W. v. W.* [1993] 2 I.R. 476, Blayney J. relying upon *Travers v. Holley* [1953] P. 246 and *Indyka v. Indyka* [1969] 1 A.C. 33.

30   [1969] 1 A.C. 33, which Blayney J. had cited with approval in *W. v. W.* [1993] 2 I.R. 476.

been rectified by the Supreme Court in *W. v. W.*[31] McGuinness J. went on to analyse section 5 of the Domicile and Recognition of Foreign Divorces Act, 1986[32] which she found to omit the phrase 'if , but only if'. Thus, in her view, the Act did not preclude the court from 'developing the rules of recognition in reliance on the decision of the Supreme Court in *W. v. W.*,[33] that common law rules are judge-made law and be modified depending on the current policy of the court'.[34] This is clearly a strained interpretation of the Act intended to achieve the desired result.

McGuinness J. further examined the judicial separation and divorce legislation[35] under which proceedings may be instituted on the basis of domicile or ordinary residence for a period of at least one year prior to the institution of the proceedings. Here the learned judge's reasoning is particularly suspect in that the Family Law Act, 1995 is a major piece of reforming family law legislation which specifically deals with the enforcement of orders consequent upon the grant of a foreign judicial separation and divorce.[36] Had the legislature intended to amend the rules on recognition of foreign divorces contained in the 1986 Act, Part III of the Family Law Act, 1995 was the appropriate time and opportunity to do so.

Whilst this is disturbing, perhaps the most unsatisfactory part of the judgment is the fact that the case was not contested by the defendant wife and both parties argued for the same result. McGuinness J. acknowledged this and relied upon her own extensive knowledge and practice in the area to overcome the fact that the action had not been a 'fully fought case'.[37] This in a way is a case of forcing the square peg into the round hole with the judge holding the hammer.

Undoubtedly there is need for our family law legislation to be uniform and it is nonsensical that a domestic divorce only requires one year's residency whereas to recognise a foreign divorce either party must be domiciled in the jurisdiction granting the divorce. Perhaps there is some practical merit in the decision as the legislature is often very slow at introducing family legislation[38] and this decision will avoid that delay. There is on the other hand some potential mischief in this decision. The so-called 'clean break' divorces are not possible under the Family Law (Divorce) Act, 1996 but they are in England. The unscrupulous spouse could, if he or she so wished, acquire the necessary residency to obtain an English divorce, and seek to have recognised in Ireland that divorce. This would be particularly disadvantageous for the financially dependent spouse where the other spouse has moved capital and assets from this jurisdiction. In this regard, whilst commentators have welcomed the decision,[39] the parameters and consequences of it have not been set. The effect of this decision is to alter the common law rules of recognition of foreign divorces for divorces granted in another jurisdiction prior to October 2, 1986. The consequence of this is that there are now currently two differing

---

[31] [1993] 2 I.R. 476.

[32] Section 5(1) provides: 'For the rule of law that a divorce is recognised if granted in the country where both spouses are domiciled, there is hereby substituted a rule that a divorce shall be recognised if granted in the country where either spouse is domiciled'.

[33] [1993] 2 I.R. 476.

[34] Unreported, High Court, January 14, 1999, McGuinness J. at 14.

[35] The Judicial Separation and Family Law Reform Act, 1989, the Family Law Act, 1995, and the Family Law (Divorce) Act, 1996.

[36] Part III, sections 23–28 of the Family Law Act, 1995.

[37] Unreported, High Court, January 14, 1999, McGuinness J. at 17.

[38] For example the Child Care Act, 1991 only fully came into effect in October 1996 and the Children Bill, 1996 which will reform the juvenile justice system remains on the back burner.

[39] Power, 1999 Vol.1 *Irish Journal of Family Law* at 26.

sets of recognition rules, residency for pre-October 2, 1986 and domicile for post-October 2, 1986 divorces. Such a scenario is plainly unacceptable and perhaps the greatest mischief when the judiciary attempt to legislate. In effect, this decision has undone the work of the Supreme Court in *W. v. W.*[40] by restoring the pre- and post-October 2, 1986 anomaly but to a greater extent.

Issues of this nature are, it is suggested, best dealt with by those whose responsibility it is to legislate. In any event, the decision is under appeal to the Supreme Court where the matter will be resolved.

III ADOPTION AND THE RIGHT TO KNOW YOUR MOTHER

I.O'T. v. B.[41] is perhaps the most interesting decision in the last year. The Supreme Court held that a natural child has an unenumerated constitutional right to know the identity of his or her natural parent. The right, however, is somewhat difficult establish and is dependent upon the child adopting the correct procedural approach and, more importantly, from the substantive constitutional point of the natural parent's attitude to having their identity disclosed. Whilst the case is of great constitutional importance, in practical terms its significance is of more academic interest as very few individuals may attempt to rely upon their newly declared constitutional right.

The case arose out of two applications before the Circuit Court brought by two adult daughters I.O'T. and M.H. Both women were seeking to have disclosed the identity of their natural mothers. Both women had been informally adopted in 1941 and 1951 respectively. The adoptions were informal as the Adoption Act, 1952 was not introduced until January 1953. Thus the Adoption Acts, 1952–1991 did not govern the applications. Parent tracing under the Adoption Act, 1952 is theoretically possible but disclosure of information is subject to an application to the Adoption Board. The Adoption Board cannot disclose information that would identify the natural mother unless a court makes an order so directing. In an application to a court for such an order, the court can only make the order if it considers that it is in the child's best interests to do so.[42] In all cases where a child or parent has sought access to documents in the Adoption Board's possession, the courts have declined to grant the order[43] or have granted an order for discovery but provided that the information furnished must not reveal the identities of the parent or child.[44]

In the present case, both plaintiffs instituted separate and distinct proceedings to reveal the identity of their natural mothers. In the first application, I.O'T. sought an application under section 35 of the Status of Children Act, 1987[45] which necessitated bringing a motion for discovery against the notice parties to disclose the identity of her natural mother, I.O'T. being unaware of her natural mother's identity. This ignorance

---

[40] [1993] 2 I.R. 476.
[41] [1998] 2 I.R. 321.
[42] Section 8 of the Adoption Act, 1976.
[43] *P.C. v. An Bord Uchtála*, Unreported High Court, April 1980, McWilliam J.; *P.B. v. A.L.* [1966] I.L.R.M. 154; and *C.R. v. An Bord Uchtála* [1993] 3 I.R. 535.
[44] *S.M. and M.M. v. G.M. and Ors* [1985] 5 I.L.R.M. 186.
[45] Section 35(1)(a) provides: 'A person (other than an adopted person) born in the State, or (b) any other person (other than an adopted person) may apply to the court in such manner as may be prescribed for a declaration under this section that a person named in the application is his father or mother, as the case may be, or that the persons so named are his parents'.

proved to be fatal to the application which was struck out as I.O'T. failed to comply with the strict wording of the section. In order for a successful application, the applicant must state the name of the individual whom they claim to be their natural parent. As I.O'T. was unable to provide the name of her natural mother the Circuit Court judge struck out the application which the Supreme Court upheld as a correct decision.[46] The consolation for I.O'T. was that section 35 of the Status of Children Act, 1987 was held to amount to a legal right to know the identity of her mother but subject to the requirements of the section and the Act. In addition, I.O'T. was declared to have an unenumerated constitutional right to know the identity of her mother. Hamilton CJ described the right in the following manner:

> 'The right to know the identity of one's natural mother is a basic right flowing from the natural and special relationship which exists between a mother and her child, which relationship is clearly acknowledged in the passages quoted from the judgements in *The State (Nicoloau) v. An Bord Uchtála* [1966] I.R. 567 and in *G. v. An Bord Uchtála* [1980] I.R. 32.'[47]

The State (Nicoloau) v. An Bord Uchtála[48] held that an unmarried mother has a constitutional right to custody and care of her child and this a personal right of the individual which falls to be protected and vindicated by Article 40.3.1 of the Constitution rather than Article 41 which affords protection only to the marital family. *G. v. An Bord Uchtála*[49] expanded upon the earlier statement in holding on the facts of this disputed adoption case, that an unmarried mother enjoys the constitutional right to protect and care for, and to have custody of, her infant child. The right stems from motherhood, nature and the natural relationship between mother and child and from the infant's total dependency and helplessness.

The Chief Justice noted a number of important points in relation to this right. First, caution should be exercised in declaring what are the personal rights of the individual and where a right is declared it should be done so in clear and explicit terms. In this regard, whilst the right to know the identity of one's parent is readily and easily inferable from the above authorities, the right cannot be held to exist until so declared by either the High or Supreme Court.[50] Secondly, the rights of the mother as declared and the right of the child to know the identity of one's natural parent are neither inalienable nor imprescriptible. Both natural mothers, by their action of placing informally for adoption, had relinquished their rights and duties in regard to their children. This alienation of their rights would in turn impact upon the child's right to know the identity of their parent. In terms of prescribing the rights of the child, the Status of Children Act, 1987 had erected a barrier in this regard as evidenced by I.O'T.'s difficulty in obtaining the order sought. More importantly the rights of the natural child could be prescribed by the natural mother's rights to privacy and anonymity which she acquired by placing for informal adoption. Thirdly, as neither plaintiff had been formally adopted, both remained the natural child of their respective mothers and were thus entitled to the benefit of that right,[51] even as adult women. Such was the position in relation to I.O'T. and a further

---

[46] Per Hamilton CJ, [1998] 2 I.R. 321 at 344.
[47] Ibid at 348.
[48] [1966] I.R. 567.
[49] [1980] I.R. 32.
[50] [1998] 2 I.R 321 at 345.
[51] Ibid at 348.

assessment and adjudication of the competing constitutional rights of the child and the mother could not occur.[52]

The position of the second plaintiff, M.H. was different, as she had instituted different proceedings which did require the court to consider the respective polarised constitutional positions of the plaintiff and her natural mother. M.H. circumvented section 35 of the Status of Children Act, 1987 by issuing an equity civil bill seeking an order for discovery against the defendants. Having overcome a procedural argument relating to making order of discovery against third parties,[53] the Chief Justice went on to consider the right of the child to know the identity his or her natural mother in the light of the competing constitutional rights of the mother. Ordinarily in assessing constitutional rights that potentially conflict, the Superior Courts will first seek to harmonise those rights rather than prioritise.[54]

The Chief Justice acknowledged that the natural mother did have a constitutional right to privacy but that this was not an absolute right.[55] The natural mother could also rely upon the fact that information in the possession of the adoption society and individuals involved in the informal process was privileged, but this was likewise not an absolute right.[56]

If the right of the child was to take precedence over the rights of the mother, then the mother's constitutional rights would be infringed and *vice versa*. The Chief Justice provided some guidance on how to resolve this problem. He identified seven factors that the trial judge should consider in attempting to balance the competing rights of the mother and child. The factors, which are not exhaustive, are: the circumstances giving rise to the natural mother relinquishing custody of the child; the present circumstances of the natural mother and the effect thereon (if any) of the disclosure of her identity to her natural child; the attitude of the natural mother to the disclosure of her identity to her natural child, and the reason therefor; the respective ages of the natural mother and her child; the reasons for the natural child's wish to know the identity of her natural mother and to meet her; the present circumstances of the natural child; and the views of the foster parents if alive.[57]

These factors, however, cannot be considered until the natural mother is first given an opportunity to assert a claim of privilege and privacy. Such an opportunity presupposes the involvement in legal proceedings by the natural mother and the stress and anxiety that such may cause. This must be alleviated by an independent and appropriately qualified individual first approaching the natural mother and compiling a report for the trial judge in advance of adjudicating upon the factors outlined above. It should be noted that, whilst these procedural steps and some of the considerations appear to favour the anonymity of the mother to the disadvantage of the child, the mother cannot object or refuse to consent to her identity being revealed by an adoption society to the

---

[52]   Had the position been otherwise, the investigation of the respective rights of the child and mother would have been futile, as the mother could not be traced.

[53]   *Megaleasing UK Ltd v. Barrett* [1993] I.L.R.M. 497, applying the House of Lords decision in *Norwich Pharmacal v. Customs & Excise* [1974] A.C. 133, held that an order for discovery could be made against a non-wrongdoing third party in order to give effect to a legal right of a plaintiff. The Chief Justice had no difficulty in extending this principle to the vindication of a constitutional right.

[54]   [1998] 2 I.R. 321 at 349.

[55]   Ibid at 352.

[56]   Ibid.

[57]   [1998] 2 I.R. 321 at 355.

court. In relation to revealing her identity to the natural child, such may occur only, if at all, after a determination of all rights of the parties concerned.

From the child's perspective there are two important constitutional rights that could be asserted in seeking to disclose the identity of the natural mother. The right to know the identity of one's natural mother is not dependent upon the constitutional rights[58] to bodily integrity[59] or the right to own property.[60] The former would be particularly relevant where the child wishes to marry and avoid the risk of marrying a blood relative or in the case of genetic disorders. The latter right to inherit property might cause some theoretical constitutional difficulties. Keane J. noted that the right to know the identity of one's natural mother would be essential to enforce the right to inherit property from that parent. By vindicating the right to inherit property, this would in turn effect a discrimination between *de jure* adopted children, whose right to inherit from the natural parents is severed on the making of an adoption order, and the *de facto* adopted plaintiffs in the present case whose right to inherit[61] remained intact.[62] Barron J. also noted these rights of the child but placed more emphasis on the practical execution of them were they to arise. In this regard he advocated that the plaintiffs be treated as if they were lawfully adopted children and to remain so until any genetic or property issues arose. At that juncture, as with lawful adoptions, intermediaries should be used.[63] He did stress, as Keane J. had also indicated, that the right to privacy should prevail over any property right asserted by the plaintiffs.[64]

Keane J. departed from the majority on the substantive constitutional issue of the right to know the identity of one's natural parent. This dissenting judgment succinctly identified the crux of the issue in this case and opted for a bold course that avoided what would be the the plaintiff's ultimate stumbling block, namely the insistence of a natural mother to retain her anonymity. Keane J. stated that if the plaintiffs had a right to know the identity of their natural mothers, that right was dependent upon the duty of the mothers to disclose their identities.[65] The former right would be meaningless unless either the natural mothers or the notice parties were compelled to disclose the information sought. Keane J. further questioned whether the right to know the identity of one's natural mother existed at all. He rejected the notion that the right of the child could stem from 'realising his or her full personality and dignity as a human being'.[66] The plaintiffs were two mature women cared for, nurtured and educated from birth by informal adopters. Whilst they had been deprived of the nurture of their natural mothers, the information they now sought could not and would not fill that void in their lives and the failure to have the society of one's natural parent could not in Keane J.'s view amount to

---

58   As stressed by the Chief Justice at [1998] 2 I.R. 248 and elaborated upon in detail by Keane J. in his dissenting judgment at 375–377.

59   *Ryan v. The Attorney General* [1965] I.R. 294.

60   Amongst the personal constitutional rights guaranteed by Article 40.3 is the right to inherit property.

61   Either on the intestate death of the natural parent or by will so devised by the natural parent to the child. There may even be the possibility of a section 117 application under the Succession Act, 1965 where a parent has failed to provide properly for a child.

62   [1998] 2 I.R. 321 at 376.

63   Ibid at 381.

64   Ibid at 381 and 376 respectively.

65   Ibid at 368.

66   Ibid at 370 quoting O'Higgins C.J. in *G. v. An Bord Uchtála* [1980] I.R.32 where the personal rights of the child were outlined.

a failure to realise their personality and dignity. If that was the correct position, it was a 'grave overstatement'.[67]

In relation to the majority's view, Keane J. doubted the origin of the right as one stemming from the special relationship between mother and child. If the right existed, it existed from birth until the child was informally adopted and not thereafter as the children had been cared for and nurtured by their informal adoptive families.[68] The reality of the situation was thus. If the natural mothers refuse to disclose their identities, then the child must seek to enforce the right. This necessarily required the right not only to be acknowledged but to take precedence over 'the established right to privacy, recognised in the decisions of the High Court and this Court'[69] which Keane J. could not countenance. Keane J. systematically rejected the existence of the right being based upon an expressly guaranteed constitutional right or an unenumerated right so declared by the courts. Keane J. acknowledged the force of an argument based upon the right to inherit property but dismissed this, as it had not been the motivation of the plaintiffs in maintaining their actions.[70] Arguments that the plaintiffs were denied access to justice because of the requirement of section 35 of the Status of Children Act, 1987 that the parent be named, failed as the plaintiffs failed to question the constitutionality of the 1987 Act which benefited in any event from the presumption of constitutionality. As to the right to bodily integrity, Keane J. stated that to recognise the right on this basis would in turn render the whole system of lawful adoption inoperative. Ultimately the need for judicial restraint justified refusing to recognise the right to know the identity of one's natural parent.

IV   THE UNMARRIED FATHER, GUARDIANSHIP AND ADOPTION

The preceding summary links appropriately with recent legislation concerning the single or unmarried father and his rights in relation to the adoption process and guardianship, the Adoption Act, 1998. The Act had to be introduced as a result of the European Court of Human Rights (ECHR) decision in *Keegan v. Ireland*[71] which held Ireland to be in breach of Articles 6 and 8 of the Convention.[72]

To place the Adoption Act, 1998 and ECHR decision in some context, the history of the Keegan saga is worthy of note. In late 1988 a daughter was born to Mr. Keegan and his partner. The relationship had been a stable one for the best part of a year but, following the discovery of the pregnancy, the relationship deteriorated and the parties went their separate ways. The mother wanted to have the child adopted and had expressed the clear intention not to keep her daughter. When Mr. Keegan discovered this he immediately instituted proceedings under section 6A of the Guardianship of Infants Act, 1964.[73] The purpose of the application was to prevent the proposed adoption

---

67   Ibid at 371.

68   Ibid.

69   Ibid at 374.

70   Ibid at 375–376.

71   (1994) 18 EHRR 342. For a case more in point see *W.O'R. v. E.H. and The Eastern Health Board*, unreported, Supreme Court, July 23, 1996 discussed below.

72   The denial of and breach of the rights to a fair and public hearing and the respect for family life respectively.

73   Section 12 of the Status of Children Act, 1987 conferred upon the single father the right to apply for guardianship of his child, which right also automatically confers the right to custody.

proceedings as, if Mr. Keegan was appointed a guardian of his child, his consent would be essential for a valid adoption to occur.

The initial application eventually wound its way to the Supreme Court for its interpretation of section 6A in light of the particular facts of the case.[74] Mr Justice Barron in the High Court was of the view, in light of the stable relationship between the parties and Mr. Keegan's strong and genuine desire for guardianship, that section 6A[75] was to be interpreted by asking whether the applicant father was a fit person to be appointed a guardian and, if that was the case, whether there were any welfare considerations against him being so appointed. In essence, Barron J. was of the view that section 6A presumed that father should be appointed as of right.

The Supreme Court rejected such an interpretation and held that section 6A merely granted to the single father the right to apply to be appointed a guardian of his child. The father possessed neither a constitutional nor a natural right in relation to his child, and the position in *The State (Nicoloau) v. An Bord Uchtála*[76] and *G. v. An Bord Uchtála*[77] prevailed. The Supreme Court did, however, acknowledge that there were a number of factors to be considered in a section 6A application. Where a child was born of a stable relationship and even more so where the conception was a planned decision of the couple, then the father would enjoy very extensive rights in a section 6A application.[78] McCarthy J. was of the view that section 6A must have had some intended purpose otherwise it would not have been introduced. In circumstances of a stable relationship or a planned pregnancy where the father has a genuine desire to have custody, McCarthy J. indicated subtly to the trial judge that it was open to him to make the order sought and stated that the father must have a substantial right, which he reasoned by saying:

'I find it difficult to accept that a loving father, who with the mother wanted to have a child, has not a natural right to the society of his child.'[79]

By the time the case was remitted to the High Court for determination, the short-term trauma risk of transferring the child from the prospective adopters to Mr. Keegan had changed to a substantial long-term psychological risk to the child. In those circumstances, Barron J. had no option but to deny Mr. Keegan the order on the basis of the child's welfare.

Having exhausted every domestic remedy and having presented cases in every court, Mr. Keegan brought his action before the ECHR where he was successful. The main objective of Mr. Keegan's case was not to have declared a right to family life with his daughter as a single father, but more so the infringement of that right by the Irish adoption law and process. The legal attack on the adoption process was twofold. First his right to family life, for which there were existing precedents in the ECHR,[80] was violated in that his child could be placed for adoption without either his consent or his knowledge, thus preventing him from establishing a relationship with his daughter and enjoying the right guaranteed by Article 8 of the Convention. Further, the only way in which the

---

[74] *J.K. v. V.W.* [1990] 2 I.R. 437.

[75] Section 6A states: 'Where the father and mother of an infant have not married each other, the court may, on the application of the father, appoint him to be a guardian of the infant'.

[76] [1966] I.R. 657 denying the single father any legal or constitutional right to the custody of his child.

[77] [1980] I.R. 32 conferring exclusively upon the single mother the constitutional right to the custody of her child.

[78] [1990] 2 I.R. 437 at 447.

[79] Ibid at 449.

[80] *Johnston v. Ireland* (1986) 9 EHRR 103 and *Berrehab v. The Netherlands* (1988) 11 EHRR 322.

adoption process could be prevented, and thereby vindicating his rights, was by Irish law conferring a right to custody or guardianship, which it had failed to do. Secondly, even once the adoption process was underway, Mr. Keegan had no *locus standi* in the process and his objections could not be heard. Both arguments successfully led to the ECHR holding that Mr. Keegan's rights under Articles 6 and 8 had been violated. He was awarded £12,000 and his costs. It should be noted that Mr. Keegan did not seek to have the adoption order declared invalid and his daughter returned to him. He had resigned himself to the fact that her welfare was better served by her remaining with the adopters.

Before the Adoption Act, 1998 was introduced, an even more alarming case came before the Supreme Court. *W.O'R. v. E.H. and The Eastern Health Board*[81] concerned an 11-year relationship between the unmarried parents of two children, a daughter aged 14 and a son aged 5. After the relationship broke down the mother left and married in June 1993 and sought to adopt the two children with her new husband in July 1993. The father instituted section 6A proceedings and continued to enjoy access to the children even while the adoption was being processed. The Adoption Board refused to make the adoption order until access to the children by their natural father was terminated.

At the hearing of the Circuit Court appeal, a case was stated for the Supreme Court's opinion on the position of the natural father and his rights under section 6A where he objected to the adoption. The Supreme Court reiterated the principles outlined in *J.K. v. V.W.*[82] but in the context of the adoption problem posed by the case, the trial judge was obliged to consider a number of factors in determining the section 6A application. These were: the fact that an application for adoption had been made but also that the father was not seeking custody of the children; the father's opposition to the adoption; that the nature and extent of the rights accruing to the father are dependent upon securing the children's welfare and in this regard the blood link is an important factor; that the effect of the adoption order would be to terminate the father's right to apply under section 6A.

These factors indicated by the Supreme Court seem to advance the position of the single father and afford him considerable rights in relation to his children. The justification for this lies in the child-orientated approach or as Denham J. stated:

> 'The rights of interest and concern of the father are directly in proportion to the circumstances that exist in the case between the father and the children. The greater the beneficial contact for the children there has been the more important it is to the welfare of the children and so the higher the rights of interest and concern for the father.'[83]

Denham J. identified rights of 'interest' and 'concern' but an adoption order could abolish those rights and she cautioned the loss of such by rights by advising that:

> '[Adoption] procedures must provide adequate protection for the welfare of the child, including an appropriate process to enable a natural father to make application for guardianship at a time within which the scales concerning the child's welfare have not been titled inevitably in another's favour.'[84]

---

[81]   Unreported, Supreme Court, July 23, 1996.

[82]   [1990] 2 I.R. 437.

[83]   Unreported, Supreme Court, July 23, 1996, Denham J. at 4.

[84]   Ibid at 6.

The advice given was not of much concern to the father in this case owing to the extensive relationship with his children and *vice versa*. It was intended more for a father in Mr. Keegan's position and this had been reflected in the Adoption Act, 1998.[85]

These judicial comments and advancements are encouraging for the single father but the dissenting judgment of Barrington J. is even more so. This may seem contradictory but this is not the case. Barrington J. vehemently objected to the unequal treatment of single fathers by denying them any substantive legal or constitutional right to the guardianship or custody of their children.[86] He stated that the *Nicoloau* decision[87] was fundamentally flawed and in a similar fashion to Denham J. advanced the position of the single father by relying upon the relationship between parent and child that should not be dependent upon marriage.[88]

These two cases provided the necessary impetus to rectify in some way the danger of a child being adopted without the single father's consent and or knowledge. The simplest means of achieving this would have been to confer an automatic right to custody or guardianship. Opposition parties in the passing of the Children Act, 1997 attempted this in both houses of the Oireachtas[89] but to no avail as this would create constitutional difficulties in the light of the current wording of Article 41 of the Constitution and would in effect place on a par the single father with that of the marital family. In addition there was statistical evidence indicating that such a change was not necessary.[90]

The necessary changes were brought about by the Adoption Act, 1998, which to a certain extent enables the single father to prevent the adoption of his child if he so wishes. There are a number of safeguards in the Act. The most notable is that the single father is now recognised as a parent of his child but only for the purposes of being heard by the Adoption Board at an adoption hearing.[91] Coupled with this, to strengthen the single father's position, is the right to notify the Adoption Board of his wish to be consulted in the proposed adoption.[92] Both the Adoption Board and any adoption society are respectively statutorily obliged to furnish and request such notification. Further, where an adoption agency is aware of the identity of the father, they are obliged to consult with him in the proposed adoption.[93] The consultation must inform the father of the proposed adoption, the legal consequences of such and ascertain his objection or approval of the placement. Depending upon the father's views the placement may proceed unless objected to, in which case the agency must not place the child for 21 days

---

[85] Section 2 of the Adoption Act, 1998 now includes the single father in the list of individuals who may be heard at the adoption hearing in addition to obligations to consult with the father at both pre- and post-placement stage imposed upon the adoption board and adoption societies, as appropriate, in sections 7D and 7E.

[86] Barrington J. was counsel for Nicoloau as acknowledged by him in the preface to his judgment.

[87] [1966] I.R. 657.

[88] Unreported, Supreme Court, July 23, 1996, at p.37.

[89] 480 *Dáil Debates* Cols. 1348 *et seq.* and 152 *Seanad Debates* Cols. 815 *et seq.*

[90] 480 *Dáil Debates* Cols. 1467–1469 where Minister O'Donoghue outlined the 1996 statistics that there were 12,500 births to single mothers. There were 750 applications for guardianship by single fathers of which 90 per cent were granted. Of those 750 applications, 400 were with the consent of the mother.

[91] Section 2 of the Adoption Act, 1998 inserting a new definition section into section 3 of the Adoption Act, 1952.

[92] Section 4 of the Adoption Act, 1998 inserting a new section 7D(1)(a) into the Adoption Act, 1952.

[93] Section 4 of the Adoption Act, 1998 inserting a new section 7E(2) into the Adoption Act, 1952.

to enable a section 6A application to be made.[94] If a section 6A application is made, the placement cannot proceed until that application is determined.[95]

These safeguards go a very long way to protect the rights of a single father where the vehicle for the adoption is an adoption society. They do nothing to protect a single father at the placement stage where the mother places her child privately with a relative or attempts to adopt her own child with her husband as in *W.O'R. v. E.H. and the Eastern Health Board*.[96] Provided that the single father is aware of a secret and private adoption, he may still notify the Adoption Board of his wish to be consulted and object to the adoption at the hearing. There is the ultimate protection in section 6 of the Adoption Act, 1998 which provides for adoptions other than through an adoption society where the Adoption Board is obliged to take all reasonable steps to consult the father of the child but in practical terms this is dependent upon the Board being aware of the identity of the father.

A further safeguard incorporated is where the father is uncontactable. The Adoption Board may not authorise the placing of a child for adoption unless the Board is satisfied that the adoption agency has taken such steps as are reasonably practicable to consult the father.[97] Whilst this appears to afford the single father some protection, there is the danger that the mother might wilfully refuse to reveal the identity of the father. Despite an obligation on the adoption agency to counsel the mother in such circumstances to obtain her co-operation,[98] the placement may still proceed if all such reasonably practicable steps have been taken to obtain that co-operation and there is no other practical way of ascertaining the father's identity.[99]

The Adoption Board, however, retains discretion to exclude the father from consultation where, owing to the parental or paternal relationship, it would be inappropriate to contact the father.[100]

Overall the Adoption Act, 1998 does remedy the positions of the fathers in *J.K. v. V.W.*[101] and *W.O'R. v. E.H. and the Eastern Health Board*[102] but it does contain some failings which a vindictive mother could abuse to the detriment of the single father in denying him any rights whatsoever. The only means of closing potential loopholes is to place the single father on an equal legal and constitutional basis with the mother but this will have to await a constitutional referendum and a rewording of Article 41.

V   HEARSAY EVIDENCE AND ALLEGATIONS OF CHILD SEXUAL ABUSE

In the 1995 edition of this *Survey*[103] I noted two decisions of the then President of the High Court, Mr Justice Costello, *Re M. S. and W. (Infants)*[104] and *Southern Health Board*

---

94   Section 4 of the Adoption Act, 1998 inserting a new section 7E(3)(b) into the Adoption Act, 1952.
95   Section 4 of the Adoption Act, 1998 inserting a new section 7E(4) into the Adoption Act, 1952.
96   Unreported, Supreme Court, July 23, 1996.
97   Section 4 of the Adoption Act, 1998 inserting a new section 7F(1) into the Adoption Act, 1952.
98   Section 4 of the Adoption Act, 1998 inserting a new section 7F(3) into the Adoption Act, 1952.
99   Ibid.
100   Section 4 of the Adoption Act, 1998 inserting a new section 7F(2) into the Adoption Act, 1952.
101   [1990] 2 I.R. 437.
102   Unreported, Supreme Court, July 23, 1996.
103   Ward, 'Life, Death and Divorce', A. Bainham (ed.) *The International Survey of Family Law 1995*, 287–319, at 308–309.
104   [1996] 1 I.L.R.M. 370.

v. C.H.[105] Both cases were appealed with two conflicting Supreme Court decisions resulting.[106] In 1996 the central and simple issue in both cases was whether hearsay evidence was admissible in what were in essence child care cases.[107] Costello P. held that the evidence in question, a video-taped recording of an interview with a senior social worker during which allegations of sexual abuse were made by children against their father, was hearsay evidence but admissible. By 1999, this simple issue had been exposed to reveal a very detailed, complex and difficult issue which had serious consequences for the three children in *Re M. S. and W. (Infants)*.[108] In the interim, however, confusion abounded with the unanimous Supreme Court decision in *Southern Health Board v. C.H.*[109] O'Flaherty J. held that the evidence in the case was not hearsay evidence in nature, but corroborative evidence that the social worker would rely upon in giving expert oral testimony as to the veracity of the allegations made by the child. O'Flaherty J. clearly overruled Costello P. as to the nature of the evidence but upheld the decision to admit the evidence in any event. To this extent the contrast in judicial opinion and criticisms that could be levelled are only of academic interest. At this juncture, the matter, even if not entirely correct,[110] at least appeared settled.

The legislature intervened to clarify the matter with the Children Act, 1997, section 23 of which makes admissible the hearsay evidence of children.[111] More recently the Supreme Court in *Re M. S. and W. (Infants)*[112] endorsed Costello P.'s original view on the nature of such evidence. There is at least consensus between the legislature and the Supreme Court on the issue of the nature of such evidence. There is, however, a degree of divergence in the approach to the admission of such evidence between the requirements of the Children Act, 1997 and the criteria and conditions recommended by the Supreme Court.[113] As the Act is not retrospective in effect, which the Supreme Court noted, it did not apply in the instant case.

At the outset, I should stress that the analysis that follows is confined to the narrow area of hearsay evidence in the context of allegations of child sexual abuse and not to the admission of hearsay evidence generally and that I am focusing exclusively upon the judgment of Keane J. Four other judgements were delivered[114] but in my view the judgment of Keane J. is the most comprehensive and authoritative.

The first point of divergence between the Children Act, 1997 and the Supreme Court, specifically the judgment of Keane J., is that the Act does not distinguish between the different forms of hearsay evidence that can arise in allegations of child sexual abuse.

---

[105] Unreported, High Court, January 23, 1996.

[106] [1996] 1 I.L.R.M. 370, and unreported, Supreme Court, January 29, 1999 respectively.

[107] The former case concerned wardship proceedings and the latter section 58 care proceedings under the Children Act, 1908, the latter of which Costello P. considered to be identical to the former as being in essence investigative of the child's welfare as opposed to being accusatorial of the alleged wrongdoer which justified the admission of the hearsay evidence.

[108] Unreported, Supreme Court, January 29, 1999.

[109] [1996] 1 I.L.R.M. 370.

[110] See the detailed and comprehensive judgment of Ward L.J. in *Re N. (A Minor) (Sexual Abuse: Video Evidence)* [1997] 1 W.L.R. 153, who came to the same conclusion as Costello P. that video-recorded evidence of allegations of child sexual abuse was hearsay evidence but admissible subject to strict guidelines and criteria. Ward L.J.'s decision was handed down three days after O'Flaherty J.'s judgment.

[111] Section 19 of the Children Act, 1997 defines 'statement' as 'any representation of fact or opinion however made'. The 'statement' if video-recorded may be admitted under section 23 which provides for the admission of hearsay evidence in the form of 'any statement' made by a child.

[112] Unreported, Supreme Court, January 29, 1999.

[113] See in particular the judgment of Keane J. which relies upon that of Ward L.J. in *Re N (A Minor)* (above).

[114] Denham, Barrington, Lynch and Barron J.J.

Keane J. noted that hearsay evidence of this nature could take the form of either the oral testimony of an expert witness, in this particular case, a speech therapist, as to what the child related to the speech therapist or it could take the form of a video-taped interview during which the allegations of sexual abuse are made. The second point of divergence is the fact that different considerations and criteria apply to the different categories of hearsay evidence according to the Supreme Court, but only one set of criteria apply to both forms of hearsay evidence according to the Act. The third point of divergence is that the Supreme Court criteria as to admissibility appear much more stringent than the Act.

Section 23 of the Children Act, 1997 permits the admission of hearsay evidence if the court considers that the child is unable to give evidence by reason of age or that it would not be in the interests of the child's welfare to give oral testimony in person or through a live television link[115] with or without an intermediary.[116] The court may refuse to admit the evidence where it is not in the interests of justice to do so, which consideration is guided by the general concept of 'all the circumstances of the case' including any risk of unfairness to the parties.[117] The section is somewhat sparse in setting the criteria applicable to the decision to admit the hearsay evidence and specifically on the fundamental issue of the child's competency. This contrasts with the detailed pre-admissibility procedure outlined by Ward L.J. in *Re N. (A Minor)*[118] and endorsed by Keane J.[119] Arguably, section 23 could be interpreted to include this detailed procedure and it is suggested that it is highly advisable in cases of allegations of child sexual abuse.

In relation to video-taped interviews during which allegations of sexual abuse are made, Keane J. identifies this as a different and distinct category of hearsay evidence to which different criteria apply as to its admissibility. As the judge can view the tape and hear and see the allegations made, the judge can thus assess the weight and credibility to be attached to it. The admissibility is, however, subject to the three principles set down by Ward L.J. in *Re N. (A Minor)*.[120] In relation to the third principle, Keane J. did not wholly endorse this requirement but he did favour it.[121] It should be noted that the Act does oblige the court to consider both the weight and credibility of hearsay evidence[122] but these considerations arise only once the decision to admit the evidence has been made whereas Ward L.J. advocates the assessment of weight and credibility at the admissibility stage. Again, and most appropriately in sexual abuse cases, the Act could be and should be interpreted along these lines.

---

[115]   Section 21 of the Children Act, 1997.

[116]   Section 22 of the Children Act, 1997.

[117]   Section 23(2)(a) and (b).

[118]   [1997] 1 W.L.R. 153.

[119]   The preliminary inquiry should be in private with the judge to assess the competence of the child and the reliability of child's evidence. Relevant factors are: timing; demeanour; personality; intelligence and understanding and the absence of any reason to fabricate the allegation. At this juncture, it is then further necessary to ascertain the expertise of the interviewer, which is recommended to be that of a child psychologist or psychiatrist.

[120]   [1997] 1 W.L.R. 153. The principles are: that the evidence is hearsay and subject to whatever weight and credibility that the judge ascribes to it, being vigilant for pressure in questioning and the use of leading questions; that expert evidence will have to be given to explain and interpret body movement, language, intonation and signs of fantasising; that the expertise of the expert would have to be to a very high standard.

[121]   Unreported, Supreme Court, January 29, 1999 at 34.

[122]   Sections 24 and 25.

In the present case, the wardship order had to be set aside as it was based exclusively upon the hearsay evidence of a speech therapist[123] to whom the allegations were made but not repeated subsequently in a video-taped interview with a senior social worker. This made the allegations inconsistent and thus unreliable. The videotaped interview was likewise inadmissible as the speech therapist was present and the interview was conducted in a pressured fashion.[124] There was a further fundamental defect in admitting the hearsay evidence. The trial judge had not conducted a preliminary inquiry as to the competence of the child to give evidence but had instead decided that the giving of oral testimony would be traumatic for the child.[125]

One final point of note in this case is the adoption of the test set out in *Re W. (Minors) (Wardship: Evidence).*[126] Owing to the defects in the evidence, it could not thus be established that there was a substantial risk to the child by leaving the child in the custody of the alleged perpetrator. Here the only evidence against the mother's failure to prevent the abuse was given by the child in the interview with the speech therapist and was not recounted in the subsequent videotaped interview with the social worker. Like the other hearsay evidence, this was unsupported hearsay evidence, which could not justify a positive finding against both parents. The court reluctantly discharged the wardship order but made no order as to custody, which enabled the High Court to reassess the making of a wardship order.

VI   OTHER ASPECTS OF THE CHILDREN ACT, 1997

The introduction of the Children Act, 1997[127] has also improved the law concerning children. The procedures for single fathers seeking to be appointed guardian with the consent of the mother may now occur informally and without the need for a court application and approval.[128] Where the parents of a child are unmarried and make a statutory declaration that they are the parents of the child concerned and have agreed to appoint the father a guardian and agree arrangements as to custody and or access, then the father becomes a legal guardian of his child. This entitles him to custody and access and prevents the child being adopted with his prior consent. This is sensible for co-habiting couples in stable relationships who are now no longer obliged to have a court approve their decision.

Section 8 of the Children Act, 1997 standardises the upper age of dependency for children in all maintenance applications. The only applications by children for maintenance which did not benefit from the upper age limits of 18 or 23 if in full-time third-level education were under section 11 of the Guardianship of Infants Act, 1964. Section 11 applications are the means by which an unmarried mother obtains maintenance for the benefit of her child against the natural father. Other improvements

---

123 Allegations of sexual abuse against the child were revealed to the speech therapist who was treating the child for speech impediment difficulties.

124 These defects were identical to the ones in *Re N. (A Minor)* [1997] 1 W.L.R. 153 in which a similar interview, where the estranged wife and mother of the child was present at the interview, was held inadmissible for the objections outlined by Ward L.J.

125 Section 23 of the Children Act, 1997 allows this as a basis for admitting hearsay evidence.

126 [1990] 1 F.L.R. 203.

127 For a detailed consideration of the Act, see the annotation by Ward in *Irish Current Law Statutes Annotated,* Children Act, 1997.

128 Section 4 of the Children Act, 1997 inserting new section 2 of the Guardianship of Infants Act, 1964.

are the conferring of express authority on the courts to grant joint custody orders[129] and enabling relatives to apply for access.[130] An important provision in the context of applications by the single father under section 6A is section 9 inserting section 11D of the Guardianship of Infants Act, 1964. This expressly requires the court to consider whether it is in the child's best interest to maintain personal relations and direct contact with his parents.[131]

Parents or relatives involved in custody and access disputes, as applicant or respondent, must be advised of alternative dispute resolution methods.[132] This is in keeping with the mainstream family legislation dealing with judicial separation[133] and divorce.[134] This provision seeks to remove acrimony from custody disputes and thus safeguards the welfare of children during the procedural mechanisms of such applications. The incentives for alternative dispute resolution methods is that any agreement reached may be made a rule of court,[135] proceedings may be adjourned without prejudice to achieve an agreement,[136] and evidence of any attempt to reach such an agreement is inadmissible.[137]

Children have specifically benefited by not having to take part in custody proceedings,[138] and where appropriate to have a guardian *ad litem* appointed[139] with legal representation if necessary.[140] The court can also hear the wishes of the child[141] and order social reports.[142] Two important legislative changes are the abolition of the oath for children under the age of 14,[143] whose evidence can be given through a live television link[144] and with an intermediary.[145]

Finally, as an update on last year's contribution,[146] the State continues to fail its children in need of secure protective care. The instances of this failure are numerous in the past year[147] but the most troubling is the case of a 12-year-old boy with a severe

---

[129] Section 9 inserting new section 11A of the Guardianship of Infants Act, 1964. There appeared to be uncertainty in this regard but this was not universal as joint orders were made in *R.F. v. J.F.* [1995] 3 *Fam, L.J.* 90 and *M.M. v. C.M.* unreported, High Court, July 1994.

[130] Section 9 inserting new section 11B of the Guardianship of Infants Act, 1964. The application is conditional on leave to apply first being granted which in turn requires the court to consider: all the circumstances of the case; the connection between the relative and the child; the risk the application would pose to the child; and the wishes of the child's guardians.

[131] The inclusion of this provision was prompted by the U.N. Convention on the Rights of the Child and is reflected in the two Supreme Court decisions *J.K. v. V.W.* [1990] 2 I.R. 437 and *W.O'R. v. E.H. and the Eastern Health Board*, unreported, Supreme Court, July 23, 1996.

[132] Sections 20 and 21 respectively of the Children Act, 1997.

[133] The Judicial Separation and Family Law Reform Act, 1989 and the Family Law Act, 1995.

[134] The Family Law (Divorce) Act, 1996.

[135] Section 11 of the Children Act, 1997, inserting new Section 24 of the Guardianship of Infants Act, 1964.

[136] Ibid new Section 22.

[137] Ibid new Section 23.

[138] Ibid new Section 27.

[139] Ibid new Section 28.

[140] Ibid.

[141] Ibid new Section 25, as was the position under section 18 of the Guardianship of Infants Act, 1964.

[142] Ibid new Section 26.

[143] The Children Act, 1997, Section 28.

[144] Ibid Section 21.

[145] Ibid Section 22.

[146] Ward, 'Children: Detention and Abortion', in A. Bainham (ed.) *The International Survey of Family Law* 1997, 355–377.

[147] See *Irish Times*, October 28, 1998; March 25, 1999; April 14, 26, and 27, 1999 and May 11, 1999 for a select few instances.

personality disorder. The child in question revealed to psychologists that if young girls refused him sexual intercourse he would kill them.[148] Over a year has elapsed since Kelly J.[149] injuncted the Minister for Health to provide the necessary funds for the building, opening and maintaining of a high support unit for extremely disturbed children. With close on £IR5 billion excess in the Irish exchequer already this fiscal year, it is a grave and gross, but necessary, embarrassment to reveal this inexcusable inactivity to the international community.

---

[148]   *Irish Times*, August 6, 1999.
[149]   [1999] 1 I.L.R.M. 93.

ITALY

INTERCOUNTRY ADOPTION REFORM IN ITALY: FROM 'ADOPTIVE NATIONALISM' TO GLOBAL HARMONIZATION?

*Elena Urso**

I   INTRODUCTION

In the area of Italian family law one of the most important events of 1998 was the long-awaited reform of intercountry adoption. The new Act (no. 476/1998), enacted on December 31, authorized the ratification of the Convention on the Protection of Children and Co-operation in respect of Intercountry Adoption (hereinafter 'the Convention'), concluded at the Hague on May 29, 1993. The same Act gave full and complete effect to the Convention, from the date of its entry into force.[1] However, this welcome legislative intervention cannot be properly described as restricted to 1998 only. In the first place, it should be emphasized that the transitional period will not end before the first half of 2000. Furthermore, there are additional reasons why the recent reform may be considered only a partial and initial (though decisive) contribution to the modification of this field of family law.

This Article will attempt to examine these reasons and, specifically, some of the controversial issues with regard to adoption from the perspective of Italian law and practice. The discussion will start with an analysis of the problems raised by intercountry adoption. A brief description of the most prominent innovations introduced by the 1998 Act will be followed by a general overview, devoted principally to some contradictory aspects of the present situation, which will need to be carefully dealt with by the Italian legislature.

Finally, the paper will try to underline the urgency for a wider and more coherent reform of adoption law, based on coordination between the national and international perspectives. If Italy really aims to be part of the large group of countries that favour (and lead) the modern trend towards a 'globalization of child law',[2] other concrete efforts are necessary. That is to say, it is not sufficient to sign and ratify a Convention to achieve its purposes. In this specific case, further initiatives need to be taken by national legislatures

---

*   Lecturer, Faculty of Law, University of Florence.

[1]   This will take place for Italy pursuant to Article 46, para. 2(a) of the Convention (Articles 2 and 8, para. 3, of the 1998 Act). The Italian Parliament definitively approved the text of the unitary Bill on the implementation of the Convention (no. 4626/1998, which unified some previous ones: nos. 130, 160, 445, 1697 and 2545) on December 15, 1998. This Bill had been introduced in the Senate by the government. It was transmitted subsequently to the Camera dei Deputati – after receiving the approval of the Senate on February 26, 1998 – and was finally approved with some limited amendments only. A regulation – whose enactment is now expected for the beginning of September 1999 – will be necessary to complete the legal framework. See text at note 23. This paper has been updated at the end of July 1999.

[2]   This expression clearly depicts the modern trend that favours not only the recognition of the universal rights of children, but also the creation of instruments of protection which may be effective also across national frontiers. See for an in-depth analysis, S. Detrick, P. Vlaardingerbroek (eds), *Globalization of Child Law – The Role of the Hague Conventions*, (1999) The Hague.

to reduce the total number of children-in-need inside and outside their boundaries. This implies the adoption of social measures aiming to strengthen international co-operation.

All in all, a renewed interest seems to characterize the present Italian debate about adoption law. At this point, it is appropriate to assign responsibility for further action to the legislature, trusting that its declared 'platform' will soon become clearer and – more importantly – that its plans will be accomplished effectively in the future.

II   THE INTERCOUNTRY ADOPTION ACT 1998: THE AIM AND THE TIMING OF A LONG-AWAITED REFORM

The first attempts to reform adoption law in Italy were made several years ago. There can be no doubt that these efforts were in fact aimed at instituting a wide reform, as they were not limited to intercountry adoption only. Therefore, the decision to implement the Convention and to postpone the general reform of adoption can be explained only in the light of the urgent need to ensure that Italian statutory instruments are in conformity with the principles affirmed by the Hague Convention – signed by Italy in 1995 and ratified by an increasing number of States in recent times.[3]

Some of the solutions embodied in the previous Italian reform of adoption law (i.e. in the 1983 Act, no.184) often proved to be too rigid, although these provisions were perhaps momentarily appropriate to cope with the difficult situation faced by the legislature at the beginning of the 1980s. Prior to this, the lack of a set of legal rules devoted expressly to intercountry adoption had meant that a 'judge-made' procedural mechanism was followed which seriously lessened the safeguards for foreign children entering Italy.[4] Thus it was extremely simple to give effect to adoptions that had taken place abroad, following the ordinary *exequatur* procedure – at that time regulated by the Code of Civil Procedure (Articles 797 ff., 801 ff.). The problem was that no provision for specific requirements or control devices was made to prevent abuses. The legislative answer, provided in 1983, to the social demand of protection for foreign children, was

---

[3]   The Convention entered into force on an international level on May 27, 1995. It has been ratified by most of the Member States (i.e. by those which are members of the Hague Conference and which are mainly 'receiving countries'). A high number of 'sending countries' which participated in the preparatory and the final meetings have ratified it too. It is worth noting that they were allowed to take part in these meetings on the same conditions as Member States (i.e. they could exercise the right to vote). This is perhaps the main reason for the great success of the Convention. Twenty-five States have ratified and twelve have signed it to this day. Italy is still inserted in the list of the signatory States. See on this issue, E.D.Jaffe (ed), *Intercountry Adoption: Laws and Perspectives of 'Sending Countries'*, (1995) Dordrecht-Boston-New York; J.H.A.Van Loon, *L'enfant et les Conventions internationales*, (1996) Presses Universitaires de Lyon.

In recent Italian legal writing see T. Ballarino, *Diritto Internazionale Privato*, (1999) Padova, 3rd, 470 ff.; M.Finocchiaro, 'Adozione internazionale', in *Guida al Diritto – Il Sole 24 Ore*, no.4, 1-30-1999, 14 ff.; L.Fadiga, *L'adozione*, (1999) Bologna, at 63; F.Zacco, 'Tutela dei minori: cosa cambia in tema di adozione di minori stranieri', in *Nuove Leggi Civili Commentate*, (1999) 84 ff.; M.Brienza, 'La nuova disciplina dell'adozione internazionale', in *Gazzetta Giuridica*, no.10/1999, 7 ff.; *Adozione internazionale e Convenzione dell'Aja – Contributi interdisciplinari*, A.Dell'Antonio (ed), (1997) Milano; A.Beghé Loreti, 'Adozione internazionale', in *Enciclopedia del Diritto, Aggiornamento*, I, (1997) Milano, 43 ff. at 54; B.Poletti di Teodoro, 'L'adozione internazionale', in *Il diritto di famiglia*, III, G.Bonilini, G.Cattaneo (eds), (1997) Torino, 404 ff.; L.Rossi Carleo, 'Adozione internazionale', in *Trattato di diritto privato*, 4, IV, P.Rescigno (ed), 2nd, (1997) Torino, 405 ff. See, more generally, V.Librando, F. Mosconi, D.Rinoldi, *Tempi biblici per la ratifica dei trattati: i diritti dei minori e la storia infinita della partecipazione italiana a quattro Convenzioni internazionali*, (1993) Padova.

[4]   It was the Court of Appeal that gave effect to foreign adoption orders. See G.Franceschelli, 'Adozione internazionale e nazionalismo adottivo', in *Giurisprudenza Italiana*, (1982) I, 2, 755 ff.

intended to improve both the substantive and procedural guarantees through the introduction of new and rigorous regulation.

Credit must of course be given to the aims of this law. Indeed, the core of the 1983 Act expressed a modern, child-oriented approach. However, some of the choices made by the legislature reflected a very restricted vision that often caused serious problems in international relations concerning intercountry adoption cases.[5] The main difficulties were due to the decision to regulate this social institution by giving absolute priority to Italian law as well as to Italian jurisdiction, without taking into account the profound differences which existed in comparison to other legal systems, especially those of the so-called 'sending countries'. Most of these problems can be seen as the inevitable consequences of the extremely narrow conception of adoption prevailing in 1983, which can be critically described as an expression of 'adoptive nationalism'.[6]

The dangers linked with such a statutory approach – expressed by the first complete regulation of adoption of children in Italy, and clearly differentiating itself from the traditional 'conflict of laws' solutions – became clear at the end of the 1980s, only a few years after the enactment of 1983 Act. The Italian legislature began to show its awareness of the need to develop a new and coordinated intervention which could be applicable on an international level as the trafficking of children became increasingly common the world over. Added to this was the awareness of other forms of severe abuses, the abolition of which called for stricter co-operation amongst States. In brief, the need for strong preventive efforts became increasingly evident in order to stop these crimes.

At this point, during the late 1980s, a wide number of States were already on the point of reaffirming their commitments in this direction. However, generally speaking, the fundamental perspective centering on criminal enforcement presupposes, both on the international and national level, the presence of an efficient system of protection based on private law rules. Furthermore, efforts to sanction violations may sometimes prove to be useless and even dangerous. On the one hand, punitive reactions simply increase the harm already done to the child because they are often directed towards the prospective adoptive parents as well, with whom the foreign child has probably established a close bond of affection. On the other, since these protective techniques should play, above all, a preventive role, they cannot operate alone in the absence of effective civil measures. Therefore, the coordination of these kinds of remedies became central in planning a new international intervention.

It was felt that the premises for reciprocal and trusting relationships between foreign States, imperative to avoid 'child-markets', could be set only by favouring a possible renewal in international co-operation. The most rational way of coping with these

---

[5]   F.D. Busnelli, 'Luci ed ombre nella disciplina italiana dell'adozione di minori stranieri', in *Rivista di Diritto Internazionale Privato e Processuale*, (1986) 255 ff. at 274; A.Davì, 'Problemi di diritto internazionale privato e processuale relativi all'applicazione della nuova legge italiana sull'adozione', in *Diritto di Famiglia e delle Persone*, (1988) 481 ff.; G.Panzera, 'L' "adozione internazionale": alcune osservazioni di diritto internazionale privato e processuale', in *Giustizia Civile*, (1988) I, 77 ff.; R.Baratta, 'La giurisdizione italiana in materia di adozione internazionale di minori', in *Rivista di Diritto Internazionale*, (1988), 48 ff. See, in comparative literature, 'L'adoption dans les principales législationes européennes', (eds) J.M.Bishoff, A.Rieg, in *Revue Internationale de Droit Comparé*, (1983), E.Brand, 631 ff., G.Kojanec, 817 ff. and J.M.Bishoff, 'Introduction comparative', 703 ff., at 705 and 710. See also V.Varano, 'L'adoption internationale', in *Italian National Reports to the XIIIth International Congress of Comparative Law* – Montreal 1990, (1990) Milano, 157 ff. at 160. For more recent accounts, see J.H.Van Loon, 'International Co-operation and Protection of Children with Regard to Intercountry Adoption', in 244 *Recueil des Cours*, (1993) VII, 191 ff. at 284 and at 327.

[6]   This trend was criticized even before the 1983 reform. See G. Franceschelli, 'Adozione internazionale e nazionalismo adottivo', in *Giurisprudenza Italiana*, (1982) I,2, 755 ff.

problems consisted of accepting the idea of 'flexibility' and abandoning any unilateral, 'national-oriented' dimension. Social, cultural, religious and legal differences need of course to be respected for the purpose of ensuring a decisive mutual collaboration between 'sending countries' and 'receiving countries'. This perspective was subsequently enshrined in the Hague Convention on Intercountry Adoption, approved at the XVII session of the Conference in 1993, the year of the celebration of its centenary.[7]

It should be remembered that, during a meeting of the Special Commission that took place in 1988, it was the government of Italy that proposed giving prominence to the discussion of issues connected with intercountry adoption. 'This was all the more interesting because Italy had only quite recently introduced strict regulations on intercountry adoption.'[8] This proposal was immediately accepted and the Permanent Bureau opened a debate on a wide scale soon afterwards, the large number of participants being deemed necessary to reach an extensive and effective agreement. One of the concrete aims of the Secretary General to the Conference was to widen the scope of the discussion, with a view to understanding the social, economic and political diversities that usually play a decisive role in the area.[9]

III   THE NEED TO STRENGTHEN THE 'DUE PROCESS' OF ADOPTING A CHILD ABROAD

The efforts towards harmonizing intercountry adoption law made by the Hague Conference were extremely successful. One of the immediate effects was that this initiative received great attention in the sense that the number of countries taking part in the meetings that led to the final draft of the Convention was higher than in any other project. Not only did all the Member States of the Conference participate in the complex preparatory work, but also some other States (mainly the so-called 'sending countries') as well as the most important non-governmental organizations.

The main aspects of the Convention are well known. Firstly, both national and intercountry adoption should be regulated following the same general principles. The fundamental aim is to ensure that adoption law respects the principle of *'subsidiarity'*, also affirmed by the 1989 United Nations Convention on the Rights of the Child.[10] Adoption may take place only if the competent authority in the State of origin has verified the impossibility of helping the biological parents with effective measures, and has also given due consideration to the child's placement in the home State. Therefore, each Member State has the duty *'as a matter of priority'* to make efforts to enable the child to remain in the care of the family of origin. If this is not possible, or it is not

---

[7]   The subject was submitted on January 19, 1988 by the Permanent Bureau to the Special Commission. 'On this occasion the Secretary General, taking into account the formal proposal made by Italy', introduced the Preliminary Document prepared by the Permanent Bureau. Cf. G.Parra Aranguren, *Explanatory Report on the Convention on Protection of Children and Co-operation in Respect of Intercountry Adoption*, Permanent Bureau, (1994) The Hague, 1 ff. at 1.

[8]   Cf. J.H.Van Loon, in 244 *Recueil des Cours*, (1993) VII, 191 ff. at 327, note 323.

[9]   See the report of the then First Secretary to the Permanent Bureau, and now Secretary General to the Conference, J.H.A.Van Loon, *Proceedings of the Seventeenth Session 10 to 29 May 1993, Adoption-Co-operation*, Permanent Bureau of the Conference, II, (1994) The Hague; by the same author, for a brief account, see *Introductory Note on the Hague Convention of May 29 1993 on the Protection of Children and Co-operation in Respect of Intercountry Adoption*, in *Uniform Law Review*, 1993, 76 ff.

[10] This leading principle is embodied in Article 21(d) of the 1989 New York Convention – which has been ratified by Italy (Act no. 176, May 27, 1991) – and also mentioned in the Preamble of the 1993 Hague Convention.

possible to find a suitable adoptive family in the State of origin of the child, intercountry adoption will be allowed, but it should take place following the safeguards established by the Convention and, in any case, in compliance with '*the best interests of the child*' and '*his or her fundamental rights as recognized in international law*'. A further object of the Convention is the creation of a system of co-operation that can properly protect children and effectively prevent their abduction, sale or traffic. A third aim consists in securing that the recognition of adoption orders is made in accordance with the Convention (i.e. in conformity with all its fundamental guarantees).[11] A key feature was the idea of accepting some inevitable differences on a national level. In fact, experience had taught that, given the impossibility of reaching uniform solutions in contexts characterized by deeply rooted conceptions such as family relationships, the best way of achieving harmonization was to start from common and shared fundamental values.

As a rule, technicalities should be set aside, at least at the beginning of the harmonization work, when they can irretrievably obstruct the target. Only when a certain degree of uniformity has been reached and when there is also a growing awareness of the practicability of detailed regulations, can efforts be directed towards legal plans for uniformity. This said, a variety of solutions usually present themselves when a common set of principles is settled. This is simply viewed, in this case, as an unmodifiable 'marking trait', typical of most family law institutions.

Looking at the 'structure' of the 1993 Convention, it is possible to observe that it was ideated in order to leave enough scope for future specifications within the different national legal systems. In so doing, a leading role is given to the competent authorities of each Member State, and in particular to those of the 'sending countries'.[12] That is to say, they are called on to establish if, in respect of the principle of '*subsidiarity*', intercountry adoption is in the best interests of the child. Moreover, they must ascertain that all the necessary consents (including the child's consent) have been freely expressed in the required legal form and in writing after complete information has been given about the termination of the relationships with the family of origin and after verifying that there has been no kind of inducement or undue influence wielded. Furthermore, national authorities need to be sure that the consent of the mother was given after the child's birth, and not before.[13]

The same clarity is apparent in the actions of the '*receiving State*'. The appropriate authorities must determine the suitability of the prospective adopters and ensure that they have been adequately counselled in order to be able to give its authorization for the entrance and permanent residence of the child in the State.[14] Foreign authorities have also been entrusted with responsibility for procedural requirements.[15] The powers conferred on (and the complex duties imposed on) the Central Authorities operating in each Member State are very wide; thus co-operation has to be achieved – in the 'framework' of the Convention – through the correct exercise of discretion as well as through the full accomplishment of these commitments. Great importance has been attributed to reciprocal reliability amongst States, in the sense of giving, receiving and keeping

---

[11]   Article 1 of the Convention.

[12]   See W.Duncan, 'The Hague Convention on the Protection of Children in Respect of Intercountry Adoption 1993. Some Issues of Special Relevance to Sending Countries', in *Intercountry Adoption*, Jaffe (ed), 217 ff. at 227, note 14.

[13]   Article 4 of the Convention.

[14]   Article 5 of the Convention.

[15]   Articles 14–22 of the Convention.

information.[16] All these aims might of course be better achieved if they entered into agreements, both bilateral and multilateral. In this way the application of the Convention would be improved through the mutual relationships set up between them. Moreover, according to the Convention, the derogations contained in these agreements – which need to heighten the level of protection – are admissible within a very limited scope, embracing only a few procedural provisions.[17]

Last but not least, the mechanism for the recognition of adoption reveals an even wider respect for decisions taken abroad: whenever an adoption is certified by the competent authority of the State of origin as having being made in accordance with the Convention, it must be recognized '*by operation of law*' in other States parties to the Convention (i.e. without any further ascertainment). The recognition may be refused only if adoption is '*manifestly contrary*' to the public policy of a contracting State, but it is always necessary to take into consideration the best interests of the child.[18] For the purpose of protecting these interests, the Convention also admits the possibility of converting an adoption that, in the State of origin, does not sever pre-existing legal ties of kinship, into an adoption that produces these effects, if this is permitted in the State of origin and if all the necessary consents have already been given to completing such a different kind of adoption.[19]

In the new vision that has emerged from the Convention, 'new rights' have also been expressly recognized: the right of the child to be informed about his or her origin, the right of prospective adopters to pay no more than '*costs and expenses, including reasonable professional fees*', and the right to an '*expeditious*' process of adoption.[20] Finally, it is worth noting that the Convention does not permit reservations, lest they open the 'floodgates' to a new diversification process.

The Italian reform of 1998 has, of course, been greatly inspired by these principles and directives. It generally reflects the most important substantive and procedural indications given by the Convention.[21] It does not therefore seem very useful to enter into details or to describe analytically all the provisions embodied in the new Act. It seems better to focus on some aspects of the Italian reform only, those that reveal the intention of the legislature not to depart completely from the 'nationalistic' approach which prevailed in 1983. Interestingly, such a critical choice was partially 'concealed'. Thus, as we shall see, the 1998 Act apparently respects the guide-lines given by the Convention, but the real meaning of certain new provisions is, in some cases, in contrast with them, at least in part (i.e. when the statute refers to some criticized solutions adopted by the previous reform, which is still in force). One can find several examples of this 'resistance

---

[16]   Articles 7 and 10 of the Convention.

[17]   See Article 39 of the Convention. Even if the positive effects of the Convention can be fully produced only through its ratification, accession or implementation, it is worth emphasizing that the idea of instituting a Central Authority, which is called to play a leading role in this field, has been widely accepted even before (or independently of) the signature or ratification of the Convention. This happened in some countries which are not likely to become parties to the Convention too, at least in the immediate future (e.g. by India and Russia).

[18]   Article 24 of the Convention.

[19]   Article 26, para. 2 of the Convention.

[20]   Articles 30–35 of the Convention.

[21]   As far as the scope of applicability of the 1998 Act is concerned, it should be stressed that it will also regulate adoptions of foreign children who reside abroad if the prospective adopters are Italians who are resident in a foreign country. However, where they have been resident in that foreign country for more than two years they can adopt according to the law of the State where they reside. The Italian *Tribunale* will give effect to this adoption order in Italy if it has been issued in conformity with the Convention (Article 36, para. 4).

to change' in the new Act. However, before considering these statutory contradictions let us complete the description of the present legal background.

IV NEW PRINCIPLES AND OLD PROBLEMS: WAITING FOR A NEW REFORM

The Hague Convention entered into force on the international level only a few years ago, in 1995. In this period (i.e. in the second half of the 1990s) severe criticism of some of the legislative choices adopted by the Italian legislature in 1983 started to be expressed by the Constitutional Court. In a growing number of decisions, the Court made it clear that, while respecting the legislative positions, it was necessary to evaluate the profound influences engendered by progressive social modifications of family relationships. As a result, some rigorous requirements, uniformly provided for both national and intercountry adoption, were declared incompatible with fundamental constitutional principles.[22] These decisions were mainly related to cases of intercountry adoptions, but their effects were extended to national adoption too, since – in most cases – they were referable to the same legislative provisions. A common foundation characterizes these decisions: they are based on the idea that the same level of protection should be afforded to all adoptees. What is innovatory is that they clearly reject the assumption that it is only statutory limitations of a severe and absolutely inflexible nature which can adequately protect children-in-need.

The 'constitutionalization' of adoption law instead conferred a more decisive role on the courts, in order that they establish the best interests of the child in individual cases. In this way, a new and more 'open' vision of adoption was thereby affirmed. This new trend has been slow but progressive and it is still in the course of realization. It must surely be considered as the most significant outcome of the intervention of the Constitutional Court. It should also be remembered, however, that some commentators manifested their strong dissent in this regard. In other words, they saw these developments as examples of a 'judicial substitution' of the legislative functions, i.e. as an inadmissible interference with Parliamentary prerogatives. Moreover, other critical remarks underlined the risks

---

[22] It can be said, more precisely, that the first decisions date back to the early 1990s. This trend has been confirmed, however, in more recent years. See e.g. Corte Costituzionale, decision n.148, 4-1-1992, in *Diritto di Famiglia e delle Persone*, (1992) 504 ff. and in *Giustizia Civile*, (1992) I, 1415 ff.; decision no 303, 7-24-1996, in *Foro Italiano*, (1997) I, 51 ff.; decision no 349, 10-9-1998, in *Guida al Diritto – Il Sole 24 Ore*, n.41, 10-24-1998, 30 ff. and, for a comment, U.Bellini, in *Nuova Giurisprudenza Civile Commentata*, (1998) 1142 ff.; decision n. 283, 7-9-1999. The latter decision has not yet been published in legal reviews. See however *Il Sole 24 Ore*, 7-11-1999, at 16; *Il Corriere della Sera*, 7-11-1999, at 15; *La Repubblica*, 7-12-1999, at 21. All these decisions declared Article 6, para. 2 of Act no 184/1983 partially incompatible with fundamental constitutional principles because this provision did not contemplate any possibility of derogating from the strict requirements established for the minimum and the maximum difference of age limits. In brief, the first (no. 148/1992), the second (no 303/1996) and the fourth (no. 283/1999) decisions eliminated the rigidity of the maximum limit. In the first case, the Court affirmed that Article 6 was unconstitutional because it did not allow the adoption of children who were brothers or sisters, even when for one of them only the limit was not respected, and when their separation would cause them serious harm as a consequence of the severing of their contact. The second decision declared the unconstitutionality of the same provision because it absolutely precluded adoption when the maximum difference of age between one of the adopters and the adoptee was higher than the limit established by the law (i.e. 40 years). The latter decision extended this principle to cases in which the maximum limit is not respected by both adopters. However, it should be stressed that the Court introduced only one exception to the rule, since the maximum difference of age should in any case be as similar as possibile to the common difference that exists between biological parents and their children. Furthermore, the exception is possible only if the refusal of adoption may cause serious harm to the child and which cannot be avoided otherwise. The same criterion was followed by the third decision (no 41/1998), which declared the unconstitutionality of the rule which strictly provided for the inflexible minimum difference of age (i.e. 18 years).

inherent in eliminating clear-cut statutory requirements (e.g. those concerning the maximum and minimum difference of age between adopters and adoptee).

Some of these concerns are, however, unjustified. Excessive freedom in the evaluation of the prospective adopters' suitability may lead to great uncertainty, which is unacceptable, but it has now been well established that a certain margin of judicial discretion has to be recognized, at least as far as age limits are concerned. That is to say, the idea of strictly abiding by these limitations in any situation has been replaced by a positive attitude towards more flexible 'guide-lines'. In fact, the departure from some of the rigorous rules originally established by the legislature in 1983 does not mean that the judge has complete discretionary powers. On the contrary, it is necessary to follow foreseeable and uniform criteria, which, however, must always be applied in the best interest of the child.

V   THE CURRENT PERSPECTIVE: A FORTHCOMING REGULATION AND THE NEED FOR A GENERAL STATUTORY FRAMEWORK

Of course, these judicial decisions cannot be considered exhaustive. Indeed, new plans for another legislative intervention have been proposed recently; these however I shall deal with below, after a brief description of the current legal position.

It should be stressed at the outset that further steps are still necessary to implement the Convention in Italy. This is another reason that has led me to specify that the process of reforming adoption law received a decisive impulse only in 1998, although it was, in fact, neither definitive nor complete, not even in the area of intercountry adoption. In order for this latter phase of implementation to take place, a specific regulation has to be enacted. This will contain detailed provisions about the organization and functions of the Italian Central Authority (*Commissione per le adozioni internazionali*), which will be constituted three months after the enactment of the regulation. The reform will enter into force only when the Central Authority starts performing its functions, and after the publication of the list of Accredited Bodies.[23] In the meantime, the old rules will continue to govern adoption procedures. It should be pointed out, however, that the first deadline has already elapsed, and that the regulation – expected by the end of May 1999 – has not been enacted, given that its text has still to be examined by the *Consiglio di Stato*. Following this, the regulation will hopefully be approved with no further delay. In any case, the reform will not enter into force before 2000.

It is also worth noting that the general situation worldwide has changed in the first six months of 1999; that is to say, the number of States which have ratified the Convention has suddenly grown.[24] This ongoing harmonization process has thus become

---

[23]   See Articles 31 and 39-ter of the 1998 Act. The Italian legislature has already designed a peculiar role for Accredited Bodies. In order to obtain the accreditation they should comply, *inter alia*, with the duty to participate in activities favouring the promotion of the rights of children. This should happen preferably through co-operation towards development programs and in collaboration with non-governmental organizations too, in conformity with the principle of subsidiarity of intercountry adoption in the countries of origin of the children (Article 39-ter, para. 1 [f] of the 1998 Act). The regulation mentioned in the text – instituting the Central Authority – is not likely to be enacted, however, before September 1999.

[24]   This process still appears to be ongoing. See, e.g., among the most recent implementation Acts, the British *Adoption (Intercountry Aspects) Act*, which received the Royal Assent on July 27, 1999, after being passed by the House of Commons (on June 11, 1999) and by the House of Lords soon afterwards. The first major 'receiving State' which ratified the Convention was Spain (November 1, 1995). See, for a clear overview, H.Van Loon, 'Transnational Family Care for Children: Adoption, Foster Care and Temporary Care – The

increasingly evident over this time span. The phenomenon has however determined an understandably cautious approach by the Italian authorities dealing with pending procedures. Especially given the continuous growth of the number of ratifications, and in view of the entry into force of the Convention in Brazil (on July 1, 1999), the practice which most of the subjects involved in these procedures have adopted (i.e. lawyers, judges, public servants, social services employees, and prospective adoptive parents as well) has attempted to follow as closely as possible the principles contained in the Convention.[25]

The fear of frustrating any legislative attempts, during the long transition period, is absolutely justified, in that serious difficulties may be faced if the new solutions are not accepted gradually. It is obvious however that the situation will become clearer as soon as the legal framework is built up. In any event, this transition period may last for several months and, as a result, there is the concrete danger that some of the aims of the reform may be jeopardized. To eliminate this risk, an increasing number of prospective adopters have started to contact voluntarily the existing authorized bodies (i.e. those that have been authorized following the 1983 Act). This practice is, however, simply a welcome anticipation of the mechanism that will become obligatory in the near future. On the contrary, other aspects of the reform have created situations which are paradoxical and which appear to be characterized by a trend of 'chaotic inactivity'.

Given the absence of any clear guidance from the competent authorities, and given the high number of foreign children coming from countries that have already ratified the Convention, there is a strong - and reasonable - reluctance to accept the idea that the 'old rules', still in force, can be applied without giving rise to substantive (even if not to formal) violations of the principle of equality.[26] A new Act, as a rule, has no retroactive

---

(Potential) Significance of the Hague Convention', in *Europe Meets in Florence for a Workshop on Intercountry Adoption*, EurAdopt meeting, Florence, April 24, 1998, CIAI (1998) Milan, 18 ff. at 22.

The concrete interest which has been shown in common law systems towards the implementation of the 1993 Hague Convention is significant. While many civil law countries have had no particular difficulty in accepting its approach, it is more difficult for common law countries to do this, given the different modalities for implementing international Conventions, and in particular, given the need (and the difficulty) to enact a federal statute in the U.S.A. in order to do so. The Bill which has been introduced in the U.S. Senate (on March 26, 1999, by Senator J. Helms – S. 682) after being presented to the House of Representatives (on June 24, 1999, by Mr. Traficant), has been immediately referred to the competent Committees (respectively, on International Relations and on the Judiciary) and to the Subcommittee on Immigration and Claims (on July 23, 1999). For this specific problems, see e.g. H.C. Kennard, 'Curtailing the Sale and Trafficking of Children: A Discussion of the Hague Conference Convention in Respect of Intercountry Adoption, in 14 *Pennsylvania Journal of International Business Law*, (1993) 623 ff. at 639, and P.H.Pfund, 'The Hague Intercountry Adoption Convention and Federal International Child Support Enforcement', in 30 *University of California, Davis LR*, (1997) 647 ff. at 655; by the same author, see also 'Intercountry Adoption: The 1993 Hague Convention: Its Purposes', in 28 *Family Law Quarterly*, (1994) 53 ff.

[25] This trend can be confirmed, so far, only by informal interviews with these subjects. It is worth noting, however, that many initiatives have been taken in order to collect and publish data about adoption in recent years. See e.g. the report drafted by the competent office of the *Ministero di Grazia e Giustizia* in 1998 on the state of application of the current Act and the trends in this area, 'L'applicazione della Legge 4.5.1983 no. 184 "Disciplina dell'adozione e dell'affidamento dei minori" nel quinquennio 1993–1997', (1998) Roma. An important statutory intervention which, *inter alia*, favours this kind of activity dates back to 1997. The legislature enacted an Act – no. 285, on 28 August – to improve the rights of children and their opportunities. A new Act (no. 451) was enacted soon afterwards, on December 23, which instituted the Parliamentary Commission and the National Observatory for Children. These statutes gave a great impetus to the new trend which favors the drafting of complete and up-to-date reports and the continuous contacts amongst groups and individuals which are involved in several activities aiming at the protection of children.

[26] Article 3, para. 2, of the Italian Constitution.

effects.[27] However, substantive guarantees such as those envisaged in the 1998 reform are closely intertwined with procedural modifications. Thus, equal protection can be substantially denied in the case of the completely different treatment of similar situations, due only to the different moment at which the prospective adopters sent in their applications.

Furthermore, attempts to adjust immediately practice to the requirements set up by the Convention may well produce great uncertainty as a consequence of the currently incomplete legal background. Therefore, at least in some cases, the sceptical and cautious behaviour shown recently by the Central Authorities of some 'sending countries' is surely to be applauded.[28] For example, most States of Latin America and Eastern Europe have ratified the Convention; nevertheless, given the high number of foreign adoptees that they send their authorities cannot be blamed if they hesitate before starting an intercountry adoption procedure with Italy today. The outcome of this process is still not clear: the current Italian situation is extremely confused and, of course, uncertain indications (the only ones that can be given at this point) are absolutely unacceptable and even dangerous. The only thing that can be said is that the objective of the Italian legislature to adhere completely to the spirit of the Hague Convention risks being disavowed unless there is a rapid acceleration in the process of clarification still in course.

VI   HOW TO PROTECT THE BEST INTERESTS OF THE CHILD: THE MAIN PHASES OF ITALIAN STATUTORY DEVELOPMENTS

To describe the fundamental phases of the modernization process of Italian adoption law that should soon culminate in the implementation of the Convention, it may be useful briefly to survey the spectrum of the main legislative developments which have taken place over the last few decades.

First of all, it should be pointed out that, notwithstanding the numerous statutory interventions in this field of child law, intercountry adoption was not expressly regulated in Italy before the 1983 reform. The previous private international law system – which was modified by the legislature in 1995[29] – contained a very limited provision devoted to adoption. Article 20, para. 2, of the preliminary provisions to the Civil Code enacted in 1942, dealt only with the 'relationships between adopters and adoptee'. According to the 'choice of law' rule embodied in this provision, these relationships had to be regulated by 'the national law of the adopter, at the time of adoption'. Such a concise indication led to

---

[27]   This solution might be considered unconstitutional, because it is in conflict with a fundamental procedural principle (*'tempus regit actum'*) as well as to the aim of fully protecting foreign adoptees. A similar choice – which has been made by the 1983 Act (Article 76) – was declared unconstitutional. See Corte Costituzionale no. 199, 7-18-1986, in *Rassegna di Diritto Civile*, (1987) 1972 ff. (annotated by A.Procida Mirabelli di Lauro).

[28]   On the contrary, a clear example of unjustified distrust towards Italian authorities is given by the reactions of the authorities of Peru, which signed a bilateral Convention with Italy in 1993. This Convention entered into force on March 1, 1995 (without the enactment of an Italian Act of authorization of the ratification, and in the presence of a Peruvian Act: no. 2638, November 8, 1994). However, these difficulties seem now to be coming to an end. See *Adozione intenazionale e Convenzione dell'Aja*, A.Dell'Antonio (ed), (1997) Milano, 137 ff.

[29]   Act no. 218, enacted on May 31, 1995.

some interpretative problems and it was deemed unsatisfactory especially when, in the late 1960s, the phenomenon of intercountry adoption took on its present features.[30]

However, focusing on the legislation enacted in this period, there are no indications of a new approach towards intercountry adoption. The first reform of adoption law (i.e Act no. 431, enacted on July 5, 1967) changed the Civil Code system extensively. It introduced several Articles (314/2–314/28) on full adoption, which was defined as 'special' in order to be differentiated from simple adoption – the only form of adoption previously accepted by Italian law, and now limited to adults. Some years later, in 1974, when Italy ratified the European Convention on the Adoption of Children concluded at Strasbourg on April 24, 1967, the legislature did not insert new provisions in the Code in order to deal specifically with intercountry adoption.[31] Thus, although both these innovations were very important, they were clearly and necessarily limited to domestic adoption. Such a perspective tended to appear too narrow as soon as it became clear that prospective adopters of foreign children could easily by-pass the strict requirements established by Italian law, since the recognition of adoptions that took place abroad was then allowed without any particular difficulty. At the same time, it was evident that the attempts towards harmonization which had been instituted by the 1967 European Convention – based on the aim of favouring the acceptance of the same legal rules and principles in each Member State – were not successful.

This situation gave rise to the idea of a new reform at the end of the 1970s. The lack of rules regulating intercountry adoption, on the one hand, and the need to follow the directives of the European Convention, on the other, were the conclusive reasons in the decision to enact a statute (*legge speciale*) which was expressly devoted to all kinds of adoption of children. Its provisions were not intended to be included in the Civil Code, although some of them (i.e. the final provisions) contained some rules that coordinated the new regime with the old one.

This was not an easy task, and the debate about the new reform lasted for many years. Indeed, it was only in 1983 that the Italian Parliament approved the Adoption of Children Act. Apart from specific procedural aspects, domestic and intercountry adoption were regulated in the same way to ensure the same level of protection in both situations. In addition, all the requirements and effects provided for full adoption were identical, whatever the nationality of the child. Adoption could take place only if the court (*Tribunale per i Minorenni*) had ascertained that the prospective adoptive parents were married, that three years had passed since their marriage, that they were not separated, and that they were suitable to bring up, educate and maintain a child. Furthermore, the law set up age limits, which were originally absolute before the above-mentioned decisions taken by the Constitutional Court. The maximum difference of age between adopters and adoptee, was thus fixed at 40 years and the minimum at 18 years. As far as the effects of adoption were concerned, it should be emphasized that adoptees acquired the same *status* as legitimate children and that their legal ties with their biological parents and with their family were severed definitively. Adoptive origins could not be revealed, except in the case of express judicial authorization.[32] The adoption order, after being

---

[30]   See A.Davì, *L'adozione nel diritto internazionale privato italiano, I- Conflitti di leggi*, Milano, (1981) 66 ff.; and by the same author, 'Adozione nel diritto internazionale privato', in *Digesto delle Discipline Privatistiche, IV, Sezione Civile*, I, (1987) Torino, 131 ff.

[31]   See Act no. 357 enacted on May 22, 1974, which authorized the ratification that dates back to May 25, 1976.

[32]   Violations of the duty to respect secrecy have been criminally sanctioned (Articles 28, 70 and 73 of 1983 Act).

registered in the office of records of the *Tribunale per i Minorenni,* had to be sent to the registry office (*Ufficio dello Stato Civile*), in order to be annotated at the margin of the birth certificate. However, the law forbade any information concerning the adoptive relationship to be communicated. Thus, certificates contained indications of the new surname only.

All these requirements have remained unchanged since then. However, there is a general impression and hope in Italy today that the adoption law will be reformed soon. Even without following the legal discussions, it is possible to see in the media that attitudes are changing. Of course, some of the features of the 1983 Act are likely to be modified when the 1998 Act comes into force but a wider intervention has already been planned. Before dealing with the expected reform, it is necessary, however, to complete the description of the current statutory frame.

A further reform that dealt with adoption before the 1998 Act dated back to 1995.[33] In that year the Italian system of private international law was completely modified by the legislature. The 1995 Act contained four provisions devoted to adoption; it introduced new rules to determine the applicable law and the scope of Italian jurisdiction, as well as to regulate the recognition of adoptions that took place in a foreign State. Even if many of these rules will now be replaced by the new ones provided for by the 1998 reform, it is worth noting that the new system of private international law already started to express a changing attitude towards the previous choices made in 1983: 'adoptive nationalism' began to show signs of coming to an end.[34]

It is true that the insertions into the 1995 Act of specific rules about adoption did not produce any substantive modifications. That is to say, the legislature did not alter the role played by special legislation, since it made direct reference to the rules contained therein. Not only did Italian law maintain its wide scope of applicability, because it continued to regulate all cases of full adoption orders requested of Italian judges, but the extensive 'boundaries' of Italian jurisdiction were also left substantially unmodified, together with the vast power of control given to Italian courts.[35] The general mechanism of so-called

---

[33]   Act no. 218, enacted on May 31, 1995.

[34]   See Bonomi, 'La disciplina dell'adozione internazionale dopo la riforma del diritto internazionale privato', in *Rivista di Diritto Civile,* (1996) I, 363 ff.; T.Ballarino, *Diritto Internazionale Privato,* (1996), 2nd, 457 ff., and (1999), 3rd, Padova, 470 ff.

[35]   The Act that reformed the system, no. 218, was enacted on May 31, 1995. For a general account, see *e.g. La riforma del diritto internazionale privato e processuale – Raccolta in ricordo di Edoardo Vitta,* G.Gaja (ed), (1994) Milano; and A.Davì, 'Le questioni generali del diritto internazionale privato nel progetto di riforma', 45 ff. at 128, note 129.

        Article 38 of the 1995 Act relates to the requirements of adoption, to its constitution and its revocation. According to this provision, these aspects are to be regulated by the national law of the adopter or by the law (if it is common) of both adopters or by the law of the State in which both of them reside or where their matrimonial life is established substantially, at the moment of adoption. Article 39 sets up the same choice of law rule to determine the applicable law regulating personal and economic relationships between the adoptee and the adoptive family. A final rule – embodied in the same provision – introduces an exception that plays a leading role if compared with the previous conflict of laws criteria. In fact, Article 38, in its ending part, reads as follows: 'Italian law shall be applicable whenever there is an application to obtain, by an Italian judge, the full adoption of a child'.

        The scope of Italian jurisdiction has been defined by Article 40. According to this provision, in the case of establishment and of revocation of the adoptive relationship, the Italian judge is competent when both adopters (one of them or the adoptee) have Italian citizenship, or if the adoptee is a child in state of abandon in Italy, or, finally, if the adopter or the adopters are foreign persons who reside in Italy. As far as the personal and economic relationships between adopters and adoptee are concerned, Italian jurisdiction is established not only in conformity with the general rule provided for by Article 3 of the 1995 Act, but is also affirmed in every case in which adoption has taken place in application of the Italian law. Finally, Article 41 deals with the recognition of adoption that takes place abroad. In the first place, this provision makes reference to the new, general system which has been introduced by the 1995 reform (Articles 64–

'automatic recognition' – introduced by the 1995 reform and which substituted the *exequatur* procedure – was not extended to the adoption of children, which remained regulated by the special legislation. Italian judges could continue, therefore, to ascertain if full adoption orders were issued by foreign authorities in conformity with both their law and with the fundamental principles affirmed in Italy in that field.

However, on the other hand, it is possible to perceive a 'changing mood' in this legislative approach. Thus, the solution that finally prevailed was clearly linked with the hope that a future reform of adoption law would be made. Indeed, a special Commission – which had been appointed in 1989 to draft a Bill to reform adoption law – had already concluded its work. In this period, Italy was approaching the signature of the 1993 Convention too. The decision was in fact taken only a few months after the enactment of the 1995 reform: in December of the same year, Italy was inserted into the list of signatory States. Of course, the reference in the 1995 Act to the special legislation in force, regulating the adoption of children, would necessarily acquire a different meaning as soon as the contents of that legislation altered entirely. The legislative intention was, therefore, to avoid decisive choices and to adopt an easy and 'neutral' position.

At this point, a twofold question may be asked: one may wonder why the legislature waited so long and why it did not coordinate its interventions. There is a first, possible answer: no one could have foreseen, only a few years ago, that the Convention would have been so successful. Instead of adopting sudden modifications, it appeared more prudent to 'wait and see'. Furthermore, it is also likely that after the implementation of the Hague Convention any previous contrary provision would have had to be abrogated. In other words, the Italian Parliament preferred a 'step by step' approach, instead of following the example of other European legislatures, which partially reformed their national laws in order to adapt them to the new 'adoptive system' created by the Convention through statutory modifications previously or contemporaneously enacted with respect to its implementation.[36]

All things considered, such a solution might have been logical if the 1998 Italian reform had given clear answers to many unresolved questions. In reality, a lack of co-ordination and in some cases open contradictions, between Italian law and the Convention, now exists. However, as we shall see further below, the general principles expressly affirmed by the new system of private international law will play a leading role, in solving some complex interpretative problems that have already arisen in reading (and, in the near future, applying) the 1998 reform. In fact, in any case of conflict between the

---

66), and which has abrogated the previous *exequatur* procedure in favor of a non-judicial ascertainment of some fundamental requirements. The second provision embodied in Article 41 has expressly affirmed, however, the applicability of the 'special legislation regulating the adoption of children' . Therefore, the specific mechanism provided for by the law in force has not been altered. See e.g. on the latter issue S.Bariatti, 'Sentenza straniera', in *Digesto delle Discipline Privatistiche*, IV, Sezione Civile, XVIII, (1998) Torino, 330 ff. at 333, 337–341; by the same author see 'Riflessioni sul riconoscimento delle sentenze civili e dei provvedimenti stranieri nel nuovo *ius commune* italiano', in *Collisio Legum – Studi di diritto internazionale privato in onore di G.Broggini*, (1997) Milano, 29 ff. at 37. More generally, see F.Mosconi, *Diritto internazionale privato, Parte speciale*, (1997) Torino, 81 ff.; R.Cafari Panico and S.Bariatti, in 'Commento alla riforma del diritto internazionale privato', in *Rivista di Diritto Internazionale Privato*, (1995), respectively 907 ff. (Articles 38–41) and 1221 ff. (Articles 64–67).

36   For example, the French legislature enacted in the same month some provisions regulating specific aspects of adoption law and the statutory instrument necessary for the ratification of the Convention. See Decret n°. 98-771, September 1, 1998 and Decret n°. 98-815, September 11, 1998, in *Recueil Dalloz*, (1998) – Legislation, respectively at 349 and 353. About the previous situation, see e.g. B.Sturlese, 'La Convention de La Haye du 29 mai 1993 sur la protection des enfants et la coopération en matière d'adoption internationale', in *Juris Classeur Periodique*, (1993) I, Doctrine, 427 ff. ; J.Rubellin-Devichi, 'Permanence et modernité de l'adoption après de la loi du 5 julliet 1996', in *Juris Classeur Periodique*, (1996) I, Doctrine, 449 ff.

national provisions and those contained in international Conventions in force for Italy, it is possible to assert that – in conformity with the clear indication given by Article 2, Act no. 218/1995 – the application of the latter '*cannot be prejudiced*' and that they are to be construed in consideration of both their international character and the need of their uniform application. This will be the last aspect to be considered in concluding this brief survey of Italian adoption law.

VII THE SCOPE OF 'ITALIAN HARMONIZATION': A GLANCE AT SOME 'RELICS OF THE PAST'

The Hague Conference had to resolve some difficult problems before achieving the final draft of the 1993 Convention. However, the positive outcomes obtained over a rather brief period encouraged its wider plans for the 'globalization' of child law. At the end of the XVIII session, the 1996 Convention on Jurisdiction, Applicable Law, Recognition, Enforcement and Co-operation in respect of Parental Responsibility and Measures for the Protection of Children was presented at the Hague.[37]

The common thread running through these initiatives is evident: the unitary goal is to set up minimum procedural guarantees on an international level. However, harmonization or 'globalization' are not magic words, and clearly there are pros and cons in favouring international co-operation through the establishment of a system based on Central Authorities – as happened with the recent Hague Conventions. Indeed an excessive concentration of functions might be set in train.

Of course, the main questions were whether and to what extent harmonization is practicable and in what way. Closely related to these questions were some others. Why abandon the traditional private international law perspective based on conflict of laws rules? Why not propose once more the solution expressed by the 1965 Hague Convention, based on the so-called 'jurisdictional approach' (i.e. on the applicability of the *lex fori* by the competent judge[38])? Which of the mechanisms can best raise the level of civil protection? Which functions should be conferred on the judiciary and which responsibilities on other agencies?

The Hague Conference followed one particular path towards harmonization, which consists in selecting a set of fundamental directives and principles and in giving rise to a common system of inderogable procedural guarantees to ensure the automatic recognition of foreign decisions. Summing up the 1993 Convention, it is possible to say that a fundamental role was designated to the Central Authority, to be established by every contracting State. In fulfilling its duties, it was to take all appropriate measures, directly

---

[37] This Convention will replace the 1961 Hague Convention on the Protection of Minors. However, only four States have signed it and only one (Monaco) has ratified it to this day. See, in Italian legal writing, P.Picone, 'La nuova Convenzione dell'Aja sulla protezione dei minori', in *Rivista di Diritto Internazionale Privato e Processuale* (1997) 705 ff. The Council of Europe also recently intervened in this field. On January 1, 1996 the European Convention on the Exercise of Children's Rights was presented at Strasbourg, but this is not however yet in force.

[38] The Convention on Jurisdiction, Applicable Law and Recognition of Decrees relating to Adoptions, concluded at the Hague on November 15, 1965 was signed and ratified by only three States. It entered into force in Austria, in Switzerland and Great Britain (10-23-1978). The 1965 Convention has influenced national legal developments, but commentators are unanimous in saying that it did not achieve its purpose which was to harmonize different European 'adoptive systems'. See, in Italian legal literature, A.Davì, *L'adozione nel diritto internazionale privato, I, Conflitti di leggi*, (1981) Milano, at 50–62. See also R.De Nova, 'Adoption in comparative private international law', in 104 *Recueil des Cours*, (1961) III, 75 ff.; D.Opertti Badan, 'L'adoption internationale', in 180 *Recueil des Cours*, (1983) II, 303 ff.

or through the public authorities or other duly accredited bodies, to the extent permitted by the law of its State (Articles 8-11, 21). The Convention contains a detailed description of these functions, but it gives rather limited indications about substantive and procedural requirements concerning adoption, as well as with regard to the role of the judiciary. As we have seen, this synthesis reflects the aim of leaving enough freedom to each State to discharge its own duties. However, in exercising these discretionary powers national authorities should not distort the fundamental choices made by the Convention.

It is worth noting that also the mechanism of implementation may differ. First, it is possible to insert the conventional rules into the national system. Many States that have ratified the Convention have adopted this solution. Another way – preferred by Italy – is based on the enactment of a statute devoted expressly to adapting national rules to international ones. Each method may prove effective and has its advantages. In all cases, however, any conflict between national and international laws is to be avoided.

If we look at the Italian 1998 Act, the grounds of criticism are not limited only to the peculiar 'timing' followed by the reform so far – after all, within a few months Italy will be one of the ratifying States. Instead they are founded on the fact that the new Act perseveres unequivocally in confirming some of the features of the 'old adoptive system'. Indeed, the intention of implementing the Convention through the 'modification' of the 1983 reform is expressed not only in the last part of the long title of the 1998 Act but also in one of its introductory provisions. Thus it is that Article 3 specifies that the previous rules will be 'substituted' by the new statute. Moreover, it reads as follows: '*Intercountry adoption takes place in conformity with the principles and following the directives of the Convention [...], according to the provisions embodied in this Act*'. In sum, the legislature, after paying lip service to the Convention, limits the scope of the changes which will take place at the very start. The point being made here is that it is easy to single out several points of divergence with the Convention in the 1998 Italian reform. This seems to be in direct contradiction to its declared aims.[39]

A brief list of the major examples of such incongruity may be useful to understand their scope and importance. First, the substantive requirements and the effects of adoption have remained completely unchanged because the reform refers to some current provisions, contained in the 1983 Act, which have not yet been modified.[40] This situation gives rise to a great number of potential difficulties. For instance, unless there is a further modification in this statute, no importance is attached to the biological parents' consent to adoption (which is not necessary according to Italian law, but it is fundamental, in the perspective of the Convention).[41] Single persons will not be allowed to adopt fully in any

---

[39] The applicability of Italian law to foreign children in state of abandon in Italy (Article 37-*bis*) is not, however, crucial.

[40] For instance, it refers to Article 6 of the 1983 Act, which lists the conditions to adopt. See above text at note 32.

[41] On the contrary, consent played a central function in the traditional vision of adoption which was expressed by the Italian Civil Code enacted in 1942. More generally, it was a fundamental requirement in the early conception of the institution, which was considered as a means of ensuring the continuation of family lines and the transmission of property. It is well known, however, that consent has a central function also in the modern, child-centered vision of adoption (both simple and full) in most civil law systems – which had accepted in the past the previous 'patrimonial' approach – as well as in common law countries, where the full adoption of children has been recognized only more recently, as the only form of adoption. According to current Italian law, this element is fundamental only in cases of the adoption of adult persons (i.e. of simple adoptions regulated by the Civil Code). Full adoptions of children may take place only if there is a total state of abandon (*stato di abbandono morale e materiale*) which must be ascertained by the *Tribunale per i Minorenni*. See Article 8, Act no. 184/1983. However, it should be noted that in some proposals advanced to reform the 1983 Act, the biological parents' consent to adoption has been deemed as a significant element in proving abandonment. See e.g. the text drafted by a special

case.[42] Moreover, the right of adoptees to know their identity will be regulated by provisions which are not inspired by the principle of openness – adopted by the Convention – but by the opposite idea of absolute secrecy.[43]

Looking now at the procedural aspects, a significant element of departure from the Convention is the aim of maintaining the central role of the *Tribunale per i Minorenni*. In fact, its intervention is too wide with respect to the expectations of the Convention. In the three-phase procedure provided by the new Act, the *Tribunale* is called on to ascertain the prospective adopters' suitability after examining their declaration of availability to adopt a foreign child.[44] It also intervenes in the final stage of the procedure, when the accredited bodies have already played their part and the Central Authority has already expressed its decision in favour of the intercountry adoption – deemed to be in the best interest of the child, whose arrival and permanence in Italy is therefore authorized.[45]

However this is not the most critical aspect of the new Act. The fact that the judiciary still plays a leading role can be considered, of course, as another point of contrast with the indications given by the Convention, especially if the Italian choice is compared with other solutions, followed by several Member States.[46] In this regard it should be remembered, anyhow, that lay experts, and not only professional judges, are members of the *Tribunale*.[47] Furthermore, the Convention does not preclude the intervention of courts

---

Commission in 1992 and the explicatory report, in *Diritto di Famiglia e delle Persone*, (1993) 883 ff. For some indication about more recent Bills see note 57. On these issues see also Corte Costituzionale, no. 536, 12-11-1989, in *Giurisprudenza Italiana*, (1990) I, 2, 681 ff. at 686.

[42]   A single person is allowed to adopt, in fact, in some special cases of simple adoptions (whenever a full adoption is not possible) or if the child – who is an orphan – is a relative of the adopter, or if he already has a close relationship with the child before his or her parents' death. Furthermore, one member of a married couple may be authorized to adopt fully in very limited cases (i.e. if separation intervened during the probatory period, or in the case of death or incapacitation of the husband or the wife during this period, and in any case if there is an express request and adoption is deemed to be in the best interests of the child). See Articles 44 and 25 of 1983 Act. The current solution has not been deemed unconstitutional. See Corte Costituzionale, no. 184, 5-16-1994, in *Giurisprudenza Costituzionale*, (1994) 1642 ff. and subsequently Corte di Cassazione, no. 7959, 7-21-1995, in *Diritto di Famiglia e delle Persone*, (1995) 995 ff.

[43]   Article 37 of Act no. 476/1998 confers on the Italian Central Authority the power to communicate to adopters information that is deemed important for the state of health of the adoptee through the intervention of the *Tribunale per i Minorenni*, where it is appropriate. Both these authorities must keep information that has been acquired, concerning the origin of the child, his biological parents' identity and the sanitary conditions of his or her family.

[44]   Article 29-*bis*, para. 4 of the 1998 Act.

[45]   This decision cannot be taken (a) if the child was not abandoned or if adoption could not take place in the sending country, or (b) if adoption does not create a permanent parent–child relationship and does not terminate pre-existing legal ties – unless the biological parents have consented to these effects (Article 32 of 1998 Act).

[46]   According to Article 35, para. 4, the *Tribunale* plays a central role also when the adoption procedure must be completed after the child's arrival in Italy. In fact, the foreign decision is considered as an authorization for a probationary period (which cannot last more than one year). After this, an adoption order can be issued by the *Tribunale* – unless it decides that this is not in the best interests of the child. In the latter case, Italian authorities should follow a procedure which respects Article 21 of the Convention.

[47]   The appellate courts also decide these cases in a special panel: *Corte d'Appello-Sezione specializzata per i Minorenni*. The presence of a lay panel in a Tribunal aiming at the protection of children has never been a matter of debate, even in the perspective of a general reform of civil justice in Italy. On this issue see e.g. *Le procedure giudiziarie civili a tutela dell'interesse del minore*, (ed) P.Dusi, and for more recent accounts, devoted to the debate about a possible reform, see A.Proto Pisani, 'Per un nuovo modello di processo minorile', in *Foro Italiano*, (1998) V, 124 ff.; S.Gustavo, 'Tutela dei minori e garanzia dei diritti nel processo camerale minorile: interazione ed interferenze fra amministrazione e giurisdizione', in *Diritto di Famiglia e delle Persone*, (1998) 1585 ff.

to uphold its guarantees, although it favours the delegation of many tasks to 'non-jurisdictional subjects'.[48]

VIII THE ITALIAN APPROACH IN IMPLEMENTING THE HAGUE CONVENTION

One of the most contradictory choices is expressed in Article 35, nos. 3 and 6 of the 1998 Act. First of all, the *Tribunale* must ascertain not only that adoption is in the best interests of the child and that it has taken place in conformity with the Convention, but also that it is not in conflict with the 'fundamental principles' of Italian family and child law (no. 3). The registration of foreign adoption orders cannot be authorized by the *Tribunale, inter alia,* if the adopters do not meet the requirements *'provided for by Italian adoption law'*, if *'the indications contained in the declaration of suitability to adopt are not respected'* and if it is not possible to transform the adoption that has taken place in a foreign State into a full adoption (no. 6).[49]

Given the present situation, it is clear that this approach may lead to difficulties.[50] There is a risk of reintroducing a control mechanism which is very similar to the previous one contained in Article 32, para. 1, [c] of the 1983 Act. This contradicts the clear indication expressed by the Convention. As I have stated, recognition may be refused – according to the Convention – only if adoption is manifestly contrary to the public policy of the receiving State, taking into consideration the best interests of the child.

The Italian legislature does not reject, of course, the mechanism of automatic recognition – which will operate not only among ratifying countries, but also among other States,[51] but there is no doubt that it has substantially limited it. Moreover, it should be emphasized that even if the same rights that are *'attributed to an Italian child'* for whom a temporary custody order has been issued (*affidamento familiare*) are also conferred on a foreign child – for whom a foreign adoption order or a custody order authorizing a probationary period has been issued – Italian citizenship will be conferred on him or her only after the registration of the adoption in the registry office (Article 34). The consequences of a denial of registration are therefore very dangerous.

The first reactions of legal commentators have underlined these difficulties.[52] Notwithstanding the complexity of the inconsistencies it seems possible, however, to solve them by giving priority to the Convention principles, which must not be 'prejudiced' by Italian national law.[53] This general interpretative rule will surely be helpful in dealing with other aspects of the reform too – for instance, through the specification of some criteria for selecting the personnel of accredited bodies[54] and in

---

[48]   Article 39 has introduced a control mechanism which might give rise to frequent repetitions of the first phase of the procedure. Prospective adopters can ask the *Tribunale* to re-examine their case, in order eventually to modify the adverse decision taken by the accredited body. If the *Tribunale* does not confirm this decision, it can decide directly or through other bodies (*'altro ente o ufficio'*).

[49]   Article 32, para. 3 gives the *Tribunale* the power to transform an adoption which does not sever family ties in the sending country into a full adoption, if it has taken place in conformity with the Convention. Registration is thereby authorized. This choice may be considered however inconsistent with Articles 23 and 27 of the Convention.

[50]   For example, in cases of a full adoption that took place abroad in favour of a single person, a hypothesis which is still precluded in Italy. See above text at note 25.

[51]   Article 35 of the 1998 Act does not aim at prejudicing the general provision about it (i.e. Article 36).

[52]   See Ballarino, (1999) 3rd, at 486 and Finocchiaro, (1999) at 70.

[53]   Article 2, Act. no. 218/1995.

[54]   For instance, according to Article 31 [b], not only experts in social and psychological fields, but also those who work in the legal field – *'in campo giuridico'* – have to be members of their respective professional

substantially increasing the role of representatives of the public administration who have a long experience in the field of intercountry adoption (e.g. of the Ministry of Foreign Affairs).[55]

The Italian Parliament should complete the evolution of adoption law following these fundamental guidelines. Many points still need to be regulated in order to render uniform the level of protection in the adoption field. Indeed, it would seem necessary for some of the innovations introduced by the legislature in 1998 to be extended to cases of domestic adoptions too. Reductions in taxation, the possibility of obtaining specific leave of absence for workers and wide support from social services, the obligatory intervention of accredited bodies and the right to be refunded for expenses sustained must not be limited to the field of intercountry adoption only. More generally, the traditional perspective centreing on the idea of interventions made in single areas should be abandoned in favour of a wider approach. For instance, the prospect of a 'legal aid' system is also welcome: it might solve many problems, not only during the eventual trial phase but also in the prior (non-judicial) stages of the adoption procedure.[56]

Finally, the enforcement mechanism should be the object of much reflection. Instead of reaffirming the central role played by criminal measures, by simply increasing their harshness, it might be more useful to introduce concurrent private law remedies.[57] These are usually more effective as deterrents when compared with severe punitive reactions. Other points also need to be carefully considered by the legislature. In the present situation, in Italy, however, it is still the judiciary that plays a decisive role.

IX CONCLUSION

Judicial decisions often have a strong impact, especially when they refer to a social institution such as adoption, and they have played a vital role in the field of Italian child law. Maybe a foreign observer would find the wide attention that has been devoted in recent years in Italy to this phenomenon 'outside the field' of legal writings unusual. For

---

roll – '*albo professionale*'. However, in Italy this necessarily means at present that they have to be inserted in the 'Law List', i.e. '*albo degli avvocati*'. Especially in view of a wide modification of this field, in the direction of a liberalization of legal professions, it might be wiser to correct such a generic provision in the forthcoming regulation. A deep knowledge of the problems concerning intercountry adoption due to a long (professional or personal) experience should be the fundamental requirement.

[55] Article 38, in listing the members of the Italian Central Authority, gives wide prominence to the executive. That is to say, the Prime Minister will designate the President, two of the ten members of the Authority will be selected from among representatives of the Prime Minister's Office, and some of the personnel who co-operate with the Authority will also come from the same Office. Some other members – who will co-operate with the *Commissione* – will be selected from 'other public administrations'. The generality of this last indication is likely to prove useful: it allows for considerable flexibility.

[56] According to the 1998 Act, it will be possible to appeal to the *Corte d'Appello* against the decision of the *Tribunale* (the appeal is called, in this case '*reclamo*', and is regulated by Article 739 of the Code of Civil Procedure). As far as the problem of access to justice is concerned, the current Italian legislative trend does not favor a general perspective, being limited to single areas, which are comprehensive, however, of the adoption field too.

[57] Which may be similar to the civil sanctions contemplated by the bill (*Intercountry Adoption Convention Implementation Act 1999*) presented to the U.S.A. Senate on March, 26, 1999 (S.682, Sec.404), and which has been introduced subsequently, without any amendments, in the House of Representatives on June 24, 1999 (H.R.2342, Sec.404). In a few words, even if adopting the same elements which are relevant for criminal sanctions (gravity of the violation, degree of culpability, and history of prior violations) and the same level of guarantees (i.e. ensuring a written notice and the opportunity to respond) it will be possible to add a pecuniary measure which usually has a very strong preventive effect. In any case unintentional and harmless violations should be treated differently. Whenever the failure to comply with the requirements of the Convention is not due to intent, a punishment is not justified or useful.

example, it is quite common to read editorial comments about adoption law in the newspapers, after decisions have been taken not only by the Constitutional Court or the Supreme Court but also by first instance judges. The media also report detailed information about the frequent expressions of a political intention to modify – at least partially – the current statute. It is interesting to note, however, that the basic structure of the 1983 Act is not an object of criticism.

The most difficult problems in practice have arisen from the rigidity of some of its requirements, as well as from the unjustified length of the procedure. The need for comprehensive legislative reform has lately become increasingly pressing and it is very intense today, after the enactment of the Act that reformed intercountry adoption and after other recent judicial decisions. It is now clear that effective regulation of intercountry adoption cannot be achieved unilaterally by each State, and also that further measures need to be taken on a national level in order to avoid adoption being seen as a 'solution' for the problems of poor people, especially those of the so-called 'developing countries'.

These are the reasons why the Italian 1998 adoption reform should not be seen as a statutory innovation which is limited to this year. With regard to the new Act, it has its roots in legislative initiatives that started many years ago. It expresses a trend towards a more general, as yet undefined, new reform. With regard to the Bill aiming to modify the 1983 Act, it is possible to say that it is constantly announced as ready for the parliamentary agenda but the debate, to this day, is still in a preliminary phase.[58]

As we have seen, most of the interpretative problems caused by the 1998 Act are due to the fact that the legislature preferred to make reference to some of the existing, central provisions of the 1983 reform (probably in view of their modification), without taking into due consideration the contradictions between the two opposite views expressed, respectively, by the Hague Convention and the 1983 Act, at least as far as some substantive and procedural requirements are concerned. Perhaps, in the short run, a temporary solution may be considered as a satisfactory compromise, without any negative 'side-effects', not only in order to solve these problems but also to prompt to a new reforming trend. Instead of waiting for months (or even years) for the achievement of complete agreement among different political groups, it might be wiser to agree on some 'starting points' that can be generally accepted.

For instance, the modification of the rules about age requirements, the simplification and the shortening of the procedure, the introduction of a new, specific provision expressly recognizing the right of the adoptee to know about his or her origins and establishing the relative guarantees for all the subjects involved, are all aspects deserving

---

[58] The first unitary Bill was drafted by a Special Commission, in 1992. See note 41 above.

In the second half of the 1990s parliamentary attempts to reform adoption law became increasingly numerous. It does not seem very useful, however, to list all the Bills which were introduced in the Parliament in 1996. They did not express a co-ordinated vision, given the great diversities between the different plans, even between those presented by the representatives of political groups that belonged to the same coalitions. It may be remembered, however, that eight Bills on the reform of the 1983 Act were introduced in the *Senato* in 1998 (Nos. 130-*bis*, 160-*bis*, 445-*bis*, 1697-*bis*, 852, 1895, 3128 and 3228) and that a unitary Bill has been subsequently drafted (on March 26, 1999) and presented to the competent Commission on a meeting that took place on April 22, 1999. During the further debate – that took place in the period April–May 1999 – some of the members of this Commission (*Commissione Infanzia*) partially criticized this project because, even if it aims at unifying several divergent proposals and it contains some good solutions, it has been too deeply influenced by the vision of the draftsman, who presides over a special Committee which had been appointed to draft this Bill. In order to reach an agreement a wider parliamentary discussion is necessary in the near future.

immediate attention by the legislature.[59] Their reform may accelerate the very slow pace followed, so far, in the preparation of a complex, but still unfinished, 'legislative picture'.

These issues need to be dealt with carefully. While the scope and the contents of future modifications might, of course, be better defined through wider general debate, it may be that the persistence of legislative silence is not a sign of deep reflection. Sometimes, indeed, this kind of silence expresses a deliberate trend towards abstaining from responsibilities. In facing hard choices, the decision not to decide may often appear the best - and easiest - solution, at least if one adopts the point of view of those who share a common fear of endangering an uncertain 'equilibrium' (or, rather, some variable political coalitions). Naturally, very sharp contradictions may arise in the attempt to support openly new solutions. This is common in the family law context, a field that is deeply influenced by religious and social conceptions. The role of the Italian Courts has been fundamental in mitigating some rigid statutory rules in response to social changes, and in selecting clear criteria applicable for establishing when children may be considered abandoned, so that they can be declared adoptable.[60] However, it is clear that even constitutional judges cannot rewrite a statute.[61]

Of course, the idea that the child's best interest should always be the paramount consideration has never been a matter for debate, but in order to decide *who* can adopt and on *what conditions*, it is necessary to deal with very difficult social problems, given the well-known differences between conceptions of family life and relationships. The legislature should necessarily take into account these differences in setting about its

---

[59]   One of the most urgent decisions deals with the future provisions ensuring the 'openness' of adoption. A glance at some solutions taken by foreign legislatures might be useful in order to follow the principles of the Convention. Access to adoption records containing identifying information might not be afforded to children under the age of 18 years. In the absence of any contrary intention expressed by the biological parents, the disclosure of this kind of information should be allowed to adult adoptees only, in the respect of their psychological need and of the necessity to help the members of the adoptive family too.
       However, there are other questions: whether to allow single persons full adoption of children; whether to place the partners of a *de facto* family in the same position as a married couple; whether the current procedure should be simplified, whether the right of defence should be strengthened or not. Last but not least, there is a new problem concerning the regulation of the '*adoption of embryos*', which has been addressed by the Bill on 'Medical assisted reproduction', recently approved by the *Camera dei Deputati* (on May 26, 1999) and which will now be examined by the Senate (Bill, no. 4048, Article 16, para. 4 and 6). Embryos will be considered as adoptable if – after three years from their creation – their use is not requested by the partners of the interested couple, who have expressly declared their intention of abandoning them. Given that – if the Bill is approved definitively by the Senate without any amendments – unmarried partners will also be allowed assisted reproduction and they will be able to adopt embryos too, the present prohibition, with regard to unmarried couples, from the adoption of children will be rendered unjustifiable (or, rather, it will give rise to a violation of the principle of equality). It is worth noting, however, that the provision on '*adoption of embryos*' will operate only until there is a number of not yet utilized embryos in the centers for assisted reproduction. Therefore, also in this area many unresolved questions are present to this day. The international perspective, together with an effective national enforcement system, will prove the best way to cope with these difficult issues in this field too. See the European Convention for the Protection of Human Rights and Dignity of the Human Being with regard to the Application of Biology and Medicine, done at Oviedo, on April 4, 1997.

[60]   The number of judicial decisions is very high. Among up-to-date surveys, see note 3 above.

[61]   See e.g. Corte Costituzionale, decision no. 281, 7-6-1994, in *Giustizia Civile*, (1994) I, 2706 ff. at 2708. The Court examined the question concerning the constitutionality of the requirement of a three-year period of cohabitation after the marriage of the adopters (i.e. one of the fundamental elements which must be ascertained in order to consider the couple as suitable to adopt a child). It denied that the current statutory provision (Article 6, Act no. 184/1983) was unconstitutional, but underlined that, notwithstanding the 'increasing importance of cohabitation *more uxorio*', and the need to reflect on this in the light of recent social modifications, any future innovation 'is a task that belongs to the legislature, which has the responsibility of taking such difficult decisions through a complex interpretation of several elements and values expressed by a society continuously modifying itself'.

reform work. A widely shared concern about prolonging the delay in the parliamentary discussion about adoption reform is, therefore, wholly justified.

JAPAN

DEVELOPMENTS IN JAPANESE FAMILY LAW DURING 1998 – DOMESTIC VIOLENCE REFORMS

*Satoshi Minamikata** and Teiko Tamaki***

I   INTRODUCTION

In 1998, issues concerning the Public Care Insurance for the Elderly Act were widely discussed in Japan as the implications of an ageing society began to be faced. The topics and issues relating to the following were also publicly discussed: (1) the Guardianship for Dependent Adults Bill;[1] (2) violence against women, especially domestic violence between partners, sexual harassment and stalking;[2] (3) child abuse and child prostitution/child pornography;[3] (4) the revision of family law related sections in the Civil Code, including the sections relating to the change of family name at marriage, the grounds for divorce and hereditary rights of an illegitimate child.

In this paper, we concentrate on reforms in the area of domestic violence. We do not deal with an ageing society and other family law reform related issues described above, as these have already been examined very capably by Professor Matsushima.[4]

II   BACKGROUND TO DOMESTIC VIOLENCE IN JAPAN

This article is devoted to introducing developments in Japanese law concerning issues of domestic violence among family members, especially violence between partners, married couples, and cohabitants.[5] Until recently, little attention has been paid to domestic violence in Japanese families. Public concern has generally focused only on criminal cases, such as that in which a father killed his child, who perpetrated violence against the family. Largely as a result of this case, almost all discussions on violence occurring in the family have been understood to mean violence perpetrated by children towards parents. On the other hand, topics such as child abuse perpetrated by parents, abuse between

---

*   Professor of Law, Faculty of Law, Niigata University.

**   Research Assistant, Faculty of Law, Niigata University.

The authors gratefully acknowledge the editorial assistance of Mr Andrew Sulston.

[1]   The Bill was approved in Lower House Committee on July 2, 1999.

[2]   Remedies for victims of sexual harassment were reinforced in accordance with a revision of the Equal Employment Opportunity Act in April 1999.

[3]   The Prohibition of Child Prostitution and Child Pornography Act was enacted in May 1999 and provides that an offence committed outside Japanese territory will be subject to this Act.

[4]   Y. Matsushima, 'What has made family law reform go astray?' in A. Bainham (ed.), *The International Survey of Family Law 1997* (1999, Martinus Nijhoff Publishers, Hague) at 193–206.

[5]   Hereinafter the term 'violence' will be taken to include all ideas of violence: physical violence which causes mental trauma, sexual abuse and acts which limit the social life of others, for instance, restricting one's partner from seeing his/her associates freely. Couples, a husband and wife and cohabitants are termed 'partners' in this paper.

partners or abuse of the elderly were until recently not widely acknowledged or even thought about by most people in Japanese society.[6]

During the 1990s, Japanese society has gradually become aware of the seriousness of domestic violence against family members largely as the result of the feminist movement, children's human rights activists and the parties concerned about an ageing society.

III   TRENDS IN THE JAPANESE FAMILY

Before discussing violence in the family, we should start by referring to the characteristics of Japanese family life today.

First, the infant population continues to decrease. The average number of children in a family fell to 1.50 in 1994 and 1.39 in 1997.[7] It is considered that this trend resulted from an increased number of young people, especially young women, who for various reasons do not wish to have children.[8]

A second factor is the largely static marriage rate. While slight changes can be seen over the last few years, the annual marriage rate per population of one thousand has been between 6.0 and 6.4 for the same period.[9] Reflecting the fact that the incidence of cohabitation is relatively smaller than that in western countries, 73.3 per cent of men and 64.1 per cent of women think 'they should legally marry' or 'it is preferable to be married legally' before living together.[10] However, even though Japanese people seem to have a positive attitude towards marriage, as mentioned above, the marriage rate is static. The fact that men have more 'expectation' of marriage as compared to women can be pointed to as an explanation for this. In addition, a recent survey shows that 20.7 per cent of men and 31.8 per cent of women say 'they do not think they need to marry'.[11]

A third development is that the average marriage age has risen in recent years. Since the 1960s, when young people entered higher education and the style of youth culture began to change, the so-called 'moratorium' generation was developed: one which had a tendency to take a positive decision not to get married. Moreover, marriage itself is no longer taken as a 'compulsory' event in one's life because amenities for single people have expanded, for instance, there has been an increase in the number of convenience stores, their opening hours and the products they sell. Furthermore, although women still face some discrimination, it is possible for them to work and to be financially independent to a greater extent in recent years than previously. From a woman's point of view, there is a reluctance to lose her freedom and independence by getting married and establishing a household where there is no equality between the sexes: marriage itself has become less attractive for women.

The number of women who are engaged in jobs outside the household (both full-time and part-time) is rising every year which also means that women's contribution to the

---

[6]   It can be said that child abuse was regarded as much less of a problem among other competing legal issues. Only a limited number of sociologists have counted domestic violence in the family as a deviation from family life (F. Kumagai (ed.) (1981). *Gendai no Esprit No.166 – Katei to Boryoku (L'esprit d'aujourd'hui – Household and Violence)* (Shibundo, Tokyo).

[7]   Prime Minister's Office (1999) *Danjo Kyodo Sankaku Hakusho (White Paper on Gender Equality)* (Okurashoinsatsukyoku, Tokyo), at 233.

[8]   *Asahi Newspaper* July 4, 1999.

[9]   Prime Minister's Office (1999), at 233.

[10] Management and Co-ordination Agency (1998) *Dai 6kai Sekai Seinen Ishiki Chosa (the 6th Annual Survey of the World Youth Views)* (Okurashoinsatsukyoku, Tokyo).

[11] Management and Co-ordination Agency (1998).

total household economy is gradually increasing. However, women still have the primary responsibility for domestic chores and child care: that is to say, men's participation in domestic work is clearly less than that of women. With respect to shopping, for example, men spend only 33 per cent of the time on it that women do, while for child care the corresponding figure is 20 per cent, and for domestic chores the figure is only 6 per cent.[12] Clearly, if a woman wishes to continue working after marriage, she runs the risk of 'double exploitation' in her workload at work and in the home.

Fourthly, while the marriage rate remains largely static, the number of divorced couples increases every year. In 1998, 243,102 couples divorced and the number of divorces per thousand of population was 1.94.[13] These data reflect an increasing public tolerance of divorce and the widely accepted idea that one's own individual happiness should be accorded greater respect. In fact, 51.4 per cent of women and 46 per cent of men thought that divorce is acceptable, although, significantly, 39.3 per cent of women and 36.7 per cent of men agree that the existence of children would be a factor holding them back from divorce.[14]

Finally, people are becoming more concerned about the issue of child abuse. Following the reporting of numerous court cases of child abuse, the need for greater legal protection of children has been actively discussed. According to a Survey of the Ministry of Health and Welfare,[15] the child abuse cases referred to child guidance centres reached 5,352 in 1998, a five-fold increase compared with the situation in 1992. Also in a 1999 survey, 9 per cent of mothers admitted to 'having abused a child' and 30.7 per cent of mothers to 'having intended to abuse a child'.[16]

Judging from the above-mentioned factors, the features of the Japanese family can be summarised in the following.

While the equality of both sexes is declared in Articles 14 and 24 of the Japanese Constitution, it does not appear to exist either in society or in the household. Women, in particular, tend to choose not to marry or to postpone getting married in order to avoid the disadvantages and demerits which may occur in their social and family life as a result of marriage. In addition, women generally wish to be independent in their personal lives, while men are still inclined to hold a traditional view of marriage. There is, therefore, a gap between the sexes in their way of understanding family life. Moreover, if family life is regarded as leading to fulfilment and happiness, it follows that it is logical to decide to dissolve married life by seeking a divorce if it prevents a partner from pursuing their own happiness. Women need not remain married if they do not wish to, since they are able to work and to be financially independent In this sense, women are finding it easier to determine a life choice for themselves than previously, although no one can deny that discrimination against women still exists. In such circumstances, women have become more conscious of their human rights, no doubt partly because their access to higher education has increased as mentioned earlier. Accordingly, women have been more aware of their power of self-determination and are increasingly individualistic and

---

[12]   Prime Minister's Office (1999), at 46.

[13]   Ministry of Health and Welfare (1998a), *Heisei 10nendo Jinko Dotai Tokei Geppo Nenkei no Gaiyo (the Outline of Vital Statistics 1998).*

[14]   Prime Minister's Office (1999), at 44.

[15]   Ministry of Health and Welfare, Children and Families Bureau (1999) *Zenkoku Koseibukyokuchokaigi Shiryo (Materials for the National Meetings of Directors of the Department of Health and Welfare)* January 18, 1999.

[16]   *Asahi Newspaper* May 31, 1999.

mindful of the equality of the sexes. These factors are to be found behind the 1990s trend among Japanese people to be more concerned about violence against women.

IV HISTORY OF VIOLENCE AGAINST PARTNERS

Domestic violence was not considered as 'a desirable incident' in Japanese society but the idea of violence against a partner was regarded as a natural part of a quarrel between partners. Any injured party was not perceived to be a true victim.[17]

From the 1970s, however, reflecting the growth of feminism in western countries and the introduction into Japan of information concerning violence between partners, the view gradually spread that this type of violence was an infringement of one's human rights.[18]

It is clearly stated in the Constitution that the fundamental human rights of each individual must be respected and, as mentioned earlier, that equality of the sexes should exist in the household. In addition, initiatives such as The Nairobi Forward-looking Strategies for the Advancement of Women 1985 (the World Conference to Review and Appraise the Achievements of the United Nations Decade for Women; The Equality, Development and Peace), the Vienna Declaration and Programme of Action 1993 (the UN Conference on Human Rights), the Beijing Declaration and the Platform for Action (Fourth World Conference on Women), have all defined violent acts as elements of discrimination against women and stated that such violence should be eradicated. Against this background of international social change, the social and legal issues relating to violence against partners are now being discussed in Japan.

In 1992, the Research Group on Violence against Wives was established, which issued a report in April 1995. In 1996, the Headquarters for the Promotion of Gender Equality of the Prime Minister's Office resolved to prepare a 'Plan for Gender Equality 2000' partly to deal with the problem of violence against women. For its part, Tokyo Metropolitan Government published a 'Report on Violence Against Women' in March 1998 and the Prime Minister's Office held 'the Forum on Violence Against Women' in October 1998 which aimed to promote violence against partners as a matter of public concern. Most recently, in May 1999 the Council for Gender Equality whose members were appointed by the Prime Minister's Office in June 1997 issued a report entitled 'Aiming for a Society with no Violence against Women'. As a culmination of these processes there has been a new initiative for the implementation of a statute prohibiting domestic violence.[19]

V CHARACTERISTICS OF VIOLENCE AGAINST PARTNERS

The characteristics and social conditions surrounding domestic violence became clearer in 1992 when a survey of domestic violence was first made.[20] The following surveys

---

[17] Mr Eisaku Sato, a Nobel Peace Prize Winner of 1974 and a former Japanese Prime Minister, was ironically quoted as saying that 'he beats his wife *only* once a week' (M.D.A. Freeman, 'What Do We Know of the Causes of Wife Battering?' 7 *Fam.Law* 196).

[18] It is important to refer to the Japanese feminist movement which dates back to the early 20th century.

[19] *Asahi Newspaper* June 19, 1999.

[20] Survey Committee on Violence by Husbands (Partners) (1998) *Domestic Violence* (Yuhikaku, Tokyo).

compiled much detailed evidence and the points which emerged may be summarised as follows.

Violence against women was far from unusual: 38.8 per cent of women answered 'yes' to the question whether they had ever experienced physical violence by their partners,[21] and when asked whether or not they had ever heard of incidents of this type of violence, 54.8 per cent of women replied that they had.[22] In contrast, results from another survey indicated that only 5 per cent of women have suffered from serious violence by their partners, although if the total number of married women in the Tokyo area is taken into account, the numbers of such victims would not be negligible.[23] Furthermore, it is reported that 30 per cent of callers to a telephone counselling service by the Japan Bar Association asked for advice on domestic violence by partners.[24]

Various kinds of physical violence are reported, which include punching, kicking and twisting of arms. Out of 796 respondents of the 1992 survey, 467 claimed physical violence; 473 stated that their rights of self-determination in sexual matters had been infringed, for instance, by being forced to have sexual intercourse against their will, or experiencing a lack of co-operation from partners in the use of contraception; 523 pointed to their experience of psychological abuse such as swearing, threats and being restricted as to whom they might associate with; two-thirds mentioned that violence had been extended to their children.[25] In the Tokyo Metropolitan Government survey, 64.4 per cent of respondents pointed to violence against their children.[26] Violence is normally long term: 40 per cent of respondents in one survey[27] and 62.5 per cent in another survey claimed violence lasting for over 10 years.[28]

In consequence, 78.8 per cent of the respondents had suffered physical injuries, 34.0 per cent mental injury, 29.8 per cent being scared,[29] while victims generally had lost their confidence and tended to evaluate themselves negatively.[30] The effect of such abuse for victims is significant.

VI RELEVANT SOCIAL FACTORS

The social background of victims reflects the fact that, despite equality of both sexes in legal terms, discrimination against women continues to exist as a feature of society. An attitude pervades Japanese society that there is a natural division of labour between both sexes, which arguably leads to sexual discrimination.[31] People who agree to an idea of the

---

[21] Osaka Women's Centre (1998), *Josei e no Boryoku Boshi – Seishaku, Iryo, Fukushi and Keisatsu (Prevention of Violence against Women – Policy, Medicine, Welfare and Police)* at 130.

[22] Osaka Women's Centre (1998) at 135.

[23] Tokyo Metropolitan Government (1998), *A Survey Report on Violence against Women* at 49.

[24] Japan Bar Association Committee on Equality of Both Sexes (1996) *Fufukan Boryoku 110 ban Hokokusho 1995 (Report on Emergency Calls for Domestic Violence 1995)* at 1.

[25] Survey Committee on Violence by Husbands (Partners) (1998) at 28, 36, 40 and 47.

[26] Tokyo Metropolitan Government (1998) at 80.

[27] Ibid.

[28] Feminist Counselling Sakai DV Research Project Team (1998) Otto/Koibito (Partner) ra karano Boryoku ni Tsuit e Chosa Hokokusho (*A Report on Violence by Husbands/Partners*) (Osaka), at 31.

[29] Tokyo Metropolitan Government (1998) at 80.

[30] Feminist Counselling Sakai DV Research Project Team (1998) at 79–82.

[31] 64.9 per cent of men and 51.9 per cent of women agree to an idea of a division of labour (Ministry of Health and Welfare (1998b), *Heisei 10nendo Kosei Hakusho (White Paper on Health and Welfare 1998)* (Gyosei Tokyo), at 73.

division of labour also tend to accept such views as restricting a wife's action by saying 'a wife must not go out when a husband is at home', and slapping or violently forcing sex upon a wife.[32] In addition, a tolerant attitude of men's aggressive nature is commonly accepted. Accordingly, violence against women is not taken very seriously. Even some women themselves reflect this attitude; while 62 per cent of the Osaka survey respondents insisted they would never forgive violence from their partners, 29 per cent of them admitted that they think the violence is acceptable depending on its occasion.[33] Under such circumstances, victims of domestic violence will find it difficult to seek effective and appropriate help and remedies.

Meanwhile, although women have been becoming financially stronger, they are still not fully independent in terms of finance. This often prevents them escaping from problems of domestic violence.[34] Indeed, if it is remembered that the average annual income of single parent families headed by mothers is only about one third of that of ordinary families, it is clearly difficult for women as a whole to be financially independent.[35]

VII ACTIONS AGAINST DOMESTIC VIOLENCE UNDER CURRENT LAW

Current Japanese law offers measures for dealing with domestic violence through the Civil Code, the Criminal Code, indirectly through social welfare law and some other Acts. However, the emphasis of such measures is on providing a remedy rather than prevention.

A Civil law remedies

The Civil Code can provide an injunction to prevent violence. A victim may also appeal to a court for provisional resolution procedures such as a preservative measure to prohibit molesting him/her.[36] In practice, even if the violent partner breaches the terms of a civil injunction, civil law does not normally offer any compensation. Adding a clause to an injunction imposing a financial penalty on any party breaching the injunction (as is possible) is not an effective solution to violence. Occasionally, it is argued that a civil law 'ouster' injunction ordering the eviction of a violent partner from the shared house would be effective, but it is thought that no such orders have been issued in the past.

In addition, the delays involved in obtaining a civil law remedy mean that civil law is not useful in an emergency situation. Although there have been cases where orders have been issued on the same day as the application, these are rare. Moreover, the business hours of courts limit their accessibility. Inevitably courts are only called on to give remedies during their business hours which makes it difficult to prevent domestic violence and also to intervene even after the incidents are found.

Regarding remedies taken after the violence, these are normally presented as a claim for damages in tort, although such a remedy is only possible when a divorce is obtained. Even if the claim is accepted, damages are generally limited to no more than 5,000,000

---

[32]   Tokyo Metropolitan Government (1998) at 40–41.

[33]   Osaka Women's Centre (1998) at 131.

[34]   Feminist Counselling Sakai DV Research Project Team (1998) at 117.

[35]   Ministry of Health and Welfare (1998b) at 22 and 97.

[36]   Civil Proceedings Preservative Measures Act Section 24.

yen (approximately £25,000). Moreover, a claim for damages in tort is necessarily made after the fact so no protection prior to violence is possible.

B   Criminal law remedies

Similarly to civil law remedies, criminal law requires a criminal act to have taken place before it offers any remedies. The police and the courts are required to follow a strict procedure of due process, and so criminal law is often of little use in an emergency situation. Up till now, the police have insisted as a matter of principle that they will not intervene in domestic disputes. In practice, the police will try to deal with domestic abuse with circumspection, rather than to detain or prosecute an assailant as a criminal.

While a husband may be found guilty of injury, murder or manslaughter, a criminal case merely punishes the violence which has occurred in the past and does not look forward. Having injured his wife and being found guilty at trial, a husband's violence against his wife may increase by way of retribution for having put him on trial, when he returns home if his sentence is suspended or he is released. In this sense, criminal law offers limited remedies for victims of domestic abuse. Frequently, victims expect the police to offer remedies,[37] and it is reported that victims have made complaints against the police for not dealing with their request appropriately.[38]

Meanwhile, the police are becoming more concerned about domestic violence in families. Some cases of positive reaction by police to emergency calls from victims have been reported recently; for instance, police officers are dispatched to the victim's house immediately whenever they receive emergency calls and they may arrest the perpetrator if necessary.[39]

In western countries, there have been significant numbers of cases of wives who have suffered from domestic violence for a long period of time launching a counter-attack and successfully pleading a doctrine of provocation or diminished responsibility. In contrast, only one case has been reported in Japan,[40] in which a woman stabbed her partner to death after suffering from severe violence for a long time. Although the court denied her assertion of self-defence and found her guilty, it declared that the execution of punishment was remitted taking into account her partner's violence and her difficult situation.

C   Social welfare law and administrative law

For the assistance of victims, local authorities and some voluntary organisations provide nation-wide 'refuges'. Most are originally homes that were built for the purpose of prostitutes' rehabilitation or dormitories for mothers and children. These are now available to the victims of violence, who are facing further violence from their partners and might find it difficult to stay with their relatives or friends because their partners would pursue them. Data from the Osaka Counselling Centre shows that domestic

---

[37]   Tokyo Metropolitan Government (1998) at 81.

[38]   Japan Bar Association Committee on Equality of Both Sexes (1996) at 10.

[39]   Osaka Women's Centre (1998) at 92ff. With regard to marital rape, the Matsue Branch of Hiroshima High Court found on June 18, 1987 that in certain circumstances it would constitute a crime (Hanrei Jiho No.1234, at 154).

[40]   Nagoya District Court July 11, 1995 (Hanrei Jiho No.1539, at 143).

violence is the main reason for women seeking temporary protection.[41] In fact, the current refuge scheme has many problems to be resolved. For instance, protection at a refuge may be given only for a limited period, and a refuge cannot generally admit victims at night even in emergencies. Moreover, there is insufficient co-operation and dialogue between local authorities as to how they can co-ordinate efficient remedies for victims.

D   Other remedies

Divorce procedure is one of the remedies. As stated earlier, domestic violence is a ground for divorce. The divorce procedure, at first, required parties to appear in the family court for in-court mediation under the rule of mandatory family court mediation prior to divorce litigation. In cases of domestic violence, it is appropriate not to apply that rule in order to secure the spouse's safety. At present, in practice, the number of family courts tend to decide dates for in-court mediation sessions by taking a spouse's safety into consideration.

For the purpose of safety, the victims need to separate themselves (and children) from their violent partners and hide their destination from them. However, since a parent, for instance a mother, is required to register her current address in the Family Registration Book, which is as a rule open to the public, in order to allow her children to join a new school, and she must give her address to a court at the beginning of a divorce procedure, her partner may learn of her location and attempt to threaten her. Accordingly, in practice, state schools can accept a victim's children by dispensing with the address registration requirement and a court does not give her partner any information on her address.

VIII CONCLUSION

As discussed above, it could be said that the current Japanese situation concerning domestic violence is at an early stage in terms of protecting the victims. However, certain legal steps have been adopted to deal with sexual harassment[42] and stalking[43] regarded as infringements of women's human rights, while women's support groups have organised various events to focus on the issues of domestic violence and continuously made great efforts to attract the attention of the mass media to this issue. It may be suggested that the challenges in 1998 and in succeeding years must be to offer more effective and comprehensive protection for female victims.

---

[41]   51.5 per cent (119 out of 231 cases) were classified as this type (Osaka Women's Centre (1998) at 113).

[42]   More than 10 court cases on sexual harassment have been reported.

[43]   According to *Asahi Newspaper* June 10, 1999, the prosecution authorities are to take action to prevent stalking by recognising it as a criminal act.

THE NETHERLANDS

OPENING UP MARRIAGE TO SAME SEX PARTNERS AND PROVIDING FOR ADOPTION BY SAME SEX COUPLES, MANAGING INFORMATION ON SPERM DONORS, AND LOTS OF PRIVATE INTERNATIONAL LAW

Caroline Forder[*]

I INTRODUCTION

1998 was a very busy time for the Dutch legislator. Two Acts dealing with private international law aspects of the law of marriages, and the law of names, respectively, were passed. Furthermore there are a number of important measures in the bio-ethical sphere. (Although not strictly speaking family law, these provisions interrelate so closely with family law provisions that they should not be disregarded.) An Act regulating scientific research using human subjects was passed. The procedures applicable in euthanasia cases were tightened up by statutory instrument. Sex selection of foetuses on the grounds of sex in the absence of medical indications justifying sex selection was prohibited by statutory instrument. A number of Bills were introduced into the second chamber or have reached a crucial, or interesting, stage. No doubt of great interest is the Bill to allow same sex couples to contract a civil marriage, which was introduced into the Second Chamber of Parliament on the same day as the Bill to allow adoption by same sex couples. Although these two Bills only became public in 1999, they were introduced into the Council of State in 1998, and as I anticipate interest in these Bills will be very strong, they are included in this report. Another fascinating Bill will regulate the storage and disclosure of information regarding gamete donors. This Bill has been pending since 1993, and may still be rejected, but there are so few countries in the world which regulate this subject-matter that it seems essential to include it in this report. The Hague Convention on Adoption 1993 was ratified by the Netherlands in 1998.

There is intriguing case-law on the right to know one's origins and three cases, one of which is from the Supreme Court, reveal that the United Nations Convention on the Rights of the Child now has a strong hold on the Dutch courts. In a series of cases the Dutch courts thrashed out how the Dutch Civil Code could and should be adapted to the phenomenon of surrogate motherhood. Furthermore I include one case on the rights of the biological father in the light of Article 8 ECHR; it appears that the Dutch Supreme Court is applying Article 8 ECHR more strictly than the European Court for the Protection of Human Rights.

Two items on registered partnership are included. One features the experiences of partnership in the first year of operation of the Registered Partnership Act. A further section covers a report which tries to provide solutions to the multitude of private international law problems which arise in connection with registered partnership (and its non-recognition in most countries). Since people commonly exercise their freedom of

---

[*] Faculteit der Rechtsgeleerheid, Rijksuniversiteit Limburg, Maastricht.

movement, these are problems which could be presented in any country. For that reason the valuable report by the state commission on the private international law aspects of registered partnership deserves consideration. There are a number of other small reports. A report on the effectiveness of the Sham Marriages Act has revealed either, depending on one's perspective, that the Act is not working, or that there was no need for the Act in the first place.

II   PARTNERSHIP AND MARRIAGE

A   *Application of partnership registration law in practice*

In the twelve months after the possibility of registration came into force 4,556 registrations took place, of which 1,550 were between partners of opposite sex.[1] According to an investigation based on the number of registrations in the first eleven months (a total of 4,237),[2] 1,577 (37%) registrations were between two men; 1,307 (31%) were between two women; 1,353 (31%) were between a man and a woman. The use of partnership registration by same sex couples is greater than expected; the Ministry of Justice had estimated 1,700 registrations by same sex couples in the first year.[3] The use is much higher, per head of population, than in the first year of partnership registration in respectively Denmark, Iceland, Norway and Sweden. Also the use of partnership registration by opposite sex couples is much greater than expected. Initially the rate of registration of all three groups taken together was more than 400 registrations per month. By the end of the year the numbers per month were closer to 300. It is impossible to conclude at the present time whether there is a downward trend, or whether the initial bulge following the introduction of registration is now over, or whether the relative drop is a seasonal drop. More people are inclined to marry in June than in December; there may be the same trend with partnership.

Registering partners are somewhat older than couples who marry. Men are on average aged 30 when they first marry; women aged 28. The pattern with first registration of partnerships in the first half of 1998 is different. Men who register are on average 45 years old; women who register, aged 43. Moreover opposite sex partners who choose to register rather than marry are older than their marrying counterparts (42 years (men) and 39 years (women) respectively). There is a concentration of registrants in the age-group 35–54 years for same sex registrations, and in the age-group 25–34 years for opposite sex registrants. The older age of registrants may be ascribed, at least in part, to the fact that many have waited some time for the possibility to register. However, the monthly pattern of registration does not so far indicate a drop in the average age of registrants.

There is typically a greater age gap between registrants than between spouses. Couples consisting of two men typically have an age difference of 7 years. Two women registering typically have an age difference of 5 years. Opposite sex registrants differ 5 years in age; marrying couples 4 years.

Of those marrying 15% were born outside the Netherlands. Only 6% of those entering a registered partnership were born outside the Netherlands. This may be

---

[1]   *Statistisch Bulletin* 10 (CBS) 11/3/1999, p. 50.

[2]   Y. Scherf, *Registered Partnership in the Netherlands. A quick scan* March 1999, (WODC) The Hague.

[3]   Second Chamber 1995–1996, 23 761 nr. 7, p. 3.

explained by the residence requirements for registration.[4] Notably persons born in Belgium, Germany and Indonesia have registered partnerships in the Netherlands. Registrations by persons born in Morocco and Turkey, which are significant population groups in the Netherlands, are negligible in number.

Of the same sex registrants 75% have not earlier been party to a marriage. In approximately 50% of opposite sex couples registering, neither partner has been party to a marriage or partnership; 33% have been divorced.

Same sex registrants are well represented in the large towns, and particularly in Amsterdam, where 500 persons concluded a partnership registration (11% of the total registrations in the Netherlands in 1998, whereas Amsterdam has only 5% of the population). 257 of the registrations in Amsterdam were between two men, reflecting the higher concentration of male same sex relationships in Amsterdam. This pattern of relatively high representation of same sex registrations is reflected in other large municipalities as well. Contrariwise, opposite sex registrants are evenly distributed over towns and the countryside. Whilst the concentration of same sex couples in the larger towns was well known, the equal use of registration by opposite sex couples regardless of location is surprising.

In the study mentioned above, in-depth interviews were conducted with 153 registered partnerships (51 male same sex partnerships, 51 female same sex partnerships and 51 opposite sex partnerships).[5] This study revealed that 60% of those interviewed did not describe themselves as religious; a figure significantly lower than the general Dutch population. The percentage of registrants with a technical or university education is higher than for the average in the Netherlands. The registrants included a higher proportion of two earners than would be found in the Dutch population. At the end of 1996 over 3.3 million of the 6.6 million households were constituted by couples. Of these 2.3 million (70%) were two income families. Of the partnership registrants 90% of the male same sex partnerships, 84% of the female same sex partnerships and 86% of the opposite sex partnerships were two income partnerships. It is accordingly not surprising that the most common reasons given by all categories of partnership for registering the partnership were inheritance, pension and the purchase of a joint home.[6]

An interesting question is why opposite sex couples choose to register rather than marry, considering the legal disadvantages which they will experience (most particularly the fact that no presumption of paternity will apply if any children are born to the female partner, and the risks of non-recognition of the relationship outside the Netherlands). One main reason was given by opposite sex couples: namely that by concluding a partnership one could avoid the cost of involving a civil law notary. However, another significant reason given by opposite sex couples was that the partnership would give the couple greater financial security. When this reason is given by opposite sex couples one can infer that they would not regard marriage as an option, since that means of achieving financial security has always been open to them. A number of respondents indicated that they had an aversion to marriage. But one quarter of respondents said they would consider entering marriage together at a later stage.[7]

More than 80% of same sex couples said they would like to convert their partnership into a marriage were such possibility to be made available to them. The reasons given

---

[4]   Each registrant must either have Dutch nationality or a valid right of residence in the Netherlands, Article 1:80a(1) and (2) Dutch Civil Code.

[5]   Scherf, *Registered Partnerships in the Netherlands. A quick scan* (fn 2 above) at 17–19.

[6]   Ibid at 23.

[7]   Ibid at 21.

were to provide greater security for children being brought up in the relationship (female couples), the greater significance of marriage as an institution and (by male couples) the desire for full equality.[8]

A CBS population survey reveals that attitudes to marriage have changed. It is expected that, of the younger generation, only 6–7 out of 10 will marry. Four out of 10 cohabitees regards marriage as a purely financial arrangement. Of those who have married and never cohabited before marriage, only 1 out of 10 holds that view.

There is no statistical evidence to suggest that registered partnership is any threat to marriage. In the same period, June 1997–June 1998, the number of marriages increased. Whereas in June 1997, 10,851 men, and 10,785 women resident in the Netherlands entered a marriage, in June 1998 11,057 men, and 11,094 women resident in the Netherlands did so.

B   Tackling private international law problems of partnership

As indicated in the previous survey, the private international law problems associated with partnership registration are formidable. During parliamentary discussions on the Bill to introduce registered partnership, questions were asked about the private international law aspects. What certainty was there that the partnership would be recognised in other countries? In the absence of such recognition one of the partners is free to travel to another country and marry there, and might, for example, escape maintenance obligations simply by going to another country. Other countries do not have jurisdiction to give financial relief in the event of breakdown, nor to grant a divorce. Some of these problems are being tackled through dialogue with the Nordic countries where partnership is already provided for. A statute passed on June 2, 1999[9] in Denmark will in the future most probably allow Dutch citizens to register a partnership in Denmark. But this statute will not enable a Danish court to give relief in the event of breakdown of a partnership concluded in the Netherlands or in any other Nordic country.

On January 16, 1997 the Secretary of Justice requested the State Committee on Private International Law to consider the private international law problems associated with partnership registration and to give advice. That committee set up a special sub-committee to investigate the problems connected with registered partnership. The sub-committee (hereafter 'the committee') gave advice in May 1998. The first point made by the committee was that there should be primary legislation on the matter, and not a series of policy rules as envisaged by the government. The proposal by the committee takes the form of a proposed Bill with explanatory notes. The committee noted that the future of registered partnership as an institution is not entirely certain. Were it to become possible for same sex couples to marry (see section II.C below), the function of registered partnership would be reconsidered after five years. This is already provided in Article III of the Bill to make marriage available to same sex couples (see section II.C below). Since it will take some time for the Bill to enable same sex couples to marry to become enacted, if at all, the State Committee suggested that its Bill could be used as a guideline for courts confronted with private international law problems in the meantime. Despite the committee's doubts about the future of partnership, the committee prepared its advice. The institution of registered partnership is not as widespread as marriage. Moreover, of the five countries which already have a registered partnership statute, the Netherlands is

---

[8]   Ibid at 22.

[9]   Act No. 360 of June 2, 1999.

out on a limb in that the Dutch institution is available to opposite sex couples as well as same sex couples (see *1997 Survey*[10]). It should be noted that there are other forms of legal protection of cohabitation relationships, whether of the same or opposite sex, to which consequences attach which are less far-reaching than those attaching to partnership. The committee's advice is confined to the private international law aspects of registered partnership.

The starting points of the committee are the following. First, the domestic approach of assimilating registered partnership to the greatest degree possible to marriage should also be followed in the international sphere. Second, and to a certain extent contrariwise, the fact that registered partnership is recognised in only a few countries means that it is impossible to apply all the private international law rules which apply to marriage to registered partnership. This limitation applies to jurisdictional as well as choice of law rules. Third, the limitation just mentioned leads to a rather one-sided approach to private international law questions. To a considerable degree the committee concentrated on rules indicating when Dutch domestic law is applicable to partnerships concluded in the Netherlands. A more international approach would frequently have the effect of reference to a legal system which does not recognise partnership. Rules with a more international character could be developed at a later date when partnership is recognised in more countries. This approach of focusing on the application of domestic law creates a problem in situations in which Dutch law has not declared itself to be applicable; for example at present it is not applicable to the recognition of partnerships registered outside the Netherlands. The choice of the committee in those cases is for the *lex loci celebrationis*, including the private international law of that system. The consequence of application of these principles is that a partnership registered in the Netherlands will be treated differently to a partnership concluded outside the Netherlands.

The committee considered the extent to which, in the light of existing private international law Conventions, the questions of choice of law, international jurisdiction and recognition and enforcement of judgments needed to be regulated. First, the choice of law questions will be considered. The committee considered the Hague Convention on Maintenance (Applicable Law) 1973[11] to be directly applicable to the maintenance obligations owed by registered partners to one another during and after termination of the relationship.[12] Accordingly the committee thought that the statute to be enacted should simply refer to this Convention. Furthermore the committee considered that the Hague Inheritance Convention 1989[13] (not yet in force) is applicable to determine the law applicable to the devolution of the inheritance of a registered partner. However the committee considered that a reference to this Convention would not be appropriate because, in contrast to the Maintenance Convention, the marital status of a person is not relevant to the subject-matter of the Inheritance Convention. Moreover, if a rule of reference resulted in reference to a legal system which does not recognise partnership, the committee thought it unlikely that the rules of intestacy of the system in question would enable the surviving registered partner to make any claim. One way of circumventing this problem on a case-by-case basis is to advise registered partners with Dutch nationality or

---

[10]   *The International Survey of Family Law 1997*, ed. A. Bainham (1999, Martinus Nijhoff Publishers, The Hague), pp. 260–261.

[11]   Opened for signature October 22, 1973 (came into force in the Netherlands on March 1, 1981).

[12]   The Convention refers the question of liability for maintenance obligations to the law of the place of residence of the person entitled to the maintenance (Article 4).

[13]   Opened for signature on August 1, 1989. (The Netherlands is currently preparing itself for ratification, see legislative proposal 23 863, (R1510).)

with ordinary residence in the Netherlands to make a choice for Dutch law as the law applicable to the inheritance. However, if the inheritance falls to be distributed outside the Netherlands, there is always a risk that the foreign court will not give effect to the choice of law clause in favour of the Netherlands. The committee considered the complications in the field of inheritance to be sufficiently serious that partners should be warned of the problems before registration. The Hague Convention on the Conclusion and the Recognition of the Validity of Marriages, March 14, 1978, was in the committee's view not applicable to the registration of a partnership in the Netherlands nor to the recognition of a partnership registered outside the Netherlands.[14] However the committee sought to draw up rules which would respect the principles laid down in that Convention. A similar approach is taken to the Hague Matrimonial Property Convention 1978.[15] In other subjects, such as the right of a partner to a share in the pension rights of the other partner, the personal obligations between the partners, the dissolution of the partnership and the law of names, no Conventions are applicable. The approach of the committee was to try to make a parallel with marriage insofar as possible. In general the committee advised that in every respect the effect of a registered partnership was less certain than in the case of a marriage, and that prospective partners should be warned of the risks.

The only aspect of international jurisdiction which is certainly provided for by treaty or Convention is the matter of maintenance, regulated by the Convention on Jurisdiction and Enforcement of Judgments in Civil and Commercial Matters (the Brussels Convention)[16] and the Convention on Jurisdiction and the Enforcement of Judgments in Civil and Commercial Matters (the Lugano Convention).[17] Article 5 paragraph 2 of the Brussels Convention declares, *inter alia*, the court of the residence or ordinary residence of the maintenance creditor competent. It is a question of interpretation in each legal system which is a member of the Convention whether the mutual maintenance obligations of the partners will be treated as falling under the maintenance obligations described in that Convention. This question could be definitively resolved by a reference to the Court of Justice of the European Communities.

Recognition of maintenance obligations is provided for in the Hague Enforcement of Maintenance Obligations Convention, October 2, 1973, which has the same geographical application as the Hague Maintenance (Applicable Law) Convention 1973. In accordance with this first-mentioned Convention, judgments from courts in other Convention countries will be recognised and enforced in the Netherlands.[18] Furthermore the Brussels and Lugano Conventions are applicable to the recognition and enforcement of judgments

---

[14] The Convention provides in Article 2 that the formal requirements will be determined by the *lex loci celebrationis*. The capacity of the parties to marry will be determined by the *lex loci celebrationis*, if one party to the marriage is a national of that country or is ordinarily resident there or if each party to the marriage satisfies the requirements of the domestic law which is applicable in consequence of the choice of law rules of the *lex loci celebrationis* (Article 3). According to Article 9, a marriage is to be recognized by the Parties to the Convention if it is valid according to the *lex loci celebrationis*.

[15] Opened for signature on March 14, 1978 (and ratified by the Netherlands on November 20, 1991 (Staatsblad 1991, 627)). Article 3 allows the parties to the marriage to choose the law applicable, within certain specified limits. If they make no choice, the law of the country where they established their first ordinary residence after concluding the marriage will be applicable (Article 4).

[16] Concluded at Brussels, January 27, 1968, amended by later Accession Conventions: Luxembourg, October 9, 1978 and October 25, 1982; Donastia/San Sebastian, May 26, 1989, Publ. EG 1989, L 285. A new Accession Convention for the accession of Austria, Finland and Sweden is in preparation.

[17] Concluded at Lugano, September 16, 1988 (EEC–EFTA Parallel Convention) Publ. bl. EG 1988, L. 319.

[18] Articles 4–8 Hague Enforcement of Maintenance Obligations Convention.

in maintenance cases. There is no Convention applicable to the recognition or enforcement of judgments terminating a registered partnership.

The committee's proposed Bill treats five questions:

(1) the scope of applicability of the proposed Bill;
(2) the conflict of law rules applicable to a partnership registered in the Netherlands;
(3) the conflict of law rules applicable to a partnership registered outside the Netherlands;
(4) international jurisdiction of a judicial termination of a partnership outside the Netherlands;
(5) recognition of a termination of a partnership obtained or carried out with mutual agreement outside the Netherlands.

1   Scope of applicability of the proposed Bill

Article 1 describes the scope of applicability of the Bill as indicated in the list above.

2   Conflict of laws rules applicable to a partnership registered in the Netherlands

Article 2 provides that it is possible to register a partnership only in accordance with Dutch law. Moreover the capacity of the partners to enter a registered partnership is determined by Dutch law.[19] The legal relationship between the partners who register their partnership in the Netherlands is regulated by Dutch law.[20] This approach is much more limited than applies to the obligations arising from marriage, which are determined by the joint nationality, ordinary residence or other legal system to which the spouses are most closely linked. The restrictive approach in the case of partnership is necessary because of the limited number of countries recognising partnership. Regarding matrimonial property the partners are free to select the law applicable, either at the moment of registration or during the partnership.[21] The validity of the choice of law will be judged according to the law which the partners have attempted to choose.[22] This approach is similar to that applying to spouses.[23] However the partners must choose a legal system which 'knows' registered partnership.[24] If the partners have not chosen an applicable law, Dutch law will be applicable.[25] Article 15 regulates the sharing of pension rights. In Dutch law this sharing is regulated by the Act of July 5, 1997. Under the Registered Partnership Act registered partners are placed in the same position as spouses regarding the sharing of pension rights. The committee decided there was no reason to treat partners differently from spouses in the international field either. The committee characterised the question of sharing of pensions as a question of matrimonial property. Furthermore the committee proposed the inclusion of new Articles in the Sharing of Pensions Act specifying the scope of application of the provisions. No attempt would be made to create general conflict rules in this field because the Dutch Sharing of Pensions Act does not resemble any known foreign scheme. The new provisions would make all pensions provided by Dutch pension schemes equally available to partners as to spouses, regardless of the law

---

[19]   Article 2(2) proposed Bill.
[20]   Article 3 proposed Bill.
[21]   Articles 4, 6 and 7 proposed Bill.
[22]   Article 8 proposed Bill.
[23]   Article 4(2) proposed Bill.
[24]   Similar to Article 6(2) of the Hague Trust Convention.
[25]   Article 5 proposed Bill.

applicable to the matrimonial property rights of the partners.[26] Furthermore, if the pension scheme is not subject to Dutch law, but the partners' matrimonial property rights are regulated by Dutch law, then the rights of the partner are equated to those of a spouse under Dutch law.[27]

The committee's proposal regarding termination of partnership is confined to termination by judicial decision or, as is permitted by Dutch law, termination by mutual agreement. Just as applies to the case of divorce, the committee proposed that Dutch law – the *lex fori* – should be applicable. Although this gives a more limited recognition than applies to divorce, the committee considered that the crucial place where the termination should have effect is the country in which the partnership was originally concluded. Article 17 regulates maintenance by declaring that the Hague Maintenance (Applicable Law) Convention is applicable. The explanatory notes to Article 1 of that Convention indicate that Article 1 is intended to apply to all maintenance obligations which arise by operation of law from family relationships.[28] The committee is of the opinion that maintenance obligations arising from registered partnership fall under this definition. Furthermore the committee considered that the Hague Convention[29] was also applicable to ex-partners as this would seem in accordance with the objectives of that Convention. In advising the inclusion of a provision stating that the Hague Maintenance Convention is applicable to maintenance obligations between partners, the Dutch committee has a different strategy to that of Denmark. The Danish Registered Partnership Act provides that Treaties and Conventions are applicable to partnership if the other Contracting Parties to the respective Convention or Treaty so agree. This 'wait and see what the others do' approach is explicitly rejected by the Dutch private international law committee.

3   The conflict of law rules applicable to a partnership registered outside the Netherlands

According to Article 18 of the proposed Bill, a partnership registered in another country will be recognised in the Netherlands on the same basis as a marriage concluded elsewhere. Recognition will be refused if such is contrary to Dutch *ordre publique*, on the same basis as a marriage might be (e.g. bigamy, non-age, lack of consent).[30] For the regulation of the personal relationship between the partners, the analogy with marriage had to be dropped. This was necessary in order to avoid a reference to a legal system in which the legal institution of registered partnership is not known. Thus the personal obligations between the partners are, according to the committee's proposal, to be regulated according to the *lex loci celebrationis*.[31] For matrimonial property questions, the partners may choose which legal system is applicable.[32] It is thought that this departure from reliance upon the *lex loci celebrationis* will increase the certainty of effect

---

[26]   Proposed new Article 1(7) in the Sharing of Pension Rights on Divorce Act, April 28, 1994, Staatsblad 1994, 342.

[27]   Proposed new Article 1(8) in the Sharing of Pension Rights on Divorce Act, April 28, 1994, Staatsblad 1994, 342.

[28]   Conférence de la Haye, *Actes et documents de la XIIème Session*, Tome IV, nr. 118, Report Explicatif, nrs. 16 and 17.

[29]   Articles 4–6 and 8 of the Convention.

[30]   Article 19 proposed Bill.

[31]   Article 20 proposed Bill.

[32]   Article 21 proposed Bill.

of the partnership. If the partners fail to make a choice, or if the choice is not made as prescribed in the Bill, the *lex loci celebrationis* will be applicable.[33]

When a partnership entered outside the Netherlands is to be terminated by judicial decision or mutual agreement Dutch law will be applicable.[34] Maintenance obligations arising from a partnership entered abroad will be subject to the rules of private international law laid down in the Hague Maintenance (Applicable Law) Convention 1973.

4 *Rules of international jurisdiction applicable to a judicial termination of a partnership outside the Netherlands*

Jurisdiction to adjudicate questions arising from a partnership which has been registered in the Netherlands will always be with the Dutch courts.[35] If a non-Dutch partner registers in the Netherlands and the partners then subsequently move abroad, it would be unreasonable were the Dutch courts to deny jurisdiction to adjudicate at the instigation of the non-Dutch partner in termination proceedings. It might not be possible, for immigration reasons, for the non-Dutch partner to establish residence, and in any case this seems disproportionate considering the probable lack of a court abroad which is likely to regard itself as competent in the matter. If the partnership was entered into abroad the Dutch court will have jurisdiction in termination matters if both partners are Dutch or one of the registered partners has lived in the Netherlands for the preceding twelve months, or if Dutch, the preceding six months.[36] The civil status registrar is bound under Article 34 to register all partnership registrations entered into in the Netherlands, quite irrespective of nationality or place of residence of the partners. Furthermore, the civil status registrar is empowered to register all partnerships entered abroad if both partners are Dutch. If only one partner is Dutch, he or she must have lived in the Netherlands for at least the preceding six months. Non-Dutch partners must have lived in the Netherlands for at least the preceding twelve months. In any case the partners who are registered abroad can request the civil status registrar in the place of partnership registration to record the registration, and then the registration can be recognised in the Netherlands in accordance with Article 35 of the proposed Bill.

5 *Recognition of a termination of a partnership obtained or carried out with mutual agreement outside the Netherlands*

Recognition of a termination obtained outside the Netherlands or of a termination by mutual agreement made outside the Netherlands should occur on the same basis as the recognition of a termination of marriage.[37]

C *Opening up marriage to same sex partners*

This legislative proposal was sent to the Council of State on December 11, 1998. The Council of State gave advice on the proposal, which was finally presented to the Second Chamber of Parliament (and thus made public), on the same day as the proposal discussed in section III.D below to introduce adoption by same sex partners, on July 8,

---

[33] Article 28 proposed Bill.
[34] Article 31(1) proposed Bill.
[35] Article 33 proposed Bill.
[36] Article 33(2) proposed Bill.
[37] Article 35 proposed Bill.

1999. There are two parts to the legislative proposal: first, the opening up of the possibility of marriage to same sex couples, and secondly, the provision of the possibility of converting a registered partnership into marriage and *vice versa*. As seen above, 80% of same sex couples registering a partnership stated that they would prefer to marry if given the choice. The initiative to open up marriage to same sex couples began with a motion accepted by the majority in Parliament on April 16, 1996 in favour of same sex marriage and the possibility for such couples of adopting children (see *1995 Survey*[38]). In response to this motion, a Commission was appointed on June 25, 1996 to investigate the effects of opening up marriage, particularly having regard to the private international law effects. The Kortmann Commission reported in October 1997, and its report is discussed in the *1997 Survey*.[39] A majority of the Commission was in favour of making it possible for same sex couples to marry, but without attaching consequences for children. There would be no presumption of legitimacy. A minority of the Commission was against opening up marriage. This group argued that registered partnership was a sufficient answer to the needs of same sex couples. The Commission was unanimous that the legal relationship between the same sex partner and any children of the other partner should be improved. Three measures were envisaged: making adoption possible, providing that joint custody would arise from the fact of registration of partnership, and extending the effects of the form of joint custody acquired by application to the court.

The Cabinet at that time decided not to follow the advice of the majority of the Kortmann Commission regarding the opening up of marriage to same sex couples, but was prepared to follow its advice regarding children. However, the elections in May 1998 brought a change of government and with it a change in policy. In the coalition pact 1998[40] it was announced that marriage would be opened to same sex partners. The arguments in favour of opening are based upon the need to avoid discrimination and the case for public acknowledgment that same sex relationships are just as worthy of State protection as are opposite sex relationships. This line of reasoning rejects the idea that the equality principle is fulfilled by a separate but equal policy. In other words, registered partnership is not enough because it treats same sex partners differently from opposite sex partners. Those holding this view are undeterred by the risk of limping relationships (see section II.B above). Indeed the presentation of foreign legal systems with the fact of a Dutch marriage between same sex couples is thought to have the desirable effect of encouraging those foreign legal systems to reconsider their stance on same sex partnerships. Opponents to the opening up of marriage to same sex couples argue that there is no discrimination since same sex and opposite sex couples are not in a similar position. This argument stresses the biological function of marriage. It is argued that registered partnership must be regarded as satisfying the needs of same sex couples. Moreover, the co-existence of marriage for same sex couples and registered partnership will only cause confusion. There is furthermore concern that the opening up of marriage to same sex couples may fundamentally change the character of the institution of marriage. Those opposed to the opening up of marriage stress moreover the seriousness of the private international law problems. It is thought undesirable for such a small country as the Netherlands to go out of step with the rest of the world.

---

[38]   *The International Survey of Family Law 1995*, ed. A. Bainham (1997, Martinus Nijhoff Publishers, The Hague) pp. 360–361.

[39]   *The International Survey of Family Law 1997*, ed. A. Bainham (1999, Martinus Nijhoff Publishers, The Hague) pp. 264–268.

[40]   Regeerakkoord 1998, Kamerstukken 1997–1998, 26 024, nr. 9, p. 68 (July 20, 1998).

The provisions opening up marriage to same sex couples are simple. In practically all respects marriage for same sex couples will be the same as marriage for opposite sex couples. The conclusion of the marriage contract by performing the marriage ceremony, the rules on capacity, the invalidation and the effects of marriage will all be the same. The differences are found in two aspects; the relationship regarding children and the international effects. Following the unanimous advice of the Kortmann Commission, a marriage between a same sex couple will have no effect upon the legal relationship with the children. The partner of the parent of a child born during the relationship will not be presumed to be the child's natural parent, as is the case through the presumption of paternity applying in marriage. The presumption of legitimacy is based upon a presumption that the husband is in fact the child's father. Admittedly sometimes this is not the case. But in the case of the same sex marriage, the partner will never be the child's natural parent, so that the application of such a presumption would be in all cases fictitious. The relationship between the child and the partner is already protected to some extent by the Shared Custody Act (see the *1997 Survey*)[41] and will be further extended by another Bill which has yet to be presented to parliament. The international effects of the marriage between a same sex couple will differ from the effects of a marriage between an opposite sex couple, but the extent of that difference depends upon the international community. It is unlikely that, for the purposes of freedom of movement of spouses, the European Community provisions will be held to be applicable to spouses of the same sex. The recent decision by the European Court of Justice in *Grant v South-West Trains*, in which an employee of South-West Trains was held not to be discriminated against by the fact that her female partner was not entitled to the travel benefits to which a male partner would have been entitled,[42] presents a most unencouraging prospect for same sex partners, whatever their marital status.

The Conventions on the private international law aspects of marriage, for example the Hague Convention on the Celebration and Recognition of Marriages, signed at The Hague on March 14, 1978, were drafted at a time when no one imagined that same sex couples would be able to marry; accordingly a sex-neutral interpretation is not indicated. The chance that another country will be prepared to accord recognition to a marriage concluded between a same sex couple is regarded by the government as slight. Even in countries in which registered partnership exists there may be difficulties about recognising such a marriage. In the absence of recognition of the marriage there is a somewhat greater chance that certain limited effects may be recognised in foreign countries. But there is no guarantee of such effects being recognised, nor that they will be the effects intended. There may, for example, be a tendency in foreign countries to accord the effects of a cohabitation rather than a marriage. It will be necessary for the Netherlands to draft special private international law rules to regulate the private international law problems arising from the possibility of same sex couples concluding a marriage. The State Committee which drafted the private international law rules on registered partnership (section II.B above) will be asked to study the problem and give advice if and when a statute making marriage available to same sex couples is passed. In any event, as with registered partnerships, the government advised that intending spouses of same sex relationships should be warned of the risk of non-recognition and lack of effect in the international sphere.

---

[41]   *The International Survey of Family Law 1997* (above) pp. 288–295.

[42]   Case C-249/96, Jur. 1998, p. 1-621, [1998] 1 FLR 839.

The relationship between the use of marriage by same sex couples and registered partnership will be reviewed after the Act has been in operation for five years. The majority of the Kortmann Commission recommended that registered partnership should be abolished at the moment that marriage became possible for same sex couples. The differences between marriage, with the modifications regarding children, and registered partnership are small. Three differences may be mentioned. First, a registered partnership can be terminated by mutual agreement of the partners. A deed must be drawn up by a notaris or advocate regulating the financial and other matters.[43] This possibility is not available for the termination of marriage; a court is always involved. Second, in relation to registered partnership no judicial separation is possible, whereas this is available for marriage. Third, Article 68 of Book 1 of the Civil Code prohibits the religious celebration of marriage before the registration by the civil status registrar; no such restriction applies to registered partnership. It might be thought confusing to have two institutions so similar to each other as marriage and registered partnership, when the differences between them seem rather marginal. But there are arguments against the abolition of registered partnership. The government mention in particular the unexpectedly high level of use of registered partnership by opposite sex couples (1550 in the first year). As mentioned in section II.A above, a reason given by many opposite sex couples for registering a partnership was the interest of those couples in regulating financial matters whilst avoiding the institution of marriage.[44] The evaluation which would take place after five years will consider the need for continuing registered partnership, especially having regard to the use of the possibility of converting a partnership into a marriage and *vice versa*.

The second part of the legislative proposal is concerned with conversion of registered partnerships into marriages,[45] and of marriages into registered partnerships.[46] Whilst the wish for the former conversion is apparent, the demand for the latter conversion must be doubted. The procedure for either form of conversion is simple. The parties must make their wish for conversion known to the civil status registrar in the place of their joint residence or the residence of one of them. If they live outside the Netherlands, and one has Dutch nationality, the request for conversion must be made to the civil status registrar in The Hague. The civil status registrar must then prepare a deed of conversion of status. The effects should be elaborated, especially if there are children involved. If an opposite sex couple were married, and the husband was, by dint of the presumption of legitimacy, father of the child, a conversion, subsequent to the birth of the child, of the marriage into a registered partnership would not alter the relationship between the father and the child. If the couple were registered partners at the time of the child's birth, and thereafter the relationship is converted into a marriage, the father will not become the father of the child by dint of conversion of the relationship. To achieve a legal filiation link to the child, the father must recognise the child. If the couple had registered their partnership in community of property, that property relationship is unchanged by the subsequent conversion into marriage. The conversion of a marriage into a registered partnership changes the possibilities for termination. A registered partnership can be terminated by mutual agreement, whereas a marriage can only be dissolved by involving the court. However this change in the possibility for termination does not apply to the regulation of

---

[43]   Article 1:80(c) in conjunction with Article 1:80d Civil Code.
[44]   Second Chamber 1998–1999, 26 672, nr. 3, p. 6.
[45]   Proposed Article 80f Book 1 Civil Code.
[46]   Proposed Article 77a Book 1 Civil Code.

the consequences of termination for any children. There is no possibility for any mutual agreement regarding the custody of the children; for a change in custody, the court must always be involved.

The introduction of the possibility of marriage for same sex couples would have one welcome consequence for transsexuals. An Act of April 24, 1985[47] provides for the birth certificate of a transsexual to be altered if two conditions are fulfilled. First, the transsexual must not be married. Second, he or she must have been operated on such that he or she is incapable of either fathering or bearing children.[48] The present legislative proposal visualises that the first requirement should be dropped. It would be illogical to require the transsexual to divorce his or her former partner if same sex couples are to be allowed to marry.[49] There are further reasons for this reform. It has always appeared to me to be particularly harsh to require the transsexual, after the ordeal which has been gone through, to divorce the former partner. In my opinion Articles 8 and 12 ECHR are violated, although at the present time the European Court is so anxious to establish common ground before it finds a violation that there is almost no chance of a judgment adverse to the Netherlands, were the question to be put to the test.

D   Validity of marriages celebrated in consulates

The Act to Amend the Conflict of Laws (Marriage) Act of December 17, 1998 came into force on the January 15, 1999.[50] This Act was passed in order to overrule a decision by the Supreme Court on December 13, 1996.[51] The applicants were a man with Moroccan nationality and a woman with Moroccan nationality who had recently additionally acquired Dutch nationality through naturalisation. The parties married in the Moroccan Consulate-General in Rotterdam. A problem arose when the husband sought to register the birth of their first child with the civil status registry. The civil status registry questioned the validity of the marriage and accordingly refused to register the male applicant as the child's father. The Regional Court 's-Hertogenbosch (*Rechtbank*) held that the marriage was valid. The appeal in Cassation to the Supreme Court 'in the interests of the law' was rejected. The appeal was founded on the proposition that it should not be possible to celebrate a marriage in a consulate if one or both parties has Dutch nationality. The normal route of marrying before the civil status registrar, with subsequent registration in the civil status registry, should be used. However this prohibition was not mentioned in the Conflict of Laws (Marriage) Act which had been in force since January 1, 1990. Moreover the explanatory notes made only oblique reference to the question of nationality and did not explicitly address the question of a possible prohibition.[52] The Hague Convention on the Celebration of Marriage 1978, Article 9, is neither for nor against such a prohibition. In the case to be decided the Advocate-General concluded that there was a prohibition against recognising a consular marriage as valid if one of the parties had Dutch nationality. But the Dutch Supreme Court held that the marriage was valid. It pointed out that the Hague Marriage Convention 1902 had

---

[47]   Staatsblad 1985, 243.

[48]   Article 28 Book 1 Dutch Civil Code.

[49]   Article 1 (C) legislative proposal 26 672.

[50]   Article III Wet van 17 december 1998 tot wijziging van de wet conflictenrecht huwelijk (an Act to amend the Marriage (Conflicts of Law) Act).

[51]   *Nederlandse Jurisprudentie* 1997, 469.

[52]   Second Chamber 1987–1988, 20 507, nr. 3, p. 7.

contained a prohibition against such marriages. It was therefore significant that the more recent Hague Convention made no reference to such prohibition. The Supreme Court further attached importance to the fact that the woman had only recently acquired Dutch nationality. The Court considered that the policy behind the Hague Marriage Convention 1978 was intended to uphold as far as possible, the validity of marriages. Articles 8 and 12 ECHR, guaranteeing respect for private and family life, and the right to marriage, respectively, were also relevant. In the light of those Articles and the proportionality principle, the Supreme Court held that the marriage should be upheld.

The Act to Amend the Conflict of Laws (Marriage) Act of December 17, 1998 overrules, in Article 4, this ruling. No consular marriage celebrated after the coming into force of this Act can be valid if either party to the marriage has Dutch nationality, including dual nationality. The reasons for this enactment are the following. First, the Supreme Court's ruling was totally at odds with consular practice. Second, there is no other country in Europe which would uphold such a marriage in comparable circumstances. Third, international law does not indicate either for, or against, such marriages. Fourth, there is good reason to keep a close check on consular marriages, since the scrutiny as to validity before the marriage is concluded is less rigorous than in the case of domestic marriages.[53] In this regard the spectre of sham marriages, a pet subject of the Dutch government in recent years (see section II.E below), was mentioned. However, when questioned, the government was unable to point to any evidence of a link between consular marriages and sham marriages.[54] Moreover the Dutch authorities have no control over the speed with which the celebration of marriage is notified to the Dutch authorities by the foreign consulate. Fifth, it is not disproportionate to expect people with Dutch nationality who are resident in the Netherlands to use the normal procedure via the civil status registrar.

Transitional provisions protect the validity of all consular marriages concluded between January 1, 1990 (the date of coming into force of the relevant Act) and January 14, 1999 (the date of the coming into force of this amending Act) in which one or both parties have dual or sole Dutch nationality.[55]

E   Sham marriages

On June 2, 1994 the Prevention of Sham Marriages Act was passed.[56] The Act provides for a marriage to be declared void if it is proved that the marriage was entered into with no other intention than to acquire a right of residence. Before the Act was passed it was thought that between 5,000 and 10,000 marriages celebrated per year were shams. In 1998 an evaluation of the effectiveness of that Act was published. On November 2, 1998 the Secretary of State of Justice made known his intentions regarding policy in the light of that evaluation. At the time that the Act was passed there were no reliable figures on the numbers of sham marriages being celebrated; there were only suspicions. The evaluation has not provided reliable statistics either. However the evaluation concludes that the Act has had a certain preventative effect. Of the 97 cases which were brought to the court, in less than half was a sham marriage found to have been established. There are

---

[53]   See Article 36a Wet gemeentelijke basisadministratie persoonsgegevens (Local Authority (Administration of personal information) Act).

[54]   Second Chamber 1997–1998, 25 703, nr. 5, pp. 8–9; 97-6459 (mw Barth (PvdA)).

[55]   Act to Amend the Conflict of Laws (Marriage) Act of December 17, 1998, Article III.

[56]   See *1994 Survey*, p. 348.

various ways of approaching the question of why the Act has had so little impact. As far as the government is concerned there is an enforcement problem. The immigration authorities rarely advise further investigation into the content of marriages and civil status registrars are thought to be unsuspicious so that they rarely refuse registration of a marriage.[57] Another approach held in the academic world is that the supposed large numbers of sham marriages do not exist. So it has been alleged that the Sham Marriages Act, which is highly intrusive into personal lives, deals with a sham problem.[58]

III PARENTHOOD

A Ratification of the Hague Adoption Convention

The Hague Adoption Convention, which was opened for signature in The Hague on May 29, 1993 was ratified by the Netherlands by a statute passed on May 14, 1998[59] which came into force on June 3, 1998. On the same day the Act to implement the Convention,[60] and the Act to amend the law regulating the acquisition of the Dutch nationality[61] were passed. The latter Act provides that a child adopted in accordance with the Convention will acquire Dutch nationality if certain requirements are complied with. At least one of the adoptive parents must have Dutch nationality and all legal filiation links with the natural family must have been broken. If the legal filiation links with the natural family have not been broken by adoption in the country of origin (known as a simple adoption), the simple adoption can be converted into an adoption according to Dutch law, thus qualifying the child for Dutch nationality.

Statistics are published each year on inter-country adoptions.[62] In 1998 there were 1,989 applications for inter-country adoption made by would-be adoptive parents. Permission to adopt was granted in 1,218 cases. 825 children were placed in Dutch families in consequence of an inter-country adoption procedure. In 616 cases the application was withdrawn, in 3 cases the application was rejected on the grounds of unsuitability of the parents and in 33 cases the application was rejected because the parents exceeded the requisite age-limits. Neither of the parents must be more than 50 years older (nor less than 18 years older) than the child. Of the 1,989 applications for permission made in 1998, 1,600 were for a first child, 302 for a second child, 75 for third child and 12 for a fourth or subsequent child. The children entering the Netherlands in 1998 came from Ethiopia (40), Nigeria (8), Poland (18), Romania (19), India (72), South Korea (42), Philippines (15), Taiwan (50), Thailand (30), China (210), Brazil (50), Colombia (178), Guatemala (11), Haiti (27) and Surinam (11). In 1998, 473 girls and 352 boys were received into Dutch families. 284 of these children were less than one year old;

---

[57] Second Chamber 1997–1998, 26 276 nr 1 (November 2, 1998).

[58] Jesserun d'Oliveira, 'Schijnhuwelijk blijkt schijnprobleem' *Volkskrant* 20 januari 1999; G.C.J.J. van den Bergh, 'Schijnhuwelijken, een pijnlijke herinnering' *Nederlands Juristenblad* 1999, pp. 683–684.

[59] Rijkswet van 14 mei 1998, Staatsblad 1998, 301 (Kamerstuk 24 810 (R 1577)).

[60] Act of 14 mei 1998, Staatsblad 1998, 302 (Kamerstuk 24 811). This Act came into force on October 1, 1998 (Besluit van 15 juli 1998, Staatsblad 1998, 475).

[61] Rijkswet van 14 mei 1998, Staatsblad 1998, 303 (Kamerstuk 24 812). This Act came into force on October 1, 1998 (Besluit van 15 juli 1998, Staatsblad 1998, 476).

[62] Statistische gegevens betreffende de opneming in gezinnen in Nederland van buitenlandse adoptiekinderen in de jaren 1994–1998, Ministerie van Justitie (Statistical information regarding the reception of foreign adoptive children into Dutch families in the years 1994–1998).

261 were aged between one and 2; 122 were 2–3 years old, 98 were 3–5 years old, and 60 were aged 5 or older.

B   Amendment to the Act on Conflicts of the Law of Names

The legislative reform to the law of names, explained in the *1997 Survey*[63] has as its key feature the right of the mother and father (whether married or unmarried) to choose which of their surnames the child shall bear. This emphasis upon choice made it desirable to regulate the scope of application of the new Dutch rules in international cases. Moreover it was thought necessary to specify how the new implementation provisions should apply to persons whose names are registered outside the Netherlands. The result was the Act to Amend the Conflict of Name Laws Act in connection with the coming into force of the Act of April 10, 1997 to amend Articles 5 and 9 of Book 1 of the Civil Code and several other provisions. The Act was passed on December 24, 1998[64] and came into force on February 15, 1999.[65] The Act divides into two parts. First, the recognition of names established under foreign legal systems is regulated in the new Article 5a inserted into the Conflict of Name Laws Act. Second, the scope of the new domestic law name provisions is regulated in the new Article 5b of the Conflict of Name Laws Act.

1   The recognition of names acquired outside the Netherlands

It needs little explanation that a person who has lived under one name will, to say the least, react unfavourably, if, on arrival in the Netherlands, he is expected to take another name. This can happen if the rules in the country of origin for determining the name of a person differ from the rules in Dutch law, and if there is no system for recognising the name acquired in the country of origin. Moreover, confusion as to a person's name can cause difficulties in establishing the identity of a person. This last consideration is usually of great interest to the public authorities. Accordingly Article 5a provides:

> 'If the family or surname of a person has been established or amended outside the Netherlands in accordance with private international law rules of that place, and is laid down in a deed in accordance with the requirements of that place, the name thus acquired by registration or amendment will be recognised in the Netherlands. Recognition cannot be denied on the ground of *ordre publique* simply because a law other than Dutch law has been applied.'

The rule laid down is in accordance with an existing policy in the Netherlands. The only question about the proposal concerns an advice given by the State Committee on Private International Law on April 15, 1997. The advice is that the proposed rule will lead to another result than that indicated by the Convention on the Law Applicable to Surnames and Christian Names, concluded at Munich on September 5, 1980. Opinions are divided as to the interpretation of that Convention, but a minority of the State Committee concluded that the rules of reference laid down in the Convention[66] should be applied also in circumstances in which a person has already acquired a name registered according to the law of origin of the person outside the Contracting State. This interpretation means that the Convention can actually cause a person's name to change from one State to

---

[63]   *The International Survey of Family Law 1997* (above), pp. 298–299.

[64]   Staatsblad 1999, 161.

[65]   Besluit van 9 februari 1999, Staatsblad 1999, 43.

[66]   Namely, that the applicable law is the law of the nationality of the person whose name is at issue.

another. Not very surprisingly, the government preferred to lay down in Article 5a the approach advocated by the majority of the committee which leads to the result that the rules of reference of the Convention are not applicable if the name has already been registered in the land of origin and avoids any change of name from State to State.[67] Only four countries are party to the Munich Convention on the Law Applicable to Names. Moreover, in at least three countries, Belgium, Germany and Switzerland, there is legislation in force which is not in conformity with the Convention. In a number of other countries, for example, France and Greece, policy rules or case-law have developed rules which depart from the principles in the Convention.[68] In response to questions in Parliament the Secretary of State stated that there is no general practice in other countries in Europe on the question of recognition of a name registered in another country. The Secretary of State admitted that the proposed rule would not produce a good result in all cases, but thought it workable, defensible on the grounds of allowing freedom of movement, and simple to operate. Moreover, as European Court on Human Rights case-law has revealed, the right to carry a particular name is protected by Article 8 ECHR.

2 Scope of the new Dutch law provisions on name

Article 5b specifies the scope of application of the Dutch domestic rules on the choice of name. The purpose of the Article is to specify the circumstances in which, despite a mixture of Dutch and foreign factors in the case, the possibility offered by Dutch domestic law of making a choice as to the child's name is offered. It should be made clear at the outset that, in the interests of unity of family name, the possibility of choosing the child's name only applies to the first-born child.

Paragraph (a) of Article 5b deals first with a non-marital child:

'This provision applies to a child which has been recognised or legitimated outside the Netherlands, and in consequence of the recognition or legitimation a legal affiliation link between the child and father has arisen causing the child to acquire or retain Dutch nationality. If a choice of the child's surname in accordance with [Dutch domestic name law] has not been made after the recognition or legitimation, the mother and the man recognising or legitimating the child may make a choice as to the child's surname within the two years subsequent to the recognition or legitimation. If the child had attained the age of 16 years at the date of recognition or legitimation, the child may in the subsequent two years choose whether to take the surname of the mother or father.'

The provision applies to a recognition or legitimisation outside the Netherlands of a child who thus acquires or retains Dutch nationality. Recognition or legitimisation of a non-Dutch child by a Dutch man will give that child Dutch nationality. If the child already has Dutch nationality, he will retain it if recognised or legitimated by a non-Dutch man. In the case of the recognition or legitimation performed abroad the foreign civil status registrar will apply private international law rules which may or may not refer the question to Dutch law. If the question is referred to another law, the name so acquired will be respected under Article 5a (explained above). If a reference is made to Dutch law, Article 5b seeks to place beyond doubt the cases in which Dutch domestic law is intended to apply. The application of Dutch law might in particular be appreciated by persons who carry out the recognition abroad, but who intend to settle in the Netherlands.

---

[67] Second Chamber 1997–1998, 25 971, nr. 3, p. 3.
[68] Second Chamber 1998–1999, 25 971, nr. 5, p. 3.

A child of Dutch nationality is always subject to the Dutch domestic law of names. This is already provided.[69] The present Act provided specially for the possibility for the mother and father to indicate their choice of the child's surname *before the child's birth*. Article 5b paragraph (b) of the present Act provides that this is possible if at least one of the parents has Dutch nationality at the moment of making the declaration. The declaration can be made to a Dutch consulate, provided that that consulate is empowered to register civil status matters.[70]

Article 5b paragraph (c) regulates the position of a marital child of Dutch nationality who is born abroad. If the parents have not availed themselves of the possibility under paragraph (b) (immediately above) of choosing before the birth whether the child should carry the name of the father or that of the mother, Article 5b paragraph (c) of the present Act gives them the opportunity to do so in the two years subsequent to the birth.

The transitional provisions allow the parents of a child who is recognised, legitimated or born after the date upon which the new Dutch domestic name law came into force (January 1, 1998) to exercise the choice of name in accordance with the present Act for a period of two years after the coming into force of this Act, i.e. until February 15, 2001.[71]

C   The right to know one's origins

1   The Bill on Storage and Disclosure of Information on Gamete Donors

On April 15, 1994 the Dutch Supreme Court ruled in the *Valkenhorst* case that the right to know one's origins was part of Dutch law. It was not an absolute right, but had to be weighed against other rights. It was already very clear from the facts of that case that the right to know would be accorded very great weight. The case is expounded in the *1994 Survey*.[72] That case did not concern a child who had been born as a result of gamete donation, and after that case there was speculation as to whether the same principles would apply. At the time of the *Valkenhorst* decision there was a legislative Bill pending which, when and if introduced, would regulate the storage and disclosure of information concerning gamete donors.[73] The Bill on Storage and Information Relating to Gamete Donors had been presented to Parliament on June 18, 1993. After several years of pondering upon the impact of the *Valkenhorst* case upon the Bill, in October 1997 the government announced that the Bill would be maintained in its original form. One change was made: whereas the original Bill had been confined to sperm donors, the Bill now applies to ovum and embryo donors too.[74] However in practice one is usually speaking of sperm donors, since the nature of ovum and embryo donation means that the donor is rarely anonymous.

The terms of this Bill should be of particular interest to the outside world. There are few other countries which have sought to regulate information relating to gamete donors at all. The countries which have done so appear to fall at one of two extremes. On the one hand there is no provision for disclosure of information which will identify the donor.

---

[69]   Wet conflictenrecht namen (Names (Conflict of Laws) Act), Article 2.
[70]   Article 5(4), Book 1 Civil Code; Consulair besluit, artikel 2.
[71]   Artikel II.
[72]   *The International Survey of Family Law 1994* (above), pp. 357–360.
[73]   Wet donorgegevens kunstmatige inseminatie (Information on donors (artificial insemination) Bill), Parliamentary proceedings 1992–1993 23 207 (presented to Parliament on June 18, 1993).
[74]   Parliamentary proceedings 23 207 (see previous note) number 9, p. 4 (October 27, 1997).

This is the case regarding the regulations in force in Victoria, Australia.[75] On the other hand, if one goes the whole hog and provides for identifying information, the Swedish experience[76] shows that there can be a disastrous decrease in the number of men prepared to put themselves forward as a sperm donor.[77] The interest of the Dutch Act is that its strategy is bolder than the Victorian Regulations, but more subtle than the Swedish Act. Bolder, because it provides for the provision of identifying information. But more subtle, because the identifying information is not provided on demand, but only after a balancing of interests has taken place.

At the present time there operates in the Netherlands a 'two-counter' system in operation in the clinics which provide sperm donation treatment. Parents wishing to receive sperm donation treatment may present themselves at counter 'A' or counter 'B'. Equally sperm donors may offer to provide sperm for the benefit of counter 'A' applicants or counter 'B' applicants. At counter 'A' a totally anonymous service is provided; the couples using those sperm donors know they cannot search for the identity of the donor, nor may the donor attempt contact with them. At counter 'B' an open service is provided; information about each party will be provided. The 'B' counter is used almost exclusively by single women and lesbian couples, who normally desire a degree of openness about the child's biological origins. It is not known to what extent the various clinics store the information regarding the identity of the sperm donors, for what period that information is stored, or whether the clinics operate a uniform policy in that matter.

The Bill proposes to regulate the information as follows. The clinics carrying out the gamete donation treatment will be obliged under the Act to supply all information regarding donation (when? by whom? to whom?) to a central information point – the Gamete Donor (Information) Foundation – (which will be set up under the Act[78]). The information need not be passed to the Foundation if it is established by the clinic that the treatment has not led to a pregnancy. The Foundation will be obliged to store the information for at least 80 years from the date of receipt.[79]

There are three categories of information relating to the gamete donor:

(1) medical information, important to the development of the child's health (for example, regarding genetically transmissible diseases). This information will be supplied upon the application of the child's G.P. The age of the person concerned is irrelevant;[80]

(2) physical characteristics, education and profession, social background of the donor (non-identifying personal characteristics of the donor). This information will be provided upon the application of a child of 12 years or older who knows or suspects that he has been born by AID or egg donation. If the child is not yet 16, the parents must be notified that the information has been disclosed to the child. The child must be notified of this communication to the parents. If the

---

[75] Infertility (Medical Procedures) Regulations 1988, Schedule 4 and Infertility (Medical Procedures) Act 1984 No. 10163, sections 19(2)(3) as amended by the Infertility (Medical Procedures) Act 1987, No. 86, sections 20(a)(b)(c). Both this and the Swedish provisions are discussed by S. Wilson, 'Identity, genealogy and the social family: the case of donor insemination', *International Journal of Law, Policy and the Family* (1997) Vol. 11, pp. 270–297.

[76] Law on Insemination No. 1140, of December 20, 1984, in force March 1, 1985, section 4.

[77] Second Chamber 1993–1994 legislative proposal 23 207, nr. 6, pp. 12–13; 1997–1998, 23 207, nr. 10, p. 8.

[78] Article 4 legislative proposal.

[79] Article 8 legislative proposal.

[80] Article 3(1)(a) legislative proposal.

child is not yet 12 years old, the information may be supplied to the parents on their application;[81]

(3) identifying information about the donor. This information will be supplied, upon the application of the child who has attained the age of 16 years, if the donor gives written permission. But if the donor withholds permission or gives no reaction, the information may be supplied if, *after weighing the interest of the applicant in the provision of the information against the interest of the donor in not providing the information, and taking account of all circumstances, the interests of the applicant weigh so heavily that disclosure should not be refused.*[82] If the institution intends to disclose the identity of the donor, he or she must be notified[83] and can lodge an objection with the Foundation within 30 days.[84] If the decision of the Foundation is adverse the sperm donor can appeal to the administrative court. And he has a further right of appeal against that decision to the Council of State, Adjudication (Administrative Decisions) Department. The same procedure must be applied if the donor is dead or cannot be found. In such a case certain close relatives are empowered to consent to disclosure of the information, and the Foundation and judicial instances must decide whether a refusal to disclose is reasonable. In this decision no account is to be taken of the interests of the relative; only the interests of the deceased or absent donor are relevant. In practice this is likely to result in disclosure in most cases when the donor is dead or missing. The procedure just described for the donor and his or her relatives is also available to the applicant, including a minor, whose application for information is refused.

The discussions are still running and the legislative proposal might be changed. The general principle is in accordance with the principles laid down by the European Court of Human Rights in *Gaskin v United Kingdom*.[85] Although some doubts have been expressed[86] as to whether the principles in *Gaskin*, which concerned information regarding the applicant's early childhood, applies to information concerning a person's biological origins, it would be quite wrong to make any distinction. Both types of information are very personal and the information regarding biological origins is clearly covered by the European Court's statement in *Gaskin*: 'In the Court's opinion, persons in the position of the applicant have a vital interest, protected by the Convention, in receiving the information necessary to know and understand [one's] childhood and early development'.[87] *Gaskin* permits a system of secrecy, but requires provision for the possibility that disputes about disclosure can be brought before an independent body (independent from the body holding the information). However there are a number of matters which will require careful scrutiny in the coming debates on the Bill. The character of the institutions which will be taking these extremely sensitive decisions needs to be examined. Doubts have been expressed as to whether the constitution of the Foundation provides sufficient guarantees that the Foundation is fitted to carry out the

---

81   Article 3(1)(c) legislative proposal.

82   Article 3(2) legislative proposal.

83   Article 3(4) first sentence legislative proposal.

84   Article 3(4) second sentence legislative proposal.

85   Eur. Court H.R., July 7, 1989, Series A Vol. 160, para. 49.

86   A.M.L. Broekhuijsen-Molenaar, 'Het wetsvoorstel donorgegevens kunstmatige inseminatie', *Tijdschrift voor familie- en jeugdrecht* 1992, pp. 205–210, p. 207; H.J.J. Leenen, 'Het recht op kennisname van de identiteit van de gametedonor en diens anonimiteit', *Nederlands Juristenblad* 1993, pp. 1101–1106, pp. 1104–1105.

87   *Gaskin*, para. 49.

task of adjudicating disputes.[88] The six-person strong Foundation will consist of three members (including a psycho-sociologist) working in the field of gamete donation, an ethicist, a lawyer and a specialist in child education and development.[89] A further question is the appeal to the administrative court. De Ruiter and the Dutch Family Council has questioned whether such a personal matter is appropriately referred to the administrative court.[90] In his view it would be better to bring the matter to the family chamber.[91]

The mother has no say in whether the information is disclosed or not.[92] The information about the sperm donor is stored in relation to the mother's name. Without this link being made to the mother it would be impossible for the child to trace the donor. The private life of the mother is affected by this linkage, but in my view the interference is entirely justified by the need to make the information accessible to the child.

The position of the minor who wishes to receive the information deserves special attention. If the child is under the age of 12, only the parents have the right to obtain information. From the age of 12 the child may obtain non-identifying information. An amendment introduced a special restriction for the child. If the child makes such application to the Foundation, the parents must be notified of the application. The parents then have the right to apply for all the information which the child has received.[93] No doubt this amendment was made with the best intentions of protecting the child, but it seems to take little account of the child's right to confidentiality. If the parents had exercised their right to obtain this information whilst the child was under the age of 12, and had shared it with him, there would have been no need for him to proceed to the Foundation. The failure of the parents to ask for the information, or the failure to share it with the child, indicates a lack of openness on the part of the parents which may entirely justify the child's need to approach the Foundation without the parents being informed. The lack of confidentiality in this matter may deter the child from approaching the Foundation at all. The concern is about the inability of the child to cope emotionally with the information acquired. However this is surely adequately covered by the duty laid down in the Bill to provide expert counselling when the information is provided.[94] Counselling the child could include urging the child to share the information with his parents, if such appears, having regard to the child's reaction, to be appropriate in order to protect his interests. When the child has attained the age of 16, he may request identifying information about the donor. It is not evident why the child must wait until the age of 16 before applying for this information. It would be better – because in accordance with Articles 3 and 5 of the United Nations Convention on the Rights of the Child – to deploy a more subtle test which takes account of the degree of understanding of the minor regarding the identity of the donor. The child must make the application

---

[88] De Ruiter, J., (1993), Manipuleren met leven, *Handelingen Nederlandse Juristenvereniging* 1993-I, p. 65.

[89] Article 5 legislative proposal.

[90] The Dutch first instance courts are divided into three chambers: administrative, criminal and civil. The family chamber is a sub-division of the civil chamber.

[91] De Ruiter, J., (1993), Manipuleren met leven, *Handelingen Nederlandse Juristenvereniging* 1993-I, p. 65; Nederlandse Gezinsraad, *Kunstmatige inseminatie en het recht op afstammingsvoorlichting*, Den Haag, (1994), p. 9.

[92] Emancipatieraad, Second Chamber 1992–1993, 23 207, nr. 3, pp. 14-15; 1993–1994, nr. 5, p. 10. Broekhuijsen-Molenaar A.M.L., 'Het wetsvoorstel donorgegevens kunstmatige inseminatie', *Tijdschrift voor familie- en jeugdrecht* 1992, p. 208.

[93] Article 3(6) legislative proposal, inserted by amendment of January 13, 1994 (Second Chamber 1993–1994, 23 207, nr. 7).

[94] Article 3(6) legislative proposal.

himself, even if a minor; the parents may not act on his behalf. If the gamete donor refuses disclosure, the Foundation must decide whether the child's interests in disclosure outweigh the interests of the donor in non-secrecy. The applicant must show 'that the applicant's interests are so great that disclosure should not be refused'. In the explanatory notes to the Bill it has been explained that the applicant must bring evidence of psychological distress or other comparable evidence.[95] It is not clear why this heavy burden is laid upon the applicant. Since the right to know one's origins has been accepted to be a basic right, why should it be necessary to bring special proof of the need, in each individual case, to exercise that right?[96]

Transitional provisions regulate the position of an applicant wishing to receive information regarding a donor who donated the gamete before the Act comes into force.[97] All information presently held by clinics and institutes must be transferred to the Foundation. Medical information will be distributed in accordance with the Act. Regarding other information, sperm donors will be invited through widely published advertisements to declare in the year following the coming into force of the Act that they do not wish information about them to be disclosed. Where such declaration is made the information will never be disclosed. If no such declaration has been made, then, when an application is made for disclosure, the gamete donor will be approached and asked whether he (or she) consents to disclosure. If he (or she) refuses, or is no longer available or is unable to consent, there will be no disclosure. This procedure will apply even if the donor gave permission to disclosure at the time of donation (counter B donation). The question is whether this regime gives sufficient scope to the rights of the applicant. If the principle in *Gaskin* is applicable, as I have defended above, then there should, also in transitional cases, be an independent body which balances the interests of the applicant in disclosure against the interests in secrecy of the sperm donor. The present transitional provisions take no account of the fact that the refusal of the donor may be unreasonable.

In the Dutch Parliament a lot of pressure was put upon the government to set up some research into the effects of disclosure and non-disclosure to children of this information. But the government was concerned about the ethical aspects of such research, particularly having regard to the small numbers of subjects likely to be available for such research. Accordingly, in October 1997 the government announced its refusal to commission such research. I think it would have been interesting to have allowed this research to be carried out, not as a pre-condition to the implementation of the Act, but as a way of evaluating the operation of it. Even though the numbers of people who could be interviewed would be small, it would still be better than nothing at all. Although the psychological effects of not knowing one's biological origins are generally assumed, there has been no serious research carried out to investigate it more deeply. The Dutch–Belgian Society for Donor Insemination had advised the Dutch government that it would be possible, under certain conditions, to carry out ethically responsible research into these psychological aspects. However research has been commissioned into another aspect of the legislative proposal, and the proposal has been shelved until that research is completed, which is expected to be at the end of 1999.[98] The research will examine the likely effects of the Bill upon the willingness of men to act as sperm donors.

---

[95]   Second Chamber 1997–1998, 23 207, nr. 10, p. 10.
[96]   Second Chamber 1993–1994, 23 207, nr. 6, p. 19 (VVD-fraction), p. 22 (D66), nr. 8, p. 11 (CDA); De Ruiter, Manipuleren met leven, *Handelingen Nederlandse Juristenvereniging* 1993-I, pp. 64–65; Raad voor het Jeugdbeleid, *De naam van de ooievaar*, Rijswijk, (1993), p. 9.
[97]   Article 14 legislative proposal.
[98]   Second Chamber 1998–1999, 23 207, nr. 12 (letter from the Minister).

Questionnaires distributed by the Academic Hospital in Leiden have revealed that 85%–90% of men who are currently donors would not be prepared to be so in the future if there was a risk that their identity could be disclosed.[99] The research commissioned by the government will establish and analyze the opinion of sperm donors regarding the desirability of the proposed Bill, in general, and having regard to their own particular situation. The purpose is to obtain an impression of the likely effect of the Bill, if enacted, upon the behaviour of potential sperm donors, and their reasons for that behaviour.

2 Case-law on the right to know one's origins

In the case before the `s-Hertogenbosch District Court (*Rechtbank*) on March 27, 1997[100] the applicant, who had serious doubts about her biological origins, requested the court to order the parents to submit themselves to a DNA test. The court agreed that a child has a right to know her origins, based on Article 7 of the United Nations Convention on the Rights of the Child. But the defendants' rights had to be weighed against that right. In particular their right to bodily integrity was at stake. In the present case the defendants' rights weighed more heavily than those of the applicant.

An interesting case reached the Zwolle District Court on July 8, 1998.[101] After the parties had divorced, a discussion arose regarding the division of matrimonial assets. The husband alleged that the wife had behaved unreasonably. Were this to be established, this would have unfavourable consequences for the wife regarding the sharing of responsibility for the household expenses, in accordance with Article 84(6) of Book 1 of the Civil Code. The unreasonable conduct in question concerned the fact that she had informed their son that he had been born as a result of artificial insemination by donor. The Court held that this was not unreasonable behaviour. On the contrary, it was well-known that the son had a strong interest in being informed of his biological origins. The wife had acted in accordance with the child's interests and could not be said to have acted unreasonably. The Court stated that its reasoning would have been the same whether or not the couple were married.

D Legislative proposal to allow adoption by partners of the same sex

On July 8, 1999 the legislative proposal to allow a couple of the same sex to adopt a child, which was submitted to the Council of State in November 1998, was presented to the Second Chamber.[102] The proposal follows the proposal of a unanimous Kortmann Commission on the Opening Up of Marriage to Same Sex couples. That commission acknowledged that extra protection was needed for the relationship between the child and the child's parent's partner when the child is being brought up in a same sex relationship. The commission recommended three proposals intended to strengthen the legal relationship between a child and his or her parent's same sex partner (see *1997 Survey*[103]); the present legislative proposal introduces the first of those recommendations. The other two proposals, which concern the attachment of automatic shared custody to registration of partnership and the providing of inheritance consequences between the

---

[99]   Second Chamber 1997–1998, 23 207, nr. 10, p. 7.
[100]   *Rechtspraak Nemesis* 1998, 855.
[101]   *Nemesis* 1999-2 nr. 1012.
[102]   Kamerstuk 26 673.
[103]   *The International Survey of Family Law 1997* (above), p. 265.

child and his or her parents' same sex partner in consequence of shared custody will be introduced in separate Bills. The introduction of the possibility of adoption for same sex couples was announced in the coalition pact of 1998.[104]

The proposal applies only to adoption of children whose ordinary residence is the Netherlands. It has no application to inter-country adoptions. In recent years only 60–100 Dutch children per year have been adopted. This approach requires explanation, as the Hague Convention, which aims almost exclusively at creating a system of co-operation between countries, and does not aspire to lay down normative values in domestic or private international law, does not prohibit adoption by same sex couples. However in the discussions leading up to the Convention, it was clear that a large number of countries objected to adoptions by same sex couples. Article 17 of the Convention, which permits either country to refuse to go ahead with an adoption without giving any reason, could clearly be used to block an adoption if it were wished to do so.[105] Accordingly it was prudent of the Dutch Ministry of Justice to investigate the likely responses of the six most important (numerically speaking) countries of origin of the children adopted in the Netherlands in recent years, and six countries to which Dutch children are sent. This investigation revealed a very strong preference for inter-country adoption by a married couple. Inter-country adoption by a single person, which is permitted by the Convention, is rare.

The Kortmann Commission had recommended that, were adoption by same sex couples to be permitted, all adoptions – also those by married couples and couples of the opposite sex – should be subject to the condition that the child cannot expect anything from his or her parents. The word 'parent' refers to the biological as well as the legal parents. Thus, according to this criterion, it must be established that that child cannot expect anything from an unmarried father who has neither recognised the child nor in any other manner established a formal legal link to the child. This approach is in accordance with the European Court of Human Rights' decision in *Keegan v Ireland*[106] in which the Court ruled that if the father has a relationship which qualifies as 'family life' within the meaning of Article 8 ECHR with the child, he cannot be entirely disregarded in any adoption procedure. It is also possible that account must be taken of what a sperm donor, if known to the mother (and any partner), has to offer the child. The question which the court will have to ask itself is not whether the 'parent' presently has contact with the child, but whether the child can expect that the parent will give some content to the 'parenthood'. Parenthood implies, according to the explanatory notes, the bearing of responsibility for the child, through care, upbringing or the exercise of custody. Furthermore, parenthood is enduring, particularly in the giving of love, attention and affection.[107] The decision whether the criterion has been fulfilled should be left up to the court. If the child has been born as a result of artificial insemination by donor, it will be relatively simple to conclude that the criterion is fulfilled. If the child was conceived by natural means, or by donor insemination by a person known to the mother, the situation is more complicated. The intentions of the man concerned will have to be established in a hearing. If the partner of the father is seeking to adopt the child it will not be a simple job to establish whether the criterion is satisfied vis-à-vis the child's mother. If she has neglected the child, it will still have to be established whether there is a chance that the

---

[104]   Second Chamber 1997–1998, 26 024, nr. 9, p. 68.
[105]   G. Parra-Aranguren, *Explanatory Report on the Hague Adoption Convention*, Permanent Bureau of the Hague Conference, May 1994.
[106]   May 26, 1994, Series A Vol. 290.
[107]   Second Chamber 1998–1999, 26 673, nr. 3, p. 4.

situation can improve in the future. Again this will have to be examined through a court hearing. Any doubt should be resolved in favour of the original parent.

According to the explanatory notes, the court will be entitled to hold that the child can expect nothing more from his parent whilst at the same time an access arrangement continues in force.[108] According to the explanatory notes, if the parent sees the child only once a month for an afternoon, the court would be entitled to hold that the child can expect nothing more from the parent *as parent*, so that the criteria for adoption would be satisfied without the access arrangement having to be terminated. The outcome could be different if the access arrangement is more intensive.

Adoption is granted by a ruling from the regional court, and must be in the child's interests.[109] If the application is by two persons together, they must have lived together for at least three years continuously immediately preceding the date of the application.[110] A number of other conditions apply[111] in consequence of Article 1:228 Civil Code, the most important in the present context being that neither parent objects to the adoption,[112] and that a sole adoptive parent has cared for the child for a continuous period of at least three years, or, in the case of adoption by two persons, they have cared for the child for at least one year.[113] The fact that the parent objects to the adoption does not automatically mean that the child can expect something from the parent; whether such is the case will have to be investigated. Conversely the fact that the parent states that he or she does not wish to retain the link to the child does not always mean that the child has nothing to expect from that parent. The statement might be a reaction to a difficult situation through which the parent could be helped.

A couple adopting a child will have to show they have lived together for three years continuously and they have cared for the child together for one year. Under current law the adoption by the parent's partner (hereafter 'a partner-adoption') is characterised as a single person adoption, in consequence of which applies the requirement that the partner has cared for the child for a continuous period of at least three years. The requirement of cohabitation does not apply, as this would not be logical in the case of a single person adoption. However the outcome, that such a long period of care is required whilst the couple have no possibility to demonstrate that their relationship is stable, is considered unsatisfactory. Accordingly these requirements have been amended in the case of partner-adoptions. Two considerations apply: first, to establish that the family situation is sufficiently stable to give the child a good home, second, to treat two-person relationships equally, regardless of the sex (or sexuality) of the partners. The three-year period of care for the child is retained as a requirement in cases of genuine single-parent adoptions. Where the adoption is by the partner of the parent, such as the partner of a woman who has conceived through donor insemination, the couple will be required to show that they have lived together continuously for three years, immediately preceding the application, and that they have cared for the child together for one year.[114]

Provisions will be added to the Civil Code to block the begetter of a child from recognising the child after the child has been adopted by the mother's female partner.[115]

---

[108] I.e. repeal of Article 1:229 lid 4 Civil Code is not proposed.
[109] Article 1:227(1) Civil Code.
[110] Article 1:227(2) Civil Code.
[111] See *The International Survey of Family Law 1997* (above), pp. 279–280.
[112] Article 1:228(1)(e) Civil Code.
[113] Article 1:228(1)(f) Civil Code.
[114] Proposed amendment to Article 1:228(1)(f) Civil Code.
[115] Proposed amendment to Article 1:204(1) Civil Code (Article 1, part B).

Equally it will become impossible for the mother or child to apply for judicial establishment of paternity.[116]

If the parent and partner are not successful in their application for adoption, or do not want to adopt, there is the possibility of applying for shared custody under Article 1:253t Civil Code, described in the *1997 Survey*.[117] This might be a good solution if adoption is ruled out because the child can expect something from his other natural parent. Such a solution might be expected to be common when the child and parent have been separated from one another by divorce. There are differences between the relationship to a child established through adoption and custody. Custody ends when the child attains majority, the adoptive relationship does not. Shared custody can be terminated by application to the court, whereas parenthood arising from adoption cannot, in general, be terminated. Parenthood arising from adoption means that the child becomes part of the adoptive parent's family, whereas custody has no such effect. Parenthood and custody arising from parenthood arise from the fact of birth. Shared custody does not arise automatically, but only on application to the court by the non-parent. Inheritance rights attach to parenthood (and adoption) but not to shared custody. As mentioned above, the two last-mentioned differences will be removed in later legislative proposals. In general it is expected that the option of shared custody should be used in preference to adoption. Adoption should only be used when the child can expect nothing from his parents. Whether this result will be achieved in practice is another matter. There is no provision in Dutch law requiring the courts to prefer the option of shared custody over that of adoption.

In the explanatory notes it is acknowledged that an adoption by a same sex couple has only a slight chance of being recognised outside the Netherlands. There is no provision for the recognition of such adoptions in Article 2 of the Hague Adoption Convention 1993, which refers only to recognition of adoptions by 'spouses' or 'single persons'. This means that the current proposal will create limping relationships. There is a possibility that some countries will be prepared to recognise the custody rights created by the adoption.

It is suggested in the explanatory notes that the Act might come into force on January 1, 2001. Considerable, rather expensive, adjustments will have to be made to the system of registration of civil status and local authority databases.

The advice given by the Council of State in its scrutiny of the Bill before it was sent to the Second Chamber was extremely negative. The Council advised the Ministry not to send the legislative proposal to the Second Chamber at all. The Council, inter alia, emphasised the breach with established doctrine in the law of parenthood, by the introduction of a form of parenthood in which there could be no pretence at all of any biological link to the child. It expressed concern about the fact that the step which the Netherlands was taking is unprecedented in any other country, and about the unlikelihood that the adoptions would be recognised outside the Netherlands.

E   Legal position of the biological father

A case decided by the Dutch Supreme Court on June 5, 1998[118] examines once again the rights of the natural father in the light of Article 8 ECHR. The mother and father had a

---

[116]   Proposed amendment to Article 207(2) Civil Code (Article 1 part C). This procedure is explained in *The International Survey of Family Law 1997* (above), pp. 272–275.

[117]   *The International Survey of Family Law 1997* (above), pp. 288–295.

[118]   *Nederlandse Jurisprudentie* 1999, 129, annotated by Jan de Boer.

relationship from mid-1993 till August 1996. The child was born on April 14, 1995. The applicant is the child's biological father. He has not recognised the child. The mother has custody by operation of law. In 1995 the father was given the status of guardian (*toeziende voogd*) by the court. In the present proceedings the father applied for an access order, alleging that there was a relationship between himself and the child of such quality as to qualify as 'family life' within the meaning of Article 8 ECHR. Were the court to find 'family life' to be established, he would be eligible to apply for access. In the absence of 'family life' his application could be dismissed without investigating the merits. Case-law of the Dutch Supreme Court dating from November 10, 1989[119] established that there was no 'family life' between the biological father and his child by dint of the very fact of birth; the father would have to show extra circumstances revealing the closeness of the relationship. The extra circumstances needed to establish 'family life' can be established either on the grounds that the relationship between the mother and father is comparable to a marriage, or on the grounds of the quality of the relationship between the father and the child.

The regional court (*rechtbank*) held that there was sufficient evidence of closeness to establish 'family life', and held the father's application admissible. The Appeal Court disagreed. The father appealed to the Supreme Court. The father was present at the birth of the child. He never lived formally with the mother, but visited her mother regularly (two to three times a week). He changed the child's nappies regularly and looked after him on one occasion. The mother telephoned the father on several occasions about the hearing problems suffered by the child, and on one occasion he came to the ear clinic with the mother. The Supreme Court rejected the appeal. It was not prepared to amend its case-law on the requirements for 'family life' and it did not agree that on the facts there was sufficient evidence of 'family life' between the father and the child. The father's first argument that mere biological paternity was sufficient to establish 'family life' was based upon the interpretation of a remark by the European Court for the Protection of Human Rights in *Boughanami v France*. The European Court had said:

'In the first place, Mr Boughanemi recognised, admittedly somewhat belatedly, the child born to Miss S. The concept of family life on which Article 8 is based embraces, even where there is no cohabitation, the tie between a parent and his or her child, regardless of whether or not the latter is legitimate (...). Although that tie may be broken by subsequent events, this can only happen in exceptional circumstances (...). In the present case neither the belated character of the formal recognition nor the applicant's alleged conduct in regard to the child constitutes such circumstance.'[120]

The confusing thing about this statement is that it can be interpreted as suggesting that the tie of family life could have been broken by the lateness of the recognition by the father. This would imply that family life existed even before the recognition. This would have been a dramatic break with the European Court's earlier case-law, such a dramatic break that it would have been surprising were the Court to have announced it in such an incidental manner.

The Dutch Supreme Court held that the correct interpretation of the European Court's statement was that the fact that recognition had taken place was necessary to the conclusion in *Boughanemi* that there was family life, and that the European Court had (probably) merely wanted to add that, had family life already existed, it would not have

[119] *Nederlandse Jurisprudentie* 1990, 628 annotated by Luijten and Alkema.
[120] Eur. Court H.R. April 24, 1996, *Reports of Judgments and Decisions* 1996-II, p. 594, para. 35.

been destroyed by the lateness of the recognition.[121] Furthermore the Supreme Court held that the Appeal Court had not been too strict in holding on the facts that insufficient additional circumstances were proven to establish the 'family life' needed in order to establish admissibility in his application for access. The annotator to the case, Jan de Boer, criticised, not the finding on the general principle, but the failure of the Supreme Court to hold that sufficient extra circumstances had been established. When one compares this case to the circumstances in *Kroon v Netherlands*,[122] or *Keegan v Ireland*,[123] it is hard to understand why the Supreme Court did not consider the relationship between the mother and father in the present case to be 'family life'. Just like the couple in *Kroon*, the mother and father had had a living-apart-together relationship, which had lasted three years. Moreover the circumstances seem closely comparable to the circumstances in *Söderback v Sweden*,[124] in which the European Court had accepted that family life was established.

F   Surrogate motherhood

In the *1997 Survey* the operation of the new provisions of the Civil Code on parenthood in the context of surrogate motherhood were explained.[125] The surrogate is the legal mother of the child by dint of birth. As part of the adoption procedure by the commissioning parents the rights of the surrogate mother must be terminated. The surrogate's rights in relation to the child can be removed only by court order, under a provision normally intended for unfit parents or parents unable to carry out their obligations (Article 1: 266 Civil Code). Article 266 reads:

> 'If the child's interests are not against such action, the regional court (*rechtbank*) can relieve a parent of custody rights over one or more of his children, on the ground that he is unsuitable or unable to fulfil his duty to care for and bring up the child.'

There is a split in opinion in the Dutch courts about the deployment of this Article in surrogacy cases. Whilst some courts are happy to apply Article 1:266 Civil Code, holding that the surrogate has proved herself to be unsuitable by the lack of an emotional bond to the child and the wish to place the child with the commissioning parents,[126] other courts point out that the terms of the Article are not fulfilled, since the surrogate is neither unsuitable nor unable to carry out her duties.[127] Unwillingness to be a parent is on this view not to be regarded as evidence of unsuitability. Moreover these courts hold that there is insufficient acceptance of surrogacy in the community for a fictional application of the Article to be accepted. Nor is there clear evidence that the case-law had failed to keep up with generally accepted norms. Moreover, as appears from the first phrase in the provision, it must be established that the child's interest is not against the surrogacy. But can it be said that it is in the child's interests to be given away on the basis of a contract made before his or her birth? Furthermore the Rotterdam Regional Court relied upon the

---

[121] HR 5 juni 1998, NJ 1999, 129, consideration 3.3; Conclusie Moltmaker paragraph 2.2.5.

[122] Eur. Court H.R., October 27, 1994, Series A Vol. 294-C, paras 29–30.

[123] Eur. Court H.R., May 26, 1994, Series A Vol. 290, paras. 42–45.

[124] October 28, 1998, *Reports of Judgments and Decisions* 1998-VII, p. 3086.

[125] *The International Survey of Family Law 1997* (above), pp. 283–284.

[126] Regional court (*rechtbank*) Amsterdam April 26, 1995, *Nederlandse Jurisprudentie* 1995, 589.

[127] Regional court (*rechtbank*) Utrecht June 18, 1997, *Nederlandse Jurisprudentie* 1997, 59; Regional court (*rechtbank*) Rotterdam March 23, 1998, *Nederlandse Jurisprudentie (kort)* 1998, 33.

duty of the natural parents (the surrogate) to bring up the child, and the right of the child to be brought up by his natural parents, guaranteed in Articles 7 and 8 of the United Nations Convention on the Rights of the Child. These reasons were the ground of a refusal to remove parental rights by the Utrecht Regional Court.[128] But on appeal the Amsterdam Appeal Court came to another view. It held, following an earlier decision of the Dutch Supreme Court,[129] that special circumstances were present which made the surrogate mother and her husband unsuitable or unable to care for the child. The circumstances were the choice to have the child for the benefit of a childless couple. Moreover, were the child to be returned to the surrogate mother and her husband, the child, which was already being brought up by the commissioning parents, would suffer. The Appeal Court stated that where the application was well motivated and shown to be in the child's interests, there was no reason in general why Article 1:266 Civil Code could not be used to terminate the natural parent's rights. The Appeal Court thought the absence of any general public acceptance of surrogacy was irrelevant for the interpretation of Article 1:266 Civil Code. A similar ruling was given by the Hague Appeal Court on August 21, 1998, a case in which the genetic material came from both commissioning parents.[130] In a comment on the Amsterdam Appeal Court case, Kalkman-Bogerd points out that the recent change in policy[131] regarding the permissibility of surrogacy using the ovum of the commissioning mother indicates that a restrictive interpretation of Article 11:266 Civil Code would be inappropriate.[132] It cannot be right that surrogacy in combination with IVF is made possible through the recent policy ruling, but that it is not possible to make the full arrangements for transfer of the child to the commissioning parents via the Civil Code.

IV   CHILD PROTECTION

A   Leeuwarden Appeal Court April 1, 1998: Hague Child Abduction Convention not applicable

The parties lived on the Dutch Antilles, part of the Kingdom of the Netherlands. They had joint custody of the children. The mother brought the child to the Netherlands without the father's permission. In proceedings brought in the Netherlands the father claimed that the Hague Convention on Child Abduction, opened for signature on October 25, 1980, was applicable. The President of the Regional Court rejected the father's application, awarding interim custody to the mother pending a full hearing. On appeal to the Leeuwarden Appeal Court the court held that the Hague Child Abduction Convention was not applicable. Since the Dutch Antilles were part of the Netherlands the alleged abduction was a domestic abduction and not covered by the Convention. Moreover there was no scope for applying the Convention by analogy. Since the Convention was primarily concerned with establishing a system of co-operation, there was no way that this could sensibly apply to a domestic situation. In any event, had the Hague Abduction Convention applied, the Appeal Court noted that the father was not requesting immediate

---

[128]   June 18, 1997, *Nederlandse Jurisprudentie* 1997, 59.

[129]   Dutch Supreme Court June 29, 1984, *Nederlandse Jurisprudentie* 1984, 767.

[130]   *Nederlandse Jurisprudentie* 1998, 865.

[131]   Explained in *The International Survey of Family Law 1997* (above), pp. 283–284.

[132]   Kalkman-Bogerd, L.E., 'Ontheffing en draagmoederschap', *Familie- en jeugdrecht* 1998, pp. 198–202, p. 201.

return of the child, as one might expect, but was rather requesting that the custody rights of the mother be suspended, and the child handed over to him, pending a full hearing on the custody issues between the parties.

V   RIGHTS OF THE CHILD

A   `s-Hertogenbosch Appeal Court April 17, 1998: child's procedural rights

The Regional Court `s-Hertogenbosch (*rechtbank*) decided to grant the Foundation (responsible for child care and protection) the power to remove the 15-year-old X immediately from her home and place her in a locked institution. X appealed against this decision. Generally speaking there is no provision in Dutch legislation to allow a minor a procedural right to appeal. The right of appeal is given to the parent or other person having custody rights over the child. In X's case that was the mother. X's mother was, however, quite content with the decision to place X in a locked institution, and therefore was not intending to exercise the right of appeal which she had on X's behalf. Dutch law does have a procedural solution to the situation in which the interests of the minor and his or her legal representative conflict. Under Article 1:250 Civil Code the District Court (*kantonrechter*) is empowered to appoint a special representative for the child. But this would all take time. The `s-Hertogenbosch Appeal Court held that, in the circumstances, X had been subjected to a curtailment of freedom of movement which entitled her to immediate legal assistance, including the right to contest the legality of the curtailment of her freedom before a judge or other judicial instance and a prompt decision upon her appeal. The court based its proposition upon Article 5 paragraph 4 of the European Convention on Human Rights and Article 37 prologue and paragraph 4 of the United Nations Convention on the Rights of the Child.[133] This creative decision by the Appeal Court should be contrasted with the much criticised decision by the European Court for the Protection of Human Rights in *Nielsen v Denmark*.[134] In that case the placement of a 12-year-old in a psychiatric observation unit was held not to violate Article 5 paragraph 4 ECHR. Jon Nielsen's mother had given her consent to the placement of Jon in the institution, and this made the placement, in the eyes of the majority of the European Court, voluntary. The facts of the Dutch case are clearly distinguishable from the *Nielsen* case, but the ability of the Dutch court to separate the interests of the parent and child, appreciate the collision of interests and find a practical solution should be a valuable lesson for future instances.

B   Dutch Supreme Court September 25, 1998: right of third party to give assistance to the child without knowledge or consent of parents

In the following case an important principle is established. Dutch law provides for child protection measures to be taken. It also provided for voluntary and non-voluntary assistance to be provided, including the provision of assistance to runaway children, discussed in the *1995 Survey*.[135] But is the provision of that assistance against the will and without the knowledge of the parents a tort? This question is not answered in the

---

[133]   *Nederlandse Jurisprudentie* 1999, 80.
[134]   Eur. Court H.R., November 28, 1998, Series A Vol. 144.
[135]   *The International Survey of Family Law 1995* (above), pp. 372–373.

legislation. In the present case the Supreme Court ruled, relying on reasoning derived from the United Nations Convention on the Rights of the Child, that such assistance was not always tortious.

On September 14, 1987 a 14-year-old girl informed one of her teachers at school of repeated rapes carried out by her brother during her last years in the primary school. In subsequent talks she told about subsequent approaches by the brother and of a suicide attempt. The talks were difficult and emotional and the girl was terrified at the idea that the information would be revealed to the parents. The teacher agreed not to inform the parents. The girl handed the teacher a written description of the brother's actions. After the autumn holiday, when the girl stated that a new rape had taken place, the girl agreed that the teacher could bring the matter to the attention of the RIAGG (the Foundation for Regional Ambulant Mental Health Care). The girl insisted that the talk with the RIAGG should take place at school, without informing her parents. Two talks with the RIAGG took place at school thereafter. There was a dispute between the girl, who persisted in not wanting to tell her parents, and the teacher, who did. It was agreed that, should the brother rape again, the teacher could approach the parents. The girl, when accepting this condition, stated that in that event she would no longer be able to stay at home. On December 11, 1987 the girl reported at school that her brother had raped her again. She had brought some belongings to school, and understood that the parents would now be informed. That day the teacher informed the woman from the RIAGG that he would notify the parents, and that, since the girl did not want to go home, he would find her a temporary address. The RIAGG employee had also been informed of the earlier suicide attempt by the girl. The parents were notified and the same day the girl was placed in a home for incest victims. Once in the home she stated that not her brother, but her father, had raped her. On December 17, 1987 the RIAGG informed the parents of the new allegations. On the same day a conference took place at which several employees of the RIAGG (including a child psychiatrist who had treated the girl's brother) and the G.P. of the family, and a representative of the Child Protection Council were present. The parents visited the girl on December 14, 1987 and January 5, 1988. Early in January 1988 the girl escaped from the home, but was brought back by the police. In consequence the Child Protection Council decided to take a child protection measure. On January 12, 1988 the girl was entrusted to the Child Protection Council. Following a suicide attempt the girl was placed in the psychiatric ward of a hospital. On February 28, 1988 the parents' parental rights were suspended for a period of six months. On September 19, 1988 the Children's Judge extended the period of placement outside the home by twelve months. In June 1989 a report was presented by the home where the girl was staying, in which is stated that the alleged incest never took place. With the parents' consent, the child protection measures were continued until June 28, 1991. After that date she lived with the parents.

The parents alleged, in tort proceedings against the RIAGG, that the RIAGG had failed to take account of theirs and their daughter's interest. In particular they complained of the removal of the daughter from them without informing them or their G.P., the failure to safeguard adequate contact between them and the girl and the fact that the incest allegations were too readily accepted as true. In the view of the parents these failings led to the late discovery of their daughter's real problems, by which time they were much more difficult to treat.

At first instance the Regional Court held that the RIAGG had behaved unlawfully towards the parents. The Regional Court did not hold the failure to inform the parents at an earlier date than December 11, to be unlawful, especially in the light of the explicit wish of the girl that her parents were not informed. The Regional Court's judgment turned on the placement of the girl in a home for incest victims without consulting the parents, and the subsequent restrictions on access. On behalf of the parents it was argued that even these measures would have been justified if they had been accompanied by a thorough investigation into the truth of the incest allegations.

The Appeal Court, focusing on the same aspects as the Regional Court, stated that the placement in a home was an interference with the right of the parents to determine where their daughter should live. But this parental right was not guaranteed to the parents without limits; not every interference with it amounted to an unlawful act. The Appeal Court regarded as relevant the fact that the actions by the RIAGG took place in the context of providing help, that the girl had made repeated, very serious, allegations, and had indicated that if her parents were informed she would be unable to go home. The Appeal Court held that in the circumstances the actions were justified. It was reproachful of the fact that the parents were not informed immediately of the location of the girl (this was done the day following her removal). The later restrictions on access were also, in the Appeal Court's view, not unlawful, since they were a response to the express wishes of the girl. Moreover, the complaint by the parents that the RIAGG did not conduct an investigation into the truth of the allegations, was, in the Appeal Court's view, unjustified. The RIAGG is a crisis organisation, and, as such, must make a correct assessment of the crisis situation. It is not equipped to investigate the truth. The parents appealed to the Supreme Court against this decision. They argued that the RIAGG was not entitled to interfere with the girl and her relationship with the parents in the absence of legal child protection measures, provided by law, being taken.[136] Moreover there was alleged to be a violation of Article 8 ECHR since the parents had not been sufficiently involved in the decision-making process.

The Supreme Court,[137] upholding the decision of the Appeal Court, reasoned as follows. The parental rights are given to the parents in the child's interests and thus the rights cannot be viewed independently of the obligation to have regard to the child's interests.[138] Furthermore, in the context of the child's interests, it must be realised that the wishes of the child deserve increased weight as the child becomes older and more mature.[139] These principles are also laid down in the United Nations Convention on the Rights of the Child, which was ratified by the Netherlands on March 8, 1995.[140] The parents have the right to determine where the child shall stay. But if the child, being at an age and degree of maturity at which account should be taken of his opinions, has reasons for not living at the place determined by the parents, a third party who assists the child without consulting the parents or seeking their consent will not necessarily be acting unlawfully. This applies even though the third party giving help may not be one of the organisations charged with statutory child protection functions and powers. The assistance provided by the third party will, in particular, not be tortious if the third party has reasonable grounds to believe that the child is in an emergency situation, requiring that the child be given short-term assistance, and that the third party informs the parents

---

[136] The RIAGG had no statutory power (or duty) to take child protection measures; that is the job of the Child Protection Council.

[137] *Nederlandse Jurisprudentie* 1999, 279, m. nt. Wortmann.

[138] Eur. Court H.R. November 28, 1988, Series A Vol. 144, para. 61 (Nielsen).

[139] Eur. Court H.R. April 22, 1992, Series A Vol. 226-B, (*Hokkanen v Finland*), para. 73; Eur. Court H.R. June 9, 1998, *Reports of Judgments and Decisions* 1998-IV, p. 1476 (*Bronda v Italy*), para. 62.

[140] Tractatenblad 1990, 46 and 170; Tractatenblad 1995, 92.

as promptly and as fully as is reasonably possible.[141] Accordingly the Supreme Court held that the actions by the RIAGG were not tortious.

The impact of this decision is potentially far-reaching. First and foremost the case acknowledges the impact of the United Nations Convention on the Rights of the Child, especially Articles 3 and 5, upon parental rights, since the wishes and opinions of a child of sufficient age and understanding are explicitly recognised as a reason for justifying the third party in not involving the parents in the first resort. Moreover, the case recognises a right to confidentiality of a child, a right which is frequently overlooked (see for example the legislative proposal discussed in section III.C.1 above). The decision creates scope for assistance to be given to minors by third parties, even though those third parties are not specifically charged with bringing legal child enforcement measures. The organisation in question did, however, have a special status, in that it was named as one of the organisations entitled to seek suitable places for children.[142] Furthermore, in the words of the Supreme Court, the special circumstances which may protect the third party from an action in tort include, but are not confined to, the circumstances in which the child is in an emergency situation. It is not certain how wide the application of the principle might go. The Supreme Court gives a broad statement of general principle before referring specifically to the situation before it of a child who no longer feels able to live with her parents. The broader principles regarding the relationship between the parent and a third party assisting the child might be applicable to other cases not so close to the facts of this case. It might, for example, be arguable that a doctor who performed an abortion on a minor without consulting the parents might, in certain circumstances, be able to rely on the principles expounded in this case regarding the relationship between third parties, parent and children. If the minor was in a state of emergency, and if the child had good reasons for not informing the parents before the operation was carried out, the doctor could be protected from an action in tort under this principle. A condition would be that the doctor informed the parents as soon and as fully as reasonably possible, and probably that the child's G.P. was consulted before carrying out the operation.

VI HEALTH ISSUES

A *New procedures for euthanasia*

On November 1, 1998 new rules regulating the procedures to be followed by doctors in euthanasia cases came into force.[143] The existing procedure is replaced by two new procedures: one to apply in cases of euthanasia and assistance with suicide and another to apply to cases of termination of life not requested by the patient. To deal with euthanasia and suicide assistance cases five new regional committees, each to be staffed by one lawyer, one medical expert and one ethical expert, will be appointed. These committees will decide in individual cases whether the doctor concerned has acted in accordance with the standards required. The committee must send its judgment on each individual case to

---

[141] A strong parallel is made with the requirements laid down in the case of help supplied to runaway children and the present case, where in fact all the requirements of that Act were complied with, in the conclusion of Advocate-General Langemeijer, para. 3.11. These requirements are laid down in the Runaway Children Act, discussed in *The International Survey of Family Law 1994* (above), pp. 372–373.

[142] Wet op de Jeugdhulpverlening, Article 27.

[143] Besluit van 19 november 1997, 1997, Staatsblad 550; Inwerkingtredingsbesluit van 11 mei 1998, Staatsblad 1998, 280.

the public prosecutor and the regional health inspector within six weeks of the notification by the treating physician of his or her actions. The physician will be informed of the committee's judgment on the case. If the committee concludes that the required standards have not been met, it may recommend the initiation of criminal proceedings. In the normal case the public prosecutor will not prosecute, unless the committee of public prosecutors concludes that prosecution should take place. The public prosecution service must notify the treating physician within three weeks. A more intense scrutiny is applied to cases of termination of life not requested by the patient. In these cases a central committee will examine the case, and make a recommendation to the public prosecutor. The committee of public prosecutors must decide whether a prosecution should follow. The regional committees are to report to the respective ministers at the end of each year. The reports will be public, except to the extent that the privacy of individuals must be protected. This amendment to procedures is not accompanied by any change in the criminal law. The government has not followed suggestions that a new defence should be created for doctors administering euthanasia.

The new procedures follow an investigation carried out in 1996 which revealed that, although many doctors met the standards laid down in the Disposal of the Dead Act (see *1994 Survey*[144]), in more than half of the cases the doctor who took action leading to termination of the patient's life did not report his actions as the law requires. In response to this finding the government resolved that more emphasis should be placed on palliative care. The patient should understand that everything would be done to alleviate pain, that he would be cared for to the best possible standards, and would not be let down. The purpose is of course to ensure that the patient makes a free choice for euthanasia. Furthermore, the need to consult a second independent doctor in all euthanasia cases should be stressed, and there should be medical-professional scrutiny of compliance with the prescribed procedures after the event.[145]

B   Cloning

After some initial hesitation it has been decided that the Netherlands will sign the Anti-cloning Protocol, the fifth Protocol to the Convention on Human Rights and Bio-medicine, opened for signature at Strasbourg on April 4, 1997. The Anti-cloning Protocol was opened for signature on January 12, 1998. Originally the Ministry of Health, Welfare and Sport objected to the Protocol because of the diverse interpretation of the word 'human being' in the Member States. The Protocol requires the Member States to give their own interpretation to that concept. In some countries a fertilised ovum is already characterised as a human being, whilst other countries do not characterise the human embryo as a human being until it has been born. If the first construction is used, signing the Protocol could block cloning for the purposes of embryo research even during the first 14 days after fertilisation. In the Netherlands this would be regarded as an objectionable result. However, in a letter of January 28, 1998[146] the Minister announced that the words 'human being' must be interpreted so as to permit research into the early stages of development of the embryo. According to this letter, the Protocol is not concerned with the technique of cloning as such. The Medical Procedures Involving

---

[144] *The International Survey of Family Law 1994* (above), pp. 349–350.
[145] Letter from the Ministers of Justice and Health, Welfare and Sport, January 21, 1997; letter and proposal November 24, 1997.
[146] Second Chamber 1997–1998, 25 835, nr. 2.

Reproductive Cells and Embryos Bill, which is still in preparation,[147] will prohibit, in accordance with Article 1 of the Protocol of the Human Rights and Biomedicine Convention, actions carried out with the intention of causing a person to be born who is genetically identical to another person (including the case in which the last-mentioned person is dead). Signature of the Protocol by the Netherlands on May 4, 1998 was accompanied by an interpretive declaration in the following terms:

> 'In relation to Article 1 of the Protocol, the government of the Kingdom of the Netherlands declares that the term "human being" is understood as being exclusively applicable to a human being which has been born.'

The Medical Procedures Involving Reproductive Cells and Embryos Bill (in preparation) will permit the development of the foetus outside the mother's body for a period not exceeding 14 days. During that period cloning techniques may be applied, for example for the purposes of transplantation.[148]

C   The Foetal Tissue Bill

The Foetal Tissue Bill was presented to the second chamber of Parliament on June 25, 1995.[149] The Bill regulates one aspect of a much wider topic – that of medical procedures involving reproductive cells and embryos – which will be regulated by a complete statute (the Medical Procedures Involving Reproductive Cells and Embryos Bill) which is currently in preparation. It was thought desirable to hive off this one aspect and get it passed in advance of that Act. The purpose of the Foetal Tissue Bill is to permit a restricted and closely regulated application of the use of foetal tissue. The tissue may only be used after the foetus is dead. Foetal tissue is used for three therapeutic purposes: the treatment of immune deficiencies, of irregularities in blood cell structure and blood-producing organs, and of neuro-degenerative conditions. Foetal tissue is also removed for diagnostic purposes, particularly in the case of a miscarriage. Research applications of foetal tissue are concerned primarily with developmental biology and the way in which harmful conditions arise in the human body. At present all these procedures are forbidden by law;[150] this Act will make it possible to carry out these useful procedures lawfully.

According to Article 2 of the Foetal Tissue Bill the preservation and use of foetal tissue is only permitted for medical purposes, medical and biological research and medical-biological educational purposes. Foetal tissue may not be used for medical treatment of persons indicated by the woman from whom the tissue originates. Preservation or use of foetal tissue may only take place with the prior written (and signed) permission of the woman from whom the tissue originates.[151] If the woman is at least 12 but not yet 18 years old, the permission of a person exercising custody over her is also needed.[152] If she is 12 or older but not able to appreciate her interests in the matter,

---

[147] An earlier Bill on this subject (Second Chamber 1994–1995 23 016 nr. 1 (February 4, 1993)) was withdrawn on March 16, 1995.

[148] Letter from the Minister of Health, Welfare and Sport, Second Chamber 1988–1999, 25 835 nr. 5 (April 28, 1999).

[149] Second Chamber 1998–1999, 26 639, nrs. 1–3 (Regels betreffende terbeschikkingstelling en gebruik van foetal weefsel).

[150] Wet op de orgaandonatie van 24 mei 1996, Staatsblad 1996, 370, Artikel 13 (gewijzigd Staatsblad 1997, 600) (gedeeltelijk inwerkingtreding door koninklijke besluit van 26 januari 1998, Staatsblad 1998, 42).

[151] Article 3(1) proposal.

[152] Article 3(2) proposal.

permission is needed from the person exercising custody or, if she has attained majority, her legal representative or spouse, registered partner or other life partner. The foetal tissue may not be used if the spouse, registered partner or life partner objects.[153] This is an interesting acknowledgment of the husband's or partner's interest.[154] Before permission is sought, the woman must be properly informed by and under the responsibility of the treating physician, in accordance with Article 4, of the exact purposes for which the tissue will be used. The permission given by the woman and any objection to it is to be filed and preserved. The woman can withdraw her permission at any time, but the withdrawal will only have effect regarding tissue used after the date of withdrawal of permission.[155] Once permission to use has been withdrawn or an objection has been lodged by the spouse or partner, the tissue must no longer be preserved.[156] The tissue is to be preserved in such way that it cannot be traced to the woman or her spouse or partner, unless such tracing is necessary for the intended use.[157] No payment may be made or received for the making available of foetal tissue.[158] It is forbidden to preserve reproductive cells which originate from a human foetus and use them for reproductive purposes.[159] It is forbidden to store or use cells which have been cultured from foetal tissue for any purpose except medial purposes, medical and biological research or medical and biological educational purposes.[160] It is forbidden to remove parts of a living foetus which has been born with the purpose of using such tissue.[161] Violations of Articles 2, 3, 4, 8 and 11 will be punished with a prison sentence of one year maximum or a fine of 25,000 guilders. Violations of Articles 5, 6, 9 and 10 will be punished with a maximum detention of six months or a fine of 25,000 guilders.[162]

D   Prohibition of sex selection on non-medical grounds

A statutory instrument prohibiting selection of foetuses on the grounds of sex in assisted reproduction procedures was passed on May 26, 1998[163] and came into force on October 1, 1998.[164] The prohibition does not apply if, according to responsible medical opinion there is a risk that the child will be born with a serious sex-linked hereditary condition and the actions concerned aim to avoid such risk eventuating.[165] The procedures prohibited by this provision are sex-selective embryo replacement (only embryos of the desired sex are placed in the womb) and sex-selective insemination (sperm is treated such that the sperm carrying x-chromosomes are separated from sperm carrying the

---

[153]   Article 3(4) proposal.

[154]   See the European Commission's case-law on the absence of a right in the man or partner to object to the abortion: *X v U.K.* Appl. 8416/79, 19 Coll. Dec. 244 (1980); *Hercz v Norway*, Appl. 17004/90 unrep.

[155]   Article 5(2) proposal.

[156]   Article 5(3) proposal.

[157]   Article 6(1) proposal.

[158]   Article 8 proposal.

[159]   Article 9 proposal.

[160]   Article 10 proposal.

[161]   Article 11 proposal.

[162]   Article 12 proposal.

[163]   Besluit van 26 mei 1998, houdende een verbod op geslachtskeuze om niet-medische redenen, Staatsblad 1998, 336.

[164]   Besluit van September 24, 1998 tot vaststelling van het tijdstip van inwerkingtreding van het Besluit verbod geslachtskeuze om niet-medische redenen, Staatsblad 1998, 567.

[165]   Article 1(2).

y-chromosome). In the longer term it is intended that this prohibition will be included in the Medical Procedures Involving Reproductive Cells and Embryos Bill (see section VI.B above). But because there was a clinic in the Netherlands which was actually practising sex selection, it was thought necessary to introduce a temporary prohibition by statutory instrument, the power to do which is conferred by the Special Medical Procedures Act,[166] rather than waiting for the Medical Procedures Involving Reproductive Cells and Embryos Bill to be passed. The clinic in Utrecht which had been offering sex-selection techniques was forced to cease all those activities in consequence of the provision. Objections to the sex selection of embryos are two-fold. First, it is thought undesirable to disturb the balance in the male–female population. Second, the procedures are perceived as reducing a child to a pure object of its parents' desires. The Convention on Human Rights and Bio-medicine includes a prohibition on sex selection in Article 14. Although the prohibition involves a restriction in the free access of services as required by Article 59 of the EEC Treaty, the restriction is justified in the interest of a pressing reason of public interest. Justification on the grounds of public interest is not provided for in the Treaty, but has been accepted in the case-law of the European Court of Justice. The Court of Justice has not decided on a case of sex selection, but did hold in the *Grogan*[167] case that the decision on the morality of carrying out abortion is up to the member states. Ten member states have signed the Convention on Human Rights and Bio-medicine. For these reasons the Dutch government concluded that the prohibition was likely to be upheld by the European Court of Justice.

E   Medical-Scientific Research with Humans Act

On February 26, 1998 the Medical-Scientific Research with Humans Act was passed.[168] The Act came into force in phases. Articles 14 and 15, which set up a central committee, came into force on April 1, 1999.[169] Articles 16–18 and 24–26 (setting up of control committees) came into force on May 17, 1999.[170] The remaining provisions are expected to come into force on October 1, 1999. The Medical Procedures Involving Reproductive Cells and Embryos Bill will regulate medical procedures concerning embryos; this Act is intended to complement that Bill by regulating medical research procedures with human beings after birth. Until the first-mentioned Bill comes into force, there is no legislative regulation of procedures concerning embryos. Because such a gap is thought undesirable, the Minister has requested that guidelines be drawn up to regulate such procedures pending the coming into force of that Act.[171]

In order to carry out research in which human beings are used a protocol must be drawn up by the researching institution. That protocol must be approved by either the central committee or a local committee. The local committee may handle all cases except:

---

[166] Of October 24, 1997, Staatsblad 1997, 515, Article 3(1). The prohibition in the statutory instrument will lapse within two years of coming into force unless a legislative provision containing the same prohibition is introduced into Parliament within two years.

[167] ECJ, October 4, 1991, case C-159/90, *Society for the Protection of Unborn Children v Ireland*, Jur. 1991, p. 1-4685.

[168] Staatsblad 1998, 161.

[169] Besluit van 23 maart 1999, houdende gedeeltelijke inwerkingtreding van de Wet medisch-wetenschappelijk onderzoek met mensen, Staatsblad 1999, 145, article 1.

[170] Besluit van 23 maart 1999, houdende gedeeltelijke inwerkingtreding van de Wet medisch-wetenschappelijk onderzoek met mensen, Staatsblad 1999, 145, article 2.

[171] Letter from the Minister of Health, Welfare and Sport, Second Chamber 1998–1999, 22 588, nr. 27, p. 3.

an administrative appeal; an investigation which is not to the benefit of the person investigated and which deliberately changes his condition; certain categories of investigation which, according to Article 19 must be referred to the central committee and certain categories of research with respect to which expertise is scarce.[172] The commission should only approve a proposed research protocol if the following conditions are satisfied: it is reasonable to assume that the research will lead to new insights in the field of medical treatment, and those insights cannot be acquired by other methods; the gains to be made are in proportion to the risks to the persons to be tested; the research satisfies certain standards regarding methodology; the researchers have the necessary expertise; it is reasonable to assume that the payments made to the persons tested have not influenced their decision to submit to the research; the protocol specifies the extent to which the research may be expected to benefit the person tested; other reasonable requirements are fulfilled.[173]

It is forbidden to carry out research with persons who have not attained the age of 18 years or who are not able to understand their interests in the matter. However, this prohibition does not apply if the research can benefit the person tested or the research can be carried out only with the co-operation of persons in the category to which the persons tested belong, and the risks are negligible.[174] In no circumstances may the research be carried out under this Article if the person concerned objects.[175]

It is forbidden to carry out research on persons who, in the light of their relationship to the researchers, cannot be expected to decide freely whether to participate. However, this prohibition does not apply if the research can benefit the person tested or the research can be carried out only with the co-operation of persons in the category to which the persons tested belong.[176]

It is prohibited to carry out research without the tested person's written consent, if the person is an adult. If the tested person is minor, but older than 12 years and is capable of appreciating his interests in the matter, the written consent of the minor and those exercising custody is required. If the person is older than 12 years but incapable of appreciating his interests in the matter, the consent of his guardian or custodian (in the case of a minor) or legal representative or spouse or other life partner is required. If the person is under the age of 12, the written consent of the parent or guardian is required.[177] If the research can be carried out only in an emergency situation, making it impossible to obtain the permission required as detailed above, and the research can benefit the person tested, the research may be carried out without consent for as long as the situation making it impossible to obtain consent continues.[178] It is the responsibility of those carrying out the research to ensure that the persons to be tested are fully informed, before giving consent, as to the purpose, character and duration of the research and any risks involved. The person must be given a period of time between being informed and the giving of consent. The person carrying out the research has in particular responsibility for ensuring that persons under the age of 12 are informed in a manner which they can understand,

---

[172] Article 2.
[173] Article 3.
[174] Article 4(1).
[175] Article 4(2).
[176] Article 5.
[177] Article 6(1).
[178] Article 6(2).

about the research and the risks for them. The person tested can always revoke the consent and is not liable for any damages caused by the revocation of consent.[179]

---

[179] Article 6.

NEW ZEALAND

GO-SLOW ON NEW LEGISLATION

*Bill Atkin**

I   NEW LEGISLATION INTRODUCED

Three significant pieces of legislation, sponsored by the Government, were introduced into Parliament in 1998. These are the Matrimonial Property Amendment Bill, the De Facto Relationships (Property) Bill, and the Assisted Human Reproduction Bill. They stand out as the year's family law highlights, but in all three instances, progress through Parliament has been slow. It is anticipated that they will eventually be enacted in the latter half of 1999, but, with a general election looming and a minority Government kept in power by a rag-bag collection of independent Members of Parliament who might force an early election at any point, doubt still hovers over the fate of the three Bills. At the time of writing, they are before parliamentary select committees. Public submissions on the first two have been heard and the committee is now deliberating on the issues raised. Submissions have been received on the Assisted Human Reproduction Bill but they have yet to be considered by the select committee. There has been a frustrating sense of 'go-slow' about these Bills.

All three Bills deal with important social and ethical questions. They impact on a wide cross-section of the population. One deals primarily with the rights of widowed spouses when their husband or wife has died. Another deals with the growing phenomenon of unmarried cohabitation. The rapidly increasing numbers of couples living in de facto relationships indicate a massive shift in values and social practice. The law is being forced to catch up. The third piece of legislation – on assisted reproduction – deals with fundamental questions about human life, personal identity and the public interest. The lack of international consensus on many of these matters is probably reflected in the New Zealand proposal, which some may consider controversial and inadequate.

II   WIDOWED SPOUSES

The current law dealing with the division of property on marriage breakdown is found in the Matrimonial Property Act 1976. In broad terms, that Act provides for the classification of property as 'matrimonial' or 'separate', for the equal division of matrimonial property between the estranged spouses (separate property falling outside the jurisdiction of the Act), for some specific exceptions to the equal sharing rule, and for sundry supplementary orders which a court can make, such as an order for the occupation of the matrimonial home. At the time when the Act was passed, now well over two decades ago, the Government foreshadowed that the legislation would in the near future be extended to cover the situation where one spouse had died. In principle, it was

---

*   Reader in Law, Victoria University of Wellington.

accepted that a widowed spouse should be treated no worse than a separated or divorced spouse, but the government of the day wanted more time to examine how to implement the extended cover. In the meantime, the old law found in the Matrimonial Property Act 1963 was saved to cover the succession situation. The 1963 Act, which, in marked contrast to the equal division rules of the 1976 Act, operates largely on the basis of judicial discretion and has been criticised for its lack of certainty, thus still exists for a narrow band of cases but will be finally repealed when the Matrimonial Property Amendment Bill is passed.

One of the main goals of the 1998 Amendment Bill is therefore to bring the position of surviving spouses into line with separated spouses. The survivor will be able to apply for division of the matrimonial property and will be granted the equal share to which spouses are prima facie entitled on separation. This entitlement takes priority over beneficiaries under a will or under the intestacy rules. There are however certain distinctive features of the new proposals and these are discussed next.

The threat of a matrimonial property claim is a potential problem for anyone administering an estate. Executors and administrators need to be confident that there are no outstanding claims on an estate before distributing it. The Amendment Bill deals with this in two ways. First, there are time limits on making a matrimonial property application. Broadly speaking, an application must be brought within 12 months of the grant of administration of an estate. Where an estate is sufficiently small that formal grant of administration is not required, the time limit is 12 months from the deceased's death. The 12-month period reflects the rule for divorced persons – a divorced person must bring an application within 12 months of the date of dissolution of the marriage but the court has a discretionary power to extend this period, a power also now provided for in the régime for surviving spouses.

Despite the time limits just mentioned, distribution of the estate can commence much earlier. Apart from situations where, for example, the survivor consents, the estate can be distributed after a 6-month delay from the grant of administration or as soon as the survivor chooses either 'option A' or 'option B'. These options represent the second important way in which administrators of an estate can plan what to do. Under the Amendment Bill, a surviving spouse is required to indicate within 6 months of the grant of administration whether or not a matrimonial property claim will be pursued. 'Option A' represents an intention to make a formal matrimonial property claim. 'Option B' represents a waiver of such a claim in favour of benefits under a will or under the intestacy rules. If no formal election is made, a survivor is presumed to have chosen option B, ie it is presumed that there is no intention to make a matrimonial property claim. Once a choice between the two options has been made, the choice cannot be revoked but if there is evidence of duress or lack of understanding about the process, a court may set the choice aside. In one important situation, a choice need not be made. This is where the spouses were already divorced or separated under a separation order from the court. Presumably the reason for this exception is that the administrator of an estate might expect some claim in any event and the choosing of an option would be otiose.

The system of electing one of the two options may at first appear to add unnecessary complexities. However, it does provide the administrator of an estate with a clear and hopefully early indication of what to expect. It also gives the surviving spouse a mechanism to forgo matrimonial property entitlements. This may be desirable for several reasons, eg the survivor may be amply provided for under the will anyway, or the survivor may be already well off and prefer that other family members take under the will. The Amendment Bill grants entitlements, but not automatic or 'forced' entitlements.

The rules for determining a matrimonial property claim on death are very similar to those applying inter vivos. There are however several significant differences. First, an application can normally be made only by the survivor and not by the estate of the deceased spouse. While this may seem anomalous at first sight, the object of the reform is to ensure that the survivor is no worse off than a separated or divorced spouse. It is not intended to benefit the estate, which ultimately means to enhance the shares of residuary beneficiaries under the estate. Further protection is given to the survivor by a rule which prevents an order being made which divests the survivor of any property already vested in the survivor's name or which forces the survivor to make a payment to the estate.

Secondly, in order to preserve parity between the surviving and separated spouse, ordinary rules of survivorship are abandoned. Thus, property the subject of a joint tenancy does not pass to the survivor as usual but instead is brought back into the pool of property to be classified as either matrimonial or separate. On the other hand, because evidence cannot be obtained from a deceased spouse, the Amendment Bill provides another rule which will advantage the widowed party. All property owned by the deceased is presumed to be matrimonial property and is thus divisible under the scheme. The estate can produce evidence to the contrary to rebut the presumption but clearly the onus is on the estate to satisfy the court that an item of property should be reclassified as separate.

The rules determining the parties' shares in matrimonial property are largely the same whether the division is inter vivos or after death, ie prima facie equal sharing. There is however one difference. Normally, where a marriage is one of short duration, defined in the Matrimonial Property Act as lasting less than three years, the house and chattels are divided according to contributions to the marriage partnership. This rule will not apply when determining how property should devolve on death. The reason for this is that a marriage ending in death after such a short time has probably been the result of some tragedy such as an accident or unexpected illness. There is no sense that the marriage has failed or that one of the parties has entered the marriage to collect a valuable dowry, only then to depart. The court will however be able to divide the house and chattels according to contributions if having regard to all the circumstances the court considers that to be just. An example might be where the parties had in fact already separated when the death occurred.

The new rules for devolution of property on death will ensure greater symmetry in the law. The anomalous situation where a divorced spouse may be in a much better position than a widowed spouse will be removed. To what extent the new provisions will be used is another question. That many survivors will be content to rely on their ordinary inheritance rights is implied by the system of electing option A or option B. The choice of proceeding under the Matrimonial Property Act will have to be carefully thought through to see whether it really does benefit the spouse. The reason for this is that a matrimonial property claim deprives the spouse of intestacy rights or entitlements under the will 'unless the will (if any) of the deceased spouse expresses a contrary intention' (clause 73). A widowed spouse's advisors will therefore have to be sure that the matrimonial property claim will reap more than would otherwise be received under an inheritance. This may well occur in a clear minority of cases.

III   TRUSTS AND COMPANIES

While the extension of the matrimonial scheme to cover survivors is the major reform proposed in the 1998 legislation, other changes are made, many of them of a technical nature. Noteworthy however are new rules dealing with assets which have been syphoned off to trusts and companies, thus ostensibly placing them outside the reach of the matrimonial property scheme. At present, the court has some limited powers under section 44 of the Matrimonial Property Act 1976 to trace such property but only if an intention to defeat the other party's matrimonial property interests can be proven. With respect to trusts, the courts have also latched on to a fairly obscure provision in the Family Proceedings Act 1980, section 182, to order payments to the spouse disadvantaged by the trust's existence. Section 182 refers to 'ante-nuptial' and 'post-nuptial settlements' in respect of which a court may make such orders as it thinks fit. The concept of such a settlement has been liberally interpreted to include family trusts but, anomalously, the power can be used only after the marriage has been dissolved. A recent example of the use of the section was *A v A*[1] where the couple had a farm originally owned by a family company. The farm was later sold to a discretionary family trust, the beneficiaries of which were the husband, wife and their two children. The Family Court granted the wife $27,000 from the trust, a figure which the High Court on appeal set aside for further argument because of other complications about a debt which the trust owed to the husband.

Amendments proposed in the 1998 Bill leave section 182 intact but may have the effect of making it largely redundant. The court will have new powers with respect to trusts and 'qualifying companies'. Any trust will qualify unless it was established under a will or other testamentary disposition. A 'qualifying company' is one where at least half of the shares are held by or for the benefit of one spouse. This formula may of course invite structuring of family companies so as to avoid the jurisdiction of the Act and yet retain effective control in the hands of one spouse. It remains to be seen whether such devices will render the new powers with respect to companies nugatory.

The court will have power to order the disclosure of information relating to the disposition of matrimonial property to a trust or company since the marriage. This provision which the court can invoke on its own motion or on application by either party may be drafted too narrowly, because it does not take account of the transfer of separate property. In contrast, section 44, the existing 'tracing' provision, refers to any disposition of property and is thus not limited to matrimonial property.

The more important new provision is the power the court will have to compensate a spouse whose claim or rights under the Matrimonial Property Act have been defeated by the disposition of matrimonial property to the trust or company. The test is much wider than has hitherto existed. It will no longer be necessary to prove an intention to defeat the other spouse's claim. Rather, it will be sufficient to show that the effect of the disposition of property, irrespective of intention, is to defeat such a claim. This will for instance enable a court to trace property into a family trust even though the trust was created for a perfectly legitimate reason. The court's power to compensate may take the form of an order requiring one spouse to pay the other a sum of money or requiring the transfer of property (matrimonial or separate) to the other spouse. As a last resort in the cases of trusts, the trustees can be ordered to pay the other spouse out of the trust's income.

---

[1]   [1998] NZFLR 330.

How successful these new provisions will be in effectively broadening the base from which a property settlement can be made remains to be seen. The power to compensate is discretionary and will depend on the justice of making an order, taking into account such things as the value of the property disposed of, when the disposition occurred, whether consideration was given for it, the amount of the rest of the matrimonial property, and, in the case of trusts, whether the spouse or children have been beneficiaries of the trust. So there will be instances where the court may decline to make any award. But a classic scenario justifying compensation is where there is little other matrimonial property and the matrimonial home has been vested in a trust or company, thus falling outside the court's usual jurisdiction. The court is highly likely in this situation to compensate the spouse who would otherwise miss out on an appropriate share of the property.

IV DE FACTO RELATIONSHIPS

A companion piece of legislation to the Matrimonial Property Amendment Bill is the De Facto Relationships (Property) Bill. This is a large Bill of 201 clauses and deals with a growing social phenomenon. Since statistics were first collected in the 1981 census when 87,960 people were living in de facto relationships, the numbers have risen sharply, so that by 1996, 236,397 people (out of a total population of around 3.5 million) stated that they were living in a de facto relationship. Many such relationships are ending either in separation or death, with consequent legal problems. The present law, in the absence of a cohabitation contract, depends largely on the complicated and unpredictable rules of trust law.

The De Facto Relationships (Property) Bill will replace the rules of common law and equity. It mirrors in many respects the matrimonial property régime. Thus, for example, the new matrimonial property rules relating to devolution on death and relating to trusts and companies are directly reflected in the new de facto legislation. There are however some significant differences which are worth noting.

First, the Bill applies to a former 'de facto relationship' which is defined as one 'where a man and a woman are living together in a relationship in the nature of marriage, although not married to each other'. This somewhat convoluted phrase has been used in other New Zealand legislation and has been interpreted by the courts.[2] While there will doubtless be litigation over relationships which fall on the borderline of this expression, most ought to be straightforward. In addition, the relationship must normally have lasted at least three years, but the court has a discretion to accept applications in relation to shorter relationships if serious injustice would otherwise occur and if there has been a child of the relationship or the applicant has made a substantial contribution to the relationship.

The most controversial aspect of the definition of 'de facto relationship' as presently drafted is that it is heterosexual. Same-sex relationships fall outside the jurisdiction of the court and, as in *Julian v McWatt*,[3] will have to continue to rely on the general law. When the Bill returns to the House of Representatives from the select committee, it is almost

---

[2]   See for instance the Court of Appeal decision in *Ruka v Department of Social Welfare* [1997] 1 NZLR 154.

[3]   [1998] NZFLR 257. In that case, Judge Kerr accepted that the relationship between the two men was 'in the nature of marriage' and, on the basis of a constructive trust, awarded the plaintiff a 45% share in the defendant's property. Why he thought he had to determine whether the two men's relationship was in the nature of marriage is unclear. The existence of a constructive trust does not depend on such a finding.

certain that there will be an attempt to alter the definition of 'de facto relationship' and, on a free vote of Members of Parliament, same-sex relationships may well be included. Under New Zealand law, gay and lesbian couples cannot marry.[4] This might justify a narrow approach being taken to property issues, especially as the Court of Appeal, by a majority, has said that the present marriage restrictions are not discriminatory against homosexual people. A property law which excluded homosexual relationships may likewise be regarded as non-discriminatory. On the other hand, the trend in New Zealand law, illustrated by two recent cases, is to recognise the reality of same-sex relationships. In *P v M*,[5] the issue was whether a woman's lesbian partner and the woman's brother were 'family members'. If so, then the brother and the lesbian partner were in a domestic relationship which provided the court with jurisdiction to consider the brother's application for a protection order under the Domestic Violence Act 1995. Fisher J answered in the affirmative:

'... one would expect the Act to be concerned with the functional realities of a relationship, not its formal legitimacy under other statutes ... it is difficult to see any policy reasons for distinguishing between homosexual and heterosexual relationships for the purpose of protecting against domestic violence.'

Arguably, these same points could be made with respect to a property statute.

The second case arose under the Child Support Act 1991. Although under that Act, liability to pay child support rests almost exclusively on biological or adoptive parents, a special exception enables the court to declare a person to be a step-parent, who will then also be liable to pay child support.[6] Until 1998, this power was hardly ever used, but a case, *A v R*,[7] arose where the applicant had lived in a lesbian relationship for 14 years. The three children, conceived by artificial insemination, treated both women as their mothers and the respondent had taken, up to the separation, a full part in their upbringing. The court had no hesitation in declaring the respondent a step-parent and stated:[8]

'... it is difficult to see why, as an ordinary matter of construction, the term ['step-parent'] should not also apply to lesbian or homosexual relationships, where there are dependent children. For that may also be a relationship "in the nature of marriage", although it is not formally so.'

Again, if the law recognises same-sex relationships for child support purposes, is it a very big leap to do so to resolve property disputes?

Another difference between the matrimonial property laws and those proposed for de facto relationships relates to the time limit within which an inter vivos application must be brought. A de facto partner has two years after the ending of the relationship within which to file a claim. This compares with an unrestricted time-frame for a separated

---

[4]   *Quilter v Attorney-General* [1998] 1 NZLR 523; [1998] NZFLR 196. This case was discussed in the New Zealand chapter of *The International Survey of Family Law 1997* (Martinus Nijhoff Publishers, 1999).

[5]   [1998] NZFLR 534.

[6]   Section 99, Child Support Act 1991.

[7]   [1999] NZFLR 249, on appeal from the Family Court judgment reported as *T v T* [1998] NZFLR 776. By coincidence, there was another step-parent case in 1998, *BPS v MNS* [1998] NZFLR 289. The facts were unusual: the child had been born by 'donor insemination' after the wife had intercourse with a friend. The marriage ended not long after the child's birth and the husband then had virtually nothing to do with the child for the next six years. In the circumstances, the court declined to make a step-parent declaration against the husband.

[8]   *A v R* [1999] NZFLR 249, 255.

spouse as opposed to one year after dissolution of marriage for a divorced spouse. Under both régimes, the court has power to extend the time limits.

Perhaps the most important way in which the marriage and proposed de facto relationship rules part company is in respect of the régime for division. Under both systems, the division of the home and chattels is on a different basis from the division of the remaining matrimonial or relationship property. For both married and de facto partners, the house and chattels are prima facie divided equally,[9] but while the principal exception to this for married persons is a stringent rule that requires the proof of 'extraordinary circumstances' which render equal sharing 'repugnant to justice', an ostensibly much more lenient test will apply to de factos. If the court considers that equal sharing would cause 'serious injustice', then the home and chattels of a de facto relationship are divided according to contributions to the relationship. The phrase 'serious injustice' is vague, is not elaborated upon in the statute, and will doubtless be the subject of litigation. The Bill uses the same words in relation to the setting aside of agreements. Mirroring the matrimonial property legislation, de facto partners will be able to contract out of the new legislation. Under the Matrimonial Property Act, the court can set agreements aside if it would be 'unjust' to give effect to the agreement taking into account a range of factors such as changed circumstances. The proposed test for de facto agreements is simply that 'giving effect to the agreement would cause serious injustice'. It remains to be seen how the courts interpret this phrase.

The rules for married and unmarried partners differ even more significantly when the balance of the property, ie other than the home and chattels, is considered. For married couples, there is a prima facie rule of equal sharing which may be departed from if one of the parties can show a clearly greater contribution to the marriage. There is no equal sharing rule proposed at all for de facto partners. The balance of the relationship property will be divided in every case according to contributions to the relationship.

The differences between the rules for married and unmarried couples are doubtless designed for ideological and political reasons to avoid complete identification of the two kinds of relationships. There is still a desire to place a premium on marriage even though New Zealand's human rights laws are hostile to discrimination on the grounds of marital status. There is also an anti-paternalistic voice inside and outside Parliament which opposes legislation for de facto relationships – on this view, people should be free to opt into a scheme such as the Matrimonial Property Act either by marrying or entering into a cohabitation scheme with appropriate terms but should not be forced by law to do so. Given that the De Facto Relationships (Property) Bill is sponsored by the Government, it is safe to predict that it will eventually be passed, but its precise form may yet change.

V   ASSISTED REPRODUCTION

The third piece of legislation which the Government introduced into Parliament in 1998 and which is still making very slow progress is the Assisted Human Reproduction Bill. Apart from earlier legislation dealing with the status of the child following the use of donor gametes,[10] this is the first attempt in New Zealand to legislate in the area of

---

[9]   Unless the relationship is one which lasted less than three years, in which case the home and chattels are divided according to contributions to the relationship. This rule is similar to the one which applies to marriages of short duration under section 13 of the Matrimonial Property Act 1976.

[10]   The Status of Children Amendment Act 1987. Under this Act, the legal parents of a child conceived through artificial donor insemination will be the birth mother and her husband, so long as the husband

assisted reproduction. It is based in part on a 1994 report of the Ministerial Committee on Assisted Reproductive Technologies.[11] The Bill has three main aspects to it: banning certain procedures; placing the national ethics committee on a statutory basis; and creating a new information régime where gametes have been donated.

The Bill bans human cloning, fusing human and animal gametes, and implanting a human embryo in an animal and vice versa. An offence is also created to outlaw trading in gametes and embryos. The latter is unlikely to cover surrogacy which is not expressly regulated by the Bill. IVF surrogacy where the commissioning couple are the genetic parents has only recently been granted ethical approval in New Zealand. Given the state of flux with respect to surrogacy it has probably been thought unwise to tackle it by legislation.

The Bill provides a statutory basis for the National Ethics Committee on Assisted Human Reproduction. This body in fact already exists but its precise legal status and authority are somewhat problematic. The Ministerial Committee had recommended the creation of a watchdog to oversee the often rapid and controversial developments in this area. The ethics committee will fulfil something of a similar function, because, apart from giving ethical approval to proposals for reproductive procedures and research, it will be able to develop protocols and guidelines and proffer advice to the government. A novel feature of the rules is a procedure involving an interplay between the committee and the government. Recognising the political implications of some of the issues, the Bill provides that the committee must refer any proposal which 'is new to New Zealand' to the government which then has two months to express a view. If the committee wishes to approve an application contrary to the views of the government, the Bill insists on a 6-month hiatus from the date when the government informed the committee of its views before the approval takes effect. This gives the government time to act, eg by bringing the issue before Parliament, if it considers the matter of sufficient importance.

An area of concern relating to the role of the committee is its lack of enforcement powers. There is no system of licensing providers, as in some other countries, and there is no statutory obligation to seek ethical approval for assisted human reproductive procedures or trials. Strong professional incentives will ensure that the main providers apply to the ethics committee, but these may not influence fringe health providers and researchers such as scientists who fall outside the health sector. The Bill also lacks any rules for ensuring that the committee's decisions are complied with. It is unclear what happens if an applicant who has been denied approval proceeds in the face of such denial.

One of the themes reported by the Ministerial Committee on Assisted Reproductive Technologies was the importance people attached to knowledge of genetic origins. This is especially precious for the indigenous Maori who use the word 'whakapapa' to describe ancestral lineage. One of the problems with donated gametes is the chance that the child will never know its true origins or whakapapa. While, in practice, clinics in New Zealand have been counselling donors and parents to accept an open approach to genetic information (made easier because of the rules which exclude the donor from any liability for things such as child support[12]), the Assisted Human Reproduction Bill now takes this a step further by setting up an official information régime for donations made after the relevant part of the Bill comes into force.

---

consented. In *W v CIR* [1998] NZFLR 817, the husband argued that either the insemination had occurred without his consent or the child had been conceived by an extra-marital affair. The court however rejected these arguments on the evidence and held the husband to be the legal father.

[11] The author was one of the two members of the Committee.

[12] The Status of Children Amendment Act 1987. See also section 7(4), Child Support Act 1991.

In broad terms, the Bill provides for two depositories of information about donors and donor children: the clinics and the Registrar-General of Births, Deaths and Marriages. The clinics must keep the information for 50 years, the Registrar-General indefinitely. A child will have access to identifying and other information about the donor from the age of 18 but the legal parents will have access prior to that. The only ground for refusing access is where there is a likelihood of danger to some other person. Donors will have access to full information about the child once the child reaches the age of 25. When the child is aged between 18 and 25, such access will be granted only if the child consents. Access by donors to information about the child is again subject only to the danger exception.

The rules on access to donor and donor child information echo the open approach nowadays taken to adoption information. They place the interest of the donor child to personal identity ahead of the anonymity of the donor. This emphasis reflects changing attitudes in New Zealand. These rules are nevertheless of restricted impact. They do not pick up donations made outside the health sector, eg 'do-it-yourself' donations whether by artificial means or natural intercourse. Nor do they have retrospective effect. Access to information relating to past donations will continue to be informal.

VI CONCLUSION

The process of law reform is often slow. In the family law context, reform can be even slower because of political agendas which place such issues as law and order and economic changes ahead of personal matters. The shape of family law reform can also be controversial, with competing personal values rising to the surface when proposals are aired. It is not therefore altogether surprising, even if disappointing, that the three areas of family reform initiated in New Zealand in 1998 – matrimonial property rights for widowed spouses, de facto relationships, and assisted reproduction – have not been enacted rapidly.

PALESTINE

PRE-STATE POSITIONING ON FAMILY LAW

*Lynn Welchman**

I   INTRODUCTION

On a Monday morning at the end of December 1998, in downtown Gaza City, an articulate professional woman from a prominent local family stood to address assembled journalists, politicians, women's rights activists, human rights workers, lawyers and other concerned (read: outraged) members of Palestinian civil society:

> 'Instead of giving me justice, the court has decided I should return in shackles ... I appeal to you today, in the name of all Palestinian women who have passed through this bitter experience, to stand with us, side by side. Support us in our demand to eliminate this contemptible measure and review all other legal procedures that undermine the dignity and freedom of women!'[1]

Married for 25 years, this woman had spent several months seeking a divorce through the Islamic courts which apply Islamic family law to Muslims in Gaza, only to be served with a notice ordering her to appear to answer a claim submitted by her husband for her to return to the matrimonial home, 'the house of obedience'. Outraged, Shadia Sarraj, herself the director of a women's education project, gathered considerable support around herself and took her case to the wider forum of social and political opinion. At the end of the press conference, heralded as the first of its kind, over 60 institutions signed up to the petition, beside the numerous individual signatories; a committee was set up and a popular campaign announced to remove the rules concerning the house of obedience from the law books.[2]

This article considers the rules on the house of obedience as an illustration of the current status and potential future development of Islamic family law in Palestine. After briefly considering the rules on the house of obedience, it describes the development of family law under the different regimes that ruled Palestine during the course of the twentieth century, and then critically compares the content of the two different laws that currently govern Muslim personal status in the West Bank and the Gaza Strip. The likely framework of a future unified Palestinian law of personal status is then considered in the light of recent legal and political developments and of the intense interest this subject is currently generating in various sectors of Palestinian civil society.

---

*   Director, Centre of Islamic and Middle Eastern Law, Department of Law, School of Oriental and African Studies, University of London.

1   Urgent Appeal to Public Opinion by S. Sarraj, reproduced in *Sawt al-Nisa'*, (*Women's Voice*) no. 62, 12/31/98 [author's translation].

2   *Sawt al-Nisa'* no. 62, 12/31/98.

II   THE HOUSE OF OBEDIENCE

The 'house of obedience' is a standard concept in traditional Islamic family law as codified and applied over much of the Middle East including the Occupied Palestinian Territory of the West Bank (including East Jerusalem) and the Gaza Strip. In the gender-specific balance of rights and duties allocated by law to husband and wife, the wife owes her husband the duty of obedience in return for his financial support and protection. The 'house of obedience' is the marital home, the physical location where the wife makes herself available to her husband, the legal assumption being that she must be present in the marital home unless she has left it for a legitimate reason or with her husband's consent. The assumption of the law is that the husband is the wage-earner and provider, since he has absolute financial responsibilities towards her under classical Islamic law: she is to be housed, clothed, fed and generally maintained at his expense regardless of her own financial means. The link between maintenance and 'obedience' is explicit: the only time a woman is not due maintenance from her husband is when she is found to be 'disobedient' (*nashiz*), and the only time a woman divorced by *talaq* (unilateral 'repudiation' by the husband) is not due maintenance during her *'idda* (waiting period during which she may not remarry) is when she is 'divorced in disobedience'.[3] The maintenance/obedience equation is affirmed within the gendered balance of spousal rights and duties by all the classical jurists on whose opinions the family laws of the Middle East are still, for the large part, based. There is also a link between dower and obedience, since a woman cannot be called to the house of obedience if her prompt dower has not been paid: her rights to dower precede her duty of obedience.

The classical Muslim jurists set limits on the husband's right of 'obedience' (*ta'a*), and these rules are stressed by writers defending the institution in recent times. The husband is not supposed to abuse his wife, or be arbitrary in his exercise of the right to her obedience. The modern jurist Abd el-Hamid identifies three conditions for the husband's invocation of obedience:

(1) that the commands given by the husband concern marital affairs (not, for example, his wife's personal financial affairs);

(2) that they accord with the *shari'a*; and

(3) that the husband has himself fulfilled his *shar'i* obligations towards his wife.[4]

Within these limits, the wife is expected to be 'obedient'. Quite what such 'obedience' involves is not always clear. In a discussion on Palestinian women and family law in the Gaza Strip, a Gazan lawyer gives the following explanation part based on law and part on customary expectations:

'By obedience is meant: that she obeys him in all lawful things, looks after herself and his property, doesn't do things that annoy him, doesn't scowl and doesn't present herself [in public] in a manner displeasing to him.'[5]

She further points out that a wife is not due maintenance if she leaves her husband's house for no [good] reason or without permission, travels in similar circumstances, goes

---

3   Unless she has waived this right in a *khul'* agreement in which the couple divorce by mutual consent by a *talaq* from the husband in exchange for compensation from the wife – most commonly, in the West Bank and Gaza Strip, renouncing her rights to her deferred dower and maintenance during the *'idda*.

4   M. M. Abd el-Hamid, *al-ahwal al-shakhsiyya fi al-shari'a al-islamiyya* (Personal status in the Islamic *shari'a*), Beirut (1984) at 116.

5   Tarazi, Hassaniyya, Mukhallalati, and Sayigh, *al-mar'a al-falastiniyya wa'l-qanun fi qita' ghazza*, (Palestinian Women and the Law in the Gaza Strip) Gaza (UNWRA) (1994) at 53–54.

to prison for crime or debt, or is a professional woman who goes out to work after her husband has told her not to. It is this latter range of situations involving the physical whereabouts and movements of the wife that is the most significant in terms of court consideration of the duty of obedience: 'the most obvious manifestation of obedience is that the wife lives in the marital home which the husband has prepared for her.'[6] It is when his wife has actually left the marital home that the husband may have recourse to the *shari`a* court to seek an award ordering her return to the 'house of obedience'. Within the home, the jurists generally considered that the husband should be able to deal with his wife's 'disobedience' as a private matter.[7]

Until relatively recently, in the West Bank and Gaza Strip as elsewhere, the authority of the State could be employed to implement a ruling for *ta`a* from the court, and the 'disobedient' wife might be escorted back to her husband's house by the local police. The institution of the 'house of obedience' has been criticised for some time by reformists in Arab States in recent years, but in law it has mostly been addressed through removing the possibility of enforcement of this kind, rather than through addressing the concept of 'obedience' as such. The tendency has been to tackle the latter question by whittling down the reach of the principle rather than eliminating it entirely, relying as much on the courts and on public opinion as on law.

The outrage voiced in Gaza at the invocation of the house of obedience resonates with debates elsewhere in the region where personal status law has long been a focus of attention for civil society.[8] Writing in 1988, Egyptian commentator Fawzi Najjar observed that '[i]n recent years, most Egyptians have regarded the institution of the 'house of obedience' as a crude and embarrassing violation of civilised norms.'[9] Najjar describes the frustration of various attempts to 'abolish the house of obedience' up until February 1967, when a ministerial decree suspending the enforcement of rulings for *ta`a* was issued: 'in actual practice, this meant that the police would refuse to drag a woman back to her husband against her will'.[10] There was opposition to both the 'tactic' (which opponents claimed was effectively amending the law through decree) and the implications of the decree, but it also found substantial support. Prominent lawyer and commentator the late Dr. Gamal al-Otaifi, for example, cited the supporting views of several *shar`i* scholars in Egypt, and stated that the forcible execution of *ta`a*

---

[6] This was the explanation in the Explanatory Memorandum to the 1979 Egyptian legislation: B.A. Badran, *huquq al-awlad fi al-shari`a al-islamiyya wa'l-qanun* (Child rights in the Islamic *shari`a* and in law) Alexandria (1981) at 214. Compare the formulation in the Code Napoléon, the husband owing protection to his wife and she owing obedience to him: Mayer notes that it was only in 1965 that married women in France got the right to work without their husband's permission: A.E. Mayer, 'Reform of Personal Status Laws in North Africa: A Problem of Islamic or Mediterranean Laws?' (1995) 49 *Middle East Journal* 432–446, at 436.

[7] They sought to regulate this by describing limits on the husband's employment of three successive stages of 'chastisement', culminating under the classical interpretations in the use of 'moderate' force.

[8] There is extensive material on the history and development of the Palestinian women's movement and the challenges it faced – and continues to face – in seeking to promote a gender-sensitive social agenda within the framework of the national struggle. See for example E.S. Kuttab, 'Palestinian Women in the Intifada: Fighting on Two Fronts,' (1993) 15,2 *Arab Studies Quarterly* at 69–85; and N. Abdo, 'Nationalism and Feminism: Palestinian Women and the Intifada – no going back?' 148–170 in V.M. Moghadam (ed.) *Gender and National Identity*, London (1994).

[9] F. M. Najjar, 'Egypt's Laws of Personal Status' (1988) 10, 3 *Arab Studies Quarterly* 319–344, at 331. See also the article by M. al-Nowaihi, 'Changing the Law on Personal Status in Egypt with a Liberal Interpretation of the *Shari`a*', *Middle East Review*, 11/4, (1979) 40–49, at 44, referring to 'the iniquitous Bayt al-ta`a'.

[10] Najjar, 'Egypt's Laws of Personal Status' (above), at 332; and see also al-Nowaihi,'Changing the Law on Personal Status in Egypt with a Liberal Interpretation of the *Shari`a*' (above).

contradicted the general principles of the Egyptian Constitution regarding personal freedom and respect for the family.[11] After the passage of the 1979 personal status legislation and replacement law in 1985[12] there was some claim that the institution of the 'house of obedience' had been eliminated, 'to the great relief of many Egyptian women'.[13] However, in effect it is only the forcible implementation that has actually been eliminated. In particular, the relationship between a married woman's right to work and her 'duty of obedience' to her husband is not fully resolved in the 1985 Egyptian law.[14]

It remains similarly unresolved in the laws governing personal status for Muslims in the West Bank and Gaza Strip. The event in Gaza was significant in its own right as a forum for drawing attention to and mobilising sectors of civil society around the issue of 'the house of obedience'. It also reflects the intense interest around personal status law that has built up in Palestine since the coming of the Palestinian Authority in 1994, when the space for the social struggle really opened up from the national struggle, reaching the streets in particularly heated debates in 1998. Finally, it illustrates the way in which the majority of those seeking to reform the law are approaching both the issue of framework as a whole, and particular issues of law. Palestine is poised on the brink of statehood, and the battle for the main ground in family law is increasingly waged by alliances who see in the outcome a stake in what sort of State it is going to be.

III   HISTORICAL DEVELOPMENT OF PERSONAL STATUS LAW IN PALESTINE

Personal status law in the West Bank, including East Jerusalem, and the Gaza Strip reflects the complex legal and political history of Palestine since the beginning of this century. The legacy of centuries of Ottoman rule, perpetuated by the British Mandate authorities, remains in the system of separate communal jurisdiction over personal status matters for the majority Muslim community and for the five recognised Christian sects. The religious courts function alongside a system of regular civil and criminal courts and are served by the same execution offices.[15]

Ottoman heritage can also be traced in the laws that govern Muslim personal status. The Ottoman Law of Family Rights of 1917, the first codification of Islamic family law,

---

[11]   In *al-Ahram*, 6/3/67, reproduced in the compilation of his articles, G. al-`Otaifi, *ara' fi al-shar`iyya wa fi'l-hurriya*, Cairo (1980) at 355–359.

[12]   A number of proposals to reform Islamic family law in Egypt were frustrated before finally in 1979 then President Anwar Sadat issued Law no.44 of 1979 by presidential decree. The constitutionality of the law was challenged (see below) and it was repealed in May 1985, to be replaced in July the same year by Law 100/1985 which incorporated most but not all the reforms of the 1979 law. See N. Hijab, *Womanpower: The Arab debate on women at work*, Cambridge (1988) at 29–35; M. Hatem, 'Economic and Political Liberalism in Egypt and the Demise of State Feminism', (1992) 24 *International Journal of Middle East Studies* at 231–251; and Najjar, 'Egypt's Laws of Personal Status' (above).

[13]   Najjar, 'Egypt's Laws of Personal Status' (above), at 332.

[14]   Articles 1 and 11 bis 2 of Law 100/1985.

[15]   From 1967, the military courts of the Israeli occupation authorities also functioned in the Occupied Palestinian Territories. Since 1994 the jurisdiction of the regular court system has been transferred to the Palestinian Authority under the terms of the various instruments of the Oslo Accords. For its part, the Palestinian Authority has set up and made use of a State Security Court much criticised by Palestinian and international human rights organisations. For legal jurisdictions and the legislative process under Oslo, see R. Shehadeh, *From Occupation to Interim Accords: Israel and the Palestinian Territories*, The Hague (1997).

was applied under the British mandate authorities in Palestine[16] and continued to govern personal status matters for Muslims until after what is called the *nakba* (disaster) of 1948, when during the war that followed the British withdrawal, hundreds of thousands of Palestinians fled, to become refugees in neighbouring Arab States. The State of Israel was declared holding possession of 70% of Mandatory Palestine, and what was left of Palestine came under Jordanian rule in the case of the West Bank and Egyptian administration in the case of the Gaza Strip. Jordan moved to 'unify' the West Bank with the East Bank (Jordan proper), issued national legislation to apply to both banks on the basis of its purported annexation, and integrated the court system into its own. Egypt on the other hand maintained the status of an administrator, appointing a Governor General to the Gaza Strip and issuing legislation specific to the Gaza Strip.[17] Unlike the courts in the West Bank, the Gaza courts were not integrated into the Egyptian national system. The *shari`a* courts in the Gaza Strip thus retained their jurisdiction over Muslim personal status matters when in 1956 the *shari`a* and other communal courts in Egypt were abolished and had their jurisdiction transferred to the national courts.[18]

Today, the *shari`a* courts in the West Bank apply the Jordanian Law of Personal Status (JLPS) of 1976 which replaced the 1951 Jordanian Law of Family Rights (JLFR).[19] The fact that the *shari`a* courts in the West Bank (including East Jerusalem) apply legislation issued in Jordan after the 1967 Israeli occupation is an anomaly, since in all other areas the law was 'frozen' in its pre-occupation state, and Israeli military orders took the place of legislation.[20] The West Bank *shari`a* courts however refused to have anything to do with the Israeli authorities, protesting at Israel's illegal annexation of East Jerusalem, the extension of Israeli municipal law to East Jerusalem and Israel's refusal to recognise the validity of rulings from the Jordanian-administered *shari`a* courts situated there, which comprised the first instance *shari`a* court for East Jerusalem and the *Shari`a* Court of Appeal with jurisdiction for the entire West Bank. The picture is further complicated by the fact that the Israeli authorities insisted (as they continue to do now) that East Jerusalem Palestinians regulate their personal status affairs according to Israeli municipal law as applied by the Israeli *shari`a* court system, which for example prohibits polygamy, while for business anywhere else in the Arab world they would have to have their personal status affairs regulated by the East Jerusalem Jordanian-administered

---

[16] By virtue of the Muslim Family Law (Application) Ordinance 1919, implementing both the OLFR and its accompanying Law of Procedure for *Shari`a* Courts. The British repealed the sections in the OLFR relating to Christians and Jews; recognised non-Muslim communities were expected to apply their own personal laws: C. A. Hooper, *The Civil Law of Palestine and Transjordan*, Volume II, Jerusalem (1936) at 59.

[17] From 1962 this legislation was passed by a Legislative Council and approved by the Governor General, in accordance with a Basic Law issued for the Gaza Strip by the Egyptian Prime Minister: Shehadeh *From Occupation to Interim Accords: Israel and the Palestinian Territories* (above), at 77.

[18] For a full account of the abolition of the communal court system see N. Safran, 'The Abolition of the Shari`a Courts in Egypt' (1958) 48 *Muslim World* 20–28 and 125–135. Brown calls the Egyptian method 'amalgamation' of the *shari`a* courts by the State, while acknowledging that it amounted to abolition, and notes opposition to this move at the time by the Muslim Brotherhood and the personnel of the *shari`a* courts. N.J.Brown, (1997) 29 'Shari`a and State in the Modern Muslim Middle East', *International Journal of Middle East Studies*, 359–376, at 370.

[19] See J.N.D. Anderson, 'The Jordanian Law of Family Rights' (1952) 42 *Muslim World* 190–206. For a comparison of the JLFR provisions with those of the 1976 Jordanian Law of Personal Status, see L. Welchman, 'The Development of Islamic Family Law in the Legal System of Jordan' (1988) 37 *International and Comparative Law Quarterly* 868–886.

[20] See R. Shehadeh, *Occupier's Law: Israel and the West Bank*, Washington (1988) for an account of the legal changes enacted by the Israeli occupation authorities after the 1967 occupation.

shari`a* court applying Jordanian law.[21] The *shari`a court system and the Israeli occupation authorities settled into a pattern of mutual non-recognition within which the *shari`a* courts continued to be administered by the Department of the Qadi al-Quda (Chief Islamic Justice) in Amman while the occupation authorities administered the regular court system and the execution offices until the Oslo arrangements were put in place in the 1990s.

The *shari`a* courts in the West Bank thus continued to apply any legislation issued in Amman for the Jordanian *shari`a* courts, including the JLPS when it was promulgated in 1976. The JLPS made a number of significant amendments to the previous JLFR, and has itself been the subject of review and draft proposals for amendment since the 1980s.[22] In the Gaza Strip, the courts apply the Law of Family Rights (LFR) of 1954, issued by the then Egyptian Governor of the Strip.[23] The *shari`a* courts in Gaza do not apply post-1967 Egyptian law, so the personal status law promulgated in Cairo in 1979 and subsequently amended in 1985 has not been applied; nor did the 1954 Law of Family Rights constitute a codification of the then existing Egyptian personal status legislation. The LFR bears a much closer resemblance to the Ottoman Law of Family Rights 1917 (OLFR) which was applied in Palestine but not in Egypt.

IV CONTENT OF THE APPLICABLE FAMILY LAW

In line with the OLFR, both the Jordanian law applied in the West Bank and the Egyptian-issued law applied in the Gaza Strip make use of rulings from other schools of law,[24] although Hanafi law remains the residual school of reference in the absence of a particular provision in the codified law.[25] In their general sweep, the West Bank and Gaza codes are as similar to each other as to those of other Arab States, and maintain the characteristic, sturdily patriarchal and patrilineal outline of the classical Islamic rules. Thus, marriage is presented as a contract giving rise to rights and duties specific to each

---

[21] On the implications of these jurisdictional complexities for the work of the West Bank and East Jerusalem *shari`a* courts, see L. Welchman, 'Family Law under Occupation: Islamic Law and the Shari`a Courts in the West Bank' pp 93–115 in C. Mallat and J. Connors (eds.), *Islamic Family Law*, London (1990). On the family law applied to Palestinian Muslims inside Israel, see A. Layish, *Women and Islamic Law in a Non-Muslim State*, Jerusalem (1975).

[22] Published as Temporary Law no. 61 1976 in the Jordanian *Official Gazette* (*al-jarida al-rasmiyya*) no. 2668 12/1/76. The latest draft text for a law to replace the JLPS appears to date from September 1996: I am indebted to attorney Reem Abu Hassan for the text.

[23] Published in the *Palestine Official Gazette* (*al-waqa'i` al-falastiniyya*) no.35 6/15/54 as Order no.303 of 1954.

[24] The 'selection' (*takahyyur*) of rules from other Sunni schools and less frequently of individual jurists is a method of effecting reform within personal status law without appearing to depart from the rulings of classical Islamic jurisprudence. The OLFR was the first codification of Islamic family law and relied heavily on selection to widen the grounds on which a woman could seek divorce, for example. Extensive examples of the use made of this method of developing family law are given in J.N.D. Anderson, *Law Reform in the Muslim World*, London (1976). There is jurisprudential criticism that 'the device of selection and amalgamation' is not 'sustained by any type of cohesive legal methodology' – see W. Hallaq, *A History of Islamic Legal Theories*, Cambridge (1997) at 210–212. Nevertheless, *takhayyur* as a method of effecting change in the rules governing various areas of Muslim family law is widely accepted and relied on by Arab legislatures.

[25] This is stated explicitly in Article 183 of the JLPS. Although there is no equivalent in the LFR, the Egyptian-issued Law of *Shari`a* Court Procedure (no.12/1965, published in a 'special edition' of the Palestinian Official Gazette on 5/22/65) requires the *shari`a* courts in the Gaza Strip to issue rulings in accordance with the strongest Hanafi opinion unless there is a particular provision in the law stipulating the application of other rules (Article 187).

spouse; the husband must pay dower and maintenance to his wife, treat her well and provide a home for her; the wife must obey her husband in lawful matters, including moving to live with him if he moves, while maintaining freedom of disposal over her private income and property. Polygyny is permitted to a maximum of four wives. The marriage can be dissolved extra-judicially by the unilateral repudiation of the husband; by court decision on specific grounds presented by the wife[26] or if the marriage has been concluded irregularly; or by mutual consent involving a final *talaq* by the husband in exchange for a financial consideration by the wife.[27] The mother is recognised as the natural custodian of her children until they reach specific ages, at which point, if their parents are separated, they are to return to the house of their father, who is recognised as their natural guardian. Guardianship by the father (or other close male agnate) over females in marriage continues to be required in court if not unambiguously in law. Succession is mostly governed by the classical Sunni rules which recognise female as well as male heirs but generally give males double the share of females.

A   Succession rights

Beyond this general picture, the separate post-1948 legal histories have meant different rules applying to the Muslim Palestinians of the West Bank and Gaza. For example, in 1962 the 'obligatory bequest' became part of the succession law applied in Gaza. This bequest addressed the problem posed by the fact that under the rules of classical Sunni inheritance law, the living sons of a parent who dies will exclude from succession any grandchildren of the dead parent through a son or daughter who has predeceased that parent. If the propositus has not thought to leave them a bequest within the third of the estate that may be bequeathed, the orphaned grandchildren will receive nothing from the grandparent's estate. The 'obligatory bequest', first introduced in Egypt in the Law of Testamentary Dispositions of 1946, made orphaned grandchildren entitled to take the amount their dead parent would have inherited had he or she been alive, provided that this does not exceed one third of the estate.[28] In 1953, the Syrians took up this idea in their Law of Personal Status, but restricted it in two ways, applying it only to grandchildren through a predeceased son, and allowing them to inherit only the share they would have received out of their father's portion.[29] In 1962, the Egyptian rules were introduced in the Gaza Strip under Egyptian administration.[30] The West Bank, however, had no equivalent legislation until the JLPS 1976, which combined the Egyptian and Syrian versions, restricting the obligatory bequest to grandchildren through a dead son as

---

[26]   And in certain circumstances (eg breach of a stipulation in a marriage contract, or a disease preventing consummation of the marriage) by the husband.

[27]   Recent research indicates that this is the most common form of divorce registered in both the West Bank and Gaza Strip. The *shari`a* courts in Hebron, Dura, Nablus and Ramallah in the West Bank, and Gaza City and Rafah in the Gaza Strip, in the years 1989 and 1992–1994, recorded an overall breakdown of deeds of or claims for divorce as follows: 67% *khul`*, 26% unilateral *talaq*, and 7% judicial divorce involving litigation (*tafriq/faskh*). Figures from field research by Fatima Mukhallalati, Reem Jabr, Hiyam Karkour and Ghada Shaheed for the Palestinian Women's Centre for Legal Aid and Counselling.

[28]   Welchman, 'The Development of Islamic Family Law in the Legal System of Jordan' (above), at 880. See N.J. Coulson, *A History of Islamic Law* Edinburgh (1978 edition), at 103 *et seq*.

[29]   Article 257 of the Syrian Law of Personal Status, Law no. 59 of 17/9/53. On the obligatory bequest in this law, see J.N.D. Anderson, 'The Syrian Law of Personal Status' (1955) 17 *Bulletin of the School of Oriental and African Studies*, at 47. The 1953 law has since been replaced with Law no.35 of 1975.

[30]   Law no.13/1962, issued by the Governor General on 12/2/62.

in Syria, but allowing these to take the full amount of their father's share, as in Egypt, provided it does not exceed one third of the estate.

Another change in the laws of succession that reached Gaza earlier than the West Bank was the application of the Islamic law of succession to the category of immovable property know as *miri* holdings, where the title is held by the ruler. In 1923 the British had implemented a 1913 Ottoman Law of Inheritance which gave males and females equal rights of inheritance to *miri* property, while leaving all holdings of *mulk* (absolute private) property to devolve in accordance with the classical rules of Islamic law.[31] In 1965 the Egyptian Governor General of the Gaza Strip reversed this by ordering that the Islamic law of succession henceforth govern *miri* property, a step which was not taken in Jordan until 1991 but which was then applied in the West Bank also.[32]

B   Post-divorce maintenance

If women's property rights ended up being similarly affected in both the West Bank and Gaza by the above regulations on succession, a particularly significant difference remains in the rules on post-divorce maintenance for a wife divorced 'arbitrarily', or without reasonable cause. The classical Hanafi rules require a man who divorces his wife unilaterally by *talaq* to pay her maintenance during the *'idda,* the 'waiting period' after divorce during which the woman may not remarry, a standard period of three menstrual cycles or until childbirth if she is pregnant. He also has to pay her deferred dower. This is the end of his financial obligations towards her, unless she is undertaking custody of their children.[33] The question of post *'idda* provision for divorcées was first taken up by Syria in its 1953 Law of Personal Status in an innovative provision which provided for compensation for the wife in the event of a *talaq* without reasonable cause that gives rise to damage and poverty for the wife; the maximum compensation was to be equivalent to her maintenance for a year, and was in addition to the maintenance that the husband was to pay during the *'idda.*[34] Subsequently a number of Arab States took up this provision in

---

[31]   The British also sought to extend the application of the Ottoman law. The Succession Ordinance required that the Ottoman law giving equal shares to males and females be the law applied by all religious and civil courts for all *miri* holdings. For *mulk* property the religious courts were expected to apply their own personal law, but while for Muslims *mulk* property could only be distributed according to traditional Islamic law, in the other communal courts the consent of all parties involved was required for the application of the personal law in intestacy, so that on the request of one of the parties the issue would be regulated under the terms of the Ottoman Law of Inheritance for *miri* property. The Ottoman law thus became the only law applicable to *miri* land, and the residual law for *mulk* land of non-Muslims. F. M. Goadby, *International and Inter-religious Private Law in Palestine,* Jerusalem (1926) at 121–124. For an explanation of land law written during the Mandate see F. M. Goadby and M. Doukhan, *The Land Law of Palestine,* Tel Aviv (1935).

[32]   In Gaza, Law no.1/1965 of 1/9/65; in the West Bank, Law no.4/1991 of 2/20/91. I am indebted to advocate Firas Bakr for the Jordanian text. In the 1920s, Goadby reported being 'informed that in fact daughters having a right to share under the Ottoman law frequently renounce' (*International and Inter-religious Private Law in Palestine* (above) at 121). The same phenomenon remains commonplace today in relation to the reduced rights of inheritance for females under the classical Islamic rules of inheritance. It was for this reason that the Palestinian Model Parliament in 1998 (see below) proposed administrative measures be devised by the *shari'a* courts to ensure that women were not pressured into unwillingly giving up their share on inheritance in favour of (usually) their brothers.

[33]   In which case he must pay for the children's maintenance and pay his ex-wife a fee or wage for her services in undertaking custody.

[34]   The 1975 Syrian Law of Personal Status revised the maximum level of compensation upwards to three years' maintenance: see Article 117.

various ways in their codifications of Islamic family law[35] including the Jordanians, who included a provision similar to the Syrian one in the JLPS, allowing a maximum of one year's maintenance as compensation to a woman divorced arbitrarily. Egypt however did not legislate on this matter until 1979; the replacement legislation in 1985 maintained the same provision, allowing for maintenance of at least two years to be awarded as financial consolation[36] to a woman divorced without her consent for no reason on her part. There is no maximum limit set, and practice in the Egyptian courts has given the provision broader application than the Jordanians have contemplated.[37] Coming as it did long after the 1967 war, the Egyptian provision is not applied in the Gaza Strip, while the Jordanian law does apply to the benefit of divorced wives in the West Bank. This means, in effect, that a husband unilaterally divorcing his wife in the West Bank – but not in the Gaza Strip – risks having his motivation scrutinised and a financial penalty imposed by way of compensation to the divorcée.[38]

C   Judicial divorce

Divorce law in Gaza, on the other hand, provides a remedy for abused wives that is denied in the West Bank, by providing for 'injury' or prejudice as grounds on which the wife is entitled to petition the court for judicial divorce. This provision in the Gaza law, and its counterpart in the West Bank, are based on standard Maliki rules, but both provisions have adopted incomplete versions of the Maliki position. In the West Bank, the JLPS allows either spouse to apply for divorce on the grounds of 'discord and strife' (fundamental breakdown of the marriage), in line with the classical Maliki rules, while in the LFR in the Gaza Strip only the wife may apply on these grounds. On the other hand,

---

[35]   Morocco, Tunisia, Algeria, Libya, Kuwait, and Yemen all have variations of the provision, as well as the Jordanian and Egyptian provisions discussed here. Post-`idda maintenance has also been considered in South Asia: notably, in India, the Shah Bano case (*Ahmad Khan v. Shah Bano Begum* A.I.R.1985 S.C.945) followed by the Muslim Women (Protection of Rights on Divorce) Act 1986; and in Bangladesh, *Hezfur Rahman v. Shamsun Nahar Begum* (1995) 15 B.L.D. 34, overturned in 1998. On the South Asian developments, see D. Pearl and W. Menski, *Muslim Family Law*, London (1998) at 201–226.

[36]   The Jordanian and Syrian laws use the term *ta`wid*, translated here as 'compensation', while the Egyptian term is *mut`a*, translated here as 'consolation'. The institution of *mut`a* has origins in classical interpretations of Islamic law justifying what could otherwise be seen as additional financial obligations on the Muslim husband: this is the case in the Explanatory Memoranda to both the JLPS and the Egyptian legislation. The Syrian and Jordanian approach stresses also however the idea of a financial penalty levied on the husband for his abuse of a right – that is, his right of *talaq*. See A. Al-Qasem, 'The Unlawful Exercise of Rights in the Civil Codes of the Arab Countries of the Middle East', (1990) 39 *International and Comparative Law Quarterly*, 396–412, where he considers the issue of compensation for abuse of the right to divorce, at 400.

[37]   Notably, in allowing *mut`a* to be awarded to women who have obtained a divorce through the court on the grounds of injury; the courts have argued that the judge is in effect acting in place of the husband in such cases, in divorcing the woman from him, and the fact that she has sought the divorce on the grounds of injury makes it against her consent. See Dawoul El Alami, 'Mut`at al-Talaq under Egyptian and Jordanian Law', (1996) 3 *Yearbook of Islamic and Middle Eastern Law* 54–61, at 57.

[38]   According to the classical interpretations of Islamic law, the husband has the power of *talaq* and need not in law provide a reason for exercising it; though in the 'disapproved' category of acts, an unjustified *talaq* is nevertheless legally valid. It should be noted that an award to the divorced woman for compensation for arbitrary *talaq* depends upon a claim being submitted by her. Court practice both in Jordan and in the West Bank has established a legal presumption that unilateral repudiation (*talaq*) is arbitrary, since there is no record of the wife's consent, and have placed the burden of overturning that presumption firmly with the husband, who must establish to the court's satisfaction that there was a good reason for the *talaq*. This principle was established soon after promulgation of the JLPS: see for example ruling no.19859/78, in M. al-`Arabi, *al-mabadi' al-qada'iyya li mahkamat al-isti'naf al-shar'iyya* (Judicial Principles of the *Shari`a* Appeal Court) Volume II Amman (1984) at 59.

the LFR takes another Maliki rule in allowing the wife to be granted a divorce by the court on establishing her husband's injury of her. It is only in the event of her failure to prove this injury that the case may be referred to arbitrators by the judge and proceed to a divorce on the grounds of strife or breakdown if the arbitrators are unable to reconcile the couple. In the West Bank, by contrast, if a woman successfully establishes her husband's injury of her, the judge is to 'warn the husband to improve his behaviour' and if he does not, then to transfer the matter to arbitrators.[39] In both cases, if their attempts at reconciliation fail, the arbitrators are empowered to recommend that the judge divorce the couple, specifying the proportions of blame attached to each spouse so that the judge can order a proportionate financial settlement.

Here, the significance in the difference between the laws does not appear to extend to practice. In an examination of the records of four *shari`a* courts in the West Bank for the years 1989 and 1992–1994, claims for judicial divorce based on the grounds of 'discord and strife' accounted for 8% of all claims for judicial divorce, behind the more common grounds of failure of the husband to maintain the wife and the injurious absence of the husband for over a year.[40] On the other hand, the *shari`a* courts records in Gaza City and Rafah for the same four years failed to reveal a single claim for divorce submitted on the grounds of injury. Nevertheless, the fact that divorce for injury is on the books in Gaza holds a certain protective potential: by contrast, in Egypt and Morocco, where provisions similar to that in the Gaza law are included in the personal status legislation, injury appears as the second most common ground on the basis of which women submit claims for divorce to the courts.[41]

D   Ages of marriage and custody

Finally, there are significant differences between the law governing both the maximum age of custody and the minimum age of marriage. For the first, classical Hanafi law

---

[39]   JLPS Article 132 a): 'If the application [for divorce] is from the wife and she establishes her husband's injury of her, the judge shall do his utmost to reconcile the couple. If he fails, then he shall warn the husband to improve his behaviour with his wife, and shall postpone the claim for a period of not less than one month; and if reconciliation has not occurred, then the matter shall be transferred to two arbiters ...'.

LFR Article 97: 'If the wife claims that her husband has inflicted injury upon her to an extent that persons like her cannot continue in the marriage, she may seek divorce from the judge. If the injury is established and the judge is unable to reconcile the couple, he shall divorce her [from her husband] by a final *talaq*. If her application is rejected but subsequently [her] complaints are renewed, yet the injury is [still] not proven, the judge shall appoint two arbitrators and proceed in the manner set out in Articles 98–102 ...' [author's translation].

[40]   Respectively, 59% and 27.5% of claims. The remainder of claims for judicial divorce were submitted on grounds of a prison sentence against the husband for three years or more, and dangerous and contagious disease. See L. Welchman, *Islamic Family Law: Text and Practice in Palestine*, Jerusalem (1999) (Women's Centre for Legal Aid and Counselling).

[41]   Mir-Hosseini found in two Moroccan courts that the most common basis for judicial divorce was absence of the husband causing injury to the wife (47% of all claims) with injury as the second most common claim (21% of claims): Z. Mir-Hosseini, *Marriage on Trial: A Study of Islamic Family Law, Iran and Morocco Compared*, London (1993) p 102 table 3:7. Shmais found 24% of claims for divorce by women in Cairo 1972–1982 to be based on grounds of injury, second to those for absence of the husband causing injury to the wife at 49.9%: A. Shmais, 'al-`aqabat allati tu`awwiq husul al-mar'a al-muslima `ala al-talaq al-qada'i fi misr' (Obstacles to Muslim women getting judicial divorce in Egypt), unpublished paper based on Ph.D. thesis at the University of Paris 1987. Shaham, in a study of applications for divorce by women in Egypt in earlier decades found about 50% to be based on the grounds of injury, concluding that 'the Egyptian qadis fulfilled the expectation of the legislators by interpreting injury broadly', with the grounds of general injury in his view providing 'residuary grounds for divorce'. R. Shaham, 'Judicial Divorce at the Wife's Initiative: The Shari`a Courts of Egypt 1920–1955' (1994) 1,2 *Islamic Law and Society* 217–253 at 251.

presumes the mother to be the natural custodian of her minor children until the boy reaches the age of seven and the girl nine, after which the children return to their father as the natural guardian (*wali*).[42] In 1976 the Jordanians extended the custody of the mother 'who has devoted herself to the upbringing and custody of her children' to the age of puberty – that is, when the children physically reach puberty. The custody of a woman other than the mother was extended to the ages of nine for boys and 11 for girls.[43] In the Gaza Strip, on the other hand, the classical Hanafi rules are maintained, allowing only the limited extension of the custody of the mother for a girl up to eleven years and a boy up to nine.[44] In Egypt, the Hanafi position has been amended to allow for the extension of custody until the boy reaches 15 years old (the presumed maximum age of puberty according to the classical law) and for the girl until she marries (the standard Maliki position), in cases where the interest of the ward requires it.[45]

While in regard to the age of custody, the Egyptian reforms were not enacted until after the Israeli occupation, in the case of the age of capacity for marriage Egypt had promulgated substantial reforms in 1923 and 1931, establishing 16 for females and 18 for males as the minimum ages at which marriage could be registered and recognised by the State.[46] However, in the LFR 1954, rather than codifying these rules, the Egyptian authorities reproduced the existing provisions of the OLFR of 1917. The Ottoman law, in provisions that were innovative for their time, had set capacity for marriage at the ages of 18 for the male and 17 for the female, but allowed the judge to give permission for marriage below that age provided the applicant had reached puberty and in the case of the female her guardian gave permission for her marriage.[47] No marriage was allowed below the ages of 12 for the boy and nine for the girl. By the time these rules were reproduced in the law the Egyptians issued for Gaza, Jordanian law had already raised the minimum age to 15 for both spouses, with the judge being allowed to authorise marriage from that age up to the ages of full capacity of 18 for males and 17 for females – again, provided the female had the consent of her guardian.[48] In 1976 this was amended to 16 for the male, who no longer needs the judge's permission to marry once he has reached that age, while the female of 15 has reached capacity for marriage but is still required to have

---

[42] Provided the mother meets certain conditions related to mental, physical and moral capacity to bring up children, and does not marry a man outside certain very close degrees of relationship to the child. The strict gendering of the parental roles between the mother as custodian (physically nurturing and looking after the child for a temporary period in their youth), and the father as guardian (wielding more enduring authority and decision-making over the persons and property of his children), has historically been able to accommodate a certain degree of flexibility with a view to the welfare and best interest of the child as evaluated by the (male) judge within his culture and community. See J. Tucker, *In the House of the Law: Gender and Islamic Law in Syria and Palestine 17th–18th Centuries*, Berkley (1997) at 113–147.

[43] JLPS Articles 161 and 162.

[44] LFR Article 118.

[45] Article 20 of the Egyptian Law no.25/1929 as amended by Law no.100/1985.

[46] This was done through procedural means rather than as a matter of substantive law, through Law no.56/1923 and Law no.78/1931. Marriages below this age are not per se invalidated. For a review of Egyptian law and practice 1920–1955 see R. Shaham, 'Custom, Islamic Law, and Statutory Legislation: Marriage Registration and Minimum Age at Marriage in the Egyptian Shari'a Courts' (1995) 2,3 *Islamic Law and Society* at 258–281. Kuwait has taken the Egyptian procedural approach in its 1984 law, but most other codifications in the Arab world have set specific ages as a matter of substantive law – although not necessarily rendering marriages below the set minimum ages invalid in all cases. A common exception is where the wife in such a marriage has fallen pregnant, or, as in Jordanian law, where both parties are of the legal minimum age by the time they come to court. In such cases criminal penalties may still apply.

[47] OLFR Articles 4–7.

[48] JLFR Article 4.

either her guardian's or the court's consent until she is 18.[49] One final point that needs to be made here is that according to the explicit text of both the LFR and the JLPS, the ages are calculated according to the lunar year – so the minimum age of marriage for the female in the West Bank is around fourteen years and seven months by the solar calendar.

The disparity in the ages of marriage at which Muslim Palestinians in the West Bank and Gaza Strip were allowed to marry was the first (and at least until the end of 1998 the only) area of Muslim family law to be addressed by the Palestinian Authority, or more specifically by one of its ministers, the Chief Islamic Justice (Qadi al-Quda).[50] Appointed from the Tunis base of the Palestine Liberation Organisation shortly after the signing of the Gaza–Jericho Agreement which paved the way for Yasser Arafat's triumphal entry into Gaza to head the Palestinian Authority,[51] Shaykh Muhammad Sardane set about rehabilitating the *shari`a* court system and the *shar`i* judiciary, particularly in the Gaza Strip, and made a number of statements about the need to unify the laws in the two regions.[52] In December 1995 he issued an administrative decision which in its preamble drew attention to the 'social, medical and humanitarian injury that results from the marriage of youngsters below the age of puberty as occurs in the *shari`a* courts of the Gaza Strip' and proceeded to set the minimum age of marriage for females at 15 and

---

[49]   JLPS Articles 5 and 6. There is a confusion in the JLPS on whether in fact the *wali's* consent is required by the female up to the age of 17 or 18 – see Articles 6, 13 and 22, and whether his consent, or that of the court in the event that he is wrongly withholding his consent, continues to be required in every case of a woman's first marriage. Two commentators on the law come to opposite conclusions in this regard: M. Samara, *sharh muqarin li-qanun al-ahwal al-shakhsiyya* (Comparative commentary on the law of personal status) Jerusalem (1987) at 119 on the basis of Articles 9, 10 and 13; and M. Sirtawi, *sharh qanun al-ahwal al-shakhsiyya al-urduni* (Commentary on the Jordanian Law of Personal Status) Amman (1981) at 115, on the basis of Articles 13 and 22. The one point on which the JLPS is explicit is that a sane adult previously married woman aged over 18 does not need the consent of a guardian to her marriage. In practice, this makes very little difference: the *shari`a* courts routinely record the consent of the woman's guardian to her marriage whether or not it is technically required and indeed in cases where it unequivocally is not. This clearly indicates that custom is stronger than law in upholding the authority of the patriarch over the females of his family: for comparison in Pakistan see S.S. Ali, 'Is an Adult Muslim Sui Juris? Some Reflections on the Concept of "Consent in Marriage" without a Wali, with particular reference to the Saima Waheed Case' (1996) 3 *Yearbook of Islamic and Middle Eastern Law* 156–174, at 165. However, women may also perceive and exploit the involvement of their guardian as representing the support and strength of their own families vis-à-vis that of the husband's, adding to their weight and position in their new family. I am indebted to students on the Gender, Law and Development course at Birzeit University for enlightening discussions of this and other areas of law in April 1999.

[50]   This does not include the issue and distribution to the *shari`a* courts under the Palestinian Authority of unified forms of standard documents used by the courts such as marriage contracts, deeds of agency, deeds of increase in dower and so forth. In a 1996 interview, the Qadi al-Quda stated that 27 separate standard forms had been issued under his supervision: *Al-Hayat al-Jadida* 26/1/96.

[51]   Shaykh Muhammad Abu Sardane was originally appointed as *wakil* responsible for the *shari`a* courts within the Ministry of Justice, but by October Yasser Arafat agreed that there be a post of Qadi al-Quda with the rank of Minister, directing a Department separate from the Ministry of Justice. Respectively, decisions of 6/5/94 and 10/18/94, reproduced in M.H. Abu Sardane, *al-qada al-shar`i fi `ahd al-sulta al-wataniyya al-falastiniyya* (The Shar`i judiciary under the Palestinian National Authority) Gaza (1996) at 53 and 93. I am indebted to His Honour Shaykh Taysir Tamimi, current Acting Qadi al-Quda, for this material.

[52]   The PA declared its intention to take over the *shari`a* court system in the West Bank and Gaza Strip as of 10/1/98 (Abu Sardane, *al-qada al-shar`i fi `ahd al-sulta al-wataniyya al-falastiniyya* (above), at 67). The Jordanian government responded by formally cutting its administrative links with the *shari`a* system in the West Bank, with the exception of East Jerusalem where it insisted in maintaining its administration of the *shari`a* court of first instance, the *Shari`a* Court of Appeal and the *Waqf* (Islamic holy endowment) sites. Occupied East Jerusalem was not included under PA jurisdiction in the Oslo Accords, but remained on the list of 'final status issues'. Jordan's insistence on its 'special role' in Jerusalem regarding the Islamic holy sites there (formally acknowledged by Israel in the Israel–Jordan peace treaty of 10/26/94) substantially complicated PLO–Jordanian relations in the autumn of 1994 and is still not entirely resolved. The PA finally established its own *Shari`a* Court of Appeal for the West Bank which currently sits in Nablus but has Jerusalem as its permanent seat.

males at 16 lunar years and to prohibit judges from marrying any persons below these ages.[53]

Basically what the Qadi al-Quda did here was to bring the law in Gaza into conformity with the law in the West Bank,[54] his tendency being clearly to take the Jordanian law applied there as the model for a unified and modernised Palestinian law.[55] For a number of groups in Palestinian civil society, however, the standards set in Jordanian law are not those to which they aspire. In particular, concern over the early marriage of women has included examination of the socio-economic and health ramifications as well as attempts to assess the extent of the phenomenon. In 1998, an extensive study of the phenomenon of early marriage in Gaza found that 41.8% of females in the survey married between the ages of 12 and 17, with 13.3% marrying under the age of 15.[56] In the summer of 1998 the Women's Affairs Technical Committee (WATC), an umbrella group representing a number of politically affiliated women's organisations, launched a national campaign to raise the age of marriage to 18.[57]

V THE FUTURE OF PERSONAL STATUS LAW IN PALESTINE

Just as the Qadi al-Quda sought to raise the minimum age of marriage in the Gaza Strip by means of an administrative decision, it is theoretically possible that another administrative decree could be issued raising it further; or that the Palestinian Legislative Council could pass a law addressing this specific area of personal status law. Since the establishment of the Palestinian Authority (PA) and the election of the Palestinian Legislative Council (PLC), a number of lobbying targets have been achieved by the women's movement as a result of high-profile and energetic issue-specific campaigns. By way of example, these include a directive circulated by the Ministry of the Interior in the PA clarifying that a married woman does not need her husband's approval to apply for a Palestinian passport, nor an adult (over 18) single female her (male) guardian's consent; and, on a more local level, the Ministry of Transport's climbdown over requiring unmarried women to be accompanied by a relative for driving lessons in Ramallah.[58] The vulnerability of these achievements lies in the fact that most have been effected by way

---

[53] Administrative Decision of the Qadi al-Quda no.78/95 of 12/25/95, valid as of 1/10/96; text reproduced in M. Abu Sardane, *al-qada al-shar`i fi `ahd al-sulta al-wataniyya al-falastiniyya*, (above) at 185.

[54] Except that the administrative decision in Gaza required a male aged 16–18 and a female aged 15–17 to have their marriage authorised by the *qadi*, in a provision resonant of the JLFR 1951 rather than the current JLPS provision.

[55] See M. Abu Sardane, *al-qada al-shar`i fi `ahd al-sulta al-wataniyya al-falastiniyya*, (above) at 49; and interviewed in *Al-Quds* 8/14/94 and *Al-Hayat al-Jadida*, 1/26/96. He himself had been an employee in the Jordanian *shar`i* system, clearly regarded the Law of Family Rights applied in Gaza as inferior to the JLPS and blamed neglect of the Gazan system under the Israeli occupation for a deterioration of *shar`i* affairs there compared to the West Bank where the *shari`a* courts had maintained 'direct links' with the Jordanian *shari`a* system.

[56] Mundhir 'Imad and Iman Radwan, 'al-zawaj al-mubakkir fi'l-mujtama` al-falastini' (Early marriage in Palestinian society – summary) Women's Affairs Centre, Gaza City (1998).

[57] *Sawt al-Nisa'* 62 12/31/98. Just after the election of the PLC in 1996 the WATC had issued a statement identifying the marriage age of 18 as a lobbying priority. Their activists seek to work through awareness-raising and consensus-building throughout broad sectors of society, in order to bring the authority of the community as well as the law to efforts to prohibit early marriage.

[58] Respectively, PNA Ministry of Interior, Passports and Nationality Department, General Directive of 3/12/96; and PNA Ministry of Transportation, Directive 913 of 7/18/96. I am indebted to Suheir Azzouni, Director of the WATC, for the texts.

of regulations or directives issued by PA officials, rather than by way of law passed by the PLC.

Partly this is due to the PLC's 'inability to assume the responsibilities granted to it by the Palestinian people and to have a meaningful effect on Palestinian life', as described by the Palestinian Independent Commission for Citizens' Rights, which has severely criticised the executive for impeding the activities of the PLC.[59] The clearest example of this is the fate of the 'flagship' Basic Law for the transitional period. The Basic Law, a sort of draft interim constitution, attracted wide-ranging discussions in Palestinian civil society, particularly on the guarantee of human rights and the rule of law, and the structuring of relations between the executive, legislative and judicial authorities. It was widely seen not only as vital for the transitional period but as indicative of things to come in a future Palestinian State, and it proved highly contentious for the executive.[60] Despite having passed its third reading by the PLC in October 1997, by the formal end of the interim period on May 4, 1999 the Basic Law had still not received ratification by the head of the Palestinian Authority, Yasser Arafat.

As for family law, a number of issues come together when those who wish to see changes consider their strategies. These can be illustrated by the current debate over the house of obedience. As noted above, Egypt put an end to the forcible execution of obedience rulings by ministerial decree a few months before the war in 1967,[61] and while the 1985 legislation does not 'eliminate' the house of obedience, it clearly does not contemplate forcible implementation. In 1976 the Jordanians effected the same change in legislation, with the substitution of one verb in Arabic, changing the 1951 text from 'the wife shall be obliged to obey her husband' to 'the wife shall obey her husband' in the JLPS.[62] Thus the effect of a ruling for his wife to return to the house of obedience obtained by a husband from the *shari`a* court is most immediately confined to implications for her maintenance rights, which are suspended until she can establish she

---

[59] See for example the PICCR's Third Annual Report covering calendar year 1997, at 55:
'The relationship between the PLC and the Executive Branch was not properly defined during 1997. Rather, the Executive Branch acted to impede the PLC's activities by failing to implement legislation or fully acceding to the PLC's recommendations in connection with PLC oversight of the Executive Branch.'

[60] The Basic Law was first drafted under the supervision of Anis al-Qasem, Chair of the Legal Committee of the Palestinian National Council following the Declaration of Independence by the PLO in 1988. After the Gaza-Jericho Agreement was signed in 1994, the draft was subjected to widespread consultation and public debate in Palestine and went through a number of different drafts until the elections for the Palestinian Legislative Council in January 1996. In the summer of 1996 the PLC published its own first draft in the local and international Arabic press, and the final version passed its third reading on 2/10/97. See J. Oyediran and M. Gangat, *huquq al-insan fi muswada mashru` al-nizam al-daturi li'l-sulta al wataniyya fi'l-marhala al-intiqaliyya* (Human rights in the draft constitution of the National Authority in the transitional period) al-Haq (Ramallah) (1996); A.B.T. Chase, 'The Palestinian Authority Draft Constitution: Possibilities and Realities in the Search for Alternative Models of State Formation', IPCRI Law and Development Program paper no.4, Jerusalem (1997); A. Al-Qasem, 'Commentary on the Draft Basic Law for the Palestinian National Authority in the Transitional Period' (1992–4) 7 *Palestine Yearbook of International Law* 187–211; and for comparison, A.C. Wing, 'The New South African Constitution: An Example for Palestinian Consideration', (1992–4) 7 *Palestine Yearbook of International Law* 105–130. Unofficial English translations of the final (4th) draft under al-Qasem's supervision and the final text passed by the PLC are published respectively by Jerusalem Media and Communication Centre (Draft Basic Law, February 1996) and LAW – Palestinian Society for the Protection of Human Rights and the Environment (Basic Law Draft Resolution, October 1997).

[61] According to Najjar, when the Minister was challenged on the admissability of this action, the speaker asked the National Assembly if there was anyone present who would support forcible execution of a *ta`a* ruling by police action, whereupon everybody in the chamber shouted 'No, no!' Najjar comments that '[n]o one wanted to go on record as being in favour of such a shameful institution!' F. Najjar, 'Egypt's Laws of Personal Status' (1988) 10, 3 *Arab Studies Quarterly* 319–344, at 331.

[62] Compare JLFR Article 33 and JLPS Article 37.

has complied with the *ta'a* ruling and her status as a 'disobedient' wife (*nashiz*) has thereby been removed. If her husband in the meantime divorces her, she will not be due maintenance during the *'idda*.

Applications by a husband to the court to order his wife back to the house of obedience appear to have been on the decrease in recent decades, probably as a result both of the impossibility of physical enforcement and of the growing social disapproval of the institution noted above. Thus, research in West Bank *shari'a* court records for 1965, 1975 and 1985 showed claims for *ta'a* constituting 16%, 11% and 5% respectively,[63] while research from the 1990s including two courts in Gaza found them constituting 3.5% of claims.[64] In most cases a *ta'a* claim is submitted by the husband in defence to a maintenance claim by the wife, or as part of a series of other claims between the two in the *shari'a* court – in other words, as a negotiating tool, for example during the proceedings of a claim by either party for divorce on the grounds of 'discord and strife'.[65] However, in 1994, the summer the PLO forces marched into Gaza and Jericho, there was an upsurge in both maintenance claims and in claims for *ta'a*, the one clearly related to the other and both possibly to be traced to a perception that with the Palestinian Authority there was more possibility of enforcement, particularly of financial claims.[66]

For clarification purposes, it would be well within the power of the executive to ensure that *ta'a* rulings in the Gaza Strip are not forcibly executed by giving appropriate administrative instructions to the police. This would not however 'eliminate the house of obedience', since the wife's duty of obedience is affirmed in both the JLPS and the LFR,[67] still balancing his unilateral financial obligations towards her. This is where a second very significant aspect of the Shadia Sarraj example comes in: namely, the way in which the arguments were addressed by supporters of the campaign she mobilised. In its fortnightly women's supplement, *Sawt Al-Nisa* (Women's Voice), the WATC devoted several column inches to exponents of the view that the concept of the house of obedience is not based on explicit texts of the Qur'an nor the practice of the prophet Muhammad (the two textual sources of Islamic law) but is rather a matter of human interpretation. The extensive examination of the Islamic law argument is indicative of recent debates in Palestine regarding the nature of a future Palestinian law of personal status, debates which focus on the authority or authorities from which such a law should be drawn and within the limits of which it must be framed.

The spring of 1998 saw a series of high-profile and carefully prepared activities by wide sections of the women's movement, which drew attention to areas of gender inequality in law. Of particular significance was the culmination of a wide-ranging project called the Palestinian Model Parliament: Women and Legislation (PMP), organised by a non-governmental women's centre, the Women's Centre for Legal Aid

---

[63] Courts of Bethlehem, Ramallah and Hebron. L. Welchman, *The Islamic Law of Marriage and Divorce in the Occupied West Bank*, Ph.D. London (SOAS) (1992) table 16 at 219.

[64] Statistics from data collected by WCLAC researchers.

[65] Court practice has established that consideration of a claim for *ta'a* by the husband will be suspended if the wife claims the existence of strife, until the wife's claim has been investigated. M.H. al-'Arabi, *al-mabadi' al-qada'iyya li mahkamat al-isti'naf al-shar'iyya* (above), at 227, ruling no. 18906/1976. Compare Mir-Hosseini on *ta'a* and maintenance claims in Morocco: 'Women resort to court to improve their bargaining position vis-à-vis their husbands. Men come to court to offset – or pre-empt – their wives' actions.' Z. Mir Hosseini *Marriage on Trial: A Study of Islamic Family Law, Iran and Morocco Compared*, London (1993), at 50.

[66] Although the Gaza City court showed an increase in maintenance claims, it was only the Rafah court that showed a surge in *ta'a* claims, and a more informed understanding of that phenomenon awaits further research.

[67] JLPS Articles 37 and 39; LFR Article 40.

and Counselling (WCLAC). Running over a period of nearly two years, the prize-winning project had sought to identify in all areas of the law those provisions discriminatory to women's rights and to draft, debate and build consensus on proposed amendments to those provisions, to be forwarded for the attention of the Palestinian Legislative Council. A study by a lawyer published by the WCLAC in the lead-up to the final sessions of the Model Parliament in the West Bank and Gaza,[68] and a set of draft proposals for modifications to personal status law drawn up for discussion in the Gaza final session,[69] received particular attention in the press and in meeting halls. The vehemence of the reaction from particular individuals and groups identified broadly as 'Islamist' against the questions being raised in these documents, and in the debates in the Model Parliament as a whole, translated into personal attacks on many of the women involved and provoked a counter-mobilisation of support across broader areas of civil society. Those joining the debate from various perspectives raised issues related to the place of Islam and Islamic law in the cultural heritage of Palestine, the meaning of democracy and pluralism and its history in Palestinian society and in the revolution, the protection of freedom of expression, women's rights and the nationalist struggle.

In the meantime, and in direct response to the activities of the PMP, the Acting Qadi al-Quda, undertaking the functions of the Qadi al-Quda during the latter's extended absence from the country, announced the establishment of a committee to draw up a draft personal status law as a matter of priority.[70] He invited submissions from all those concerned with the matter, although not apparently addressing the women's organisations that had been involved in the PMP. The question of authoritative framework is not an issue for this committee, which will draw on the rules of classical Islamic law while asserting its right to exercise independent judgement on matters traditionally held to be matters of human interpretation.

For those who were involved in the PMP, the political women's movement and other sectors of civil society involved in parallel discussions on the way forward in family law, the options are more complex. One of the reasons the study published by WCLAC was attacked was that it argued that optimally a unified civil code embodying the principle of gender equality should regulate family affairs for all Palestinians regardless of religion, and that the religious authorities should maintain a guiding and counselling role but no longer have a legislative or judicial role in personal status matters.[71] Although the author conceded that this was not going to happen in the short term,[72] she insisted on the principle of gender equality as the basic authoritative principle in reformulating family

---

[68] A. Khadr, *al-qanun wa mustaqbil al-mar'a al-falastiniyya* (*The law and the future of Palestinian women*) WCLAC (1998).

[69] K. Nashwan, 'muswada muqtadayat li-qanun ahwal shakhsiyya falastini muwahhad' (draft requirements for a unified Palestinian personal status law), discussion paper presented to the Palestinian Model Parliament, Gaza City, April 1998; I am grateful to Karam Nashwan for the text and to Marwa Qasim and Maha Abu Dayyeh for inviting me to attend the final session of the PMP in Gaza. Much of the argumentation of the Gaza PMP document is reproduced in Z. Uthman, 'al-barliman al-falastini as-suri: al-mar'a wa'l-tashri`, bayn al-tajdid wa'l-quliba' (The Palestinian Model Parliament: Women and Legislation – between renewal and stereotyping) (1998) 5,9 *al-siyasa al-falastiniyya (Palestine Policy)* 57–85.

[70] *Al-Ayyam* 4/4/98.

[71] Khadr, *al-qanun wa mustaqbil al-mar'a al-falastiniyya* (*The law and the future of Palestinian women*) (above), 118–120.

[72] Compare the failure that same summer of 1998 of the Lebanese Bill for 'optional civil marriage': C. Mallat, 'Lebanon', 297–301 in (1997–8) 4 *Yearbook of Islamic and Middle Eastern Law*, and N.M. El-Cheikh, 'The 1998 Proposed Civil Marriage Law in Lebanon: The Reaction of the Muslim Communities', paper for the Islamic Marriage Contract conference hosted by the Islamic Legal Studies Program of Harvard Law School, January 1999.

law. In the Gaza PMP discussion document, a similar emphasis was laid on the fact that the personal status laws being criticised are 'inherited laws' – that is, not issued by Palestinians for Palestinians – and that a Palestinian law must conform to the spirit of the 1988 Declaration of Independence and to the guarantee of gender equality made in the draft Basic Law,[73] as well as having regard for international human rights law in general and the Convention of the Elimination of All Forms of Discrimination against Women in particular. At the same time, the document proposed development of Muslim family law within the Islamic framework, stating that the *shari`a* is a principal source of personal status law and claiming the space for interpretations of the sources beyond the classical rules to give substance to the principles of equality and justice.

The majority tendency among activists outside the *shar`i* system itself thus appears to favour working within the broad limits set by tradition and culture, which includes a role for religion in personal status law: a 'Muslim feminist' approach as defined in the Egyptian context by Azza Karam.[74] The internal cogency of this approach is illustrated by what happened with the relevant provisions in the draft Basic Law. Commenting on the extensive debates on the draft text that he had originally presented in 1994, Chair of the PNC's Legal Committee Anis al-Qasem noted that women's organisations had raised questions to do with personal status issues, but that '[i]t was explained and accepted that a basic law was not the place for such subjects and that that had to be attended to in special legislation.' In similar vein he explained the absence, in his draft texts, of any reference to the place of Islamic law in the Palestinian legislative process:

'The Draft intentionally avoided the inclusion of issues that may be divisive at this stage within the Palestinian community, such as the religion of the state, the sources of legislation and boundaries. It has been the regular practice in the Arab states to declare that Islam is the religion of the state and *shari`a* the main source or a source of its legislation. Within the Palestinian community, there are various trends on the subject: the secular, the modernist and the fundamentalist. It was thought that such an issue should be decided upon in an atmosphere of freedom when the time comes for the preparation of a permanent constitution.'[75]

At the same time, the recently appointed Qadi al-Quda was having discussions with top officials in the PLO, including Arafat, during which he objected *inter alia* to the absence of any mention of the *shar`i* judiciary in the draft text of the Basic Law for the interim period.[76] Predictably, when the PLC published its own draft version in the summer of 1996, and began discussions of it in the Council, the place of *shari`a* gave rise to impassioned interventions.[77] The published discussions did not reach the intensity or

---

[73] Article 9 of the draft passed by the PLC: 'All Palestinians shall be equal before the courts and the law without discrimination on any ground such as race, sex, colour, religion, political opinion or disability'. There is no equivalent of Article 10 of the earlier draft: 'Women and men shall have equal fundamental rights and freedoms without any discrimination'. On this article, the drafter Anis al-Qasem noted that it was inserted as a result of interventions by women's organisations: al-Qasem, 'Commentary on the Draft Basic Law for the Palestinian National Authority in the Transitional Period' (1992–4) 7 *Palestinian Yearbook of International Law*, at 201.

[74] A. Karam, *Women, Islamisms and the State: Contemporary Feminisms in Egypt*, London (1998) at 11–12.

[75] Al-Qasem, 'Commentary on the Draft Basic Law for the Palestinian National Authority in the Transitional Period' (1992–4) 7 *Palestinian Yearbook of International Law*, 198.

[76] As he reports in his book: Abu Sardane, *al-qada al-shar`i fi `ahd al-sulta al-wataniyya al-falastiniyya* (above), at 44–46.

[77] In a packed meeting in Nablus, one speaker called for the implementation of 'a full Islamic constitution as the source of legislation in Palestine': *al-Quds* 24/7/96. *Al-Quds* (9/6/96) also reported 'heated discussions' on this topic in the PLC during the first reading of the draft Basic Law.

depth of the debates in Egypt in earlier decades, but they revolved around similar issues: the role of Islam and whether the *shari`a* – or 'the principles of *shari`a*' – were to be 'a source', 'a principal source' or 'the principal source' of legislation.[78] In its very first reading of the text the PLC overturned al-Qasem's cautionary position regarding legislating these issues at this time, and by the time of its third reading the text stated that 'the principles of Islamic *shari`a* are a principal source of legislation' and that 'matters of personal status are to be dealt with by *shari`a* and religious courts'.[79] This firm indication that communal jurisdiction over personal status matters is set to continue for the foreseeable future puts Palestinian personal status law firmly within the pattern of neighbouring Arab States.[80]

It remains to be seen whether there will also be a pattern in procedure. The notorious sensitivity of the issue of personal status law has traditionally been one reason for the use of less than democratic means to legislate changes.[81] In Egypt, commentators note the dilemma of 'Egyptian feminists and progressives' who, while desirous of the type of reforms legislated in the 1979 law, were sympathetic to the argument that Sadat's use of presidential decree had bypassed democratic debate and was an abuse of process.[82] In Jordan, the JLPS was issued as a temporary law during a ten-year suspension of parliament, and parliament is still reviewing draft texts for a permanent law.[83] In Tunisia, the 1956 law is still hailed by many as the Arab law that goes the furthest towards legislating equality between the spouses in family law. Promulgated right at the dawn of independence, its political significance was clear, but once again, President Bourghiba issued it by decree.

In Palestine, Yasser Arafat has already issued many decrees but so far has given no indication of intending to emulate Bourghiba, at least not in respect of issuing a radical personal status law when Palestine finally does achieve independent statehood. The Legislative Council, albeit fettered as it is by the neglect and insolence of the executive, may well turn its attention to family law and can expect to be lobbied intensively by advocates of all the different approaches to personal status law. It may on the other hand decide to leave such a fundamental (and at the same time, for many, non-priority) matter for what many current PLC members will argue will be the more authoritative legislative body that will succeed it in the State of Palestine. Provided that the Legislative Council or its successor is given its proper place in the system of government in Palestine, it may well be that the first Palestinian law of personal status is issued by parliamentary process. The discussions are guaranteed to be long and heated. As for the campaign to eliminate

---

[78] See selections of the debate in the Egyptian press in 1971, particularly the pieces by al-`Otaifi and his critics, translated in J. O'Kane, 'Islam in the new Egyptian Constitution: some discussions in *Al-Ahram*' (1972) 26 *Middle East Journal* 137–148.

[79] Respectively, Articles 4(2) and 92(1).

[80] Chase notes that continuing separate communal jurisdiction 'impel a consideration of a number of issues which stand at the junction of individual human rights, groups rights and Islamic family law.' A.B.T. Chase, 'The Palestinian Authority Draft Constitution: Possibilities and Realities in the Search for Alternative Models of State Formation', IPCRI Law and Development Program paper no.4, Jerusalem (1997) at 47. The defeat of the Lebanese Bill for optional civil marriage has not however deterred Palestinian supporters of this approach.

[81] See for example A. Karam, *Women, Islamisms and the State: Contemporary Feminisms in Egypt*, London (1998), at 145.

[82] Hijab, *Womanpower: The Arab debate on women at work*, Cambridge (1988) at 31; Hatem,'Economic and Political Liberalism in Egypt and the Demise of State Feminism', (1992) 24 *International Journal of Middle East Studies* at 240–241.

[83] Welchman,'The Development of Islamic Family Law in the Legal System of Jordan' (1988) 37 *International and Comparative Law Quarterly* 868–886, at 872.

the house of obedience, it has not begun before its time: even in Tunisia, the law retained the concept of the wife's duty of obedience until 1993, when an amendment also removed the wife's absolute exemption from any financial obligations. If the prospective Palestinian legislation does in fact abolish the house of obedience in one fell blow, that will indeed be breaking the pattern.

PAPUA NEW GUINEA

OBSTACLES TO THE RECOGNITION OF CUSTOMARY FAMILY LAW

Owen Jessep[*]

I   INTRODUCTION

Papua New Guinea, a Pacific nation of some four million people, is a former Australian colony which became independent in 1975. A distinguishing characteristic of Papua New Guinean family law is the contrast and conflicts which are evident between family law legislation, on the one hand, and customary family law, on the other.[1] The statute law is mostly old Australian colonial legislation, which has continued in force notwithstanding almost a quarter of a century of independence.[2] At the same time, customary family law is also recognised (subject to certain qualifications) under the Constitution and several other statutes.[3] In the result, in some areas of family law a 'dual' system operates, in which persons can choose whether to follow statute or custom. In relation to marriage, for example, a person may either make a monogamous statutory marriage by satisfying the formalities of the Marriage Act (Chapter 280 of the Revised Laws), or instead make a customary marriage formed in accordance with the relevant custom.[4]

In the eight years or so since the last survey of developments in family law in Papua New Guinea,[5] there has been no family law legislative activity to speak of. As a result, developments in family law in this decade have very largely come from the judiciary. One feature of the case-law in recent years has been the readiness of National Court judges to challenge aspects of customary family law. In some instances, this has led to denial of recognition and enforcement of custom, on the basis that certain constitutional or legislative safeguards have been infringed. These challenges to customary family law, and especially the leading 1997 case of *Re Willingal*,[6] will provide the focus for this review.

---

[*]   Associate Professor of Law, University of New South Wales, Sydney, Australia.

[1]   See generally, O. Jessep and J. Luluaki, *Principles of Family Law in Papua New Guinea*, 2nd ed (UPNG Press, 1994).

[2]   These pre-Independence statutes are continued in force by virtue of the Constitution of Papua New Guinea, Schedule 2.6.

[3]   Customary family law claims can be instituted at all levels of the legal system, from the Village Courts, to the Local and District Courts, and even (depending on the amount and issues involved) in the National Court. See O. Jessep and J. Luluaki, note 1 above, at Chapters 4 and 5.

[4]   For discussion see O. Jessep and J. Luluaki, note 1 above, at Chapter 2.

[5]   See O. Jessep, 'Papua New Guinea – Adultery Legislation and the Jurisdiction of the Village Courts', (1991–92) 30 *Journal of Family Law* 367–379. An earlier outline of elements of Papua New Guinean family law is given in C. Bradley and S. Tovey, 'Papua New Guinea – Lo Bilong Famili', (1988–89) 27 *Journal of Family Law* 261–273.

[6]   *Re Willingal* (1997) N 1506.

II   CONSTITUTIONAL AND STATUTORY PROVISIONS

By section 9 of the Constitution of Papua New Guinea, the laws of the country include the Constitution itself, various categories of legislation, and the 'underlying law'. According to section 20, until such time as an Act of Parliament provides otherwise, the underlying law is to be understood as set out in Schedule 2 of the Constitution. By that Schedule, the two principal sources of the underlying law are custom,[7] and the common law. In relation to custom, Schedule 2.1(1), so far as relevant, states that 'custom is adopted, and shall be applied and enforced, as part of the underlying law'. This is however made subject to subsection (2), which provides as follows:

> '(2) Subsection (1) does not apply in respect of any custom that is, and to the extent that it is, inconsistent with a Constitutional Law or a statute, or repugnant to the general principles of humanity.'

One further important statutory provision dealing with the recognition of custom needs to be mentioned. Section 3(1) of the Customs Recognition Act (Chapter 19 of the Revised Laws) is in the following terms:[8]

> '(1) Subject to this Act, custom shall be recognized and enforced by, and may be pleaded in, all courts except so far as in a particular case or in a particular context –
>
> (a) its recognition or enforcement would result, in the opinion of the court, in injustice or would not be in the public interest; or
> (b) in a case affecting the welfare of a child under the age of 16 years, its recognition or enforcement would not, in the opinion of the court, be in the best interests of the child.'

III   LIMITATIONS ON THE RECOGNITION OF FAMILY LAW CUSTOM

It follows from the constitutional and statutory provisions outlined above that, in relation to a family law custom that appears to be relevant in a legal context, there are potentially six grounds for refusing to adopt that custom as part of the underlying law. These six grounds (three from the wording of Schedule 2.1 of the Constitution, and three from section 3 of the Customs Recognition Act) are the following:

(i)   inconsistency with the Constitution;
(ii) inconsistency with a statute;
(iii) repugnancy to the general principles of humanity;
(iv) resulting in injustice;
(v)   contrary to the public interest; and
(vi) contrary to the best interests of a child under 16 years of age.

Of these possible reasons for impugning family law custom (reasons which in practice may be expected to overlap to some extent), several decisions of the National

---

[7]   In Schedule 1.2 of the Constitution, the term 'custom' is defined to mean:
       'the customs and usages of indigenous inhabitants of the country existing in relation to the matter in question at the time when and the place in relation to which the matter arises, regardless of whether or not the custom or usage has existed from time immemorial'.

[8]   Some further limitations concerning the applicability of custom in criminal and civil cases are found in sections 4 and 5 of the same statute (Chapter 19). Those sections are not relevant for the purposes of this survey.

Court in the early 1990s had resorted to grounds (i) and (iii), that is to say by referring to custom in relation to the Constitution, and also in regard to the 'general principles of humanity'. Brief examples of each approach will now be given.

In the 1991 case of *Re Wagi Non and the Constitution Section 42(5)*,[9] the husband had left his wife and their four children in the care of his relatives when he travelled to another province for employment. After he had been away for five or six years without making contact with his family or relatives, the wife eventually formed a relationship with another man. The husband's relatives then complained in the Village Court that the wife had committed adultery, in breach of customary expectations, and obtained an order for compensation against her. When she failed to pay the amount required, the Village Court ordered her imprisonment. In the National Court, Woods J ordered her release, stating (among other reasons) that the custom relied on by the relatives of the husband should not be recognised, as it infringed section 55 of the Constitution. In substance, this section provides that 'all citizens have the same rights, privileges, obligations and duties irrespective of race, tribe, place of origin, political opinion, colour, creed, religion or sex'. In the opinion of the court:

> 'I cannot help feeling that the going off and leaving the wife and children without his support and protection yet expecting her to remain bound by custom is a custom that must be denigrating to her status as a woman. It is denying her the equality provided in the *Constitution*, s 55. ... I am not saying that a man cannot have several wives and cannot travel but if he chooses to have wives and travel elsewhere he must accord them equality in care and participation and she must have the same freedoms that he has. ... The facts of this case suggest that this woman is bonded, almost in slavery, to the husband even when the husband neglects her. This must clearly be a denigration of the woman's humanness.'[10]

Again, in *Re Kepo Raramu and the Yowe Village Court*,[11] a Village Court had sentenced a woman to a term of six months' imprisonment for commencing a new relationship after her husband had died. On appeal, the National Court ordered her immediate release. One of the grounds relied on for this decision by Doherty J was the following:

> 'I am well aware of the custom in many areas that says women whose husbands have died are not to go around with another man. ... I do not know of any equivalent custom that says a man whose wife died is not allowed to go around with other women, and, as such, I consider this custom strikes against the basis of equality provided in s 55 of the *Constitution*.'[12]

Despite the lack of any clear judicial definition in Papua New Guinea of what might be meant by 'the general principles of humanity' (a legislative expression that first appeared during colonial times), the notion of 'repugnancy' to these principles has featured in several National Court family law cases. The first such instance occurred in *Re Kaka Ruk and the Constitution Section 42(5)*,[13] on facts notably similar to those in *Re Wagi Non* (see above). In *Kaka Ruk*, a husband had complained to the Village Court that his wife had committed adultery with the husband's brother. After being unable to pay the

---

9   [1991] PNGLR 84.

10 [1991] PNGLR 84, Woods J at 86–87.

11 [1994] PNGLR 486.

12 [1994] PNGLR 486, Doherty J at 486.

13 [1991] PNGLR 105. For a discussion of this case, see J. Zorn, 'Women, Custom and State Law in Papua New Guinea', (1994–95) *Third World Legal Studies* 169–205.

compensation ordered by the court, she was gaoled. When the matter came to the attention of the National Court, Woods J found that the husband had neglected her during the time when he had been absent at work on a plantation, and this had led to her associating with his brother, by whom she was now pregnant. After referring to paragraph 2(12) of the National Goals and Directive Principles in the Preamble to the Constitution (equality of spouses' rights and duties in marriage), and the 'repugnancy' test in Schedule 2.1 of the Constitution, Woods J stated:

> 'This custom that the husband is seeking to apply which leads to her gaoling when he is in the dominating position and where the situation has been partly caused by his behaviour must be a custom that denigrates women and is thus repugnant to the general principles of humanity and should be denied a place in the underlying law. ... In this situation before me now the wife [was] caught between bride price problems and an unhappy marriage which has produced no children. She almost [had] no way out. ... People in Papua New Guinea must come to terms with the law that women are not chattels that can be bought and thus bonded forever. They are equal participants in the marriage and in society ...'[14]

Marital problems of this sort should be resolved, the court added, by discussion and mediation rather than by the precipitate application of criminal sanctions.[15]

A final illustration, also with reference to the 'repugnancy' doctrine, is found in the 1994 case of *Ubuk v Darius*.[16] This was a dispute over custody of a child aged 20 months, whose parents had lived together in a de facto relationship for about two years. When the relationship broke up, the man (who had been previously married by custom) returned to live with his customary wife and their children. He sought custody of the ex-nuptial daughter, and emphasised his wife's apparent willingness to look after her. He relied on evidence of local custom to the effect that if an informal relationship did not progress to the status of a customary marriage, the father was entitled to automatic custody of any child born in the meantime, subject to a payment of compensation to the woman for having borne the child. The court was not impressed. In the words of Sevua J:

> 'Whether one views it subjectively or objectively, the woman is a sex object. So where is the morality and value of humanity in this woman? ... How does a woman in such a situation free herself from this seemingly sexual domination? I consider [these] customs repugnant to the general principles of humanity and, therefore, inapplicable to the present case. The applicant can gain no assistance from that customary law.'[17]

In the event, custody of the child was given to the mother, with access to the father.[18]

IV   THE DECISION IN *RE WILLINGAL* (1997)

In cases like those so far mentioned, the court typically relied on one or another of the requirements of Schedule 2.1 of the Constitution, or of section 3 of the Customs Recognition Act, to deny recognition to some aspects of family law custom. Several of

---

[14]   [1991] PNGLR 105, Woods J at 107.
[15]   Ibid.
[16]   [1994] PNGLR 279.
[17]   [1994] PNGLR 279, Sevua J at 283–284.
[18]   Ibid at 284.

these cases arose from competing expectations about the respective behaviour and duties of the parties to a customary marriage, in which the National Court felt obliged to intervene to protect women from excessive punishment at the hands of Village Courts.[19] The 1997 case of *Re Willingal*,[20] in contrast, reached the National Court after publicity in one of Papua New Guinea's national newspapers, which in turn led to the institution of proceedings by a non-governmental human rights organisation. These proceedings featured a whole battery of challenges against a custom requiring a woman's forced marriage.

As mentioned in the judgment of Injia J in this case, the PNG Post Courier of May 3, 1996 ran an article beginning with the chilling headline of 'Girl Sold in Death Compensation'.[21] The story dealt with the unfortunate situation of Ms Miriam Willingal, an 18-year-old high school student from the Western Highlands area of Papua New Guinea.

In brief, the problem for Miriam Willingal began when her father was killed, apparently by mistake, during a police operation designed to apprehend a known criminal. The deceased man's mother's clan members (of 'Clan X') were upset about the death, which they felt had been brought about by the father's clan members (of 'Clan Y') liaising with and assisting the police to enter the territory of Clan Y in a night time raid. Without this assistance, the argument of Clan X continued, the police operation would not have been possible, and the accidental shooting would not have occurred. Accordingly, Clan X (which historically had a rather special relationship with Clan Y, both through marriage ties and through the provision of refuge for Clan Y members during tribal fighting with other groups) felt entitled to receive compensation from Clan Y. The members of Clan Y were in evident agreement with the basis of the claim by Clan X, and the only real point for negotiation was the amount of compensation to be paid. As noted by Injia J, 'the payment of compensation by the deceased's tribe to the deceased's mother's tribe for the death caused by unnatural causes is widely practised in [this] area'.[22]

Unlike the common practice in other types of compensation claims, where recompense is made merely by the handing over of pigs, money, and various personal items of value,[23] in this case the compensation being discussed between Clan X and Clan Y also included the transfer of two young women, who might then be expected to marry men from the deceased's clan. Since Miriam Willingal (also a member of Clan Y) was, for various reasons, one of the most likely candidates to be pressured into taking part in this arrangement, she began to object. It is not entirely clear how the information reached the newspaper, although Miriam's affidavit, quoted in the judgment, ends with the statement: 'For the reasons stated ... I went public hoping that somebody might help me'.[24]

In response to the publicity, the Individual and Community Rights Advocacy Forum Inc (ICRAF) instituted proceedings in the National Court under section 57 of the Constitution, claiming that Miriam's constitutional rights were being infringed by the proposed compensation arrangements between Clan X and Clan Y. Section 57 grants

---

[19]   For discussion, see O. Jessep, 'Village Courts in Papua New Guinea: Constitutional and Gender Issues', (1992) 6 *International Journal of Law and the Family* 401-16.

[20]   *Re Willingal* (1997) N 1506.

[21]   Ibid, at 7.

[22]   Ibid, at 14.

[23]   Ibid, at 34–35.

[24]   Ibid, at 34.

standing to any person with an interest in the protection and enforcement of constitutional rights to seek appropriate National Court orders. As a preliminary step, the court found that ICRAF, a community interest group in Papua New Guinea with a history of human rights advocacy, was entitled to make the application on behalf of Miriam.[25] Interim injunctions and protective orders were made by the court, pending a proper hearing of the matter which took place during the following month.[26]

At the trial, there was some disagreement among the witnesses over the details of the customary compensation claim. The broad outlines of the claim referred to 25 pigs, 20,000 kina, and two women.[27] Some witnesses said that no particular women were identified in the negotiations, that no woman would be pressured to comply with the arrangement, and that the marriages might not take place until some years in the future. Other witnesses, including Miriam, gave a contrary impression, to the effect that pressure could be or had been brought to bear on individual women by the clan leaders, and that a delay in arranging the marriages would cause aggravation and ill-feeling between the two groups. In his findings on this crucial point, Sevua J stated:

'I find that because [Miriam] was of marriageable age and the daughter of the deceased, immediate pressure was brought to bear on her. ... Miriam did not consent to the request and felt unhappy and depressed ... She also felt at a loss because she did not know who her bridegroom was. She felt humiliated in the eyes of the public because she did not like the idea of being used as a form of payment. I find that Miriam is living in fear and feels threatened by men from both [groups, who] may get too impatient and try to enforce the commitment on her.'[28]

Turning to the relevant law, Sevua J had no doubt that Miriam's constitutional rights had been infringed, and gave multiple reasons for this conclusion. His general approach to the issue of recognition of custom appears in the following passage:

'The traditional customs of the people of [this area] like the rest of PNG have existed from time immemorial and they serve complex value systems which only they themselves best know. It is not easy for any outsider to fully understand the customs and the underlying values and purposes they serve. Any outsider including the modern courts must not be quick to extract those customs and their values and pass judgments on their soundness or otherwise. ... But it is clear to me that the framers of our Constitution and modern day legislators were thinking about a modern PNG based on ethnic societies whose welfare and advancement was based on the maintenance and promotion of good traditional customs and the discouragement and elimination of bad customs as seen from the eyes of an ordinary modern Papua New Guinean. No matter how painful it may be to the small ethnic society concerned, such bad custom must give way to the dictates of our modern national laws.'[29]

The court accordingly held that a number of provisions of the Constitution and of other statutes would be infringed were the custom to be enforced. To begin with, section 32 of the Constitution, which guarantees basic freedoms in accordance with the law, would be infringed if Miriam was not free to choose whom to marry.[30] Further, a forced

---

25   Ibid, at 6.
26   Ibid, at 7–8.
27   Ibid, at 24. At this time, the value of the kina was approximately equal to $Aust 0.92c.
28   Ibid, at 42.
29   Ibid, at 51–52, 54–55.
30   Ibid, at 45–46.

marriage in these circumstances would amount to a breach of section 55 (here, discrimination on the basis of sex), 'because there is no evidence that the same custom which targets young women from the deceased's tribe also targets eligible men from the deceased's mother's tribe'.[31]

Turning to other legislation, the court found that the proposed marriage would also breach section 5 of the Marriage Act (Chapter 280 of the Revised Laws), which was designed to protect women from being pressured into customary marriages.[32] As to the criteria and requirements of section 3 of the Customs Recognition Act (Chapter 19), the court found that the custom in question was not only repugnant to the general principles of humanity, but would also, if carried out, produce injustice and be contrary to the public interest. The custom was repugnant to the general principles of humanity because 'living men or women should not be allowed to be dealt with as part of compensation payments under any circumstances'.[33] Further, it would be unjust for any woman from this area to live under the compulsion and fear of a forced marriage, while 'men from [the same area] and other men and women in other parts of Papua New Guinea live, associate and marry freely'.[34] Finally, and for similar reasons, to recognise the custom would not be in the public interest, because it would 'subject Miriam or any other woman from the [same] area to unnecessary life-time obligations, pressure and [they would] live under threat and fear in their young and single life'.[35]

For all of these reasons, the court then proceeded to issue permanent injunctions and restraining orders against the various groups and their members.[36] With such an array of provisions all leading to the same result, the court stated that it was therefore unnecessary to consider additional arguments presented on behalf of the plaintiff. These further points turned on whether the relevant custom also infringed other provisions in the Constitution, such as section 36 (freedom from inhuman treatment); section 42 (liberty of the person); section 49 (right to privacy); and section 52(1) (freedom of movement).[37]

V   DISCUSSION AND CONCLUSION

There is little doubt that *Re Willingal* will be a leading case for years to come whenever aspects of customary family law are in issue. For any legal context involving family law custom, the case contains a bundle of potential weapons for future plaintiffs seeking to prevent the enforcement and recognition of particular customs. The reasoning in *Re Willingal* drew on earlier decisions of the National Court, but at the same time extended the range and scope of the arguments available to challenge family law custom, especially where the custom appears to be one-sided, oppressive or patriarchal in its application. The possibility of additional forms of argument is also suggested in those points upon which the court in *Re Willingal* found it unnecessary to rule.

---

[31]   Ibid, at 48–49.

[32]   Ibid, at 47, 49. Section 5 empowers a Local Court Magistrate, on complaint by a woman, to forbid a prospective customary marriage, or annul a customary marriage which has already occurred, where the court finds that the woman has been subjected to 'excessive pressure', or that it would otherwise be a hardship on the woman to compel her to comply with the relevant custom.

[33]   Ibid, at 50–51.

[34]   Ibid, at 50.

[35]   Ibid, at 50.

[36]   Ibid, at 56–57.

[37]   Ibid, at 49.

In recent years in Papua New Guinea, the most controversial family law topic has been that of polygamous marriage. Even more than the perennial controversy over elements of customary bride price, the practice of polygamy (which in practice means polygyny, that is the right of a man to have more than one customary wife) has produced a constant flow of public debate.[38] While polygamy is virtually unknown in many parts of the country today, it remains a relatively common practice among leaders from the Highlands provinces. In legal terms, a polygamous customary marriage has generally been regarded as valid by virtue of section 3(1) of the Marriage Act (Chapter 280 of the Revised Laws), which allows customary marriages 'in accordance with the custom prevailing in the tribe or group to which the parties or either of them belong or belongs'. Thus, in the passage previously quoted from *Re Wagi Non and the Constitution Section 42(5)*,[39] Woods J stated plainly: 'I am not saying that a man cannot have several wives …', but went on to insist that all the wives must be treated fairly and equally.

Against advocates of the practice, who rely on the Constitution's support for traditional customs, objections have come from community and church groups, as well as magistrates and judges dealing with the frequent financial and custody disputes as well as criminal assaults and murders (whether between spouses, or between co-wives) arising from polygamous arrangements.[40] Since 1996, private members' Bills designed to abolish or ban polygamy have been circulated on at least two occasions in Parliament, so far without any collective response. Indeed, a parliamentary response is unlikely in the foreseeable future. This is due not only to the lack of unanimity on the issue, but also to the obvious fact that a government trying to deal with mounting problems of social, economic and political instability (such as those currently facing Papua New Guinea) is unlikely to see family law reform as very high on its list of priorities.

It is interesting to speculate on whether, assuming the absence of any parliamentary legislative initiative, a court in Papua New Guinea might be faced with an objection to some aspect of customary polygamous marriage, based upon one or more of the arguments considered in *Re Willingal* and earlier cases. Such a claim might be ventilated in any context in which a party's rights or responsibilities will vary according to whether the marriage is legally valid or not (such as spousal maintenance, property claims, inheritance, fatal accidents, and so on). Some years ago, it may be noted, a Task Force of the PNG Law Reform Commission expressed the view that the custom of polygamy was 'unconstitutional', because the freedom to have more than one spouse was only extended to males. Rather than argue for a similar liberty to be extended to females, however, the Task Force concluded that Parliament should insist on monogamy for everyone.[41]

In its claim that polygamy was unconstitutional, the Task Force presumably had in mind the prohibition on discrimination contained in section 55 of the Constitution, which was also one of the grounds for the decision in *Re Willingal*. While it is not necessary to go into the point here, there are in fact some complex problems of interpretation involved

---

[38] For discussion, see for example O.Jessep, 'The Governor-General's Wives – Polygamy and the Recognition of Customary Marriage in Papua New Guinea', (1993) 7 *Australian Journal of Family Law* 29–42. Analogous contemporary discussions in various African jurisdictions are referred to in several papers in J. Eekelaar and T. Nhlapo (eds), *The Changing Family – Family Forms and Family Law* (Hart 1998).

[39] [1991] PNGLR 84, Woods J at 86–87.

[40] Among the frequent references in the press, the Catholic Church of PNG has recently called for 'a total ban on polygamy' (PNG Post Courier, April 21, 1999), and a National Court judge has called for legislation to punish husbands when co-wives are led to injure or kill one another (PNG Post Courier, May 7, 1999).

[41] PNG Law Reform Commission, Task Force on Family Law Reform, *Press Release*, June 20, 1990.

in applying section 55 to a customary practice which appears to be justified by a statute of pre-Independence origin (such as the Marriage Act).[42] Leaving aside these complications, nevertheless, it is obvious that arguments based on some of the other grounds canvassed above might just as easily come to the fore: for instance, that customary expectations and practices relating to polygamy in a particular Papua New Guinean community might be inconsistent with other rights guaranteed to women by the Constitution, or might produce injustice or be contrary to the public interest (thereby infringing the terms of section 3 of the Customs Recognition Act).

A court's decision invalidating, on any of the grounds mentioned, a particular polygamous marriage (that is, by denying recognition and enforcement to the relevant custom) might well be dependent upon the precise legal context in which the issue arose, as well as the nature of the evidence adduced in the instant case. That is to say, the decision would not automatically spell invalidity for polygamous marriages in general. Such a general consequence would most likely require legislative intervention.[43] On the other hand, the presence of a single National Court decision concerning a polygamous marriage, in which arguments of this sort were successful, might well provide an impetus for further developments by encouraging other plaintiffs to mount similar actions. In this event, the case of *Re Willingal* may come to represent a turning point in the history of customary family law in Papua New Guinea.

---

[42] For example, subsection (3) of section 55 states that the prohibition on discrimination contained in sub-section (1) 'does not affect the operation of a pre-Independence law'. See O.Jessep, note 38 above, at 38–39.

[43] On the difficulties inherent in any legislative attempt to ban or discourage polygamy, see O.Jessep, note 38 above, at 40–41.

POLAND

FAMILY AND CHILD IN THE LIGHT OF
THE NEW CONSTITUTION OF THE REPUBLIC OF POLAND

*Wanda Stojanowska**

Every constitutional legislator attaches much importance to the role of the family which is the natural environment for the birth and development of man, source of satisfaction of basic human needs and a significant element in an ordered society. Hence it is natural that the State is vitally interested in marriage and the family and particularly in the family fulfilment of its functions both towards society and individual family members. This interest of the State appears to be independent of particular socio-political systems as evidenced by comparing the new Constitution of Poland passed on April 2, 1997 with the former one of 1952 which – generally speaking – ensured due protection of the family. The new Constitution extends that protection either in its direct provisions or, indirectly, by its general objectives. It may be worth illustrating the foregoing opinion with the provisions of the new Constitution which create certain important rules of law. These include protection of the good of the child (Section 72), stability of marriage (Section 18), autonomy of the family in relation to society, the equal rights of spouses and parents (Section 32), family protection (Section 71), etc.

The 'rule of law' constitutes a certain, especially significant, directive which is of superior character in relation to other norms within a particular system of law. The constitutional rule of law expresses a certain value assumed by the legislator.[1]

The new Constitution includes principles directly referring to marriage and the family, privacy and autonomy. When evaluating and interpreting those norms we may also consider the preamble to the Constitution which to a certain extent indicates the axiological grounds for the constitutional principles.[2]

The new Constitution provides in Section 18 for a legal model of marriage which incorporates the principle that the spouses must be of the opposite sex. This means that marriage may be concluded exclusively by a man and woman, and that only such matrimony is protected by the State.[3]

Reference should also be made to common law marriage. People living in that kind of union do not enjoy the advantages of the legal status of matrimony – nevertheless that does not affect the legal relationship which they have with their common children. Although the common law union is not regulated by family law it may, however, give rise to legal effects in civil law relations.[4]

---

[*]   Institute of Justice, Warsaw. Judge of the Voivodeship Court in Warsaw. Translated by Hanna Wacinska.

[1]   Z. Ziembinski: *Constitutional Values. A Sketch on the Problem.* Warsaw, (1993) p. 55; W.J. Wolpiuk: *The Kind of Constitution against the background of Principles and Values.* [W:] Quality of law, Warsaw (1996), p. 98.

[2]   T. Smyczynski: *Family and Family Law in the light of the new Constitution,* 'State and Law', note-book 11–12, (1997), p. 187.

[3]   *Ibid.*

[4]   A. Szlezak: *Property Relations between Common Law Husband and Wife,* Poznan (1992), pp. 9–11.

Evidently, parenthood means both motherhood and fatherhood. In Section 18 of the Constitution, motherhood is mentioned along with parenthood and is protected jointly with marriage and the family. Section 71 para 2 of the Constitution provides for the particular protection of the mother by public authorities. In para 1 thereof this protection is guaranteed not only in relation to a regular family but also to single parent families.

Owing to the biological aspects of motherhood, a woman is given special protection under labour law and social regulations which implement the principles included in the Constitution.

Protection of motherhood in the Polish Constitution (Section 71 para 2) refers not only to the mother and her living child but also to a pregnant woman.

Neither the new Constitution, nor other laws, define what the family actually is. This may be gleaned by interpretation in the context of the whole legal system as it bears on family questions and, in particular, of those provisions included in the family law (Sections 23, 24, 27, 30) which imply that it is the nuclear family, resulting from marriage, that is under consideration.

The new Constitution in Sections 18 and 71, however, provides for family protection irrespective of whether a family is established within marriage, or whether it contains two parents or consists of one parent and children.

It is worth mentioning that Section 23 of the new Constitution stipulates that the family is the basis of a free society. Members of the family are thus given constitutional protection.

Questions relating to children are deserving of detailed provision in the new Constitution. It must be said the new Constitution provides for protection of the child's welfare much more widely and clearly than the former one.

The good of the family, as mentioned above, is provided for in Section 71. The recent legislators were not satisfied with that wording to the same extent as their predecessors were with the Constitution of 1952. Hence, in Section 72 para 1, it is expressly stressed that 'the Republic of Poland ensures protection of the child's rights. Everyone has the right to demand protection of the child by the public authorities against violence, abuse, unfair exploitation and moral danger'. It also declares in para 2 that 'any child deprived of parental care is entitled to the care and help of the public authorities'. Para 3 of the Section makes reference to Section 12 of the Convention on the Rights of the Child stipulating that in the course of the determination of the child's rights, public authorities and persons responsible for the child will be obliged to listen to and take into consideration the child's opinion.

In para 4 of Section 72, the new Constitution provides for the appointment of a Commissioner for the Protection of Children's Rights in order to safeguard the protection of the child's welfare and enforcement of his/her rights.[5]

Incorporation of the Convention on the Rights of the Child in the Polish system is effected by Section 91 para 1 of the new Constitution which stipulates that 'any ratified international agreement shall be part of the Polish legal system and be directly applied upon publication in the Journal of Laws of the Republic of Poland unless application thereof is subject to enactment of Law'. This view was expressed as early as June 12, 1992 by the Supreme Court of Justice by the decision of a panel of seven judges.[6]

---

[5] The institutional way of protecting the child's rights, suggested by the author see: W. Stojanowska: *The Protection of the Child against the Negative Effects of Conflict between Parents*, Warsaw (1997), pp. 117–118.

[6] III CZP 48/92, OSNCP 1992 No 10 item 179.

Parental autonomy in relation to their child's upbringing is provided for under Section 48 of the Constitution. This stipulates the following:

> '1. Parents have the right to bring up their child according to their own convictions. This upbringing must be appropriate to the stage of their child's development as well as his/her freedom of conscience and religion and also his/her convictions.
> 2. Limitation or deprivation of parental rights may take place in the circumstances determined by law and only by a legally valid court judgement.'

The purpose of this provision is to prevent indoctrination of children by the State against their parents' will and convictions.

This regard for the degree of the child's development complies with the laws of nature, i.e. with the natural growth of the child's autonomy, and parents are required to use methods of persuasion rather than those of repression in the process of upbringing. If the parents, however, come to the conclusion that their child's behaviour is contrary to his/her welfare (e.g. the child damages his/her health by taking drugs), they must take all necessary legal measures to counteract this threat to their child's welfare. They may also apply for help from the appropriate public institutions.[7]

This obligation of parents results from the fact that, in the final analysis, they have responsibility for their child until he/she comes of age, under state supervision, as the court may deprive them of their parental rights if necessary.

From the provisions of the Constitution under consideration we may observe the State's relationship to the family. The State supports the family in the fulfilment of its various functions but, by no means, does it act in place of the family or interfere in the sphere of family life without necessity.[8]

The new Constitution creates a democratic legal order including international Conventions which become a part thereof upon ratification (eg. the above-mentioned Convention on the Rights of the Child). The State's objectives include protection of the family against outside threats as well as protection of particular members of the family against the danger they may represent to one another. Particular protection must be ensured for the child if his/her welfare is threatened by his parents.[9]

Another kind of family protection is provided by Section 47 which ensures legal protection of private and family life for every citizen.

Every citizen has the right to refer directly to the Constitution as the fundamental Law, especially when it is necessary to support interpretation of other legislation.[10] Should any inconsistency arise between any legislative provision and the Constitution, it is for the Constitutional Tribunal to resolve it.

---

[7] T. Smyczynski: op cit., p. 193.
[8] Ibid.
[9] Ibid.
[10] Ibid.

RUSSIA

THREE YEARS AFTER THE ADOPTION OF THE NEW RUSSIAN FAMILY CODE

Olga Khazova[*]

Since the adoption of the new Russian Family Code[1] nearly three years have elapsed. This period is clearly not enough to see properly how the new law operates and what are the trends in judicial practice. Nevertheless the period is long enough to see the shortcomings of the new Code, or at least some of them, to see provisions in which the wording might be better, or, perhaps, should even be completely different. An attempt to improve those that relate to adoption procedure has already been made by the RF Parliament, and the amendments to the Code were enacted recently. As regards the others, in particular those that concern property relations between the spouses, establishment of paternity matters and those that concern surrogacy provisions – these are now being discussed among scholars and family lawyers and solutions are not so easy to find.

I   ADOPTION – AMENDMENTS TO THE NEW FAMILY CODE

One of the main innovations of the new Family Code in matters connected with the adoption of children left without parental care was the introduction of a judicial procedure for adoption instead of the former administrative one. This means that now, under the new law, to adopt a child it is necessary to get a court decision, and not merely a decision of an appropriate department of the Ministry of Education, as it was before. Corresponding amendments were made to the legislation on civil procedure six months after the adoption of the Family Code,[2] and now in the Code of Civil Procedure there is a special chapter devoted to adoption proceedings.[3]

Under the Family Code, Russian citizens have the advantage over foreigners in adopting Russian children. Section 124 (para 3) provides that intercountry adoption of Russian children is permitted only if there is no possibility of these children being adopted by the families of RF citizens, permanently residing on the RF territory, or by the relatives of the children, irrespective of the relatives' citizenship and their place of residence (domicile). Russian citizens whose domicile is outside the Russian federation, foreign citizens, and stateless persons who are not related to the children can adopt children upon the expiration of a three-month period from the day of centralized registration.

To make the search for children for adoption easier, to help adopters to find a child for adoption, and simultaneously to put the pre-judicial stage of adoption procedure under

---

[*]   Institute of State and Law, Russian Academy of Sciences, Moscow.

[1]   *Sobranije Zakonodatel'stva RF*, 1996, No. 1, it. 16.

[2]   Civil Procedure Code (Changes and Amendments) Law 1996 (August 21) – *Sobranije Zakonodatel'stva RF*, 1996, No. 35, it. 4134.

[3]   Chapter 29-1.

the proper control of competent authorities, the Family Code provided for the creation of a system of centralized registration of children without parental care at the local, regional and federal levels and formation of federal and regional data-banks of neglected children. The system was enacted in August 1996 by the Decree of the RF Government[4] which, among other provisions, contained those that defined the order of centralized registration of children without parental care. Administrative and criminal responsibility have also been established for illegal adoption; responsibility of the heads of children's homes and other special institutions for children left without parental care for failure to place the information about such children into the data-banks; for other actions violating the established order of adoption, and for criminal responsibility for the sale of children.

However, the new adoption procedure did not operate properly, especially in its pre-judicial aspect, and there appeared to be a lot of shortcomings in the new system of centralized registration of children without parental care. As a result Russian citizens, in contradistinction to foreigners, have nearly no access to the data-bank. During the 18 months in which the system has operated, there were only 138 applications by Russian citizens to the federal data-bank. In contrast there were 7454 applications by foreigners (mostly representatives of foreign adoption agencies). The situation can be explained in a number of ways, including the absence of an established order of access to these data, incompleteness of the information available through the bank, absence of necessary computer facilities in all regions, uncertainty concerning the relationship between the regional banks and the federal one and between the regional banks themselves, and by the fact that Russian citizens are not well informed about the existence of such a data-bank in general.

There was an urgent necessity to put the whole process of adoption in Russia into good order, taking into account the danger of commercialization of the adoption process in this country and the great number of violations of law that have already taken place in this field. With this aim in view, a set of legislative acts were adopted recently by the RF Parliament which introduced changes into the Family Code, the Civil Procedure Code, and the Administrative Offences Code.[5] The new laws, amongst others, have provided for the following.

Under the amendments to the Family Code, the order of registration of children left without parental care and their placement in families is now defined more clearly. The Law has stipulated that the formation and use of the State data-bank should be determined by the special federal law (work on which has already begun).

The Law forbids activity by intermediaries in the field of adoption, which is defined as any activity aiming to find children for adoption on behalf of and in the interests of people seeking to adopt a child (section 126-1). The activity of those bodies and organizations specially authorized by foreign States to act in the field of adoption, which is carried out on RF territory by virtue of an international agreement or on the principle of reciprocity, is not regarded by the Law as an intermediary activity. These bodies and organizations must not, however, pursue commercial purposes in their activity.

In accordance with the new provisions, prospective adopters are obliged to take part personally in court proceedings for adoption (section 125); under the previous law adoption cases were heard only with the participation of a custody and guardianship

---

[4]   RF Government Decree No. 919, August 3, 1996 – *Sobranije Zakonodatel'stva RF*, 1996, No. 33, it. 3995.

[5]   RF Family Code (Changes and Amendments) Law 1998 (June 27) – *Rossiiskaja Gazeta*, 01.07.98; RSFSR Civil Procedure Code (Changes and Amendments) Law 1998 (June 25) – *Rossiiskaja Gazeta*, 30.06.98, p. 4; RSFSR Administrative Offences Code (Changes and Amendments) Law 1998 (June 25) – *Rossiiskaja Gazeta*, 30.06.98, p. 4.

agency and a public prosecutor. The requirement for adopters to participate personally in adoption proceedings does not prevent them from being represented simultaneously by their legally authorized representative.

The new Law also provides that the parents' consent to adoption of their child may be given only after the birth of the child (section 129, para 3).

The Civil Procedure Code (Changes and Amendments) Law has changed the competence of Russian courts in matters connected with intercountry adoption – now they fall within the jurisdiction of the higher courts (supreme courts of Russian Federation subjects, i.e. republics, territories, autonomous regions), and not within the local courts, as it was before (section 263-1 of the Civil Procedure Code). In accordance with the new wording of section 263-3, before hearing a foreign adoption case, a custody and guardianship agency must present to the court, together with the other documents, a document which proves that the information about the child has been actually in the data-bank of children left without parental care, as well as the documents which prove the impossibility of placing the child in a Russian family.

As to the Law amending the Administrative Offences Code, it has raised the level of administrative fines for breach of the procedure of registration of children without parental care and for their placement in families, as well as for unlawful intermediate activity in the field of adoption. The federal officials who deal with registration of neglected children are now liable for any actions designed to prevent the children from being placed in a family (sections 193-1 and 193-2).

II MARITAL PROPERTY

Under the new Family Code, as it was before, the regime of common joint property is recognized in law. It means that in the absence of a marriage contract between the spouses it operates from the moment of conclusion of marriage.

Common joint property of the spouses (marital property for short) consists of the property acquired by the spouses during the marriage.[6] As to the personal property of each of the spouses, which they own separately, this consists of the property which belonged to each of them before marriage, as well as property acquired during the marriage as a gift, by inheritance, or through other uncompensated transactions.[7]

The wording of the corresponding section shows that the legislator tried to define the items of marital property and personal property as clearly as possible, aiming to avoid disputes and uncertainty in the future. However, it is already evident that there are provisions which can be interpreted differently, and there are different opinions among lawyers on these matters. In particular, a lot of questions arise in connection with income derived from the economic use of a spouse's personal property. Does this form part of the personal property of the spouses, or does it constitute part of spouses' common property? There is no clear answer to this question in the Code. Section 34 of the Code, which lists items of marital property, stipulates that 'wage and salary income, income from business (entrepreneurial activity) and income derived from intellectual activity' constitute marital property. This means that if a business asset, which was acquired by a spouse before marriage and which therefore falls within his personal property, brings in an income, this income will become spouses' joint property (if a marriage contract does not provide

---

[6] RF Family Code, section 34.

[7] Ibid., section 36.

otherwise). However, what regime will operate towards the income derived from securities or bank interest, if the securities or money deposited in a bank form part of the personal property of one of the spouses, since, for example, placing money at the bank could hardly be considered as entrepreneurial activity if the words are interpreted literally? There are no definite answers to these questions, and there could be different approaches to their resolution.[8]

A lot of questions will definitely arise in connection with division of marital property and, particularly, division of stocks and other securities. There is a lot of uncertainty with regard to the management of marital property. There are also no clear rules concerning the spouses' rights to plots of land. The list of such examples could be continued. Obviously, it will be the courts which will give answers to most of these questions, and the role of the judiciary will inevitably increase.

III   ESTABLISHMENT OF PATERNITY IN COURT

In accordance with the new Family Code, a court when considering a paternity case takes into account any evidence that may prove a child's filiation in relation to a particular person (section 49). If it is necessary to answer questions connected with a child's filiation a court may order genetic testing to be performed. Under the civil procedure rules,[9] genetic testing results are to be considered as just one of the pieces of evidence of a person's paternity presented to a court and are to be evaluated together with the other circumstances of the case. No evidence can be recognized in advance as established fact without being considered by a court.[10] In the present context this means, however, that if a court comes to a conclusion that a child's paternity is proved by DNA analysis, and consequently there is no doubt about who is the child's biological father, the court will make a positive paternity decision. Moreover, the court does not seem to be entitled to make a different decision, even if, in its opinion, it is not a proper conclusion, taking into account the other circumstances of the case.

No doubt, in the situation when there are no clear guidelines except genetic testing, it will be difficult for a court to solve complicated legal and psychological problems connected with paternity. If, for example, there are two persons claiming to be the legal father, one of whom is a biological father and another who has raised and maintained the child for years and treated the child as his own, what decision will a court make? What will be the court's answer if a biological father contests the paternity of the husband of a child's mother? Who will be recognized as the legal father in all these cases? Though such situations may be rare, and setting aside what might be a proper solution of these cases, the existence of a general rule which would give the court some space for manoevre is important in this connection. At present, except where a person's paternity is proved by genetic testing, Russian courts cannot make a choice in favour of 'social parentage', irrespective of the circumstances of a case and the child's interests, at least if they follow the literal interpretation of a corresponding section of the Family Code.

The child's best interests must be a decisive factor in the process of application of legal rules to real life situations, including paternity disputes. A priority for the defence of minor children's rights and interests is stipulated in the Family Code as one of the main

---

8   E.A. Chefranova, Imushchestvennye otnoshenija v Rossiiskoi semije. – Moscow. Jurist. 1997, p.20.

9   RSFSR Code of Civil Procedure, section 78.

10   Ibid., section 56 (para. 2).

principles of Russian family law.[11] Apart from this, there is the UN Convention on the Rights of the Child with its 'best interests of the child' principle which should be applied directly. Notwithstanding this, at present the section of the Family Code on judicial establishment of paternity is formulated in such a way that it leaves a court no flexibility for interpretation, which does not sit well with the UN Convention on the Rights of the Child. What should have been done with this provision of the Family Code to improve its wording? A few words on the child's best interests should have been added to it, the final wording of which would then be as follows: 'a court when considering a paternity case should take into account any evidence that proves the child's filiation to a particular person and should make a decision that is in the best interests of the child'.

IV SURROGACY PROVISIONS

From a legal and ethical point of view the practice of surrogate motherhood is complicated since it involves the splitting of genetic and physiological maternity (at least, when we speak about gestational surrogacy) and permits the carrying of a child 'on order' for a childless couple. In its regulation of surrogate motherhood, Russia has followed the European model, trying to avoid the problems of the 'Baby M. Case'. Under Russian family law, it is the surrogate mother who is treated in law as the mother, at least until she gives her consent to registration of a childless couple as the child's parents. It is the surrogate mother who has the right to decide whether to keep the child or not.

However, this is only one part of the problem. We have to decide as well whether free admission to artificial reproduction techniques for those who want them, should be permitted irrespective of marital status or, on the contrary, it is necessary to restrict it to the cases which are recommended for medical reasons. And how should we interpret these 'medical reasons'? Should we open new reproductive techniques to single women and to cohabiting couples? If 'yes', what should we do with same-sex couples? Of course, same-sex couples are not the main problem in Russia today. But they might become a problem quite soon, taking into account our rapid development in general, and the situation in Moscow in particular.

As to our legal rules in this connection they are unclear and controversial. On the one hand there is a new Family Code, stipulating that 'a married couple who have agreed to the implantation of an embryo in another woman (surrogate mother) can be registered as the child's parents only if the surrogate mother gives her consent to such a registration', and that 'a married couple who have agreed to the transfer of an embryo to another woman, as well as the surrogate mother, are not entitled to refer to these circumstances after the registration of the child's birth when contesting paternity or maternity'. Thus, in both cases reference is made to a married couple. On the other hand, there is another law, 'The Basic Principles of Russian Legislation on Protection of Citizens' Health', adopted two years earlier, in 1993, under which every woman has the right to benefit from treatment, to conceive a baby through methods of artificial procreation. So, there is a contradiction between our Family Law and the Law on Protection of Citizens' Health. As to the Family Code, the legislator's intention was not to open the new reproductive technologies to same-sex couples. However, the final wording turned out to be far from the best.

---

[11] Section 1, para.3.

In fact, the question whether we should permit same-sex couples to have access to the artificial reproduction technologies is the crucial point in defining family policy. It will have more far-reaching consequences than, perhaps, even the introduction of the institution of registered partnership. A lot will depend on whether or not the law ignores the same-sex phenomenon and the desire of such couples to have babies, and prevents (or not) the application of artificial reproduction techniques to same-sex couples. Obviously, we are on the eve of great changes in family forms, taking into account the recent advancements in biology, especially cloning. How far is it in our power to stop these changes? I am afraid that we will just postpone the making of a final decision.

There is another set of problems in connection with surrogacy that we also need to solve. At present there are no provisions in our law, except those I have already mentioned, which would define the relations between the childless couple and the surrogate mother. There are no clear rules that would provide the answer to the question what we should do with the paternity presumption, if a surrogate mother is married. There are no rules which would provide the answer to a more difficult question – whether surrogate motherhood on a commercial basis is permitted or prohibited. Generally speaking, there is no special prohibition in our civil and criminal law – this means that surrogacy contracts may be concluded in Russia. If we go further, given the legality of such contracts, we ought to define the main terms of surrogacy contracts and the rights and duties of those involved in the process. Finally, we should decide whether we admit the activities of special agencies dealing with surrogacy arrangements or, on the contrary, prohibit such activities.

Whether we want it or not, and depending on our attitude, we shall have to make proper provision in law. Taking into account the economic and social situation in this country, the great number of childless couples all over the world, and our sad experience in the field of intercountry adoption, we should be aware of the real danger of unregulated surrogacy practices, commercialization of surrogate motherhood and the sale of children born through artificial reproduction. These domestic difficulties will be compounded by international surrogacy.

SCOTLAND

CONSOLIDATION AND ANTICIPATION

Elaine E. Sutherland[*]

I   INTRODUCTION

The most significant legal developments for Scots family law in 1998 will probably prove to be the passing of two statutes which make no specific mention of family law at all – the Scotland Act 1998 and the Human Rights Act 1998. The Scotland Act 1998 brings a type of federalism to the UK with the creation of a Scottish Parliament, sitting in Edinburgh. While the UK Parliament will continue to sit at Westminster, complete with representatives of Scottish constituencies, its jurisdiction to legislate for Scotland will be confined to 'reserved matters'.[1] All other matters will be the province of the Scottish Parliament and most legislation in the family law area will fall into this category.[2] Thus, the future of Scots family law lies with the Scottish Parliament.

What difference will this make? First, and most obviously, this should result in family legislation which is tailor-made to the needs of the Scottish people.[3] Of course, views about the functions and goals of family law are no more homogenous in Scotland than in any other jurisdiction and it is expected that rigorous debate will be a feature of any reform. The second anticipated effect of devolution relates to parliamentary time. Regular readers of the *International Survey* will be familiar with the complaint that insufficient time has been found at Westminster for reform of Scots family law.[4] This should cease to be a problem once there is a legislature devoted wholly to legislation for Scotland. It is hoped that one result will be that the excellent proposals for reform of aspects of family law contained in the Scottish Law Commission's *Report on Family*

---

[*]   Senior Lecturer, School of Law, University of Glasgow and Professor, Lewis and Clark School of Law, Portland, Oregon.

[1]   Scotland Act 1998, sections 29 and 30 and Schedule 5.

[2]   There are exceptions here and, for example, the provision of State benefits will continue to be determined from Westminster. Abortion, unlike most other health matters, will not be devolved to the Scottish Parliament and, arguably, the real reason for the UK Parliament retaining control of abortion lies in the strength of the anti-abortion lobby in parts of Scotland and a desire to avoid the unseemly future prospect of a trail of pregnant women heading over the border to England in pursuit of terminations.

[3]   This is not to suggest that legislation on family law was unsuited to the needs of the Scottish people in the past, simply because it was passed at Westminster. Most legislation in this area applied to Scotland only and, over the last quarter of a century, much of it has been a product of the Scottish Law Commission.

[4]   Whereas the concept of no-fault divorce was introduced in England and Wales by the Divorce Reform Act 1969, it was not until the Divorce (Scotland) Act 1976 that similar provision was made for Scotland. Reform of child law in England and Wales was effected by the Children Act 1989, with the relevant Scottish legislation being the Children (Scotland) Act 1995 and parliamentary time was only found for the latter when it became clear that the then government's plans for water privatisation in Scotland would not succeed. It should be noted that, in both cases, the legislation is not in identical terms.

Law[5] will finally find their way into legislation.[6] Perhaps the real question is whether the Scottish Parliament will produce 'better' family law than has been the case henceforth. Undoubtedly, enormous hopes attach to the new arrangements and there are opportunities to change the whole way we approach legislation.[7] Whether any difference will result will depend on a whole host of factors, including the calibre of the representatives elected. Certainly, there is no reason to suppose that Members of the Scottish Parliament will necessarily prove any more or less 'enlightened' (whatever that means) than their counterparts at Westminster.

Essentially, the Human Rights Act 1998 incorporates the European Convention on Human Rights into the law of the UK. It should be remembered that the Convention has always been relevant to Scots law. Where any provision of domestic law is ambiguous, it will be interpreted by the courts in a manner which will ensure compliance with the UK's international obligations.[8] Thus, in cases of ambiguity, the interpretation favouring the Convention would often prevail. That was no help, of course, where the domestic provision was unambiguously inconsistent with the Convention or, indeed, any other international instrument. Certainly, Scotland has provided its share of cases going to the European Court of Human Rights.[9] The passing of the Human Rights Act 1998 will make a difference on three levels. First, proposed legislation will be subject to pre-scrutiny. Where it is being introduced at Westminster, any incompatibility with the Convention must be declared.[10] In Scotland, the Parliament will be unable to legislate in a manner inconsistent with the Convention.[11] Secondly, the courts will be able to issue a 'declaration of incompatibility'[12] in respect of Westminster legislation, while Acts of the Scottish Parliament will be declared unlawful if they are inconsistent with the provisions of the Convention.[13] Thirdly, acts of public authorities may be challenged and declared unlawful where they violate the Convention.[14] In short, no lawyer's education will be complete without a thorough understanding of the European Convention.

For the present, we return to reviewing developments in Scots family law over the last two years. Discussion will concentrate on two broad themes – ante-natal issues and adult relationships. For once, child law will not feature and the decision to omit it is, in part, an attempt to redress the balance in reporting on Scottish family law developments. The, very considerable, reform of child law over the past few years has meant that much of the recent entries from the present contributor has been devoted to the subject. Furthermore, while the Children (Scotland) Act 1995 appears to be operating well, it is

---

[5]   Scot. Law Com. No. 135, 1992.

[6]   Such has been the delay that the Scottish Office has taken the opportunity to produce a further consultation paper, *Improving Scottish Family Law* (March 1999), seeking current views on these and other possible reforms.

[7]   For an excellent discussion of how the Scottish Parliament might approach legislation, see E.M. Clive, 'Lawmaking in Scotland: From A.P.S. to A.S.P.' (1999) 3 *E.L.R.* 131. This fascinating title may need some explanation for readers outside Scotland. 'A.P.S.' is the abbreviation for the Acts of the Parliament of Scotland which was dissolved on March 25, 1707 when the Parliaments of Scotland and England united. 'A.S.P.' indicates legislation to be passed by the new Scottish Parliament.

[8]   *T, Petitioner* 1997 S.L.T 724.

[9]   See, for example, *Campbell v Cosans v UK* [1982] 4 E.H.R.R. 293 (the parental right to prohibit corporal punishment in schools) and *McMichael v UK* [1995] 20 E.H.R.R. 205 (child protection procedures and parental rights). The fact that Scotland was a source of such cases is hardly a matter for national pride.

[10] Human Rights Act 1998, section 19.

[11] Scotland Act 1998, section 35.

[12] Human Rights Act 1998, section 4.

[13] Scotland Act 1998, section 29.

[14] Human Rights Act 1998, section 6.

still 'bedding down' and it would be premature to attempt an in-depth analysis of it at this time. That is a task which will be undertaken in the future.

II   ANTE-NATAL ISSUES

A   Abortion

Legal abortion has been available throughout the UK, in certain circumstances, since the passing of the Abortion Act in 1967.[15] It was well established in other jurisdictions,[16] that the pregnant woman's partner has no standing to prevent her going ahead with a termination and commentators were confident that this was the position in Scotland, albeit the matter had not been litigated here. Consequently, a shudder ran through the legal community or, at least, sections of it, when a Mr. Kelly sought interdict to prevent his estranged wife having a termination.[17] Given the clear indications from elsewhere that he had no standing, *qua* husband, to achieve his goal, his case was argued on a different, rather ingenious, basis. For Mr. Kelly it was argued that a child can claim damages for ante-natal injury, that such claims could be made by the child's guardian, that interdict was competent to prevent a wrong occurring, and that he was therefore entitled to seek interdict to prevent this particular wrong (as the potential child's guardian). The Second Division rejected his claim on the basis that, while a living child had a right of action in respect of injuries sustained in the womb, the foetus has no legal *persona* and, thus, can have no rights which are capable of being protected by interdict. In particular, the Court took the view that Scots law confers no right on the foetus to a continued existence in the womb, since such a right would conflict with the woman's right to seek a termination under the 1967 Act. The position of at least one Scottish court in the 'foetal rights v women's rights' debate seems clear and refreshingly insightful. In passing, it should be noted that an aggrieved husband, like Mr. Kelly, would almost certainly have an action for divorce on the basis that his wife's behaviour, in having a termination against his wishes, made it unreasonable to expect him to continue to live with her.[18]

B   Wrongful birth

Regular readers of the *International Survey* will recall the surprising decision, at first instance, in *McFarlane v Tayside Health Board*.[19] The case involved a failed vasectomy and the couple involved being advised that the operation had been a success and that they need no longer use contraception. When the wife subsequently gave birth to a healthy

---

[15]   Prior to the Act, procuring an abortion was an offence, subject to the defence that it was necessary to save the life or preserve the health of the pregnant woman; G.H. Gordon, *The Criminal Law of Scotland* (W. Green, 1978), at paras 28-01-28-04.

[16]   See, for example, *Paton v Trustees of the British Pregnancy Advisory Service* [1979] Q.B. 276, where a husband in England was unsuccessful in seeking an injunction to prevent his wife from having an abortion. He also failed in his claim that his rights under Article 8 (respect for family life) of the European Convention on Human Rights and Fundamental Freedoms had been violated; *Paton v United Kingdom* (1980) 3 E.H.R.R. 408. See also *Tremblay v Daigle* (1989) 62 D.L.R. (4th) 634 (Canada).

[17]   *Kelly v Kelly* 1997 S.L.T. 896. While the couple had separated by the time the action was raised, it was not disputed that the pregnancy had resulted from relations between them.

[18]   Divorce (Scotland) Act 1976, section 1(2)(b).

[19]   1996 S.L.T. 211. The decision of the Outer House of the Court of Session is discussed more fully in E.E. Sutherland, 'From Birth to Death' 1996 *International Survey of Family Law* at 384–386.

daughter, the couple sought to recover damages for the wife's pain, suffering and distress, her loss of earnings, the cost of moving to a larger house and the cost of raising the child. In a decision which astounded commentators, who had predicted confidently that the Scottish courts would take the approach arrived at eventually elsewhere, their action failed. The Lord Ordinary rejected their claim on the basis that pregnancy was not a form of personal injury; that the benefits of a child outweighed the costs involved (the 'joys and blessings' argument); and that, were he wrong on these points, the case would still fail on the issue of causation.

Prior to the appeal in *McFarlane* being heard by the Inner House of the Court of Session, another case, presenting rather different circumstances, was heard in the Outer House. In *Anderson v Forth Valley Health Board*,[20] the pursuers, a married couple, had two sons. When the elder boy was about four years old, it was discovered that he suffered from a form of Duschene muscular dystrophy, a genetically transmitted condition which affects only males, but can be passed on through the female line. Further tests revealed that the younger boy also suffered from the condition. The parents raised an action against the health board alleging that, on the basis of information about her family history disclosed by the wife, they ought to have been referred for genetic counselling. Had this been done, they alleged that they would have opted to have only female children and, thus, have avoided giving birth to two children suffering from Duschene muscular dystrophy. They sought damages for anxiety, upset and distress, caused by the birth of their two children, and for the patrimonial loss caused by the wife having to give up work to look after the children and the husband being unable to work overtime as a result of the additional child care responsibilities involved in looking after the boys. Allowing a proof before answer, the Court rejected the 'joys and blessings' argument in the following terms:

> 'The birth and upbringing of a child no doubt bring both advantages and disadvantages, both happiness and distress; and most people most of the time would regard the former as outweighing the latter. But it seems to me to be a question of fact and degree in the circumstances of any particular case where the balance rests. It may be regarded as being within the range of reasonable responses to the birth of a child that in one case his parents may accept it as an unmixed blessing ... while in another it is seen as nothing less than an unmitigated disaster.'[21]

It was in the context of these widely divergent views from the lower courts that the Inner House heard the appeal in *McFarlane* and was able to reach unanimity in overturning the Lord Ordinary's decision.[22] Turning first to Ms. McFarlane's claim in respect of the pregnancy, the Court took the view that it was unnecessary to categorise it as personal injury since it constituted 'manifestations of *damnum* to an interest'.[23] On the issue of the cost of raising the child, the Court noted the parental obligation to do so. Finally, on the issue of children as an unmitigated blessing, the Court gave what can be regarded for the time being, at least, as the definitive view, in the following words:

> 'The proposition that the blessing of a child is an overriding benefit is one-sided. It ignores the fact that couples such as the pursuers can and do seek sterilisation and

---

[20]   1998 S.L.T. 588.

[21]   Ibid, at 605D–E.

[22]   1998 S.C. 389.

[23]   Ibid, at 393B–394B.

rely on its effectiveness precisely in order to avoid the additional expenditure which the birth of another child will entail.'[24]

Thus, the position in Scotland at present is that, while children may be a blessing, that blessing is not necessarily unmitigated. Consequently, where the parents have sought to avoid the child's conception and there has been negligence on the part of health care professionals resulting in the birth of a child, the health board responsible for the professionals will be liable. This is so regardless of the fact that the resulting child is healthy. In addition, it should be noted that the health board may be liable in a second situation. Where a child is born with disabilities that could have been foreseen in the circumstances, and the parents were not warned, they have an action in delict (= tort) against whoever failed to inform them of the risk, their measure of damages being the additional cost of raising the child.[25] Cases here include both pre-conception harm, for example, negligent screening of the parents who then pass a genetic condition on to the child, and negligence that occurs post-conception, for example, a failure to diagnose the pregnant woman as having been infected with rubella (German measles). Essentially, by not being informed of the likely dangers, the pregnant woman (and to some extent her partner) has been deprived of the opportunity to seek a termination.

III   ADULT RELATIONSHIPS

How adults in Scotland organise or, often, fail to organise, their personal relationships today does not differ from developments in many other post-industrial western societies. Thus, in 1997, the latest year for which statistics are available, the number of marriages celebrated reached an all-time low[26] and the number of divorces, while down slightly on the previous year, continued the general trend over the recent past.[27] Nonetheless, marriage remains an important form of adult relationship and has significant legal consequences, particularly in the context of property. Spouses gain a right to live in the family home on marriage, irrespective of which of them owns or rents the home and, in certain circumstances, can have a violent partner ordered out by the court.[28] Spouses are obliged to support one another during the marriage.[29] On divorce, a whole system of regulation kicks in if the parties are unable to resolve disputes over property.[30] Heterosexual cohabitation remains popular, either as an alternative or as a prelude to marriage, and the legal system accords limited recognition to such relationships. On the one hand, the right to live in the family home and have a violent partner excluded is available to such cohabitants, albeit in more limited circumstances.[31] On the other hand,

---

[24]   Ibid, at 395I–396A.

[25]   In *McLelland v Greater Glasgow Health Board*, unreported, September 24, 1998, available on Lexis, the health care professionals were aware that there was a history of Down's Syndrome in the mother's family. Despite this, they failed to diagnose the condition in the foetus she was carrying. When the parents sued the hospital board after she gave birth to a son with Down's Syndrome, liability was not denied and the case was disputed only on the issue of damages.

[26]   In 1997, there were 29,611 marriages; *Registrar General's Annual Report 1998* (General Register Office for Scotland, 1998), Table 7.1. This figure should be understood in the context of a country with a population of about 5 million.

[27]   12,222 decrees of divorce were granted in 1997; *Registrar General's Annual Report 1998*, Table 8.1.

[28]   Matrimonial Homes (Family Protection) (Scotland) Act 1981.

[29]   Family Law (Scotland) Act 1985, section 1.

[30]   Divorce (Scotland) Act 1985, sections 8–16.

[31]   Matrimonial Homes (Family Protection) (Scotland) Act 1981, section 18.

cohabitants are not obliged to support one another financially and, should they separate, no special regime applies to resolving property disputes. Since marriage is not available to same-sex couples,[32] and Scotland has no concept of the registered partnership, as an alternative method of recognising personal relationships, same-sex couples gain virtually no acknowledgement from the legal system.

In terms of what people choose to do, diversity is the order of the day, but the legal system has been slow to respond to this diversity. As long ago as 1992, the Scottish Law Commission proposed modest law reform designed to give slightly more recognition to heterosexual cohabitation but made no proposals in respect of same-sex couples. As we have seen, given the lapse of time and the inertia that followed, it has been felt necessary to re-examine these proposals.[33] When a relationship sours, problems arise in two distinct contexts – children and property. It should be noted that, as far as the future arrangements for the care of children are concerned, the legal system is there for all children and is capable of stepping in, irrespective of the marital status or sexual preference of the adults involved.[34] However, when we turn to property, we find that unmarried couples are poorly served and are thrown on the general provisions of the law when disputes arise. Presently, we will examine how the general law can help, before considering how the regime for financial provision on divorce is working. First, however, we will consider the ancient concept of marriage by cohabitation with habit and repute, since it has sometimes been used as a mechanism for obtaining relief in this context.

A   Common law marriage – Marriage by cohabitation with habit and repute

Marriage by cohabitation with habit and repute is the only remaining valid form of irregular marriage (i.e. marriage without complying with the statutory formalities[35]) in Scotland. It probably has its roots in pre-tridentine canon law and was later acknowledged by a 1503 statute dealing with widows' succession rights. Whether it was simply a method of *proving* that consent to marriage had been exchanged or developed into a method of *constituting* marriage has been the subject of considerable debate.[36] While it is often helpful to seek declarator of marriage from the courts, such a declarator is simply confirmation that the marriage exists and not something which creates it, a point best illustrated by the fact that many declarators are granted after the death of one of the spouses. Establishing a date on which such a marriage was constituted caused some problems in the past and the difficulty was largely remedied by the 1977 Act,[37] which provides for registration of the marriage.[38]

For a valid marriage by cohabitation with habit and repute to exist, the couple must have lived together in Scotland as husband and wife for a sufficiently long time and have

---

[32]   Marriage (Scotland) Act 1977, section 5(4)(e).

[33]   See note 6 (above).

[34]   Children (Scotland) Act 1995.

[35]   Marriage (Scotland) Act 1977.

[36]   See E.M. Clive, *The Law of Husband and Wife in Scotland* (4th ed, 1997, W. Green), paras 05.022–05.027; D.I.C. Ashton-Cross, 'Cohabitation with Habit and Repute' 1961 *J.R.* 21; D.P. Sellar, 'Marriage by cohabitation with habit and repute: review and requiem?' in D. Carey Miller and D. Meyers, *Comparative and Historical Essays in Scots Law* (1992).

[37]   See Clive (above), paras 05.040–05.048 for a discussion of the problem and the solution.

[38]   Marriage (Scotland) Act 1977, section 21. Where a decree of declarator of marriage has been granted, the Principal Clerk of Session transmits the relevant particulars to the Registrar General who arranges for the marriage to be registered.

been generally regarded by those who knew them as a married couple. Instantly, two things are apparent. First, the definition is flexible and vague, and this probably explains its popularity with academics and law students. The result has been that the concept has been stretched by the courts in individual cases. Only periods of cohabitation when the couple were free to marry can be taken into account and, while a period of years was required at one time,[39] more recently the courts have granted declarator on the basis of a few months, provided that the requisite repute could be established.[40] It was always the case that 'although repute need not be universal it must be general, substantially unvarying and consistent and not divided'.[41] Certainly, it is not fatal that some people knew the couple were not married, even where those individuals are relatives.[42] It might be thought that, where the couple planned to have a wedding, they are indicating that they do not regard themselves as married, but the courts have not always taken this approach.[43]

Secondly, the concept is inapplicable to people who live together in the thoroughly modern form of relationship; what might be described as 'open cohabitation'. For this reason, declarator of marriage, in this context, is very rare and is usually sought where one of the parties has died and the survivor is seeking to establish rights of succession. The Scottish Law Commission has recommended the prospective abolition of this kind of marriage, not least because of the uncertainty surrounding the concept and the fact that it puts a premium on deception.[44] However, this recommendation should be read along with the Commission's other recommendations on void marriages and the rights of cohabitants, since they form part of an inter-related package.

In *Walker v Roberts*[45] the courts had the opportunity to consider the concept again. Here both parties were alive and it was being used, by Mr. Walker, as a means of resolving a dispute over property. Discounting the time when he was married, and one year when they lived together abroad, the period of cohabitation taken into account was about five years. While Ms Roberts sometimes helped to serve in Mr. Walker's bar and some of the customers thought they were married, she had not given this impression to her colleagues at work. Relatives were divided on the question of repute. The court was influenced by the fact that the parties had separate bank accounts and acquired property individually and that Ms Roberts had not changed her name, although these factors are present in many regular marriages in Scotland today. In addition, it appears that the couple had initially indicated that they were opposed to marriage and, latterly, had contemplated marrying in the future. As a result, the court held that Mr. Walker had failed to establish a marriage by cohabitation with habit and repute. Given the indulgence shown by earlier courts, not only in respect of short periods of cohabitation, but of

---

[39] *Mackenzie v Mackenzie* March 8, 1810 F.C. (10 years was enough); *Campbell v Campbell* (1866) 4 M 867 (views expressed that three years would probably be enough but one year would not).

[40] *Shaw v Henderson* 1982 S.L.T. 211 (11 months sufficient); *Mullen v Mullen* 1991 S.L.T. 205 (six months enough); *Kamperman v McIver* 1994 S.L.T. 763 (six months not 'necessarily insufficient').

[41] *Low v Gorman* 1970 S.L.T. 356, at 359.

[42] *Shaw v Henderson* (above); *Donnelly v Donnelly's Executor* 1992 S.L.T. 13; *Gow v Lord Advocate* 1993 S.L.T. 275. It is worth remembering that family members may have a pecuniary interest in disputing the marriage of a deceased relative.

[43] *Mackenzie v Scott* 1980 S.L.T. (Notes) 9 (couple had discussed getting married, declarator refused); *Shaw v Henderson* (above) (couple had made arrangements for a wedding, declarator granted); *Dewar v Dewar* 1995 S.L.T. 457 (couple had discussed formal ceremony, declarator granted).

[44] *Report on Family Law*, paras 7.1–7.13 and Rec.42. The Commission emphasised that a marriage contracted prior to any legislation implementing its abolition should be valid, whether or not declarator had already been sought.

[45] 1998 S.L.T. 1133.

divided repute, it may be that this case simply illustrates a court which was faced with an attempt to stretch the concept too far. However, one wonders to what extent it was influenced by the fact that Mr. Walker, whom the court had found to be neither reliable nor credible, was seeking not only to establish a marriage but to move on swiftly to divorce and financial provision. A grieving 'widower' seeking succession rights inevitably elicits greater sympathy than a spurned lover seeking financial advantage. Certainly, it does appear that this is not a way for cohabiting couples to resolve property disputes, save in the most exceptional of cases.

B   Cohabitation proper

What of the couple who have lived together, quite openly, without any pretence that they are married? How can they resolve property disputes? Clearly, the routes of negotiation and mediation, which are open to married couples, are also available to them. Usually, avoiding the acrimony and cost of litigation is to be recommended, particularly where the couple will have to co-operate over future arrangements for children. However, confrontation cannot always be averted and *Shilliday v Smith*[46] provides a rare example of a cohabitant finding assistance from the provisions of the general law. There, Ms Shilliday moved into her fiancé's home which was in need of considerable renovation. She contributed some £10,000 towards the renovation project and, after it was completed, he terminated their relationship and evicted her. She sought to recover the money on the basis that the payments were made because the couple were planning to marry and that they would not have been made had matrimony not been in prospect. General principles of unjust enrichment were applied and she succeeded. While that case helped one former cohabitant to achieve what many would regard as substantial justice, the limits of applying unjust enrichment should be noted. Ms Shilliday was only successful because she could demonstrate that the payments were made in contemplation of marriage. Had she simply been cohabiting with Mr. Smith, her generosity would have been regarded as just that, and recovery would not have been possible. Other concepts which might be employed by an aggrieved former cohabitant include agency, implied contract[47] or implied trusts,[48] but each would involve extensive examination of the relationship and could prove something of a blunt instrument in resolving disputes over what would sometimes be comparatively small sums of money.

Thus, cohabitants should consider other ways of protecting their interests and one possibility is a cohabitation contract, a solution which has gained popularity in other jurisdictions but is not without problems.[49] In Scotland, it has been suggested that such a

---

[46]   1998 S.L.T. 976.

[47]   Some US courts have accepted the use of implied contracts in this context, at least in principle: *Beal v Beal* 4 *Family Law Reporter* 2462 (Ore., 1978); *Watts v Watts* 13 *Family Law* 1367 (Wis., 1987). Others have rejected it: *Morone v Morone* 413 N.E. 2d 1154 (NY, 1980), where the court described the implied contract theory as 'conceptually so amorphous as practically to defy equitable enforcement'.

[48]   See, K.McK. Norrie, 'Proprietary Rights of Cohabitants' 1995 *J.R.* 209 for an excellent discussion of why the law of trusts could be used more effectively.

[49]   This issue came to the fore in the USA in a long-running battle between the actor Lee Marvin and his former cohabitant Michelle Triola Marvin. The cases are usually cited as follows: *Marvin I* 557 P. 2d 106 (Cal. 1976), *Marvin II* 5 Fam. L. Rep. (1979) and *Marvin III* 179 Cal. Rptr. 555 (Cal. Ct. App. 1981). The issue of inequality of bargaining power sometimes arises in such cases. See, for example, *DeLorean v DeLorean* 511 A. 2d. 1257 (N.J., 1986) (23-year-old wife with limited business experience and 48-year-old husband who was a senior executive with a large commercial organisation) and *Simeone v Simeone* 525 A. 2d. 162 (Pa., 1990) (wife was a 23-year-old unemployed nurse and husband was a 39-year-old neurosurgeon).

contract might be struck down as illegal and unenforceable on public policy grounds because its object was 'the furtherance of illicit sexual intercourse'.[50] However, as the Scottish Law Commission pointed out when it examined the issue,[51] the cases supporting such a view of cohabitation contracts date from the nineteenth century or earlier and it is to be hoped that such a view would not be taken today. Further support for the validity of cohabitation agreements can be found in the fact that the law already recognises cohabitation for a variety of purposes, the changed nature and increased incidence of cohabitation itself and the recommendation of the Committee of Ministers of the Council of Europe that such agreements should be upheld.[52] Thus, it is less likely that cohabitation agreements would be struck down by the courts. Nonetheless, the Commission felt that it would be wise to put the matter beyond doubt and recommended that legislation should provide:

> 'A contract shall not be void or unenforceable solely because it is a contract between cohabitants or between prospective cohabitants who entered into the contract in contemplation of cohabiting with each other.'[53]

Whatever the present or future validity of cohabitation contracts, the point is that most couples will simply not be sufficiently organised to make them. It is axiomatic that people often do little to make prudent arrangements in respect of personal relationships while all is going well. Once the relationship begins to sour, it is too late.

Of course, some couples do not marry because they are rejecting the concept of marriage and all its attendant consequences quite expressly. In such cases, imposing a marriage-like regime on them would deny them freedom of choice. However, cohabitation is often a product of inertia and, in any event, many couples will not understand the legal implications. Arguably, the legal system is abdicating its responsibility in simply leaving such cohabitants to their own devices. The Scottish Law Commission sought to steer a middle course here. It recommended that the courts should have the power to order financial provision on the termination of the relationship but only in respect of economic advantages and disadvantages resulting from the relationship.[54] With hindsight, it may be that this recommendation does not go far enough and, certainly, the opportunity is there for the Scottish Parliament to adopt a more radical approach. Whether it will do so is, at best, doubtful.

C   *Financial provision on divorce*

Scots law on financial provision on divorce has remained relatively settled since the passing of the Family Law Act 1985 and the cases have been devoted to working through some of the provisions of the Act.[55] Briefly,[56] either spouse may apply to the court for

---

50   W.M. Gloag, *Law of Contract* (2nd ed, 1929, W. Green) at 562.
51   *The Effects of Cohabitation in Private Law* (Scot. Law Com., Discussion Paper No.86, 1990), para. 9.1; *Report on Family Law*, para. 16.46.
52   On March 7, 1988, the Committee recommended that member states should take steps along the lines ultimately recommended by the Commission; R(88)3.
53   *Report on Family Law*, Recommendation 87.
54   Ibid, Recommendation 82. This recommendation was preceded by a process of consultation. See *The Effects of Cohabitation in Private Law* (Scot. Law Com. Discussion Paper No. 86, 1990).
55   See, for example, *Fulton v Fulton* 1998 GWD 15-768 and *Bye v Bye* 1998 GWD 32-1668.

financial provision on divorce and the general guidance given to the court is to make such orders as are *both* justified by the five principles set out in the Act *and* reasonable having regard to the resources of the parties.[57] The principles are as follows: the net value of the matrimonial property should be shared fairly between the parties to the marriage; fair account should be taken of any economic advantage derived by either party from contributions by the other, and of any economic disadvantage suffered by either party in the interests of the other party or of the family; any economic burden of caring, after divorce, for a child of the marriage under the age of 16 years should be shared fairly between the parties; a party who has been dependent to a substantial degree on the financial support of the other party should be awarded such financial provision as is reasonable to enable him to adjust, over a period of not more than three years from the date of the decree of divorce, to the loss of that support on divorce; and a party who at the time of the divorce seems likely to suffer serious financial hardship as a result of the divorce should be awarded such financial provision as is reasonable to relieve him of hardship over a reasonable period.[58]

In *Dougan v Dougan*,[59] the court had its first opportunity to consider the issue of a pre-marital sacrifice. There, the woman had taken a demotion in her company in order to relocate to be with her fiancé. When the marriage foundered, she sought a financial adjustment to take account of her loss of career position and the court, quite correctly, had no hesitation in building this into its package of financial provision in the divorce.

One problem relates to property acquired by way of gift or succession from a third party. It is expressly excluded from the definition of matrimonial property.[60] Thus, if a wife inherits a large sum of money and puts it in the bank, the money is not subject to division in any subsequent divorce, albeit it will be taken into account as part of her overall resources. However, if she converts the money into some other kind of property, like a house, the house does become matrimonial property and is subject to division,[61] although the court can take account of the source of the funds used to purchase the property.[62] Reference to 'wise and foolish virgins' is tempting, if not wholly appropriate, here. Another difficulty can arise over property acquired prior to marriage which increases dramatically in value during the marriage. Again, pre-marital property is largely excluded from the definition of matrimonial property[63] and, again, it is not subject to division. As things stand, the increased value of such property remains with the owner.

The courts themselves have sometimes worked through apparent injustices resulting from earlier decisions under the Act. For the purpose of division, property is valued at the 'relevant date' (i.e. the date of separation or service of the divorce summons, whichever is earlier[64]) and the problem is exemplified by *Wallis v Wallis*,[65] a case which generated

---

[56] For a full discussion of financial provision on divorce, see E.M. Clive, *The Law of Husband and Wife in Scotland* (4th. ed, 1997, W. Green), chapter 24 and E.E. Sutherland, *Child and Family Law* (T. & T. Clark, 1999), chapter 14.

[57] Family Law (Scotland) Act 1985, section 8(2).

[58] 1985 Act, section 9(1).

[59] 1998 S.L.T. (Sh. Ct.) 27. That decision was affirmed on appeal and a further appeal is pending.

[60] 1985 Act, section 10(4).

[61] *Latter v Latter* 1990 S.L.T. 805.

[62] 1985 Act, section 10(6)(b).

[63] 1995 Act, section 10(4). An exception covers property acquired prior to the marriage for use as a matrimonial home or furniture for such a home.

[64] 1985 Act, section 10(3).

[65] 1992 S.L.T. 676 (IH), 1993 S.L.T. 1348 (HL).

considerable academic debate.[66] There, the couple co-owned a house and it increased in value very substantially between separation and the case being heard. The husband sought an order transferring his wife's share of the home to him. The Inner House and the House of Lords rejected the sheriff's solution in granting the order, and making an adjustment of capital payable to the wife to take account of the increase in value, since valuation was tied to the date of separation. Effectively, the husband reaped the benefit of the increase in value. The solution found in a later case was to refuse to transfer the property and, instead, to grant an incidental order for division and sale, thus enabling both spouses to share in the increase in value.[67] This might not suit a spouse, like Mr. Wallis, who wanted to remain in the home. However, if threatened with sale, such an individual would then have had every incentive to negotiate a fair price for the transfer.

These occasional problems suggest that minor refinements to the 1985 Act may be warranted. However, the overall verdict on the Act is very positive. It does appear to provide the courts with a principled approach to financial provision on divorce and sufficient flexibility to meet most cases.[68] In addition, the clarity of the system enables practitioners to advise clients on what is a reasonable settlement to agree, thus avoiding much costly and acrimonious litigation.[69] For couples who are initially disinclined to reach agreement, the increased use of mediation can often help them resolve their disputes without resort to the courts. If we can provide this sort of comprehensive system for married couples, with a little imagination, we can do the same for cohabitants.

IV CONCLUSIONS

1998 has been a year of consolidation and, to some extent, marking time, in anticipation of the Scottish Parliament. Case-law, most notably in the areas of abortion and ante-natal injury, simply confirmed what many commentators predicted would happen once the courts had the opportunity to consider issues which had already been resolved in other jurisdictions. However, this confirmation should not be seen as some kind of negative reinvention of the wheel. Decisions in Scotland must be based on Scots law which, ideally, should be a reflection of the will of the Scottish people. While much can be learned from solutions found elsewhere, these solutions must be examined in the domestic context in order to establish whether they are, indeed, appropriate here. It was entirely fitting that new legislation affecting Scottish child and family law should not be introduced at Westminster when the Scottish Parliament was about to take over responsibility in these fields. What will result from that new body is a matter for speculation but it is clear that a number of areas, most notably non-marital parenthood

---

[66] E.M. Clive, 'Financial Provision on Divorce' 1992 SLT (News) 241; J.M. Thomson, 'Financial Provision on Divorce: Not Technique but Statutory Interpretation' 1992 SLT (News) 245; 'Dr. Clive Replies' 1992 SLT (News) 247. See also, A. Bissett-Johnson and J.M. Thomson, 'Sharing Property in a Fluctuating Market' 1994 SLT (News) 248.

[67] *Jacques v Jacques* 1995 S.L.T. 963 (IH), 1997 S.L.T. 459 (HL).

[68] A study of how the system was working, F. Wasoff, R.E. Dobash and D.S. Harcus, *The Impact of the Family Law (Scotland) Act 1985 on Solicitors' Divorce Practice* (Central Research Unit, Scottish Office, 1990), found a very positive reaction from the legal profession.

[69] Research has demonstrated that couples are increasingly reaching agreement on financial provision: S. Morris, S. Gibson and A. Platts, *Untying the Knot: Characteristics of Divorce in Scotland* (Central Research Unit, Scottish Office, 1993) and F. Wasoff, A. McGuckin and L. Edwards, *Mutual Consent: Written Agreements in Family Law* (Central Research Unit, Scottish Office, 1997).

and non-traditional adult relationships, are in need of urgent attention. At present, these aspects of the law lie in darkness but, then, it is always darkest before the dawn.

SOUTH AFRICA

GIVING EFFECT TO THE SPIRIT OF THE CONSTITUTION

June Sinclair[*]

I   INTRODUCTION

The last chapter on South Africa in the *Survey*[1] covered the years 1995 and 1996, during which the interim Constitution was in operation. The final Constitution came into force on February 4, 1997.[2] Comparisons between the two constitutions were made and a selection of the cases and legislation concerning the application of the final Constitution and affecting children was offered. It is now possible to reflect on the events of 1997 and 1998, insofar as they have seen changes to family law. Again, the chapter will not seek comprehensively to cover every piece of legislation and all the cases. A selection has been made covering, again, the law relating to children, and a number of important developments dealing with marriage. It will be clear that several of the cases and enactments have their rationale in the provisions of the Constitution. Attempts are being made by the courts and the legislature to bring the internal rules of private law governing the family into line with the rights enshrined in the Constitution. In particular, instances of unfair discrimination are being identified, and appropriate, albeit belated, recognition of African customary marriages has received attention.

II   CHILDREN

A   The Hague Convention

The Hague Convention on the Civil Aspects of International Child Abduction Act[3] incorporated the Hague Convention of 1980 into South African municipal law, as from October 1, 1997.

B   Fathers and their extra-marital children

Reference was made in the 1996 *Survey*[4] to the spate of cases in which the natural fathers of children born out of wedlock were attempting to challenge the common-law rule that denies them rights of guardianship, custody and access (visitation). Giving expression to this rule, the Child Care Act of 1983[5] had provided that the consent of the natural father

---

[*]   Executive Director, Honorary Professor of Law, University of Pretoria.

[1]   A. Bainham (ed) *The International Survey of Family Law 1996* (1998) Martinus Nijhoff, 435–449.

[2]   The Constitution of the Republic of South Africa Act 108 of 1996.

[3]   Act 72 of 1996.

[4]   Op cit note 1 above, at 444.

[5]   Act 74 of 1983, in section 18(4)(*d*).

of such a child was not required for the child's adoption, and the constitutionality of this provision was successfully challenged as being unfairly discriminatory in the case *Fraser v Children's Court, Pretoria North.*[6] The Natural Fathers of Children Born out of Wedlock Act of 1997[7] represents the legislature's first attempt to rectify the situation. It is regarded by some, however, as a disappointment, even a non-event.[8] The Act does not alter the assumption inherent in the Roman-Dutch law that *een moeder maakt geen bastaard.* It retains the preferential status accorded to mothers of extra-marital children and amounts to not much more than a codification of the common-law principles which always entitled a court, on application of the father, to grant him guardianship, custody and access if to do so would be in the child's best interests.[9] To rectify the unconstitutionality of the provision in the Child Care Act, relating to consent for adoption, the 1997 Act[10] requires that the father be given notice of the impending adoption, but it does not require his consent. Regarded barely a year after its enactment as deficient, this weak change in the law had to be amended by the Adoption Matters Amendment Act of 1998.[11] It demands that the father's consent to the adoption be obtained, but only provided that he has acknowledged himself in writing to be the father and has made his identity and whereabouts known, as provided for in the Act.[12] The need to obtain the father's consent is dispensed with if the required acknowledgement has not been made, if the father has not discharged his parental duties to the child, if the child was conceived as a result of incest, or if the father of the child has raped or assaulted the child's mother.[13]

C   Custody

Parental responsibility for children in South African law, conventionally referred to as the 'parental power', comprises guardianship and custody. Prior to the enactment of the Guardianship Act of 1993[14] fathers of marital children were considered to be their guardians although, for certain special matters such as consent to the child's marriage or adoption, the consent of both parents was required. On divorce, custody was, except in highly unusual circumstances, granted to the mother, while the father retained guardianship and was usually granted a right of access to the child. The 1993 Act conferred joint and equal guardianship on both parents of a 'legitimate' child.[15] Custody

---

[6]   1997 (2) SA 261 (CC).

[7]   Act 86 of 1997.

[8]   See June Sinclair 'From Parents' Rights to Children's Rights' in C. J. Davel (ed) *Children's Rights in a Transitional Society* (1999) Protea Book House, Pretoria, 62 (in press).

[9]   The Act lists the circumstances the court must take into account in making a determination, but most of these are obvious and would feature in any event in any court's consideration of these matters (see section 2). The persisting assumption that an unwed father does not deserve equal treatment in respect to his child is criticised by me (op cit note 8) as being an instance of insistence on special treatment by women that may be inimical to the attainment by them of real equality.

[10] Section 6.

[11] Act 56 of 1998.

[12] Section 4 of the 1998 Act amends section 18 of the principal Act.

[13] Section 5 of the 1998 Act, amending section 19 of the principal Act.

[14] Act 192 of 1993.

[15] It was confined to creating equality between the parents of children whose parents were married to each other at the time of conception, or at birth or at any time between those dates, and between parents whose extra-marital children had become legitimated by the subsequent marriage of their parents to each other. It did not address the matter of parental responsibility for extra-marital children.

is still predominantly given to the mother on divorce, which means that the child lives with her, she controls its daily life, but she shares guardianship with the father, who is usually granted access.[16] In the case of *Stassen v Stassen*,[17] an uncontested divorce, the mother asked for 'custody and control' of the minor children. The judge refused to grant the order in these terms, on the ground that the implications of the term 'control' were unclear. Awards of custody to mothers while fathers retained guardianship, under the pre-1993 dispensation had often been described as a splitting of 'control' over the children, and something peculiar to South African law. The case itself is of no great moment. But it does highlight the difficulties being experienced in this country as we move closer to the notion that parents should share responsibility towards their children and that issues of 'control' exclude from the conversation the child's own rights. Now that both equality and children's rights to parental care are enshrined in the Constitution, we need to shift our focus from the exclusive pre-occupation with parental rights to a child-centred approach that would ensure that children's interests remain paramount. The shift is occurring, and is evident from the increase in the number of cases in which joint custody is asked for on divorce and also from the approach to child-care law being pursued by the South African Law Commission.[18]

V v V[19] is an important case on joint custody, which also involved the highly controversial issue of gay and lesbian rights. The action was one in which the husband sought a divorce and custody of the children of the marriage, a son and a daughter, aged 12 and 13 years. The defendant wife had suffered what the court described as 'ritual sexual abuse ... in the context of a misuse of the Catholic religion'[20] as a child, in Ireland. She had also manifested a behavioural disorder during the marriage, which had resulted in her covertly ingesting rat poison, which contains the decoagulant, Warfarin. Her husband had spent substantial sums of money and considerable effort to discover the cause of the subcutaneous bleeding and skin disorders that had ensued from his wife's secret substance abuse, which doctors had diagnosed as a rare disease. Through psychiatric help, the woman had overcome her substance dependence, but the marriage had by then disintegrated. The parties had been living apart for some two years prior to the action and had been exercising joint custody, in that the children had lived at times with their father and at other times with their mother, who had formed a lesbian relationship with a woman who was living with her as her partner. The husband was agreeable to a right of access being granted to his wife, either under his supervision, or provided that no other person would sleep in the same residence except with his consent when the children were with their mother. The court found that he genuinely and deeply believed that he had a duty to protect his children from the harmful effects of exposure to their mother's lesbianism, and feared also a recurrence of the substance abuse. The wife contended during the trial that she had recovered from her drug dependence. Although she would have liked to be awarded custody of the children, she stated that she would be content with a joint custody order, since that had been the *de facto* situation for some

---

[16]   See, for example, the case of *van Pletzen v van Pletzen* 1998 (4) SA 95 (O), where the court stated that the assumption that a mother is better able to care for a child than its father is one that belongs to the past but, nevertheless, granted custody of a girl aged four to her mother.

[17]   1998 (2) SA 105 (W).

[18]   A detailed documentation and analysis of the shift is offered in the work cited in note 8 above, where several recent and important contributions in the literature are referred to. The cases on joint custody are also discussed there, as is the commendable work being undertaken by the Law Commission, reflected in its Issue Paper 13, Project 110 on The Review of the Child Care Act, dated April 1998.

[19]   1998 (4) SA 169 (C).

[20]   At 175.

time before the divorce action, and her children had indicated joint custody as their preference. She did not consider her sexual orientation to be a threat to her children.

The court analyzed the evidence of several psychiatrists and experts who had expressed opinions on the possible effects of the mother's lesbianism on the children. It rejected the husband's insistence on access under his supervision and refused to incorporate the condition that he sought to have imposed. Confirming strongly the shift away from parental power in favour of parental responsibility and children's rights, it held that the children had a constitutional right to parental care. The parents had both demonstrated that they cared deeply for their children. Although they were at arm's length, they remained civil to each other, and the mother's resilience and ability to deal with her husband's categorization of her lesbianism as an unhealthy practice from which the children should be protected impressed the judge. He concluded that the children's best interests would be served by allowing them to continue their relationship with both parents, To this end, he awarded joint custody.[21]

The decision is the most recent and clearest manifestation of the commitment of the courts to give effect to rights enshrined in the Constitution that impact on family law. In particular, the emphasis placed on the equality clause,[22] which outlaws unfair discrimination on a number of grounds, including sexual orientation, and which led the court to declare that homosexual orientation cannot be declared abnormal, reveals a marked change in attitude in relation to joint custody orders on divorce. In 1994, in the case of *van Rooyen v van Rooyen*,[23] another division of the High Court had held that lesbianism sends 'the wrong message' to children. Belinda van Heerden and Julia Sloth Nielsen[24] describe what is happening in child and family law as 'an impending revolution'.[25]

III   REPRODUCTIVE RIGHTS

A   *Abortion and the constitutionally enshrined right to life*

It was probably inevitable that the pro-life lobby would challenge the response by the legislature to calls for the liberalization of South Africa's abortion laws. In order to comply with the equality clause and the constitutional provision guaranteeing reproductive rights,[26] which clearly brought into question the restrictive 1975 Abortion

---

[21]   The order was unusually detailed, and it might be questioned whether the attempt via such regulation to avoid some of the conflict that seemed likely to ensue between the parents pursuant to the order would be effective. The order that the children would spend equal time with the parents, to be arranged between them, may reveal a misunderstanding of the implications of joint custody orders. They need not entail the children moving from one parent to the other on a regular, and perhaps undesirably frequent, basis. Joint custody can imply shared legal custody, while the children live physically with one or other parent – see June Sinclair (assisted by Jacqueline Heaton) *Law of Marriage Volume I* (1996) Juta & Co, Cape Town, 155 and note 411, citing the important work of Ivan Schafer 'Joint Custody' (1987) 104 *SALJ* 149.

[22]   Section 9.

[23]   1994 (2) SA 325 (W).

[24]   'Putting Humpty Dumpty Back Together Again: Towards Reconstructing Families' and Children's Lives in South Africa' (1998) 115 *SALJ* 156.

[25]   Ibid.

[26]   Discussed in the 1996 *Survey*, op cit note 1 above, at 445–449, and contained in section 12(2) of the Constitution. Writers on the subject of abortion have adduced other constitutional rights that demanded a change in the law, such as the right to dignity, security of the person, privacy, and freedom of religion, belief and opinion – see Sinclair (assisted by Heaton), op cit note 21 above, at 93–110.

and Sterilization Act,[27] the Choice on Termination of Pregnancy Act[28] was enacted in 1996. The constitutionality of the new Act was in issue in *Christian Lawyers Association of SA v Minister of Health*.[29] The plaintiffs sought an order declaring the Act invalid in its entirety. It provides for abortion on request of the pregnant woman during the first 12 weeks of the gestation period. It also permits abortion during the thirteenth and up to and including the twentieth week, provided that termination is supported by the opinion of a medical practitioner that the pregnancy resulted from rape or incest, that the continuation of the pregnancy entails risk of injury to the mother's physical or mental health, risk of physical or mental abnormality of the unborn child, or on the strength of the catch-all ground that the continuation of the pregnancy would significantly affect the social or economic circumstances of the mother.

The Constitution declares that 'everyone has the right to life'.[30] The court in this case was required to pronounce on whether a foetus is included among those persons who enjoy such a right. It canvassed authority from other jurisdictions, notably the United States and Canada, and found that the drafters could not have intended implicitly to enlarge the category of rights-bearers by including an unborn child within the purview of this or any other constitutional right. The court correctly, it is submitted, declined to consider medical, moral, religious or other arguments on the meaning of human life and the date of its commencement. The question was a legal one, requiring a proper interpretation of the Constitution. Nothing within the document suggested that unborn children, not enjoying legal personality in our law, qualified for the protections contained in it. The operation of the Roman *nasciturus* rule, which fictionally antedates the acquisition of legal personality for the purpose of benefiting a child subsequently born alive by, for example, allowing one who suffered pre-natal injury to claim compensation from a wrongdoer, properly had no effect on the finding of the court. The legislation stands.[31] Provision of adequate health care to women seeking termination of their pregnancies, however, remains a social and economic problem.

B   Sterilization

Sterilization of a person capable of consenting to such a procedure was regarded as unlawful in Roman-Dutch law, and the Abortion and Sterilization Act of 1975[32] did nothing to change that. It regulated sterilization of persons incapable of giving their consent. The Sterilization Act of 1998[33] brings the law into line with the reproductive rights contained in the Constitution by declaring that no person who is capable of consenting and is 18 or more years of age is prohibited from being sterilized.[34] The Act

---

[27]   Act 2 of 1975.

[28]   Act 92 of 1996.

[29]   1998 (4) SA 1113 (T).

[30]   Section 11.

[31]   The case for enacting remedial legislation to permit abortion was made and the contention offered that to do so would not infringe upon the constitutional right to life, by Sinclair (assisted by Heaton) in 1996, op cit note 21 above, at 93–110, but the work was not referred to by the court.

[32]   Note 27 above.

[33]   Act 44 of 1998.

[34]   Section 2. The Act also provides for sterilization of a person under the specified age where failure to perform the procedure would jeopardise the person's life or seriously impair his or her physical health.

also regulates the sterilization on eugenic grounds of persons incapable of consenting 'due to severe mental disability'.[35]

IV MARRIAGE AND THE CONSTITUTION

A *Same-sex unions*

Marriage in South African private law is conventionally confined to a union between one man and one woman, but the question of gay and lesbian marriages (and the rights of such couples) is one assuming prominence as a constitutional issue. The Constitution expressly forbids unfair discrimination on the ground of sexual orientation.[36] In *Langemaat v Minister of Safety and Security*,[37] the definition of 'dependant' within the regulations promulgated in terms of the South African Police Service Act[38] and contained in the rules of the relevant medical-aid scheme were attacked. They confined the term to the legal spouse or widow/er or dependent child of the member. The applicant was a female police captain who had for over ten years been living in a stable, marriage-like relationship with a woman with whom she jointly owned a house, operated a joint bank account and whom she had named as her beneficiary in certain insurance policies. The court held that the refusal of the chairperson of the medical-aid scheme to register the captain's partner as a dependant amounted to unfair discrimination.

The judge explained correctly that the legal duty to maintain rests upon proof of need on the part of the alleged dependant, and upon whether the relationship between the parties creates a duty of support. (The legal relationships which create such a duty flow either from the common law or from statute.[39]) On the latter question, he had no difficulty declaring that the answer 'must take account of the times and society in which we live'.[40] Far-reaching consequences may be taken to flow from the broad, if not loose, language of the decision. It appears to cover not only same-sex couples, but also, for example, the large number of heterosexual cohabitants who live in stable, marriage-like relationships. Nowhere did the court limit its finding to the fact that gay and lesbian couples are denied the right to marry and thus to bring themselves within the purview of the statutory term 'legal spouse'. Exclusion of such persons from the protection of the rules of the law of husband and wife flows from such denial, and it is this fact that would form the basis of a claim of unfair discrimination. The finding in the instant case rests upon the loose statement that the definitions under attack excluded 'a great number of persons who are *de facto* dependants of ... members'.[41] It was the *de facto* financial status of the captain's partner that won the day. While the decision's implications may be desirable on the facts, they seem not to be based on sound legal reasoning. Cohabitants are not denied the right

---

[35]   Section 3.

[36]   Sections 9(3) and 9(4). See also Angelo Pantazis 'An Argument for the Legal Recognition of Gay and Lesbian Marriages' (1997) 114 *SALJ* 556, who contends, beyond an argument for equality, that the right to privacy includes the right to marry.

[37]   1998 (3) SA 312 (T).

[38]   Act 68 of 1995.

[39]   The current rule governing post-divorce maintenance, for example, resides in section 7 of the Divorce Act 70 of 1979. At common law, the termination of the marriage ended the relationship upon which the duty to maintain was founded. Thus, the court's power to award maintenance to an ex spouse had to be created by legislation.

[40]   At 315H.

[41]   At 316A.

to marry. They may choose not to do so, while in fact being dependent on each other for financial support. Is this circumstance enough to confer upon them the protection confined in law to spouses, children, siblings and divorcees? I think not. If there is a case for extending the protective and supportive rules of family law to cohabitants, it would require legislative intervention.[42]

A massive broadening of the right to claim damages for loss of support resulting from the unlawful killing of a person obliged to maintain one – the so-called dependant's action – is an inescapable consequence of the judgment. It will undoubtedly be vigorously resisted by insurers.

B   Muslim marriages and African customary marriages

Because Muslim and African customary marriages are potentially polygynous, they have both been refused legal recognition as valid marriages, equal in status to those celebrated according to the civil law in terms of the Marriage Act.[43] Our highest court held in 1983, in *Ismail v Ismail*,[44] that polygyny (common to both Muslim and African customary marriages) is 'contrary to the accepted customs and usages which are regarded as morally binding upon all members of our society'.[45] No distinction was made by the court between *de facto* monogamous and *de facto* polygynous Muslim marriages. The implicit definition of 'society' to exclude Black people and Muslims is manifestly discriminatory and amounts to foisting the values of one section of the South African population on other groups.

Ryland v Edros[46] refused to accept the approach in *Ismail,* the court concluding that while the Muslim marriage was not valid in our law, contractual obligations flowing from the marriage, including a duty of the husband to maintain his wife, could be enforced. The judge stressed, however, that his view was confined to a *de facto* monogamous marriage and should not necessarily be taken to cover the case of a polygynous Muslim marriage.[47] The placing of this constraint upon the finding about public policy was, it is submitted, unfortunate. The judgment has been hailed as progressive, sensitive and in keeping with the altered approach to the determination of public policy demanded by the Bill of Rights.[48] But entailed in that altered approach must surely be tolerance for a system of religious personal law that does *not* accord with the Christian principle of monogamy. After all, it is precisely the polygynous nature of Muslim and African customary marriages that has been the basis of the denial of recognition. To confine acceptance and tolerance of Muslim marriages to cases that *in fact comply* with the

---

[42]   Chapter 4 of Sinclair (assisted by Heaton), op cit note 21 above, is dedicated to the issue of cohabitation. The implications for the duty of support are covered at 284–285, and the vexed question of whether the legislature should intervene is traversed at 291–296.

[43]   Act 25 of 1961.

[44]   1983 (1) SA 1006 (A).

[45]   At 1026.

[46]   1997 (2) SA 690 (C).

[47]   At 709D.

[48]   See for example Joan Church 'The Dichotomy of Marriage Revisited: A Note on *Ryland v Edros*' (1997) 60 *THRHR* 992, who commends the decision and highlights the contrast between this case and not only *Ismail,* but also *Kalla v The Master* 1995 (1) SA 261 (T), which accepted the view on public policy espoused in *Ismail* although it was decided after the enactment of the interim Constitution; I. P. Maithufi 'Possible Recognition of Polygamous Marriages' (1997) 60 *THRHR* 695; G. M. Ferreira and J. A. Robinson 'Reflections on the *Boni Mores* in the Light of Chapter 3 of the 1993 Constitution' (1997) 60 *THRHR* 303.

Christian notion of monogamy, and hence to indicate a different outcome for a similar dispute involving a *de facto* polygynous Muslim marriage, on the ground of the polygyny, reduces our newfound tolerance to symbolism. Such an approach serves merely to entrench the discredited view of public policy taken in *Ismail*. It continues to foist the values of one section of the society on other sections.

The decision in *Ryland* must now be viewed against the enactment of The Recognition of Customary Marriages Act of 1998,[49] which recognizes and permits polygyny, but only within African customary marriage. The Act does not deal in any way with Muslim marriages. If no equivalent legislation is enacted to recognize Muslim marriages, and if the constraint imposed by the judge in *Ryland* is followed, the resentment, already substantial, flowing from the unequal treatment of the two types of potentially polygynous marriages, will be reinforced.[50]

The Recognition of Customary Marriages Act confers full recognition on African customary marriage and regulates celebration, registration, proprietary consequences and dissolution. It permits polygyny within customary marriage and declares that a customary marriage celebrated prior to its enactment (regardless whether the marriage was celebrated in accordance with its provisions) is for all purposes recognized as a valid marriage.[51] It provides further that a customary marriage entered into after the commencement of the Act, and which complies with its requirements, is for all purposes recognized as a valid marriage.[52] Among the several requirements for the validity of customary marriages is that both spouses must be above the age of 18 years, failing which the Minister may give written permission for the marriage to take place if he or she considers the marriage to be in the interests of the parties, that both spouses must consent to the marriage, and that the marriage must be entered into in accordance with customary law.[53] The spouses to a customary marriage are placed under a duty to register their marriage,[54] but the Act goes on to state that failure to register a customary marriage does not affect its validity.[55] While spouses married at customary law may marry each other at

---

[49] Act 120 of 1998 which, as at September 1999, had not been brought into operation. It is discussed below.

[50] A different question is whether a court should accept that polygyny does not infringe the constitutional right of sex equality, that is, that it does not unfairly discriminate against women. Within the context of this difficult question, there may be more justification for distinguishing between marriages that are potentially polygynous but *de facto* monogamous, and those that are *de facto* polygynous. On the difficult choices that may confront a court concerning competing claims about culture, religion and sex equality, see below. It should be noted that the Marriage Act 25 of 1961, in section 3, provides for the appointment of priests of any Indian religion as marriage officers. If a marriage of an Indian couple is solemnized in accordance with the Act, a valid, but *monogamous* marriage comes into existence.

[51] Section 2(1) of Act 120 of 1998.

[52] Section 2(2).

[53] Section 3.

[54] Section 4(1).

[55] Section 4(9). The proprietary consequences of a customary marriage are set out in detail in the Act. The provisions are complex and must be seen against the background of the rules that have previously governed the interface between civil and customary marriages. For an explanation of these rules see Sinclair (assisted by Heaton), op cit note 21 above, chapter 3, and for comment on the draft Bill which preceded the Recognition of Customary Marriages Act, and is substantially the same, see Sinclair, in Belinda Van Heerden, Alfred Cockrell and Raylene Keightley (eds) *Boberg's Law of Persons and the Family* 2ed (1999) Juta & Co, Cape Town, chapter 8, especially notes 19 and 20. The proprietary consequences of a customary marriage entered into prior to the commencement of the Act remain unchanged, and continue to be governed by customary law (section 7(1)); and those of a marriage entered into after the commencement of the Act are community of property and of profit and loss, provided that neither spouse is a partner in another existing customary marriage. Community can be excluded by antenuptial contract. This dispensation mimics that of civil marriage.

civil law, provided that neither is a party to a customary marriage with another person, those who have married at civil law are not competent to enter into any other marriage.[56]

The Recognition of Customary Marriages Act falls clearly within the purview of section 15(3)(*a*) of the Constitution, which permits legislation recognizing 'systems of personal and family law under any tradition ...'. The difficulty with the legislation is that it has also to be tested against the statement in section 15(3)(*b*) of the Constitution, which requires legislation granting recognition of a system of personal and family law to be consistent with the other provisions of the Constitution. Section 9(4) outlaws unfair discrimination or, put another way, guarantees equality.[57] The complex question that has to be confronted is whether polygyny is a violation of a woman's right to equality or, put another way, whether polygyny discriminates against women. Opinions on this issue are anything but a harmonious chorus.[58] In terms of the interim Constitution, legislation recognizing a system of personal or family law was sanctioned by section 14(3) and, if passed, would have had the implicit effect of trumping the issue of sex equality because the section did not require the recognizing legislation to comply with the anti-discrimination/equality clause. The final Constitution does. Thus, when a court is confronted with a claim that polygyny discriminates against women and therefore that the Recognition of Customary Marriages Act is unconstitutional, it will have to make a finding on a highly sensitive issue that, it would seem, has implicitly been pronounced upon by the legislature. By enacting a statute which sanctions polygyny, the legislature can be taken to have expressed its view on two points: first, the right protecting against unfair discrimination on the ground of culture (in this case) required it to end the refusal by the courts to recognize African customary marriages. (The Act may be seen to be the legislature's response to the injunction in section 9(4) to enact legislation to eradicate unfair discrimination (on the ground of culture, in this case).) Secondly, polygyny either does not discriminate against women or, if it does, freedom from unfair discrimination on the ground of culture trumps the right to sex equality. Not a happy choice for the courts, is this one. Similar questions arise in respect of Muslim marriages, although here the legislature is displaying a reticence to intervene that is hard to reconcile with its apparent willingness to intervene in respect of African customary marriages.[59]

The enactment of the Recognition of Customary Marriages Act highlights the different treatment of African customary and Muslim marriages. If the legislature fails to enact legislation envisaged in the Constitution to recognize Muslim marriages, it seems likely that a constitutional challenge could be mounted, on the basis of unfair discrimination between African customary marriages and Muslim marriages, on the basis of culture, and on the basis of religion. There seems to be no sound reason for accepting the validity of one type of potentially polygynous marriage but not another. The fact that the Muslim population is minuscule compared to that of Africans will not pass muster.

---

[56] Section 10(1) and (4). The language suggests that such a subsequent marriage would be void.

[57] Section 9 is often referred to as 'the equality clause'.

[58] See the discussion of the issue and the views of a number of writers in Sinclair (assisted by Heaton), op cit note 21 above, at 164–170.

[59] Although *Ryland v Edros* (note 46 above) permitted enforcement of a contractual claim arising from a Muslim marriage, it did not find that such a marriage was valid. Furthermore, no legislation to recognize Muslim marriages is currently under consideration, although the Constitution (section 15(1) and (3)) expressly provides that the right to freedom of religion, belief and opinion does not prevent legislation recognizing marriages concluded under any tradition, or a system of religious, personal or family law. Section 15(3)(*b*) demands that such legislation be consistent with other provisions in the Constitution. Section 9(4), prohibiting unfair discrimination on a variety of grounds, including culture and religion, declares that national legislation *must* be enacted to prevent unfair discrimination (on any ground).

But can it be doubted that this fact has influenced the legislature's timely attention to the matter of African customary marriages and its dilatory response regarding the marriages of a small minority?

Within African customary law, the hallowed rule governing intestate succession is one of male primogeniture. It provides another possibility for conflict between customary law and the equality provision in the Constitution. There is academic writing to the effect that this rule is discriminatory against women.[60] A recent case, however, concludes that the rule differentiates, but does not unfairly discriminate: *Mthembu v Letsela*[61] concerned the devolution of the deceased's house. The applicant claimed to be his customary wife and launched an attack on the rule of customary law that identified the respondent, the deceased's father, as his intestate heir. The constitutionality of the male primogeniture rule, which excludes women from inheriting from a person who dies intestate, was not the only point at issue. Central to the dispute was the existence of the alleged customary marriage between the deceased and the applicant. This matter was referred by Roux J. for oral evidence; hence the second reported decision, by Mynhardt J. In the first of the two decisions, Roux J. concluded that the rule of succession has much to commend it, for its corollary is the duty of the heir to provide 'sustenance, maintenance and shelter'[62] to the widow of the deceased. He declined to find that the rule was 'unfairly' discriminatory and compared it to other rules which differentiate, without being unfair, such as separate toilet facilities for men and women.[63] There are, however, powerful reasons for disagreeing with the view of Roux J. The fact that women married at customary law are excluded from inheriting, but acquire as a *quid pro quo* a right to maintenance against the male heir, may well not rescue a rule that denies them rights that men have solely on the ground of their sex. The arguments on unfair discrimination put forward by counsel for the applicant are compelling, and ought to have been accepted. In the second of the two cases, which entailed a final determination of the facts relied upon by the applicant, Mynhardt J. found that there had been no customary marriage. The applicant's claim, therefore, and her attack on the constitutionality of the male primogeniture rule, had to fail. The learned judge acknowledged that the court should 'develop' the rule to render it consonant with the Constitution, that the customary law of succession required reform, and that its 'development' should be undertaken by the legislature rather than the court.[64]

The Intestate Succession Act 81 of 1987 is the current regulating statute. The draft, remedial legislation is the Amendment of Customary Law of Succession Bill.[65] The Bill overrides customary rules of succession by providing that, despite any other law to the contrary, the estate of a person must devolve in accordance with the person's will or according to the law of intestate succession as regulated by the Intestate Succession Act.

---

[60] A. J. Kerr 'Customary Law, Fundamental Rights and the Constitution' (1994) 111 *SALJ* 720 at 725–756; 'The Bill of Rights in the New Constitution and Customary Law' (1997) 114 *SALJ* 346 at 350–352; T. W. Bennett 'The Equality Clause and Customary Law' (1994) 10 *SAJHR* 122 at 128–129.

[61] 1997 (2) SA 936 (T) and 1998 (2) SA 675 (T).

[62] At 945G.

[63] At 946A. Extensive and technical comment on the cases is offered by A. J. Kerr 'Inheritance in Customary Law under the Interim Constitution and under the Present Constitution' (1998) 115 *SALJ* 262. I. P. Maithufi 'The Constitutionality of the Rule of Primogeniture in Customary Law of Intestate Succession' (1998) 16 *THRHR* 142 at 146 welcomes the decision.

[64] At 686–687.

[65] B109-98.

SWEDEN

PATERNITY AND CUSTODY

Åke Saldeen[*]

I   INTRODUCTION

In my report on Swedish family law in 1995 I described, among other things, a report submitted in April 1995 by the National Council for Medical Ethics on the permissibility of egg donation in Sweden.[1] However, no legislation has yet (April 1999) been introduced on the basis of this proposal.[2] I also described the report 'Custody, Residence and Access' (Official Government Report – SOU 1995:79), submitted in August 1995 by the Custody Disputes Commission, which proposed, *inter alia*, various amendments to the rules concerning custody and access. During 1997, the Swedish government submitted a Bill 1997/1998:7 'Custody, Residence and Access'. This government Bill was dealt with by the Riksdag (Swedish Parliament) during 1998 and resulted in legislation, which entered into force that same year on October 1 (Swedish Code of Statutes – SFS 1998:319). I shall describe this legislation in Part III. However, I will first deal with the issue of DNA technology and determination of paternity in Swedish law, referring to an important case decided by the Supreme Court in 1998, and reported in Nytt Juridiskt Arkiv – NJA 1998, at page 184.

II   DNA TECHNOLOGY AND DETERMINATION OF PATERNITY

There is a so-called legal presumption in Swedish law concerning the determination of the paternity of children born to unmarried mothers.[3] In accordance with an amendment made in 1969, this presumption, contained in Chapter 1, Section 5 of the Code on Parents, Children and Guardians, means that if the plaintiff (the child) succeeds in proving that the mother and the respondent man had sexual intercourse with each other during the period when conception was possible (presumed fact), the action will succeed provided that it is probable, having regard to all the circumstances, that the child was fathered by the respondent, or, in other words, if the alleged paternity (the presumed relationship – legal fact) appears probable. In legal literature it has been claimed for many years – by myself among others – that, in parallel with this statutory presumption of paternity, there must be assumed to exist a more general, primary (unwritten) rule of paternity. According to this, the paternity action should succeed if the plaintiff is able to prove directly paternity, irrespective of the position concerning evidence on the issue of

---

[*]   Professor of Private Law, Faculty of Law, Uppsala University, Sweden. Translated by James Hurst.

[1]   See A. Bainham (ed.) *The International Survey of Family Law 1995* (Martinus Nijhoff, 1997).

[2]   According to information from the Ministry of Health and Social Affairs, a government Bill concerning this matter may be presented during the autumn of 1999.

[3]   C.f. Saldeen. 'DNA-teknik och fastästallande av faderskap' [DNA Technology and Determination of Paternity], *Juridisk Tidskrift* 1998–99, p. 174 ff.

sexual intercourse in the case in question.[4] This really means nothing more than that it must be considered possible to determine paternity not only by applying the said rule of presumption in the Code on Parents, Children and Guardians (with its requirements on proof of sexual intercourse) but also by applying general principles of evidence. In comparison with the general, primary (unwritten) rule on paternity, the presumption thus involves a relaxation of evidential requirements as regards proof of legal facts, i.e. paternity: subject to the requirement concerning proof of sexual intercourse, it is not necessary to prove paternity according to the presumption, but is sufficient if the alleged paternity is shown to be probable.

In Sweden, DNA technology started to be used in 1991 to a limited extent in the forensic genetic investigation of paternity matters.[5] However, as of 1994, this technology has always been used in such investigation. (It should be mentioned that every year about 2,000 paternity matters are registered by the Forensic Genetics Institute, which corresponds to only 2% of the number of children born in Sweden per annum).

The ability of a plaintiff in a paternity action to prove paternity directly was, of course, extremely limited before DNA technology began to be used in medical paternity diagnostics during the 1990s. The issue of the possibility of determining paternity by applying general principles of evidence, instead of applying the above-mentioned presumption, was also very seldom raised in legal practice. However, it was raised in the cases NJA 1984, page 49, and NJA 1985, page 236, I and II, where the oral evidence concerning sexual intercourse was not considered sufficient to prove sexual intercourse but the probability of the respondent's paternity, on the basis of the so-called blood group statistics paternity index, was relatively high.

In all three cases mentioned here the Supreme Court (Högsta Domstolen (HD)) was not unanimous. In the first two cases (i.e. NJA 1984, page 49, and NJA 1985, page 236, I), the minority (two Justices) wished to apply the presumption found in Chapter 1, Section 5 of the Code on Parents, Children and Guardians and in that connection use the forensic genetic evidence as supplementary evidence concerning the issue of proving sexual intercourse: a method that I myself for various reasons claim should not be used. However, the majority applied the above-mentioned general, primary (unwritten) paternity rule and thus found that paternity was proved. However, in the latter case, as a consequence of the voting rules in the Code of Judicial Procedure, the view that was represented by the minority in both of the previous cases prevailed.

In the 1998 case (i.e. NJA 1998, page 184), the HD considered for the first time the evidential value of the results of forensic genetic investigation conducted using DNA technology. The respondent man's paternity index in that connection amounted to 255,000, meaning a paternity probability exceeding 99.999%. The total exclusion factor amounted to 99.997, which theoretically meant that out of 100,000 incorrectly identified men all but three could be excluded from paternity according to the results of the forensic genetic investigation. However, the District Court, whose decision was confirmed by the Court of Appeal, strangely enough, disallowed the action as the oral evidence of sexual intercourse, in accordance with the presumption in Chapter 1, Section 5 of the Code on

---

4   See Saldeen, *Faställande av faderskap* [Determination of Paternity], 1980, p. 54 ff. and p. 78 f., and also Ekelöf, *Rättegång* [Law of Judicial Procedure] IV, 5 ed., 1982, p 94.

5   Forensic genetic investigation of paternity matters is conducted centrally in Sweden at the Forensic Genetics Institute in Linköping. This Institute is accredited in accordance with EN (European Norm) 45001 for the forensic genetic analysis with DNA technology, an accreditation that requires that the Institute conduct special quality controls. The taking of the blood samples themselves is conducted by a physician or at a health clinic.

Parents, Children and Guardians, was not considered sufficient. However, a unanimous Supreme Court revoked the Court of Appeal's judgment and granted the paternity action since paternity was deemed proved by the forensic genetic evidence. In its judgment, the HD, *inter alia*, issued a reminder of the discussion conducted in the above-mentioned cases of 1984 and 1985 and stated that the DNA method provides a 'significantly more reliable statistical evaluation (on the basis of the paternity index) of a non-excluded man's probability of paternity than previous methods of investigation'.

The outcome of the case NJA 1998, page 184, may raise the issue of whether or not the time is now ripe for the Swedish legislator to alter the legislation on the determination of the paternity of children born to unmarried mothers, for example in the same way that has already taken place in Norway or as is proposed for Danish law. Nowadays, the applicable rule in Norwegian law, according to legislation from 1997, is that if a putative father after a DNA analysis may be considered to be the father, he shall be declared by the court to be the father. If, however, DNA analysis has not taken place, or if there is reason to believe that the DNA analysis yielded an incorrect result, or if some close relative of the putative father is also possibly the father of the child, the former rules on the determination of paternity apply, i.e. the rule of presumption requiring proof of sexual intercourse during the possible period for conception and an assessment of probability on the paternity issue (Chapter 2, Section 9, Children and Parents Act (*barneloven*)). In a Danish Report of 1997,[6] the introduction of a rule with, *inter alia*, the following content (Chapter 3, Section 19) was proposed: if the results of a forensic genetic examination show undoubtedly who is the father of the child, he shall be declared to be the father by the court (Section 1). In other cases, a man shall be declared to be the father if he has had sexual intercourse with the mother during the period of possible conception and no circumstances exist whereby it is improbable that he is the father and provided the mother, during the said period: (1) did not have sexual intercourse with another man; (2) has had sexual intercourse with one or several men but none of these, as a result of forensic genetic examination, could come into question as the father; or (3) has had sexual intercourse with one or more men but it is most probable that none of these is the father (Section 2).

I have, myself, in other connections asked the question whether one should not consider taking an even more daring step in the development of this field within the not too distant future. This would quite simply involve the Swedish municipal social welfare boards, which have a statutory duty to ensure that the issue of paternity is investigated when an unmarried woman gives birth to a child and also to consider approval of acknowledgements of paternity, together with the courts no longer dealing with issues concerning the determination of paternity in those cases where the forensic investigation gives a clear answer to the paternity issue. In such cases, the issue of paternity could instead be a matter to be dealt with solely by the Forensic Genetics Institute and the civil registration authorities.

III CUSTODY, RESIDENCE AND ACCESS

As mentioned in the introduction, the so-called Custody Disputes Commission submitted their report 'Custody, Residence and Access' (SOU 1995:79) in 1995. On the basis of

---

[6] Report no. 1350 on the *Legal Status of Children*. Preliminary report issued by Ministry of Justice, Children and Parents Act.

this proposal for legislation, the government introduced the Bill 1997/1998:7 'Custody, Residence and Access' in October 1997. However, this government Bill deviated from the proposals of the Custody Disputes Commission on certain items, as indicated in more detail below. The Riksdag adopted the proposal in the Bill in 1998 and new legislation entered into force on October 1 of the same year (SFS 1998:319).[7]

According to the Bill, the reform aims, *inter alia*, to place greater emphasis in the legislation on the principle of the best interests of the child and also on the importance of finding solutions through discussion and to assist parents in reaching agreements to the greatest extent possible on how custody and access, etc. should be resolved. The new legislation also aims to pave the way for increased use of joint custody.

In more concrete terms, the legislation in question means, *inter alia*, the following. By an introductory section inserted into the Code on Parents, Children and Guardians, Chapter 6, Section 2A, it is explained that the best interests of the child shall be a primary consideration in determinations made under the Chapter concerning all issues of custody, residence and access. A previous rule has also been linked to this rule whereby, when assessing what is in the best interests of the child, particular attention should be paid to the needs of the child for close and good contact with both parents. Finally, the introductory section in question has been supplemented with a rule that any risk of the child being exposed to abuse, unlawful abduction or detention or of otherwise being harmed should be taken into account when determining the above-mentioned issues.

In the government Bill it was stated that the objective should be that parents, even if they do not cohabit with each other, should have joint custody in all cases where this form of custody is found to be in the best interests of the child in the individual case. However, according to the wording of the legislation prior to the reform in question, the situation was that joint custody always had to be dissolved if one of the parents requested this and opposed the continuation of joint custody. Furthermore, the rule was that if only one of the parents had custody, the court could not order reinstatement of joint custody on the application of one parent if the other parent opposed this. The new legislation means, as regards this item, that the court can order joint custody even if one of the parents opposes it. However, according to the Bill, the power to order joint custody in a case where a parent opposes joint custody should be used with great caution and sensitivity. If the person opposing joint custody provides substantial reasons for his or her standpoint, it will often be desirable not to go against his or her wishes. If the opposition is based on circumstances such as assault or harassment or other forms of molestation by the other parent, it may, according to the government Bill, be in the best interests of the child that one of the parents is awarded sole custody.

It was concluded in the course of the preparatory work for the legislation that the introduction of a power to order joint custody even against the wishes of a parent necessitated the introduction of the power to prescribe a right of access even when there is joint custody. Similarly, it was thought necessary to have a power to prescribe rules concerning the child's residence, i.e. deciding with whom the child should mainly live when the parents have joint custody but do not live together. Previously, it had not been possible to make orders for access rights when the parents had joint custody – it being assumed that the parents would be capable of reaching agreement on such matters if custody was joint.

As regards access, it should be mentioned that a rule has been introduced which emphasises that the parents of a child have a joint responsibility to ensure that the child's

---

[7]   Parliamentary Standing Committee on Civil Law Legislation Report 1997/98:LU12.

needs for access to the parent with whom the child does not live are met. Furthermore, it should be mentioned that the Custody Disputes Commission made a proposal concerning the introduction of a rule whereby a court, in certain circumstances, would in addition be empowered also to decide on other kinds of contact, in addition to physical contact, between the child and the parent with whom the child does not live (for example, contact by correspondence or telephone). However, this proposal was not adopted. Such a possibility already exists in our neighbouring countries Finland and Denmark. One of the reasons why the proposal to introduce this rule was not adopted by the government Bill was that we did not have any experience of how such a rule functioned in those two countries. Another reason for the proposal not being implemented was that one could not, according to the government Bill, ignore the risk of detailed over-regulation possibly reducing the parents' preparedness to co-operate.

Finally, in this connection, it should be mentioned that the Custody Disputes Commission also proposed the introduction of a rule into the Code on Parents, Children and Guardians providing that a sole custodian should not be allowed to take a child out of Sweden for a longer period than 30 consecutive days without the permission of the other parent, but the proposal was not implemented. One reason for this was that there was considered to be a risk that the proposed rule might in many cases lead to further conflicts between the parents. Another reason was the conclusion that it was likely that the proposed rule on the requirement of permission would seldom have the desired effect as it was not supported by any sanction.

Finally, it should be mentioned here that through this legislation a rule was introduced on parents sharing the travel costs connected with the exercise of access. Although the parent whom the child is to meet has the primary responsibility for such expenses, following an amendment to the Code, the other parent must bear part of these costs according to his or her capacity. According to the government Bill, the sharing of travel expenses should not come into question unless the costs involved are reasonably substantial. Not only expenses for domestic travel, but also foreign travel should be shared. However, in principle, only necessary expenses are payable, in which connection one should proceed on the basis that the least expensive means of travel by public transport are used.

For the parents themselves, but not least for the child, it is of course of great importance to avoid both judicial hearings and contentious negotiations, which are often heart-rending. Thus, for quite a number of years some municipalities (district councils) in Sweden have offered parents the opportunity of so-called divorce conflict resolution by co-operation talks aimed at working through parental conflicts in order to find, hopefully, solutions by consensus to the various problems relating to children concerning, for example, custody after divorce. Co-operation talks mean detailed and structured discussions under expert guidance with parents who, in conjunction with or after a separation, cannot reach agreement on issues concerning the children regarding, for example, custody and access. The purpose of these talks is that the parents should reach agreement on these issues and, consequently, it is not a form of family advice. As a result of the positive experience gained from these operations, municipalities were, by legislation in 1990 (Section 12a, Social Services Act, Swedish Code of Statutes SFS 1980:620), placed under a duty to make provision to enable them to assist parents through the opportunity of such talks. The Custody Disputes Commission, whose terms of reference included the important task of endeavouring to investigate how co-operation talks work, found that such talks yielded good results in practice. On the proposal of the Commission, a new statutory rule was introduced into the Code on Parents, Children and

Guardians, acting as a reminder of the opportunity for co-operation talks. According to the *travaux préparatoires*, the new rule should also be seen as an encouragement to attorneys and other legal representatives not to institute proceedings without substantial reasons before efforts have been made to urge the parents to reach a solution by consensus.

It must be said that a very novel feature of the new legislation was the introduction of an opportunity for parents to be able to conclude an extrajudicial agreement concerning custody, residence and access. Such an agreement is valid if it is in writing and is also approved by the municipal social welfare board. The board should grant its approval provided that what the parents have agreed is in the best interests of the child, or – if the agreement is based on custody being joint – provided that what the parents have agreed is not manifestly incompatible with the best interests of the child. The wishes of the child, having regard to the age and maturity of the child should, among other things, be taken into account when making this assessment. It should be added that the social welfare board is only empowered to approve or disapprove the agreement of the parents. Thus the board cannot adjust the content of an agreement or decide a contentious issue.

An agreement between the parents concerning custody, residence and access, which is in writing and approved by the social welfare board, may be enforced in the same way as a determination of a court that has entered into final legal force. The agreement can be amended by a new agreement or by a determination of the court. It should be emphasised that a determination of a court can also be amended, not only by a new determination but also by a written agreement approved by the social welfare board.

Finally, it should be mentioned that Finnish law served as a model as regards this opportunity to conclude agreements on custody, residence and access. This possibility has existed in Finland for many years.

SWITZERLAND

A NEW DIVORCE LAW FOR THE NEW MILLENNIUM

*Olivier Guillod**

I INTRODUCTION

Most of the Bills that were alluded to in the latest survey of Swiss law have now been passed. On June 26, 1998, the Swiss Parliament adopted the Act reforming several chapters of the Civil Code, especially on the requirements for contracting a marriage, on void marriages and on divorce. On December 18, 1998, it adopted a new Federal Constitution and the Federal Act on Medically Assisted Procreation as well as the Federal Act on Maternity Leave. The first part of this survey will present these new laws, their content, scope and fate.[1]

By contrast with the wealth of new statutes touching on family law, there have been few important judicial decisions. Courts have been rather conservative during the period under review, simply affirming a number of previous holdings. Part III of the present survey will briefly report on two of the most significant cases from the Federal Court.[2]

II STATUTORY LAW

A *Marriage and divorce*

On January 1, 2000, the latest in a series of reforms of Swiss family law comes into force.[3] This broad enterprise started in 1956(!), when a committee of experts was nominated under the chairmanship of Prof. Jacques-Michel Grossen (who wrote for several years the Swiss report to the *International Survey of Family Law*). At the time, it was decided to split the reform of Swiss family law into several slices: first, the child–parent relationship (achieved in 1973 for adoption and 1978 for all other aspects), then the effects of marriage and matrimonial property law (achieved in 1988), followed by marriage and divorce (2000) and finally guardianship (a committee of experts has just been entrusted with the task of preparing a first draft that can be expected within two

---

[*] Professor, University of Neuchâtel Law School.

[1] All federal laws (statutes, regulations and other legislative acts) that are in force can be found in French, German or Italian on the Internet site (http://www.admin.ch) of the Swiss Confederation: see http://www.admin.ch/ch/f/rs/rs.html (for the French version of the *Recueil systématique du droit fédéral [RS]*) and http://www.admin.ch/ch/f/as (for the French version of the *Recueil officiel des lois fédérales [RO]*, i.e. the chronological Digest of Swiss laws). Parliamentary debates (published in the *Bulletin officiel des délibérations des Chambres Conseil National + Conseil des Etats [BO CN and BO CE]*) may be found at http://www.parlament.ch. Bills and Federal Council reports that introduce them (published in the *Feuille Fédérale [F.F.]*) may be accessed at http://www.admin.ch/ch/f/ff/index.html.

[2] The Federal Court decisions from 1975 on, published in the *Recueil officiel des arrêts du Tribunal fédéral [ATF]* are to be found at http://www.eurospider.com/BUGE.

[3] Federal Act of June 26, 1998 reforming the Civil Code, RO 1999 1118ff. See also the Federal Council report of November 15, 1995, F.F. 1996 I 1ff.

years). Such a slicing might have endangered the global coherence of the whole reform. This danger has not materialized: on the contrary, each step has been in line with the previous ones and has even made it possible to fine-tune the previous reforms after a few years of implementation.

Remarkably (for Switzerland!), the latest reform of the Swiss Civil Code was widely accepted throughout the country as well as by parties covering the whole political spectrum. There was no successful request for a referendum, contrary to what had happened for instance to the previous reform (on the effects of marriage and matrimonial property law). Such a wide acceptance may be explained by the fact that the reform basically adapted the 'law in the books' to the 'law in action' on the most sensitive topic of the reform, i.e. divorce. For the last twenty years or so, the gap between the practice of divorce and the formal provisions that could be read in the Civil Code has indeed grown ever wider. In addition, divorce has been commonly viewed by the population as a morally and socially acceptable option for spouses whose marriage has become an empty shell.

In 1998, there were in Switzerland 17,800 divorces, a figure that has been consistently increasing since the 1980s (for instance up 40% from 1990 to 1998). The rate of divorce (i.e. the proportion of marriages contracted in 1998 that would end up in a divorce if the number of divorces remained stable in the future) amounted therefore to 42%, one of the highest figures in Europe. Marriage, on the contrary, seems less attractive: the numbers have been declining for the last ten years or so, from a peak of 47,567 in 1991 to 38,500 in 1998. It nevertheless remains by far the favourite option of couples who want to have children: only 8.7% of children were born out of wedlock in 1998, a rate that has been slowly increasing for the last ten years but remains one of the lowest in Europe.[4]

Despite calls for abolishing any statutory provision on betrothal, the reform left almost intact the material rules of the present Civil Code (Articles 90–93 of the new Civil Code (nCC) replacing Articles 90–95 of the present Civil Code (CC)). Betrothal is defined as an agreement to marry but it does not give rise to an action for specific performance of the agreement. In the case of breach of the agreement to marry, each party can claim the return of the presents he or she gave to the other; upon request, the court may also grant fair compensation to the party who incurred *bona fide* expenses in expectation of the marriage. Both claims must be filed within one year from the date of the breach.

The personal requirements for contracting marriage have been modified in a number of respects (Articles 94–96 nCC replacing Articles 96–104 CC). A man or woman who has attained his or her eighteenth year and has discretion according to Article 16 CC[5] can contract a marriage. The requirement of sanity (Article 97 para 2 CC) has been abandoned because of its eugenic connotation and because requiring discretion was deemed sufficient. The reform has preserved only two impediments: a previous, undissolved, marriage and a close relationship, which encompasses relations in the direct ascending or descending line and between brothers and sisters as well as between parents-in-law and sons-in-law or daughters-in-law. The period of delay (300 days) that Article 103 CC imposed on women who wanted to remarry (because of the presumption of paternity extending until 300 days after the dissolution of the marriage: Article

---

4   All these figures are taken from *Annuaire statistique de la Suisse* 1999, Zurich (1999).

5   Discretion is defined as the situation of somebody 'who is not incapacitated from acting rationally through tender age, insanity, feeblemindedness, drunkenness or other similar cause' (Article 16 CC).

255 CC) was rightly quashed since Article 257 CC already solves the problem by providing that the second husband is taken to be the child's father. Similarly, the period of delay that the divorce judge could impose on a divorced person according to Articles 104 and 150 CC was abandoned. It had anyway been ruled contrary to Article 12 of the European Convention on Human Rights by the European Court of Human Rights a long time ago.[6]

If the material conditions for marriage have been made more simple, the procedure leading to the solemnization of marriage has been even more relaxed (Articles 97–103 nCC replacing Articles 105–119 CC). There will be only two steps: first, the *fiancés* make a request to the registrar of civil status who controls the validity of marriage and delivers an authorization to solemnize the marriage. Secondly, the marriage is solemnized publicly within the next three months by the registrar of civil status chosen by the *fiancés* anywhere in Switzerland. The procedure for publication of the planned marriage, in order to allow any interested person to oppose the marriage by alleging a disability or a legal impediment, has not been kept. Irrespective of the opinion one may have on the desirability of this kind of public control over the contracting of marriages, it has proved totally inefficient. Another point was more controversial: after some debate in Parliament, it was eventually decided to keep the prohibition on celebrating a religious ceremony of marriage before the civil ceremony (Article 97 para 3 nCC corresponding to Article 118 para 2 CC).

The chapter on voidable marriages (Articles 104–110 nCC replacing Articles 120–136 CC) has not been significantly altered in substance but its structure and wording have been clarified. The law still makes a distinction between so-called 'absolute' and 'relative' grounds for annulment. The former (bigamy, permanent incompetence, impediment based on relationship) differ from the latter (temporary incompetence, mistake, fraud and duress) on three points: 'absolute' grounds may be invoked by any interested party whereas 'relative' grounds may only be invoked by one of the spouses; a suit for a declaration of annulment should be instituted *ex officio* by the competent authority in case of 'absolute' grounds only; there is no period of limitation for 'absolute' grounds whereas a suit to annul the marriage based on 'relative' grounds must be brought within six months from the date when the plaintiff discovers the existence of a ground and in any case within five years of the date of the marriage.

The core of the reform deals with divorce (Articles 111–149 nCC replacing Articles 137–158 CC). The drafters of the new law have borrowed from reforms which have taken effect in other European countries during the last 25 years, notably from the French and the German divorce law. The Swiss reform is not, therefore, terribly original. It adheres to a number of basic ideas that have already inspired reforms previously enacted abroad. One could mention at least the following nine points:

(1) *liberalisation*: the grounds for divorce have been made less restrictive and legal obstacles preventing a spouse from getting a divorce have been removed;

(2) *privatisation*: the judge will normally no longer enquire into the private life of spouses before granting them a divorce; the mutual agreement of the spouses has been made the fundamental ground for divorce;

(3) *decriminalization*: fault has been abandoned as a ground for granting, or not granting, a divorce as well as for awarding alimony;

---

[6]   Decision of December 18, 1987 (*F. v. Suisse*), *Publications de la Cour Européenne des Droits de l'Homme*, Série A, vol. 128.

(4) *simplification*: though retaining a judicial process, the reform has taken account of the new nature of divorce based on the spouses' mutual agreement and made the procedure leading to a divorce less cumbersome;

(5) *post-divorce solidarity*: if one spouse is unable to maintain himself or herself at the time of the divorce, he or she has a right to be financially supported by the other until he or she can be expected to be financially autonomous;

(6) *balancing the economic situation of the spouses*: through the division of matrimonial property as well as through a compulsory system of pension sharing, the economic situation of divorced spouses is adjusted in order to ensure that both spouses benefit to a similar extent from the wealth accumulated during marriage;

(7) *separating the matrimonial and parental roles*: divorced parents may in future keep joint parental power in relation to their children;

(8) *protecting the children*: the child's best interest will be the paramount principle in all matters concerning the divorcing couple's children (parental power, guardianship, visitation rights, maintenance, etc.);

(9) *a right to be heard for children*: children are to be be heard by the court in the divorce of their parents and may even be represented in the procedure through a 'curator'.[7]

The basic ground for divorce will be the mutual agreement of both spouses. Even if it sounds new for Switzerland, it is in fact no revolution. Indeed, the solution worked out in practice for many years simply finds legal recognition, accompanied with procedural simplifications. Today, a couple gets a divorce in less than 6 months (2 or 3 months is not a rarity) in two thirds of cases. In future, a divorce sought by both spouses will also be granted quickly: spouses who have signed a written agreement dealing with all subsidiary effects of the divorce will submit their agreement to the judge at a single hearing. After two months, they will have simply to confirm their decision in writing and the judge will grant them a divorce. One feminist member of Parliament criticized such a quick process, which she labelled a 'Nescafé divorce', i.e. an instant divorce, noting that lawyers would probably prepare a posdated writ and have it signed by their clients before the first judicial hearing. All would be done at the same time, which could prove, she said, without convincing a majority of her colleagues, detrimental to the economically weaker party, usually the wife.

Divorce may also be sought by a single spouse in two cases: where the spouses have led a separate life for more than four years[8] or when serious grounds not attributable to the plaintiff make the continuation of life in common intolerable. Unlike French and German law, for instance, no hardship clause is provided which, it is submitted,[9] is the more appropriate solution. One should stress that the ground on which the divorce decree

---

[7]   There have already been a number of books written on the new divorce law even though it is not yet in force. See for instance J. Micheli, P. Nordmann, C. Jaccottet Tissot, J. Crettaz, T. Thonney, E. Riva, *Le nouveau droit du divorce*, Lausanne (1999); R. Pfister-Liechti (Ed.), *De l'ancien au nouveau droit du divorce*, Berne (1999); H. Hausheer (Ed.), *Vom alten zum neuen Scheidungsrecht*, Berne (1999); Stiftung für juristische Weiterbildung (Ed.), *Das neue Scheidungsrecht*, Zurich (1999), all with numerous further references.

[8]   The federal Parliament was divided on that issue: the upper Chamber voted for three years and the lower Chamber for five years, as proposed by the government; after long and unexpectedly passionate debates, they finally settled on four. One MP criticized the decision and said that passing a statute should not be like negotiating at a souk.

[9]   See O. Guillod, 'La clause de dureté dans quelques législations européennes sur le divorce', *Revue internationale de droit comparé* (1983), n° 4, p. 787ff.

is based bears no influence on the subsidiary effects of divorce, especially on financial consequences.

When marrying, a woman normally takes the name of her husband ('family name') but she may keep her former name and place it before the family name. On grounds worthy of consideration, the engaged couple may request that the bride's name be the name of the family (Articles 160 and 30 CC).[10] Upon divorce, the spouse who acquired a new name by her marriage retains it, unless she (or he) asks within one year after the divorce the registrar of civil status that he or she should regain the name she (or he) bore before the marriage (Article 119 nCC). A divorced person loses the statutory right of inheritance towards her or his ex-spouse and cannot claim any benefits from testamentary dispositions made before the suit for divorce was brought (Article 120 nCC).

The reform gives the court power to issue rules for the future use of the family home, on the basis of the situation of the family, especially the children. The court will not be bound by contractual or property rights relating to it (Article 121 nCC). The judge can, for instance, transfer the lease from the husband to the wife who gets sole parental power over the minor children and lives with them. In such a case, the husband would nevertheless be severally and jointly liable for paying the rent for a maximum period of two years. The judge may also grant the use of the home owned, for instance, by the husband to the wife, by way of a right to residence fairly limited in time (presumably at the latest until the youngest child living with his mother attains 18, but it will be up to the courts to decide).

Not unlike the position under German law, old-age entitlements accumulated in a pension fund by the spouse who earns a salary during the marriage (through fixed payments deducted monthly from the wages) must be divided in half upon divorce (Article 122 nCC). The other spouse will not get money in cash but the amount will be put in a pension fund which will pay retirement benefits in the future. The finality of the rule is, of course, to secure a better position for social security of the spouse (usually the wife still today[11]) who did not earn a living during the marriage but who looked after the children and kept the household. Such compulsory pension sharing will not occur in only two situations: when the home-keeping spouse renounced it during the divorce proceedings[12] (provided her or his maintenance during old age is secured in another way) and where the division would prove grossly unfair (Article 123 nCC).[13] When the working spouse is already retired, the division of future entitlements becomes impossible and that spouse must then pay a fair contribution in cash to the other (Article 124 nCC). The system is consistent with the legal regime ('participation in acquisitions', Articles

---

[10] The Swiss system pertaining to the family name is clearly contrary to the equal treatment clause. See the case *Burghartz v. Suisse, Publications des arrêts de la Cour européenne des droits de l'homme*, Série A, n° 280. This is one of the main reasons why it was recently proposed to change it (parliamentary initiative *Sandoz*): according to the proposal submitted to Parliament, the spouses would be entitled to choose the name of the bride or that of the groom as the common family name or to keep one's name after getting married. If they could not agree, they would keep their original name. The name of the children born during the marriage would be either the common family name of their parents or the name the latter would have chosen for them (either the mother's or the father's names). All children would bear the same name. See the Federal Council report of 31 August 1998, F.F. (1999) 4894.

[11] Statistics indicate that between 41% and 64% of women aged 20 to 59 are professionally active whereas between 96% and 99% of men aged 20 to 59 are professionally active. Among so-called 'active' women, between 72% and 82% have a full-time activity (as against between 96% and 98% of men).

[12] Any previous renunciation, e.g. in a marriage covenant, would be invalid.

[13] For instance when a professionally low-qualified wife has worked hard to pay for the higher education of her husband who 'dumps' her as soon as he gets his diploma, no pension sharing might be ordered by the court.

196ff CC) of matrimonial property division upon divorce and should prove an efficient tool in reaching a fairer balance between the economic situation of both ex-spouses.[14]

The reform has substantially changed the system of post-divorce maintenance. Under present law, only the 'innocent' spouse can be awarded alimony (Articles 151 and 152 CC) unless, of course, the other spouse agreed to pay it. In future, financial contributions from one ex-spouse to the other will not depend any more on fault but will be based on need. As long as a divorcing spouse is unable to maintain herself or himself properly after divorce, she or he will be entitled to a fair contribution from the other spouse (Article 125 nCC). The amount and the duration of the contribution will be agreed upon by the divorcing spouses (under the supervision of the judge who must ratify their written agreement) or decided by the court after adequate consideration of all relevant circumstances (the duration of the marriage, the way each spouse contributed to the maintenance of the family, the standard of living enjoyed, the age, health, earnings, education and professional activity of each spouse, etc.). In the normal case, monthly instalments will be ordered (Article 126 nCC), adjusted yearly for inflation (Article 128 nCC) but a cash settlement is also possible. In order to secure payment, the court may issue an injunction to the debtor's employer to pay each month part of the salary directly to his employee's ex-spouse or decide on other security (Article 132 nCC). Public services in each canton will continue to provide assistance in getting the alimony paid and will give advance payments (Article 131 nCC). If the party entitled to the annuity later remarries, she or he forfeits her/his right to it, unless the spouses agreed in the divorce agreement that the annuity would be paid for a longer period (Article 130 nCC). The contribution to maintenance may be diminished, suppressed or suspended if the personal circumstances of one of the parties change significantly, for instance where the party entitled to it cohabits with a stable partner. Within 5 years of the date of the divorce, a contribution could be awarded or increased by the court if it had not been possible at the time of the divorce to grant a contribution large enough to cover one spouse's basic needs and if the financial situation of the other has notably improved since the divorce (Article 129 nCC).

The consequences of divorce for the children have not been seriously modified, save for the possibility given to the court under Article 133 nCC to grant shared parental power to the divorcing spouses. Switzerland is therefore one of the last countries in Europe to accept the idea that divorce breaks the spousal link but not the parent–child relationship. However, the Swiss Parliament did not fully endorse this idea: shared parental power is not the rule but may be decided by the court only when three conditions are met: the spouses jointly request it, they have agreed in writing on all aspects of the future care of their children, including maintenance, and shared parental power appears to be in the best interests of the children. Whatever solution was reached by the divorce court it can be modified if there is a significant change of circumstances (Article 134 nCC).

The children must be heard on all matters that directly concern them, either by the court or by an appropriate third party designated by the court (Article 144 nCC). This principle was already derived from Article 12 of the Convention on Children's Rights, which was deemed directly applicable by the Federal Court.[15] Of course, application of the provision will depend on personal circumstances, especially the children's age and

---

[14]   For a critical analysis of the law in that respect, see A. Leuba, *La répartition traditionnelle des tâches entre les conjoints, au regard du principe de l'égalité entre homme et femme*, Berne 1997.

[15]   ATF 124 III 92.

understanding. It is up to each canton to implement the principle set forth in Article 144 nCC. For instance, the canton of Neuchâtel decided[16] that children under eight years would normally not be heard. Older children would be heard, first by a specially trained person then by the judge outside the courtroom, and in the absence of the parents and their lawyers. Where serious grounds make it desirable (for instance when the parents disagree on who should keep parental power after divorce), or where the child asks for it, the court must appoint a curator with the task of speaking for the child (Article 146 nCC). The curator will be able to take part in the procedure with respect to all matters concerning the child and will have standing to appeal.[17]

To end on a less positive tone regarding the presentation of the new divorce law, I would deplore the erasure by Parliament of two provisions from the draft law: the first made it an obligation for all cantons to set up family mediation services and the second encouraged the cantons to create family courts to decide divorce and other family law cases. Both ideas were, it is submitted, worthy of approval. Petty concerns about cost and about cantonal sovereignty in procedural matters rallied a majority of deputies against the two provisions. However, I am convinced that this parliamentary *faux-pas* will not stop mediation services from developing, either on a private basis or with the direct assistance of a number of cantons.

The Parliament took the opportunity of the reform of the Civil Code to amend a number of other provisions dealing with the parent–child relationship and a few other topics. It resisted calls to create a legal status for cohabitants[18] but nevertheless modified the rules on parental power to allow cohabitants to share it (Article 298a nCC), something that has been impossible under present law. It also recognized a right of information from third parties, especially schoolteachers and physicians, in the parent who does not hold parental power (Article 275a nCC).

To sum up, I would say that, as far as one can assess a law before it takes effect, the reform of divorce law appears a balanced and thoroughly thought out reform. It remains to be seen, however, how courts will implement it.

B   *A new Federal Constitution*

On April 18, 1999, an overwhelming majority of Swiss citizens and all cantons accepted a new, updated version of the Federal Constitution that will take effect presumably on January 1, 2000. It is not really a new text from a substantive point of view, even though a few amendments have been brought to the text of 1874 (which had already been amended more than 100 times as a result for the most part of popular initiatives). But formally, it is an entirely restructured version[19] which is much more readable than the older one. I shall limit myself to mentioning a few provisions dealing with the family.

A complete list of individual rights and freedoms (which are not new in Swiss law but were not necessarily written in the Constitution earlier) appears now in Articles 7ff. Among them, one could stress the right of children and young people to have their

---

[16]   Draft law adapting the cantonal legislation to the new federal divorce law, May 1999.

[17]   On the general issue of the implementation of the child's right to be heard, see the contributions collected in *Revue suisse de jurisprudence* 1999, n° 14 (July 15, 1999), p. 309ff.

[18]   A Report from the Swiss Ministry of Justice was made public in June on the issue. It contains several proposals for legislation. This might be the main topic of a future Survey.

[19]   Federal Act concerning the up-dating of the Federal Constitution, of 18 December 1998, F.F. 1999 176. See also the Federal Council report of November 20, 1996, F.F. 1997 I 1.

integrity specially protected (Article 11), the right to private and family life (Article 13) and the freedom to marry and have a family (Article 14).

Article 41 provides that the State must pursue a number of social goals including the protection and promotion of the family, which is defined merely as 'a community of adult people and children'. Article 116 directs the State to take into account adequately family needs in all its policies. More specifically, Article 116 para. 3 provides that 'the Federal State shall set up a system of maternity leave'. This constitutional mandate given to the Swiss Confederation was originally put into the Constitution in 1945. We shall see in the next paragraph how it has been carried out.

C   The Still-Born Federal Act on Maternity Leave

Maternity leave is a sour story in Switzerland.

The number of births has been slowly decreasing for many years: in 1998, 78,300 children were born, which represents the lowest fertility rate ever observed in the country. It means that 100 women aged between 15 and 49 give birth to 146 children (or 128 children if only Swiss women are included).[20] Now, one knows that in order to secure the renewal of the population, there should be 210 children for every 100 women. In such a context, one might think that a system of maternity leave would be welcome, even though its impact on natality is not clear.

As it was mentioned before, the Federal State had received the constitutional mandate to set up a system of maternity leave in 1945. It is the start of a long story that I shall make here as short as possible.[21] A draft proposal was circulated in 1946 and quickly shelved ; a second proposal was made in 1954 and drew mixed reactions, so it was shelved again. A third, very generous, proposal made through a constitutional initiative, was rejected by Swiss citizens in 1984. A fourth, more modest, proposal joined to a controversial reform of the national health insurance scheme was rejected again in a popular vote in 1987. The fifth attempt, in the 1990s, appeared finally to be on course for success. After a lengthy preparation, the Bill was largely accepted in Parliament which passed the Federal Act on Maternity Leave on December 18, 1998.[22] However, the national organization of employers and conservative parties launched a referendum.[23] On June 13, 1999, 66% of citizens from the French-speaking part of Switzerland accepted the Federal Act on Maternity Leave while 68% of voters in the German-speaking part of the country rejected it. The global result was therefore a clear 'no' (61%)[24] and many hard feelings in the French-speaking part of Switzerland.

Nobody thinks that a sixth attempt will be made soon. A system of maternity leave will probably exist in Switzerland only when, sometime during the next millennium,[25] the country will join the European Union and be bound to implement EC Directive 92/85. Until then, it means that in one of the wealthiest countries in Europe, it will be forbidden for young mothers to work during the eight weeks after delivery (a period that can be

---

[20] *Annuaire statistique de la Suisse*, note 4 (above).

[21] For more details, see the Federal Council report of June 25, 1997, F.F. 1997 IV 881. See also F. Coda-Jaques, *La protezione della maternità e della paternità nell'ottica del principio costituzionale della parità dei sessi*, Bellinzona (1998).

[22] F.F. 1998 4973 and F.F. 1999 2864 for an *errata*.

[23] F.F. 1999 2767: approximately 70,000 people participated in it (constitutional requirement: 50,000).

[24] See the detailed results in the newspaper 'Le Temps' of June 14, 1999, p. 3.

[25] A majority of Swiss citizens (again from the German-speaking part of the country ...) refused to join the European Economic Area in December 1992: see F.F. 1993 I 147 for the detailed results.

reduced to six weeks if the woman so asks) but a number of working women will get a salary for only three or four weeks.

D   The Federal Act on Medically Assisted Procreation

Under pressure from a popular initiative seeking to ban altogether in-vitro fertilization (IVF) and all heterologous methods of artificial reproduction,[26] the Swiss Parliament adopted a very restrictive regulation of medically assisted procreation.[27] One must stress, however, that the federal legislator was not completely free since Article 24[novies] of the Federal Constitution[28] imposed a number of strict substantive principles, such as the limitation of artificial procreation to cases of infertility or serious genetic risk impossible to avert in any other way, the prohibition of surrogate motherhood, of cryo-conservation of embryos as well as of embryo research and embryo donation. Article 24[novies] also affirms the extra-commercial nature of gametes and asserts the individual right to know one's origins.

The Federal Act on Medically Assisted Procreation (AMAP) passed on December 18, 1998, will come into force after the popular referendum on the above-mentioned initiative and provided, of course, that the initiative is rejected, which is not sure as yet. In addition to the constitutional prohibitions, AMAP outlaws egg donation, post-mortem artificial procreation, mixing the sperm from several donors, sex selection, germ-line gene therapy, cloning and pre-implantation genetic diagnosis. It also limits access to heterologous methods of artificial reproduction to married couples and sets up a system of licensing for practicing IVF and artificial insemination by donor (AID) as well as for storing human gametes (only specially trained physicians may get the licence). The prohibition of pre-implantation diagnosis is especially surprising since prenatal genetic diagnosis is largely available, and performed, in Switzerland, even for very basic indications. A draft law on genetic testing made public in September 1998[29] would affirm this situation: it prohibits prenatal diagnosis only when it aims at knowing features unrelated to the health of the foetus or at determining *per se* the sex of the foetus. In other words, prenatal diagnosis may be performed for detecting any health problem of the foetus. It is paradoxical, to say the least, to outlaw on a two-cell or four-cell embryo what is allowed on a 12-week foetus.

Article 27 AMAP entitles any child born of artificial procreation to access the data, filed at the Federal office for civil status and kept for 80 years from his birth, on the sperm donor, i.e. on his biological father. The child's right of access is unconditional as to the donor's identity and physical appearance as soon as he is 18 years old. Whatever his age, the child may also access all data regarding the donor if he can show a material ground. The data include the full identity, residence, education and profession of the donor, the date when sperm was donated, the result of medical tests performed as well as information on the donor's physical appearance.

---

[26]   'Initiative for a procreation respecting the human dignity', F.F. 1992 V 877. See also F.F. 1996 III 197ff. The popular vote should be held in 2000. Parliament recommends rejection of the initiative.

[27]   F.F. 1998 4992. See also the Federal Council report of June 26, 1996, F.F. 1996 III 197.

[28]   See F.F. 1991 II 1433. Article 24[novies] was accepted in a popular vote on May 18, 1992. This provision was split into two Articles in the new federal Constitution, without changing its content: Article 119 dealing with human procreation and genetics and Article 120 dealing with gene technology applied to animals and plants.

[29]   Draft Federal Law on Human Genetic Testing, reproduced in *Revue de droit suisse* (1998), I, p. 473ff.

A child born of artificial procreation using the sperm of a donor will be the lawful child of his mother's husband, according to the basic principle spelled out in Article 255 CC (presumption of paternity of the mother's husband when the child was born during the marriage or within 300 days of its dissolution).[30] The child will be barred from bringing an action to contest the presumption of paternity (Article 256 CC as amended by the AMAP). It means that nobody will have standing to disavow the child's paternal link with his mother's husband, since the latter cannot bring the action himself when he consented to the heterologous method of artificial procreation (which is required by Article 7 AMAP). Besides, a paternity suit against the sperm donor is excluded by Article 23 AMAP, unless the donor knowingly gave his sperm to somebody who does not hold a licence to practise IVF or AID.

At a time of the Internet and cheap travel, it remains to be seen whether the prohibitions and limitations set forth in the Federal Act on Medically Assisted Procreation will prove really effective. Other countries in Europe have more liberal legislation or no legislation at all. In the not so distant past, there have been migratory divorces and abortions; there will be (and probably there is already) migratory artificial reproduction.

III   CASE-LAW

A   *A child has the right to be heard about visitation rights*

The Convention on the Rights of the Child adopted by the United Nations General Assembly on November 20, 1989 was signed by Switzerland on April 10, 1991. After a long parliamentary process,[31] the Convention was eventually ratified on February 24, 1997 and took effect for Switzerland on March 26, 1997.

Ratification was achieved with five reservations dealing with Article 5 ('the Swiss legislation on parental power is reserved'[32]), Article 7 (Swiss law does not grant a right to acquire Swiss nationality), Article 10 para. 1 (certain categories of foreigners are not entitled to family reunion), Article 37 litt. *c* (the right of children to be detained separately from adults is not recognized in full) and Article 40 (the law in a few cantons does not recognize in full the right of a child to have legal assistance and the free assistance of an interpreter; the juvenile court consists in most cantons of a judge who exercises the functions of examining magistrate as well as of sitting judge; cases may arise where no appeal can be lodged against a criminal sentence because the child is directly tried before Switzerland's highest criminal court).[33]

---

[30]   This is why, so it was said by deputies, heterologous methods of reproduction were limited to married couples. The presumption of paternity does not apply outside marriage, of course. But it would have been easy to amend the Civil Code in order to accommodate the situation of cohabitants. See for instance M. Madofia Berney, 'Vérités de la filiation et procréation assistée', Bâle (1993), p. 189f. The Federal Parliament simply did not want to.

[31]   To get an idea of its difficulty, see O. Guillod, 'Swiss Law and the United Nations Convention on the Rights of the Child', *Children's rights. A comparative Perspective*, M. Freeman (Ed.), Aldershot-etc., (1996), p. 223ff. Ratification was proposed by the Swiss government in a 1994 report: F.F. 1994 V 1. For the parliamentary debates, see BO CN 1996, p. 1679ff, 2148ff, 2369 and BO CE 1996 342ff, 359ff, 900ff, 1048ff.

[32]   I haven't so far understood the meaning of this reservation added by a group of deputies.

[33]   For an assessment of the scope of these reservations, see St. Wolf, 'Die UNO-Konvention über die Rechte des Kindes und ihre Umsetzung in das schweizerische Kindesrecht', *Revue de la Société des Juristes Bernois* (1998), p. 113ff.

Once an international treaty is ratified, the main question is to determine whether its provisions are self-executing or not. It is well known that national courts have answered the question differently throughout Europe. On December 22, 1997, the Second Civil Chamber of the Federal Court had the first opportunity to give its own answer.[34]

The issue was to determine whether a six-year-old little girl ought to be heard on the issue of a visitation right claimed by her father, whom she barely knew. A preliminary question was to assess the nature of Article 12 of the Convention on the Rights of the Child. The judges stressed the fact that Article 12 was a central provision of the Convention. Taking into account the clear wording and concrete scope of this provision as well as the possibility for a judge to apply it, the Federal Court ruled that it was indeed self-executing. Consequently, a violation of Article 12 could be invoked in an appeal to the Federal Court against a decision from a cantonal court. The court went on to examine whether the child in the case should have been heard personally. It answered negatively because the girl was very young and did not know her father.[35]

This ruling is of great importance for the rights of children and will apply in many disputes beyond visitation rights. It has also prompted cantons to amend their procedural laws to implement fully the right of the child to be heard. And it is totally in line with the new provisions of the Civil Code on the right of the child to be heard personally or through a curator in the divorce proceedings of his parents.

B The dark side of cohabitation

Cohabitation has no legally organized status in Switzerland but the problems confronting cohabitants have been solved by the courts on a case-by-case basis. The legal provisions on marriage have usually not been applied in favour of cohabitants, for instance to grant them the same rights as those of married people in relation to social security. By contrast, the courts have frequently applied rules framed for married people to cohabitants (arguing by analogy) to prevent situations from arising where cohabitants would be treated better than married couples. For instance, when a divorced woman who was granted alimony lives with a partner in a durable and stable relationship, she loses the alimony as if she remarried (Article 153 para 1 CC). This ruling was logically extended to the situation where the wife was already cohabiting at the time of divorce: the Federal Court decided that the wife had forfeited her right to financial contributions from her ex-husband.[36]

In one area, the situation has been very complex: taxation. More than ten years ago, married couples successfully claimed that they were not treated on an equal footing with cohabitants as to the taxation of income (largely ruled by cantonal law). This was due to the fact that married people formed a single entity for tax purposes whereas cohabitants were taxed separately. The Federal Court noted that it was impossible to ensure equal treatment in each individual case and 'to prevent that some advantages be granted to married couples or to cohabitants'. The Court added that 'the legal status of marriage and its social significance require that the tax legislator favor married couples over cohabiting couples'.[37] In other words, limited fiscal disadvantages to the detriment of cohabiting couples are compatible with the equal treatment clause. But the tax authority must

---

[34]   ATF 124 III 90.

[35]   ATF 124 III 90, at 93f.

[36]   ATF 124 III 52.

[37]   ATF 110 Ia 7, ATF 118 Ia 1, at 5. See also ATF 120 Ia 343.

consider in all cases the financial capability to pay taxes ('*capacité contributive*') and must tax similarly people with the same capability, comparing the situation of spouses, cohabitants and single people.

It is generally admitted that the legal principles developed by the Federal Court about income tax do not apply fully to taxes of a special nature, like inheritance tax or taxes on the selling of real estate, where the capability to pay taxes is not relevant. A recent case was a good opportunity to test where the Federal Court stood on the issue.[38]

A man died and left no widow, children or parents. A will was found that made his long-time companion his sole heir. Since the estate amounted to SF 405,000.–, the canton of Neuchâtel asked her to pay SF 145,800.–, or 36% of the total estate, as inheritance tax, on the basis of the cantonal law. She contested the decision, arguing that it was arbitrary and violated the equal treatment clause of Article 4 of the Federal Constitution on two counts: first, a spouse would be exonerated from the tax (if she had children) or would have to pay only 6% (i.e. SF 24,300.–); secondly, the law is more favourable to relatives,[39] although they may have no personal bond with the deceased, than to the long-time partner: a brother or sister would have to pay 9%, uncles and aunts 12%, cousins 15%, etc. Since her claim was rejected by the cantonal administrative court, she appealed to the Federal court.

The Federal court refused to strike down the cantonal law. It stressed that the amount of the tax was based on the formal degree of relationship, in accordance with the system of the Civil Code (Article 20 CC) that also uses it to define the order of succession (Article 457ff CC). It is a simple and easy to control criterion that cannot be deemed contrary to the equal treatment clause. The cantonal law did not take into account the real intensity of the relationship, as the appellant would have liked. Such a criterion, that would favour personal over family ties, would be too difficult to implement (anybody could claim he or she was quite close to the deceased ...) and would therefore raise too much uncertainty. The court concluded that the system adopted in the cantonal law, which also exists in numerous other cantons, aimed at protecting family values and was therefore legitimate. It is up to the cantonal lawmaker and not to the courts to modify the system by taking into consideration the situation of cohabitants.

The rationale of the court's decision is not entirely persuasive, but it is fairly typical. As in several other decisions dealing with cohabitation, the court couldn't help but give a short lesson on morals. It remarked that the appellant had a paid job during the time when she lived with the deceased and that, under cantonal law, she benefited from a lower income tax than that of a married couple. 'She therefore is not in a position to question a legal status that she has freely chosen with her partner now that this status proves detrimental to her'.[40] This sentence is more telling than all the legal arguments used in the decision as to the position of the Federal Court towards cohabitation.

---

[38]   ATF 123 I 241.
[39]   In the sense of Articles 20 and 21 CC.
[40]   ATF 123 I 241, at 247–248.

UKRAINE

JUVENILE PROPERTY RIGHTS IN UKRAINE

Irina Zhylinkova[*]

I INTRODUCTION

A basic task of a socially oriented State is to satisfy juvenile interests in the maximum possible way, to protect juvenile rights as well as to fulfil the obligations prescribed by the UN Convention on the Rights of the Child.[1] The situation with respect to juvenile development in Ukraine may be characterized as desperate. This is accounted for by the general demographic crisis in the country reflected in the deterioration of both quantitative and qualitative characteristics of the population including the juvenile section, which amounts to about 13 million in Ukraine. A juvenile is a young person under the age of 18. Over four million juveniles are living in poor conditions. These are primarily orphans, juveniles temporarily lacking parental support, the disabled, juvenile delinquents and children from poor families. The general economic crisis in the country, major ecological problems, lack of resources, inefficiency in the old system of social protection and medical care seriously infringe the rights of the juveniles mentioned above.[2]

The Children of Ukraine National Programme was approved by the country's President on January 18, 1996 to solve the juvenile protection problems. It provided for measures to improve the situation and to ensure the right to social protection of each child. The programme is based on the assumption that the family is a natural medium for the physical, psychological and spiritual development of the child. The family provides for the child's material living conditions, is a principal source of his/her financial support and is responsible for fulfilling this obligation.

The law relating to juvenile property rights has become a major problem lately. The deterioration of the economic situation in Ukraine increases the number of cases where parents do not provide for the child's proper living conditions, do not pay alimony, illegally sell the child's property and deprive children of their dwelling space. Thus, the UN Convention on the Rights of the Child (Article 27, paragraph 2) as well as the requirements of the Ukrainian legislation are violated. All these cases call for immediate action on the part of State and volunteer organizations which provide for the protection of juvenile rights.

---

[*]   Professor in the Civil Law Department at the National Law Academy of Ukraine (Kharkiv).

[1]   Ukraine ratified the Convention on the Rights of the Child on February 27, 1991.

[2]   Z.Kolesnichenko, 'Uzhodzhennia zakonodavstva Ukrainy z vymohamy Konventsii OON pro prava dytyny – vymoha chasy'. *Pravo Ukrainy*. No 6. S.39 (1997).

II   BASIC JUVENILE PROPERTY RIGHTS WITHIN A FAMILY

Juvenile property rights constitute an element in the whole array of juvenile rights which have to be guaranteed within a family. Among the basic ones are the following:

- the right of the child to be supported by his/her parents and other members of the family;
- the right to the property acquired as a result of civil legal transactions (donation, sale or purchase, exchange, inheritance, etc.);
- the right to the property acquired as a result of the privatization of State property;
- the right to the profit accumulated from the property owned by him/her;
- the right to the proper management of the property on the part of his/her parents, other members of the family as well as guardians;
- the right to deposit money in a bank and to hold the corresponding income (juveniles above the age of 15 years);
- the right to control his/her own wages/salary, stipend, royalties and any other income acquired as a result of his/her work, intellectual or business activity (juveniles above the age of 16 years);
- the right to use the dwelling and other property which is in legal ownership of his/her parents or other member of the family.

III   THE PARENT–CHILD PROPERTY RELATIONSHIP

The parent-child property relationship has two aspects:

(1) the parent–child property relationship;
(2) the parent–child alimony relationship.

In both types of relationship the parents must act in such a way as to ensure the best interest of the child. Father and mother have equal rights and obligations as regards their children (Article 59 Marriage and Family Code of Ukraine).[3] Ukrainian law has always been based on the principle of the parents' equal rights and obligations and has not imposed a discriminatory support duty on the father.

A   *The parent–child property relationship*

The child may own a wide range of things: houses, apartments, cars and other valuables. According to Article 13 of the Law Concerning Property[4] the composition, amount, and cost of private property is not restricted. Property may be acquired by the child through inheritance, donation or other transactions. According to Article 77 of MFC of Ukraine the parents have no right to the child's property as long as the child is alive. The parents may own the child's property only in the case of the child's death as his/her heirs.

Juveniles are divided into two categories: those under the age of 15, and those aged 15 to 18. The extent of juvenile capacity is determined depending on their age. Juveniles under 15 may of their own volition conduct minor everyday transactions. Apart from that a child may on his own deposit and withdraw money from a bank (Article 14 of the Civil Code of Ukraine). Parents manage the property of their children under the age of 15 and

---

[3]   The Marriage and Family Code of Ukraine hereafter referred to as 'MFC of Ukraine'.
[4]   Vidomosti Verhovnoi Rady Ukrainy. 20. St.249 (1991).

are responsible for any damage inflicted on the property by their children. The parents conduct all actions their child would conduct himself/herself assuming he/she had full capacity. While managing their children's property the parents must act within certain limits provided by the law. A sale of the real estate and other valuable property belonging to a juvenile can be conducted only with the permission of specially designated State bodies. The donation of a child's property is forbidden altogether.

A child under the age of 16 may not be employed. Children (between the ages of 16 and 18) may work and retain their own wages. They can be in control of their wages/salary, a stipend or any other income acquired by their labour. If juveniles between 15 and 18 get financial support from their parents, it is necessary to obtain the parents' consent where those juveniles wish to conduct a transaction. Third parties bear their own responsibility for damage caused to property. Parents may be made responsible where their child did not have enough money to compensate fully for damage he/she has inflicted. The parents have no right to demand the reimbursement of sums paid as compensation for damage inflicted by their children after the latter have reached the age of 18.

Emancipation occurs by operation of law when: (a) a minor reaches the age of majority; and (b) a minor marries (Article 11 of the Civil Code of Ukraine).[5] If a juvenile gets married he/she automatically acquires full capacity without a judicial hearing. If a person gets divorced before he/she reaches the age of 18, his/her capacity does not decrease. There have been suggestions in legal literature that full capacity should be given to juvenile mothers and fathers who are not legally married. The mere registration of a juvenile as the mother and/or father of a child should, it is argued, be a sufficient ground for the juvenile's emancipation.[6] However the existing legislation does not confer full capacity on a single mother or father.

An order that a minor is emancipated has the following effect: the minor may buy and sell movable and not immovable property; the minor may enter into property contracts; the minor may sue and be sued in his own name. The parents of minors will no longer be the guardians of their child. But the parents are not relieved of the obligation to pay maintenance to their juvenile children even if their daughter/son gets married before she/he is 18.

The property rights of juveniles are protected by civil, family and other branches of Ukrainian legislation. Civil law provides two main methods for the protection of ownership: the negatory suit and the suit of vindication. The negatory suit is applicable if any person hinders the normal exercise of the child's property right. The vindication suit is used where the child-owner is not in possession of his/her property but another person has this property in his/her possession without a legal title. The parents of minors should file a legal suit to protect the children's property rights; if a juvenile has full capacity, he/she speaks in the court of law in his/her own name.

---

[5] According to Article 16 of MFC of Ukraine men are allowed to get married at the age of 18 and women at the age of 17. In exceptional cases those age limits may be disregarded on the decision of the corresponding State bodies.

[6] Z.V. Romovska, 'Tsivilna diyezdatnist hromadyanyna (fizychnoyi osoby) (do rozroblennia novoho Tsyvilnoho kodeksu)' *Pravo Ukrainy*. No 2. C.25 (1995).

B   The parent–child maintenance relationship

Parents must support their minor children. According to Article 80 of MFC of Ukraine, the parental maintenance obligation extends to the child's age of majority (18 years). This obligation terminates upon the death of either the child or the parent. The parents themselves decide on the way in which they will pay maintenance to support the child. However the amount of money which is due to be paid cannot be smaller than that prescribed by the law. If the mother/father evades her/his obligation, the money to support the child is exacted from them through a court.

The general rule is that a certain proportion of the parent's income is exacted to support the child depending on the number of children: 1/4 for one child, 1/3 for two children, 1/2 for three or more children. Maintenance has a periodic character and must be paid every month. The parents' property division after separation does not influence the amount of maintenance to be paid. If the parent the child is going to live with receives a larger amount of property after the divorce, it does not give the right to the other parent to demand a decrease in the amount of maintenance to be paid.

This maintenance enforcement system was established long ago.[7] It suited the situation where the wages/salaries in the country were low and fixed. But it does not make much sense at present. Nowadays the parents' income may be large. Correspondingly 1/4 of a parent's income, to be paid to the child every month, may constitute a fairly large sum of money. The transfer of those sums to the parent with whom the child lives (mostly mothers) may not always be in the child's interests. Therefore it is now proposed to introduce a limit on the maximum amount of money which can be exacted from a parent as maintenance to be paid for the child's support.

In some cases a court may decrease the amount of maintenance to be paid for the child's support. This may happen where:

(a) the payer is a disabled person;
(b) the child works and has his/her own income;
(c) the child has state support;
(d) the parents have other minor children who are less well supported than those for whom the maintenance is exacted (Article 82 of MFC of Ukraine).

However, even when one of the above-mentioned conditions is present, the decrease in the amount of maintenance does not occur automatically. For example, a juvenile works and has his/her own income. However, during the hearing in the court it is discovered that the juvenile had to quit school because of financial difficulties in the family. In this case, the decrease in the amount of maintenance would not be in the interests of the child.

According to the present law, parents are not obliged to provide educational support for their children past the age of majority. This rule has been in effect for many decades and was explained by the fact that education in the soviet period in Ukraine was free. Now a juvenile may be obliged to pay for his/her higher education. Correspondingly the idea of prolonging the period until the child's time of graduation is being discussed at the moment. This obligation however should not be imposed on parents automatically but only where the juvenile, on reaching the age of 18, is not able for some reason to provide financial support for himself/herself unaided. In such cases the parents would have to continue paying maintenance but would not be obliged to pay for the child's tuition.

---

[7]   The existing MFC of Ukraine came into effect on January 1, 1970.

According to the present law, in exceptional cases, parents may be made to provide additional support for their minor children (Article 86 of MFC of Ukraine). This may be the case with a serious disease or severe injuiry of the child. As a rule parents pay for the treatment of the child on a voluntary basis. However, if they do not, the required amounts may be exacted through a court. In that case the court specifies the amount of money required at the moment or to be required for the child's treatment in the future. Those amounts may include expenses for medicine, medical care, prosthetic appliances, additional nutrition, etc. Such expenses may be covered by a lump sum or on a monthly basis, depending on the circumstances.

If circumstances change, either side may apply to the court to vary the decision concerning the enforcement of periodic payments. If the child's health has deteriorated, the amount of payments may be increased. If the opposite has happened, the court may decrease the amount of payments for the child's treatment, or it may terminate such payments altogether.

THE UNITED STATES

THE ADOPTION AND SAFE FAMILIES ACT: A MAJOR SHIFT IN CHILD WELFARE LAW AND POLICY

Barbara Bennett Woodhouse[*]

I   INTRODUCTION

This past year has seen numerous developments in family law in the United States, but I will focus on one that I believe has sweeping policy implications – the recent amendments of State child welfare laws in response to the Adoption and Safe Families Act. These changes to the laws governing protective interventions were intended to establish child safety as the paramount concern, accelerate termination of parental rights to free children for adoption, and shift government subsidies from foster care and family preservation to adoption. This shift of resources into promoting adoption, as opposed to State-managed foster care, as a solution for children in 'dysfunctional' families can be seen as a form of 'privatizing' child welfare.[1] This policy shift was initiated by Congress in the Adoption and Safe Families Act of 1997 (hereinafter 'ASFA').[2] ASFA took effect in 1998, and during that year its policies were extended nationwide, by legislation enacted at the State level. In order to place this development in context, the next section will provide some background on child welfare laws and the child welfare system in the United States.

A   Welfare, child welfare, and foster care

'The child welfare system' is the name we use to refer to a network of laws and government agencies intended to protect and shelter children who are at risk of abuse and neglect and to care for 'dependent children', i.e. children who are dependent on the community because they lack proper parental care and supervision.[3] 'Child welfare' is different from 'welfare', the term Americans use to describe a system of income supports

---

[*]   Professor of Law, University of Pennsylvania Law School. This article is dedicated to the memory of James Lafferty, Esq., who headed the Family Unit at Community Legal Services of Philadelphia, until his untimely death in June 1999. Jim devoted his career to helping poor families, and was instrumental in educating the Philadelphia legal community, including myself and my students, about the implications of the Adoption and Safe Families Act. He was a devoted family man, deeply religious, a committed social activist, a gifted lawyer and an inspiring teacher. He will be missed.

[1]   I use 'scare quotes' around each of these terms intentionally. The concept of 'dysfunction' is strongly contextual and depends on cultural assumptions that are often hard to defend. The notion of 'privatization' is also contextual – and here I use the term to describe the shifting of actual operational responsibility for a task previously performed by government to some private sector entity. The private sector entities, in this case, are the families who adopt children out of foster care.

[2]   Public Law 105-89, amending the Adoption Assistance and Child Welfare Act, codified at 42 U.S.C. 671 & ff.

[3]   For a comprehensive set of essays on the U.S. child welfare system see *The Future of Children: Protecting Children from Abuse and Neglect* (Spring 1998). This volume is the eighth one in a series of studies commissioned by the David and Lucille Packard Foundation on key children's issues.

for the poor. Although rates of poverty and rates of child abuse and neglect are interconnected, law-makers often act as if 'welfare' policy and 'child welfare' policy were entirely unrelated.[4] As I will argue later, it is no accident that, a year before enactment of ASFA, Congress replaced the primary 'welfare' program, Aid to Families with Dependent Children (AFDC) with a new program called Temporary Assistance to Needy Families (TANF).[5] In both the welfare and child welfare contexts, the recent reforms effectively limited the time during which families that lack monetary or parenting resources may be maintained at taxpayers' expense.

Child welfare policy traditionally has focused on protection of dependent children and children at risk of abuse or neglect through means other than providing income supports for their parents. Many child welfare services indirectly benefit parents and are provided to children in their own homes.[6] In Philadelphia, for example, 'SCOH workers' can be assigned to provide family preservation services including parenting training, play therapy, and homemaking.[7] However, between 1985 and 1995 the population of children removed from home and placed in 'substitute' care almost doubled, from 276,000 to 494,000, and it continues to increase.[8] Of the more than three million children reported abused and neglected each year, approximately 250,000 are taken into protective custody, under the control of county or State agencies with names like Administration for Children's Services, Department of Human Services, or Department of Youth and Family Services.[9] While their parents retain vestigial rights, for all intents and purposes the State has become responsible for rearing the child. State and county agencies, either directly or through contracts with private non-profit organizations, employ social workers to manage the children's cases, and supervise their placement with licensed foster families who are paid to care for them.

How did these half a million children enter 'State care'? Some were surrendered voluntarily by parents who could not cope, due to mental or physical illness, addiction, family dissolution, or other disruptive circumstances. Others were involuntarily removed by court order under State child protective laws empowering police and child protective workers to intervene in cases of abuse and neglect, often because of drug involvement of the parent. Sometimes a 'voluntary' placement is made under threat of coercive court intervention, making it difficult for policy analysts to determine how many children are removed under duress.

---

[4]   Bernadine Dohrn and Dorothy Roberts have both pointed out this anomaly in articles to be published in the 1999 symposium issue of *St. John's Journal of Law Reform* (forthcoming 1999) and in the 1999 symposium issue on children's rights of the *University of Pennsylvania Journal of Constitutional Law* (forthcoming 1999). *The University of Pennsylvania Journal of Constitutional Law* publishes electronically and articles can be located at http://www.law.upenn.edu by clicking on 'publications' and accessing the Journal's home page.

[5]   In 1996, the primary federal 'welfare' program AFDC was replaced by TANF, Title III, Pub. L. No. 104-193, 110 Stat. 2105 (1996). TANF limits time on welfare and emphasizes programs intended to move unemployed mothers into the work force.

[6]   See generally Jacquelyn McCroskey & William Meezan, 'Family-Centered Services: Approaches and Effectiveness' at p. 54 in *Protecting Children* (note 3 above).

[7]   SCOH is an acronym for Services to Children in their Own Homes.

[8]   See Jill Duerr Berrick, 'When Children Cannot Remain Home: Foster Family Care and Kinship Care' at p. 72, in *Protecting Children* (note 3 above). For an excellent book of research papers on these issues, see *Young Children and Foster Care: A Guide for Professionals* (Judith A. Silver et al, eds.) (Brookes Pub. 1999).

[9]   Douglas Besharov, 'Commentary: How We Can Better Protect Children from Abuse and Neglect?' at pp.120, 122 in *Protecting Children* (note 3 above).

Foster care has long been conceptualized as a temporary measure providing respite and support, and giving families time to rebuild and reunify. The classic role of the foster family is not to provide a permanent home but merely to house, feed, and clothe the child while the State or local agency works with the child's parents to resolve whatever issues necessitated placement. Foster families enter into a contract with an agency which sets forth their duties and gives them only a limited form of custody and no parental rights. Typically, they are urged to avoid becoming too attached or allowing the child to become too attached, so as to avoid disrupting bonds with the biological family with whom the child will be reunited. In short, foster families are discouraged from becoming the child's 'real' family.

This makes sense if the foster care system functions simply as a temporary safe haven. For too many children, the reality has not matched this aspiration. Many children have spent the bulk of their lives moving from temporary foster placement to foster placement – a syndrome critics have described as 'foster care drift'.[10] These children suffer developmental and emotional damage from a loss of trust in adults and from a lack of stability and continuity. The child welfare system also has had a disparate impact on racial minorities. Black children are three times as likely to be in foster care as white children and stay in care on average twice as long.[11] Many children – again, disproportionately minority children – spend their entire childhoods in foster care only to 'age out' of the system at 18 or 21, without ever being reunified with their families of origin. Many became 'state orphans' when the courts terminated the rights of their biological parents to pave the way for an adoption that never materialized. Case workers assigned to assist these youths in the transition to 'independent living' face the task of re-establishing ties with family members whose legal relationship has long ago been terminated.[12] Without such ties, the young person lacks the family support network necessary to survival once he exits the child welfare system.

For all its costs and detriments, the child welfare system does not ensure children's safety. Shockingly, 48% of child abuse deaths in 1995 involved children previously known to the authorities.[13] Sometimes it is a story of under-intervention – of a child left in his home after reported abuse only to be beaten to death. Sometimes it is a story of over-intervention – of a child removed from home only to be abused by a foster parent. As the National Commission on Children reported, 'If the nation had deliberately designed a system that would frustrate the professionals who staff it, anger the public who finance it, and abandon the children who depend on it, it could not have done a better job than the present child welfare system'.[14]

---

[10] Besharov reports that of 400,000 children in foster care in 1990, 40% had been in care for more than two years, half of these had been in at least two foster homes, a quarter of these in three or more foster homes. Besharov in *Protecting Children* (note 3 above) at 122.

[11] Children's Defense Fund, *Black and White Children in America*: Key Facts (Washington, D.C., 1985). For a comprehensive discussion of black children in the welfare system, see Joyce E. Everett, Sandra S. Chipungyu, & Bogart R. Leashore, eds, *Child Welfare: An Africentric Perspective* (1991).

[12] For a thoughtful discussion of the implications for youths of policies favoring terminations of parental rights, see Marsha Garrison, 'Parents' Rights v. Children's Interests: The Case of the Foster Child', 22 *N.Y.U. Rev. L. Soc. Change* 371 (1996).

[13] See Besharov in *Protecting Children* (note 3 above), citing National Committee to Prevent Child Abuse, *Current Trends in Child Abuse Reporting and Fatalities: the Results of the 1995 Fifty-State Survey*, (Chicago: NCPCA, April 1996, p. 3).

[14] National Commission on Children, *Beyond Rhetoric: A New American Agenda for Children and Families* 293, U.S. Govt Printing Office (1991).

B   *The federal role in setting child welfare policy*

Unfortunately, the complexities of the federal system allowed scant opportunity for 'deliberate design' on a national scale. Authority for child welfare policy and implementation in the U.S. remains fragmented between federal, local and State authorities. The federal Constitution reserves to the States all powers not specifically delegated to the federal government.[15] Family matters, including child welfare laws, have historically been a state preserve. Thus, the actual laws that govern protective interventions in the family are written at the state level by State legislatures. These laws are often administered by courts and agencies operating at the county or municipal level.

State legislatures and local courts do not operate in a vacuum, however. The federal Constitution places important limitations on State and local authorities. The Constitution has been interpreted by the Supreme Court as requiring that the State show a compelling reason for infringing on rights of family privacy and for overriding parental autonomy, since these are fundamental liberties protected by the Fourteenth Amendment guarantees of due process.[16] As long as State and local authorities do not unlawfully burden those rights protected by the Constitution, they are theoretically free to formulate their own child protection and child welfare policies.

Even more importantly, however, about half of the funding for child protective programs comes from federal tax dollars.[17] While Congress has limited authority to intervene directly in child welfare law, it has virtually unlimited authority under the 'Spending Clause' to fund programs for the general welfare.[18] By attaching conditions to receipt of federal funds, or creating incentives through federal grants linked to performance measures, Congress uses the power of the purse to shape state and local policies. By choosing to fund some programs (for example, reimbursing States for payments to foster families and adoptive families) and not other programs (for example, restricting reimbursements to States for in-home services or welfare subsidies), Congress, in effect, is dictating social welfare policies.

Beginning with the Social Security Act of 1935, Congress has passed a sequence of federal laws that conditioned the receipt of funding to defray the costs of child welfare

---

[15]   United States Constitution, Amendment X. For a discussion of the historical tensions between the constitutional limits on federal action and the desire of children's rights advocates to mandate nationwide compliance with child labor laws and education laws, see Barbara Bennett Woodhouse, 'Who Owns the Child?: Meyer and Pierce and the Child as Property', 33 *Wm. & Mary L. Rev.* 995 (1992). See also, Jill Elaine Hasday, 'Federalism and the Family Reconstructed', 45 *UCLA L. Rev.* 1297 (1998).

[16]   Although the term 'family' is nowhere mentioned in the U.S. Constitution, the United States Supreme Court has interpreted the scope of the 'liberty' protected by the Fourteenth Amendment as reaching the rights to marry and form a family, rights of family privacy, and the rights of parents to custody and control of their children. In addition, the Court has applied other provisions of the Constitution in contexts relevant to child welfare laws. See, e.g., *Meyer v. Nebraska*, 262 U.S. 390 (1923) (vindicating parents' substantive due process rights to control the upbringing of their children); *Stanley v. Illinois*, 405 U.S. 645 (1972) (recognizing unmarried biological father's rights to raise his children); *Wisconsin v. Yoder*, 406 U.S. 205 (1972) (protecting parents' First Amendment right to keep children out of school in order to inculcate them with their own religion). For a discussion of the process of constitutionalization of family rights, see Barbara Bennett Woodhouse, 'Constitutional Interpretation and the Re-Constitution of the Family,' in *New Family Forms* (John Eekelaar, ed. 1998). For a persuasive argument that in America these rights are rooted in the history of the Civil War Amendments, which repudiated slavery as an assault on basic human rights of family integrity, see Peggy Cooper Davis, *Neglected Stories: The Constitution and Family Values* (1997).

[17]   See generally Mark E. Courtney, 'The Costs of Child Protection in the Context of Welfare Reform', in *Protecting Children* (note 3 above), at 88.

[18]   Article I, section 7, U.S. Constitution ('Congress shall have the power to lay and collect taxes to … provide for the common defense and general welfare of the United States.').

programs on the State's conformance with certain standards and procedures. For purposes of this discussion, the most important federal initiative prior to ASFA was the Adoption Assistance and Child Welfare Act of 1980 (hereinafter 'AACWA'). AACWA was passed in response to concerns that children were being removed unnecessarily from their homes and then left to drift in foster care. In AACWA, Congress created strong incentives for States to pass child welfare laws that would emphasize family preservation and reunification.[19] In the scheme envisioned by this reform measure, children were not to be separated from their families unnecessarily. AACWA offered federal funds to the States for foster care and other services, but only if the State enacted laws guaranteeing that 'in each case, reasonable efforts will be made (A) prior to placement of a child in foster care to prevent or eliminate the need for removal of the child from his home, and (B) to make it possible for the child to return to his home'.[20] Under the laws enacted by States to conform with AACWA, agency social workers and families, together with their lawyers, would participate in drawing up a Family Service Plan (commonly referred to as the 'FSP') identifying a goal for the child and outlining programs and services the State must provide to the family. It was hoped that periodic court reviews of these FSPs would speed reunification. Only if a family showed no progress over an extended period of time despite the State's best efforts, would it be appropriate to terminate the parent–child relationship to free the child for adoption by a new family.

In practice, the initial goal for almost every child was 'reunification'. The issue of 'permanency' – whether or not the parents could realistically care for the child in the foreseeable future and, if not, who would care for him on a permanent basis – was supposed to be addressed 18 months after placement, but often was delayed well beyond this time. A goal change to 'adoption' at 18, 24 or 48 months did not provide permanency, but merely shifted the focus from reunification to the long and arduous process of terminating parental rights and searching for an adoptive home.[21]

After almost 20 years of AACWA, calls for reform were universal. Critics from both right and left believed the child welfare system was failing in its most important purposes. More children were streaming into the system, entering younger and remaining longer, and still the national rates of child abuse and fatality were rising. As popular sentiment turned against big government and social welfare programs and in favor of privatization and personal responsibility, the child welfare pendulum swung away from family preservation and reunification, and toward more aggressive child protection and a greater emphasis on moving children out of the child welfare system into permanent adoptive homes where they would no longer be wards of the State. Some believed that AACWA was being misinterpreted and employed in ways that institutionalized foster care as a 'way of life' for both parents and children.[22] They charged that the laws valued

---

[19] AACWA or PL 96-262, is codified at 42 U.S.C. sec. 620-629a. 670-679a. The Family Preservation and Support Initiative, PL 103-66, granted funds to States for family preservation and support.

[20] This passage of the Adoption Assistance and Child Welfare Act of 1980 was singled out for criticism by Congress. See 143 Cong. Rec. S.12198.

[21] The Supreme Court held in *Santosky v. Kramer*, 455 U.S. 755 (1982), that States must have 'clear and convincing evidence' that the parents would be unable to care for the child before terminating parental rights. Any lesser standard would violate the parent's constitutional rights to due process under the Fourteenth Amendment. Under *Stanley v. Illinois*, (above), unmarried fathers as well as mothers were entitled to notice and could claim constitutional rights to raise their offspring.

[22] The comments of Senators in the Congressional Record illustrate their belief that past measures had failed and new policies were required. See, e.g., 143 Cong. Rec. S. 12210 & ff. Adopting the rhetoric of recent 'welfare reform' aimed at weaning adults from the dole, Senator Grassley of Iowa stated, 'Set up to serve as a temporary emergency situation for children, the foster care system is now a lifestyle for many kids.' 143 Cong. Rec. S. 12211.

parents' rights and preservation of the biological parent–child relationship more than the welfare and safety of children. Critics pointed out that the average child who entered foster care would have to wait three years before any decision was made about his future and 'twenty-one states' were failing so badly in managing their child welfare systems that they had been forced to enter into consent decrees.[23] An over-emphasis on 'reasonable efforts' was preventing children who would never realistically be reunited with their parents from moving on to find safe, permanent families through adoption.[24] AACWA, its critics contended, encouraged authorities to return children prematurely to unsafe families and prevented their timely removal from dangerous situations.

Advocates for parents countered that far too many children were being removed in the first place.[25] These children were being removed not because of gross abuses but because of more nebulous concerns about 'neglect'. Child protective workers who were fearful of making a fatal mistake, or who viewed the world through white middle-class spectacles, saw danger where no real danger existed. Moreover, critics charged that funding policies set at the national level skewed State policies. Congress was willing to reimburse foster care outlays but was slow to fund basic income support or in-home services, with the result that many children were removed because of their parents' poverty and lack of education, when appropriate income transfers and social supports might have prevented removal.[26]

II   THE ADOPTION AND SAFE FAMILIES ACT OF 1997

A   *The basic provisions of ASFA*

In 1997, Congress passed the Adoption and Safe Families Act (ASFA) which did not repeal but rather amended the Adoption Assistance and Child Welfare Act (AACWA).[27] Any State that wished to share in federal funds earmarked for foster care and child protective services must pass laws embodying a new set of priorities. As described by Senator Rockefeller of West Virginia, 'The major objective of this Bill is to move abused and neglected kids into adoption or other permanent homes and to do it more quickly and more safely than ever before'.[28] In the following sections I will summarize ASFA's basic goals and operational language.[29]

---

[23] Senator Grassley, 134 Cong. Rec. S. 1221.

[24] This case has been made most forcefully by Dr. Richard Gelles, in his book detailing the failures of the child welfare system, *The Book of David: How Preserving Families Can Cost Children's Lives* (New York: Basic Books 1996). See also remarks of Senator Craig of Idaho, quoting from the Adoption Assistance and Child Welfare Act, 143 Cong. Rec. S. 1219.

[25] Martin Guggenheim presents a powerful case in the 1999 Symposium issue of the *University of Pennsylvania Journal of Constitutional Law* (note 4 above), commenting on a paper by Dr. Gelles.

[26] This position is forcefully argued by Professor Dorothy Roberts in a forthcoming article in the *University of Pennsylvania Journal of Constitutional Law* (forthcoming 1999).

[27] For a discussion of the legislative history, see Cecile Pagano, 'Recent Legislation: Adoption and Foster Care', 36 *Harv. J. on Legis.* 242 (1999).

[28] Senator Rockefeller, 143 Cong. Rec. 12199.

[29] This list of goals and others similar to it were used by proponents of ASFA and by President Clinton when he signed the legislation into law. See 143 Cong. Rec. S. 12210; 'Remarks on Signing the Adoption and Safe Families Act of 1997', 33 Weekly Comp. Pres. Doc. 1863, 1864 (Nov. 19, 1997).

1 Making children's safety and health the paramount concern

Critics of AACWA had focused on the 'reasonable efforts' language, arguing that it encouraged courts and agencies to initiate efforts at reunification or preservation in circumstances which placed children at unacceptable risk. Under ASFA, the State scheme is eligible only if it provides that 'in determining reasonable efforts ... to be made with respect to a child, and in making such reasonable efforts, the child's health and safety shall be the paramount concern'.[30] This language shifts the emphasis from balancing of various values such as family autonomy and child safety to a priority of child safety over competing values such as family preservation or parental rights. ASFA also provides that 'not later than January 1, 1999, the State shall develop and implement standards to ensure that children in foster care placements in public or private agencies are provided quality services that protect the safety and health of the children'.[31] In addition, ASFA requires States to perform police and child abuse registry checks not only of foster and adoptive parents but of all adults in the household.[32] This measure addressed growing concerns about abuse inflicted by non-relative males living in the child's household.

2 Moving children more rapidly out of foster care and into permanent homes

A second major goal of ASFA was to shorten children's stays in foster care. AACWA emphasized permanency through reunification and the mandate of 'reasonable efforts'. Before ASFA, some States adopted the higher standard of 'diligent' efforts. AACWA mandated six-month reviews of the FSP and set 18 months as the time at which permanency planning should be initiated. ASFA mandates a permanency hearing at 12 months. After a child has been in care for 15 out of 22 months, ASFA shifts the burden to the State to show why a TPR petition should *not* be filed. The key ASFA language reads:

'in the case of a child who has been in foster care under the responsibility of the State for 15 of the most recent 22 months ... the State shall file a petition to terminate the parental rights of the child's parents (or, if such a petition has been filed by another party, seek to be joined as a party to the petition), and, concurrently, to identify, recruit, process, and approve a qualified family for an adoption.'

ASFA carves out three situations in which the State need not petition for TPR:

'(i) at the option of the State, the child is being cared for by a relative;
(ii) a State agency has documented in the case plan (which shall be available for court review) a compelling reason for determining that filing such a petition would not be in the best interests of the child; or
(iii) the State has not provided to the family of the child, consistent with the time period in the State case plan, such services as the State deems necessary for the safe return of the child to the child's home, if reasonable efforts ... are required to be made with respect to the child.'

To speed permanent placement, ASFA introduces two new concepts: (1) a duty upon the state to make reasonable efforts at *permanency planning*, once adoption or permanent guardianship become the goal, and (2) the concept of 'concurrent planning' – the practice of planning simultaneously for two mutually exclusive alternative goals such as adoption and reunification.[33] The operative language reads:

---

[30] 42 U.S.C. 671 Section 15.
[31] 42 U.S.C. Section 671 (22).
[32] 42 U.S.C. Section 673 (20).
[33] 42 U.S.C. Section 675 (E).

'(E)   if continuation of reasonable efforts [at reunification/preservation] is determined to be inconsistent with the permanency plan for the child, reasonable efforts shall be made to place the child in a timely manner in accordance with the permanency plan, and to complete whatever steps are necessary to finalize the permanent placement of the child.

(F)   reasonable efforts to place a child for adoption or with a legal guardian may be made concurrently with reasonable efforts of the type described in subparagraph (B).'

3   Removal of barriers to adoption

A third goal of ASFA was to remove barriers to adoption, including geographic, racial and economic barriers. Racial barriers had already been addressed in laws that Congress enacted pursuant to its Fourteenth Amendment powers. The ASFA language tracks these recently enacted civil rights laws which prohibited the delay or denial of placement based on racial matching polices.[34] Geographic barriers plague the current systems for adoption not only because of the complexity of interstate adoption and the lack of uniformity in adoption laws across the United States, but also because local agencies may have fiscal and political incentives to place children locally. The language of ASFA would prohibit policies that impeded cross-jurisdictional adoptions.[35]

Perhaps the most significant policy shift of ASFA is contained in the provisions reducing economic barriers to adoption. The federal government has been subsidizing private adoption of children in foster care since at least the mid 1980s. However, ASFA significantly increases funding of adoption assistance agreements guaranteeing cash subsidies and other benefits to adoptive families, to encourage and support adoption of 'special needs' children.[36] The term 'children with special needs' may sound like a small subset, but in practice it covers the great majority of children in foster care. 'Children with special needs' is child welfare jargon for children who are hard to place. It acknowledges the barriers to adoption faced by children with neurological, physical and emotional disabilities, children over the age of five, children from minority racial groups, children in sibling groups – in brief, the typical child at risk of drifting indefinitely in foster care.[37] ASFA addresses these barriers not only by encouraging and funding cash

---

[34]   The language of 42 U.S.C. 671 (18), applying to foster care funding, and 42 U.S.C. § 1996b, enforceable via the Civil Rights Act, and thus applicable regardless of whether the actor receives federal funding, are virtually identical. They provide that covered entities may not: '(A) deny to any individual the opportunity to become an adoptive or a foster parent, on the basis of the race, color, or national origin of the individual, or of the child, involved, or (B) delay or deny the placement of a child for adoption or into foster care, on the basis of the race, color, or national origin of the adoptive or foster parent, or the child, involved'.

[35]   42 U.S.C. Section 671 (23) provides that the State shall not: '(A) deny or delay the placement of a child for adoption when an approved family is available outside of the jurisdiction with responsibility for handling the case of the child'.

[36]   42 U.S.C. Section 671 (21) provides for health insurance coverage for any child who has been determined to be a child with special needs, regardless of the income of the adoptive family. 42 U.S.C. Section 675 (3) defines the term 'adoption assistance agreement' as 'a written agreement, binding on the parties to the agreement, between the State agency, other relevant agencies, and the prospective adoptive parents' which defines what payments and services will be provided.

[37]   42 U.S.C. Section 673 defines eligibility for 'special needs' subsidies, requiring in part that:

'(1) the State has determined that the child cannot or should not be returned to the home of his parents; and

(2) the State had first determined (A) that there exists with respect to the child a specific factor or condition (such as his ethnic background, age, or membership in a minority or sibling group, or the presence of factors such as medical conditions or physical, mental, or emotional handicaps) because of which it is reasonable to conclude that such child cannot be placed with adoptive parents without providing adoption assistance under this section or medical assistance under title XIX ...'.

subsidies to adoptive parents to defray some of the extra costs of rearing these children, but also by insuring that children will remain eligible for government-funded health care and mental health services after they are adopted. Ordinarily, families must be extremely poor to qualify for government-paid health care. After ASFA, a middle class adoptive family need not fear bankrupting itself to care for a disabled child and will not be financially ruined if the child needs residential care.

To break down bureaucratic inertia and give the States a fiscal stake in encouraging adoptions, ASFA creates a system of 'adoption incentive payments' for the States. Once a State exceeds a certain baseline quota of adoptions, the State is eligible to receive a $4,000 bounty for each additional adoption. Finally, ASFA requires that States make funding for family support and preservation programs available to families who adopt children to support their post-adoption needs. In essence, ASFA shifts money and services from biological families and foster families to adoptive families.

4 Fast tracking severe or repeat abusers

One major concern with AACWA was the presumption favoring reunification or preservation of a child with his family even though the parents had already severely harmed a child in their care. ASFA envisions that parents should be judged according to past conduct rather than being given a fresh start with each new child.[38] Parents who have severely abused or killed any of their children, or who had a prior involuntary termination of parental rights with respect to another child, are to be placed on a 'fast track' to termination of their rights as parents, so their children can be freed for adoption. ASFA provides that in cases involving a parent who has murdered the child's sibling, or committed a felony resulting in serious bodily injury to the child or his sibling, the case must be listed for a permanency hearing within 30 days. ASFA leaves to each State to decide what additional 'aggravated circumstances' will trigger assignment to the fast track but the statute provides examples such as torture and abandonment. In this subset of cases, the State should not be required to expend any time or resources attempting to preserve or reunify a family.[39] Overall, the Bill reflects a growing conviction on the part

---

[38]   Kathleen Haggard, 'Note: Treating Prior Terminations of Parental Rights as Grounds for Present Terminations', 73 *Wash. L. Rev.* 1051 (1998).

[39]   As amended, the statute reads:

'reasonable efforts of the type described in subparagraph (B) shall not be required to be made with respect to a parent of a child if a court of competent jurisdiction has determined that–

   (i) the parent has subjected the child to aggravated circumstances (as defined in State law, which definition may include but need not be limited to abandonment, torture, chronic abuse, and sexual abuse);

   (ii) the parent has–

      (I) committed murder (which would have been an offense under section 1111(a) of title 18, United States Code, if the offense had occurred in the special maritime or territorial jurisdiction of the United States) of another child of the parent;

      (II) committed voluntary manslaughter (which would have been an offense under section 1112(a) of title 18, United States Code, if the offense had occurred in the special maritime or territorial jurisdiction of the United States) of another child of the parent;

      (III) aided or abetted, attempted, conspired, or solicited to commit such a murder or such a voluntary manslaughter; or

      (IV) committed a felony assault that results in serious bodily injury to the child or another child of the parent; or

   (iii) the parental rights of the parent to a sibling have been terminated involuntarily;

(E) if reasonable efforts of the type described in subparagraph (B) are not made with respect to a child as a result of a determination made by a court of competent jurisdiction in accordance with subparagraph (D)–

of policy makers that many families simply cannot be fixed and therefore courts must terminate parental rights early in the process, while children are still young enough to be adopted by new families.[40] Many parents' advocates protest that ASFA goes too far. Most controversial is the idea that one involuntary termination, no matter how long ago or for what reason, would mandate fast-tracking without any reunification efforts in any subsequent case involving that parent.

B   State implementation of ASFA principles

During 1998, State legislatures around the country were engaged in revising their existing laws to bring them into conformity with ASFA. A full review of these amendments is beyond the scope of this article; however, the overall impression gleaned from a quick review is one of diversity bordering on chaos. Recall that each State had its own juvenile and child welfare laws prior to the entry of the federal government into the arena. These laws differed from State to State not only in the terminology employed but also in their underlying emphasis on principles such as family preservation, parents' rights, and child safety. After the passage of AACWA in 1980, a flurry of amendments at the State level institutionalized the principles of 'reasonable efforts' at family preservation and reunification, FSPs, six-month status reviews and permanency planning at 18 months. Post ASFA, a new flurry of amendments introduces new language superimposing ASFA on the language reflecting AACWA's principles. States vary substantially in how they interpret and implement ASFA requirements and whether they simply add the ASFA concepts or also repeal the AACWA concepts.

For example, States vary in the ways in which they modify the principle of family preservation reflected in AACWA to make the health and safety of the child paramount, as mandated by ASFA. Arkansas, in a Bill signed by the Arkansas Governor in March 1999, amended its child welfare law so that the goal of 'preserving family ties whenever possible' now applies only 'when it is in the best interest of the juvenile'.[41] Colorado, by contrast, interprets ASFA as merely a clarification of AACWA. Colorado lawmakers retained the old AACWA 'reasonable efforts' language but added the idea that 'reasonable efforts' to prevent or eliminate the need for removal might be 'unnecessary due to the existence of an emergency situation that requires immediate removal of the juvenile from the home'. Colorado also added provisions protecting parents' rights.[42]

(i) a permanency hearing (as described in section 475(5)(C) [42 USCS § 675(5)(C)]) shall be held for the child within 30 days after the determination; and

(ii) reasonable efforts shall be made to place the child in a timely manner in accordance with the permanency plan, and to complete whatever steps are necessary to finalize the permanent placement of the child.'

42 U.S.C. Section 671 (D)–(E).

[40]   'If the window of opportunity is missed the child leaves the system as a legal orphan.' 143 Cong. Rec. S 12211.

[41]   See Arkansas Code 9-27-302 (1999).

[42]   1999 Colo. H.B. 1146, amending 19-1-103 Colo. Rev. Stat (1999) requires the fact-finder to determine: '(B) Whether reasonable efforts have been made to prevent or eliminate the need for removal of the juvenile from the home or whether such efforts are unnecessary due to the existence of an emergency situation that requires the immediate removal of the juvenile from the home; and (C) whether procedural safeguards to preserve parental rights have been applied in connection with the removal of the juvenile from the home, any change in the juvenile's community placement, or any determination affecting parental visitation.'

New Jersey, in response to ASFA, changed the phrase 'life and health' to 'life, safety and health' in various statutory provisions, replaced the term 'diligent efforts' with 'reasonable efforts,' and inserted the phrase 'the safety of the child shall be of paramount concern' in numerous places throughout its statute. Reflecting the new emphasis on adoption, the New Jersey legislature also amended its statute to add to the purposes of 'supportive services' (previously described as insuring the child's best interest and promoting reunification) the purposes of insuring the child's 'safety', and 'promoting placement for adoption or an alternative permanent placement. Services to facilitate adoption or an alternative permanent placement may be provided concurrently with services to reunify the child with the parent or guardian.'[43] The ASFA concepts that petitions for TPR must be filed after findings of 'aggravated circumstances' or after 15 months in care appears in New Jersey's amendments, but the pre-existing language of the New Jersey statute preserves a distinctive qualification. Prior to ASFA, New Jersey law articulated an important limiting principle: a TPR is only 'appropriate' if 'termination of parental rights will not do more harm than good'.[44] This phrase remains in the amended statute, clarifying that a court should not order a TPR without examining its effects. By contrast, many States' laws contain no such clarifying language and therefore may be be interpreted by judges, post ASFA amendments, as allowing or even mandating termination without an individualized inquiry into the costs and benefits.

These few examples illustrate how the principles of ASFA can be misinterpreted, exaggerated, distorted, diluted or mitigated as they are translated by State legislatures into amendments to existing statutory schemes. The chaotic process of 'law reform' at the State level that follows a major Bill attaching conditions to federal funding raises constitutional concerns as well as policy concerns. State legislatures that depend heavily on federal subsidies to operate their child welfare systems have no realistic choice but to amend them, and often do so without confronting or taking responsibility for the underlying policy implications of what they are doing. The spending clause, if overused, can create distortions in the constitutional balance of federal and State authority and contributes to sloppy and illogical State laws.

III SOME THOUGHTS ON REDEFINING FAMILY AND PRIVATIZING CHILD WELFARE

ASFA and its State law counterparts clearly signal some major shifts in child welfare law and policy. Explicitly aimed at providing 'safe and stable homes' for children at risk, they also represent a critical moment in the process of defining and redefining the meaning and role of the 'family' as a basic unit of society. In this section, I will argue that ASFA reflects a merging of two contemporary trends evident in the United States. First, is the trend, in culture and in law, away from defining family around the biological nuclear family (those who bear and beget the children) and towards supporting and recognizing the 'functional family' (those who are actually engaged in or are willing and able to do the work of parenting).[45] The biological family is linked by ties of blood and marriage,

---

[43] See 1999 N.J. ALS 53; 1999 N.J. Laws 53; 1999 N.J. Ch. 53; 1998 N.J. S.N. 1705, amending P.L.1977, c.367.

[44] Section 7(4) of New Jersey's Public Law 1991, Ch. 53 (1999).

[45] See Barbara Bennett Woodhouse, 'It All Depends on What you Mean by Home?: Towards a Communitarian Theory of the "Non-Traditional" Family', 1996 *Utah L. Rev.* 569 (1997). See also Karen Czapanskiy, 'Interdependencies, Families, And Children', 39 *Santa Clara L. Rev.* 957 (1999)

while the functional family may be linked by looser kinship bonds or by no blood or legal ties at all. Second is the political trend toward privatization of many functions assumed by government in the New Deal and Great Society eras, including the function of providing a safety net to preserve the poor family.[46]

It is axiomatic in a democratic society that the family is the unit entrusted with nurturing and acculturating each new generation of citizens.[47] Family, however, can have many meanings. Each society determines how to balance the mix of blood relationship, legal formality, religious meaning, social investment, community continuity, and nurturing care that constitute what we consider the defining attributes of 'the family'. Each society also allocates between public and private spheres the responsibility for supporting family functions – public education, school lunches, public health care, mothers allowances, are examples of this public/private partnership in child-rearing.

In comparative law terms, a distinguishing feature of United States family policy is our delegation of the work of child rearing to the private sphere of family life where it is performed as unpaid labor primarily by women.[48] Welfare – using taxpayer dollars to help poor parents support their children – has been stigmatized as a 'handout' and not viewed or structured as an entitlement. Child welfare has long been an exception to this rule – children are perceived as having a right to protection at the public expense. Abused and abandoned children escape the stigma of shiftlessness and dysfunction attached to poor parents, allowing a major commitment of government resources without serious protest from the right. ASFA represents a turn toward privatization – reducing the role of 'public' child welfare programs while incentivizing formation of 'private' adoptive families to take on this role. Under ASFA, long-term State-managed fostering is discouraged and ASFA promotes permanency primarily in terms of getting kids out of the system through adoption, whether with kin, with foster families willing to adopt, or with strangers. This privatization of welfare, which first emerged in 'welfare' reform, has spread to 'child welfare' reform. In the context of 'welfare', TANF shifted responsibility for providing income for poor mothers to the private sector, where mothers who do not have a breadwinner mate must 'earn' enough to support themselves and their children through employment or rely on private charity. In the context of 'child welfare', ASFA enlists the private sector (potential adoptive parents) to reduce the involvement of government in providing care for dependent children.

The idea that the 'private' sphere of family operates independently of the public sphere is, of course, an illusion. Government and family always have been partners in child rearing, to the extent that government invisibly subsidizes middle-class families through tax breaks, social insurance, and public services. The notion of subsidized 'special needs' adoptions opens a new chapter in the history of how the private sphere of 'family' and the public sphere of 'government' interact in raising children. In the post-

---

(commenting on changing theories of family focusing on interdependency rather than purely biology); Naomi R. Cahn, 'Review Essay: The Moral Complexities of Family Law', 50 *Stan. L. Rev.* 225 (1997) (discussing the changing normative framework for valuing diverse family forms).

[46] I place this term in 'scare quotes' because dysfunction is partially a social construct and often has been defined by a majority community in ways that have disparate impact on minority communities. See Robin D. G. Kelly, *Yo' Mama's Dysfunktional* (Beacon Press: 1997).

[47] *Prince v. Massachusetts*, 321 U.S. 158 (1944) ('It is cardinal with us that the custody, care and nurture of the child reside first in the parents.')

[48] See Martha Fineman, *The Neutered Mother, the Sexual Family, and Other Twentieth Century Tragedies*; Mary Ann Glendon, *The Transformation of Family Law: State, Law and Family in Western Europe and the United States* (1989); Barbara Bennett Woodhouse, 'Who Owns the Child?' (note 15 above).

ASFA scheme of child welfare laws and policies, we continue to subsidize a child's 'family' but now 'the family' is defined not by biology but by function.

These two trends – redefinition of family and privatization of child welfare – intertwine in ASFA. In a society where widespread divorce and geographic mobility make family relationships highly fluid, families seem endlessly malleable, even fungible. Families are made and unmade not by God and Nature, but by personal choice. Thus reunification services and professional foster care to preserve 'failed' birth families are seen as endangering children and wasting money for no good reason. These supports merely contribute to a 'lifestyle' of dependency, with no gains for the children whose formal birth family is preserved but who continue to lack what Americans increasingly describe as a 'real' family. Taxpayers' money should be used not to support failed families but to incentivize the creation of new and presumptively 'functional' adoptive families, bound together by demonstrated commitment and ability to provide the time consuming and emotionally taxing work of child rearing.

Riding this sociological shift in how we conceptualize the family, government can 'get out of the business' of fostering displaced children. By redefining what counts as 'family', government can redistribute resources to private entities who can accomplish the work of the 'family' within the private sphere. The family remains the basic unit for child-rearing, but the legally autonomous family has been recreated out of the ashes of the dysfunctional biological family, through adoption.

There is much in this vision of a Brave New World for children that I find appealing. I generally support a focus on family functions as opposed to forms because it recognizes the reality of children's lives. However, I find the notion of the fungible family unsettling and in tension not only with pluralist democracy but also in tension with a child-centered policy. Families are not fungible to children, once they form attachments to parenting figures. I would argue that children have a right to be safe and secure but in their own homes, if possible. I also welcome the notion of government subsidies for special needs children, as a recognition that all children are 'our' responsibility. By creating a public–private partnership in rearing dependent children, the subsidy model departs from the tradition of privatizing the social costs of dependency within 'the family'. I would argue, however, that all children, not just those whom the State seeks to shift off its child welfare rolls, should be eligible for needed medical care and support services. The work of all parents, not just those recruited to adopt children with special needs, ought to be given appropriate public support.

V CONCLUSION

ASFA is a sweeping reform yet to be fully implemented. Was reform of the child welfare system necessary? The consensus view, which I share, holds that child welfare reform was imperative. The system's critics – on all sides – were right. Too many children not truly at risk were being removed, especially within the African American community. However, those left in their homes or reunified with abusive parents were too often the very children most at risk of harm. Clearly, the toughest challenge for child welfare was, and remains, the difficulty of measuring the level of risk presented in each individual case. Until we can master that art, we will continue to fail the children we seek to protect.

Was ASFA the right path to reform? To the extent that ASFA funds research on risk assessment, it is surely a step in the right direction. To the extent it frees children whose families are irretrievably broken to find new safe and permanent families, it serves the needs of children for real homes and gets the State out of mismanaging their lives. To the extent it forces bureaucrats to respond to children's needs in a timely manner, employing both sticks and carrots, it offers some hope of breaking the log jam of inertia that has plagued child welfare systems for so long. To the extent that subsidized adoption provides a revitalized model of public–private partnership with children's care givers, ASFA contributes to rethinking family policy.

But ASFA also poses great risks. Are its time frames so short that it will destroy families that should, for children's sake, be preserved? Many advocates for parents worry that a year is not sufficient to rehabilitate a drug-involved parent, even when that parent is committed to changing. Parent advocates are sure to challenge the new State laws in court, based on constitutional claims that they infringe parental rights. Children's advocates may also have reason to challenge ASFA as applied in various settings. ASFA's time lines tend to lead to a 'one size fits all' approach. A child-centered policy would reflect a child's changing sense of time. For an infant who desperately needs to form a stable parenting relationship, a year is arguably too long to wait for an addicted or mentally ill parent. For a child of ten, who knows and loves an addicted or mentally ill parent, a year is not long enough.

Will courts and legislatures read ASFA's provisions without fully understanding them?[49] For example, many workers seem to be interpreting ASFA as mandating the cessation of reasonable efforts or mandating the filing of a TPR, without evaluation on a case by case basis of whether the action is truly in the best interest of the child. Will case workers and courts apply culturally and ethnically sensitive methods to measuring whether a family is so dysfunctional that it cannot serve the needs of its children? The law reports abound with stories of children removed from homes that are dirty or disorganized, judged by middle-class standards, but not dangerous. When race and poverty combine, families are at heightened risk of inappropriate interventions. Every parent advocate has seen cases in which parents lost their children because of circumstances beyond their control, such as being burned out of their homes or driven out by domestic violence.[50] ASFA's short time frames and fast-tracking will reduce drift, but they will also make it harder for parents' advocates to combat unjust interventions. Will the value to children of attachments to kin and foster parents who cannot, for some reason, adopt, be ignored in the rush to promote adoptions? ASFA encourages explorations of kinship placements, foster family adoption, and open adoption but it does not fund long-term guardianship with a family member or foster parent. The model of the infant who needs to be freed quickly in order to find a safe and permanent home – the image of permanency that clearly drove the drafters of ASFA – may not fit the older child who has already formed attachments with family and substitute care givers. For such a child, stability and permanency may mean preserving the status quo.[51]

Perhaps the biggest unanswered question is what will happen to children after a TPR is entered. How many of these 'State orphans' will realize the goal of finding adoptive

---

[49]   Marcia Robinson Lowery argues that this tendency to oversimplify – seeing only binary choices where choices are far more complex – is the fatal flaw of all child welfare reform. See Commentary: 'How We can Better Protect Children from Abuse and Neglect', in *Protecting Children* (note 3 above), at 123.

[50]   Kathleen A. Bailie, 'Note: the Other "Neglected" Parties in Child Protective Proceedings: Parents in Poverty And The Role of The Lawyers Who Represent Them' 66 *Fordham L. Rev.* 2285 (1998).

[51]   See Courtney (note 17 above), for a description of how federal funding has tended to skew the incentives to favor out of home care and adoption over family services. While, under ASFA, States can apply for waivers to allow funds to be used to subsidize permanent guardianship – for example, in cases where a grandparent has actual custody but is reluctant to push a TPR against his or her own child – the built-in incentive is towards TPR and adoption.

homes? How many will continue to drift in foster care until they 'age out'? How many will be adopted into unsafe and impermanent homes, with kin or with strangers, only to arrive back in the child welfare system as cases of abuse or disrupted adoptive placement?[52]

Let us hope that the goal articulated by President Clinton of doubling the number of children adopted out of foster care by the year 2000 can be accomplished. Let us hope it is accomplished in a way that serves the best interests of children, including their interests in retaining family, cultural and community ties. The best reform of all would adopt a child-centered perspective on issues like timing, attachment, and risk, and it would define the family through the child's eyes. We continue to struggle for the magic formula that will guarantee to all children the right to grow up safe and secure in their own homes.

---

[52] Robert M. Gordon, 'Drifting Through Byzantium: The Promise and Failure of the Adoption and Safe Families Act of 1997', 83 *Minn. L. Rev.* 637 (1999) (expressing concern that ASFA fails adequately to fund the resources needed to assure adoption of so many children).